GW00758522

Ramban

Commentary on the Torah

Commentary on the Torah

ספר בראשית
GENESIS

Translated and Annotated *with* Index
by Rabbi Dr. Charles B. Chavel, PH.B., M.A., LL.B., D.H.L., D.D.

Shilo Publishing House, Inc.
New York, N.Y. 10002

by Shilo Publishing House, Inc.

Library of Congress Catalog Card No. 71-184043

Standard Book No. 0-88328-006-X

MANUFACTURED IN THE UNITED STATES OF AMERICA

Preface:

Rabbi Moshe ben Nachman,[1] one of the most illustrious Jewish personalities, was active in the age immediately following that of Maimonides,[2] and he attained wide renown as a scholar, physician, sage, philosopher, poet, orator,[3] and defender of the faith. In addition, he was the *ish hama'aseh* (man of action) for he was the official spokesman for Jewry before the ruler of his country, the king of Aragon,' as well as being a pioneer and builder. It was he who laid the foundation for the Jewish community in Jerusalem "on the ninth day of the month Ellul, in the year five thousand twenty-seven" (1267 C.E. - as he states it in his letter to his son Nachman), about seven years after the destruction of the Holy City by the Mongols. Despite of the many adverse conditions which afflicted this Jewish community during

(1) Also known as Ramban, an acrostic of the full Hebrew name. (This is not to be confused with Rambam, the acrostic for Rabbi Moshe ben Maimon, or Maimonides.) In English, Ramban is known as Nahmanides or Nachmanides. (2) Ramban was born to a prominent family of the city of Gerona, in the kingdom of Aragon in northern Spain, in the year 4955 (1195 C.E.). He was thus nine years old when Maimonides passed away in the year 1204. The year of Ramban's death is not precisely known; it is generally assumed to have been in the year 5030 (1270 C.E.). He died somewhere in the Land of Israel to which he journeyed at great risk in his old age. He left Spain because of his role in the historic disputation in Barcelona, which commenced on July 10, 1263, at which he spoke in defense of Judaism. His spirited presentation placed him in mortal danger from the Church, and he decided to seek refuge in the land of his ancestors. (3) Four major sermons delivered by Ramban have been preserved. (See my Kithvei Haramban, I, pp. 129-252). The one entitled *Torath Hashem Tmimah* ("The Law of the Lord Is Perfect") is reputed to have been delivered by Ramban in the presence of the king and high dignitaries of the government on the Sabbath following the Barcelona disputation.

succeeding generations, its revival by Ramban imbued it with sufficient strength and endurance to enable it to continue to our present day without further interruption.[4]

Elsewhere[5] we have detailed the biography of this great Rabbi of Spanish Jewry. In this preface, however, we will attempt to delve into the unique qualities of Ramban's Commentary on the Torah, which constitutes a major portion of his legacy, and to gauge the extent of its influence on Jewish thought.

When, in the latter part of his life,[6] Ramban turned his attention to the task of writing a commentary on the Five Books of Moses[7] he found two prior major works which had already gained wide acceptance. These were the commentaries of Rabbi

(4) In our own times, the sacred city of Jerusalem did "sit solitary" for nineteen years (5708-5727: 1948-1967 C.E.) while the Jordanians not only refused access to Jews, who wished to pray at the Western Wall of the ancient Temple, but, like the barbarian Vandals of old, destroyed every Jewish house of worship, including the synagogue founded by Ramban. The day of Iyar 28, 5727, when the Jews recaptured the old city of Jerusalem from the hands of the enemy will thus forever live in the annals of our history. [Ramban's synagogue, incidentally, has already been cleared and restored.] (5) See Ramban, His Life and Teachings, published by Feldheim, N.Y. 1960, and Rabbeinu Moshe ben Nachman, published by Mosad Harav Kook, Jerusalem. 1967. (6) Ramban's Commentary on the Torah is the culminating work of a life-long literary activity which began when he was sixteen years old. Where was the Commentary written? An examination of the text reveals these facts: (a) Ramban wrote the bulk of the work while still in Spain, and he took the manuscript with him on his journey to the Holy Land (b) There, he not only made emendations on certain points which he now perceived in a new light because of his newly acquired knowledge of the geography of the Land, (see 35:16), but he also made inquiries concerning ancient Hebrew coinage, cities of the Near East, etc. (See his comment on Genesis 11:28: "Furthermore, we have investigated and know it from the word of many students who lived in that country, etc.") (c) Whether any part of the Commentary was originally written in the Land of Israel remains a moot question. This writer has expressed the opinion that certain parts of the commentary on the books of Numbers and Deuteronomy were penned in the Holy Land. See my article in Hamayon, Jerusalem, Tammuz 5728. This much however is certain: To the end of his days, Ramban was steadily engaged in refining and perfecting his work. (7) Another major work by Ramban in the field of Biblical studies is his commentary on the book of Job. He obviously chose to write on this book because it discusses the apparent contradiction between the basic principle of Divine justice and the harsh facts of human experience. In view of the continued persecution of Israel by the nations throughout the Medieval Ages, Ramban's attempt to fathom the mystery of the suffering of the

Shlomo ben Yitzchak [Rashi] and Rabbi Abraham ibn Ezra. In a very profound sense these are among the greatest literary products of Medieval Jewry. Ramban expressed his position with regard to the works of these two masters in his Opening Verses to his Commentary:

"I will place as an illumination before me
The lights of *the pure candelabrum*,
The commentaries of our Rabbi Shlomo [Rashi],
A crown of glory, and a diadem of beauty,
Adorned in his ways,
In Scripture, Mishnah and Gemara,
The right of the first-born is his.
In his words will I meditate,
And in their love will I ravish,
And with them we will have
Discussions, investigations and examinations...
And with Abraham the son of Ezra
We shall have open rebuke and hidden love."

The significance of these words should be evaluated within the context of certain facts.

At the time Ramban penned the above lines, Rashi's pre-eminent position in all Talmudic study had been firmly established. For a century and a half preceding the lifetime of Ramban, French and German Rabbis had developed in their schools a system of learning known as *Tosafoth,* (literally, 'Additions'), in which Rashi's exegesis of the Talmud served as the seed from which sprouted extensive critical studies.[8] No advanced student of the Talmud

righteous as revealed in the book of Job is comprehensible. Ramban may also have written a commentary on the Psalms – (see my Peirushei Haramban al Neviim Ukethuvim, p. 5) – but if so, that work has been completely lost.
(8) Ramban lived toward the end of the *Tosafoth* period. He was a younger contemporary of Rabbi Yechiel of Paris, whose activity flourished in the first half of the thirteenth century, and whom he mentions in his Sermon on Rosh Hashanah. Rabbi Yechiel left for the Land of Israel in the year 5017 (1257 C.E.), and established his school in Acco. It was there that Ramban some twelve years later, delivered his Sermon on Rosh Hashanah. See my Hebrew work on the life of Ramban, pp. 60-61, 200-201. It is noteworthy that Ramban also wrote *Chidushim* on certain tractates of the Talmud similar in spirit and method to that of the French and German masters of the *Tosafoth.*

who has ever delved into the profound discussions of the masters of the *Tosafoth* can forget the thrill of coming in contact with the creative thinking that is the essence and life-soul of the *Tosafoth.* Ramban was now to introduce this new dimension into the field of Biblical study. Showing the greatest respect for Rashi's commentary on the Torah, he adopted an approach analogous to the one used by the masters of the *Tosafoth* when they analyzed and dissected Rashi's commentary on the Talmud.

Specifically, Ramban's undaunted and penetrating analysis of Rashi's commentary developed three areas in which he differed with Rashi's approach to the sacred text.

a) The first was their respective attitudes towards the Agadic material of the Sages of the Talmud and Midrash. Rashi, a native of France and a product of its schools of learning, selected Agadic material illuminating the ethical stance implicit in the Scriptural texts and used it as a source of moral inspiration. Ramban, a product of Spanish Jewry, approached the same homiletic material in a more analytic and intellectual manner. A case in point is the opening of Rashi's commentary on Genesis which commences with a statement by Rabbi Yitzchak which questions the necessity of beginning the Torah with the account of creation. Rashi accepts Rabbi Yitzchak's question at face value, and proceeds from there; Ramban makes some profound and penetrating remarks about the question itself, which lead to a different interpretation of the entire matter.

b) In many places, Rashi explains the text in accordance with the principle that "There is no 'earlier' or 'later' in the Torah," meaning that the order of Scripture is often not chronological. Ramban's position is that "the whole Torah is written in chronological order except where Scripture itself tells us differently,[9] in which case it was done with a

(9) See Numbers 1:1 and 9:1. Some of the other exegetic principles established by Ramban are these: (a) Scripture speaks briefly of matters which are self-evident; (b) It cuts short the genealogy of people with whom it is not concerned; (c) It speaks only in hints of hidden and future matters; (d) It does not desire to speak at length about the ways of idolatry; (e) A sequence of events is sometimes attributed to the one who caused them, and sometimes to the agent who performed them.

specific purpose." It is evident that Ramban's approach makes the text simpler to comprehend, for according to him, verse and chapter follow each other in logical sequence.

c) In explaining obscure Hebrew words, Rashi was not averse to relating them to foreign words, from languages such as Aramaic, etc.[10] Ramban was opposed to this in principle for the language of the Torah is the Sacred Tongue. "It is the language in which the words of the Torah and prophecies and all sacred matters were expressed; moreover, it is the language in which the Holy One, blessed be He, speaks with His congregation." How then can that language be explained on the basis of Aramaic, Greek or Persian? In these linguistic encounters with Rashi, Ramban displays a phenomenal knowledge of the entire field of Hebrew literature.[11]

Ramban's scrutiny of Rashi's commentary on the Torah was to bear fruit in the sixteenth century when a group of scholars continued his approach and produced a series of exhaustive works on Rashi.[12] Every word of Rashi was pondered, and with respect to those points wherein Ramban differed with Rashi, many came to the defense of Rashi while others sided with Ramban.[13] Thus it may truly be said that Ramban's Commentary on the Torah gave a

(10) See Genesis 44:20. See also Ramban on Exodus 30:13, where he differs with Maimonides as to why the Sages refer to the language of the Torah as the Sacred Tongue. (11) Ramban's knowledge of Hebrew literature was not limited to that of the past. He was also fully acquainted with the works of his contemporaries, such as Joseph and David Kimchi. Their names appear in his Commentary on Genesis (1:26 and 35:16) and their influence is felt throughout the work. (12) This period of activity began with Rabbi Eliyahu Mizrachi (1455-1526), chief Rabbi of Turkey, and spread from there to the northern countries, such as Austria, where the famous Maharal of Prague devoted his work Gur Aryeh to a study of Rashi's commentary, and Poland, where Rabbi Mordechai Jaffe wrote L'vush Ha'orah for that same purpose. (13) A notable example of this type of effort is the Nimukei Shmuel by Rabbi Shmuel Tzarfati. It is devoted entirely to a defense of Ramban's teachings as regards the points of criticism raised against them by Mizrachi in his defense of Rashi. In our times there has been a great revival of interest in Ramban's Commentary. It was begun by the great Chasam Sofer (1763-1839), the foremost Rabbinic authority of his time, who set the example of studying Ramban's work regularly in his academy with his pupils.

new impetus to Hebrew Biblical scholarship, the influence of which has not ceased to this day.

With reference to the second major commentary of the era, that of Rabbi Abraham ibn Ezra, Ramban's attitude, as we have seen, was ambivalent; "open rebuke and hidden love." Ramban directed the open rebuke towards Ibn Ezra whenever his independent views brought him into conflict with traditional authority,[14] while his hidden love for him was in recognition of his mastery of language and grammar, and his understanding of Biblical syntax.

Maimonides' Moreh Nebuchim (The Guide of the Perplexed) also comes in for some sharp criticism in this work of Ramban.[15] Despite of his unbounded admiration for the author – in whose behalf he had penned his famous letter to the French Rabbis which confirmed *all* of Maimonides' works as being the authoritative voice of Judaism[16] – Ramban, nevertheless, proceeds to reject some interpretations of Biblical texts by Maimonides. It is noteworthy that, as in the case of Rashi, an entire literature has evolved in defense of the master of "the Guide" in those instances in which Ramban rejected his views. Of special interest is the work of Rabbi Yom Tov ben Abraham (Ritba), a disciple of the famous Rashba,[17] who dedicated his Sefer Hazikaron to a rejection of

(14) See Ramban's comments on Genesis 46:15, also 25:34. A detailed study of Ramban's comments on Ibn Ezra conclusively bears out this point: For every case of critical comment that Ramban directed against Ibn Ezra he made many more that express his esteem for him. See Kithvei Haramban, II, pp. 591-592, for a full list of citations of Ramban's attitude towards Ibn Ezra. (15) The main reproof appears at the beginning of *Seder Vayeira,* where the entire nature of prophetic vision and esoteric experiences are discussed. Another main point of divergence between Ramban and Rambam appears in their explanation of the reason behind Onkelos' unique rendition of certain passages of the Torah. See Ramban on Genesis 46:1. (16) For the text of the letter, see Kithvei Haramban, I, pp. 336-351, and also the English biography of Ramban, pp. 31-41. This letter forms a landmark in Jewish history. "It gave the historic stamp of approval upon *all* works of Rambam, leaving no longer a shade of a doubt that in *all* the works of Rambam the eternal voice of Judaism is heard." (*Ibid.* p. 36). (17) The best-known pupil of Ramban, Rashba (Rabbi Shlomo ben Aderet) of Barcelona (1235-1310) was the towering personality of the coming generation. He is especially known for the thousands of responsa on every aspect of Jewish law which he sent to inquiring communities throughout the world.

Ramban's criticism of the Moreh Nebuchim. The following excerpt is most revealing. After defending Maimonides' words, the Ritba concludes: "Nonetheless, it is fitting to say concerning this matter that I have extended myself in order to defend that to which I do not subscribe, for the way of Ramban, of blessed memory, is the traditional and paven way, from which one is not to turn aside right or left. Yet I have had compassion for the master [Maimonides], of blessed memory, and for his effort, for all his words were motivated by a desire to glorify the Name of Heaven, and in addition, they contain great wisdom. It is not for me to question them. And even though our Rabbi, of blessed memory, [i.e., Ramban], has found it necessary to speak and do as he did, for those who come after him [to speak likewise against Maimonides] is a sin and a guilt."[18] The great esteem of future generations for both Rambam and Ramban has never been more clearly enunciated.

While Ramban was concerned with all the problems of philosophy, science, and ethics which engaged the minds of his generation, he never constructed an integral system as did other major Jewish philosophers of the Middle Ages. Yet it may be said that his nearest approach to such a philosophic work is his Commentary on the Torah. There is no major problem that does not occupy his attention: creation, man, the nature of the human soul,[19] freedom of will, Providence, miracles – both apparent and

(18) Sefer Hazikaron, edited by Kalman Kahana, p. 44. The standard Hebrew edition of the Moreh Nebuchim also contains a number of other commentators who defend Maimonides against the critical remarks of Ramban. (19) Ramban's understanding of the working of the human mind are especially noteworthy. See p. 259 where he touches upon some modern aspects of psychoneurosis. From his writings on the Talmud (Chullin, Chapter 3) we learn that Ramban in seeking to establish the guiding principles by which we may distinguish between birds that are clean and unclean went out into the forest with hunters in order to gain first-hand knowledge of these matters. A keen awareness of the effect of the physical environment upon the human organism is definitely discernable in his remarks on Leviticus 26:4. "G-d commences the blessings with the matter of the rains, because in coming in their season the air will be pure and good, the springs and rivers will be full-flowing, and these in turn will cause the growth of healthy plants and fruits... Living in such an environment no man will be susceptible to sickness etc., and man will fulfill his days. For when the physical bodies of men are tall and healthy they may indeed exist as in the days of Adam. This indeed is the greatest of blessings." Also interesting is Ramban's concept of the nature

concealed – the roots of Israel's history as reflected in the lives of the patriarchs, the uniqueness of the Land of Israel – all these and others come to light in this work. And to the glory of Ramban, it should be noted, that in his consideration of all these problems the unique Torah perspective is always preserved.

An element of pervasive influence in this work is that of the Cabala – the mystic teachings of the Torah – which Ramban was the first to introduce into Biblical Commentary. The great Cabalist of the sixteenth century Rabbi Yitzchak Luria[20] spoke of Ramban's presentation of Cabalistic principles of thought in the highest terms: "Deep they lie, exceedingly deep; who can grasp them?"[21] The wide extent of Cabalistic influence on the coming generations can be traced to Ramban, for despite of the word of caution included at the end of his introduction to the Commentary which warns against reaching into the Cabala on one's own initiative, the study of Cabalistic doctrines received a great impetus and became widely diffused because of him.

The present volume, a translation of Ramban's Commentary on the entire book of Genesis,[22] is based on the Hebrew text which I was privileged to publish a few years ago on the basis of manuscripts and first editions.[23] The printed editions of Ramban had become seriously corrupted, and it was necessary to establish

of time. Thus he writes: "From the moment some substance came into existence, time was already part of it" (p. 32). One wonders if there is not implicit in this statement an awareness of the principle that time and matter are interdependent and that the nature of one is dependent upon the other. (20) One of the greatest Cabalists of all times whose teachings mark the high point in the classic period of Cabala. (21) There are a number of works which help explain Ramban's mystic references. The earliest was written by a pupil of Rashba, Meir Abusaula. Rabbeinu Bachya ben Asher, another pupil of Rashba, also explicates a good part of Ramban's Cabala in his lengthy commentary on the Torah. At about the same time, Menachem of Ricanti, of Italy, also used Cabala selections of Ramban in his work on the Torah, with some explanatory comments. (22) In the year 1960, in Leyden, Jacob Newman published "The commentary of Nachmanides on Genesis, Chapters 1-6," which only covers *Seder Bereshith.* The present volume is thus the first of its kind since it covers the *entire* book of Genesis. (23) The first edition of this Hebrew text appeared in the year 5719 (1959), and was published by the Mosad Harav Kook in Jerusalem. A fifth printing appeared in 5730 (1970).

the pure text of Ramban. In the task of translation I have aimed principally at clarity, in order to convey the true thoughts of Ramban in the clearest language possible.[24] The notes appended show the sources of Ramban's words, and also serve to clarify matters with which Ramban dealt succinctly.

In closing, I wish to record my thankfulness to SHILO PUBLISHING HOUSE, INC. for sponsoring this Torah-project. For the painstaking care which Mr. Henry Petzenbaum and Mr. Joseph Salomon have devoted to the production of a book so technically complicated I express my deep appreciation. I am also thankful to Rabbi Eliezer Gewirtzman for his invaluable suggestions on reading the manuscript. At the same time I wish to express my gratitude to Mr. Alan Augenbraun for his technical assistance with the preparation of the manuscript.

I conclude with a fervent prayer that this translation serve as a significant aid to people who seek the light of the Torah in this troubled age, and that they find in it a key to unlock the rich treasure-house which is Ramban's Commentary on the Torah.

C. B. Chavel

21 Tammuz, 5731
July 14, 1971
Edgemere, N.Y.

(24) To have the intent of Ramban made perfectly clear and the translation more readable, I have included minor explanatory phrases which are not offset from the actual text. Major explanatory notes are offset by brackets. All Cabalistic texts have been translated except for a very few passages, which because of their great profundity would have required too lengthy explanations. In general the present translation is based wholly upon my Hebrew commentary on Ramban's text. In my notes I have made several references to it for further enlightenment about specific problems.

A SHORT NOTE TO THE SECOND EDITION

The need to reprint the English translation of Ramban's Commentary on the Book of Genesis within a year of its first appearance demonstrates the lasting attraction of the word of Ramban. It is seven hundred years since the Sage of Gerona penned his commentary; but his word remains as relevant to the modern Jew as it was to the Jew of old.

In my preface to this translation, I made an attempt to summarize the special qualities of Ramban's contribution to Biblical studies. In this connection I wish to quote a passage from the Magen Avoth of Rashbatz (Rabbi Shimon ben Tzemach, one of the great Rabbis of the fourteenth century) which has recently come to my attention and which illustrates the esteem in which Ramban has been held by all generations. After quoting certain words of Ramban, he follows the citation with this comment: "These are the words of the holy Rabbi, our master Rabbi Moshe ben Nachman, of blessed memory. They are pure, sacred words, befitting an angel of G-d, as he was."

C. B. C.

Chanukah 5753

Contents

COMMENTARY ON THE TORAH

BY OUR MASTER

RABBI MOSHE THE SON OF NACHMAN

THE GERONDITE

Introductory Verses

In the name of *the great G-d, and the fearful,*[1]
I will begin to write novel interpretations
On the explanation of the Torah,
With terror, with fear,
With trembling, with sweat, with dread,[2]
Praying and confessing
With a humble heart and a broken spirit,
Asking forgiveness,
Seeking pardon and atonement,[3]
With bowing to the ground,
With kneeling, with prostration,
Until all the vertebrae of the spine
Seem to be loosened.[4]
And that my soul knoweth right well,[5]
In clear awareness,
That the egg of the ant is not as small
In comparison to the outermost sphere

(1) Daniel 9:4. It could not be Deuteronomy 10:17 since there the attribute *mighty* is mentioned. It is possible that the author chose the verse from Daniel rather than that of Deuteronomy in order to allude to the rest of the verse there: *And I prayed unto the Eternal my G-d, and made confession and said, O, Eternal the great and fearful G-d, and Who keepest the covenant and mercy with them that love Thee and keep Thy commandments.* There is thus here an allusion to a prayer for G-d's mercy in the author's work before him. (2) See Berachoth 22 a, where it is explained that these are the ways in which the Torah was given and by which it was studied. (3) That is, in case he errs in his interpretations and especially in his refuting the opinions of the other masters. (4) Berachoth 28 b. (5) Psalms 139:14.

As is my little wisdom
And brief knowledge
Against the hidden matters of the Torah[6]
That lie hidden in her house,
Concealed in her room;
For every precious thing and every wonder,
Every profound mystery and all glorious wisdom
Are stored up with her,
Sealed up in her treasure
By a hint, by a word,
In writing and in speaking;
Just as the prophet – who was adorned
With royal garments and a crown,
The annointed of the G-d of Jacob,[7]
The author of the sweetest of songs – said:
I have seen an end
To every purpose;
But Thy commandment
Is exceedingly broad,[8]
And it is said,
Thy testimonies are wonderful;
Therefore doth my soul keep them.[9]
But what shall I do
Since my soul craves for Torah
And she is in my heart
As a consuming, burning fire[10]
In my kidneys restrained;
To go forth in the steps
Of the former ones,
The lions of the group,[11]
The exalted of the generations,

(6) A reference to the Cabala – the mystic teachings of the Torah – elements of which the author intends to include in his commentary, but here he confesses his brief knowledge thereof. (7) II Samuel 23:1. (8) Psalms 119:96. (9) *Ibid.*, Verse 129. (10) See Jeremiah 20:9. (11) A reference to the most distinguished scholars of the generations.

The men of might;[12]
To enter with them
"The thickest part of the beam,"[13]
To write as they did
Explanations of the verses,
And Midrashic interpretations
On the precepts,
And the *Agadah* [homily],
Ordered in all things, and sure.[14]
I will place as an illumination before me
The lights of *the pure candelabrum,*[15]
The commentaries of our Rabbi Shlomo [Rashi],
A crown of glory, and a diadem of beauty,[16]
Adorned in his ways,
In Scripture, Mishnah and Gemara.
The right of the first-born is his.[17]
In his words will I meditate,
And in their love will I ravish,[18]
And with them we will have
Discussions, investigations and examinations,
In his plain explanations
And Midrashic interpretations,
And every difficult *Agadah*
Which is mentioned in his commentaries.
And with Abraham the son of Ezra
We shall have open rebuke and hidden love.[19]

(12) That is, in their knowledge of the Torah. "A man of might" is he who knows to answer in a discussion of the Torah. (Sanhedrin 93 b.) (13) The heart of the problem. (14) II Samuel 23:5. The preceding part of the verse reads: *For an everlasting covenant he hath made with me.* Ramban thus suggests that his part in the Torah was assured from on high, and therefore he need not fear to go forth in the steps of the former giants of the Torah. (15) Exodus 31:8. (16) Isaiah 28:5. (17) Deuteronomy 21:17. A reference to the fact that Rashi's commentary to the Torah was the first great commentary to be accepted by all Israel. (18) See Proverbs 5:19. (19) *Ibid.*, 27:5. The exact quotation: *Better is open rebuke than love that is hidden.* Ramban thus suggests that while he will criticize Ibn Ezra openly on many of his interpretations, yet his admiration of his work will not be lessened.

And G-d Whom alone I shall fear
He shall save me from *the day of wrath.*[20]
He shall keep me from mistakes
And from all sin and transgression,
And He shall lead me in the straight way
And open for us the gates of light,
And He shall deem us worthy
To see the day of tidings,[21]
As it is written:

How beautiful upon the mountains
Are the feet of the messenger of good tidings
That announceth peace,
The harbinger of good tidings
That announceth salvation,
That saith to Zion:
'Thy G-d reigneth.'[22]

Thy word is tried to the uttermost,
And Thy servant loveth it.[23]
Thy righteousness
Is an everlasting righteousness,
And Thy law is truth.[24]
Thy testimonies are righteous forever;
Give me understanding,
And I shall live.[25]

(20) Zephaniah 1:15. (21) "The day of tidings" was to Ramban a reality which was to transpire in the very near future. See his commentary further, 2:3, towards the end of the verse. (22) Isaiah 52:7. (23) Psalms 119:140. (24) *Ibid.*, Verse 142. (25) *Ibid.*, Verse 44. (See my Hebrew commentary, p. 20, for the reason why Ramban mentions these three verses from Psalms.)

The Book of Genesis

Moses our teacher wrote this book of Genesis together with the whole Torah from the mouth of the Holy One, blessed be He.

It is likely that he wrote it on Mount Sinai for there it was said to him, *Come up to Me unto the mount, and be there; and I will give thee the tablets of stone and the Torah and the commandment which I have written, to teach them.*[1] *The tablets of stone* include the tablets and the writing that are the ten commandments. *The commandment* includes the number of all the commandments, positive and negative. If so, the expression *and the Torah* includes the stories from the beginning of Genesis [and is called *Torah* – teaching] because it teaches people the ways of faith. Upon descending from the mount, he [Moses] wrote the Torah from the beginning of Genesis to the end of the account of the tabernacle. He wrote the conclusion of the Torah at the end of the fortieth year of wandering in the desert when he said [by command of G-d], *Take this book of the law, and put it in the side of the ark of the covenant of the Eternal your G-d.*[2]

This view accords with the opinion of the Talmudic sage who says[3] that the Torah was written in sections.[4] However, according to the sage who says that the Torah was given in its entirety,[5] everything was written in the fortieth year when he [Moses] was commanded, *Now write ye this song for you and teach it unto the*

(1) Exodus 24:12. (2) Deuteronomy 31:26. (3) Gittin 60 a. The name of the authority is Rabbi Yochanan. (4) When a section was declared to Moses, he immediately wrote it down. When all the sections were completed, he compiled them together into one Torah. Rashi, *Ibid.* (5) Resh Lakish is the authority who maintains that Moses wrote the whole Torah at one time after all sections had been given to him intermittently during the forty years and were properly systematized in his mind.

children of Israel; put it in their mouths,[6] and, as he was further instructed, *Take this book of the law, and put it in the side of the ark of the covenant of the Eternal your G-d.*[2]

In either case it would have been proper for him to write at the beginning of the book of Genesis: "And G-d spoke to Moses all these words, saying." The reason it was written anonymously [without the above introductory phrase] is that Moses our teacher did not write the Torah in the first person like the prophets who did mention themselves. For example, it is often said of Ezekiel, *And the word of the Eternal came unto me saying: 'Son of man,'*[7] and it is said of Jeremiah, *And the word of the Eternal came unto me.*[8] Moses our teacher, however, wrote this history of all former generations and his own genealogy, history and experiences in the third person. Therefore he says *And G-d spoke to Moses, saying to him*[9] as if he were speaking about another person. And because this is so, Moses is not mentioned in the Torah until his birth, and even at that time he is mentioned as if someone else was speaking about him.

Now do not find a difficulty in the matter of Deuteronomy wherein he [Moses] does speak about himself – [as he says,] *And I besought the Eternal;*[10] *And I prayed unto the Eternal,*[11] – for the beginning of that book reads: *These are the words which Moses spoke unto all Israel.*[12] Thus throughout Deuteronomy he is like one who narrates things in the exact language in which they were spoken.

The reason for the Torah being written in this form [namely, the third person] is that it preceded the creation of the world,[13] and, needless to say, it preceded the birth of Moses our teacher. It has been transmitted to us by tradition that it [the Torah] was written with letters of black fire upon a background of white fire.[14] Thus Moses was like a scribe who copies from an ancient book, and therefore he wrote anonymously.

(6) Deuteronomy 31:19. (7) Ezekiel 3:16–17; 12:1, etc. (8) Jeremiah 1:4. (9) Exodus 6:2. (10) Deuteronomy 3:23. (11) *Ibid.*, 9:26. (12) *Ibid.*, 1:1. (13) Shabbath 88 b. (14) Yerushalmi Shekalim 13 b. See also Rashi on Deuteronomy 33:2.

However, it is true and clear that the entire Torah – from the beginning of Genesis to *in the sight of all Israel*[15] [the last words in Deuteronomy] – reached the ear of Moses from the mouth of the Holy One, blessed be He, just as it is said elsewhere, *He pronounced all these words unto me with his mouth, and I wrote them with ink in the book.*[16] G-d informed Moses first of the manner of the creation of heaven and earth and all their hosts, that is, the creation of all things, high and low. Likewise [He informed him of] everything that has been said by prophecy concerning the esoterics of the Divine Chariot [in the vision of Ezekiel][17] and the process of Creation, and what has been transmitted about them to the Sages. [Moses was informed about these] together with an account of the four forces in the lower world: the force of minerals, vegetation in the earth, living motion, and the rational soul. With regard to all of these matters – their creation, their essence, their powers and functions, and the disintegration of those of them that are destroyed[18] – Moses our teacher was apprised, and all of it was written in the Torah, explicitly or by implication. Now our Sages have already said:[19] "Fifty gates [degrees] of understanding were created in the world, and all were transmitted to Moses with one exception, as it is said, *Thou hast made him but little lower than the angels.*"[20] [Concerning this statement of the Sages] that in the creation of the world there are fifty gates of understanding, it is as if it said that there is one gate of understanding pertaining to the creation of the minerals, their force and their effects, one gate of understanding pertaining to the creation of the vegetation in the earth, and similarly, as regards the creation of trees, beasts, fowl, creeping things and fish, that there pertains to each of these one gate of understanding. This series culminates in the creation of the rational soul [for the gate pertaining to this latter creation]

(15) Deuteronomy 34:12. (16) Jeremiah 36:18. Baruch, Jeremiah's scribe, is explaining the manner in which he wrote down his master's prophecies: *he* [Jeremiah] *pronounced all these words*, etc. (17) Ezekiel, Chapter 1. (18) The rational soul in man is not subject to destruction. Hence Ramban writes of "*those of them* that are destroyed," not all. (19) Rosh Hashanah 21 b. (20) Psalms 8:6.

enables man to contemplate the secret of the soul, to know its essence and its power in "its palace" [namely, the body][21] and to attain [that degree of understanding] which is alluded to in the saying of the Sages:[22] "If a person stole, he [who has the aforesaid understanding] knows and recognizes it on him; if a person committed adultery, he knows and recognizes it on him; if one is suspected of having intercourse with a woman in her state of uncleanness, he knows and recognizes it on him. Greater than all is he who recognizes all masters[23] of witchcraft." And from [that level of understanding] a man can ascend to the understanding of the spheres, the heavens and their hosts, for pertaining to each of these there is one gate of wisdom which is unlike the wisdom of the others. The total number of different gates as ascertained by tradition is fifty less one. It is possible that this fiftieth gate concerns a knowledge of the Creator, blessed be He, which is not transmittable to any created being. Pay no regard to the Sages' saying that ["Fifty gates of understanding] *were created,*"[24] for that statement relates to the majority even though one gate was indeed not created. This number [49] is clearly alluded to in the Torah in the counting of the *Omer,*[25] and in the counting of the Jubilee,[26] the secrets of which I will disclose when I attain thereto by the Will of the Holy One, blessed be He.

Everything that was transmitted to Moses our teacher through the forty-nine gates of understanding was written in the Torah explicitly or by implication in words, in the numerical value of the letters or in the form of the letters, that is, whether written normally or with some change in form such as bent or crooked letters and other deviations, or in the tips of the letters and their crownlets, as the Sages have said:[27] "When Moses ascended to heaven he found the Holy One, blessed be He, attaching crownlets

(21) See Ibn Ezra's commentary on Deuteronomy 32:2, which states that the body is the palace of the soul. (22) Heichaloth Rabboth 1:3. (23) "Masters"; in Heichaloth Rabboth: "kinds." (24) Since the fiftieth gate of understanding was never transmitted to any created being, how could the Sages say that fifty "were created"? The answer is that the statement relates to the majority of the gates. (25) Leviticus 23:15: *Seven weeks shall there be complete....* (26) *Ibid.* 25:8. (27) Menachoth 29 b.

to certain letters of the Torah. He [Moses] said to Him, 'What are these for?' He [G-d] said to him, 'One man is destined to interpret mountains of laws on their basis.' "[28] " 'Whence dost thou know this?' He [Rabbi Akiba] answered them: 'This is a law given to Moses on Mount Sinai.' "[29] For these hints cannot be understood except from mouth to mouth [through an oral tradition which can be traced] to Moses, who received it on Sinai.

Based on this tradition, the Sages have said in Shir Hashirim Rabbah[30] concerning King Hezekiah [when he was visited by a delegation from the king of Babylon]:[31] "He showed them the Book of *Tagin* [crownlets]." This book is known and is available to everyone. In it is explained how many crownleted *alephs* there are in the Torah, how many *beths,* and the [frequency of the] rest of the letters and the number of crownlets on each one. The praise which the Sages bestowed on this book and the disclosure of Hezekiah's secret to the delegation were not for the crownlets themselves but rather for a knowledge of their essence and their meanings, which consist of many exceedingly profound secrets.

There, in the Midrash Shir Hashirim Rabbah,[32] they [the Sages] have also said: "It is written, *And He declared unto you His covenant,*[33] which means: *He declared unto you* the Book of Genesis, which relates the beginning of His creation;[34] *which He commanded you to perform, even the ten words,*[33] meaning the ten commandments, ten for Scripture and ten for Talmud.[35] For

(28) *Ibid.* Moses said to G-d: "Show me this man." G-d showed him Rabbi Akiba sitting with eight ranks of disciples. Moses sat down in the eighth rank but was not able to follow the discussions, a fact which deeply grieved him. But then he heard the disciples asking Rabbi Akiba, "Whence dost thou know this?" See now in text of Ramban. (29) Now Moses was content. *Ibid.* (30) Not found in our text. See, however, Shir Hashirim Rabbah 3:3, and see also my Hebrew commentary, p. 4, for further reference on this matter. (31) Isaiah, Chapter 39. (32) 1:28. (33) Deuteronomy 4:13. (34) The interpretation is based upon the similarity between the words *b'riyah* (creation) and *b'ritho* (His covenant). (35) "Ten for Scripture and ten for Talmud." Thus the Oral Law is made equal to the Written Law. The basis for the interpretation seems to be the extra word *la'asoth* (to perform), which is taken to refer to the Oral Law since it teaches us how to perform the commandments.

from what source did Elihu the son of Barachel the Buzite [36] come and reveal to Israel the secrets of the behemoth [37] and the leviathan? [38] And from what source did Ezekiel come and reveal to them the mysteries of the Divine Chariot? [17] It is this which Scripture says, *The king hath brought me into his chambers,"* [39] meaning that everything can be learned from the Torah.

King Solomon, peace be upon him, whom G-d had given wisdom and knowledge, derived it all from the Torah, and from it he studied until he knew the secret of all things created, even of the forces and characteristics of plants, so that he wrote about them even a Book of Medicine, as it is written, *And he spoke of trees, from the cedar that is in Lebanon even unto the hyssop that springeth out of the wall.* [40]

Now I have seen the Aramaic translation of the book called *The Great Wisdom of Solomon,* [41] and in it is written: "There is nothing new in the birth of a king or ruler; there is one entrance for all people into the world, and one exit alike. Therefore I have prayed, and the spirit of wisdom was given to me, and I have called out and the spirit of knowledge came to me; I chose it above scepter and throne." And it is further said there: "It is G-d alone Who gives knowledge that contains no falsehood, [enabling one] to know how the world arose, the composition of the constellations, the beginning, the end and middle of the times, the angles of the ends of the constellations, and how the seasons are produced by the movement of heavens and the fixed positions of the stars, the benign nature of cattle and the fierceness of beasts, the power of the wind and the thoughts of man, the relationship of trees and the forces of roots; everything hidden and everything revealed I know."

(36) Job 32:2. (37) *Ibid.,* 40:15. See following note. (38) *Ibid.,* 40:25. The Behemoth and the Leviathan are mentioned in G-d's response to Job (Chapter 40) and are not found in Elihu's speeches. Rabbi David Luria (in his notes to the Midrash) amends the text of the Midrash to read: "the secrets of the winds and the rains." These are mentioned by Elihu in Chapter 37. (39) Song of Songs 1:4. (40) I Kings 5:13. (41) One of the books of the Apocrypha. In Weisel's Hebrew edition, Verses 4-6 in Chapter 7 come close to the text here mentioned.

All this Solomon knew from the Torah, and he found everything in it – in its simple meanings, in the subtleties of its expressions and its letters and its strokes, as I have mentioned.

Scripture likewise relates concerning him, *And Solomon's wisdom excelled the wisdom of all the children of the east.*[42] That is to say, he was better versed than they in divination and enchanting, for this was their wisdom, as it is said, *For they are replenished from the east, and with soothsayers like the Philistines.*[43] (The Sages similarly said:[44] "What was the wisdom of the children of the east? They knew and were crafty in the divination of birds.") *And all the wisdom of Egypt*[42] means that Solomon was better versed in sorcery, which is the wisdom of Egypt, and in the nature of growing things. As is known from the Book of Egyptian Agriculture,[45] the Egyptians were very well versed in the matters of planting and grafting different species. Thus the Sages have said:[46] "Solomon even planted peppers in the Land of Israel. How was he able to plant them? Solomon was a wise man, and he knew the essence of the foundation of the world. Why was this? [It is written] *Out of Zion, the perfection of beauty, G-d hath shined forth.*[47] Out of Zion the whole world was perfected. How is this known? Why was it called 'the Foundation Stone?' Because the world was founded from it. Now Solomon knew which of its arteries extends to Ethiopia, and upon it he planted peppers, and immediately it produced fruits, for so he says, *And I planted trees in them of all kinds of fruit.*"[48]

We have yet another mystic tradition[49] that the whole Torah is comprised of Names of the Holy One, blessed be He, and that the letters of the words separate themselves into Divine Names when divided in a different manner, as you may imagine by way of

(42) I Kings 5:10. (43) Isaiah 2:6. (44) Pesikta of Rabbi Kahana, *Parah.* Bamidbar Rabbah, Chapter 19. (45) Mentioned in Rambam's Moreh Nebuchim III, 29-30. Ramban also mentions it further, 11:28. Abraham ibn Ezra refers to it in his Commentary to Exodus 2:10. (46) Tanchuma, *Kedoshim* 10. (47) Psalms 50:2. (48) Ecclesiastes 2:5. (49) Zohar *Yithro* 87a: "The whole Torah is the Name of the Holy One, etc." See also my Hebrew commentary, p. 6 for a broader discussion of this matter.

example that the verse of *Bereshith* divides itself into these other words: *berosh yithbare Elokim*. This principle applies likewise to the entire Torah, aside from the combinations and the numerical equivalents of the Holy Names. Our Rabbi Shlomo [Rashi] has already written in his commentaries on the Talmud[50] concerning the manner in which the Great Divine Name of seventy-two letters is derived from the three verses: *And he went,*[51] *And he came,*[52] *And he stretched out.*[53] It is for this reason that a Scroll of the Torah in which a mistake has been made in one letter's being added or subtracted is disqualified [even though the literal meaning remains unchanged], for this principle [that the whole Torah comprises Names of the Holy One, blessed be He], obligates us to disqualify a scroll of the Torah in which one letter *vav* is missing from the word *otham* – of which there are thirty-nine fully-spelled ones in the Torah – [despite the fact that the same word appears many times without a *vav*], or if he [the Scribe] were to add a *vav* to any of the other deficient ones [that is, words which could be written with an additional *vav* but are not so written]. So it is in similar cases even though it matters not one way or another on cursory thought. It is this principle which has caused the Biblical scholars to count every full and defective word in the Torah and Scripture and to compose books on the Masoretic text, going back as far as Ezra the Scribe and Prophet,[54] so that we should be heedful of this, as the Sages derived it from the verse, *And they read in the book in the Law of G-d, distinctly; and they gave the sense, and caused them to understand the reading.*[55]

It would appear that the Torah "written with letters of black fire upon a background of white fire"[14] was in this form we have mentioned, namely, that the writing was contiguous, without break

(50) Sukkah 45 a. (51) Exodus 14:19. (52) *Ibid.*, Verse 20. (53) *Ibid.*, Verse 21. (54) Megillah 15 a. Malachi (the prophet) is identical with Ezra. (55) Nehemiah 8:8. The Sages' interpretation is found in Nedarim 37 b: "*And they read in the book in the law of G–d,* this means the written text; *distinctly,* this is the Targum [translation]; *and they gave the sense,* this has reference to the division in verses; *and they caused them to understand the reading,* this means the punctuating signs [or accents], and some Rabbis say that this is the *Masoreth* [the traditions regarding the full or defective words]."

of words, which made it possible for it to be read by way of Divine Names and also by way of our normal reading which makes explicit the Torah and the commandment. It was given to Moses our teacher using the division of words which expresses the commandment, and orally it was transmitted to him in the rendition which consists of the Divine Names. Thus masters of the Cabala [56] write the letters of the Great Name I have mentioned [namely, the Name containing seventy-two letters] all close to each other, and then these are divided into words consisting of three letters and many other divisions, as is the practice among the masters of the Cabala.

And now, know and see what I shall answer to those who question me concerning my writing a commentary of the Torah. I shall conduct myself in accordance with the custom of the early scholars to bring peace of mind to the students, tired of the exile and the afflictions, who read in the *Seder* [57] on the Sabbaths and festivals, and to attract them with the plain meanings of Scripture and with some things that are pleasant to the listeners and which give grace [58] to the scholars. And may the gracious G-d *be merciful unto us and bless us* [59] so that we shall *find grace and good favor in the sight of G-d and man.* [60]

Now behold I bring into a faithful covenant and give proper counsel to all who look into this book not to reason or entertain any thought concerning any of the mystic hints which I write regarding the hidden matters of the Torah, for I do hereby firmly make known to him [the reader] that my words will not be comprehended nor known at all by any reasoning or contemplation, excepting from the mouth of a wise Cabalist

(56) Literally, "reception." In the Talmud the word *cabala* denotes the whole body of the oral tradition in contrast to the written word of G–d, the Torah. Here, however, as well as in later Hebrew usage the word denotes the system of mystic lore and philosophy which constitutes a distinctive body of esoteric thought. (57) The portion of the Torah assigned for reading on a particular Sabbath or festival. (58) The Hebrew word *chein* (grace) is here an abbreviation for the Hebrew words *chochmah nistarah* [the hidden wisdom or the Cabala]. (59) Psalms 67:2. (60) Proverbs 3:4.

speaking into the ear of an understanding recipient.[61] Reasoning about them is foolishness; any unrelated thought brings much damage and withholds the benefit. *Let him not trust in vanity, deceiving himself,*[62] for these reasonings will bring him nothing but evil as if they spoke falsely against G-d, which cannot be forgiven, as it is said, *The man that strayeth out of understanding shall rest in the congregation of the shades.*[63] *Let them not break through unto the Eternal to gaze,*[64] *For the Eternal our G-d is a devouring fire, even a G-d of jealousies.*[65] And He will show those who are pleasing to Him wonders from His Torah. Rather let such see in our commentaries novel interpretations of the plain meanings of Scripture and Midrashim, and let them take moral instruction from the mouths of our holy Rabbis:[66] "Into that which is beyond you, do not seek; into that which is more powerful than you, do not inquire; about that which is concealed from you, do not desire to know; about that which is hidden from you, do not ask. Contemplate that which is permitted to you, and engage not yourself in hidden things."

(61) The Hebrew is *Mekabel mevin,* which may also mean "an understanding Cabalist," thus suggesting that the recipient too has already been initiated into these mysteries to a lesser degree. (62) Job 15:31. (63) Proverbs 21:16. (64) Exodus 19:21 and 24. (65) Deuteronomy 4:24. (66) Bereshith Rabbah 8:2.

Bereshith

1 1. IN THE BEGINNING G-D CREATED. Rabbi Yitzchak said: The Torah, which is the book of laws, should have begun with the verse, *This month shall be unto you the first of the months,*[1] which is the first commandment given to Israel.[2] What then is the reason that it begins with the creation? Should the nations of the world say to Israel, "You are robbers because you took unto yourselves the lands of the seven nations of Canaan," they [Israel] may reply to them, "The whole world belongs to the Holy One, blessed be He. He gave it to whom He pleased, and according to His Will, He took it [the land] from them and gave it to us."

This is a homiletic exposition[3] as quoted by Rabbi Shlomo [Rashi] in his commentaries.

One may object that it was indeed very necessary to begin the Torah with the chapter of *In the beginning G-d created* for this is the root of faith, and he who does not believe in this and thinks the world was eternal denies the essential principle of the [Judaic] religion and has no Torah at all.[4]

(1) Exodus 12:2. (2) It is true the book of Genesis contains three commandments (1:28; 17:10; 32:33), but after the Revelation on Sinai these laws became incumbent upon Israel. Hence the verse *this month*, etc., is "the *first* commandment given to Israel" as a people. (3) Found in Tanchuma (Buber), *Bereshith* 11. See also Rashi (Berliner) p. 424. (4) A person who thinks the world is eternal cannot believe in miracles since, if G-d did not create the world, He cannot possibly change it. Ramban explains in many places (e.g., see further, 17:1; 46:15) that all Divine promises concerning the blessings or imprecations which will follow upon our observance or disregard of the Torah are miraculous in nature of "invisible miracles." A person who believes that the world is eternal thus has "no Torah at all." See further my English work, Ramban: His Life and Teachings, Chapter 13.

The answer is that the process of creation is a deep mystery not to be understood from the verses, and it cannot truly be known except through the tradition going back to Moses our teacher who received it from the mouth of the Almighty, and those who know it are obligated to conceal it.[5] It is for this reason that Rabbi Yitzchak said that it was not necessary for the Torah to begin with the chapter of *In the beginning G-d created* and the narration of what was created on the first day, what was done on the second and other days, as well as a prolonged account of the creation of Adam and Eve, their sin and punishment, and the story of the Garden of Eden and the expulsion of Adam from it, because all this cannot be understood completely from the verses. It is all the more unnecessary for the story of the generations of the flood and of the dispersion to be written in the Torah for there is no great need of these narratives, and, for people who believe in the Torah, it would suffice without these verses. They would believe in the general statement mentioned to them in the Ten Commandments: *For in six days the Eternal made heaven and earth, the sea, and all that is in them, and rested on the seventh day,*[6] and the knowledge of the process of creation would remain with individuals as a tradition from Moses who received the law on Sinai together with the Oral Torah.

Rabbi Yitzchak then gave a reason for it. The Torah began with the chapter of *In the beginning G-d created* and recounted the whole subject of creation until the making of man, how He [G-d] granted him dominion over the works of His hands, and that He put all things under his feet;[7] and how the Garden of Eden, which is the choicest of places created in this world, was made the place of his abode until his sin caused his expulsion therefrom; and how the people of the generation of the flood were completely expelled from the world on account of their sin, and the only righteous one among them — he [Noah] and his children — were saved; and how the sin of their descendants caused them to be scattered to various places and dispersed to different countries, and how subsequently

(5) Chagigah 11 b: "The process of Creation may not be expounded before two." (6) Exodus 20:11. (7) See Psalms 8:7.

they seized unto themselves places *after their families, in their nations,*[8] as chance permitted. If so, it is proper that when a people continues to sin it should lose its place and another people should come to inherit its land, for such has been the rule of G-d in the world[9] from the beginning. This is true all the more regarding that which is related in Scripture, namely that Canaan was cursed and sold as a servant forever.[10] It would therefore not be proper that he inherit the choicest of places of the civilized world. Rather, the servants of G-d – the seed of His beloved one, Abraham[11] – should inherit it, even as it is written, *And He gave them the lands of the nations, and they took the labor of the peoples in possession; that they might keep His statutes, and observe His laws.*[12] That is to say, He expelled those who rebelled against Him, and settled therein those who served Him so that they know by serving Him they will inherit it, whereas if they sin against Him, the land will vomit them out, just as it vomited out the nation before them.[13]

Elucidating the explanation I have written are the words of the Sages in Bereshith Rabbah, wherein they say as follows:[14] "Rabbi Yehoshua, of the city of Siknin, in the name of Rabbi Levi opened [his discourse on this chapter of Creation with the verse]: *He hath declared to His people the power of His works.*[15] Why did the Holy One, blessed be He, reveal to Israel what was created on the first day and what was created on the second day? It is on account of the seven nations who inhabited the land of Canaan, so that they should not taunt Israel and say to them: 'Are you not a nation of robbers?' Israel could then reply to them: 'And you, is it not booty in your hands? *Have not the Caphtorim that came forth from Caphtor destroyed them and dwelt in their stead?*[16] The world and the fullness thereof belong to the Holy One, blessed be He. When He willed it, He gave it to you, and when He willed it, He took it from you and gave it to us.' It is this which Scripture

(8) Genesis 10:5. (9) The Hebrew word *ba'aretz* (world) may also refer here to "the land," especially the Land of Israel. See Ramban further, 26:5. (10) Genesis 9:25. (11) See Isaiah 41:8. (12) Psalms 105:44-45. (13) See Leviticus 18:28. (14) 1:3. (15) Psalms 111:6. (16) Deuteronomy 2:23.

says, *To give them the heritage of the nations.*[15] *He hath declared to His people the power of His works* in order *to give them the heritage of the nations*. Hence He told them the account of creation."

There is yet another source for the subject I have mentioned: the mysteries in the process of creation. It is what our Rabbis of blessed memory have said:[17] *"He hath declared to His people the power of His works.*[15] To declare the power of the process of creation to a mortal being is impossible. Therefore, Scripture closed the matter: *In the beginning G-d created.*" Thus is elucidated what we have said on this subject.[18]

IN THE BEGINNING G-D CREATED. Rashi wrote: "This verse calls aloud for elucidation,[19] as our Rabbis have explained it:[20] "For the sake of Torah which is called *reshith,* as it is said, *The Eternal made me as 'reshith'* (the beginning) *of His way.*[21] and for the sake of Israel who is called *reshith,* as it is said, *Israel is the Eternal's hallowed portion, the 'reshith'* (first-fruits) *of His increase.*"[22]

(17) This Midrash is quoted by Rambam in his Preface to Moreh Nebuchim. See Batei Midrashoth, ed. Wertheimer, I, p. 251. (18) That the details in the process of creation and the settlement of the earth were written for the purpose of justifying Israel's possession of the land while the essential process of creation itself remains a mystery. (19) The difficulties in the verse are: (a) The word *bereshith* (in the beginning) appears throughout the Bible in a construct form such as: *In the beginning of the reign of Jehoiakim* (Jeremiah 27:1). But here it cannot be in construct form since such a form can be used only in connection with a noun, and the word *bara* (He created) is a verb. (b) Again, it cannot be said that here *bereshith* is actually in a construct form and that a missing noun is implied, thus making the sense of the verse, "in the beginning of all, G—d created...," for if so, the following difficulty presents itself: since Scripture, according to this interpretation, sets out to tell us the order in which things were created, why does it say in Verse 2 *And the spirit of G-d hovered over the face of the waters* when it has not yet told us when water was created? Hence Rashi turns to a Midrashic interpretation in which the word *reshith* is another name for the Torah and Israel. The word *bereshith* is thus not in a construct form but stands by itself, and the sense conveyed is: "For the sake of that which is *reshith* [Torah and Israel] G-d created." (20) Bereshith Rabbah 1:6; Tanchuma (Buber) *Bereshith* 3. (21) Proverbs 8:22. (22) Jeremiah 2:3.

This Midrash of our Rabbis is very hidden and secret for there are many things the Rabbis found that are called *reshith* and concerning which they give Midrashic interpretations, and those wanting in faith count their multitude. For example, they [the Rabbis] have said:[23] "For the merit acquired by [fulfilling the commandments associated with] three things has the world been created: for the merit of the Dough-offering, for the merit of Tithes and for the merit of the First-fruits. *In the beginning G-d created. Reshith* surely signifies the Dough-offering, as it is said, *The first of your dough.*[24] *Reshith* surely signifies the Tithes, as it is said, *The first of thy corn.*[25] *Reshith* surely signifies the First-fruits, as it is said, *The first-fruits of thy land.*"[26]

The Rabbis have further said:[23] "For the merit acquired by Moses [the world has been created], as it is said, *And he chose a first part for himself.*"[27]

Their intent in the above texts is as follows: the word *bereshith* alludes to the creation of the world by Ten Emanations, and hints in particular to the emanation called Wisdom, in which is the foundation of everything, even as it says, *The Eternal hath founded the earth by wisdom.*[28] This is the Heave-offering [referred to in the Midrash mentioned above], and it is holy; it has no precise measure,[29] thus indicating the little understanding created beings have of it. Now just as a man counts ten measures – this alludes to the Ten Emanations – and sets aside one measure of the ten as a Tithe, so do the wise men contemplate the tenth Emanation and speak about it. The Dough-offering, which is the single commandment pertaining to the dough, alludes to this. Now Israel, which is called *reshith* as mentioned above, is "the

(23) Bereshith Rabbah 1:6. (24) Numbers 15:20. (25) Deuteronomy 18:4. (26) Exodus 23:19. (27) Deuteronomy 33:21. Reference here is to Moses who took the territory of Kings Sihon and Og as he knew that his grave was to be therein. (See Rashi, *ibid.*) It was thus for the sake of this meritorious person, of whom *reshith* was said, that the world was created. (28) Proverbs 3:19. (29) By law of the Torah, the Heave-offering given to the priest has no fixed measure; the owner may give according to his discretion. "Even one grain frees the whole mound" (Kiddushin 58 b). Similarly, our conception of Divine wisdom is infinitesimal in relation to its true scope.

congregation of Israel," which is compared in the Song of Songs to a bride and whom Scripture in turn calls "daughter," "sister" and "mother." The Rabbis have already expressed this in a homiletic interpretation of the verse, *Upon the crown wherewith his mother hath crowned him,*[30] and in other places. Similarly, the verse concerning Moses, *And he chose a first part for himself,*[27] which they [the Rabbis in the above Midrash] interpret to mean that Moses our teacher contemplated [the Deity] through a lucid speculum,[31] and he saw that which is called *reshith* (the first) for himself, and therefore he merited the Torah. Thus all the above Midrashim have one meaning. Now it is impossible to discuss this explanation at length in writing, and even an allusion is dangerous since people might have thoughts concerning it which are untrue. But I have mentioned this [i.e., the above brief explanation] in order to close the mouths of those wanting in faith and of little wisdom, who scoff at the words of our Rabbis.

IN THE BEGINNING. Rashi wrote: "If you wish to explain it [the word *bereshith*] in accordance with its plain meaning, explain it thus: at the beginning of the creation of the heaven and earth, and the earth was formless and void and there was darkness, the Holy One, blessed be He, said, *Let there be light.*" If so, the whole text leads into the creation of light.

Rabbi Abraham ibn Ezra explained it in an identical way. However, he established that the letter *vav* in the word *veha'aretz* (and the earth) does not serve [as a connecting letter as it normally does and which would mean "and," but it serves rather as the word "when."] There are many such examples in Scripture. The meaning then according to Rabbi Abraham would be: at the beginning of the creation of heaven and dry land, there was no habitable place on earth; rather, it was unformed and void and covered with water, and G-d said, *Let there be light.* According to Abraham ibn Ezra's opinion, only light[32] was created on the first day.

(30) Song of Songs 3:11. (31) So clearly stated in Yebamoth 49 b. (32) According to Rashi in Verse 6 (also 2:4), the sun, etc., was also created on the first day.

The difficulty which Rabbi Shlomo [Rashi] had which led him to the above interpretation is, as he said: For if Scripture intended to teach the order in which the acts of creation took place, it should have written *barishonah* [instead of *bereshith*], since wherever the word *reshith* occurs in Scripture it is in the construct state. But there is the verse, *Declaring the end 'mereshith' [from the beginning].*[33] And if one will connect it with the missing word *davar* [thing – thus making the verse read:"Declaring the end of a thing from the beginning of a thing"–] here too it could be connected to a missing word.[34] There is also the verse, *And he chose 'reshith' (a first part) for himself.*[27] [Here again the word *reshith* is not used in the construct state.] And Rashi raised other objections.

Now listen to the correct and clear explanation of the verse in its simplicity. The Holy One, blessed be He, created all things from absolute non-existence. Now we have no expression in the sacred language for bringing forth something from nothing other than the word *bara* (created). Everything that exists under the sun or above was not made from non-existence at the outset. Instead He brought forth from total and absolute nothing a very thin substance devoid of corporeality but having a power of potency, fit to assume form and to proceed from potentiality into reality. This was the primary matter created by G-d; it is called by the Greeks *hyly* (matter). After the *hyly,* He did not create anything, but He formed and made things with it, and from this *hyly* He brought everything into existence and clothed the forms and put them into a finished condition.

Know that the heavens and all that is in them consist of one substance, and the earth and everything that is in it consist of one substance. The Holy One, blessed be He, created these two substances from nothing;[35] they alone were created, and everything else was constructed from them.

(33) Isaiah 46:10. Here the word *reshith* is not in the construct state. (34) Thus reading: *Bereshith kol,* (In the beginning of everything [G–d created]). (35) Such is also the theory of Rambam: "All things on earth have one common substance; the heavens and the things in them have one substance different from the first" (Moreh Nebuchim II, 26).

This substance, which the Greeks called *hyly*, is called in the sacred language *tohu*, the word being derived from the expression of the Sages:[36] "*betohei* (when the wicked bethinks himself) of his doings in the past." If a person wants to decide a name for it [this primordial matter], he may bethink himself, change his mind and call it by another name since it has taken on no form to which the name should be attached. The form which this substance finally takes on is called in the sacred language *bohu*, which is a composite word made up of the two words *bo hu* (in it there is [substance]). This may be compared to the verse, *Thou art not able 'asohu' (to perform it),*[37] in which case the word *asohu* is missing a *vav* and an *aleph* [and is a composite of the two words] *aso hu*. It is this which Scripture says, *And he shall stretch over it the line of 'tohu' (confusion) and the stones of 'bohu.'*[38] [The *tohu* in Hebrew or *hyly* in Greek] is the line by which the craftsman delineates the plan of his structure and that which he hopes to make. This is derived from the expression, *Kavei (Hope) unto G-d.*[39] *The stones* are forms in the building. Similarly it is written, *They are accounted by Him as nought and 'tohu,'*[40] as *tohu* comes after nothingness and there is nothing yet in it.

So the Rabbis have also said in Sefer Yetzirah:[41] "He created substance from *tohu*, and made that which was nothing something."

They have furthermore said in the Midrash of Rabbi Nechunya ben Hakanah:[42] "Rabbi Berachyah said: 'What is the meaning of the verse, *And the earth was 'tohu' (without form) 'vavohu'* (*and void*)? What is the meaning of the word "was?" It had already been *tohu*. And what is *tohu*? It is a thing which astonishes

(36) Kiddushin 40 b. (37) Exodus 18:18. (38) Isaiah 34:11. "The stones," which are forms in the building (as explained later on by Ramban), thus constitute substance as expressed in the Hebrew *bohu*. (39) Psalms 27:14. (40) Isaiah 40:17. (41) 2:6. Sefer Yetzirah (Book of Creation) is one of the earliest Hebrew books of the Cabala tradition. (See introduction to Bereshith, Note 56.) Some of the profoundest mystic commentaries have been written on this book. See my Hebrew work, Kithvei Haramban, Vol. 2, pp. 451-461. (42) Called also Sefer Habahir (Book of the Bright Light), 2. This book too is a classic in the mystic teachings of the Cabala. It was written in the style and manner of the Midrashim.

people. It was then turned into *bohu*. And what is *bohu*? It is a thing which has substance, as it is written, [*bohu* is a composite of the two words] '*bo hu*' (in it there is substance).' "

3. AND 'ELOKIM' (G-D) SAID. The word *Elokim* means "the Master of all forces," for the root of the word is *e-il*, meaning force, and the word *Elokim* is a composite consisting of the words *e-il heim*, as if the word *e-il* is in a construct state, and *heim*, [literally] "they," alludes to all other forces. Thus *Elokim* means "the Force of all forces." A secret will yet be disclosed in connection with this.[43]

If so, the simple correct explanation of the verse is as follows: *In the beginning*[44] *G-d created the heavens* means He brought forth their matter from nothing; *and the earth* means that He brought forth its matter from nothing. *And the earth*, includes all the four elements,[45] [not merely the land] as in the verse, *And the heaven and the earth were finished,*[46] which includes the entire lower sphere, and in *Praise the Eternal from the earth, ye sea-monsters, and all deeps,*[47] and as in many other verses. Now with this creation, which was like a very small point having no substance, everything in the heavens and on the earth was created. The word *eth* –[*eth hashamayim ve'eth ha'aretz*] – is like "the essence of a thing." The Sages have always set it forth as serving to include,[48] since it is derived from the expression, *The morning 'atha' (cometh), and also the night.*[49] And so did our Rabbis say:[50] " *'Eth hashamayim (the heavens)' – eth* includes the sun, moon, stars and constellations. '*Ve'eth ha'aretz (and the earth)' – ve'eth* includes the trees, herbs, and the Garden of Eden." These include all created things which are corporeal.

Now after having said that with one command G-d created at first the heavens and the earth and all their hosts, Scripture returns and explains that the earth after this creation was *tohu*, that is,

(43) See Ramban, Exodus 20:3. (44) Ramban thus indicates his opinion that the word *bereshith* is not in a construct state. This is contrary to Rashi, as explained above. (45) Fire, wind, water, and earth. (46) Genesis 2:1. (47) Psalms 148:7. (48) Pesachim 22 b. (49) Isaiah 21:12. (50) Bereshith Rabbah 1:19.

matter without substance. It became *bohu* when He clothed it with form. Then it [Scripture] explains that in this form was included the form of the four elements: fire, water, earth, and air. The word *ha'aretz* (the earth) includes these four elements. In this verse, the element of fire is called "darkness"[51] because the elemental fire is dark. Were it red, it would redden the night for us. The element of water with which the dust was kneaded is here called "deep."[51] This is why the waters of the oceans are called "the deeps," as it is written, *The deeps cover them;*[52] *The deeps were congealed;*[53] *The deep was round about me.*[54] The bottom of the ocean is also referred to as "deep:" *And He rebuked the Red Sea, and it was dried up, and He led them through the depths, as a wilderness;*[55] *He led them through the deep as a horse in the wilderness.*[56] And the element air is here called "spirit."[57]

Now it is already known that the four elements fill up the whole space with matter.[58] That which stands still is the sphere of earth. The waters surround the earth, the air encompasses the waters, and the fire envelopes the air.[59] Scripture thus states that the earth took on form, and the fire above enveloped the intermingled waters and dust, and the wind blew and rose in the darkness and hovered over the waters.

It appears to me that this [primeval] point, [which G-d created out of absolute nought], which took on form and became *bohu*, is what the Sages call:[60] " 'The rock of foundation' from which the world was founded."

(51) *And darkness was upon the face of the deep.* So also explained in the Moreh Nebuchim, II:30: "By *Choshech* the element fire is meant, nothing else." Ramban's reasoning on this point is also found there. (52) Exodus 15:15. (53) *Ibid.*, 8. (54) Jonah 2:6. (55) Psalms 106:9. (56) Isaiah 63:13. (57) *And the spirit of G-d hovered over the face of the waters.* (58) "This sphere in its totality is composed of the celestial orbs, the four elements and their combinations; there is no vacuum whatever therein, but the whole space is filled up with matter." (Guide of the Perplexed, Friedlander's translation, I, 72.) (59) From the language of Rambam, *ibid.* It is to be noted that Ramban follows Yehudah al Charizi's translation of Rambam's philosophic work and not that of Shmuel ibn Tibbon. See my Hebrew work, The Life of Ramban, pp. 23-24, on the far-reaching significance of this point. (60) Yoma 54 b. This "foundation rock" is the stone on which the Ark of the Covenant rested in the Holy of Holies in King Solomon's Temple.

The purport of the verses is thus: In the beginning G-d created the heavens from nought, and He created the earth from nought. The earth, when created, was *tohu* and then it became *bohu*, and in these there were "darkness" [i.e., fire, as explained above], water, dust and the wind blowing upon the water. Thus everything was created and made. The reason why *ruach* (wind) is attached to the name of G-d [as it says, *and the spirit of God*] is that it is the least substantial of all elements [61] and is above them, hovering upon the face of the waters only by command of the Holy One, blessed be He.

In case you seek information concerning the creation of the incorporeal angels, you will not find it explained in the Torah. The Sages, however, have explained concerning them that they were created on the second day, so that you should not say that they assisted in the creation of the world. [62] But if you will merit and understand the secret of the word *bereshith* and why Scripture does not begin by saying, "G-d created in the beginning," you will know that, in the way of truth, [63] Scripture tells about the lower creations and alludes to the higher ones and that the word *bereshith* refers covertly to the Emanation called Wisdom, which is the head of all beginnings, as I have mentioned. This is why they translated *bereshith* in the Jerusalem Targum to mean "in wisdom," and the word is adorned in the Torah with a crown on the letter *beth*. [64]

AND G-D SAID, 'LET THERE BE LIGHT.' The word "saying" here indicates Will, as in the verse, *What dost thy soul say, that I should do it for thee?* [65] which means, "What do you want and desire?" Similarly, *And let her be thy master's son's wife, as the Eternal hath spoken* [66] means, "...as He hath willed, for such is the

(61) Although fire is thinner than wind, since the element of fire is alluded to in the verse by the word "darkness," as explained above, it would not be fitting to attach it to the name of G–d. (Bachya). (62) Bereshith Rabbah 3:11. (63) A reference to the true wisdom of the Cabala which enables one to grasp the mysteries of the Torah. (64) The adornment on the top of the letter *beth* hints at the *Kether* (Crown) above, from which all emanations issue. It is also referred to as *Ein Sof* (the Infinite). See my Hebrew commentary, p. 15. (65) I Samuel 20:4. (66) Genesis 24:51.

Will before Him." Or, it may be [that the word "saying" here means] "thinking," as in the verses, *Thou sayest in thy heart;*[67] *And the chiefs of Judah shall say in their heart.*[68] The purport is to state that the creation was not done with toil. Our Rabbis have also called this "thought." Thus they have said:[69] "The thought [concerning what was to be created on a particular day] was during the day; the deed itself was at sunset." This teaches that creation was thought out, that there is a reason for everything created, that creation was not a simple manifestation of mere Will alone.

The word "being" [*Let there 'be'*] indicates a deed for the present time,[70] just as: *And thou wouldst be their king*[71] [meaning: their king from this moment on]. Therefore Scripture says that when He created the substance of the heavens, He said that from that substance there should come forth a shining matter called "light."

AND THERE WAS LIGHT. The verse does not say, "And it was so," as it is said on other days, because the light did not remain in this state all the time, as did the other creations. Concerning this matter, our Rabbis have an interpretation with a profound secret.[72]

Know that the term "day" as used in the story of the creation was, in the case of the creation of heaven and earth, a real day, composed of hours and seconds, and there were six days like the six days of the workweek, as is the plain meaning of the verse. In the profounder sense, the Emanations issuing from the Most High are called "days," for every Divine Saying[73] which evoked an existence is called "day." These were six, for *Unto G-d there is the*

(67) Isaiah 47:8. (68) Zechariah 12:5. (69) Bereshith Rabbah 12:14. (70) Thus unlike Rashi and R'dak (Rabbi David Kimchi), who hold that the reference here is to the creation of the luminaries, such as the sun, moon, etc., which were not suspended in the firmament until the fourth day (see Rashi, Verse 14), Ramban explains that the light of the first day was of a special substance; hence Scripture does not say, *And it was so*, since that light did not remain forever in its original state. (71) Nehemiah 6:6. (72) Ramban's hint here is to the Sefer Habahir, 190. See my Hebrew commentary pp. 15–16. (73) The tenfold expression, *And G-d said*, found in the chapter of Creation.

greatness, and the power, etc.[74] The Sayings,[73] however, are ten because regarding the first three Emanations, the term "day" does not apply at all. The explanation of the order of the verses in terms of this profound interpretation is sublime and recondite. Our knowledge of it is less than that of a drop from the vast ocean.

4. AND G-D SAW THE LIGHT, THAT IT WAS GOOD. Rabbi Shlomo [Rashi] wrote: "Here too[75] we must depend on the words of the homiletic Agadah G-d saw that the wicked were unworthy of using the light, and so He set it aside for the righteous in the World to Come. But according to the plain meaning of the verse, explain it thus: He saw that the light was good, and that it was not seemly for it and the darkness to function in a confused manner. He therefore assigned the one's sphere of activity to the daytime and the one's sphere of activity to the nighttime."

And Rabbi Abraham ibn Ezra said: "The word *vayar (and He saw)* has the same meaning here as in *Vera'iti ani (And I saw),*[76] which refers to the thought in the heart. *And He divided* refers to His giving them different names."[77]

But the words of both Rashi and Ibn Ezra are incorrect for if they were, it would appear that there was on the part of G-d a

(74) I Chronicles 29:11. (75) A reference to Rashi's similar comment on the first word of the Torah – *bereshith* (see above). The difficulty here in the text is twofold: (a) It is first written, *and darkness was upon the face of the deep,* and then G–d said, *Let there be light.* Thus there already was a separation between light and darkness. Why then does Scripture continue by stating, *and G–d divided the light from the darkness?* (b) Concerning all other acts of creation, the expression "And G–d saw that it was good" is found at the completion of the act of creation, while here this phrase is written (in the beginning of Verse 4) *before* the completion. The Agadah, which Rashi quotes, answers: (a) *vayavdel* means here that He set apart the light for the righteous in the world to come. (b) *ki tov* (that it was good) could not have been written *after* the separation of the light for the righteous from the ordinary light, since the remaining light was no longer perfect. Therefore, *ki tov* is mentioned *before* the setting aside of the light. (76) Daniel 10:7. (77) Ibn Ezra's opinion is thus that the division was not because it was unseemly that the light and darkness function in a confused manner, but it was for the purpose of assigning each one a separate name.

change of mind and new counsel, as if to say that after G-d said, *'Let there be light' and there was light*, He saw that it was good, and therefore He divided between it and darkness just as a human being who does not know the nature of something until it comes into existence! Rather, the order followed in the process of creation is that the bringing forth of things into actual existence is called *amirah* (saying). Thus: *And G-d said, 'Let there be light;' And G-d said, 'Let there be a firmament;'* [78] *And G-d said, 'Let the earth put forth grass.'* [79] And the permanence of things called forth into existence is called *re'iyah* (seeing), as *And I saw* in Ecclesiastes,[80] and similarly, *And the woman saw that the tree was good for food.*[81] In the language of the Rabbis we also find, "I see the words of Admon."[82] Likewise, *And the king said unto Zadok the priest, 'Seest thou? return into the city in peace.'* [83] The purport of the word "seeing" is thus to indicate that their continuing existence is at His Will, and if that Will should for a second depart from them, they will turn into nought. Now just as Scripture says in connection with the work of each day, *And G-d saw that it was good* and on the sixth day when everything was completed it says, *And G-d saw everything that He had made, and behold, it was very good,*[84] so does it say on the first day when light came into existence, *And G-d saw ... that it was good*, meaning He desired its existence forever. The verse adds "the light" [*And G-d saw 'the light' that it was good*], because had it just said, "And G-d saw that it was good," it would have referred to the creation of the heaven and the earth, and at that time He had not yet decreed for them permanence, as they did not remain as they were. Instead, from the substance created on the first day, the firmament was made on the second day, and on the third the waters and the dust were separated and the dry land – which He called "earth" – was formed. He then decreed for them permanence, and said concerning them, *And G-d saw that it was good.*[85]

(78) Verse 6. (79) Verse 11. (80) 2:13. (81) Genesis 3:6. (82) Kethuboth 109 a. (83) II Samuel 15:27. (84) Verse 31. (85) Verse 10.

AND G-D DIVIDED THE LIGHT FROM THE DARKNESS. This is not "the darkness" mentioned in the first verse[86] which, as explained above, refers to the element of fire; rather, the "darkness" mentioned here means the absence of light, since G-d gave a length of time to the light and decreed that it be absent afterwards until it returns.

Now some commentators[87] have said that this light was created in front of the Holy One, blessed be He, that is to say, in the west,[88] and He immediately caused it to disappear for the period of the night, and afterwards it gave light for the period of the day. This is the reason for the verse, *And there was evening and there was morning*, since the night came first and afterwards the day, and both of them came after the existence of the light.

But this is not correct at all, for in this way they might add a short day to the six days of creation.[89] It is possible, however, to say that the light was created in front of Him, blessed be He, but did not extend over the four elements mentioned [in the second verse, as explained above] and then He divided between it and the darkness by assigning to each a certain period. Light now remained before Him for the length of night, and then in the morning, He caused the light to shine upon the elements. In this way night preceded day.

It is further possible that we should say that when the heavens and the earth came forth from nought into existence, as mentioned

(86) "First verse." It is actually mentioned in Verse 2. However, in view of Ramban's interpretation above that the first two verses tell of everything else to come, he refers to Verse 2 as "the first verse." (87) Reference here is to Yehuda Halevi who, in his philosophic work Al Khazari, sets forth this theory: The first light was created at the time of sunset, and it was an illumination which soon passed away, leaving the world in darkness. The established order was then that night preceded day, as it is written, *It was evening and it was morning* (2:20, Hirschfeld's translation). See also my Hebrew commentary, 2d edition, p. 547, that Ramban may also refer here to Rabbeinu Zerachyah Halevi, who was of a similar opinion. (88) In accordance with the opinion of Rabbi Abahu who says, "The Divine Presence is in the West" (Baba Bathra 25a). (89) Since night and day were *after* the creation of light, and light was created at the time of sunset, it follows that there was a short day (that is, light without darkness) preceding the *first* day. Thus a short day is added to the six days of creation.

in the first verse, time came into being, for although our time consisting of minutes and hours is measured in light and darkness, yet from the moment some substance came into existence time was already part of it. If so, after the heavens and the earth were created they so remained for the length of a night without light. Then He said, *'Let there be light,' and there was light*, and He decreed that it remain the same period as the first, and that after that it be absent from the elements. Thus, *there was evening, and there was morning.*

5. AND G-D CALLED THE LIGHT DAY. The verse states that time was created, and G-d made the length of the day and the length of the night.

The purport of the word *vayikra (And He called)* is [to indicate that] since Adam later gave names [to all the beasts, the fowl, etc.],[90] it states that those things which were made before his existence were given names by G-d. This is the opinion of Rabbi Abraham ibn Ezra.[91]

The correct interpretation is that the matter of calling a name here indicates the division which bounded them when they assumed their form. Thus did the Rabbis say:[92] "[G-d said to the light,] 'The day shall be your boundary,' [and to darkness He said,] 'The night shall be your boundary.' "

AND THERE WAS EVENING AND THERE WAS MORNING. There was evening and there was morning of one day. The beginning of the night is called *erev* [which also means "mingling"] because shapes of things appear confused in it, and the beginning of the day is called *boker* [which also means "examining"] because then a man can distinguish between various forms. This coincides with the explanation of Rabbi Abraham ibn Ezra.

By way of the simple explanation of Scripture, it could not have said, [*And there was evening and there was morning*] "the first

(90) Further, 2:20. (91) In Verse 8. (92) Bereshith Rabbah 3:7.

day,"[93] because the second had not yet been made; "the first" precedes a "second" in number or degree but both exist, whereas "one" does not connote the existence of a second.

Some scholars explain[94] that *one day* is a reference to the rotation of the sphere upon the face of the whole earth in twenty-four hours, as every moment thereof is morning in some different place and night in the opposite place.[95] If so, the verse alludes to that which will take place in the firmament after the luminaries will be placed in the firmament of the heavens.

6. LET THERE BE A FIRMAMENT. G-d now said that the substance which had come into being first – that which He created from nought – should be a firmament, stretched as a tent in the midst of the waters, separating between waters and waters. It is possible that this is what the Rabbis intended by their saying,[96] "Rav said, 'The heavens were in a fluid form on the first day, and on the second day they solidified.' Rav thus said, '*Let there be a firmament* means let the firmament become strong.' Rabbi Yehudah the son of Rabbi Shimon said, 'Let the firmament become like a plate, just as you say in the verse, *And they did beat* – *[vayerak'u* contains the same root as *raki'a*, firmament] – *the gold into thin plates.*' "[97]

IN THE MIDST OF THE WATERS. This means in the center of the waters, between the higher waters and the lower waters. For there is the same distance between the firmament and the waters upon the earth as between the higher waters and the firmament.

(93) Instead, it says *one day*. See Rashi who says that according to the regular mode of expression it should have really said "the first day." He explains, however, the expression "one day" on the basis of the Midrash: It is "because the Holy One, blessed be He, was then the Only One (the Sole Being) in His universe, since the angels were not created until the second day." *One day* thus means "the day of the One Being." It is this interpretation of Rashi that Ramban alludes to when he comments that according to the simple meaning of Scripture it could not have said, "the first day." (94) Ibn Ezra, Verse 5, and Rambam, Moreh Nebuchim, II, 30. (95) *One day* thus means that the entire day consists of evening and morning occurring simultaneously in different places. (96) Bereshith Rabbah 4:1. (97) Exodus 39:3.

Thus you may infer that the upper waters are suspended in space by the command of G-d. Thus it is explained in Bereshith Rabbah[98] and in Rashi's commentary. This is part of the process of creation [which those who know it are obliged to conceal]; so do not expect me to write anything about it, as the subject is one of the mysteries of the Torah, and the verses in their plain meaning do not require such an interpretation since Scripture itself did not go into it at length, and to give the interpretation is forbidden even to those who know it, and so much the more to us.

7. AND G-D MADE THE FIRMAMENT. The word *asi'yah* (doing) always means adjusting something to its required proportion.

AND IT WAS SO. On the first day, *And there was light* is written after *And G-d said, 'Let there be light,'* in order to explain that after the command of G-d, it [the light] came forth into actuality and was as He decreed it to be. But here, after the command, *Let there be a firmament,* it is written, *And G-d made the firmament, and divided,* etc.; why then has Scripture added here, *And it was so?* It is to tell us that it was to be ever so, for all times.

But Rabbi Abraham ibn Ezra explained that the expression *and it was so* is attached to the verse which follows, meaning *when* it was so, G-d called the firmament Heaven. That is not correct.

In Bereshith Rabbah[99] the Rabbis have said: "*And G-d made the firmament.* This is one of the verses which Ben Zoma[100] found difficult:[101] *And G-d made,* etc. But was not [the world created] by command, as it is written, *By word of the Eternal were the heavens made?*"[102] Now Ben Zoma's difficulty was not only on account of the word *vaya'as (And He made),* since on the

(98) 4:2. (99) 4:7. (100) A colleague of Rabbi Akiba. He was one of the four men of his time who were deeply engaged in the interpretation of the mystical doctrine of creation. See Chagiga 14 b. (101) Literally: "caused the world to shake." (102) Psalms 33:6.

fourth,[103] fifth,[104] and sixth day,[105] *vaya'as* is also written. Rather, his difficulty was, as I have said, that on the other days, immediately after G-d's command, it is written, *And it was so*, indicating that it came into being immediately after the command, but here on the second day, after it says, *And G-d said – vaya'as (And He made)* is written! This was his question. Perhaps Ben Zoma had some secret interpretation which he did not want to reveal. This is the explanation of the cause of his difficulty.

8. AND G-D CALLED THE FIRMAMENT HEAVEN. On the second day He gave them this name when He clothed them with the form of the firmament for on the first day the heavens were still in the process of creation, but the name was not attached to them until they took on this form.

The meaning of this name [*shamayim* – heavens] is as if it had the sign of a *segol* under the letter *shin* [the prefix *shin* thus voweled means "that" or "for"] just as in *Shalamah (For why) should I be as one that veileth herself?*[106] It is thus as if He said that they [the heavens] are waters which have congealed and stretched like a tent in the midst of the upper and lower waters. By this name *shamayim* He has made known the secret of their creation.

In the *Gemara* Tractate Chagigah,[107] the Rabbis have said, "What is the meaning of the word *shamayim*? It means *shem mayim.*"[108] If so, there is one *mem* missing here in the word *shamayim* on account of the adjoining of two similar letters, just as in the word *yeruba'al* [which stands for *yareb bo ba'al* – let Baal contend against him].[109] The word *shamayim* is thus as if it said *shem mayim*, meaning that "heaven" is the name given the

(103) Verse 16. (104) Verse 21. On the fifth day the word *vaya'as* is not found; only *vayibra (and He created)*. (105) Verse 25. (106) Song of Songs 1:7. The letter *shin* there stands for *asher - asher lamah* (for why). Similarly in Ibn Ezra, *ibid.* Likewise here, the word *shamayim* is as if it said *asher mayim* (that waters), as is explained further in the text. (107) 12a. (108) "It is a name for water." So clearly explained further on by Ramban. (109) Judges 6:32.

waters when they took on a new form. This is the plain meaning of the verses in accordance with the way of Rashi's writing,[110] and it conforms with the opinion of Rav[111] which we have mentioned. Thus the names "heaven" and "earth" mentioned in the first verse point to the names by which they would be called in the future, as it would be impossible to make them known in any other manner. It is, however, more correct in accordance with the meaning of the verses that we say that the heavens mentioned in the first verse are the upper heavens, which are not part of the lower spheres but are above the *merkavah* (the Divine Chariot), just as it is stated, *And over the heads of the living creatures there was the likeness of a firmament, like the color of the transparent ice, stretched forth over their heads above.*[112] It is on account of these higher heavens that the Holy One, blessed be He, is called *He Who rideth upon the heavens.*[113] Scripture, however, did not relate anything concerning their creation, just as it did not mention the creation of the angels, the *chayoth* of the *merkavah*, and all Separate Intelligences which are incorporeal. Concerning the heavens, it mentioned only in a general way that they were created, meaning that they came forth from nought. On the second day He said that there should be a firmament in the midst of the waters, meaning that from the waters, the creation of which had already been mentioned, there should come forth an extended substance separating them [into two distinct waters]. These spherical bodies He also called "heavens" by the name of the first upper heavens. This is why they are called in this chapter "the firmament of the heaven" [rather than "heavens"] – *And G-d set them in the firmament of the heaven*[114] – in order to explain that they are not the heavens mentioned by that name in the first verse but merely the firmaments *called* "heavens."

This likewise is the opinion of our Rabbis mentioned in Bereshith Rabbah,[115] who state, "All Rabbis say it in the name of

(110) "The word *shamayim* [may be regarded as made up of either of these words]: *sa mayim* (carries water), etc." Rashi. (111) Mentioned above: that the heavens were in a fluid form on the first day, and on the second day they solidified. (112) Ezekiel 1:22. (113) Deuteronomy 33:26. (114) Verse 17. (115) 4:1.

Rabbi Chananyah the son of Rabbi Pinchas, and Rabbi Yaakov the son of Rabbi Avin says it in the name of Rabbi Shmuel the son of Rabbi Nachman: *Let there be a firmament in the midst of the waters* – the middle drop of water congealed, and the lower heavens and the highest heaven of heavens were formed." This saying of the Rabbis refers to the spherical bodies in which there are the lower heavens and the upper ones, called "the heavens of heavens," as it is written: *Praise ye Him, sun and moon; praise Him, all ye stars of light. Praise Him, ye heavens of heavens, and ye waters that are above the heavens.*[116] The heavens mentioned here in the first verse, in which is the Throne of the Holy One, Blessed be He, as it is written, *The heaven is My throne,*[117] are the ones mentioned in the beginning of that Psalm: *Praise ye the Eternal from the heavens; praise Him in the heights. Praise ye Him, all His angels.*[118]

This interpretation is correct as far as the simple meaning of the verses is concerned. But there is yet a sublime and hidden secret in the name "the heaven" and in the name "the throne" for there is a heaven to the heavens, and a throne to the throne. Based on this, the Sages use the expressions, "In order that a man may first take upon himself the yoke of the kingdom of Heaven,"[119] and "the fear of Heaven."[120] Scripture likewise says, *That the heavens do rule.*[121] The Sages also have a remarkable Midrash on the verse, *And Thou hear in heaven.*[122] The worthy one will see all this alluded to in the first verse.

Thus the verses have explained that the first created things were from nought, and the rest were derived from the first created substance.

See no objection to this explanation from the saying of Rabbi Eliezer the Great,[123] who states, "Whence were the heavens

(116) Psalms 148:3-4. (117) Isaiah 66:1. (118) Psalms 148:1-2. (119) Berachoth 13 a. (120) *Ibid.*, 7 a. (121) Daniel 4:23. (122) I Kings 8:32. The Midrash referred to is in Sefer Habahir, 100, and found in Zohar 2, p. 271. See my Hebrew commentary, p. 19, note 58. (123) Found in Pirke d'Rabbi Eliezer, 3. See also Moreh Nebuchim II, 26, where Rambam discusses this saying of Rabbi Eliezer and concludes that he is not able to explain it sufficiently. Ramban, however, explains it further on in the text in a way which makes it consistent with the theory of creation from absolute nought.

created? From the light of the garment of the Holy One, blessed be He." [This would apparently indicate that the heavens were not created from nought but from another preceding substance.] This opinion is also found in Bereshith Rabbah.[124] Since the Sages wanted to elevate the first substance to the utmost and make it ethereal, they did not find it feasible that the heavens, which are moving corporeal bodies possessing matter and form, were created from nought. Instead, they said "the light of the garment" was created first, and from it came forth the real substance of the heavens. And to the earth He gave another substance,[125] not as minute as the first [substance from which the heavens were formed], and that is "the snow under the Throne of Glory," for the Throne of Glory was first created, and from it came forth "the snow" under it, and from it [the "snow"] was formed the substance of the earth, which was third[126] in the order of creation.

9. LET THE WATERS UNDER THE HEAVEN BE GATHERED TOGETHER. The deep, which is water and sand, was like turbid waters, and He decreed concerning the waters that they be gathered together in one place, surrounded on all sides, and He further decreed concerning the sands that they rise up until they be seen above the waters and that they become dry, so that there be a stretch of dry land suitable for settlement thereon. And so it is written: *To Him that spread forth the earth above the waters.*[127] Or perhaps G-d's decree was that the earth be spherical, partly visible and mostly submerged in the waters, as the Greeks imagine in their proofs, apparent or real. Thus there were two decrees, that is, two matters done by the Will of G-d that are contrary to their natural inclination. For in view of the heaviness

(124) 12:1. (125) This is based on the concluding statement of Rabbi Eliezer the Great: "Whence was the earth created? From the snow under the Throne of Glory." (See Note 123.) (126) The Throne of Glory, the snow, the earth. In the case of the heavens, however, creation was completed in the second stage: 'the light of the garment' and then the heavens. This accords with the theory explained above (see Note 35) that the substance of the heavens is unlike that of the earth. (127) Psalms 136:6.

of earth [which would cause it to sink] and the lightness of the waters [which would cause them to rise], it would have been natural that the pillar of the earth be in the center and that the waters should cover it, thus surrounding it from all sides.[128] Therefore, He said, *Let the waters under the heaven be gathered together,* that is to a lower place, and then He said, *And let the dry land appear.* He gave them names as they assumed these forms, for at the beginning their collective name was "the deep."

10. AND G-D CALLED THE DRY LAND EARTH. The verse states that the proper name for it would be *yabashah* (dry land) for as the waters are separated from the sand it becomes dry. However, He called it *eretz* (earth) as the name which included the four elements created on the first day. The reason for this is that they were all created for the sake of the earth in order that there be a habitation for man, since among the lower creatures no one but man recognizes his Creator.[129]

And the gathering together of the waters He called '*yamim*' *(seas).* It is as if [the word *yamim*, (seas) combines the two words] *yam* and *mayim* (a sea of waters), for the bottom of the ocean is called *yam*, as it is written, *As the waters cover the sea,*[130] and likewise, *And he took down the sea from off the brazen oxen.*[131] It is called "sea" because there was a large gathering of water in it.

AND G-D SAW THAT IT WAS GOOD. This means that their continued existence was by His Will, and the purport is that when He clothed them with this form He desired them to be so and their existence was thus established as I have explained.[132] This conforms to what our Rabbis have said:[133] "Why is it not stated in reference to the work of the second day *that it was good?*

(128) But instead He decreed that the waters which filled the whole world should go down as would be natural for the earth, and that the earth should come up as would be natural for the water. (129) This is a major principle in Ramban's thought, that the purpose of all existence is that man acknowledge his Creator. "We have no other reason for the Creation." (See end of *Seder Bo* in the Book of Exodus). (130) Isaiah 11:9. (131) II Kings 16:17. (132) In Verse 4. (133) Bereshith Rabbah 4:8.

Because the work associated with the waters was not completed until the third day. Therefore on the third day, [the words *ki tov – that it was good*] are repeated, once in reference to the completion of the work associated with the waters, and once in reference to [the completion of the other work of] that day."

11. AND G-D SAID: 'LET THE EARTH PUT FORTH GRASS.' He decreed that there be among the products of the earth a force which grows and bears seed so that the species should exist forever. It is possible that the name "earth" mentioned in the first verse already contains a hint that a force which causes things to grow should spring up from the earth, and it was from this force that the foundations of all vegetations according to their kinds emanated. From them sprang the grass and trees in the garden of Eden, and from them came those in the world. This is what the Rabbis have said:[134] "On the third day He created three creations: trees, grass, and the garden of Eden." They have also said:[135] "There is not a single blade of grass below [that does not have] a constellation in heaven that smites it and says to it, 'Grow.' It is this which Scripture says, *Knowest thou the ordinances of the heavens? Canst thou establish 'mishtaro' (the dominion thereof) in the earth?*[136] – [*mishtaro* being derived from the root] *shoter* (executive officer)."

And He said that all this vegetation should be *after its kind.* This is the basis of the prohibition of sowing mixed kinds of seeds,[137] since he who sows them works contrary to the power of the work of creation. I will yet explain this [137] with the help of G-d.

Now Rabbeinu Shlomo [Rashi] wrote: "*Deshe essev (grass, herb). Deshe* does not mean the same as *esev* and *esev* does not mean the same as *deshe*, for by *deshe* is meant that which forms the covering of the ground when it is filled with vegetation, and it is not linguistically correct to say 'this or that *deshe*.' Each by itself is called this or that *esev*."

(134) The source is not definite. See Pirke d'Rabbi Eliezer, Chapter 3. (135) Bereshith Rabbah 10:7. (136) Job 38:33. (137) Leviticus 19:19.

This interpretation of Rashi is not correct. For if it were so, the word *deshe*[138] could have no plural, and yet we find the Sages saying, "If a person grafted together two kinds of *deshaim,* what should the law be?"[138] And the Rabbi himself[139] mentions *deshaim.*[140] Rather, *deshe* is the young growing plant, and *esev* is the mature product which produces seeds. This is why Scripture says, *'tadshei ha'aretz' (let the earth put forth) 'deshe' (young plants),* and it would not be correct usage to say *ta'asiv* [for the word *esev* applies to mature products which produce seeds]. And every young thing that grows from the earth is called *deshe,* even trees. Therefore *tadshei ha'aretz* in the verse extends also to the expression *etz pri* (the fruit-tree). [This interpretation is necessary] since He did not say, "Let the earth put forth *deshe esev* and *let it bring forth* the fruit-tree." The word *deshe* thus has the same meaning as *tz'michah* (growing). Similarly we find: *For the pasture of the wilderness 'dash'u' (do spring), for the tree beareth its fruit.*[141]

I wonder why Scripture did not mention the creation of fruitless trees, and how is it that He commanded only concerning fruit-trees? Perhaps this is what induced our Rabbis to say,[142] "Even the presently barren trees at first bore fruit." If so, we must say that since the imprecation [which was visited upon Adam for his sin] – *Cursed be the ground for thy sake*[143] – barren trees came into existence. But it is possible that the explanation of the verse before us is as follows: "Let the earth bring forth growing things, and herbs which yield seed and trees which bear fruit." Thus He decreed at first the creation of barren herbs and barren trees in general, and then He specified herbs which yield seed and trees which bear fruit. From what He said later on – *bearing fruit... wherein is the seed thereof* – we may derive that all trees were to grow from their seed although it is the custom with some trees to be propagated by planting a branch.

(138) Chullin 60 a. (139) Rashi. The title *Harav* (the Rabbi, the Master) without specification of the name is used by Ramban only with reference to Rashi or Rambam. It is the highest mark of respect. Precedent for it is found in the Talmud where just the title *Rabbi* meant Rabbi Yehudah Hanasi, redactor of the Mishnah, and the title *Rav* was a reference to Abba Arucha, founder of the Babylonian Academy of Sura. (140) That is, when Rashi writes, "For the species of *deshaim* are different; each by itself called this or that *esev.*" (141) Joel 2:22. (142) Bereshith Rabbah 5:9. (143) Genesis 3:17.

12. AND G-D SAW THAT IT WAS GOOD. This affirms the existence of the various kinds forever.

There was no special day assigned for this command for vegetation alone, since it is not a unique work. The earth, whether it brings forth anything or is salt land, is one.

14. LET THERE BE LIGHTS. Now the light was created on the first day, illuminating the elements, but when on the second day the firmament was made, it intercepted the light and prevented it from illuminating the lower elements. Thus, when the earth was created on the third day there was darkness on it and not light. And now on the fourth day the Holy One, blessed be He, desired that there be in the firmament luminaries, the light of which would reach the earth. This is the meaning of the words, *in the firmament of the heaven to give light upon the earth,*[144] for there already was light above the firmament which did not illuminate the earth.

The meaning of the words, *Let there be lights,* is as follows: He decreed on the first day that from the substance of the heavens there should come forth a light for the period of the day, and now He decreed that it become corporeal and that a luminous body come forth from it which would give light during the day with a great illumination, and that another body of lesser light [should come into existence] to illumine at night, and He suspended both in the firmament of the heavens in order that they illumine below as well.

It is possible that just as He endowed the earth with the power of growth in certain places thereof, so He placed in the firmament certain areas that are prepared and ready to receive the light, and these bodies which receive the light reflect it, just as window-panes and onyx stones. This is why He called them *me'oroth* and not *orim.* [*Orim* would imply that they have their own light; *me'oroth* on the other hand implies that they reflect the light which they receive], even though they are called *orim,* in the Psalm.[145]

(144) Verse 17. (145) Psalms 136:7. *To Him that made great 'orim' (lights).*

TO DIVIDE THE DAY FROM THE NIGHT. Rashi wrote: "This took place after the primeval light was concealed for the righteous, but during the six[146] days of creation the [primeval] light and darkness functioned, one by day and one by night."[147]

Now I do not see that this is the opinion of our Rabbis who mention concealment in connection with the primeval light. In their opinion, rather, the primeval light functioned for three days, and on the fourth an emanation took place from which was formed these two luminaries, just as the Rabbis have said,[148] "The sphere of the sun is an offshoot of the upper light." For since this world was not deserving of being served by this primeval light without an intermediary, He concealed it for the righteous in the World to Come, and He made use of this offshoot of the upper light from the fourth day on. Thus the Rabbis said in Bereshith Rabbah:[149] "It was taught: The light which was created during the six days of creation could not give light at daytime because it would then dim the sphere of the sun; at night it could not give light, since it was created to light only at daytime. So where is it? It was concealed. And where is it? It is prepared for the righteous in the hereafter, as it is said, *And the light of the moon shall be as the light of the sun, and as the light of the seven days.*[150] 'Seven?' I wonder! Were they not three?[151] It is like a man who says thus: 'I am keeping this for the seven days of my wedding feast.' " That is to say, it is common parlance that one say: "I am keeping and guarding this meat for the seven days of my wedding festivity." It is not that this would suffice him for all seven days, only that he will use it during that time. In the same way the Rabbis explained the expression *seven days,* meaning as the light which functioned during some of those days.

(146) In our text of Rashi: "seven." See my note to Berliner's edition of Rashi (p. 436) that both texts can be explained as correct. (147) In our text of Rashi: "functioned together both by day and by night." However, during the seven days of creation it was the primeval light that functioned, its concealment taking place on the eve following the Sabbath (so clearly explained in Maharal's commentary on Rashi – Gur Aryeh). (148) Bereshith Rabbah 17:7. (149) 3:6. (150) Isaiah 30:26. (151) For since the present light was created on the fourth day, the primeval light functioned only for the first three days during Creation.

There in Bereshith Rabbah the Rabbis also said:[152] *"And He separated the light.*[153] Rabbi Yehudah the son of Rabbi Simon said, 'He separated it for Himself.'[154] And the Rabbis say, 'He separated it for the righteous in the hereafter.' " Now if you could know the intent of the Rabbis in their saying in the Blessing of the Moon,[155] "A crown of glory to those borne by Him from the birth," you would know the secret of the primeval light, the conserving thereof, and the matter of separation mentioned [in the words of Rabbi Yehudah the son of Rabbi Simon] – i.e., "He separated it for Himself" – as well as the secret of "the two kings making use of one crown,"[156] as will indeed be the case at the end when *the light of the moon shall be as the light of the sun* after *the light of the sun shall be sevenfold.*[150]

AND THEY SHALL BE FOR SIGNS. These are the changes which they will bring forth, making signs and wonders *in the heavens and in the earth, blood, and fire, and pillars of smoke.*[157] This is similar in meaning to the expression, *And be not dismayed at the signs of heaven.*[158]

AND FOR SEASONS. This means *seedtime and harvest, and cold and heat, and summer and winter.*[159]

AND FOR DAYS. This means the length of day and the length of night.

AND YEARS. The luminaries are to complete their orbit and then traverse again the same course they followed, thus making the solar year consist of 365 days and the lunar year consist of [lunar cycles, each approximately] 30 days.

(152) 3:7. (153) Verse 4. (154) Just as the verse says, *And the light dwelleth with Him.* (Daniel 2:22). (155) Sanhedrin 42 a. (156) Chullin 60 b, and mentioned in Rashi here, Verse 16: "The sun and the moon were created of equal size. When the moon complained, 'It is impossible for two kings to make use of one crown,' G-d said to it, 'Go and diminish thyself.' " (157) Joel 3:3. (158) Jeremiah 10:2. (159) Genesis 8:22.

15. AND THEY SHALL BE FOR LIGHTS IN THE FIRMAMENT OF THE HEAVEN TO GIVE LIGHT UPON THE EARTH. He added here that their light should reach the earth since it is possible for the light to be seen in the heavens and perform all mentioned functions without lighting upon the earth. Hence He said that it *be for lights in the firmament of the heaven,* directed toward the earth and shining upon it.

16. AND G-D MADE. 17. AND G-D SET THEM. This teaches us that these lights were not made from the body of the firmament, rather, they were bodies set into it.

18. AND TO RULE OVER THE DAY AND OVER THE NIGHT. The matter of rulership is a different matter from the function of light which He mentioned, since it includes that which He stated at first, *And they shall be for signs, and seasons.* Their rulership over the earth comprises the changes which they cause in it and the power of bringing about the existence and deterioration of all things in the lower world since the sun, by its rule during the day, causes the sprouting, the propagation and the growth of all the warm and dry things, while the moon by its rule increases the springs and the oceans, and all liquid and cold things. Therefore He said in a general way, *And to rule over the day and over the night,* because theirs is the dominion over things in the lower world.

It is possible that the rulership given to them contains also a power of emanation for they are the leaders of things in the lower world, and with their power, every ruling power in nature holds sway. Thus the constellation which comes up by day rules during it, even as it is written, *The sun and the moon and the stars... which the Eternal thy G-d hath allotted unto all the peoples.* [160] And this is what Scripture means when it says, *He counteth the number of the stars; He giveth them all their names,* [161] likewise, *He calleth them all by name.* [162] For the calling of names signifies the differentiation in their respective powers, giving to this one the power of justice and

(160) Deuteronomy 4:19. (161) Psalms 147:4. (162) Isaiah 40:26.

righteousness, and to that one the power of blood and the sword, and similarly all other powers, as is known in astrology. And all is done by the power of the Most High and in accordance with His Will. Therefore it says, *Great is our Lord, and mighty in power,*[163] for He is greatest of all and mightiest in power over them. And similarly it says, *He calleth them all by name by the greatness of His might and the strength of His power.*[162] In accord with the secret I have hinted to you, the matter of rulership is completely true.

AND TO DIVIDE THE LIGHT FROM THE DARKNESS.Rabbi Abraham ibn Ezra said: "By the coming forth of the sun at daytime and the light of the moon at night, they shall divide the light from the darkness."[164] In my opinion, the light mentioned here refers to the day, and the darkness is the night for such are their names, as it says, *And G-d called the light Day, and the darkness He called Night.*[165]

Now in connection with all the works of creation, Scripture mentions the Divine command and then tells of the deed. And here too He commanded, *And they shall be for lights,*[166] and then it relates, *And G-d set them.*[167] He further said, *And to rule over the day and over the night,*[168] meaning that one is to rule by day and the other by night, the rulership being that which He commanded when He said, *And they shall be for signs, and for seasons.*[169] And now He related that the rulership of the two is not alike but instead consists of dividing the darkness from the light. The greater luminary will rule by day and light will be everywhere, even where the sun does not reach, and the smaller luminary will rule by night, and there will be darkness except that the moon will lighten its darkness. This then is the command He gave in order *to divide the day from the night,*[169] as it says, *And G-d divided the light from the darkness.*[153]

(163) Psalms 147:5. (164) Ibn Ezra's opinion is that the word *ul'havdil* (and to divide) refers to both the sun and moon, that each in coming forth separates between light and darkness. (Tur.) (165) Verse 5. Thus according to Ramban, the meaning of the verse is: "and to divide *the day* from *the night*," meaning, that light is to serve at daytime and darkness at night. (Tur.) (166) Verse 15. (167) Verse 17. (168) Verse 18. (169) Verse 14.

20. LET THE WATERS SWARM WITH 'SHERETZ' (SWARMS) OF LIVING CREATURES. Rashi wrote: "Every living creature that does not rise much above the ground is called *sheretz,* [e.g., species] of winged creatures such as flies; of abominable creatures such as ants and worms; of larger creatures such as the mole and the mouse and others of the same kind, and all fishes."

But what will the Rabbi[170] say of the verse, *And you, be ye fruitful, and multiply; 'shirtzu' (swarm) in the earth and multiply therein,*[171] which was said to Noah and his sons? Likewise, the verse stating, *which 'hamayim' (the waters) swarmed,*[172] should, according to this opinion of Rashi, read: "Which swarmed *bamayim* (in the waters)."[173] Again there are many winged creatures that do not rise in height above the ground even as much as the mole and mouse, and the bat has very small legs, so why should it not be called *sheretz ha'oph* (a winged swarming thing)?

Onkelos' opinion is that the term *shritzah* (swarming) has an implication of movement. Thus he says of both *sheretz* and *remes: richasha d'rachish* (moving things that move).[174] He has explained it correctly. *Shratzim* are so called because of their constant movement. It is possible that it is a composite word: *sheretz, shehu ratz* (that which runs). *Remes* is so called because it creeps upon the earth and is never quiet or at rest.

Know that every winged creature that has four legs is called *sheretz ha'oph* (a winged creeping[175] thing) because it leans on its legs and moves like *shratzim,* and a winged creature which is not so is called *oph kanaph* (winged fowl) because its main method of movement is flying. The meaning of the verse, *'Veshartzu' in the earth and be fruitful, and multiply upon the earth*[176] is thus: that

(170) Rashi. See Note 139. (171) Genesis 9:7. (172) In Verse 21. (173) Since, according to Rashi, they swarm *in* the waters. (174) This expression of Onkelos is found in Leviticus 11:44, where the Hebrew reads, *hasheretz haromes,* which Onkelos translated, *richasha d'rachish.* Thus it is obvious that Onkelos understood both words *(sheretz* and *remes)* as conveying a sense of movement. (175) "Creeping," according to Rashi, would be "swarming." (176) Genesis 8:17.

they may walk[177] upon the entire earth, and be fruitful and multiply upon it. *'Shirtzu' in the earth and multiply therein*[171] means "move about the entire earth and multiply thereon." This is the reason for the repetition of the word *ur'vu (and ye multiply)* in the verse.[178] This being so, we will explain the expression, *which the waters 'shartzu,'*[172] as meaning "which the waters have moved and brought forth." Similarly, the expression, *'Vesharatz' the river with frogs*[179] [means that the river moved and brought forth frogs]. Also, *And the children of Israel were fruitful 'vayishr'tzu,'*[180] means that they were fruitful and they multiplied and moved about because of their multitude until the land was filled with them.

Onkelos, however, interpreted the verse, *'Shirtzu' in the earth,*[171] as having reference to propagation. He thus translated, "Propagate in the land," since he understood the word *shirtzu* – a verb – as being borrowed from the noun *shrátzim* (reptiles). [The verse, according to Onkelos, thus states:] "And you, be ye fruitful and multiply, as the prolific creatures in the earth, and multiply therein." Similarly, *And the children of Israel were fruitful 'vayishr'tzu'*[180] means they brought forth progeny abundantly as the prolific creatures.

AND LET FOWL FLY ABOVE THE EARTH. On this fifth day the command of creation was given to the waters, and on the sixth day it was given to the earth. If so, the expression, *and let fowl fly above the earth,* must be interpreted as being connected with [the beginning of the verse which has the following meaning]: "Let the waters swarm with swarms of living creatures and with fowl that will fly." And the verse stating, *And the Eternal G-d formed out of the ground every beast of the field, and every fowl of the air,*[181] [which

(177) Translations which read "that 'they may swarm' in the earth" are thus according to Rashi's interpretation. Ramban, as here explained, understands the sense of the verse to be: " 'that they may move about' the earth." (178) Quoted above: *And you be ye fruitful and multiply, 'shirtzu' in the earth and multiply therein* [9:7]. Thus the first expression *and multiply* establishes the commandment of procreation; the second refers to the duty of making the whole earth habitable for people. (179) Exodus 7:28. (180) *Ibid.*, 1:7. (181) Genesis 2:19.

seems to indicate that the fowl were created from the ground, not from the water, must be understood] as if it said: "And the Eternal G-d formed out of the earth every beast of the field, and He also formed every fowl of the air out of the water." There are many verses like this. So also is the opinion of Rabbi Eliezer the Great in his Chapters,[182] where he says: "On the fifth day he caused all winged fowl to swarm from the waters." However, in the *Gemara*[183] the Sages differ on this point. Some, agreeing with the previously mentioned interpretation, say that all winged fowl were created from the waters, and some say that they were created from both – in their words, "they were created from the swamps." If so, since the fowl sprang from the waters, and the swamps are at the bottom of the ocean, this is why the command concerning their creation took place on the fifth day.

Similarly He said, *Let the waters swarm with swarms of living creatures,* since both the body and soul of fish come from the waters by word of G-d Who brought upon them a spirit from the elements, unlike man, in whom He separated the body from his soul, as it is said, *And the Eternal G-d formed man of the dust of the ground, and breathed into his nostrils the breath of life.*[184] On the third day of creation when the plants came into being, He mentioned nothing at all concerning a soul because the power of growth which resides in plants is not a "soul;" only in moving beings is it a "soul." And in the opinion of the Greeks, who say that just as in moving beings the power of growth is only through the soul, so also in the case of plants is the power of growth through a soul. The difference between them will be that the one [the moving being] is a *nefesh chayah (a living soul),*[185] that is, a soul in which there is life, for there is a soul which has no life and that is the soul of plants. Our Rabbis have mentioned "desire" in connection with date trees.[186] Perhaps this is a force in growth, but it cannot be called "a soul."

(182) Beginning of Chapter 9. (183) Chullin 27 b. (184) Genesis 2:7. (185) In Verse 20: *Let the waters swarm with swarms of 'nefesh chayah' (a living soul).* Same in Verse 24, in the creation of beasts, etc. (186) Bereshith Rabbah 44:1.

21. AND G-D CREATED THE GREAT SEA-MONSTERS. Because of the great size of these creatures, some consisting of many Persian miles – the Greeks in their books even relate that they knew some of them to be 500 Persian miles long, and our Rabbi likewise spoke of them in magnifying terms[187] – on account of that, Scripture explicitly ascribes their creation to G-d for He brought them forth from nought from the beginning, as I have explained the expression *b'riyah* (creation). Similarly, Scripture does so in the case of man[188] on account of his exaltedness, thus informing us that man, with his mind and reason, also came forth from nought.

I wonder why it does not say "and it was so" on this day? Perhaps it would not have been possible to mention *And He created* after saying, "and it was so," since it refers to the preceding.[189]

Our Rabbis have said[190] that *the great sea-monsters* are the Leviathan and its mate which He created male and female. He then slew the female and preserved it in salt for the benefit of the righteous in the hereafter. It is possible that on account of this it would not have been appropriate to say concerning their creation, "and it was so," since they did not continue to exist [in the form in which they were created].

22. AND G-D BLESSED THEM SAYING. He decreed the blessing on them and said of them that they should be fruitful and multiply, meaning that they should bring forth abundantly, that one creature should bring forth many like itself. The purport of the blessing is procreation, even as it says, *And I will bless her, and she shall be a mother of nations.*[191] In connection with plants also, the term "blessing" applies: *Then I will command My blessing upon you in*

(187) Baba Bathra 73 b. (188) Verse 27: *And G-d created man in His own image.* (189) If Verse 20 (*Let the waters swarm with swarms of living creatures*, etc.) would have concluded with the expression *and it was so*, it would have implied the creation of the sea-monster, since they also swarm in the waters. How then could it say in the following verse, *And G-d created the sea-monster*, as if it were another act of creation? To say, *and it was so* after *vayibra* (And He created) is also not possible for this would be redundant. Hence on the fifth day, the expression *and it was so* does not appear in Scripture. (190) Baba Bathra 74 b. (191) Genesis 17:16.

the sixth year.[192] However, it does not say so on the third day [when the plants and trees were created] because all created *living* beings were only a single pair, male and female, according to their kind, and therefore they were in need of a blessing to bring forth abundantly; but in the case of plants, they sprang up over the face of the entire earth in great abundance, just as they exist today. Nor did He mention a blessing on the sixth day for cattle and beasts because in the decree of abundancy which He decreed for the moving souls in the waters there were included the moving souls on the earth, as all living souls that do not speak are in the same class of creation. And our Rabbis have said[193] that they [the fish and fowl] were in need of a blessing because people hunt them and eat them.[194]

AND FILL THE WATERS IN THE SEA. He blessed them that in their abundancy they would fill the seas, the streams and the pools. Or it may be that their "filling" is to be in the seas only for in the streams they are few.

AND LET FOWL MULTIPLY IN THE EARTH. Although the fowl were created out of the waters, their blessing – that they be fruitful and multiply – was to be on the earth for there is no fowl that lays its eggs in the waters and has them grow there. Even those fowl which abide always in the waters and derive their food from them lay their eggs on the earth, and there they are born.

24. CATTLE. These are the species that eat grass, whether domestic animals or those of the wilderness.

AND BEAST OF THE EARTH. Those which eat flesh are called *chayoth* (beasts), and they all seek and seize prey.

(192) Leviticus 25:21. (193) Bereshith Rabbah 11:2, and quoted here in Rashi. (194) "Beasts also were in need of a blessing [for the same reason, namely, that people decrease their numbers by hunting them and eating them], but on account of the serpent that was to be cursed in the future, G-d did not bless them, in order that it might not be included in the blessing." Rashi.

'VAREMES' (AND CREEPING THING). Rashi wrote: "These are creeping swarms that creep low upon the earth, appearing as though they are dragged along." Now in this chapter we find: *And over every animal 'haromeseth' (that creepeth) upon the earth;*[195] and it is further written, *And all flesh 'haromes' (that moved) upon the earth perished, both fowl and cattle, and beasts, and every swarming thing that swarmeth upon the earth;*[196] also, *Wherein all the beasts of the forest 'tirmos' (do creep forth).*[197] But the meaning of *r'misah* is as if it were written with the letter *samech,* as in *The foot tirm'senah (shall tread it down),*[198] and other related expressions. He thus says of beasts and cattle, *'romes' (that tread) on the earth,*[199] and of creeping things that drag along, *'remes' (that creep) upon the ground,*[200] because they tread on the ground with their entire body.

26. AND G-D SAID: 'LET US MAKE MAN.' There was a special command dedicated to the making of man because of his great superiority since his nature is unlike that of beasts and cattle which were created with the preceding command.

The correct explanation of *na'aseh (let us make)* [which is in the plural form when it should have been in the singular] is as follows: It has been shown to you that G-d created something from nothing only on the first day, and afterwards He formed and made things from those created elements.[201] Thus when He gave the waters the power of bringing forth *a living soul,*[202] the command concerning them was *Let the waters swarm.*[202] The command concerning cattle was *Let the earth bring forth.*[203] But in the case of man He said, *Let us make,* that is, I and the aforementioned earth, let us make man, the earth to bring forth the body from its elements as it did with cattle and beasts, as it is written, *And the Eternal G-d formed man of the dust of the ground,*[204] and He, blessed be He, to give the spirit from His mouth, the Supreme One, as it is written, *And He*

(195) Verse 28. Here Rashi's interpretation could not apply to animal. (196) Genesis 7:21. (197) Psalms 104:20. (198) Isaiah 26:6. (199) Verse 26. (200) Verse 25. (201) Fire, wind, water, and earth. (202) Verse 20. (203) Verse 24. (204) Genesis 2:7.

breathed into his nostrils the breath of life.[204] And He said, *In our image, and after our likeness,* as man will then be similar to both. In the capacity of his body, he will be similar to the earth from which he was taken, and in spirit he will be similar to the higher beings, because it [the spirit] is not a body and will not die. In the second verse, He says, *In the image of G-d He created him,*[205] in order to relate the distinction by which man is distinguished from the rest of created beings. The explanation of this verse I have found ascribed to Rabbi Joseph the Kimchite,[206] and is the most acceptable of all interpretations that have been advanced concerning it.

The meaning of *tzelem* is as the word *to'ar* (appearance), as in *'Vetzelem' (And the appearance) of his face was changed;*[207] similarly, *Surely 'b'tzelem' (as a mere appearance) man walketh;*[208] *When Thou arousest Thyself 'tzalmam' (their appearance) Thou wilt despise,*[209] that is, the appearance of their countenance. And the meaning of the word *d'muth* is similarity in form and deed, as things that are akin in a certain matter are called similar to each other. Thus man is similar both to the lower and higher beings in appearance and honor, as it is written, *And Thou hast crowned him with glory and honor,* [210] meaning that the goal before him is wisdom, knowledge, and skill of deed.[211] In real likeness his body thus compares to the earth while his soul is similar to the higher beings.

AND LET THEM HAVE DOMINION OVER THE FISH OF THE SEA. On account of his [man's] being male and female, he said, *And let 'them' have dominion over the fish of the sea,* in the plural.

In Bereshith Rabbah, the Rabbis have said:[212] "*Let the earth bring forth a living soul after its kind.*[203] Said Rabbi Elazar: '*A living soul* – this has reference to the spirit of the first man.' " Now it is impossible that Rabbi Elazar should say that the expression, *Let*

(205) Verse 27. (206) The father of Rabbi David Kimchi (R'dak, the famous grammarian and commentator of the Bible). The explanation is found in R'dak's commentary to the Torah here as well as in his Sefer Hamichlal. In his works on Hebrew grammar and Bible, R'dak often mentions the interpretation of his father. Moses Kimchi, a second son to Joseph, also continued the tradition of the family. (207) Daniel 3:19. (208) Psalms 39:7. (209) *Ibid.*, 73:20. (210) *Ibid.*, 8:6. (211) Ecclesiastes 2:21; 4:4. (212) 7:7.

the earth bring forth, be explained as having reference to the soul of the first man at all.[213] Instead, his intent is to say what I have mentioned, that the formation of man as regarding his spirit, namely, the soul which is in the blood, that was done from the earth, just as in the command of formation of the beasts and cattle. For the souls of all moving things were made at one time, and afterwards He created bodies for them. First He made the bodies of the cattle and the beasts, and then the body of man into whom He imparted this soul [which resides in the blood, and is akin to that of the cattle and beasts], and afterwards, He breathed into him a higher soul. For it is concerning this separate soul that a special command was devoted by G-d Who gave it, as it is written, *And He breathed into his nostrils the breath of life.*[204]

The way of truth in this verse [as to why Scripture begins with "man" in the singular – *let us make 'man'* – and then uses the plural, *let 'them' have dominion*] will be known to him who understands the following verse [27, where the same change appears. It begins by stating, *in the image of G-d He created 'him,'* and then uses the plural: *male and female He created 'them'.*]

It is possible that Rabbi Elazar meant to explain the expression *Let the earth bring forth* as meaning "the earth of eternal life," that it bring forth a living soul after its kind that will exist forever. Similarly, [we explain that when Scripture] said, *male and female He created them,*[205] it is because man's creation at first was male and female, and His soul was included in both of them. However, in the formation, man was formed first, and then He built the woman from the rib of man, as Scripture tells later. Therefore Scripture mentioned here the term "creation," and in the chapter below it mentioned "formation."[204] The person learned [in the mysteries of the Torah] will understand.

The meaning of *let them have dominion* is that they shall rule vigorously over the fish, the fowl, the cattle, and all creeping things – "the cattle" here includes the beast.

(213) Since man did not at all derive his higher soul from the earth at all.

And He said, *And over all the earth,* to indicate that they are to rule over the earth itself, to uproot and to pull down, to dig and to hew out copper and iron. The term *r'diyah – ['v'yirdu' over the fish ... and over all the earth]* – applies to the rule of the master over his servant.

28. AND G-D BLESSED THEM. This is an actual blessing [unlike Verse 22 where the blessing of the fish and fowl consisted of bestowing upon them the power of procreation]. Therefore, it is written here, *And G-d blessed them, and G-d said unto them.* But above in Verse 22 it is written, *And G-d blessed them, saying,* [the word *saying* indicating] that the blessing is the command of procreation, that He gave them the power of bringing forth offspring, and no other command with which they are to be blessed. [But in the case of man, in addition to the power of being fruitful, he was also blessed that he have dominion over the earth, hence Scripture continues, *and G-d said unto them.*]

AND REPLENISH THE EARTH. This is a blessing that they fill the earth because of their numbers. In my opinion, He blessed them that they fill the whole earth, and that the nations should disperse according to their families and should populate the far ends of the world because of their numbers and not be concentrated in one place, as was the thought of the men of the generation of the dispersion.

AND SUBDUE IT. He gave them power and dominion over the earth to do as they wish with the cattle, the reptiles, and all that crawl in the dust, and to build, *and to pluck up that which is planted,*[214] and from its hills to dig copper, and other similar things. This is included in what He said *and over all the earth.*[199]

AND HAVE DOMINION OVER THE FISH OF THE SEA. He said that they should also have dominion over the fish that are concealed from them, *And over the fowl of the heaven* which are not on the

(214) Ecclesiastes 3:2.

ground, and also *over every wild animal.* He thus mentioned them in the order of their creation: first the fish and fowl, and afterwards the animals. So likewise Scripture says, *Thou hast made him have dominion over the works of Thy hands; Thou hast put all things under his feet: sheep and oxen, all of them, yea, and the beasts of the field, the fowl of the air, and the fish of the sea.*[215] Our Rabbis, however, have made a distinction between *kvishah* (subduing) and *r'diyah* (having dominion).[216]

29. BEHOLD, I HAVE GIVEN YOU EVERY HERB YIELDING SEED. He did not permit Adam and his wife to kill any creature and eat its meat, but all alike were to eat herbs. But when the era of "the sons of Noah" came, He permitted them to eat meat, as it is said, *Every moving thing that liveth shall be for food for you; as the green herb have I given you all;* [217] even as the green herb that I permitted to the first man, so do I permit you everything. Thus is the language of Rashi. And so did the Rabbi[218] explain it in Tractate Sanhedrin:[219] *"And to every beast of the earth* [220] – to you and to the beasts I have given the herbs and the fruits of the trees, *and every green herb for food."*[220]

But if so, then we must explain the expression, *every green herb for food,*[220] to mean *"and* every green herb."[221] But this is not so.

(215) Psalms 8:7-9. In Keseph Mezukak the author notes that this Scriptural quote should be preceded by the expression, "even if Scripture elsewhere does *not* state them in this order" since in this quotation fowl and fish are after all mentioned last in order. (216) Thus the Rabbis, in Bereshith Rabbah 8:12, say that while the terms *kvishah* and *r'diyah* imply power and dominion, *r'diyah* also suggests *yeridah* (sinking low). Thus, if man is worthy he dominates (*rodeh*) over the beasts and cattle; if he is not worthy, he sinks lower (*yarud*) than they, and the beasts rule over him. (217) Genesis 9:3. (218) Rashi. (219) 59 b. (220) Verse 30. (221) The intent of Ramban's remark is as follows: if, as according to Rashi, man and beast were made alike with respect to their permitted food, then Verse 29, which specifies the food for man, and Verse 30, which begins with *and to every beast of the earth* and concludes with *every green herb for food,* are to be understood as one command since both man and beast were permitted the same food. In that case, Verse 30 should read: *"and* every green herb," that is, in addition to *every herb yielding seed... and every tree, in which is the fruit of a tree yielding seed* mentioned in Verse 29, they could also eat *every green herb.*

Rather, He gave to man and his wife every herb yielding seed and all fruit of the trees [as mentioned in Verse 29], and to the beasts of the earth and the fowl of the heaven He gave all green herb [as mentioned in Verse 30] but neither the fruit of the tree nor the seeds. The food of all of them was thus not the same. However, meat was not permitted to them until the time of the "sons of Noah,"[222] as is the opinion of our Rabbis. And this is the plain meaning of the verse.

The reason for this [prohibition of eating meat] was that creatures possessing a moving soul have a certain superiority as regards their soul, resembling in a way those who possess the rational soul: they have the power of choice affecting their welfare and their food, and they flee from pain and death. And Scripture says: *Who knoweth the spirit of man whether it goeth upward, and the spirit of the beast whether it goes downward to the earth?*[223]

But when they sinned, and *all flesh had corrupted its way upon the earth,*[224] and it was decreed that they die in the flood, and for the sake of Noah He saved some of them to preserve the species, He gave the sons of Noah permission to slaughter and eat them since their existence was for his sake.[225] Yet with all this, He did not give them permission regarding the soul thereof, and He prohibited them from eating a limb cut off from a living animal, and in addition He gave us [the children of Israel] the commandment prohibiting the eating of all blood because it is the basis of the soul, as it is written: *For the life of all flesh, the blood thereof is all one with the life thereof; therefore I said to the children of Israel: Ye shall eat the*

(222) After the flood all people of all time were commanded to observe as a minimum the following seven precepts: (a) to establish courts of justice; (b) to abstain from idolatry; (c) incest; (d) murder; (e) robbery; (f) blasphemy; and (g) eating flesh cut from living animals. These are the laws of Noachids, or "sons of Noah." (See further Ramban 34:13.) At that time permission was given them to eat meat, the reason for which is explained in the text. (223) Ecclesiastes 3:21. (224) Genesis 6:12. (225) That is, Noah's sake. The Tur's version reads "*their* sake," a reference to all three sons of Noah who were also righteous. See Ramban further, 2:3, where he discusses the profounder meanings of the elements created on the second day, and he writes that they symbolize Noah and his sons as all having been *tzadikim* (righteous men).

blood of no manner of flesh; for the life of all flesh is the blood thereof.[226] Thus He has permitted the eating of the body of dumb animals after death, but not the soul itself.

This indeed is the reason for the commandment of killing [animals in the prescribed manner before eating their flesh], and for the saying of the Rabbis:[227] "The duty of relieving the suffering of beasts is a Biblical requirement." And this is the meaning behind the benediction which we make before killing animals: "[Blessed art Thou, O Eternal our G-d, king of the universe] Who hast sanctified us by His commandments and commanded us concerning the killing [of animals]." I will yet discuss the purport of the commandment prohibiting the eating of blood when I reach thereto,[228] if G-d will reward me.

The meaning of the expression, *every herb yielding seed... and every tree, in which is the fruit of a tree yielding seed; to you it shall be for food,* is that they should eat the seeds of herbs, such as the grains of wheat, barley, beans, and the like, and that they should eat all fruits of the tree; but the tree itself was not given to them for food, nor was the herb itself until man was cursed and he was told, *And thou shalt eat the herb of the field.* [229]

31. AND, BEHOLD, IT WAS VERY GOOD. This signifies their permanent existence, as I have explained.[230] The meaning of the word *me'od* (very) is "mostly." On this sixth day He added this word because he is speaking of creation in general which contains evil in some part of it. Thus He said that *it was very good,* meaning its *me'od* is good [thus conveying the thought that even the small part of it which is evil is basically also good, as is explained further on]. It is this thought which is the basis of the saying of the Rabbis in Bereshith Rabbah:[231] "*And, behold, it was very good. And, behold, it was good* – this refers to death." Similarly the Rabbis mentioned, "This means the evil inclination in man,"[232] and, "This means the

(226) Leviticus 17:14. (227) Shabbath 128 b. (228) Leviticus 17: 14. (229) Genesis 3: 18. (230) Above in Verses 4 and 12. (231) 9:5. (232) *Ibid.*, 9. "Were it not for the evil inclination, no one would build a house or marry a woman."

dispensation of punishment."[233] Onkelos also intended to convey this thought for he said here, "And, behold, it was very orderly," meaning that the order was very properly arranged since the evil is needed for the preservation of the good, just as it is said, *To every thing there is a season, and a time to every purpose under the heaven.*[234] Some Rabbis explain[235] that on account of the superiority of man, He added special praise on his formation, i.e., that he is "very good."

2 1. AND ALL THE HOST OF THEM. "The host of the earth" are those which have been mentioned: beasts, creeping things, fish, and all growing things, and also man. "The host of the heavens" are the two luminaries and the stars, mentioned above, just as it is written: *And lest thou lift up thine eyes unto heaven, and when thou seest the sun and the moon and the stars, even all the host of heaven.*[236] It also includes the Separate Intelligences,[237] just as it is written: *I saw the Eternal sitting on His throne, and all the host of heaven standing by Him;*[238] also, *The Eternal will punish the host of the high heaven on high.*[239] It is here [in the expression, *all the host of them*], that He has hinted at the formation of the angels in the work of creation. Similarly, the souls of men are included in the host of heaven.[240]

3. AND G-D BLESSED THE SEVENTH DAY AND HE SANCTIFIED IT. He blessed it through the Manna. [On all other days of the week there fell one portion per person, whereas on the sixth day – the eve of the Sabbath – a double portion fell.] And He

(233) *Ibid.* "He considers well how to mete it out" so as to cause a minimum of suffering. (234) Ecclesiastes 3:1. (235) Bereshith Rabbah 9:14. (236) Deuteronomy 4:19. (237) Intelligences without matter, generally referring to the angels and spheres. See Rambam, Hilchoth Yesodei Hatorah 3:9. Also Moreh Nebuchim, I, 49: "The angels are likewise incorporeal; they are intelligences without matter, etc." (Friedlander's translation.) (238) I Kings 22:19. (239) Isaiah 24:21. (240) Ramban is thus inferring that the souls of all men of all generations were created at the beginning of creation. This thought is clearly expressed in the other writings of Ramban. (See Ramban's letter to Rabbeinu Yonah, Kithvei Haramban, Vol. I, 383. See also in same volume his Commentary to Job 38:21, p. 117).

sanctified it through the Manna [by not having it fall on the Sabbath]. And the verse is written here with reference to the future. Thus are the words of Rabbeinu Shlomo [Rashi] as quoted from Bereshith Rabbah.[241] In the name of the Gaon Rav Saadia[242] they have said that the blessing and sanctification refer to those who observe the Sabbath, meaning that they will be blessed and sanctified. However, from the intimation of the verse it does not appear that it refers to something which will happen in the future.

And Rabbi Abraham ibn Ezra said that the blessing signifies additional well-being, that on the seventh day there is a renewal of procreative strength in the body, and in the soul, a greater capacity in the functioning of the reasoning power. *And He sanctified it* by not working on it as He did on the other days. Now Ibn Ezra's interpretation is correct to those who believe in it for this additional well-being he speaks of is not perceptible to human senses.

The truth is that the blessing on the Sabbath day is the fountain of blessings and constitutes the foundation of the world. *And He sanctified it* that it draw its sanctity from the Sanctuary on high. If you will understand this comment of mine you will grasp what the Rabbis have said in Bereshith Rabbah[243] concerning the Sabbath: ["Why did He bless the Sabbath? It is] because it has no partner,"[244] and that which they have further related [that G-d said to the Sabbath]: "The congregation of Israel will be thy partner." And then you will comprehend that on the Sabbath there is truly an extra soul.

WHICH G-D IN CREATING HAD MADE. The work which should have been done on the Sabbath, He did in the double work which He executed on the sixth day, as it is explained in Bereshith Rabbah.[245] So says Rashi.

Rabbi Abraham ibn Ezra, however, explained simply that *His work* refers to the roots of all species to which He gave the power

(241) 11:2. (242) Mentioned in Ibn Ezra here. (243) 11:9. (244) "Because it has no..." (*l'phi sh'e*) is a direct quote from the Midrash there. (See Theodore's ed. of Bereshith Rabbah, p. 95, variants.) In the printed edition of the Midrash, the word *l'phi* (because) is missing. (245) 11:10.

to make [i.e., to produce] after their own kind. [Thus the verse would translate: *which G-d had created in order to make it.*]

To me, the explanation appears to be that *He rested from all His work which He created* out of nothing; *to make* from it all the works mentioned on the six days. Thus the verse is stating that G-d rested from creating and forming – from the creation He created on the first day, and from the formation He formed on the rest of the days. And it is possible that the word *la'asoth* (to make) is connected with the expression above in the verse, *that in it He rested from all His work which He created* from *making*, [thus making the word *la'asoth* to be understood as *mila'asoth* (from making)]. So also are the verses: *Until he ceased 'lispor'*[246] *(to count)*, which means *milispor* (until he left off counting); *And they ceased 'livnoth' (to build) the city*,[247] which means *milivnoth; Take heed to yourselves, that ye go not up into the mount;*[248] *And they departed not 'mitzvath' (the commandment of the king*,[249] which should be understood as *mimitzvath* (from the commandment); and thus in many other cases.

Know that in the word *la'asoth* (to make, to do) is also included a hint that the six days of creation represent all the days of the world, i.e., that its existence will be six thousand years. For this reason the Rabbis have said:[250] "A day of the Holy One, blessed be He, is a thousand years." Thus on the first two days the world was all water, and nothing was perfected during them. They allude to the first two thousand years when there was no one to call on the name of the Eternal. And so the Rabbis said:[251] "The first two thousand years there was desolation." However, there was the creation of light on the first day corresponding to the thousand years of Adam who was

(246) Genesis 41:49. (247) *Ibid.*, 11:8. (248) Exodus 19:12. *Aloth* (going up) should be understood as *me'aloth* (from going up). (249) II Chronicles 8:15. (250) Bereshith Rabbah 19:14. It is noteworthy here that Ramban's explanation of the history of the world in terms of the six days of Creation was regarded with approval by many later authors. Bachya ben Asher (see my edition, I, pp. 54-6) and Menachem Ricanti copied it verbatim. Surprisingly it found its way into Egypt, and was wholly incorporated into the Midrash Rabbi David Hanagid, (Book of Exodus, pp. 201-2, ed. by A. Katz), grandson of Maimonides. (251) Avodah Zarah 9a.

the light of the world[252] and who recognized his Creator. Perhaps Enosh did not worship idols[253] until the death of the first man.

On the second day G-d said, *'Let there be a firmament... and let it divide,'*[254] for on that "day" [i.e.,the second thousand-year period] Noah and his sons – the righteous ones –[255] were separated from the wicked,who were punished in water.

On the third day, the dry land appeared; plants and trees began growing, and fruits ripened. This corresponds to the third thousand-year period which begins when Abraham was forty-eight years old,[256] for then he began to call the name of the Eternal. *A righteous shoot*[257] did then spring forth in the world for he attracted many people to know the Eternal, just as the Rabbis interpreted the verse: *And the souls that they had gotten in Haran*[258] – and he commanded his household and his children after him, *and they shall keep the way of the Eternal, to do righteousness and judgment.*[259] This course continued until his descendants received the Torah on Sinai and the House of G-d was also built on that "day," and then all commandments – which are "the fruits" of the world – were affirmed.

Know that from the time twilight falls it is already considered as the following day. Therefore, the subject of every "day" begins somewhat before it, just as Abraham was born at the end of the second thousand years. And you will see similar examples for each and every day.

On the fourth day the luminaries – the large and the small and the stars – were created. Its "day," in the fourth thousand-year period, began seventy-two years after the First Sanctuary was built and continued until one hundred seventy-two years after the destruction of the Second Sanctuary. Now on this "day," *the children of Israel had light,*[260] *for the glory of the Eternal filled the house of the*

(252) Yerushalmi Shabbath 2, 6: "The first man was the light [literally: the candle] of the world." (253) See further, 4:26, Rashi. (254) Above, 1:6. (255) See Note 225 above. (256) In Avodah Zarah 9a it appears that Abraham, at the end of the first 2000 years, was 52 years old. (257) Jeremiah 23:5. (258) Genesis 12:5. "These are the converts which they converted." (Bereshith Rabbah 39:21.) (259) *Ibid.*, 18:19. (260) Exodus 10:23.

Eternal,[261] and the light of Israel became the fire upon the altar in the Sanctuary, resting there like a lion[262] consuming the offerings. Afterwards their light diminished and they were exiled to Babylon just as the light of the moon disappears before the birth of the new moon. Then the moon shone for them all the days of the Second Sanctuary, and the fire upon the altar rested on it like a dog.[262] And then the two luminaries disappeared towards eventide and the Sanctuary was destroyed.

On the fifth day the waters swarmed with living creatures and fowl flying above the earth. This was a reference to the fifth thousand-year period which began one hundred seventy-two years after the destruction of the Second Sanctuary since, during this millennium, the nations will have dominion, and man will be made *as the fishes of the sea, as the creeping things, that have no ruler over them; they take up all of them with the angle, catch them in their net and gather in their drag,*[263] and no one seeks the Eternal.

On the sixth day in the morning, G-d said: *'Let the earth bring forth the living creature after its kind, cattle and creeping thing, and beast of the earth after its kind.'*[264] Their creation took place before sunrise, even as it is written, *The sun ariseth, they withdraw, and crouch in their dens.*[265] Then man was created in the image of G-d, and this is the time of his dominion, as it is written, *Man goeth forth unto his work and to his labor until the evening.*[266] All this is an indication of the sixth thousand-year period in the beginning of which the "beasts," symbolizing the kingdoms *that knew not the Eternal,*[267] will rule, but after a tenth thereof – in the proportion of the time from the first sparklings of the sun to the beginning of the day[268] – the redeemer will come, as it is said concerning him, *And his throne is as the sun before Me.*[269] This is the son of David, who

(261) I Kings 8:11. (262) So in Yoma 21 b. Maharsha explains there the symbolism of *the lion* and *the dog*, that the first Sanctuary was built by King Solomon who was of the tribe of Judah, likened to a lion (see Genesis 49:9), while the second Sanctuary was built by the government of the Persians, symbolized by the dog (see Rosh Hashanah 4 a). (263) Habakkuk 1:14-15. (264) Above 1:24. (265) Psalms 104:22. (266) *Ibid.*, Verse 23. (267) Judges 2:10. (268) In Pesachim 94a it is so explained that the time from the beginning of the day to the first sparklings of the sun is one tenth of the day. (269) Psalms 89:37.

was formed in the image of G-d, as it is written, *And behold, there came with the clouds of heaven, one like unto a son of man, and he came even to the Ancient One of days, and he was brought near before Him. And there was given him dominion, and glory, and a kingdom.* [270] This will take place one hundred eighteen years after the completion of five thousand years, [271] that the word of the Eternal by the mouth of Daniel might be accomplished: [272] *And from the time that the continual burnt-offering shall be taken away, and the detestable thing that causeth appalment set up, there shall be a thousand two hundred and ninety days.* [273]

It would appear from the change of days – from the swarms of the waters and the fowl created on the fifth day to the beasts of the earth created on the sixth day – that in the beginning of the sixth thousand-year period a new ruling kingdom will arise, *dreadful and terrible, and strong exceedingly,* [274] and approaching the truth more than the preceding ones.

The seventh day which is the Sabbath alludes to the World to Come, "which will be wholly a Sabbath and will bring rest for life everlasting." [275]

And may G-d guard us during all the days and set our portion with His servants, the blameless ones.

4. THESE ARE THE GENERATIONS OF THE HEAVEN AND THE EARTH WHEN THEY WERE CREATED. Scripture now relates the account of the heaven and the earth as regards rain and growth after they had been created and put in proper order, *that the heavens shall give their dew*[276] and rain, *and the ground shall give her increase,*[276] these making possible the existence of all living beings. And in the word *b'hibaram* (when they were created) – [which could be read as if it were two words: *b'hei baram*] –

(270) Daniel 7:13-14., (271) This corresponds to the year 1358 C.E. See my biography of Ramban, p. 141, for further discussion of this matter. (272) See Ezra 1:1. (273) Daniel 12:11. *Yamim* here means "years." Thus 172 years after the destruction of the Second Temple, the fifth millennium began. Add this to the 118 years after the beginning of the sixth millennium, and you have 1290 years, as mentioned in the verse. (274) *Ibid.*, 7:7. Rambam refers here to rise of Islam. (275) Tamid VII, 4. (276) Zechariah 8:12.

Scripture alludes to what the Rabbis have said:[277] "He created them with the letter *hei*" [which is the last of the four letters of the Tetragrammaton]. It is for this reason that Scripture until this point mentioned only the word *Elokim*. This is explained in the verse: *For all these things hath My hand made;* [278] and so did Job say, *Who knoweth not among all these, that the hand of the Eternal hath wrought this?* [279] This being so, the expression, *in the day that the Eternal G-d made*, refers covertly to the word *bereshith* (in the beginning).[280]

5. AND EVERY SHRUB OF THE FIELD. In the opinion of our Rabbis in Bereshith Rabbah,[281] [every herb of the field created] on the third day [did not come forth above the ground but] they remained just below the surface of the earth, and on the sixth day they grew after He caused rain to fall on them.

In my opinion, in accordance with the plain meaning of Scripture, on the third day the earth did bring forth the grass and the fruit trees in their full-grown stature and quality as He commanded concerning them. And now Scripture tells that there was no one to plant and sow them for future purposes, and the earth would not produce until a mist would come up from it and water it, and man was formed who would work it – to seed, to plant, and to guard. This is the meaning of the *shrub of the field... had not yet grown*. It does not say "the shrub of the ground" for only a place which is cultivated is called "field," as in *Which thou hast sown in the field* [282] and *We will not pass through field or through vineyard.* [283] This is the course of the world that was to be following the six days of creation and forever after, that due to the mist the heavens will bring down rain, and due to the rains the earth will make the seeds that are sown in it to spring up.

(277) Menachoth 29 b. , (278) Isaiah 66:2. The last letter (*hei*) of the Tetragrammaton is in the Cabala considered the *yad hashem* (the hand of G-d). See my Hebrew commentary, p. 32. (279) Job 12:9. (280) See Ramban above at the end of 1:1 and see also Note 64. (281) See Bereshith Rabbah 12:4 for a similar text. See also Rashi here. (282) Exodus 23:16. (283) Numbers 20:17.

7. AND HE BREATHED INTO HIS NOSTRILS THE BREATH OF LIFE. This alludes to the superiority of the soul, its foundation and secret, since it mentions in connection with it the full Divine Name.[284] And the verse says that He breathed into his nostrils the breath of life in order to inform us that the soul did not come to man from the elements, as He intimated concerning the soul of moving things, nor was it an evolvement from the Separate Intelligences.[237] Rather, it was the spirit of the Great G-d: *out of his mouth cometh knowledge and discernment.*[285] For he who breathes into the nostrils of another person gives into him something from his own soul.[286] It is this which Scripture says, *And the breath of the Almighty giveth them understanding,*[287] since the soul is from the foundation of *binah* (understanding) by way of truth and faith.[288] This corresponds to the saying of the Rabbis in the Sifre:[289] "Vows are like swearing 'by the life of the King:' oaths are like swearing 'by the King Himself.' Although there is no proof for it in Scripture, there is an allusion to it: *By the living G-d, and by the life of your soul.*"[290] And in the Midrash of Rabbi Nechunya ben Hakanah we find:[291] "What is the meaning of the word *vayinafash* (and He

(284) *And the 'Eternal G-d' formed... and He breathed into his nostrils....* (285) Proverbs 2:6. (286) Similarly, since G-d breathed into man's nostrils, it follows that the soul in man is of Divine essence. (287) Job 32:8. (288) *Truth and faith* here signify Cabalistic concepts. See my Hebrew commentary, p. 33. (289) Numbers, beginning of *Seder Matoth*. (290) II Kings 4:30. Here in the verse where an oath is being expressed, it says, *by the living G-d.* It does not say "by the life of G-d," which would indicate that His life is independent of Him; rather it says, *by the living G-d,* thus indicating that life is His very essence. (The correctness of this translation is indicated by the *patach* under the word *chai*, which is not in the construct state, and therefore means "*the living* G-d.") See my Hebrew commentary, p. 33, for further elucidation of this point. Thus there is an allusion here to the teaching of the Sifre that "an oath is like swearing 'by the King Himself,' " since in this verse quoted, where an oath is being given, it says, *by the living G-d.* This is an oath "by the King Himself." In the case of a person, however, it says "by the life of your soul," thus indicating that in a human being his life and his soul are two independent things. This explains the *tzere* under the word *chei*, which indicates a construct state combining two independent nouns. Thus there is an allusion to "Vows are like swearing 'by the life of the King.' " See also Note 293. (291) Sefer Habahir, 57. See above, Note 42.

rested)?[292] It teaches us that the day of the Sabbath preserves all souls, for it is *vayinafash*" [i.e., from the word *nefesh*, soul]. It is from here that you will understand the expression, *speaking the oath of G-d.*[293] The person learned in the mysteries of the Torah will understand.

Know that those who engage in research have differed concerning man. Some say that man has three souls. One is the soul of growth, like that in a plant; or you may call this "the force of growth." Then there is also a soul of movement in him, which Scripture mentioned concerning fish, animals, and everything that creeps upon the earth. The third is the rational soul. And there are some philosophers who say that this soul in man which comes from the Most High comprises these three forces while the soul is but one.[294] This verse in its plain meaning so indicates for it states that *G-d formed man of the dust of the ground,* but he lay there lifeless like a dumb stone, and the Holy One, blessed be He, *breathed into his nostrils the breath of life, and then man became a living soul,* able to move about by virtue of this soul, just like the animals and the fish, concerning which He said: *'Let the waters swarm with swarms of living creatures,'*[295] and *'Let the earth bring forth the living creature.'*[296] This is the meaning of the expression here, *'lenefesh chayah' (into a living soul) man was made,* meaning man turned into a soul in which there is life, after having been *as a potsherd with the potsherds of the earth.*[297] For the letter *lamed* in the word *lenefesh* indicates the opposite, [namely, that from being a potsherd he became a living soul]. And so it is in the verses, *And the water shall turn 'ledam' (into blood) upon the dry land;*[298] *And it turned 'lenachash' (into a snake);*[299] *And He made the sea 'lecharavah' (into dry land).*[300]

(292) Exodus 31:17. (293) Ecclesiastes 8:2. This denotes that an oath is like swearing "by G-d Himself." See Note 290 above. (294) The division of opinion among the philosophers as to the nature of the soul is clearly marked in Jewish philosophy. Ibn Ezra (Ecclesiastes 3:7) writes at length to prove that the soul in man consists of three parts. He quotes Saadia Gaon to be of the same opinion. The poet-philosopher Solomon ibn Gabirol (M'kor Chayim 5:20) also held this theory. Rambam, however, in his Sh'monah P'rakim, Chapter 1, holds that man's soul is but one. (295) Above, 1:20. (296) *Ibid.*, Verse 24. (297) Isaiah 45:9. (298) Exodus 4:9. (299) *Ibid.*, Verse 3. (300) *Ibid.*, 14:21.

Onkelos, however, said: "And it became a speaking soul in man." From this it would appear that his opinion coincides with those who say that man has various souls and that this rational soul which G-d breathed into his nostrils became a speaking soul.

It appears to me that this also is the opinion of our Rabbis, as we may deduce from what they said:[301] "Rava created a man. He sent him to Rabbi Zeira who spoke to him but he did not answer. Said Rabbi Zeira to him: 'You are created by one of the colleagues; return to your dust.' "[302] And in Midrash Vayikra Rabbah we find written:[303] "Said Rabbi Avin: When a man sleeps, the body tells the *neshamah* (the moving spirit), and the *neshamah* tells the *nefesh* (the rational soul), and the *nefesh* tells the angel."[304] So also the verse, *He gathers unto Himself his spirit and his breath,*[305] indicates, according to its plain meaning, that *his spirit and breath* are two distinct things.

That being so, the verse, *And the Eternal G-d formed man*, states the formation of movement, that man was formed into a creature capable of movement since "formation" denotes life and perception by virtue of which he is a man and not a kneaded mass of dust, just as it is said, *And the Eternal G-d formed out of the ground every beast of the field, and He brought them unto the man.*[306] And after He formed him with the power of perception, He breathed into his nostrils a living soul from the Most High, this soul being in addition to the formation mentioned, *and the* whole *man became a living soul* since by virtue of this soul he understands and speaks and does all his deeds and all other souls and their powers in man are subject to it. The letter *lamed* in the word *lenefesh* is thus the *lamed* indicating possession, just as in the following verses: *My lord, O king, 'lecha ani' (I am thine), and all that I have;*[307] *'lakoneh' (to him that bought)*

(301) Sanhedrin 65 b. (302) This story indicates that man has various souls, since Rava was able to bestow the soul of movement upon the man he created, but he could not give him the soul of speech. (303) 32:2. (304) The Midrash there concludes that each soul in man communicates to the other its sense of agreement that G-d's judgment is just. At the same time it is obvious from this Midrash that the Rabbis are of the opinion that there are various souls in man. (305) Job 34:14. (306) Further, Verse 19. (307) I Kings 20:4.

it, throughout his generations;[308] *'lecha ani' (I am thine), save me.*[309] Or, it may be that the verse is stating that man wholly became a living soul and was transformed into another man, as all His formations were, from now on, directed towards this soul.

8. AND THE ETERNAL G-D PLANTED A GARDEN 'MIKEDEM' (EASTWARD) IN EDEN. Rashi explained that "in the east of Eden He planted the garden." But Onkelos translated *mikedem* to mean "previously," [that is, before man was created]. And so have the Rabbis said in Bereshith Rabbah,[310] and this is the correct explanation.

The meaning of *vayita* (and He planted) is not that He brought the trees from another place and planted them here for it was from that place that He caused them to grow, just as it is said, *And out of the ground the Eternal G-d caused to grow every tree.*[311] But the purport of the expression, *and the Eternal G-d planted*, is to state that it was *the planting of the Eternal,*[312] for before He decreed upon the earth, *Let the earth put forth grass,* [313] He had already decreed that in that place there be a garden, and He further said: "Here shall be this tree, and here that tree," like the rows of planters. It was unlike the rest of the places on the earth concerning which He said, *Let the earth put forth grass... and fruit-tree,* [313] and it then grew without order. Now concerning the trees of the garden of Eden He decreed that they grow branches and bear fruit forever, the root thereof was never to wax old in the earth, and the stock thereof was never to die in the ground.[314] These trees were not to need any one to tend and prune them. For if they were in need of cultivation, who tended them after man was driven therefrom? This also is the meaning of the expression, *And the Eternal G-d planted*, that they were His plantings, the work of His hands,[315] and existing forever, even as it is said, *Its leaf shall not wither, neither shall the fruit thereof fail ... because the waters thereof issue out of the sanctuary.*[316] If so, what then is the meaning of the verse: *And He*

(308) Leviticus 25:30. , (309) Psalms 119:94. (310) 15:4. (311) Verse 9. (312) Isaiah 61:3. (313) Above, 1:11. (314) See Job 14:8. (315) See Isaiah 60:21. (316) Ezekiel 47:12.

put him into the garden of Eden to cultivate it and to keep it?[317] He put him [man] there so that he should sow for himself wheat and all kinds of produce, and every herb bearing seed, and rows of spices, reaping and plucking and eating at his will. This also is the meaning of *to cultivate it and to keep it*[317] — to cultivate the ground of the garden by the rows he [man] would make there, for the part of the garden where the trees were was not to be cultivated.

It is possible that [in the words *le'ovdah uleshomrah* — literally, *to cultivate her and to keep her,*] He refers to the garden in the feminine gender, just as in the verses: *And as the garden causeth the things that are sown in her to spring forth;*[318] *And plant gardens.*[319] Our Rabbis noted this use of the feminine gender, saying in Bereshith Rabbah:[320] *"Le'ovdah uleshomrah (to cultivate her and to keep her)* — these words refer to the sacrifices, as it is said, *'Ta'avdun' (Ye shall serve) G-d upon this mountain.*[321] It is this which Scripture says, *'Tishm'ru' (Ye shall keep) to offer unto Me in its appointed season."*[322] The intent of the Rabbis in this interpretation is that plants and all living beings are in need of primary forces from which they derive the power of growth and that through the sacrifices there is an extension of the blessing to the higher powers. From them it flows to the plants of the garden of Eden, and from them it comes and exists in the world in the form of "rain of goodwill and blessing,"[323] through which they will grow. This conforms to what the Rabbis have said:[324] *"The trees of the Eternal have their fill, the cedars of Lebanon, which He hath planted.*[325] Rabbi Chanina said: Their life shall have its fill; their waters shall have their fill; their plantings shall have their fill." "Their life" refers to their higher foundations; "their waters" refer to *His good treasure*[326] which brings down the rain; and "their plantings" refer to their force in heaven, just as the Rabbis have said:[327] "There is not a single blade of grass below that does not have a

(317) Further, Verse 15. (318) Isaiah 61:11. (319) Jeremiah 29:5. *Ganoth* (gardens) is here in the feminine gender. (320) 16:8. (321) Exodus 3:12. (322) Numbers 28:2. (323) Taanith 19 a. (324) Bereshith Rabbah 15:1. (325) Psalms 104:16. (326) Deuteronomy 28:12. (327) Bereshith Rabbah 10:7. This text is also quoted above 1:11 (Notes 135-6).

constellation in heaven that smites it and says to it, 'Grow.' It is this which Scripture says, *Knowest thou the ordinances of the heavens? Canst thou establish 'mishtara' (the dominion thereof) in the earth* – [*mishtara* being derived from the root] *shoter* (executive officer)."

9. AND THE TREE OF LIFE IN THE MIDST OF THE GARDEN AND THE TREE OF KNOWLEDGE OF GOOD AND EVIL. Since Scripture says, *And the tree of life in the midst of the garden,* and does not say "in the garden," and, moreover, since it says, *But of the fruit of the tree which is in the midst of the garden, G-d hath said: 'Ye shall not eat of it,'*[328] and does not mention it or refer to it by another name, we must say, according to the simple meaning of Scripture, that it was a known place in the garden which was "in the midst" thereof. This is why Onkelos translated: "in the middle of the garden." Thus according to Onkelos the tree of life and the tree of knowledge were both in the middle of the garden. And if so, we must say that in the middle of the garden there was the likeness of an enclosed garden-bed made which contained these two trees. This "middle" means near its middle for with respect to the exact middle, they have already said[329] that no one knows the true central point except G-d alone.

And the tree of life. This was a tree the fruit of which gave those who ate it long life.

And the tree of the knowledge of good and evil. The commentators[330] have said that the fruit thereof caused those who ate it to have a desire for sexual intercourse, and therefore Adam and Eve covered their nakedness after they ate of it [the fruit]. They quote a similar expression [where "good and evil" refers to such desire], the saying of Barzilai the Gileadite: *Can I distinguish between good and bad?*[331] – meaning that this sexual desire was already removed from him. But in my opinion this interpretation is

(328) Genesis 3:3. (329) If Ramban is stating a specific mathematical principle, its source is unknown to me. His intent may, however, be general. If so, the source may be found in Berachoth 3b, where it is stated that the exact point of midnight is known only to G-d. (330) Mentioned in R'dak in the name of the "commentators." (331) II Samuel 19:36.

not correct since the serpent said, *And ye shall be as 'Elohim,' knowing good and evil.*[332] And if you will say that the serpent lied to her, now [Scripture itself attests to the truth of his statement in the verse], *And the Eternal G-d said, 'Behold man has become like one of us knowing good and evil.'*[333] And the Rabbis have already said:[334] "Three stated the truth and perished from the world, and these are: the serpent, the spies,[335] and Doeg the Edomite.[336]

The proper interpretation appears to me to be that man's original nature was such that he did whatever was proper for him to do naturally, just as the heavens and all their hosts do, "faithful workers[337] whose work is truth, and who do not change from their prescribed course,"[338] and in whose deeds there is no love or hatred. Now it was the fruit of this tree that gave rise to will and desire, that those who ate it should choose a thing or its opposite, for good or for evil. This is why it was called *'etz hada'ath' (the tree of the knowledge) of good and evil,* for *da'ath* in our language is used to express will. Thus in the language of the Rabbis: "They have taught this only with regards to one *sheda'ato* (whose will) is to return;"[339] and "his will is to clear" [the produce in the store-room in his house before Passover].[340] And in the language of Scripture, *Eternal, what*

(332) The *Elohim* here means angels, who have no such desire (R'dak). (333) Genesis 3:22. (334) In Pirka D'Rabbeinu Hakadosh, Section 3. See my Hebrew commentary, p. 36, Note 84, for variants. (335) Numbers, Chapters 13-14. Sanhedrin 108 a. (336) I Samuel 22:9-10. Sanhedrin 90 a. The Hebrew text here also contains an additional word, "the Beerothite." See II Samuel, Chapter 4. Ramban's general thought is clear: the saying of the Rabbis proves that the serpent spoke the truth. Hence the serpent's statement, *And ye shall be as 'Elohim,' knowing good and evil,* was true. Now since sexual desire is not spoken of in connection with the angels, the expression *knowing good and evil* cannot refer to such desire. (337) Who do not veer from their prescribed course (Rashi, Sanhedrin 42 a). See, however, Tosafoth there which mentions a variant reading, "A faithful Worker," which refers to G-d. Our version of this benediction in the Prayer Book is based on this reading. (338) The source of this expression, in connection with the blessing for the new moon, is found in Sanhedrin 42 a. (339) Pesachim 6a. If his will (or wish) is to return to his house during the days of Passover, then he must search his house for leaven before leaving his house even if he leaves more than 30 days before Passover. (340) *Ibid.* In that case too he must search for leaven which lies under the produce even more than 30 days before Passover.

is man 'vateida'ehu,'[341] meaning that "Thou shouldst desire and want him;" *yedaticha beshem,*[342] meaning "I have chosen thee of all people." Similarly, Barzilai's expression, *Ha'eda (Can I distinguish) between good and bad,*[331] means that he lost the power of thought, no longer choosing a thing or loathing it, and he would eat without feeling taste and hear singing without enjoying it.

Now at that time sexual intercourse between Adam and his wife was not a matter of desire; instead, at the time of begetting offspring they came together and propagated. Therefore all the limbs were, in their eyes, as the face and hands, and they were not ashamed of them. But after he ate of the fruit of the tree of knowledge, he possessed the power of choice; he could now willingly do evil or good to himself or to others. This, on the one hand, is a godlike attribute; but as far as man is concerned, it is bad because through it, he has a will and desire. It is possible that Scripture intended to allude to this matter when it said, *That G-d made man upright, but they have sought out many inventions.*[343] The "uprightness" is that man should keep to one right path, and the "seeking out of many inventions" is man's search for deeds which change according to his choice. Now when the Holy One, blessed be He, commanded Adam concerning the tree, that he should not eat of its fruit, He did not inform him that it has this quality. He told him without any qualification, *But of the fruit of the tree which is in the midst of the garden,*[328] that is to say, the one that is known by its central position, *thou shalt not eat thereof.* And this was what the woman said to the serpent. And the verse which states, *But of the tree of the knowledge of good and evil, thou shalt not eat of it,*[344] mentions it to us by its true name.

11. THE LAND OF HAVILAH, WHERE THERE IS GOLD. This is to explain that it is not the Havilah of Egypt, concerning which it is said, *And they dwelt from Havilah unto Shur, that is before Egypt,*[345] for this one [referred to here] is in the extreme east. The verse mentions also, *There is the bdellium,*[346] in praise of the river,

(341) Psalms 144:3. (342) Exodus 33:12. Literally, *I know thee by name.* (343) Ecclesiastes 7:29. (344) Further, Verse 17. (345) Genesis 25:18. (346) Verse 12.

that in the sand that is in it and on its bank there is found that good gold, the bdellium and the onyx stone. For these things are found in rivers; in some, silver can be found. Similarly, the bdellium and precious stones are found mostly in rivers.

In the opinion of former scholars,[347] Pishon is the Nile of Egypt; it compasses this entire land of Havilah, and comes from there and passes the whole land of Egypt until it falls into the great sea at Alexandria in Egypt.

17. THOU SHALT NOT EAT OF IT. He admonishes him against eating the fruit, for the tree itself is not edible. And so it says further on: *But of the fruit of the tree which is in the midst of the garden.*[328] Similarly, *And eat ye every one of his vine, and every one of his fig tree*[348] [means "of the fruit of his vine and of the fruit of his fig-tree]." Likewise, *In toil shalt thou eat it*[349] means "eat its fruit."

IN THE DAY THOU EATEST THEREOF THOU SHALT SURELY DIE. At the time you eat of it, you will be condemned to die. Similarly, we find: *On the day thou goest out, and walkest abroad any whither, thou shalt surely die.*[350] This does not mean that he [Shimi] is to die immediately on that day; nor does it refer to his mere knowledge thereof, namely that he is to know that he will die eventually *for* all *the living know that they shall die.*[351] But it does mean that at the time he [Shimi] goes forth from Jerusalem, he is liable to death at the hand of the king, and he will slay him when he pleases. [Similarly, in the verses:] *But they shall not go in to see the holy things as they are being covered, lest they die;*[352] *And they shall not bear sin for it, and die thereby.*[353] Their intent is [not that those who transgress against these prohibitions will die immediately], but only that they will be liable to death and will die on account of this sin of theirs.

(347) Rabbeinu Saadia Gaon and Rashi. (348) II Kings 18:31. (349) Genesis 3:17. (350) I Kings 2:42. Said by Solomon to Shimi, that on the day he goes outside of the limits of Jerusalem he *shall surely die.* (351) Ecclesiastes 9:5. (352) Numbers 4:20. (353) Leviticus 22:9.

Now in the opinion of men versed in the sciences of nature, man was destined to die from the beginning of his formation, on account of his being a composite [of the four elements, and everything that is composite must revert to its original components]. But now He decreed that if he will sin he will die on account of his sin, like those who are liable to death at the hands of Heaven for such sins as a non-priest eating the Heave-offering, or a priest who has drunk wine or who does not wear the [required number of priestly] garments when performing the Service in the Sanctuary, and other cases. There the intent is that they will die prematurely on account of their sin. This is why in stating the punishment [after Adam ate of the fruit of the tree of knowledge] He said, *Till thou return to the ground; for out of it wast thou taken; for dust thou art, and unto dust shalt thou return,*[354] by your nature. In the beginning before he sinned, Adam also ate of the fruit of the tree and of the seeds of the earth; and if so, there was bound to be depletion in his body, and he was subject to the cause of existence and destruction. [Thus the opinion of the men of science.]

But in the opinion of our Rabbis,[355] if Adam had not sinned he would have never died, since the higher soul bestows life forever, and the Will of G-d which is in him at the time of his formation would always cleave to him and he would exist forever, as I have explained in the verse, *And G-d saw that it was good.*[356]

Know that composition indicates destruction only in the opinion of those wanting in faith, who hold that creation came by necessity. But in the opinion of men of faith who say that the world was created by the simple Will of G-d, its existence will also continue forever as long as it is His desire. This is clear truth. That being so, *In the day thou eatest thereof thou shalt surely die* means that then you will be condemned to die since you will no longer exist forever by My Will. And the matter of eating [from the other trees] was to

(354) Genesis 3:19. (355) Shabbath 58 b. (356) Above, 1:10.

Adam at first only a source of enjoyment.[357] And it is possible that the fruits of the garden of Eden were absorbed in his limbs as the Manna, and they sustain those that eat them. But when He decreed upon him, *And thou shalt eat the herb of the field*[358] and with the sweat of his face he shall eat bread of the earth,[359] this [the food] became a cause for decomposition since he is dust, and dust he eats, and unto dust he shall return.

18. IT IS NOT GOOD THAT THE MAN SHOULD BE ALONE. It does not appear likely that man was created to be alone in the world and not beget children since all created beings – male and female of all flesh – were created to raise seed. The herb and trees also have their seed in them. But it is possible to say that it was in accordance with the opinion of the Rabbi who says:[360] "Adam was created with two faces [i.e., male and female persons combined]," and they were so made that there should be in them an impulse causing the organs of generation to produce a generative force from male to female, or you may say "seed," in accordance with the known controversy concerning pregnancy,[361] and the second face was a help to the first in the procreative process. And the Holy One, blessed be He, saw that it is good that "the help" stand facing him, and that he should see and be separated from it or joined to it at his will. This is the meaning of what He said in the verse, *I will make him a helper opposite him.*

The meaning of the expression, *it is not good,* is that it cannot be said of man that "it is good" when he is alone for he will not be able to so exist. In the work of creation, "the good" means existence, as I have explained on the text, *And G-d saw that it was good.*[362]

(357) Ramban is aiming to answer the question: If Adam was destined at first to exist forever on account of his superior soul, what purpose did his eating serve? Ramban answers that, according to this theory, he ate not out of necessity but for enjoyment. (358) Genesis 3:18. (359) *Ibid.*, Verse 19. (360) Berachoth 61 a. The name of the Rabbi is Yirmeyahu the son of Rabbi Elazar. (361) See Ramban, beginning of *Seder* Thazria concerning the opinion of the doctors and the Greek philosophers. (362) Above, 1:10.

19. AND WHATSOEVER 'YIKRA LO HA'ADAM NEFESH CHAYAH' (THE MAN WOULD CALL EVERY LIVING CREATURE). Rashi comments: "Invert [the phrasing of the sentence] and explain it thus: and every living creature to which Adam would give a name, that should remain its name forever." And Rabbi Abraham ibn Ezra said that the letter *lamed* of the phrase, *that the man called 'lo' (it),* is carried forward [to the word *nefesh*, making it *lenefesh (to* the creature), thus] : and whatever the man called *to* every living creature, that was to be its name.

It is possible that the phrase be explained in connection with the matter of "the help" that G-d gave to Adam, and the meaning is that *ha'adam nefesh chayah* (man is a living soul), as it is said, *And man became a living soul,*[363] and it is as I have explained it there. And He brought before him all species so that every one of them unto which Adam would give a name and say that it is a living soul like himself, that would remain its name and be a help to him. So Adam gave names to all, but as for himself he found no help which he would be able to call "a living soul" like his own name.

20. BUT FOR ADAM THERE WAS NOT FOUND A HELP MEET FOR HIM. Rashi comments: "When He brought them, He brought them before him as male and female. Thereupon Adam said, 'All of them have a mate, and I have no mate!' Immediately, *the Eternal G-d caused a deep sleep to fall* upon him." Rashi explained it well for by Scripture's bringing the verses concerning "the calling of names" into the matter of "the help" that G-d gave Adam, it proves that this interpretation mentioned above is correct.

"The calling of names," in the opinion of the commentators,[364] is to be understood in its plain sense, namely, that everyone should have a name for himself so that they be known and recognized in their progeny by the names Adam would call them, names which would be valid forever. Now when the Holy One, blessed be He, wanted to make "the help" for Adam He brought all species before him since He had to bring them before him in pairs so that he should also give a name to the females of the species; for in some [species,

(363) Above, Verse 7. (364) Rashi and R'dak.

both male and female] are called by one name, and in others they differ, such as bull and cow, *tayish* (he-goat) and *eiz* (she-goat), sheep and ewe, and others. When Adam saw them mating with each other, he had a desire for them, but as he found among them no help for himself, he was saddened and fell asleep. G-d then caused a deep sleep to fall upon him so that he should not feel the removal of a rib from his body.

In my opinion, however, "the calling of the names" is identical with "the help" [as I explained in the above verse], and the purport thereof is as follows: the Holy One, blessed be He, brought before Adam all the beasts of the field and all the fowl of the heavens, and he, recognizing their nature, called them names, that is, names appropriate to them. By the names it was made clear who is fit to be the help for another, meaning, fit to procreate with one another. Even if we are to believe that names are merely a matter of consensus and not of nature, [i.e., that they do not reflect the essence of the object bearing the name], we can say that "the calling of the names" means the division of the species as – male and female – they passed before Adam and he contemplated their nature as to which of them would be a help to each other in procreation so that they should beget offspring. Thus he called the large creatures by one name and the beasts by another so they would not beget offspring from one another, and so on for all species. And among them all he did not find a natural help for himself so that it could be called by his name for "the calling of the names" signifies the division of the species and the separation of their powers from each other, as I have explained above. Now it does not mean that it was in Adam's power to find a help for himself among them since they were all created with natures [different from that of man]. But it means that if Adam was to find satisfaction with one of the species and he would choose it for his help, the Holy One, blessed be He, would adapt its nature to him, as He did with the rib, and He would not have found it necessary to build "a new structure."[365] This is the meaning of the verse, *And*

(365) "A new structure" is a reference to the explanation of the Rabbis: "*Vayiven (And He built... the rib)* – this teaches us that He *built* Eve after the fashion of a store-house." (Eruvin 18 a.)

whatsoever the man would call every living creature, that was its name;[366] that is to say, that was to be its name, for the Holy One, blessed be He, would so preserve it along the lines which I have explained.

In my opinion it is correct to say that it was His will, blessed be He, not to take Adam's rib from him to make him a wife until he himself would know that among the created beings there is no help suitable for him and until he would crave to have a help suitable for him like her. This was why it was necessary to take one of his ribs from him. This is the meaning of the verse, *But for Adam there was not found a help meet for him;* that is to say, but for the name *Adam* (man), he found no help suited to be opposite him and to be called by his name so that he should beget children from that "help". We need not resort here, therefore, to the words of the commentators[367] who say that the name "Adam" comes here in place of the reflexive pronoun ["himself." The verse would thus read: "But for himself] he found no help meet for him," just as, *Ye wives of Lemech,*[368] [which should read, "*my* wives"]; *And Jephthah, and Samuel,*[369] [which should read, "and Jephthah and myself"]. This is the meaning of Adam's saying: *This is now bone of my bones;*[370] that is to say, "This time I have found a help for me which I did not find till now among the other species, for she is *bone of my bones, and flesh of my flesh,*[370] and is fit to be actually called by my name for we shall propagate together."

In the word *zoth* (this, this time) there is a secret; it will be made known from our words in the section *Vezoth habracha,*[371] if my Rock will bless me, enabling me reach thereto. This is why Adam repeats, *because 'zoth' (this) was taken out of man.*[370] [Delve into it] and understand.

(366) Verse 19. (367) Ibn Ezra and R'dak. (368) Genesis 4:23. (369) I Samuel 12:11. The words were spoken by Samuel. (370) Further, Verse 23. (371) See Ramban, Deuteronomy 33:1, in the commentary beginning, "the man of G-d."

24. THEREFORE SHALL A MAN LEAVE HIS FATHER AND HIS MOTHER, AND SHALL CLEAVE TO HIS WIFE. The Divine Spirit says this, thus prohibiting immoral relationships to "the sons of Noah."[372]

AND THEY SHALL BE ONE FLESH. The child is created by both parents, and there in the child, their flesh is united into one. Thus the words of Rashi. But there is no point to this since in beast and cattle too, their flesh is united into one in their offspring.

The correct interpretation appears to me to be that in cattle and beast the males have no attachment to their females. Rather, the male mates with any female he finds, and then they go their separate ways. It is for this reason that Scripture states that because the female of man was bone of his bones and flesh of his flesh, he therefore cleaves to her and she nestles in his bosom as his own flesh, and he desires to be with her always. And just as it was with Adam, so was his nature transmitted to his offspring, that the males among them should cleave to their women, leaving their fathers and their mothers, and considering their wives as if they are one flesh with them. A similar sense is found in the verses: *For he is our brother, our flesh;*[373] *to any that is near of his flesh.*[374] Those who are close members of the family are called *sh'eir basar* (near of flesh). Thus man will leave "the flesh" of his father and his mother and their kin and will see that his wife is nearer to him than they.

3 6. THAT THE TREE WAS GOOD FOR FOOD. She [Eve] had thought that the fruit of the tree was bitter and poisonous and this was why He admonished them against eating thereof, but now she saw that it was good and sweet food.

AND THAT IT WAS A DELIGHT TO THE EYES, i.e., that by means of its fruit, one attains desire and goes about after his own eyes.

(372) See above, Note 222. (373) Genesis 37:27. (374) Leviticus 18:6.

AND THAT THE TREE WAS TO BE DESIRED TO MAKE ONE WISE for by means of its fruit, one becomes wise to desire. Now she ascribed "delight" to the eyes and "desire" to the mind. The principle is that [by eating the fruit of the tree], one can will and desire a thing or its opposite.

7. AND THE EYES OF THEM BOTH WERE OPENED. Scripture speaks here with reference to intelligence, and not with reference to actual seeing. The end of the verse proves this: *and they knew they were naked.* [Even a blind person knows when he is naked! It must therefore refer to intelligence], as [explained in] the words of Rashi. In a similar sense is the verse, *Open thou mine eyes, that I may behold wondrous things out of Thy law.*[375]

8. AND THEY HEARD THE VOICE OF THE ETERNAL G-D WALKING IN THE GARDEN. The Rabbis have said in Bereshith Rabbah:[376] "Rabbi Chilfi said that from here we may learn that a voice 'walks,' for it is said, *And they heard the voice of the Eternal G-d walking.*" And so did the Rabbi [Moshe ben Maimon] write in Moreh Nebuchim.[377] And so is the opinion of Rabbi Abraham ibn Ezra that "walking" refers to "the voice," just as in the verse: *The sound thereof shall go like the serpent's.*[378] And Ibn Ezra further says that the meaning of *toward the cool of the day* is that they heard the voice towards evening. And he mentioned in the name of Rabbi Jonah ibn Ganach[379] that the meaning of the verse is: "and man was walking in the garden toward the cool of the day," [the sense of the verse thus being that while man was walking in the garden, he heard the voice of G-d].

In my opinion, the sense of *walking in the garden* of Eden is similar to that of the verses: *And I will walk among you;*[380] *And the*

(375) Psalms 119:18. Here too "the opening of eyes" has reference to understanding. (376) 19:12. (377) I, 24: "It is *the voice* that is modified by *walking.*" (378) Jeremiah 46:22. (379) Also known as Jonah ibn Janach (990-1050), considered the greatest Hebrew grammarian. He is the author of the Rikmah (Many Colored Web) and the Book of Roots, a lexicon. (380) Leviticus 26:12.

Eternal went as soon as He had finished speaking with Abraham;[381] *I will go and return to My place.*[382] All these verses indicate a revelation of the Divine Presence in that place or the departure from the place wherein He was revealed. The sense of the expression, *toward the cool of the day,* is that with the revelation of the Divine Presence comes a great and strong wind, even as it says, *And, behold, the Eternal passed by, and a great and strong wind rent the mountains, and broke in pieces the rocks before the Eternal.*[383] Similarly we find: *Yea, He did swoop down upon the wings of the wind;*[384] and in the book of Job it is written, *Then the Eternal answered Job out of the whirlwind.*[385] Therefore Scripture says here that *they heard the voice of G-d* as the Divine Presence was revealed in the garden approaching them in the wind of the day, *because the breath of the Eternal blew upon it,*[386] that is, in the garden, like the wind of ordinary days, not a great and strong wind as in the vision of other prophecies, in order that they should not be frightened or terrified. Yet Scripture says that in spite of this they hid themselves on account of their nakedness. In Bereshith Rabbah[387] we find that the Rabbis also said: "Said Rabbi Aba the son of Kahana: '*Mehalech* (walking) is not written here but *mith'halech* (meaning "it leaped and ascended)."[388] Rabbi Aba thus interpreted the word *mith'halech* similarly to that of *And the Eternal went,*[381] as we have explained the term "walking," except that he explained the verse before us as referring to the withdrawal of the Divine Presence that dwelt in the garden of Eden and its retiring therefrom on account of the sin of Adam, even as it says, *I will go and return to My place.*[382] We interpret it to mean the revelation of the Divine Presence in that place, which is the correct and fitting explanation of the verse.

12. THE WOMAN WHOM THOU GAVEST TO BE WITH ME. The sense of it is to say: "The woman whom Thy Honor Himself gave me

(381) Genesis 18:33. (382) Hosea 5:15. (383) I Kings 19:11. (384) Psalms 18:11. (385) Job 38:1. (386) Isaiah 40:7. (387) 19:13. (388) This means that when Adam sinned, the Divine Presence went from the earth to the first heaven, and then with every successive generation of sinners it departed to yet another higher heaven. This is so clearly explained in Bereshith Rabbah there (19:12).

for a help, *she gave me of the tree,* and I thought that whatever she says to me is a help and benefit to me." This is why He said when meting out his punishment, *Because thou hast hearkened unto the voice of thy wife,*[389] meaning "You should not have transgressed My commandment on account of her advice." Our Rabbis have called Adam "ungrateful" for this remark.[390] By this they mean to explain that the sense of his answer was: "Thou caused me this stumbling for Thou gavest me a woman as a help, and she counselled me to do evil."[391]

13. WHAT IS THIS THOU HAST DONE to transgress My commandment? For the woman was included in the admonition given to Adam since at that time she was yet bone of his bones, and similarly she was included in his punishment. The reason why G-d did not say to the woman, "and thou hast eaten of the tree," is that she was punished for both her eating and her advice, just as the serpent was punished for the advice. This is why she said, *The serpent beguiled me, and I did eat,*[392] as the punishment for the beguiling was greater than that for the eating. [Hence as soon as she mentioned that the serpent beguiled her, G-d meted out his punishment immediately, as is stated in the following two verses.] Thus we may derive from here the principle of punishment for those that cause people to sin in any matter, just as our Rabbis have derived it from the verse, *Thou shalt not put a stumbling-block before the blind.*[393]

14. FROM AMONG ALL CATTLE, AND FROM AMONG ALL BEASTS OF THE FIELD. From a study of this verse, Rabbi Yehoshua the son of Chananya derived the fact that a serpent gives

(389) Further, Verse 17. (390) Avodah Zarah 5 b. (391) He thus ascribed his sin to G-d's giving him Eve as a help. (Rashi, *ibid.*) In this he spoke ungratefully. (392) In the verse before us. Thus she mentioned both the eating and the advice. (393) Leviticus 19:14. In Pesachim 22 b, the verse is interpreted to mean: do not give a person who is "blind" in a matter advice which is improper for him. Advising or causing one to sin is thus included in this prohibition. Ramban is here suggesting that while the admonition against causing people to sin is derived from the verse in Leviticus, the principle of punishment for such advice is derived from here.

birth once in seven years;[394] this they investigated and found to be so.[395] For the Midrashic interpretations of Scripture and their allusions are all traditional, and they found in them profound secrets on procreation and all matters, as I mentioned in my introduction.

15. AND THOU SHALT BRUISE THEIR HEEL. This means man will have an advantage over you [the serpent] in the enmity between him and you for he will bruise your head but you will bruise him only in his heel, with which he will crush your brain.

16. 'T'SHUKATHECH' (AND THY DESIRE) SHALL BE TO THY HUSBAND, meaning for cohabitation. Yet you will not have the boldness to demand it by word, rather *he shall rule over thee.* It will all be from him and not from you. Thus are the words of Rashi. But this is not correct, for modesty is praiseworthy in a woman, just as the Rabbis have said:[396] "This is a good quality in women."

Rabbi Abraham ibn Ezra said: "*And thy desire shall be to thy husband*, meaning your obedience." This means you will obey whatever he commands you for you are under his authority to do his desire. However, I have found the expression *t'shukah* used only in connection with desire and lust.

The correct interpretation appears to me to be that He punished her that her desire for her husband be exceedingly great and that she should not be deterred by the pain of pregnancy and birth or that he keeps her as a maid-servant. Now it is not customary for a servant to desire to acquire a master over himself, rather his desire is to flee from him. Thus her punishment is measure for measure; she gave [the fruit of the tree of knowledge] also to her husband and he ate at her command, and He punished her that she should no longer command him, but instead he should command her entirely at his will.

(394) Bechoroth 8a. See my Hebrew commentary, p. 41. (395) See Bereshith Rabbah 20:7. (396) Eruvin 100 b.

22. AND NOW, LEST HE PUT FORTH HIS HAND. The Holy One, blessed be He, wanted His decree concerning the death of Adam to be fulfilled, and if he were to eat of the tree of life which was created to give everlasting life to those who ate of its fruit, the decree would be nullified; for either he would not die at all or his day of death would not come at the time it was decreed for him and his descendants to die. [397] And now that Adam had the power of choice, He therefore guarded this tree from him for at first Adam did only what he was commanded and he did not eat thereof as he did not need it.

Know and believe that the garden of Eden is on this earth [398] as are also the tree of life and the tree of knowledge, and from there the river comes forth and is divided into four heads [399] which are visible to us. For the Euphrates [400] is in our land and within our border,[401] and Pishon, [402] according to the words of the former scholars, is the Nile of Egypt. [402] But as these are on earth so are there also in the heavens things similarly named, and those in the heavens are the foundations of these on earth, just as the Rabbis have said: [403] "*The king hath brought me into his chambers*[404] – this teaches us that the Holy One, blessed be He, is destined to show Israel the treasures on high that are chambered in the heavens. Another interpretation of *The king hath brought me into his chambers* is that these are the chambers of the garden of Eden. It is on the basis of this that they have said: 'The work of the garden of Eden is like the work of the firmament.' " The rivers correspond to the four camps of angels on

(397) See above, 2:17, where Ramban explained two theories. The teaching of the Rabbis is that man was originally designed to live forever. By having sinned, death was decreed upon him; by eating of the tree of life, he would thus restore himself to his original position of immortality. The opinion of the philosophers, however, is that man was originally destined to die; by having sinned, it was decreed that he die before the time designated at first. By eating of the tree of life he would thus live a long time and not die at the time decreed for him as punishment for his sin. This is the deeper meaning of Ramban's words here in the text, "for either he would not die at all, etc." (398) See my Kitvei Haramban, Vol. 1, p. 309, in notes, as to why this point that the Garden of Eden is on this earth is of such vital importance to Ramban that he writes: '*Know and believe* that the garden....'" (399) Above, 2:10. (400) *Ibid.*, 2:14. (401) Deuteronomy 1:1. (402) Above, 2:11. (403) Midrash Shir Hashirim Zuta, 1:4, (Buber ed., pp. 9-10). (404) Song of Songs 1:4.

high, and it is from there that the power of the kingdoms on earth is derived, just as it is written, *The host of the high heaven on high, and the kings of the earth upon the earth.*[405] Thus the Rabbis said in Bereshith Rabbah,[406] "*Into four heads*[407] – these are the four kingdoms. *The name of the first is Pishon*[408] – this is Babylon, etc." And the things called the tree of life and the tree of knowledge on high – their secret is high and lofty. Adam sinned with the fruit of the tree of knowledge below and on high, in deed and thought.

Now if the fruit of the tree were good for food and he desired it to become wise, why did He withhold it from him? Indeed, G-d is kind and dealeth kindly; *He will withhold no good thing from them that walk uprightly!*[409] The serpent, moreover, has today no speaking faculty, and if it did have it at first, He would surely have mentioned in His curse that its mouth become dumb, as this would have been the most grievous curse of all. But all these things are twofold in meaning, the overt and the concealed in them both being true.

In Bereshith Rabbah the Rabbis say:[410] "Another interpretation of *Le'ovdah uleshomrah (to cultivate her and to keep her)*[411] is that these words refer to the sacrifices, as it is said, *'Ta'avdun' (Ye shall serve) G-d upon this mountain.*[412] It is this which Scripture says, *'Tishm'ru' (Ye shall keep) to offer unto Me in its appointed season.*"[413] By this Midrash, the Rabbis hinted that the sacrifices will cause growth and expansion in the tree of life and the tree of knowledge and all other trees in the garden of Eden. It is this which constitutes their cultivation and care.

Now Rabbi Abraham ibn Ezra denies what the scholars have said, namely, that Pishon is the Nile, because they found that the Nile comes from the Mountain of Frankincense [far south of the equator], and therefore it swells during the days of summer.[414] But

(405) Isaiah 24:21. (406) 16:7. (407) Above, 2:10. (408) *Ibid.*, 2:11. (409) Psalms 84:12. (410) 16:8. Mentioned also above, 2:8. (411) Above, 2:15. (412) Exodus 3:12. (413) Numbers 28:2. (414) For when it is summer time in the northern hemisphere, it is the time of the rainy season in the southern hemisphere. Hence the Nile, the source of which is in the southern hemisphere, swells during the summer time. And "we know that the Garden of Eden is near the equator, where day and night are always equal" (Ibn Ezra), it follows that Pishon is not the Nile, since the Nile originates far south of the equator. This is the opinion of Ibn Ezra. Ramban replies: "But it is already known, etc."

it is already known that many rivers come from their source and flow for a great distance and enter the bowels of the earth for a journey of many days, and then break forth again, and flow from under one of the mountains in a distant place. [This being the case, it is possible that Pishon *is* the Nile.]

4 1. AND SHE CONCEIVED AND BORE CAIN. The sense of it is that she gave birth to a son, and she called his name Cain [from the word *kanah*, acquisition] , because she said, *I have gotten a man with* [the help of] *the Eternal.* In a similar sense is the verse, *And she conceived and bore Enoch,* [415] and many similar verses in this chapter and in other places.

"*Eth Hashem* (with the Eternal). When He created me and my husband He created us by Himself, but in the case of this one, we are co-partners with him." Thus the words of Rashi.

The correct interpretation appears to me to be that she said: "This son will be for me an acquisition for the Eternal, for when we shall die he will exist in our stead to worship his Creator." This is also the opinion of Onkelos who translated *eth hashem* to mean "before the Eternal." [The word *eth* in the following verses is translated] in a similar sense: *And it shall be shown 'eth hakohen' (the priest),* [416] meaning to the priest; *And David came near 'eth ha'am' (the people),* [417] meaning to the people. Or it may be that *eth hashem* has the same interpretation as in the verses: *And Enoch walked 'eth ha'elokim' (with G-d);* [418] *Noah walked 'eth ha'elokim' (with G-d).* [419]

Now she [Eve] called one son by a name indicating "acquisition," and the second one she called Abel, denoting "vanity" because man's acquisition is likened to vanity. But she did not wish to say so explicitly. Therefore, no reason is written for the name of the second son. The secret received by tradition concerning Abel is very profound. [420]

(415) Further, Verse 17. (416) Leviticus 13:49. (417) I Samuel 30:21. (418) Genesis 5:22. See following note. (419) *Ibid.*, 6:9. The sense here in the verse before us would thus be: I have acquired a man to walk with G-d. (420) See my Hebrew commentary, p. 43.

3. AND CAIN BROUGHT OF THE FRUIT OF THE GROUND AN OFFERING UNTO THE ETERNAL. 4. AND ABEL, HE ALSO BROUGHT. These men [Cain and Abel] understood the great secret of the sacrifices and the meal-offerings. So also did Noah, [who likewise offered sacrifices].[421] Our Rabbis have said that the first man also sacrificed a bullock.[422] This should close the mouth of those who speak foolishness[423] concerning the reason of the sacrifices. I will yet intimate a great principle concerning this matter with the will of the Holy One, blessed be He.[424]

7. IS IT NOT THUS, IF THOU MENDEST 'SE'EITH'. In the opinion of the commentators,[425] this means there is a "lifting" or forgiveness of your sin. And in the opinion of Rabbi Abraham ibn Ezra it means a "lifting" of your face in contrast to [the question G-d asked of Cain]: *Why is thy face fallen?*[426] For he who is ashamed presses his face downward. Similarly, it is said, *And the light of my countenance they cast not down,*[427] whereas one who honors him is as if he raises his face upward. This is the sense of the verses: *Perhaps he will lift my face;*[428] *Do not lift the face of the poor.*[429]

In my opinion the verse means: "If you will mend your ways you will have your rightful superiority in *se'eith* (dignity) over your brother since you are the firstborn." And this is the meaning of [G-d's question to him]: *Why art thou wroth?*[426] For by virtue of his feeling ashamed before his brother, his face fell, and because of his jealousy of him he killed him, and now the Eternal told him: *Why art thou wroth* regarding your brother, *and why is thy face fallen* on

(421) Genesis 8:20. (422) Psalms 69:32. Chullin 60 a. (423) Reference is made here to the Moreh Nebuchim, III, 46, where it is stated that the laws concerning the sacrifices were intended as a guard against idolatry. It is this theory that Ramban intends to refute when he says that in the days of Adam, Cain and Abel, there was no idolatry and yet they brought sacrifices. There is thus a positive aspect to the sacrifices which Rambam did not take into account. (424) See Ramban on Leviticus 1:9. (425) Reference is here to R'dak. So also in Onkelos. (426) Verse 6. (427) Job 29:24. (428) Genesis 32:21. Meaning, perhaps he will accept me. (429) Leviticus 19:15. Meaning, do not respect the person of the poor in judgment, but judge in righteousness.

account of him? *Is it not thus! If thou mendest,* you will have superiority in *dignity* over your brother, *and if thou dost not mend,* evil will come upon you not only because of him [your brother], for *at the door* of your house your *sin lurks* causing you to stumble in all your endeavors.

AND UNTO THEE IS ITS LONGING, for your sin longs to cleave to you at all times. Nevertheless *thou mayest rule over it* if you so desire, for you may mend your ways and remove it from upon you. Thus He taught him [Cain] concerning repentance, that it lies within his power to return anytime he desires and He will forgive him.

8. AND CAIN SPOKE TO ABEL HIS BROTHER. He began a conversation of argument and contention with him in order to seek a pretext against him and so kill him. This is the language of Rashi. Rabbi Abraham ibn Ezra said that the interpretation that appears most likely to him is that Cain related to Abel all the chastisements with which G-d had reprimanded him [and Cain accused Abel of having brought them upon him].

But in my opinion it is connected with the following words of Scripture: *and it came to pass, when they were in the field,* meaning that Cain said to Abel, "Let us go forth into the field," and there he secretly killed him.

It is possible that his intention in killing Abel was that the world be built up from himself for he thought that his father would not have any more children. He also feared that the main building up of the world might be from his brother, [which seemed likely since it was he] whose offering had been favorably accepted.

11. CURSED ART THOU FROM THE GROUND – more than it has already been cursed on account of its sin. In this, too, it has further sinned in that *it hath opened its mouth to take thy brother's blood.* Therefore, I impose upon it an additional curse: *it shall not continue to give unto thee her strength.*[430] Thus the words of Rashi.

(430) Verse 12.

But this is not correct since here He did not curse the ground because of him as He did in the case of his father, rather He said that he be cursed through the ground. The explanation of the curse is that the earth shall not continue to give him its strength, and that he be a fugitive and a wanderer in it,[430] and He further stated, "*When thou tillest the ground*[430] with all your efforts to cultivate it properly by plowing and hoeing, *and in all manner of service in the field*[431] and by properly sowing it, *it shall not continue to give unto thee her strength.*[430] Instead, you will sow much and harvest little." This then was the curse, in the same sense as in the verse: *And I will curse your blessings.*[432] Thus He uttered the curse in connection with his occupation for *he was a tiller of the ground,*[433] and so He cursed his work. This then is the sense of the expression, *it shall not continue to give unto thee her strength,*[430] meaning, "It will no longer yield to you its full produce as it had done till now when you cultivated it." And so did Rabbi Abraham ibn Ezra explain it.

It is possible that He also cursed him though the ground in that it should no longer yield its strength to him of its own accord; the fig-tree and the vine would not yield their strength[434] in his estate, and the trees of the field would not yield him their fruit.[435] Then He added, "Even when you work the ground by plowing and sowing, it will not continue to give you its strength as before." Thus there were two curses relating to his occupation, and a third one – that he be a fugitive and a wanderer in the world. This means that his heart will not be at rest, and he will lack the tranquility to remain in one place on the earth; he will wander forever for the punishment of murderers is exile.

The expression *in that it hath opened its mouth to take thy brother's blood* means: "You have killed your brother and covered his blood with the earth, and I will decree upon it that it uncover its blood, *and she shall no more cover her slain*[436] for it will be punished together with all that is covered up in it, such as seed and plant." This is the punishment for all blood-letting on the earth, even as it is written, *For blood, it polluteth the land.*[437] The pollution of

(431) Exodus 1:14. (432) Malachi 2:2. (433) Verse 2. (434) See Joel 2:22. (435) See Leviticus 26:4. (436) Isaiah 26:21. (437) Numbers 35:33.

the land consists of a curse upon its produce, as it is written: *When one came to a heap of twenty measures, there were but ten; when one came to the wine vat to draw out fifty press-measures, there were but twenty.*[438]

13. MY SIN IS GREATER THAN I CAN BEAR. This is in the form of a question: "You bear the worlds above and below, and is it impossible for You to bear my sin?" Thus the words of Rashi quoting Bereshith Rabbah.[439]

The correct plain interpretation is that it is a confession. Cain said: "It is true that my sin is too great to be forgiven, and *Thou art righteous, O Eternal, and upright are Thy judgments*[440] even though You have punished me exceedingly. And now *behold, Thou hast driven me out this day from the face of the land*[441] for in being a fugitive and a wanderer unable to stay in one place, behold, I am driven from the land and there is no place where I can find rest. *And from Thy face shall I be hid*[441] whereas I will not be able to stand before You to pray or bring a sacrifice and meal-offering for *I was ashamed, yea, even confounded, because I did bear the reproach of my youth.*[442] But what shall I do? *Whosoever findeth me shall slay me,*[441] and You in Your manifold loving-kindness did not decree death upon me." The sense of this is that Cain said before G-d: "Behold, my sin is great, and You have punished me exceedingly, but guard me that I should not be punished more than You have decreed upon me for by being a fugitive and wanderer and unable to build myself a house and fences at any place, the beasts will kill me for your shadow has departed from me."[443] Thus Cain confessed that man is impotent to save himself by his own strength but only by the watchfulness of the Supreme One upon him.

Now because Scripture says, *And the Eternal appointed a sign for Cain,*[444] and it does not say, "and G-d gave him a sign," or "made him a sign," it indicates that He appointed for him a steady sign which would always be with him. Perhaps it indicates that as he

(438) Haggai 2:16. (439) 22:25. (440) Psalms 119:137. (441) Verse 14. (442) Jeremiah 31:19. (443) See Numbers 14:9 and Ramban there. (444) Verse 15.

wandered from place to place he had a sign from G-d indicating the way in which he should walk, and by that he knew that no misfortune would overtake him on that road.

In Bereshith Rabbah[445] the Rabbis similarly stated, "Rabbi Aba said: 'He gave him a dog.' " Since he feared the beasts, He gave him one of them to walk before him, and wherever the dog turned to go, Cain knew that G-d commanded him to go there and that he would not be killed by any living creature. Now the Sages singled out a contemptible sign [a dog] as was befitting him, but the intent is that there was with him a perpetual sign showing him the way to go for such is indicated in the word *vayasem (and He appointed).*

16. AND CAIN WENT OUT FROM THE PRESENCE OF THE ETERNAL. The sense thereof is that he never stood before Him any more, as he meant when he said, *and from Thy face shall I be hid,*[441] [as explained above].

And he dwelt in the land of Nod. The sense thereof is that Cain did not traverse the entire world, but he dwelt in that land, perpetually wandering therein and not resting at all in any one place thereof, and so it was forever called "the land of *Nod* (wandering)" after him.

17. AND HE BUILDED A CITY, AND CALLED THE NAME OF THE CITY AFTER THE NAME OF HIS SON ENOCH. For at first Cain thought that he would be childless on account of his sin, but after a child was born to him he began to build a city for his son to dwell therein. But because he himself was cursed and his works would not prosper, he called the city "Enoch," thus proclaiming that he did not build it for himself since he has no city or dwelling place in the land because he was a fugitive and wanderer; rather, the building would be for Enoch, and it is as if Enoch had built it for himself.

Now since it does not say *vayiven ir* (and he built a city) – [but rather, *vayehi boneh ir*, which literally means "and he was building a city,"] as it says elsewhere, *vayiven (and he builded) Nineveh;*[446]

(445) 22:27. (446) Genesis 10:11.

And the children of Gad built Dibon[447] – it indicates that he was building the city all his days because his works were cursed. Thus he would build a little with effort and toil, and then move and wander off from that place and return there and build a little more, but he would not prosper in his ways.

The descendants of Cain and his works were recorded in Scripture in order to make known that G-d is long-suffering and that He prolonged the time of his punishment,[448] for he begot children and children's children, and then it relates how He visited *the iniquity of the fathers upon the children,*[449] and his descendants perished. Our Rabbis say[450] that Cain lived many years and that he died in the flood. Thus his hoary head did not go down to the grave in peace,[451] rather he saw his destruction *and all his seed with him.*[452]

It would appear that Cain's descendants consisted of only six generations[453] until the flood, while among the descendants of Seth [the third son of Adam] there were an additional two generations before the flood.[454] [It may be that Cain's descendants consisted of more than six generations before the flood, but Scripture] had no need to relate anything concerning them. It recorded only the names of those who began the building of cities, the grazing of sheep, the art of music, and the skill of working with metals. Scripture also recorded Lamech's chastisement of his wives in order to tell us that he did beget children but his sons perished before they begot offspring.

22. FORGER OF EVERY CUTTING INSTRUMENT OF BRASS AND IRON. He was a forger and cutter of all brass and iron.[455] Scripture thus states that he was a forger and cutter in all works of

(447) Numbers 32:34. (448) See Exodus 34:6. This constitutes one of the Thirteen Attributes of G-d. (449) *Ibid.*, Verse 7. (450) Koheleth Rabbah 6:3. (451) See I Kings 2:6. (452) Genesis 46:6. (453) Enoch, Irad, Mehujael, Methusael, Lamech, Jabal and Jubal and Tubal-Cain (three brothers). Scripture does not relate any history beyond the children of Lamech for they all perished in the flood. (454) Enosh, Kenan, Mahalalel, Jared, Enoch, Methuselah, Lamech and Noah. (455) The translation preserving the order of the Hebrew words is: "the forger of all cutters in copper and iron." Ramban transposes the words to read: "the forger and cutter in all copper and iron."

brass and iron. A similar [usage in transposing a word is found in the verse] : *Forgive all iniquity, and accept that which is good.*[456] In the opinion of Onkelos, however, this is connected with the first verses, meaning he was the father of every forger and cutter in brass and iron.

AND THE SISTER OF TUBAL-CAIN WAS NAAMAH. This is as if Scripture would say: "and a sister was born to him and her name was Naamah." A similar sense is found in the verses: *And Lotan's sister was Timnah;*[457] *And Miriam their sister;*[458] *His sister's name was Maacah.*[459]

In Bereshith Rabbah[460] there are some Rabbis who say that Naamah was Noah's wife. "And why did they call her Naamah [which means lovely]? Because her deeds were lovely and pleasant." By this the Rabbis meant to say that she was famous in those generations because she was a righteous woman and she gave birth to righteous children. This was why Scripture mentioned her. If so, a small remembrance of Cain was left in the world. However, if we say that she was not the woman from whom Noah begot his three sons, there is no reason for Scripture mentioning her. However, our Rabbis have another Midrash[461] concerning her which states that she was the very beautiful woman in whom the *bnei ha'elohim*[462] erred. This is hinted in the verse, *And the 'bnei ha'elohim' saw the daughters of men,*[463] as mentioned in Pirkei d'Rabbi Eliezer.[461] But other sources[464] have it that Naamah was the wife of Shamdon, the mother of Ashmedai,[465] and it is from her that the demons were born for her name is indeed found in the writings of "the use of the demons." Scripture hints and deals briefly with such hidden matters.

23. AND LAMECH SAID UNTO HIS WIVES. For the sense of this verse, the commentators have depended on the opinion of

(456) Hosea 14:3. The order preserving translation of the Hebrew would be: "All forgive iniquity...." Here too a transposition of words is necessary as above. (457) Genesis 36:22. (458) Numbers 26:59. (459) I Chronicles 7:15. (460) 23:4. (461) Pirkei d'Rabbi Eliezer, Chapter 22. (462) See further 6:2, 4. (463) *Ibid.*, Verse 2. (464) Mentioned in Midrash Hane'elam. (See my Hebrew commentary, p. 46, Note 3.) (465) Chief of demons.

Onkelos who explained *therefore whosoever slayeth Cain vengeance shall be taken on him 'shivatha'im'* [466] as meaning that at the end of seven generations, vengeance shall be taken on him [Cain], but not now [467] because G-d would be long-suffering with him. Now Lamech's wives feared to bear children because they would be the seventh generation to Cain, but he comforted his wives by saying that G-d would be forbearing with him for yet seventy-seven generations because he would pray before Him, for He is long-suffering and would have mercy upon him. Or it may be that Lamech's words were an absurd *a fortiori* argument, in accordance with the Midrash that Rashi mentioned, [namely: "For if so, the Holy One, blessed be He, could never exact His debt nor fulfill His word."] If so, Scripture is stating: "Therefore whosoever slayeth Cain, vengeance shall be taken of the seventh generation" and not in his days. And this is the translation of Onkelos: "All who would slay Cain! In seven generations, punishment will be exacted of him [Cain]." But if so, it would have been proper that the verse, *And Lamech said unto his wives,* appear before [Verse 20: *And Adah* – Lamech's wife – *bore Jabal*].

In my opinion, the word *shivatha'im* does not mean "seven generations" because this word is not used for seven separate units but rather for the multiplying of one thing seven times, such as: *refined 'shivatha'im' (sevenfold);* [468] *restore 'shivatha'im' (sevenfold);* [469] *and the light of the sun shall be 'shivatha'im',* [470] meaning doubled and redoubled seven times. But the meaning of *therefore, whosoever slayeth Cain* [466] is, according to its real sense, that G-d said: "Therefore, whosoever slayeth Cain will have vengeance taken on him sevenfold, for I will punish his slayer seven times for his sin, since I have promised Cain that he will not be slain in view of his fear of Me and his confession before Me." However, the matter of Lamech and his wives is not mentioned clearly in Scripture. We could also say that they feared lest Lamech be killed as

(466) Above, Verse 15. (467) The sense of the verse, according to Onkelos, would thus be: "Therefore, all ye who would slay Cain, know that seven generations later vengeance will be taken on him (Cain), but not now." (468) Psalms 12:7. (469) Proverbs 6:31. (470) Isaiah 30:26.

a punishment for his ancestor's sin since G-d did not tell Cain, "I have forgiven you." Instead, He promised him only that he will not be slain, but He would collect His debt from his children, and they did not know when. And so indeed the matter happened. Lamech, however, comforted them by saying that G-d would have mercy on him even as He had mercy on Cain, for he had cleaner hands than Cain, and he also would pray before Him and He would hear his prayer.

However, it appears to me that Lamech was a very wise man in every craft, and he taught his eldest son [Jabal] the business of pasturing according to the nature of the cattle. To the second son [Jubal] he taught the art of music, and he taught the third one [Tubal-Cain] to forge metals and to make swords, spears, javelins, and all instruments of war. His wives were then afraid that he might be punished because he brought the sword and murder into the world, and he thus retained in his hand the evil deed of his ancestor [Cain] since he was a descendant of the first murderer and he created *the waster to destroy.*[471] But he [Lamech] told them: "I did not slay a man by wounds, nor a child by bruises,[472] as did Cain, and G-d will not punish me. Instead, He will guard me from being killed moreso than Cain" He [Lamech] mentioned this in order to say that man cannot kill only with the sword and javelin; death caused by wounds and bruises is a worse death than by the sword. Therefore, the sword is not the cause of murder, and there is no sin upon him who made it.

5 1. THIS IS THE BOOK OF THE GENERATIONS OF ADAM. These are the children He will mention in the chapter.[473] In my opinion, this alludes to the entire Torah, for the entire Torah is *the book of the generations of Adam.* Therefore, He says here "book" and does not say, "And these are the generations of Adam," as He says in other places, e.g. *And these are the generations of Ishmael;*[474] *And these are the generations of Isaac,*[475] and so in all such cases.

(471) *Ibid.*, 54:16. (472) See Verse 23 in this chapter. (473) So Rashi and Ibn Ezra. (474) Genesis 25:12. (475) *Ibid.*, Verse 19.

IN THE DAY G-D CREATED MAN. This is connected with what follows it: [*in the likeness of G-d He made him*]. He begins with Adam himself, mentioning that he was created from nothing, and therefore Scripture says: *in the day G-d created* – out of nothing – that *man* mentioned, *in the likeness of G-d He made him.* Scripture thus explains that man was the work of G-d and in the likeness of G-d, and further mentions that just as He created him out of nothing, so He created his wife.

2. AND HE BLESSED THEM. This means that He gave them the power of procreation, to be blessed forever with very many sons and daughters. The intent is to state that begetting offspring comes as a blessing of G-d, for Adam and Eve were not born but were created from nothing and they were blessed to do so [to beget offspring].

AND HE CALLED THEIR NAME ADAM. Since the name *Adam* (man) is a generic name for the whole human species, Scripture mentions that G-d called the first pair by that name because all generations were potentially in him. It is with reference to them that Scripture says, *This is the book of the generations of Adam.*[476]

Rabbeinu Sherira Gaon[477] wrote[478] that the Sages transmitted to one another [the principles of knowledge concerning] "the recognition of faces" and the arrangements of the lines in the face. Some of these principles are stated in the order of the words of the verse, *This is the book of the generations of Adam,*[476] and some in the order of the following verse, *Male and female He created them.*[479] But the secrets and mysteries of the Torah are transmitted only to those in whom we see signs indicating that he is worthy of it. These are the words of the Gaon, but we have not merited to understand them.

(476) Verse 1. (477) A famous Gaon of the academy of Pumbeditha who flourished in the second half of the tenth century. He is the author of the letter to the Jews of Kairwan giving a historical account of how the Mishna was written and how the traditions were transmitted through the generations following the era of the Mishna. He was the father of Rav Hai Gaon, the last of the Gaonim. (478) See my Kitvei Haramban, I, p. 161. (479) Verse 2.

3. AND HE BEGOT A SON IN HIS OWN LIKENESS, AFTER HIS IMAGE. It is known that all who are born from the living are in the likeness and in the image of those who give birth to them, [so why was this verse necessary?] However, because Adam was elevated in his likeness and image in that Scripture said of him, *In the likeness of G-d He made him,*[476] Scripture explains that his offspring were also in this ennobled likeness. Scripture did not state this concerning Cain and Abel for it did not want to prolong the discussion of them. It explains it, however, in the case of Seth because the world was founded from him, [Noah being his direct descendant]. Or it may be that because Adam was created with absolutely perfect form, Scripture relates concerning Seth that he was like him [Adam] in strength and beauty.

4. AND THE DAYS OF ADAM AFTER HE BEGOT SETH WERE EIGHT HUNDRED YEARS. Because of the long lives of these first men, Scripture states their ages before they begot children and also afterwards, and then sums them all up in the end until the generations which followed the flood.

The reason for their longevity is that the first man, the handiwork of the Holy One, blessed be He, was made in absolute perfection as regards beauty, strength, and height. Even after it was decreed upon him that he be mortal, it was in his nature to live a long time. But when the flood came upon the earth, the atmosphere became tainted, and as a result their days kept on decreasing. Until the flood, their days were about the length of Adam's; some even lived longer than Adam.[480] And Shem [Noah's son], who was born before the flood, lived six hundred years;[481] he benefitted from his innate strength, but the tainted air after the flood caused him harm, [hence he died at a younger age than that attained by the preceding generations]. The days of his sons who were born after the flood were still more shortened until they came down to four hundred years.[482] You can see that this degree of longevity remained with

(480) Jered lived 962 years (Verse 20), and Methuselah lived 969 (Verse 27) while Adam lived 930 years (Verse 5). (481) Genesis, 11:10-11. (482) *Ibid.*, Verses 10-17.

them until the generation of the Dispersion, when the change of climates caused by the Dispersion affected them, and their days were again shortened. Thus you find that the life of Peleg, *in whose days the earth was divided,* [483] came down to half their days, i.e., two hundred years. [484]

It would appear that in the generations of Abraham, Isaac, and Jacob, people lived seventy and eighty years, just as Moses, our teacher, mentioned in his prayer. [485] But as for the righteous ones in their generations, *The fear of the Eternal prolongeth days*[486] for them. For Pharaoh wondered about Jacob's old age, and Jacob in turn spoke to him about the long days of his fathers, even as he said, *And they have not attained unto the days of the years of the life of my fathers in the days of their sojournings.* [487]

Now what the Rabbi[488] has written in the Moreh Nebuchim [489] does not seem right to me, namely, that the longevity was only in those individuals mentioned, while the rest of the people in those generations lived lives of ordinary natural length. He further said that this exception was due to the mode of living and food of such people or by way of a miracle. But these are words without substance. Why should this miracle have happened to them since they were neither prophets nor righteous, nor worthy that a miracle be done for them, especially for generation after generation. And how could a proper mode of living and proper food prolong their years to the extent that they are so many times greater than that of the entire generation? It is possible that there were also others who observed such a mode of living, in which case all or most of them should have attained similar longevity. And how did it happen that enough of the wisdom concerning this good mode of living did not come down to just one of all the sons of Noah after the flood [to enable him to match the longevity of his ancestors], for there was among them a little wisdom of their ancestors even though it steadily decreased from generation to generation?

(483) *Ibid.*, 10:25. (484) *Ibid.*, 11:19. (485) Psalms 90:10. *The days of our years are threescore years and ten, or even by reason of strength fourscore years.* (486) Proverbs 10:27. (487) Genesis 47:9. (488) Rabbi Moshe ben Maimon (Rambam). See above, Note 139. (489) II, 47.

6 1. AND IT CAME TO PASS, WHEN MEN BEGAN TO MULTIPLY ON THE FACE OF THE EARTH. When Scripture mentioned Noah and his sons and wanted to begin the account of the flood, it said that as soon as men began to multiply they began to sin, and they continued their sinful ways for many years until Noah was four hundred and eighty years [490] of age. Then the Holy One, blessed be He, decreed against them that "His spirit will not abide in them forever,"[491] but that He will prolong their years until their measure of sin is full, for such is the way of G-d's judgment.

2. BNEI HA'ELOHIM. The sons of princes and rulers. This is the language of Rashi, and so it is in Bereshith Rabbah. [492] If so, Scripture relates that the judges whose duty it was to administer justice among them committed open violence without anyone interfering.

'KI' (WHEN) THEY WERE FAIR. [The meaning of the word *ki* here] is the same as in the verses: *'Ki' (when) thou seest the ass of him that hateth thee;* [493] *'ki' (when) a bird's nest chance to be before thee.* [494] When the daughters of men were fair, they would take them forcibly as wives for themselves. Thus Scripture tells of the violence and mentions further, *whomsoever they chose,* in order to include those who were married to others. Scripture, however, did not mention the prohibition concerning them clearly, and the punishment decreed upon them was only because of the violence, [495] because this is a reasoned concept and does not require the Torah to prohibit it.

3. 'BESHAGAM' (FOR THAT ALSO) HE IS FLESH. It is as if *beshagam* were written *beshegam* with a *segol* under the *shin.* And Rashi explained: "This quality is also in him, that he is only flesh, and yet he is not humble before Me. What would he do if he were made of fire or some hard substance." This explanation has neither rhyme nor reason.

(490) Noah begot children at the age of 500 (Verse 32 in Chapter 5). Twenty years before, G-d decreed the advent of the flood. (See Rashi here, Verse 3.) (491) See Verse 3. (492) 26:8. (493) Exodus 23:5. (494) Deuteronomy 22:6. (495) Further, Verse 13.

Rabbi Abraham ibn Ezra explained that G-d said, "My spirit will not abide in man forever because of this violence and also because man is flesh, and when he reaches a certain age he disintegrates." Ibn Ezra thus understands the verse as if it said, *gam beshehu basar* (also because he is flesh). But what need is there for stating this contention when it is known *that they were but flesh.*[496] and death had been decreed on them, as it says, *For dust thou art, and unto dust shalt thou return?*[497]

The correct interpretation appears to me to be that G-d said: "My spirit shall not abide in man forever because man also is flesh as all flesh that creepeth upon the earth in the forms of fowl and cattle and beast, and it is not fitting that the spirit of G-d be within him." The purport is to state *that G-d made man upright*[498] to be like the ministering angels by virtue of the soul He gave him. But he was drawn after the flesh and corporeal desires; *he is like the beasts that perish,*[499] and therefore the spirit of G-d will no longer be sheathed in him for he is corporeal and not godly. However, He will prolong for them [this withdrawal of spirit] if they repent. The sense of this verse is thus similar to [the verse in Psalm 49]: *So He remembered that they were but flesh, a wind that passeth away, and cometh not again.*

4. THE NEPHILIM. Rashi comments: "[They were called *nephilim* because] they fell (*naphlu*) and caused the downfall (*hipilu*) of the world." This is found in Bereshith Rabbah.[500] The masters of language[501] say that they [the *Nephilim*] were so called because the heart of man fell from fear of them. The same applies to the word *ha'eimim.*[502]

IN THOSE DAYS. Rashi comments: "in the days of the generation of Enosh. AND ALSO AFTER THAT. Although they witnessed the destruction of the generation of Enosh when the ocean

(496) Psalms 78:39. (497) Above, 3:19. (498) Ecclesiastes 7:29. (499) Psalms 49:13. (500) 26:16. (501) Found in R'dak. (502) Genesis 14:5. *Eimah* means terror. The *Eimim* thus induced terror into the hearts of those who saw them.

rose and flooded a third of the world, still they did not humble themselves and take a lesson from them."

Rabbi Abraham ibn Ezra explained: "*also after* the flood, since the sons of *Anak* [503] were of the family of *bnei ha'elohim.*" If so, we must say that either the wives of Noah's sons were of their [the *Nephilim's*] descendants and resembled them or that ibn Ezra will accept the statement of the Rabbi [504] who advanced the interpretation that Og [505] escaped from the flood, to which Rabbi Abraham will add that others too escaped with him [since the verse states: "*The 'Nephilim'* – (in the plural) – *were in the earth...and also after that*", which Ibn Ezra interprets as meaning after the flood].

The correct interpretation appears to me to be that Adam and his wife are called *bnei ha'elohim* because they were G-d's handiwork and He was their father; they had no father besides Him. And he [Adam] begot many children, as it is written, *And he begot sons and daughters.* [506] Now these men, first to be born of a father and mother, were of great perfection in height and strength because they were born in the likeness of their father, as it is written concerning Seth, *And he [Adam] begot a son in his own likeness, after his image.* [507] And it is possible that all the children of the first generations – Adam, Seth, Enosh – were called *bnei ha'elohim* because these three men were in the likeness of G-d. But then the worship of idols commenced, and there came upon men a weakness and slackness.

And so they said in Bereshith Rabbah: [508] "*This is the book of the generations of Adam.* [509] Are not the first ones *toldoth* (offspring)! But what are they? [They are in the image and likeness of] G-d. They raised a question before Aba Kohen Bardela: 'Adam, Seth, Enosh?' At first, he was silent, but then he said to them: 'Up to here [Seth] they were in the image and likeness of G-d; after that, Kenan, vexers.' " [510]

(503) Numbers 13:33. The giants. (504) Rabbi Yochanan (Niddah 61 a). (505) Og, King of Bashan (Numbers 21:33). It is he, according to Rabbi Yochanan, of whom Scripture says: *And there came one that had escaped* (Genesis 14:13); i.e., *escaped* from the flood. (506) Above, 5:4. (507) *Ibid.*, Verse 3. (508) 24:6. (509) Above, 5:1. (510) *Kenan, vexers.* Enosh's son was Kenan (Above, 5:9), which name is interpreted as having the same root as the word *kanteir* (he who makes himself disagreeable).

Now when men began to multiply and daughters were born to them, the men of these first generations were in their strength, and because of their great desire they would choose the beautiful women of tall stature and good health. Now first Scripture tells that by force they took them unto themselves as wives, and afterwards it tells that they came in a promiscuous manner to the daughters of men who were not of that high degree, and the matter was not known until they begot children for them, and everyone recognized that they were not the offspring of other people but that they had been born to these *bnei ha'elohim* because these children were very tall. They were, however, inferior to their fathers in height and strength, [This is the meaning of the name *Nephilim* – inferior ones], just as the word *Nephilim* is used in the expression: *I am not 'nophel' (inferior) to you.*[511] Still they were mighty men in comparison with the rest of the people. And Scripture tells that this happened in the first generation to those who were called *bnei ha'elohim* because they were of absolute perfection, and it is they who caused the daughters of men to beget *nephilim* (inferior ones); *and also after that,* for the *nephilim* themselves begot *nephilim* from them.

The meaning of the expression, *that were of old*, is that after the flood, the men, upon seeing the mighty, would remember these *nephilim* and say: "There have already been mightier men than these in the ages which were before us." They were *the men of* renown in all generations afterward. This is a fitting explanation of this chapter. But the Midrash of Rabbi Eliezer the Great,[512] in the chapters concerning the angels that fell from their place of holiness in heaven – as is mentioned in the Gemara of Tractate *Yoma* –[513] fits into the language of the verse more than all other interpretations. But it would necessitate delving at length into the secret of this subject.

6. AND THE ETERNAL REPENTED... AND IT GRIEVED HIM AT HIS HEART. The Torah speaks in the language of men. The purport is that *they rebelled, and grieved His holy spirit*[514] with their sins. The sense of the expression *at His heart* is that He did not

(511) Job 12:3. (512) Chapter 22. (513) 67 b. (514) Isaiah 63:10.

tell this to a prophet, a messenger of G-d. This expression is also found with respect to thinking, just as: *to speak to my heart,* [515] and other similar expressions.

In Bereshith Rabbah [516] there is a significant matter concerning this, expressed by a parable which the Rabbis bring of an agent and an architect. [517] This constitutes a great secret which is not permitted to be written down. The one who knows it will understand why here the Tetragrammaton is written while in the whole of the rest of the chapter and the account of the flood, the name *Elokim* is used.

8. BUT NOAH FOUND GRACE IN THE EYES OF THE ETERNAL. The meaning thereof is that all his deeds were pleasing and sweet before Him. Similarly: *For thou hast found grace in My sight, and I know thee by name.*[518] This is like the verses: *And He gave him favor in the sight of the keeper of the prison;* [519] *And Esther obtained favor in the sight of all of them that looked upon her.* [520] Scripture mentions this in contrast to what it said concerning his [Noah's] generation, namely, that all their deeds brought grief before Him, blessed be He. But of Noah it says that he found grace in His eyes, and afterwards it tells [521] why he was pleasing before G-d: because he was a perfectly righteous man.

(515) Genesis 24:45. (516) 27:6. (517) Rabbi Berachyah said: "It is like a king who had a palace built by an architect, and when he saw it, it displeased him. Against whom is he to complain? Surely against the architect." Rabbi Assi said: "It is like one who traded through an agent and suffered a loss. Whom does he blame? The agent. Here too *It grieved Him at His heart.*" (518) Exodus 33:17. (519) Genesis 39:21. (520) Esther 2:15. (521) In the following *Seder Noach.*

Noach

9. THESE ARE 'TOLDOTH' NOAH. Commentators[1] have explained the word *toldoth* to mean "his experiences" [or "his events"] much the same as the sense of: *what a day 'yeiled' (may bring forth).*[2]

In this way the word *toldoth* refers to the entire section [since all the events of the flood are occurrences in the life of Noah]. But this does not appear to me to be correct since the external events in the life of a person, [over which he has no control], are not his *toldoth.*

The correct interpretation is that the word *toldoth* here retains its literal meaning of "progeny," just as, *These are 'toldoth' (the progeny of) the sons of Noah;*[3] *And these are 'toldoth' (the progeny of) Ishmael.*[4] Thus Scripture is saying, "These are the progeny of Noah: Shem, Ham, and Japheth."

Scripture however repeats, *And Noah begot three sons,*[5] because [at the end of the first verse] it interrupted by saying, *Noah was a righteous man, and whole-hearted,* in order to inform us why He commanded him concerning the ark. And even though Scripture has already stated above, *And Noah was five hundred years old; and Noah begot Shem, Ham, and Japheth,*[6] it returns to mention them a second time in order to relate that Noah was unlike all his ancestors who begot daughters and sons. This is the meaning of the

(1) Ibn Ezra and R'dak. These commentators felt the difficulty in explaining *toldoth* to mean "progeny" or "generations" since it further states, *And Noah begot three sons.* (2) Proverbs 27:1. (3) Genesis 10:1. (4) *Ibid.,* 25:12. (5) Verse 10. (6) Above, 5:32.

words, *three sons;*[5] Scripture mentions their number in order to say that these three alone were his progeny, and they were saved by his merit, *and by them was the whole earth overspread.*[7]

HE WAS A RIGHTEOUS MAN AND WHOLE-HEARTED. Scripture mentions that he was guiltless and perfect in his righteousness in order to inform us that he was worthy to be saved from the flood without any punishment whatever since he was whole-hearted in righteousness. For a *tzadik* (a righteous person) is one who is found guiltless in judgment as opposed to the wicked person, as Scripture says, *And they come unto judgment, and the judges judge them, by justifying the righteous, and condemning the wicked;*[8] and also, *For Thou art just in all that has come upon us, for Thou hast dealt truly;*[9] similarly, *In righteousness shalt thou judge thy neighbor.*[10] But in the case of Abraham, concerning whom it says, *that he will command his children to do 'tz'dakah' and 'mishpat,'*[11] Scripture praises him for righteousness which is synonymous with judgment, and for mercy which is synonymous with *tz'dakah.*[12]

And Rabbi Abraham ibn Ezra said, "*Righteous* in deeds; *whole-hearted* in his heart." However, it is written, *Thou art whole-hearted in thy ways;*[13] [the term "whole-hearted" is thus used in connection with "ways" and *not* with matters of the heart].

Now after Scripture said that Noah was a righteous man, meaning that he was neither a man of violence nor one who perverted his ways as did the guilty ones of his generation, it further said that he walked with the glorious Name,[14] fearing Him alone. He was not enticed by the astrologers, enchanters and soothsayers, and surely not by idolatry, and he paid no heed to them at all; to G-d alone he did always cleave, and he walked in

(7) Genesis 9:19. (8) Deuteronomy 25:1. (9) Nehemiah 9:33. (10) Leviticus 19:15. (11) Genesis 18:19. (12) Ramban is thus saying that where Scripture uses *tzedek* alone it means "guiltless in judgment," but in the case of Abraham where in addition to *tzedek* (or *tz'dakah*) Scripture also mentions *mishpat,* (judgment) *mishpat* of necessity means "guiltless in judgment," while *tz'dakah* in this case means "mercifulness." (13) Ezekiel 28:15. (14) See Deuteronomy 28:58.

the way G-d chose or taught him for he was a prophet. This is analogous in meaning to the verse, *After the Eternal your G-d shall ye walk, and Him shall ye fear,*[15] which is stated in connection with the removal of him who prophesies to encourage the worship of idols and gives a sign or wonder to verify his words, as I will explain. I will again mention this in connection with the verse, *Walk before Me, and be thou whole-hearted,*[16] if He Who is perfect in knowledge[17] will be with me.

Now since Noah was a righteous man and undeserving of punishment, it was fitting that his sons and his household be saved by his merit for if his sons were to perish, it would have been a punishment upon him. Or it may be said that he was a perfectly righteous man, and his sons and household were also righteous since he taught them; this is analogous to that which is written concerning Abraham: *For I have known him, to the end that he may command his children and his household.*[11]

IN HIS GENERATIONS. Some of our Rabbis explained it to his credit, [i.e., he was righteous despite his generation]; it follows all the more had he lived in a generation of righteous people. Others explain it to his discredit. [In comparison with his own generation he was considered righteous, but had he lived in the generation of Abraham he would not have been considered of any consequence.] Thus the language of Rashi.

The correct interpretation according to the plain meaning of Scripture appears to be that he alone was a righteous man in those generations, there being no righteous or whole-hearted men except him in those generations. In a similar sense is the verse, *For thee I have seen righteous before Me in this generation,*[18] meaning that there is no other in the generation worthy of being saved. Scripture says, *in his generations* —[using the plural form]— because many generations passed since the time men had become corrupted, and there was no righteous man besides him. Let not the word of our Rabbis concerning Methuselah,[19] [which said that

(15) *Ibid.,* 13:5. (16) Genesis 17:1. (17) See Job 36:4. (18) Genesis 7:1. (19) Bereshith Rabbah 32:10.

he was a righteous man], cause you difficulty for Scripture tells only that there was no righteous man worthy of being saved from the flood in all those generations except Noah.

10. SHEM, HAM, AND JAPHETH. It appears to me that Japheth was the oldest, as it is said, *the brother of Japheth the elder,*[20] and so in counting their generations, Scripture mentions the children of Japheth first.[21] Ham was the youngest of all, as it is said, *And [Noah] knew what his youngest son had done unto him.*[22] Here, however, Scripture mentions Shem first because of his superiority and then Ham, for they were born in that order. Thus Japheth is left at the end. But Scripture did not want to say, "Shem and Japheth and Ham," because in that case all of them would have been mentioned out of the order of their birth, and Japheth had no outstanding quality to merit that the order of birth be dispensed with on his account. Shem, however, is mentioned here first because of his superiority even though in the account of the generations he is last.[20] Similarly, [we find the verses]: *The sons of Abraham: Isaac and Ishmael;*[23] *And I gave to Isaac Jacob and Esau.*[24]

12. FOR ALL FLESH HAD CORRUPTED THEIR WAY. If we were to explain *all flesh* in its usual sense and thus say that even cattle, beasts and fowl corrupted their way by consorting with other species, as Rashi has explained, we must then say that the expression, *for the earth is filled with violence through them,*[25] does not mean "because of all of them" but only because of some of them [since "violence" does not apply to beasts and cattle], and Scripture tells of the punishment of man alone [even though *all flesh* corrupted their way]. Or we may say that the cattle, beasts, and fowl also did not follow their natural instincts, and all cattle seized prey and all fowl became birds of prey; thus they too committed violence.

(20) Genesis 10:21. (21) *Ibid.*, 10:2. (22) *Ibid.*, 9:24. (23) I Chronicles 1:28. Here too Isaac is mentioned first because of his superiority although Ishmael was older. (24) Joshua 24:4. This also is similar to the above case. (25) Verse 13.

By way of the simple meaning of Scripture, *all flesh* means "all men." Further on Scripture says explicitly: *all flesh wherein is the breath of life;*[26] *and of every living thing of all flesh,*[27] meaning all living bodies. But here it says *all flesh*, meaning all people. Similarly [we find the verses]: *All flesh shall come to worship before Me,*[28] [meaning "all people"]; *Or when the flesh hath in the skin thereof,*[29] [where again reference is only to people].

13. VIOLENCE, that is, robbery and oppression. Now G-d gave Noah the explanation [that the flood was due to the fact that the "the earth is filled with] violence" and did not mention "the corruption of the way" [recorded in the preceding verse] because violence is a sin that is known and widely publicized. Our Rabbis have said[30] that it was on account of the sin of violence that their fate was sealed. The reason for it is that the prohibition against violence is a rational commandment,[31] there being no need for a prophet to admonish them against it. Besides, it is evil committed against both heaven and mankind. Thus He informed Noah of the sin for *which the end is come* – the doom is reached.[32]

AND BEHOLD, I WILL DESTROY THEM 'ETH' THE EARTH. This is similar to saying "*from* the earth." So also: *When I go forth 'eth' the city,*[33] [meaning "*from* the city"]; *he suffered 'eth' his feet,*[34] [meaning "*from* his feet"]. Another interpretation is that *eth ha'aretz* means "with the earth" for even the land was blotted out to the depth of a furrow of three handbreadths. Thus the language of Rashi quoting Bereshith Rabbah.[35]

(26) Genesis 7:15. (27) *Ibid.*, 6:19. (28) Isaiah 66:23. (29) Leviticus 13:24. (30) Sanhedrin 108 a. (31) Likewise Ramban above 6:2. See also Yehudah Halevi's Al Khazari, II, 48, that "the rational laws are the basis and preamble of the divine law, preceding it in character and time, and being indispensable in the administration of every human society." (Hirschfeld's translation.) (32) See Ezekiel 7:6-7. (33) Exodus 9:29. (34) I Kings 15:23. (35) 31:7.

And Rabbi Abraham ibn Ezra said that the word *mashchitham (destroy them)* draws along with it a similar word, [meaning it is as if the verb "destroy" appears twice in the verse], thus stating, "And behold, I will destroy them and destroy the earth."

By way of the truth [the mystic teaching of the Cabala],[36] this is like the verse, *eth hashamayim ve'eth ha'aretz (the heaven and the earth),*[37] thus intimating that "the earth"[38] will be destroyed, and with the destruction of the earth they too will be destroyed and thus they will be blotted out from the World to Come, just as is intimated in the verse: *and it grieved Him at His heart.*[39] It is to this that the Rabbis alluded in Bereshith Rabbah:[40] "This is like a master's son who had a wet-nurse; whenever he would commit an offense the wet-nurse would be punished."[41]

17. AND, BEHOLD, I DO BRING THE FLOOD. "Now I agree with those angels who long ago said to Me [when I was about to create man], *What is man that Thou art mindful of him.*"[42] Thus the words of Rashi quoting Bereshith Rabbah.[43]

But I wonder: in what way did He "agree" with them since He left man a remnant for a great deliverance through Noah and his sons and all living things to increase their seed as the sand! Perhaps this agreement with their opinion signified [His intent which was to come to fruition] when He would show them no mercy. [However, when the Divine quality of mercy was introduced, it resulted in the deliverance of mankind through Noah.]

By way of the truth [the mystic lore of the Cabala], *va'ani (And I)* is similar to: *And I also will chastise you;*[44] so also, *I am He! behold, My covenant is with thee;*[45] *And as for Me, this is My covenant.*[46] The verse here thus states: "I also will have My hand on them for having destroyed the earth." This is why He said

(36) See Bereshith, Note 63. (37) Above, 1:1. (38) Here referring to "the earth of immortal life." (39) Above, 6:6. See Ramban there. (40) 31:7. (41) "So, said the Holy One, blessed be He: 'I will destroy them and destroy the earth with them.'" (Bereshith Rabbah.) (42) Psalms 8:5. (43) 31:15. (44) Leviticus 26:28. The word *va'ani* (And I) thus intimates the attribute of judgment. (45) Genesis 17:4. (46) Isaiah 59:21.

[after the flood]: *This is the token of the covenant which I make.*[47] – *He maketh sore, and He bindeth up.*[48] The learned student [in the mystic lore of the Cabala] will understand.

18. AND I WILL ESTABLISH MY COVENANT. Rabbi Abraham ibn Ezra said that this is a sign that G-d had sworn to Noah that during the flood, neither he nor his children would die even though it is not clearly written at first. This is similar to what we find in Deuteronomy: *And ye came near unto me every one of you, and said: Let us send men before us, that they may search the land for us.*[49]

The meaning of *V'hakimothi (And I will establish)* is "I will fulfill My oath." It appears likely to me that this covenant mentioned here refers to the rainbow, [Thus G-d hinted to Noah that after the flood He will make a covenant with him if he will fulfill the commandment concerning the making of the ark.] The meaning of the word *b'rith* (covenant) is an agreement and accord which two have chosen, stemming from the root, *'b'ru' (choose) you.*[50] And the word *b'rith* takes the same form in construct and in separateness. A similar case is [the word *sh'vith*, captivity]: *'sh'vith' (the captivity of) Jacob;*[51] *And his daughters 'bash'vith' (in captivity).*[52] And some say that the word *b'rith* means the establishment of a boundary [to which each party to the covenant should adhere]. All these are Abraham ibn Ezra's words.

A more correct explanation in line with the simple meaning of Scripture is that the purport of the expression, *And I will establish My covenant,* is, "At the time of the coming of the flood, My covenant will be established with you so that you and your family and two of all flesh will come into the ark to remain alive, that is to say, so that you will live there and maintain yourself in order to go forth from there alive." And *b'rith* (covenant) means G-d's

(47) Genesis 9:12. (48) Job 5:18. (49) Deuteronomy 1:22. This account, narrated by Moses, is not explicitly stated in Numbers, Chapter 13, which begins with G-d saying: *Send thou men...* Ramban cites this as another case where the first account lacks some of the details of the later account. (50) I Samuel 17:8. (51) Psalms 85:2. Here the word *sh'vith* is in construct. (52) Numbers 21:29. Here the word *bash'vith* is separate.

word when He decrees something without any condition and residuary and fulfills it. Now He mentions the *b'rith* and mentions that it will be fulfilled, [which, according to the present interpretation is an apparent redundancy], just as we find the verse, *The Jews ordained and took upon them, and upon their seed,*[53] meaning they accepted upon themselves a matter which was to exist. [Thus our verse is to be explained in a similar way, i.e., He established an unconditional covenant.]

By way of the truth, [the mystic lore of the Cabala], the *b'rith* is *everlasting*, the word being derived from *In the beginning G-d 'bara' (created).*[37] Thus *brithi* (My covenant) is similar to *b'riyothi* (My creation), and the word is alike in construct form because it is adjoined to the times there were before us. He thus commanded that the *b'rith* exist and be with the righteous one [Noah]. In a similar sense are the verses: As for *Me, behold, I establish My covenant with you;*[54] *My covenant was with him.*[55] The learned student [in the mystic lore of the Cabala] will understand.

19. OF ALL FLESH. It is known that there are a great many beasts, and some of them – such as elephants, rams and others – are very large; likewise, the creeping things upon the earth are very many. Of the fowl of the heaven there are also innumerably many kinds, just as our Rabbis have said:[56] "There are one hundred and twenty kinds of unclean birds in the east, and all of them belong to the species of *ayah* (kite)."[57] Clean fowl are innumerable. Noah was thus obligated to bring all of them into the ark in order that they may beget their like. If you would gather a full year's supply of food for all of them, [you would find] that this ark and ten others like it could not hold it! But this was a miracle of a small space containing a great quantity. And in case you suppose that he should have made it [the ark] very small and rely on this miracle, the answer is that the Holy One, blessed be He, saw fit to make it large so that the people of his generation should see it, wonder at it, converse about it, and speak of the subject of the flood and the

(53) Esther 9:27. (54) Genesis 9:9. (55) Malachi 2:5. (56) Chullin 63b. However, instead of 120 kinds, the figure mentioned there is 100. (57) See Leviticus 11:14.

gathering of the cattle, beast, and fowl into it so that perhaps they would repent. Furthermore, he made it large in order to reduce the miracle for such is the way with all miracles in the Torah or in the Prophets: whatever is humanly possible is done, with the balance left to Heaven. Now be not persuaded to say as Ibn Ezra that the three hundred cubits [of the length of the ark were measured] in cubits of a man like Noah, who was unusually tall. If so, the other people were also tall, and the beasts and fowl of those generations were also tall until the world was struck by the flood! Moreover, the cubits here are the standard cubits of the Torah.[58]

THOU SHALT BRING INTO THE ARK, TO KEEP THEM ALIVE WITH THEE. G-d thus commanded Noah that he concern himself with and help them in their entering the ark and that he strive on behalf of their existence even as he would for his own life.

20. TWO OF EVERY SORT SHALL COME UNTO THEE, TO KEEP THEM ALIVE. G-d thus informed Noah that two of every sort would come of their own accord, and he would not find it necessary to hunt for them in the mountains and distant lands, and he would bring them into the ark after that. At the actual narration [of their coming, Scripture] explains[59] that they came male and female; this is implied here. After that, He commanded him to take seven and seven of every clean beast.[60] Concerning these, G-d did not say that they would come of their own accord but that Noah should take them.[61] The reason for this is that those who came to be saved and to keep their seed alive[62] did come of their own accord, but for those who were to be sacrificed as whole offerings, G-d did not decree that they come of their own accord to be slaughtered. Rather, Noah took them since the purpose of the command to take seven and seven was that Noah bring a sacrifice from them after the flood.

(58) See Erubin 3 b. (59) Genesis 7:16. (60) *Ibid.*, 7:2. (61) The verse states: *Of every clean beast thou shalt 'take' to thee seven and seven.* Noah brought sacrifices after the flood from the clean beasts and fowl. (See Chapter 8, Verse 20.) (62) Chapter 7, Verse 3.

The meaning of the word "clean" is that the Holy One, blessed be He, explained to Noah the signs of ritual cleanliness for beast and fowl. Scripture, however, refers to it briefly by saying, "clean," in accordance with the Torah.[63] But Rashi wrote: "*Clean*, meaning that which in the future will be permitted to Israel as clean; we thus learn that Noah studied the Torah."

From here we derive that the sacrifices of the sons of Noah[64] must also be only of the clean beast and the clean fowl. So also it is said of the sacrifice of Abel: *of the first-born of his flock and of the fat thereof.*[65] However, all clean species are permissible for them to bring as sacrifices as it is written: *And he took of every clean beast, and of every clean fowl, and offered burnt-offerings on the altar.*[66] [Later, when the Torah was given, G-d] added a commandment to Israel that all their sacrifices be only *of the beasts and of the herd,*[67] *of the turtledoves and of the young pigeons.*[68]

Of the fowl also of the heaven, seven and seven[69] – this means the clean fowl for the verse is a continuation of the verse above: [*Of every 'clean' beast shalt thou take to thee seven and seven*].[70]

22. AND NOAH DID THUS; ACCORDING TO ALL THAT G-D HAD COMMANDED HIM, meaning that he constructed the ark and gathered the food. Scripture's intent in saying, *And Noah did... so did he*, is to explain that he did not omit a thing from all that G-d had commanded him.

7 1. AND THE ETERNAL SAID TO NOAH. G-d informed Noah that with the attribute of mercy [as indicated by the use of the Tetragrammaton, "the Eternal,"] He will save him and his family and that He will give life to their seed for all generations. This is the meaning of the phrase, *to keep seed alive upon the face of all the earth.*[71] At first He said, *to keep them alive with thee;*[72] but now with the attribute of mercy He hinted to him

(63) See Leviticus, Chapter 11. (64) See *Seder Bereshith*, Note 222. (65) Above, 4:4. (66) Genesis 8:20. (67) Leviticus 1:2. (68) *Ibid.*, Verse 14. (69) Genesis 7:3. (70) *Ibid.*, Verse 2. (71) Verse 3. (72) Above, 6:19.

concerning the sacrifice to inform him that he will have regard for his offering and that by the merit of his offering, the world will exist, never again to be cut off by the waters of the flood.[73] This is why the Tetragrammaton is mentioned here for in all matters concerning the sacrifices, Scripture does not mention *Elokim* (G-d), as I will elucidate when I reach there[74] with the help of G-d.

COME THOU AND ALL THY HOUSE INTO THE ARK. Noah constructed the ark many days before the flood, and when the time of the flood arrived on the tenth day of the second month, He again commanded him that he and all his household come into the ark. This is why He said to him at first: *thou, and thy sons, and thy wife, and thy sons' wives with thee.*[75] He thereby informed him that on account of his merit alone they will be saved since He did not say, "Ye [in the plural] I have seen righteous before Me." And He commanded that he take and bring of the clean beasts and clean fowl seven and seven, and then He informed him of the day of the flood, at which time he was to come into the ark. And Noah did so for *in the selfsame day came Noah... into the ark.*[76] This is the meaning of [the verse: *And Noah came in... into the ark*] *because of the waters of the flood.*[77] But Rashi wrote: "Noah also was one of those who have little faith, and he did not enter the ark until the waters forced him to do so." In the words of Bereshith Rabbah:[78] "Noah was lacking in faith. Had the waters not reached his ankles he would not have entered the ark." But if so, let him say that Noah did not enter there until the waters greatly increased and covered the whole face of the earth and he saw that he was drowning!

8. OF CLEAN BEASTS, AND OF BEASTS THAT ARE NOT CLEAN. 9. TWO AND TWO THERE CAME IN UNTO NOAH. Rashi explained: "They were all equal with respect to this number for the last number of any species was two." Others[79] said that

(73) See further, 9:11. (74) See Ramban, Leviticus 1:9. (75) Above, 6:18. (76) Verse 13. This refers to the day when the rains began, namely, the seventeenth day of the second month. (77) Verse 7. (78) 32:9. (79) R'dak.

the meaning of "two" is pairs, meaning that they came couplewise, male and female together.

In my opinion, the matter was thus: two – a male and a female – came of their own accord from each species, and Noah added by bringing six additional pairs from the clean ones since those that came to be saved arrived of their own accord while he busied himself for the sake of the commandment with those that were destined for sacrifice, for so it was told to him.[80] And the meaning of the verse, *And Noah did according unto all that the Eternal commanded him,*[81] is, as the Rabbis have said in Bereshith Rabbah,[78] that he was to prepare to bring in the cattle, beast, and fowl, meaning the clean ones, those which he himself went after and brought to his house. The verse which states a third time, *as G-d hath commanded Noah,*[82] means that he did as He had commanded him concerning entering the ark, for this verse is connected with the above verse: *And Noah came in.*[77] The verse thus states that Noah and his sons and his wife and his sons' wives came into the ark along with two and two of the cattle and fowl and creeping things that came to him in order to enter into the ark. All of them came with him, entering the ark *because of the waters of the flood,*[77] as G-d commanded him. Scripture then returns and sets forth the month and the day in which the flood came[83] and how he entered the ark, stating that on that selfsame day when the rains began – and not before – Noah entered the ark, and with him were all living things.

15. AND THEY CAME IN UNTO NOAH INTO THE ARK. The intent of this is to make known that the beasts, fowl, etc., did not gather to him at all, nor did they come until that selfsame day when the rains came. And he came into the ark for it was G-d that *hath commanded and His breath which hath gathered them*[84] in one moment.

(80) See Ramban above, 6:20. (81) Verse 5. (82) Verse 9. (83) Verse 11. (84) Isaiah 34:16.

16. AND THEY THAT CAME IN, CAME IN MALE AND FEMALE OF ALL FLESH. The intent of this is that those who came into the ark were male and female for so Noah brought them in. This is why Scripture says, *as G-d hath commanded him,* since it was He who commanded him to bring them into the ark.

But the opinion of Rabbi Abraham ibn Ezra is that the verse, *And Noah came in, and his sons, and his wife, and his sons' wives with him, into the ark,*[77] does not mean that they entered it but that they all came to Noah on the tenth day of the second month for his house was near the ark. [He thus interprets the verse as meaning "to the ark," rather than "into the ark."] Ibn Ezra explains the phrase, *because of the waters of the flood,*[77] to mean "on account of the fear of the waters of the flood." At the end of the seven days came the waters of the flood, and then they all gathered in the ark, and Noah closed the door and the window.[85] But Ibn Ezra's words are not correct.[86]

It is possible that the verses, *And Noah did according to all that the Eternal hath commanded him, And Noah was six hundred years old,*[87] and the succeeding verses until, *In the six hundredth year,*[88] do not recount a narrative. Rather, *And Noah did according to all that the Eternal commanded him* generalizes the entire matter. It states that he did everything as he was commanded, not omitting a thing: he constructed the ark and assembled the food and took of the clean beasts and fowl seven and seven on the day He commanded him. When he was six hundred years old and the flood came down upon the earth, he came with his household and with the clean beasts and all living things into the ark, as G-d had commanded him. After that, Scripture narrates the event, *And it came to pass after the seven days ... in the six hundredth year,*[89] and completes the subject.

(85) See above, 6:16. (86) As explained above in Verses 1 and 8, when the time of the flood arrived G-d again commanded Noah that he and all his household come into the ark, and He further informed him of the day of the flood. (87) Verses 5-6. (88) Verse 11. (89) Verses 10-11.

18. AND THE WATERS PREVAILED ('Vayigb'ru'). 19. AND THE WATERS 'GAVRU' (PREVAILED). This means that they increased exceedingly, for the Hebrew language calls great abundance *gvurah* (strength, power). So too, *And their transgressions which 'yithgavru' (have prevailed),*[90] meaning increased exceedingly; *His mercy 'gavar' (has prevailed) toward them that fear Him,*[91] meaning increased. And so also: *If 'bigvuroth' four-score years,*[92] meaning with great abundance.

It is conceivable that the meaning of *vayigb'ru* is that the rains came in a rushing downpour, uprooting trees and toppling buildings, since power is called in Hebrew *gvurah* (strength) because strength lies in power. In a similar sense are the verses: *They also 'gavru' (wax mighty) in power;*[93] *'Vehigbir brith' (And he shall make a strong covenant) with many for one week,*[94] meaning he will establish the covenant with firmness. And in the words of the Sages, [we find the expression], *gvuroth geshamim* (the powers of the rains),[95] because they come down with strength. It is possible that the verse, *If 'bigvuroth' four-score years,*[92] is of the same sense, i.e., if his bones and body be strong, and he is a man of power, he will live four-score years. And if so, *'gavru' upon the earth*[96] will mean that the waters were in their complete strength, overcoming even the high mountains and inundating them.

23. AND HE BLOTTED OUT EVERY LIVING SUBSTANCE WHICH WAS UPON THE FACE OF THE EARTH. After having said, *And all flesh perished,*[97] and having said, *whatever was in the dry land, died,*[98] Scripture continues to say, *And He blotted out,* meaning that the bodies dissolved and became water, just as is in the verse, *And he shall blot them out in the water of bitterness*[99] — for the waters of the flood were hot, as our Rabbis have said.[100] But if so, the fish also would have died. Perhaps it was as

(90) Job 36:9. (91) Psalms 103:11. (92) *Ibid.,* 90:10. (93) Job 21:7. (94) Daniel 9:27. (95) Taanith 2 a. (96) Verse 19. (97) Verse 21. (98) Verse 22. (99) Numbers 5:23. (100) Sanhedrin 108 b.

the Rabbis have said in Bereshith Rabbah:[101] *"Whatever was in the dry land died,*[98] but not the fish in the sea. And some authorities say that they too were destined to be destroyed, but they fled to the Mediterranean."[102] Either way the fish were saved.

Both of these opinions are plausible. For it is conceivable that the hot waters of the flood mingled with the seas, heating only their upper waters, while the fish descended to the depths of the ponds and lived there. Or, in accordance with the opinion of some authorities,[103] it is possible that the fish in the waters of the countries near the Mediterranean[102] fled there when they felt the heat of the water, and were thus saved. And even if all those outside the Mediterranean died, since the majority of fish are in the Mediterranean[102] where the waters of the flood did not come down – as it is said, *And the rain was upon the earth*[104] – the fish were thus saved. For none of the fish were brought into the ark to keep their seed alive, and at the time of the covenant it is said, *I establish My covenant with you... and with every living creature that is with you, the fowl, and cattle, and every beast of the earth with you; of all that go out of the ark,*[105] but it does not mention the fish of the sea.

AND THEY WERE BLOTTED OUT FROM THE EARTH. The commentators[106] have explained that the reason for the double [expression, *And He blotted out ... and they were blotted out*], is that their remembrance was forgotten since they had no seed. But what need is there to say that after we are told that they all died? Perhaps on account of the fowl and some creeping things, Scripture tells that none of their eggs were left on any tree or under the earth for everything was blotted out. It is probable that the sense of the verse is as follows: "And He blotted out every living

(101) 32:19. (102) Literally, *Okeanus* (ocean), but usually meaning the Mediterranean Sea. (See Jastrow.) (103) Mentioned in the Midrash quoted above, that the fish too were destined to be destroyed, but they fled to the Mediterranean. (104) Verse 12. (105) Genesis 9:9-10. (106) Ibn Ezra and R'dak.

substance which was upon the face of the earth, for from man to beast to creeping things and to fowl of the heaven, they were blotted out from the earth, only Noah remaining alive." Now our Rabbis have expounded:[100] "*And He blotted out*, meaning from this world. *And they were blotted out from the earth*, meaning from the World to Come." The Rabbis thus explained "the earth" mentioned here as meaning "the land of eternal life." I have already alluded to its secret.[107]

8 1. AND G-D REMEMBERED NOAH, AND EVERY LIVING THING, AND ALL THE CATTLE. The remembrance of Noah was because he was a perfectly righteous man, and He had made a covenant with him to save him. The word "Noah" here includes his children that were there with him. Scripture did not mention them specifically, though, for they were saved by his merit. However, the remembrance stated concerning beast and cattle was not on account of merit, for among living creatures there is no merit or guilt save in man alone. But the remembrance concerning them was *Because He remembered His holy word*[108] which He had spoken, causing the world to come into existence, and the Will which was before Him at the creation of the world arose before Him and He desired the existence of the world with all the species that He created therein. Thus He now saw fit to bring them forth so that they should not perish in the ark. Scripture does not mention the fowl and the creeping things for the remembrance of *the living thing* is similar to their remembrance, and *the companion thereof telleth concerning it.*[109]

4. AND THE ARK RESTED IN THE SEVENTH MONTH, ON THE SEVENTEENTH DAY OF THE MONTH. Rashi wrote: "From here you may infer that the ark was submerged in the water to a depth of eleven cubits." This he wrote on the basis of the calculation written in his commentaries, and it is so found in

(107) Above, 6:13. (108) Psalms 105:42. (109) Job 36:33. That is, since the remembrance of the fowl and creeping things would be the same type of remembrance as that of all animals—i.e., the remembrance of His holy word—one implies the other.

Bereshith Rabbah.[110] But since in certain places Rashi minutely examines Midrashic traditions and for the same verses also takes the trouble to explain the simple meanings of Scripture, he has thus given us permission to do likewise for there are seventy ways of interpreting the Torah,[111] and there are many differing Midrashim among the words of the Sages. And so I say that this calculation which they have mentioned does not fit into the language of Scripture unless we bear with that which explains *And the ark rested in the seventh month* as referring to that day mentioned above [in Verses 2-3] when the rain was withheld and the waters receded from the earth and decreased continually. [This interpretation of the seventh month is] unlike the counting of *the second month*[112] mentioned in the beginning of the section, [which Rashi explains there as being "the second month" of the creation calendar], and unlike the counting stated at the end of the section [in Verse 13: *in the first month*, which Rashi similarly explains as being "the first month" of the creation calendar]! And how is it possible that in the second verse Scripture should immediately retract [from using the withholding of the rain as a reference point for counting] and state, *until the tenth month,*[113] and proceed to another reference point, counting it, as Rashi explains, as the tenth month with reference to the coming of the rains!

The evidence Rashi brings from the submergence of the ark in the waters is no proof for he attributes an equal decrease of water to each of the days – namely, a cubit every four days – and it is known in nature concerning the decrease of water that a great river which decreases at first a cubit every four days will at the end decrease four cubits in a day. Thus according to this calculation of Rashi, on the first day of the month of Ab the tops of the mountains were seen,[114] and on the first day of Tishri the earth dried.[115] Thus in sixty days the waters decreased the entire height of the high mountains consisting of many thousands of cubits,

(110) 33:10. (111) Midrash Othiyoth d'Rabbi Akiba. (112) Above, 7:11. (113) Verse 5. (114) Rashi, *ibid.* (115) Rashi, Verse 13.

[surely a greater rate than four cubits a day, as Rashi would have it]! Besides, when Noah sent forth the dove on the seventeenth day of the month of Ellul, [116] the waters were yet on the face of the entire earth, [117] and the trees were covered, and in a matter of twelve days [118] the whole earth dried! And by way of reason, if the ark was submerged in the waters eleven cubits, that being more than a third of its height [which was thirty cubits], [119] it would have sunk because it was wide at the bottom and finished to a cubit at the top, [120] contrary to the structure of ships, and there was also in it great weight!

From the simple interpretation of Scripture it appears that the hundred and fifty days mentioned in connection with the prevailing of the waters [121] include the forty days of the coming down of the rains [122] since the main increase and prevailing of the waters took place during these days. Thus the waters began decreasing on the seventeenth day of Nisan, [123] and thirty days later – the seventeenth day of the month Iyar, [124] which was the seventh month from the time the rain began to fall [125] – the ark rested upon the mountains of Ararat. Seventy-three days later, on the first of Ab, which was the tenth month from the time the rain began to fall, the tops of the mountains were seen. We have thus made a small correction in the interpretation of the language of Scripture, [namely, that all counting begins from the time the rain began to fall].

(116) The raven was sent by Noah forty days after the tops of the mountains were seen on the first day of Ab. (See Verses 5-6). This brings us to the tenth of Ellul. Seven days later, on the seventeenth day of Ellul, he sent forth the dove. (117) Verse 9. (118) From the eighteenth of Ellul to the first of Tishri is a period of twelve days. (119) Above, 6:15. (120) *Ibid.*, Verse 16. (121) Above, 7:24. (122) *Ibid.*, Verse 12. (123) From the seventeenth day of Cheshvan (the beginning of the rains) to the seventeenth day of Nisan there are 150 days. This is contrary to Rashi, who said that the decrease of the waters began forty days later on the first of Sivan. (124) According to Rashi this was on the seventeenth of Sivan. (125) According to Rashi, "the seventh month," mentioned in connection with the resting of the ark upon the Ararat mountains, was the seventh month after the rains stopped, as explained above.

But the correct interpretation appears to me to be that the hundred and fifty days[121] were from the seventeenth day of the second month, namely, the month of Marcheshvan, to the seventeenth day of the seventh month, namely, the month of Nisan, and that was the day when the ark rested on the mountains of Ararat.[126] For then G-d caused *a strong east wind* to pass *all the night and made* the waters *dry land,*[127] meaning that they decreased very much, and the ark rested. The proof for this is that Scripture does not say here, "and the waters decreased on such a month and on such a day and the waters decreased continually until the seventh month, and the ark rested, etc.," as it said concerning the other decrease when the tops of the mountains were seen, for on the very day the waters began decreasing, the ark rested. The order of events in this matter was thus: on the day the rain began to fall *all the fountains of the great deep were broken up,*[112] and the windows of the heavens were opened and the rain came down for forty days. During that time the waters prevailed fifteen cubits above[128] [the summits of all the mountains]. The rain stopped at the end of forty days, but "the fountains of the deep" and "the windows of the heavens" remained open. The atmosphere was very damp, and the whole earth was full of water, not like waters poured down a precipice,[129] nor ever to become dried. And they stood thus in their power until one hundred and fifty days from the day the rain began were completed. Then G-d caused a very powerful wind to pass through the heavens and over the earth, *and the fountains of the deep were stopped*[130] for the water that flowed from them returned to its place until the deep filled up as it was before the flood, and the openings of its fountains were locked, as were "the windows of the heavens." And the air was dried very much by a drying wind, and the water on the earth was licked up.[131] Thus the waters decreased exceedingly on that day, and the ark, which was submerged in the waters

(126) This is unlike his opinion above that the ark rested thirty days after the seventeenth of Nisan. (127) Exodus 14:21. Also see Verse 1 here in Chapter 8. (128) Above, 7:19. (129) See Micah 1:4. (130) Verses 1-2. (131) See I Kings 18:38.

about two to three cubits, rested. Seventy-three days after that – on the first day of the tenth month, namely, the month of Tammuz – the tops of the mountains were seen. At the end of forty additional days – on the tenth day of the eleventh month, Ab – Noah opened the window of the ark, and three weeks later the dove left him; thirty days later, he removed the covering of the ark.

AND G-D MADE A WIND TO PASS OVER THE EARTH.[132] This means that there was a great and powerful wind coming out from the bowels of the earth over the face of the deep and hovering over the waters, and the fountains of the deep were stopped thereby. This is so since Scripture does not say, "and G-d made a wind to pass over the waters."

AND THE WATERS ASSUAGED ('VAYASHOKU').[132] This means that the waters which were flowing from the deep subsided. It is the same expression as, *Then the king's wrath 'shachachah' (assuaged),*[133] meaning that his anger subsided. Or it may be that this is an expression of a thing being concealed and swallowed up. Thus the verse teaches that the waters of the deep were swallowed up in their place. And so did the Rabbis say in Seder Olam:[134] "The waters that went up were dried by the wind, and those that went down were swallowed in their place."

AND THE RAINS FROM THE HEAVENS WERE WITHHELD.[135] This means that no more rain came down until they [Noah and his family and all living creatures] went out of the ark for by this wind [which G-d made to pass over the earth] the heavens became as iron.[136] Neither dew nor rain came down, the air lost its moisture, and the waters dried up for the rain of the flood completely stopped after the fortieth day.

(132) Verse 1. (133) Esther 7:10. (134) Chapter 4. The Seder Olam (Order of the World) is a historical record of events from the time of creation to the destruction of the Second Temple. It was authored by Rabbi Yosei, a disciple of Rabbi Akiba. (135) Verse 2. (136) See Leviticus 26:19.

AND THE WATERS RETURNED FROM OFF THE EARTH CONTINUALLY.[137] The verse states that the waters decreased gradually until *the face of the ground was dried up.*[138]

And after the end of a hundred and fifty days the waters decreased.[137] This is connected with the following verse, *And the ark rested,*[139] thus stating that on that day there was a great decrease in the waters which enabled the ark to rest [on the mountains of Ararat], as I have explained.

5. AND THE WATERS DECREASED CONTINUALLY UNTIL THE TENTH MONTH. This verse is to be interpreted by transposition: the waters decreased continually until the tops of the mountains were seen in the tenth month, which is the month of Tammuz. Scripture thus informs us that during seventy-three days[140] the waters decreased fifteen cubits.[141] But we do not know the amount of the original decrease which enabled the ark to rest since Scripture did not find it necessary to inform us either of the number of cubits that the ark was submerged in the waters or of the amount of the decrease.

In the matter of the floating of the ark, it appears to me that because the waters flowed from the deeps and were hot, as our Rabbis have said,[100] the ark therefore floated upon the face of the waters. Were it not for that, it would have sunk on account of its weight for there were many living things in it, as well as a great deal of food and drink. But as soon as the waters subsided from their flowing or from their heat and they decreased on account of the wind, the ark at once entered into the midst of the waters due to the weight of its load, and it rested on the mountain.

In the opinion of the commentators,[142] the Scriptural accounts concerning the total of one hundred and fifty days during which the waters prevailed, the resting of the ark, the visibility of the

(137) Verse 3. (138) Verse 13. (139) Verse 4. (140) From the seventeenth of Nisan, which marked the end of the 150 days during which the waters prevailed, as explained above in Verse 4, to the first day of Tammuz. (141) See above, 7:20. (142) Ibn Ezra and R'dak. See my Hebrew commentary, p. 59.

tops of the mountains and the succeeding forty days – all these events we know by way of prophecy for Scripture so informs us, but Noah knew only that he felt that the ark had rested, and he waited a period of time which, in his opinion, was sufficient for the waters to abate.

Now according to our words, as well as those of our Rabbis and all commentators, the mountains of Ararat, which are among the highest mountains under the heavens, had fifteen cubits of water above their summit.[143] Therefore this difficulty is to be posed: it is known that the Greek mountain Olympus is very much higher than they, and the land of Ararat, which is near Babylon,[144] lies in the lower part of the globe! Perhaps we should then say that the decrease of waters which took place on the seventeenth day of the seventh month[145] was very much more than fifteen cubits, and at first the tops of the high mountains were seen, not the mountains of Ararat, and it just happened that the ark was in the land of Ararat during the seventh month and it rested on the tops of those mountains.

Now Noah, from the time the rains ceased, would open and close the window at his will. Seventy-three days[140] after the resting of the ark he looked forth from the window and the tops of the mountains of Ararat were visible to him, and he again closed the window. Scripture then relates that forty days later he sent forth the raven. Scripture does not say, "and it was in such-a-month and on such-a-day that Noah opened the window," but instead it says, *And it came to pass at the end of forty days,*[146] in order to declare that from the time the tops of the mountains were seen by Noah, he waited forty days for he thought that by then the towers would be seen and the trees would become visible and the fowls would thus find in them a place to nest, and so he opened the window in order to send forth the raven. In the first month, which is the month of Tishri, *the waters were dried up,*[138] and in the second month, which is the month of Marcheshvan, on the twenty-seventh day thereof, *was the earth*

(143) Above, 7:20. (144) See Ramban further 11:2. (145) That is, the seventeenth day of Nisan, on which date the ark rested. (146) Verse 6.

dry,[147] and on that day they went out of the ark. Thus all calculations of the section are in accordance with the simple explanation of Scripture and its usual sense.

Know that after the Sages agreed that it was in the month of Tishri that the world was created[148] – as [is evidenced by the text of the prayer for the New Year which] they formulated, i.e., "This day, on which was the beginning of Thy work, is a memorial of the first day," and by the fact that the Scriptural order of the seasons is *seedtime and harvest, and cold and heat*[149] – that the beginning of the year is reckoned from Tishri. And so also were the months reckoned from Tishri until we reached the exodus from Egypt. Then the Holy One, blessed be He, commanded us to reckon the months according to another count, [namely, from the going forth from Egypt, which occurred in the month of Nisan], as it is said, *This month shall be unto you the beginning of months; it shall be the first month of the year to you.*[150] Thenceforth in all of Scripture, Tishri is reckoned as the seventh month. But as far as the years are concerned, the reckoning from Tishri was still retained, as it is written, *And the feast of ingathering at the turn of the year.*[151] And so did Jonathan the son of Uziel[152] translate the verse, *In the month of Eithanim which is the seventh month,*[153] saying, "in the month which the ancients called the first month and which is now the seventh month." And in the Mechilta we also find:[154] *"This month [Nisan] shall be unto you.* But the first man did not reckon by it; [he reckoned Tishri as the first month]."

(147) Verse 14. (148) In Tractate Rosh Hashana, 11 a, it is recorded that there was a difference of opinion on this matter. Rabbi Eliezer maintained that the world was created in Tishri while Rabbi Yehoshua taught that the world was created in the month of Nisan. The consensus of the Sages conformed with Rabbi Eliezer's view (*ibid.,* 27 a). This is the intent of Ramban's saying here: "Know that after the sages agreed, etc." See also Ramban further, 17:26. (149) Further, Verse 22. Thus the winter precedes the summer. (150) Exodus 12:2. (151) *Ibid.,* 34:22. (152) A disciple of Rabbi Yochanan ben Zakkai and one of the early Tannaitic sages. He wrote a *Targum* or Aramaic version of the books of the Prophets. It is similar in scope to that of Onkelos on the Five Books of Moses. (153) I Kings 8:2. (154) Mechilta, Exodus 12:2.

9.AND THE DOVE FOUND NO REST. It is not customary for fowl to rest on the tops of the high mountains on the earth which are bare of trees and surely not when *the waters were on the face of the whole earth.* Therefore, the dove found no rest suitable for her. But as soon as she saw the trees she went her own way[155] for in their branches she would build her nest.

11. AND LO AN OLIVE LEAF. From the plain meaning of this verse it would appear that the trees were not uprooted or blotted out in the flood because there was there no flooding stream since the whole world became full of water. But in Bereshith Rabbah the Rabbis have said,[156] "From where did the dove bring the olive leaf? Rabbi Levi said, 'She brought it from the Mount of Olives since the land of Israel was not inundated by the waters of the flood. This is as the Holy One, blessed be He, said to the prophet Ezekiel: *Son of man, say unto her: Thou art a land that is not cleansed, nor rained upon in the day of indignation.'*[157] Rabbi Biryei said, 'The gates of the garden of Eden were opened for the dove and from there she brought the leaf.' " Thus the intent of the Rabbis is that the trees were uprooted and blotted out in those places where the flood was, and surely the leaf faded.[158] Similarly the Rabbis said,[159] "Even the [solid substance of the] lower stationery millstone was blotted out in the flood," and [to substantiate this statement] they expounded the verse, *The waters wore the stones,*[160] [as referring to the waters of the flood which wore down stones]. And their saying that "the Land of Israel was not inundated by the flood" is to be understood as meaning that the rain of the flood was not there, as it is written, *nor rained upon;*[157] *the fountains of the great deep*[161] were not therein. But the waters did spread over the whole world, and *all the high mountains that were under the whole heaven were covered,*[162] as it is clearly written, and there is no partition around the Land of Israel to prevent the waters from entering. And so did the Sages

(155) Verse 12. (156) 33:9. (157) Ezekiel 22:24. (158) See Jeremiah 8:13. (159) Bereshith Rabbah 28:3. (160) Job 14:19. (161) Above, 7:11. (162) *Ibid.,* 19.

say in Pirkei d'Rabbi Eliezer:[163] "The waters of the flood did not come down from heaven upon the land of Israel, but they rolled in from other lands and came there, as it is said, *Son of man, say unto her,* etc."[157] Now according to the opinion of Rabbi Levi, [mentioned above, that the dove brought the olive leaf from the Mount of Olives], it was because the torrential rain did not come down upon the land of Israel and *the windows of heaven*[161] were not opened there that the trees remained there while in the rest of the world they were broken and uprooted by the flood and *His mighty rain.*[164]

But I wonder about their saying that [the olive leaf was brought by the dove] from the garden of Eden. If it were so, then Noah did not know that *the waters abated from off the earth* for there [in Eden] the waters of the flood did not enter. But perhaps its gates were closed so that the waters did not enter there, but when the waters abated they were opened. [Thus the olive leaf indicated the opening of the gates which in turn indicated that the waters had abated.]

It is on the basis of this opinion of theirs [—that the trees were broken and uprooted in the entire world during the flood – that the Rabbis] have said there in Bereshith Rabbah,[165] *"And he [Noah] planted a vineyard.*[166] And from where did he have a branch? Said Rabbi Abba bar Kahana, 'When he went into the ark he had taken with him branches of the vine, shoots of fig trees, and stumps of olive trees.' "

'TARAPH' (PLUCKED) IN HER MOUTH. Rashi wrote: "I am of the opinion that the dove was a male and that therefore Scripture sometimes speaks of it as masculine[167] and sometimes as feminine[168] because where the word *yonah* (dove) occurs in Scripture it is spoken of as feminine. *Taraph* however means '*he* plucked.' But a Midrashic explanation takes it [*taraph*] as meaning 'food,' and the word *b'phiha* (in her mouth) it explains as meaning

(163) Chapter 23. (164) Job 37:6. (165) 36:4. (166) Genesis 9:20. (167) It is indicated by *taraph* (he plucked) rather than *tarpha* (she plucked). (168) It is indicated by the word *b'phiha* (in her mouth).

'speaking.' Thus she said: 'Rather that my food be bitter as an olive and come by the hand of the Holy One, blessed be He, than as sweet as honey and from the hand of mortal man.' "

All this does not appear to me to be correct for there is no reason why Scripture should change its reference to doves from feminine to masculine in one place in the same section. And if it is proper language to always speak of *yonah* in Scripture as feminine, why did it change here? Similarly, their Midrashic explanation does not at all make the word *b'phiha* to mean "speaking." Instead, their Midrash is based on the fact that she brought this kind of leaf for if we should say that it just happened [that she brought an olive leaf], it cannot be in vain that Scripture mentioned it since it should have said, "And, lo, in her mouth a leaf freshly plucked." Besides, the olive does not come from the very high trees that the fowl should nest there on account of its long branches. It was for this reason that the Sages said that there was in this a hint that it is more pleasing to the fowl to have their food bitter as wormwood from the hand of the Holy One, blessed be He, and not have it be good and sweet as honey from the hand of mortal man, and surely, all the more, people do not wish to be dependent for their livehood upon one another. In the words of Bereshith Rabbah:[156] "Rabbi Abahu said, 'If the dove brought the olive leaf from the garden of Eden, could she not have brought something exceptional such as either cinnamon or balsam? But it was a hint which she gave to Noah: rather something even more bitter than this from the hand of the Holy One, blessed be He, than something sweet from your hand.' " But in the Gemara[169] they [the Sages] added: "What evidence is there that the word *taraph* means food? It is written, *'Hatripheni' (Feed me) with mine allotted bread.*"[170] It is due to the reason we have stated, [namely, that Scripture mentioned the name of the tree in order to indicate this hint] for which the Rabbis found support in the word *hatripheni*, implying that it is as if Scripture said, "And, lo, an olive-leaf of *tereph* (food)[171] in her mouth."

(169) Erubin 18 b. See my Hebrew commentary, p. 61, Note 28. (170) Proverbs 30:8. (171) And not *taraph* (he plucked), as it is actually vocalized.

As for the plain meaning of Scripture, the commentators[172] have explained that the word *taraph* modifies the word "leaf," thus stating, "And, lo, a plucked olive leaf was in her mouth." Proof for this [i.e., that *taraph* modifies "leaf" rather than acting as a verb] is that *taraph* is wholly vocalized with the *kamatz*, as is the rule.[173] It is, however, found in irregular forms: *For 'taraph' (He hath torn), and He will heal us;*[174] *And he shall restore that which 'gazal' (he took by robbery);*[175] *The error which 'shagag' (he committed);*[176] and many other additional verses.

21. AND THE ETERNAL SAID IN HIS HEART. He did not reveal the matter to a prophet at that time, but on the day He commanded Moses concerning the writing of the Torah He revealed to him that as Noah brought his sacrifice it mounted pleasingly, and He decreed that He will no more smite every living thing. In this regard, I have already written of a secret[177] hinted at by our Rabbis.

The sense of the expression, *I will not again curse the ground any more for man's sake* is that they were punished because of him for if man had not sinned, they have been spared even though they had also corrupted their ways.

FOR THE IMAGINATION OF MAN'S HEART IS EVIL FROM HIS YOUTH. He ascribes merit to men because by their very creation they have an evil nature in their youthful days but not in their mature years. If so, for these two reasons,[178] it is not proper to smite every living thing. The reason for the prefix *mem* [which signifies "from" in the word] *min'urav* (from his youth) is to indicate that the evil imagination is with men from the very

(172) Ibn Ezra and R'dak. (173) If it were a verb, it would have been vocalized with a *kamatz* followed by a *patach.* (174) Hosea 6:1. Here the word is vocalized wholly with the *kamatz,* and yet it is a verb rather than an adjective. (175) Leviticus 5:23. Similar to the above. (176) *Ibid.,* Verse 18. This too is similar to the above. (177) See Ramban above, 6:6. (178) First, that by his very creation, man's heart is evil, and second, that this evil persists only when he is young but not when he matures. Therefore, for these two reasons it is not proper that every living thing be smitten on account of man.

beginning of their youth, just as the Rabbis have said:[179] "From the moment he awakes to go forth from his mother's womb the evil impulse is placed in him." It is possible that the verse is saying that it is from youth – meaning, on account of youth – that the evil inclination is in man, for youth causes him to sin. And some say[180] that it is as if it said "in his youth," [*min'urav* being interpreted as if it were *bin'urav*]. Similarly we find *'Miterem' (Before) a stone was laid upon a stone in the temple of the Eternal,*[181] [where the word *miterem* is interpreted as *beterem*]; so too, *This is the land which ye shall divide 'minachlah' (by lot) unto the tribes of Israel,*[182] [where *minachlah* is interpreted as *benachlah*].

9 3. EVERY 'REMES' (MOVING THING) THAT LIVETH. This refers to cattle, beasts and fowl – and also the fish in the sea – since all of them are called "moving things," just as it is written: *Every living creature 'haromeseth' (that creepeth) wherewith the waters swarmed.*[183]

4. ONLY FLESH WITH THE LIFE THEREOF, THE BLOOD THEREOF, SHALL YE NOT EAT. Rashi wrote: "This prohibition applies while the animal's life is still in the blood. Thus, you should not eat flesh as long as there is life in it, meaning a limb cut from a living animal, nor shall you eat its blood together with its life, meaning the blood of a living animal."[184] But if this be so Scripture should have said, "flesh, so long as there is life in it, *and* also its blood ye shall not eat." But according to the simple meaning of Scripture, this interpretation is incorrect, and according to the Midrash it is not true, for the sons of Noah[64] have been admonished against eating a limb cut from a living animal, as is the opinion of the Sages, but not the blood of a living animal, as is the

(179) Bereshith Rabbah 34:12. (180) I have not identified the source of this opinion. (181) Haggai 2:15. (182) Ezekiel 48:29. (183) Above, 1:21. (184) Rashi thus connects *b'naphsho* (with its life) with the preceding word, *basar,* and also with the succeeding word, *damo* (its blood), although the text reads, *basar b'naphsho damo.* Ramban objects that if so the text should have said, *v'damo* (and its blood), instead of *damo.*

opinion of Rabbi Chanina ben Gamliel.[185] Rather, the interpretation of the verse is as follows: "only flesh with the life thereof, which is the blood thereof, shall you not eat," *for the life of all flesh is the blood thereof.*[186]

5. AND SURELY YOUR BLOOD 'LENAPHSHOTHEICHEM' (OF YOUR LIVES) WILL I REQUIRE. This is as if it were written, *your blood 'naphshotheichem,'* [without the letter *lamed*], and meaning "your blood which is your lives." This is similar to the verse, *'Lechol' (To all) the instruments of the tabernacle,*[187] [which means all the instruments needed for the tabernacle, the letter *lamed* in the word *lechol* being redundant]. So also, *the third 'l'Avshalom' (to Absalom),*[188] [which means, "the third, Absolom," the lamed in the word *l'Avshalom* is redundant].

It is possible to explain *your blood 'lenaphshotheichem'* as meaning *benaphshotheichem* (*in* your souls), *for the life of all flesh, the blood thereof is all one with the life thereof.*[189] Likewise, *And ye shall eat no manner of blood in all your dwelling places, 'la'oph velabeheimah' (to fowl and to cattle),*[190] which is to be explained as "in fowl or in beast."

The correct interpretation is that Scripture is saying, "the blood which is the life in you I will require." He is thus declaring that the blood is one with the life, and He intimates that one incurs the death penalty for spilling the blood upon which life depends, but not for spilling the blood of those limbs on which life is not dependent. Our Rabbis have expounded this verse as an injunction against suicide,[191] the verse stating, "I will require your blood from your own souls."

AT THE HAND OF EVERY BEAST WILL I REQUIRE IT. I wonder: if "the requiring" is here meant in its usual sense, i.e., from the hand of the beast as well as from the hand of man, in both cases there will be punishment in the matter, but the beast

(185) Sanhedrin 59 a. (186) Leviticus 17:14. (187) Exodus 27:19. (188) I Chronicles 3:2. (189) Leviticus 17:14. (190) *Ibid.*, 7:26. (191) Baba Kamma 91 b.

has no reason [with which to discern between good and evil] so that it should be punished or rewarded! Perhaps this principle applies only to spilling man's blood; every beast that will devour him will itself be devoured, for such is the decree of the King. And this is the reason [why Scripture says of an ox that killed a human being], *the ox shall surely be stoned, and its flesh shall not be eaten.* [192] This is not a form of monetary punishment for the owner since even an ownerless ox is subject to the death penalty, [193] and the command applies alike to the sons of Noah [64] and to the Israelites. The meaning of *Who so sheddeth man's blood* [194] would thus be, "all shedders" whether beast or man, their blood will be required by the Court on earth and [195] by the hand of Heaven.

It is possible that the meaning of the expression, *at the hand of every beast,* is that the vengeance upon the shedder of blood will be at the hand of every beast, just as it is said, *That she hath received of the Eternal's hand double of all her sins.* [196] Thus He says, "Surely your blood will I require and avenge *at the hand of every beast* for I will send against the murderer all beasts of the earth, and I will also send against him *the hand of man,* and he will not escape them." Similarly, *Because of all mine adversaries I am become a reproach,* [197] meaning "because of the hand of all mine adversaries;" *This is the portion of a wicked man from G-d, and the heritage appointed unto him by G-d,* [198] [meaning this is the portion of a wicked man by the hand of G-d].

Perhaps the requiring at the hand of the beast means that she should not devour man for so He established their nature. The secret of the matter is that at the time of creation He gave man *every herb bearing seed... and every tree in which is the fruit of a tree... for food,* [199] and to the beast He gave *every green herb for food,* [200] and Scripture says, *and it was so,* [200] meaning that such was their nature and habit. But now when He said of man that he

(192) Exodus 21:28. (193) Baba Kamma 44 b. (194) Verse 6. (195) "And." The Tur, quoting Ramban, has "or." (196) Isaiah 40:2. (197) Psalms 31:12. (198) Job 20:29. (199) Above, 1:29. (200) *Ibid.*, Verse 30.

may slaughter the lower living creatures for food and it was so placed in nature or habit that living creatures should eat each other, it became necessary to command that the other living creatures be unto men *a prey to their teeth*[201] while they are to fear men and not devour them. And He said, *And surely, your blood of your lives will I require*, in order to hint that He will not require the blood of one beast from the hand of another. This being so, it was thus left to them to devour one another. And this is the reason why He mentioned here the prohibition of spilling the blood of man; it is on account of the permission given here for slaughtering, which became the customary way of spilling blood since in the opinion of our Rabbis,[202] Adam had already been admonished against spilling blood. But on account of the permission for slaughtering, it became necessary for Him to say, "I have permitted you to spill the blood of every living thing except your own blood. This is forbidden to you as well as to all living things for it will not be their nature to spill it."

7. AND YOU, BE YE FRUITFUL, AND MULTIPLY. The plain meaning thereof is as its Midrash, i.e., that it is a commandment.[203] A similar verse mentioned with reference to Adam,[204] also one with reference to the sons of Noah[205] in conjunction with the statement that G-d blessed them, constitutes a blessing, just as it is said concerning the fish.[206] Now because He spoke here of the other living things and said, *that they may swarm in the earth, and be fruitful, and multiply upon the earth,*[207] He said here, *And you* – man – *be ye fruitful and multiply.* He continued saying, *swarm in the earth, and multiply therein,* in order to repeat the commandment for the purpose of emphasis, thus stating that they should be engaged in it with all power [since those who came forth from the ark were few]. Perhaps He commanded them concerning the settlement of the whole earth, as I have explained in *Seder Bereshith.*[204]

(201) Psalms 124:6. (202) Sanhedrin 56 b. (203) *Ibid.,* 59 b. (204) Above, 1:28. (205) Verse 1 here. (206) Above, 1:22. (207) *Ibid.,* 8:17.

Now Rashi wrote, "According to the plain interpretation, the first time [this was said to man it was said] as a blessing; here it is a command. According to the Midrashic explanation, [this command is mentioned here after the prohibition of murder] in order to liken one who abstains from having children to one who sheds blood." Now the Rabbis have derived this Midrash only from the juxtaposition of the verses, but the verse itself was written as a commandment, and the first [time this was said to man it was] as a blessing. [This is contrary to Rashi who implies that the Midrashic explanation differs from the plain interpretation.] And so the Rabbis have said in Tractate Sanhedrin,[203] "But the commandment to be fruitful which was declared to the sons of Noah – as it is written, *And you, be ye fruitful and multiply,....*"

8. AND G-D SPOKE TO NOAH AND TO HIS SONS. The meaning thereof is that He spoke to the sons by means of their father for his sons were not prophets, and Ham did not reach the level of prophecy. Likewise, "And the Eternal spoke to Ahaz,"[208] [which means that G-d spoke to him through Isaiah].[209] And so also, *And the Eternal spoke unto Moses and unto Aaron,*[210] which according to the words of our Rabbis[211] means He spoke to Moses so that he would in turn speak to Aaron. And so Scripture makes explicit at the end of the present chapter: *And G-d spoke to Noah.*[212]

12. THIS IS THE SIGN OF THE COVENANT WHICH I MAKE. It would appear from this sign that the rainbow in the cloud was not part of creation and that now G-d created a new thing by making a rainbow in the heavens on a cloudy day. Now commentators have said[213] concerning the meaning of this sign that He has not made the rainbow with its feet bent upward because it might have appeared that arrows were being shot from heaven, as in the verse, *And He sent out his arrows and scattered*

(208) Reference is to the verse, *Once more the Eternal spoke to Ahaz.* (Isaiah 7:10.) (209) See R'dak there. (210) Exodus 7:8 and others. (211) Torath Kohanim *Vayikra,* 1. (212) Verse 17 here. (213) I have found this opinion in Chizkuni.

them [214] on the earth. Instead He made it the opposite of this – [with the feet bent downward] – in order to show that they are not shooting at the earth from the heavens. It is indeed the way of warriors to invert the instruments of war which they hold in their hands when calling for peace from their opponents. Moreover, [with the feet of the bow being turned downward towards the earth, it can be seen] that the bow has no rope upon which to bend the arrows.

We must perforce believe the words of the Greek [philosophers who maintain] that the rainbow is a natural result of the heat of the sun falling upon damp air for even in a vessel containing water which stands in the sun there is the appearance of the rainbow. When contemplating the language of Scripture we will understand that it is so, for He said, *I have set My bow in the cloud,* [215] [the use of the past tense indicating that He had already set it so from the beginning and it is not a new creation]. He did not say, "I set in the cloud," even as He said, *This is the sign of the covenant which I make.* Moreover, the word *kashti* (My bow) – [in the possessive form] – indicates that He possessed the bow previously. Therefore, we shall explain the verse thus: "The rainbow which I have set in the clouds from the day of creation will be from this day on a sign of covenant between Me and you; whenever I will see it I will remember that there is a covenant of peace between Me and you."

And should you want to know how the rainbow can be a sign, the answer is that it has the same meaning as the verse, *This stone-heap be witness, and this pillar be witness;* [216] likewise, *For these seven ewe-lambs shalt thou take of my hand, that it may be a witness unto me.* [217] Every visible object that is set before two parties to remind them of a matter that they have vowed between them is called a "sign," and every agreement is called a "covenant." Similarly, in the case of circumcision, He said, *And it shall be a token of a covenant between Me and you,* [218] because of the agreement that all seed of Abraham be circumcised *to serve*

(214) Psalms 18:15. (215) Verse 13 here. (216) Genesis 31:52. (217) *Ibid.,* 21:30. (218) *Ibid.,* 17:11.

Him with one consent.[219] Moreover, when the above-mentioned rainbow is seen in its inverted form, [namely, with the feet of the bow turned downward], it is a reminder of peace, as we have written. Thus, whether the bow was a newly established phenomenon or one that always existed in nature, the significance thereof as a sign is the same.

Our Rabbis however have a profound secret in this section. They have said in Bereshith Rabbah:[220] *"I have set 'kashti' (My bow) in the cloud.*[215] This means, 'My likeness, that which resembles Me.' But is that possible? It is possible only as the straw resembles the fruit. *And it shall come to pass, when I bring a cloud over the earth.*[221] Rabbi Yudan said in the name of Rabbi Yehudah the son of Rabbi Shimon, 'This is like one who had in his hand some heated flour which he wanted to cast upon his son, but [because of his compassion for him] he cast it upon his servant.' "[222] There in Bereshith Rabbah it also says:[223] *"And the bow shall be in the cloud, and I will look upon it, that I may remember the everlasting covenant between G-d*[224] – this alludes to the attribute of Justice on high. *And every living creature of all flesh that is upon the earth*[224] – this alludes to the attribute of justice on earth. The heavenly attribute of justice is stern; the earthly one is sparing." And you already know the saying of the Rabbis concerning one who gazes at the rainbow:[225] "Whosoever takes no thought for the honor of his Maker would have been better off had he not come into the world." And if you will be worthy to understand the words of the Rabbis, you will know that the explanation of the verses is as follows: *My bow* – [*kashti* shares a common root with the word *kasheh* (hard, stern)] – which is symbolic of the attribute of justice, set in the cloud, shall be at the time of judgment *for a token of the covenant.*[215] *And it shall come to pass when I bring clouds over the earth*[221] – meaning that when G-d will not make His countenance shine upon[226] the earth

(219) Zephaniah 3:9. (220) 35:3. (221) Verse 14 here. (222) In the same way, when the generation is wicked and deserves destruction, G-d instead punishes the fruit of the earth. (223) 35:4. (224) Verse 16 here. (225) Chagigah 16 a. (226) See Numbers 6:25.

on account of the sins of its inhabitants– "My attribute of justice will be seen in the cloud, and I will remember the covenant in a remembrance of mercy, and I will have compassion on the little ones that are on the earth." Thus, this token and the covenant are like the token of circumcision and the covenant thereof, [227] and the language of the verses is very appropriate for the subject. And thus the Rabbis in the above Midrash have explained the expression *between G-d* [224] as referring to the attribute of justice on high, which is *gevurah* (strength), and *that which is upon the earth* [224] as being the attribute of justice on earth, which is a kindly attribute, conducting the world together with the attribute of mercy, for Scripture does not say "that which is *in* the earth," [which would have alluded to "the earth above"], but only "that which is *on* the earth." I have already hinted [228] at the secret of the Rabbis concerning the name "earth." But Rashi wrote, "*Between G-d* [224]– between the attribute of justice on high and you." But our Rabbis did not intend to imply this interpretation in their Midrash.

18. AND HAM IS THE FATHER OF CANAAN. Rashi explained, "Because this section goes on to deal with Noah's family, [229] relating that Ham sinned and through him Canaan was cursed, and since the generations of Ham have not yet been mentioned [to let us know that Canaan was his son], it was necessary to state here that Ham is the father of Canaan."

And Rabbi Abraham ibn Ezra said that Ham only saw the nakedness of his father and informed his brothers while Canaan did him the evil, the nature of which Scripture does not reveal, [230] and this is the meaning of the verse, *And he knew what his youngest son had done unto him,* [230] since Canaan was the youngest of Ham's sons, as Scripture enumerates them, *And the sons of Ham: Cush, and Mitzraim, and Phut, and Canaan.* [231] [Ibn Ezra thus interprets "son" to mean "grandson."] Now here Rabbi Abraham

(227) See Ramban further, 17:13. (228) See Ramban above, 6:13. (229) "Family." The first edition of Rashi concurs with this quote. In our texts of Rashi: "drunkenness." (230) Verse 24 here. (231) Further, 10:6.

ibn Ezra abandoned his method of explaining Scripture according to its plain meaning and began to declare statements contrary to the truth.[232]

The correct interpretation appears to me to be that Ham was the youngest of Noah's sons as I have explained at the beginning of this portion of the Torah, and Canaan was Ham's oldest son. And as for the verse which states, *And the sons of Ham: Cush, and Mitzraim, and Phut, and Canaan,*[231] [which indicates that Canaan was the youngest son], this was stated after he was sold to be *a servant of servants;*[233] Scripture gave his brothers preference over him. Now when this event happened to Noah, Ham had no other children except Canaan. This explains the verse, *And Ham, the father of Canaan, saw,*[234] for Ham had no other son then, and when he sinned unto his father, he cursed his seed. Now if Noah had said, "cursed be Ham, a servant of servants shall he be," the punishment would have been only his since the seed already born to him is not part of him, and perhaps Ham would no longer beget children. In that case Noah would not have taken his vengeance of him for who knows what shall be after him.[235] Therefore, he cursed the son he had. Even if he will later beget a hundred children,[236] it is enough that the oldest son – and all his seed with him – were cursed.

The sin committed was that Ham saw the nakedness of his father[234] and did not act respectfully. He should have covered his nakedness and concealed his shame by not telling even his brothers, but he told the matter to his two brothers in the presence of many people in order to deride him [Noah]. This is the meaning of the word *outside*[237] And so did Onkelos translate it as "in the market-place." The meaning of the verse, *And* [Noah] *knew what he had done unto him,*[230] is that he knew that Ham

(232) For Scripture in no way ascribes the act of evil done to Noah by Canaan. Instead, it mentions only Ham, (Verse 22). Thus what made Ibn Ezra say that it was Canaan that did it? (233) Verse 25 here. (234) Verse 22. (235) See Ecclesiastes 3:22. (236) See *ibid.*, 6:3. (237) *And he told his two brethren outside.* (Verse 22.)

had disclosed his disgrace to many, and he was ashamed of the matter. Our Rabbis have mentioned an additional sin that Ham committed.[238]

20. 'ISH' (A MAN) OF THE GROUND. Rashi explained it as "the master [owner or lord] of the ground. This is similar to the expression, *'ish' (the man) of Naomi,"*[239] [which means the master of Naomi]. But this is not so. *'Ish' Naomi* is an expression of the marital state, just as: *'ish ve'ishto' (a man and his wife).*[240] Others[241] have said that it means "the outstanding one of the earth, and its leader," and they brought proof from similar verses: *Gideon the son of Joash, 'ish' (a man) of Israel,*[242] [meaning a chief of Israel]; *Both ye sons of 'adam' and ye son of 'ish;'*[243] *Art thou not 'ish' (a man)? And who is like to thee in Israel?*[244] And there are many other similar verses according to their opinion.

In my opinion, *Gideon the son of Joash 'ish' of Israel,*[242] refers to his genealogy, i.e., that he was an Israelite. *Art thou not a man?*[244] means that "there is no one like you in Israel." Similarly, *strengthen yourselves, and be men,*[245] means that they should not be weak like women. *Both ye sons of 'adam' and ye sons of 'ish,'*[243] [means "both ye low-born and] ye men of higher station." However, *a man of the ground* is like *the men of the city,*[246] since Noah lived all over the earth and never built a city or country to which he should relate himself. Similarly, *a man of the field*[247] means one who constantly stayed there. In the Mishnah we find:[248] "Yosei ben Yoezer a man of Tzreidah, and Yosei ben Yochanan a man of Jerusalem."

[It may be that *a man of the ground* means] that he was determined to work the ground, to sow and to plant, because he found the earth had been laid waste, for whoever dedicates himself to a certain purpose is so called, [i.e., *ish* of that purpose]. *The*

(238) Sanhedrin 70 a. See Rashi at the end of Verse 22. (239) Ruth 1:3. (240) Above, 7:2. (241) Found in R'dak's Book of Roots. (242) Judges 7:14. (243) Psalms 49:3. Translated: both low and high. (244) I Samuel 26:15. (245) *Ibid.,* 4:9. (246) Genesis 19:4. (247) *Ibid.,* 25:27. (248) Aboth, I, 4.

men of the city [246] means those that dwell in it. *The men of David* [249] are his servants, and *a man of G-d* [250] is one who is dedicated to His service. And so the Rabbis have said in Bereshith Rabbah: [251] "*A man of the ground* [is so called just] as the castle guard is called by the name of the castle." And the Rabbis also said [252] that Noah had a passion for agriculture. Thus [the word *ish* is here used to signify] a relationship.

The meaning of the word *vayachel (and he began)* is that he commenced the planting of vineyards. The preceding men had planted single vines, but Noah began to plant many rows of vines, which together comprise a vineyard. On account of his desire for wine, he did not plant the vine singly as other trees; rather, he made a vineyard.

26. BLESSED BE THE ETERNAL G-D OF SHEM, AND MAY CANAAN BE SERVANT TO THEM. Rabbi Abraham ibn Ezra explained that *to them* means that Canaan be servant to G-d and to Shem since Shem will compel him to worship G-d. And the second time [this expression is repeated – in Verse 27: *May G-d enlarge Japheth, and may He dwell in the tents of Shem, and may Canaan be servant to them* – Ibn Ezra] explained that Canaan would be a servant to Japheth and Shem. But if this be so, Noah came to curse his enemies, and behold he blessed [253] Canaan that he be a servant to G-d!

But Rashi wrote: "*Blessed be the Eternal G-d of Shem*, Who will in days to come carry out His promise to the descendants of Shem to give them the land of Canaan, and may Canaan pay them tribute. This is repeated again [in Verse 27, as explained above], in order to state that even when the children of Shem will be in exile, the children of Canaan will be sold to them as slaves." [Thus Rashi interprets *to them* as referring to the descendants of Shem.]

(249) I Samuel 23:3. (250) Deuteronomy 33:1. (251) 36:6. (252) *Ibid.*, 36:5. (253) See Numbers 24:10.

The correct interpretation appears to me to be that at first he [Noah] cursed him that he be a servant of servants to the entire world, and whosoever will find him will enslave him, for the meaning of *unto his brethren* [233] is "unto all men," just as in the verse, *For I will set all men every one against his neighbor,* [254] and as is the sense of the expression, *Every man his fellow.* [255] It may that *unto his brethren* [233] refers to Shem and Japheth for his father's brothers are called "his brothers," just as in the expression, *that his brother was taken captive,* [256] [which refers to Lot who was a son of Abraham's brother]. And some say – as found in Ibn Ezra – that *unto his brethren* means his father's children [namely, Cush, Mitzraim and Phut, who are his father's children]. [231] Thus, after being made a servant to his father's children and to Shem and Japheth, he was a servant to the whole world. Now Noah first blessed the G-d of Shem, thereby letting it be known that Shem will be a servant of G-d while Canaan will be subject to him. And *to them* alludes to the seed of Shem who were many. It is possible that *to them* reverts also to his brothers already mentioned. Then he blessed Japheth with an enlargement of the boundary, he blessed Shem with the dwelling of G-d in his tents, and finally said that Canaan be a *servant to them*, meaning to the two of them. He made Canaan subservient to Shem twice, [in Verses 26 and 27, as explained above], thus hinting that the seed of Shem will inherit his land and all that he has, for that which a slave acquires belongs to his master. [257]

This section was written in Scripture in order to make known that it was on account of his sin that Canaan became a servant forever and that Abraham was favored with his land. The subject of the wine's effect on Noah was written because it contains a greater warning against drunkeness than that of the section on the Nazirite: [258] even the perfectly righteous man – whose righteousness saved the whole world – even he sinned on account of wine, and it brought him to disgrace and the cursing of his seed.

(254) Zechariah 8:10. (255) Isaiah 3:5. (256) Genesis 14:14. (257) Pesachim 88 b. (258) Numbers 6:1-21.

10 1. AND UNTO THEM WERE SONS BORN AFTER THE FLOOD. The intent thereof is to imply that even though they were fit to have children before the flood – for in those generations it was normal to beget children at about sixty years of age [259] – these did not beget children even at the age of a hundred, only until after the flood, for G-d restrained them from having children in order that they should not perish in the flood or that it [not] be necessary to save many persons in the ark. And so also did G-d do to this entire family: Lamech was delayed in begetting Noah until more than twice the age of his ancestors, [260] and Noah much more. This is already mentioned in the commentary of Rashi [261] who quotes from Bereshith Rabbah. [262]

2. THE SONS OF JAPHETH: GOMER. Scripture begins with Japheth for he was the oldest. After him, it mentions Ham [even though he was the youngest] [263] for Scripture wanted to delay the account of the generations of Shem in order to place side by side the two sections dealing with Shem's children since it is important to dwell at length on the generations of Abraham.

5. FROM THERE WERE PARTED THE INHABITANTS OF THE MARITIME SETTLEMENT OF THE NATIONS IN THEIR LANDS. The meaning of this is that the children of Japheth are those who dwell on the isles of the sea, and they are separated, each one of his sons residing singly on another isle, and their countries are far from each other. This was indeed the blessing of their father Noah, who said, *May G-d enlarge Japheth,* [264] meaning that they be numerous in the expanses of the earth. The sons of Ham, however, are all near one another as they dwell on the continents. Therefore Scripture said, *And the boundary of the Canaanite was from Sidon...in their lands and in their nations.* [265] The same is true of the sons of Shem.

(259) See above, 5:15, 21. (260) Enoch begot Methuselah at the age of sixty-five (above, 5:21), and Lamech begot Noah at the age of 182 (*ibid.,* Verse 28). Noah begot his sons when he was five hundred years old (*ibid.,* Verse 32). (261) Above, 5:32. (262) 26:2. (263) See Ramban above, 6:10. (264) Above, 9:27. (265) Verses 19-20 here.

Now Scripture narrates all this in order to inform us of Abraham's lineage from Shem, and Ham's descendants are mentioned to inform us of those nations whose lands Abraham was favored with on account of the sin of their fathers. Therefore it tells also of Japheth and of the dispersion [266] in order to inform us of the cause of the difference in languages and the scattering of the nations to the ends of the earth in a short period of time after the first man. Moreover, this narration serves to let us know the kindness of G-d and His keeping the covenant He made with Noah that he would not destroy them.

The Rabbi [267] said in Moreh Nebuchim [268] that the genealogy of the nations verifies to those that hear it the principle of the creation of the world. [269] This also is true, for our father Abraham *will command his children and his household after him* [270] and will affirm to them the narration concerning Noah and his sons who saw the flood and were in the ark. Thus he, [Abraham, not having seen the flood but hearing of it], was witness from mouth to mouth in the whole matter of the flood, and he was a fourth witness to creation since Noah saw his father Lamech who saw Adam. Isaac and Jacob saw Shem, the witness of the flood, and Jacob told all this to those that went down to Egypt, as well as to

(266) Genesis 11:1-9. (267) Rabbi Moshe ben Maimon (Rambam or Maimonides). See *Seder Bereshith,* Note 139. (268) III, 50. (269) "It is one of the fundamental principles of the Torah that the universe has been created out of nothing, and that of the human race, one individual being, Adam was created. As the time which elapsed from Adam to Moses was not more than about two thousand five hundred years, people would have doubted the truth of that statement if no other information had been added, seeing that the human race was apread over all parts of the earth in different families and with different languages, very unlike the one to the other. In order to remove this doubt the Law gives the genealogy of the nations [Genesis 5 and 10], and the manner how they branched off from a common root. It names those of them who were well known, and tells who their fathers were, how long and where they lived. It describes also the cause that led to the dispersion of men over all parts of the earth, and to the formation of their different languages, after they had lived for a long time in one place, and spoken one language [*ibid.*, 11], as would be natural for descendants of one person." (*Ibid.*, Friedlander's translation III, p. 273.) (270) Genesis 18:19.

Pharaoh and the people of his generation. The people in every generation similarly know from their fathers who tell them the deeds and progeny of the four to five previous generations.

7. AND THE SONS OF CUSH: SEBA AND HAVILAH, ETC. These sons became the heads of nations, and the two sons of Raamah [namely, Sheba and Dedan] became two nations. Nimrod the son of Cush, however, did not become the head of a nation. Therefore, Scripture wrote afterward, *And Cush begot Nimrod,*[271] and did not say, "and the sons of Cush: Nimrod, and Seba, and Havilah" [which would have indicated that Nimrod, like Seba and Havilah, also became the head of a nation]. But Phut the son of Ham[272] became only one people, and not various nations as was the case with Mitzraim[273] and Canaan,[274] the sons of Ham.[272] Therefore, Scripture did not return [to tell of the progeny of Phut, as it did with the other sons of Ham, namely, Cush, Mitzraim and Canaan]. In Bereshith Rabbah we find:[275] "Said Resh Lakish, 'We might have thought that the family of Phut was swallowed up, but Ezekiel came and explained, *Phut, and Lud, and all the Arabians,*' "[276] The meaning of the Midrash is that because Scripture did not return to tell about Phut, we might have thought that his seed intermingled with the children of Canaan and they neither became a nation, nor did they inherit a land called by their name. [The prophet Ezekiel thus clarified that the children of Phut existed as a separate nation in their own land.] However, in the case of *Magog, and Madai...and Tubal, and Meshech, and Tiras,*[277] – the children of Japheth – Scripture also did not mention the families of their progeny. And so also with *the sons of Shem: Elam, and Asshur, and Arpachshad,*[278] *and Lud,*[279] who became heads of nations; Scripture did not mention their progeny since each one just became one people inhabiting one country, and they did not give rise to various nationalities.

(271) Verse 8. (272) Verse 6. (273) Verses 13-14. (274) Verses 15-18. (275) 37:2. (276) Ezekiel 30:5. (277) Verse 2. (278) "Arpachshad." In this case Scripture does record his progeny (Verses 24-29). The Tur in quoting the language of Ramban rightly omits Arpachshad. Neither is it found in Ramban Mss. (279) Verse 22.

8. HE BEGAN TO BE A MIGHTY ONE IN THE EARTH. Rashi wrote, "*Mighty* in causing the entire world to rebel against the Holy One, blessed by He, by the plan he devised for the generation that witnessed the dispersion of the races." But if so, *he began* means that he began after the flood [for it could not mean that he was the first ever to begin to rebel against G-d] since in the days of the generation of Enosh, such rebellion had already begun.[280] It is possible that we should say that rebellion against G-d began in the generation of the dispersion while in the days of Enosh, people were not yet among those *that rebel against the light;*[281] rather, they also worshipped other gods.

9. HE WAS A MIGHTY HUNTER BEFORE THE ETERNAL. He ensnared the minds of people by his words, misleading them to rebel against the Omnipresent. Therefore it is said regarding any man who brazenly acts wickedly, knowing his Master and yet intentionally rebelling against Him – it is said, "This man is like Nimrod." Thus the language of Rashi, and so is the opinion of our Rabbis.[282]

But Rabbi Abraham ibn Ezra explained the matter in the opposite way, by way of the plain meaning of Scripture, for he interpreted the verses thus: *He began to be a mighty one* over the animals in hunting them. *Before the Eternal,* Ibn Ezra explained, means that he would build altars and offer the animals as whole-offerings before G-d. But Ibn Ezra's words do not appear to be correct, and lo *he justifieth the wicked,*[283] for our Rabbis knew by tradition of Nimrod's wickedness.

The correct interpretation appears to me to be that Nimrod began to be a ruler by force over people, and he was the first monarch. Until his era there were no wars and no reigning monarchs; it was he who first prevailed over the people of Babylon until they crowned him.[284] After that he went to Assyria,[285] *and*

(280) See above, 4:26, Rashi. See also Rambam in the beginning of "Laws of Idolatry," wherein he describes the process of how mankind was misled into the worship of the idols during the generation of Enosh. (281) Job 24:13. (282) Bereshith Rabbah 37:2. (283) Proverbs 17:15. (284) Verse 10 here. (285) Verse 11.

he did according to his will, and magnified himself,[286] and there he built fortified cities with his power and with his might. This is what Scripture intended when it said, *And the beginning of his kingdom was Babel...and Accad...and Shinar.*[284]

11. OUT OF THAT LAND – when Nimrod reigned over it – WENT FORTH ASSHUR, meaning he went forth to Asshur for Asshur was one of the sons of Shem.[279] This usage is similar to that found in the verses: *And it shall go forth Hazar-addar, and pass along to Azmon,*[287] [which means that it shall go forth *to* Hazzar-addar]; *And Og the king of Bashan came out against us Edrei,*[288] [which means *at* Edrei]; *And he shall return his own land with great substance,*[289] [which means that he shall return *to* his own land]; and many other similar verses. This is why the land of Assyria is called the land of Nimrod, just as it is said, *And they shall waste the land of Assyria with the sword, and the land of Nimrod with the keen-edge sword,*[290] alluding to Nineveh, and the city of Rehoboth, and Calah.[285] Scripture tells yet more about Nimrod's prowess – i.e., that *he was a mighty hunter,*[291] prevailing also over the animals and ensnaring them. Scripture said, *Before the Eternal,*[291] to suggest wonderment for there was no one under the heaven like him in strength. Similarly, *And the earth was corrupt before G-d,*[292] means that everything before Him on the earth was corrupt. This is like the verse, *That soul shall be cut off from before Me,*[293] since every place is "before Him."

13. AND MITZRAIM BEGOT. Scripture mentions the descendants of Mitzraim but does not specify their habitation as it does concerning the others. With the sons of Japheth it mentioned the isles,[294] with the sons of Cush it mentioned the land of Shinar[284] and Asshur,[285] and with the sons of Canaan it mentioned the boundaries of their land,[295] and likewise with the sons of Shem.[296] This was because *Mitzraim* (Egypt), the land of

(286) Daniel 8:4. (287) Numbers 34:4. (288) Deuteronomy 3:1. (289) Daniel 11:28. (290) Micah 5:5. (291) Verse 9 here. (292) Above 6:11. (293) Leviticus 22:3. (294) Verse 5 here. (295) Verse 19. (296) Verse 30.

his habitation, was known for it was called by his name, and all his children lived around Egypt, and the names of their countries were also like their names. Thus we find for Pathrusim,[297] [one of the children of Mitzraim], the land of Pathrus, which is part of the land of Egypt, as it says, *And I will put a fear in the land of Egypt. And I will make Pathros desolate;*[298] *Into the land of their origin.*[299] Similarly, *Lud and all the Arabians*[300] were also around Egypt, and the names of their countries were like their names. So also the land of the Philistines was called Philistia, and so it is written [in Exodus 15:14], *the inhabitants of Philistia.*

But Rabbi Abraham ibn Ezra said that these [names – *Ludim, and Anamim,* etc., in Verses 13-14] – are names of countries, and in each and every country there dwelled one family. This is why the names are all in the plural form, [that is, on account of the persons in the family, hence *Ludim* and not "Lud"]. And the real proof [that these are names of countries is the expression], *'misham' (whence) went forth,*[297] for this word *misham* alludes to a place. In the opinion of the commentators,[301] the meaning of the expression, *that went forth,* is that they begot them, just as in the expression, *And kings shall come out of thy loins.*[302] Now Rashi wrote: "They [the Philistines] were descended from both of them [the Pathrusim and the Casluhim], for the Pathrusim and Casluhim used to live together in promiscuous intercourse, and the Philistines were their offspring. Thus in Bereshith Rabbah."[303]

In my opinion, by way of the plain meaning of Scripture, the Casluhim dwelled in a city of that name – which was part of the land of Caphtor where the Caphtorim their brethren were – and *they went forth from there,* meaning from the Caphtorim who were of the seed of Casluhim. And they went in order *to look for a resting-place for themselves,*[304] and they left the land to their brethren and conquered for themselves a land by the name of

(297) Verse 14. (298) Ezekiel 30:13-14. (299) *Ibid.,* 29:14. The verse reads: *And I turn the captivity of Egypt, and will cause them to return into the land of Pathros, into the land of their origin.* This shows that the land of Pathros is near Egypt. (300) *Ibid.,* 30:5. (301) Rashi and Ibn Ezra. (302) Genesis 35:11. (303) 37:8. (304) Numbers 10:33.

Philistia, after which they came to be called Philistines. This is why Scripture says, *The Caphtorim, that came forth out of Caphtor, destroyed them, and dwelt in their stead,*[305] the Caphtorim being of the sons of Casluhim, dwellers of the land of Caphtor.

15. AND CANAAN BEGOT ZIDON HIS FIRST-BORN. These were the ten[306] nations, sons of Canaan, whose lands were given to our father Abraham since all seed of Canaan were sold into servitude forever. These were the ones that were given to Abraham. Their names, however, changed for the most part in the days of Abraham; here they were inscribed according to the names their father called them on the days of their birth, but after they parted according to their lands and their nations, they were called by other names.[307] Perhaps they were called by the names of the land in which they settled, as we have explained.[308] Likewise, *Se'ir the Horite*[309] was so called because the name of the city was Se'ira. And there are many similar names. It may be that the Arkite and the Sinite[310] did beget families but were cut off from them, and their children were, for example, *the Kenite, and the Kenizzite.*[311] These became the heads of families, the entire nation being called by their name as was customary among the tribes of Israel. Now in His gift [of the land of Abraham, G-d] called the ten nations by the names by which they were known in the time of Abraham.[312]

Proof of this, [namely, that some of the names of the sons of Canaan changed in the time of Abraham], is that the Hivite mentioned here[310] is not mentioned in the gift to Abraham,[312] and yet he was among them, as it is said, *And He shall cast out many nations before thee, the Hittite, and the Girgashite, and the Amorite, and the Canaanite, and the Perizzite, and the Hivite, and*

(305) Deuteronomy 2:22. (306) "Ten." There are eleven children of Canaan mentioned here. Ramban will explain later in the text that one did not develop into a separate nation. (307) Compare Verses 15-18 here with Verses 19-21 in Chapter 15. (308) Above, at the end of Verse 13 concerning the origin of the name Philistines. (309) Genesis 36:20. (310) Verse 17 here. (311) Further, 15:19. (312) *Ibid.*, Verses 19-21.

the Jebusite, seven nations.[313] So also in every place [Scripture counts the Hivite among the nations that inhabited the land of Canaan]. Now the Canaanite is counted in the gift to Abraham among his [Canaan's] children,[314] but only ten are counted [there[312] – while eleven children of Canaan are mentioned here] –[315] because one of his sons did not prevail like his other brothers, and so he was called together with his brother [the Hivite] by the name of his father, [thus bringing to a total of ten the number of nations whose lands were given to Abraham]. It is possible also that it was Zidon, Canaan's first-born who was called the Canaanite together with his brother, [the eleventh son of Canaan], who did not become a nation, [thus making ten the total number of lands given to Abraham].

Do not find it difficult that the land of the Philistines was also given to Abraham – as it is written, *Sojourn in this land ... for unto thee, and unto thy seed, I will give all these lands*[316] – and yet the Philistines were of the sons of Mitzraim [and not of Canaan]! Scripture said, *Counted to the Canaanites were the five lords of the Philistines,*[317] because the Philistines conquered part of the land of the Canaanites and settled thereon. And here in Scripture you will see [that the Philistines captured part of the Canaanite land], *for the boundary of the Canaanite was from Sidon, as thou comest to Gerar, unto Gaza*[318] yet we find that these were Philistine cities, since Abimelech, king of the Philistines, was king of Gerar,[319] and Gaza belonged to the Gazites. Similarly, *For Gaza one.*[320] Sidon also belonged to the Philistines, for it is written, *All the Zidonians will I drive out from before the children of Israel; only allot thou it unto Israel for an inheritance;*[321] and again, *And also what are ye to Me, O Tyre, and Zidon, and all the*

(313) Deuteronomy 7:1. (314) As the verse states: *And the Amorite and the Canaanite...* . Further, 15:21. (315) Verses 15-18 here. (316) Genesis 26:3. (317) Joshua 13:3. Hence their lands were also given to Abraham even though the Philistines themselves were not of the seed of Canaan. (318) Verse 19 here. (319) Genesis 20:2. (320) I Samuel 6:17. This is counted among the guilt-offerings the five Philistine cities sent along with the Ark of G-d which they were returning. (321) Joshua 13:6.

regions of Philistia?[322] Perhaps the rest of the land of the Philistines, excluding that of these five of their lords,[323] was not given to Israel.

Know that the land of Canaan with its boundaries, *since it became a nation,*[324] was qualified for Israel, and this was the lot of their inheritance, as it is said, *When the Most High gave to the nations their inheritance, when He separated the children of men, He set the borders of the peoples according to the number of the children of Israel.*[325] But at the time of the dispersion of the nations, the Holy One, blessed be He, gave it to Canaan, on account of his being a servant, to keep it for Israel. This is just as a man who deposits for safe-keeping the belongings of the master's son with his servant until such time as the son will grow up and acquire the belongings as well as the servant. I will explain this yet[326] with the help of G-d, exalted be He.

21. AND UNTO SHEM, TO HIM ALSO WERE CHILDREN BORN. Since Scripture delayed the narration of the generations of Shem and related the generations of his younger brother as if Shem had no children, it therefore says here, *to him also.*

THE FATHER OF ALL THE CHILDREN OF 'EBER.' This means that he was the father of all who dwelled beyond (*eber*) the Euphrates River, which was the place of Abraham's family. But it is not possible that *Eber* in this context be the name of the person who was the father of Peleg[327] for why would Scripture connect the children of Eber with Shem [moreso than with any of his other offspring]?

THE BROTHER OF JAPHETH THE ELDER. It is the way of Scripture to record a younger brother beside the oldest of his

(322) Joel 4:4. (323) Joshua 13:3. (324) Exodus 9:24. (325) Deuteronomy 32:8. (326) *Ibid.,* 2:23. (327) Verse 25 here. So too the opinion of Ibn Ezra and R'dak.

brothers, and not beside a younger one than himself.[328] And similarly, we find the verse, *Miriam the prophetess, the sister of Aaron.*[329] The reason for mentioning this altogether is to state that he [Shem] is the brother of the honorable Japheth, comparable to him in distinction. Scripture thus declares that the reason it delayed telling of his genealogy is not because Ham was more distinguished than he.

It appears to me that "the elder" is descriptive of Shem,[330] meaning that he was the older brother of Japheth, as Ham was the youngest of all, even though Scripture mentioned Japheth first. So, likewise, in all places in Scripture, the descriptive noun refers to the subject spoken of, such as: *Isaiah the son of Amoz the prophet,*[331] [the term "the prophet" refers to Isaiah, who is the subject of the narration]; *Unto Hobab, the son of Reuel the Midianite, Moses' father-in-law,*[332] [here, "Moses' father-in-law" refers back to Hobab]. But Rashi wrote: "*The brother of Japheth.* It does not state "the brother of Ham" because these two [Shem and Japheth] honored their father whereas Ham put him to shame." This interpretation also declares that the sense of the verse is that Shem is the brother of the righteous brother, and not the brother of the wicked brother even though he is counted after him.

(328) See above, 6:10, that Ramban's opinion is that Noah's children were born in this order: Japheth, Shem, and Ham. Ramban thus says here that it is customary for Scripture to record a second son (Shem) beside the oldest (Japheth) even though Shem had a younger brother, Ham. Thus Scripture writes, *the brother of Japheth the elder,* rather than "the elder brother of Ham." (329) Exodus 15:20. Even though Moses was younger than Miriam, Scripture records the younger Miriam beside the elder Aaron, rather than say, "the older sister of Moses." (330) Ramban, in this final paragraph, sets forth his principle that Shem was really the oldest of the three brothers. The order of their birth was thus: Shem, Japheth and Ham. This is completely unlike the theory of Rashi (5:32; 9:24) who holds that they were born in this order: Japheth, Ham and Shem. R'dak here conforms with Ramban's theory, as is clear from R'dak's following words: "The word *hagadol (the elder)* is descriptive either of Japheth or of Shem. If so, *the elder* refers to age in years for in my opinion Shem was the oldest of the brothers while, in the opinion of most commentators, Japheth was the oldest. It is also possible to explain *the elder* as referring to distinction, and it may also be descriptive of either of them." (331) II Kings 20:1. (332) Numbers 10:29.

11 2. AS THEY JOURNEYED FROM THE EAST. Rashi comments: "They journeyed from where they were then dwelling, as it is written above, *And their dwelling was from Mesha, as thou goest toward Sephar, unto the mountain of the east.*[333] From there they journeyed to search out for themselves a place that would accomodate them all, but they found none except Shinar." But this is not correct for this is the account of the children of Shem only, concerning whom it was so said [that they dwelled at "the mountain of the east"], and why should Scripture attribute the dispersion to the descendants of Shem when the children of Japheth and of Ham were more numerous than they? Besides, their habitation in their countries was from Mesha to the mountain of the east,[333] and the dispersion of the nations took place before they settled there, for the children of Japheth surely did not come from the isles of the sea[334] to the land of Shinar; rather, it was during the dispersion that *G-d scattered them abroad upon the face of all the earth,*[335] and at that time they were settled *in their lands, after their nations.*[336]

And Rabbi Abraham ibn Ezra explained that the mountains of Ararat are in the east. [Thus the verse before us which states, *as they journeyed from the east*, means as they journeyed from the mountains of Ararat.] That which he said is correct for the mountains of Ararat are in the east near Assyria, as it is said, *And they escaped into the land of Ararat.*[337] And when Noah came down from the mountain [upon which the ark had rested],[338] he and his sons settled in those lands, and when they increased they journeyed from there to this valley called Shinar.

According to our Rabbis,[339] the men of the dispersion rebelled against their Creator. But those who pursue the plain meaning of Scripture say[340] that their idea was only to be closely united, for

(333) Above, 10:30. (334) *Ibid.*, Verse 5. (335) Verse 9 here. (336) Above, 10:31. (337) II Kings 19:37. The reference there is to the sons of Sennacherib of Assyria, who slew their father and fled to the nearby land of Ararat. (338) Above 8:4. (339) Sanhedrin 109 a. (340) This opinion is found in R'dak.

Scripture declares their intention, *lest we be scattered,*[341] and does not relate any other matter [motive] concerning them. But if it be as those commentators say, then the men of the dispersion were fools for how could one city and one tower suffice for all people of the world? Or perhaps they thought that they would not be fruitful and multiply, as it is written, *and the seed of the wicked will be cut off.*[342]

However, he who knows the meaning of the word "name" – as they said, *and we will make for us a name*[341] – will understand their intent and will know the extent of their evil intention in constructing the tower. And then he will understand the whole subject, namely, that theirs was an evil thought, and the punishment that came over them – to be dispersed in their languages and countries – was meted out measure for measure for "they mutilated the shoots" [of faith by seeking to undermine the principle of the Unity]. Thus their sin was comparable to that of their father Adam.[343] Perhaps on account of this the Sages expounded:[344] *"And the Eternal came down to see... which the children of men had built.*[345] Said Rabbi Berachyah, '[Whose children could they have been but the children of men?] Perhaps the children of donkeys or camels? Rather it means the children of the first man, etc.' " Contemplate further that in the entire subject of the flood, Scripture mentions *Elokim* (G-d), while in the entire matter of the dispersion it mentions the Tetragrammaton; the flood came on account of the corruption of the land, and the dispersion came because "they mutilated the shoots" of faith and therefore their punishment was meted out by His Great Name. This explains the "coming down"[345] and also the Divine measure meted out in Sodom.[346] The student learned [in the mystic lore of the Cabala] will understand.

(341) Verse 4 here. (342) Psalms 37:28. (343) See Ramban above, 3:22. (344) Bereshith Rabbah 38:12. (345) Verse 5 here. (346) See Ramban further, 19:24.

28. AND HARAN DIED IN THE PRESENCE OF HIS FATHER TERAH IN THE LAND OF HIS BIRTH IN UR OF THE CHALDEES. In accordance with the words of our Rabbis, Rashi wrote, "Terah accused his son Abram before Nimrod of having broken his idols, and he cast him into a fiery furnace. Meanwhile Haran waited and said to himself, 'if Abram proves triumphant I will be on his side, and if Nimrod wins I shall be on his.' When Abram was saved, they said to Haran, 'On whose side are you?' He replied, 'I am on Abram's side.' They therefore cast him into the fiery furnace, and he was burnt to death. It is to this event that the name *Ur Kasdim* (fire of the Chaldees) alludes. Menachem ben Saruk,[347] however, explained the word *ur* as meaning 'valley.' So also, *Therefore glorify ye the Eternal 'ba'urim' (in the valleys),*[348] and also, *'me'urath' (the den of) the basilisk.*[349] Every hole or deep cleft may be called *ur*." This matter received by our Rabbis through tradition is the truth, and I will elucidate it.

Our father Abraham was not born in the land of Chaldaea. His ancestors were descendants of Shem, and Chaldaea and the whole land of Shinar were countries inhabited by the sons of Ham,[350] and Scripture states, *And he told to Abram the 'Hebrew,'*[351] not Abram the Chaldean. And it is further written, *Your fathers dwelt in days of old beyond the river, Terah the father of Abraham, and the father of Nahor,*[352] the word *mei'olam (of old)* teaching that his origins were always from there. And again Scripture states, *And I took your father Abraham from beyond the river.*[353] Proof of the matter is that we find Nahor [Abraham's brother] in Haran.[354] Now if Terah's place were in Ur of the Chaldees in the land of Shinar and Scripture relates that upon Terah's going forth from Ur of the Chaldees he took with him only his son Abram, his grandson Lot the son of Haran, and Sarai his daughter-in-law,[355]

(347) Menachem ben Saruk was a great grammarian who lived in the middle of the tenth century in southern Spain. He composed the first dictionary covering the entire field of the Biblical language. His work is called Machbereth (literally, "a joining of words"). Rashi, in his commentary on the Torah and other books of the Bible, made great use of this work. (348) Isaiah 24:15. (349) *Ibid.*, 11:8. (350) See above, 10:10-12. (351) Further, 14:13. (352) Joshua 24:2. (353) *Ibid.* 3. (354) Genesis 29:4-5. (355) Verse 31 here.

then Nahor was left in the land of Chaldaea, [and yet we find that he was in Haran,[354] which is in the land of Mesopotamia, as explained further].

But the truth of the matter is that the country of the birth of Abraham's ancestors was the land of Aram, which is beyond the River Euphrates; this was always the habitat of his ancestors. Thus Scripture says concerning the children of Shem, *And their dwelling was from Mesha, as thou goest toward Sephar, unto the mountain of the east,*[333] this being a generic name applicable to all their countries, as it is written there, *in their land, after their nations,*[336] and again it is written, *From Aram Balak bringeth me, the king of Moab from the mountains of the east,*[356] [proving that Aram is in the land of "the mountains of the east"]. Thus it is clear that Abram and his ancestors always lived in the land of Aram. Furthermore, we find in the Talmud[357] that Abraham was imprisoned [by Nimrod because he broke the idols] in Cuthah, and that city is not in the land of Chaldaea, for it is written, *And the king of Assyria brought men from Babylon, and from Cuthah, and from Avva, and from Hamath,*[358] and it is further written, *And the men of Babylon made Succoth-benoth, and the men of Cuth made Nergal.*[359] But it would appear that Cuthah is a city beyond the river, in the land of Mesopotamia, for Haran is the name of a city in the land of Mesopotamia, as it is written, *And he went to Aram-naharaim* [Mesopotamia], *unto the city of Nahor,*[360] which is Haran. Furthermore, we have investigated and know it from the word of many students[361] who lived in that country that Cuthah is a large city between Haran and Assyria, far from the country of Babylon. The distance between it and Haran is about that of a six-day journey. It is, however, included in the

(356) Numbers 23:7. (357) Baba Bathra 91 a. (358) II Kings 17:24. (359) *Ibid.*, Verse 30. (360) Genesis 24:10. (361) This alludes to the time during the last three years of his life when Ramban lived in the land of Israel and there gathered around him students from nearby countries. It was from these students, who came from the eastern countries, that he sought first-hand knowledge to illumine the problems he had in his commentary. Concerning this fascinating period in the life of Ramban, see his biography, pp. 191-206 in my Hebrew work, pp. 60-65 in the English edition.

term, "beyond the river,"[353] because it lies between Mesopotamia and the River Euphrates – which is the border of the land of Israel[362] – and *the Tigris which goeth towards the east of Assyria.*[363] Thus Terah begot his older sons, Abraham and Nahor, in the area "beyond the river," the land of his ancestors. He then went with his son Abram to the land of Chaldaea, where his youngest son, Haran, was born. His son Nahor, however, remained "beyond the river," in the city of Haran. It may be that he was born there or that he came to settle there from Cuthah. This is the meaning of [the verse here which says of Haran], *in the land of his birth, in Ur of the Chaldees*, since that was the birthplace of Haran alone [among Terah's children].

This matter received through tradition [that Cuthah was the birthplace of Abraham] is also found in a book called The Antiquities of the Nations, as the Rabbi[267] wrote in the Moreh Nebuchim[364] that in the book of Egyptian Agriculture it is mentioned that Abraham, who was born[365] in Cuthah, differed with the opinion of the people who worshipped the sun, and the king put him in prison, but he continued to argue against them for many days. At last the king was afraid that he might corrupt his land and turn the people away from their religion, and so he expelled him to the far land of Canaan, after confiscating all his wealth.

Thus in any case it was in this place, the land of Chaldaea, that a miracle – or more exactly a hidden miracle[366] – was done to our father Abraham, for G-d put it into the heart of that king to save him and not to kill him, and so he released him from prison to go where he desires. It may be that it was an overt miracle,[366] i.e., that the king threw him into a fiery furnace, and he was saved, as our Rabbis have stated.[367]

(362) Genesis 15:18. (363) Above, 2:14. (364) III, 29. Ramban is following Al-Charizi's translation, and not Ibn Tibbon's. See notes in my Hebrew commentary, pp. 72-73. (365) "Born." Ibn Tibbon has, "grew up." (366) See Ramban further, 17:1, concerning the two kinds of miracles. (367) As mentioned in Rashi, quoted at the beginning of this verse.

Let not Rabbi Abraham ibn Ezra mislead you with his questions,[368] saying that Scripture has not narrated this wonder, for I will yet give you[369] a reason for the omission and proof of the verity of this and other miracles like it. These peoples, however, did not mention it in their books because they differed with his [the Patriarch's] opinion, and they thought his miracle was a deed of sorcery, just as was the case with our teacher Moses in his confrontation with the Egyptians at the beginning of his deeds. It is on account of this that Scripture no longer mentions this miracle [of Abraham] for it would have had to mention the words of those who differed with him, as it mentioned the words of the Egyptian magicians, and Abraham's words were not as openly verified to them as were ultimately the words of our teacher Moses, [which were established by ten clearly revealed miracles]. Thus Scripture says, *I am the Eternal that brought thee out of Ur of the Chaldees to give thee this land to inherit it,*[370] for the word *hotzeisicha (brought thee out)* points to a miracle. It does not say, "that took thee from Ur of the Chaldees;" instead it says, *that brought thee out*, meaning that He brought out a prisoner from the dungeon[371] just as in the verse: *that brought thee out from the land of Egypt.*[372] And He said to Abraham, *to give thee this land to inherit it,*[370] because from the time that G-d brought him out of Ur of the Chaldees, it was His Will, exalted be He, to make him into a great nation and to give him this land of Canaan. From that day on which Abraham was saved, Terah – his father – and Abraham had in mind to go to the land of Canaan, a distant point far from the land of Chaldaea, out of fear of the king, since Haran, [the city of their inhabitance], was near them [the Chaldeans], and they were one people with one language since Aramaic was their common language. They [Terah and Abraham] wanted to go to a nation where their speech would not be understood by that king and his people. This is the meaning of the verse, *And they went forth with them from Ur of the Chaldees, to go into the land of Canaan, and they came unto Haran*[373] where their families and

(368) In Verse 26. (369) See Ramban further, 46:15. (370) Genesis 15:7. (371) See Isaiah 42:7. (372) Exodus 20:2. (373) Verse 31 here.

ancestors ever lived, and they settled among them, staying there for many days. It was there that Abraham was commanded to do what he had intended, i.e., to go to the land of Canaan, and so he left his father, who later died there in Haran,[374] his country, and went with his wife and Lot, his brother's son, to the land of Canaan.[375] Thus Scripture says, *And I took your father Abraham from beyond the river, and led him throughout all the land of Canaan,*[353] for Abraham was commanded concerning this when he was yet "beyond the river," and from there G-d took him and led him throughout all the land of Canaan.

Now according to the opinion of our Rabbis [that Nimrod threw Abraham into a fiery furnace, the name] *Ur Kasdim* will be understood as the plain meaning indicates, [namely, "Fires of the Chaldees"], from the same expression: *I am warm, I have seen 'ur' (the fire).*[376] Scripture thus says, *And they went forth with them from Ur of the Chaldees,*[373] even though Terah did not go forth from the fiery furnace. However, since Abram is the main [person of interest, it mentions *Ur Kasdim* although the name has reference to him alone]. It may be that on account of the miracle the place came to be so called, just as we find, *And at Taberah, and at Massah, and at Kibroth-hattaavah,*[377] and others. Scripture thus alludes that when Abram went forth from the fiery furnace, they all fled from that country.

And the meaning of the verse, *Glorify ye the Eternal 'ba'urim,'*[348] is in my opinion consonant with that which the Rabbis have said [concerning *Ur Kasdim*, namely, that it means "the Fire of the Chaldees"], for *urim* are the high mountains on which they make fires and "kindle the flares"[378] to make the new events known quickly in distant places, even as it says [in the second half of the verse]: *In the isles of the sea, the name of the Eternal, the G-d of Israel.*[348] The sense of that verse is thus that for the glory of G-d they should let the whole world know the

(374) Verse 32. (375) Further, 12:5. (376) Isaiah 44:16. (377) Deuteronomy 9:22. – These places were so named because of the events that occurred there. See Numbers 11:3, 34. Exodus 17:7. (378) Rosh Hashana 22b. The subject there concerns the kindling of flares on the tops of the hills to declare that the day of the New Moon had been declared.

miracle and the wonder which had been done to them. So also, *'Me'urath' the basilisk*[349] means his [the serpent's] hole, where his fire and great heat are, just as he is indeed called *saraph* [the serpent, but literally, "the burning one"]. And I have seen in the Midrash:[379] *"Arise, 'uri' (shine).*[380] Therefore *glorify ye the Eternal 'ba'urim.'*[348] How do you glorify Him? Rabbi Yeivo bar Kahana said, 'With these torches such as the lanterns which burn in synagogues[381] in all places, even *in the isles of the sea,*[348] to the glory of G-d.' " Thus it is clear that the Rabbis understood the word *ba'urim* as an expression of fire, in accordance with its simple sense.

31. AND THEY WENT FORTH WITH THEM FROM UR OF THE CHALDEES. Because Abram was more important than his father and those that followed his counsel and for whose sake they went, Scripture says, *And they went forth,* [rather than "he went forth"] even though it says at the beginning of the verse, *And Terah took.* Lot and Sarai, however, went with them to the land of Canaan on account of Abram, for even after Abram separated from his father they went along with him.[382]

32. AND TERAH DIED IN HARAN. After Abram had left [Haran, as related in the next chapter, and had come to the land of Canaan], Terah remained alive for many years after that.[383] Why then does Scripture mention the death of Terah before the departure of Abram? [The answer is that Scripture does so] in order that this matter [of leaving his home during his father's lifetime] might not become publicized to all, lest people say that Abram did not show a son's respect to his father and mother[384]

(379) Pesikta d'Rabbi Kahana, 21. (380) Isaiah 60:1. (381) This is one of the earliest sources for establishing the religious duty of kindling lights in a synagogue. See my edition of Kithvei Rabbeinu Bechaya, pp. 89-90. (382) The Tur concludes: "Thus it should have said, 'and they walked with *him,*' that is with Abram. But out of respect to his father, Scripture ascribes it to both of them." (383) Abram was seventy-five years old when he left Haran (12:4), and Terah was seventy years of age when Abram was born (11:26), making Terah 145 years old at the time Abram left Haran. Terah thus lived for sixty more years as he died at the age of 205 (11:32). (384) "And mother." Not in our text of Rashi.

as he left his father in his old age and went his way. That is why Scripture speaks of Terah as dead. Moreover,[385] for the wicked, even while alive, are called dead. Thus the words of Rashi which are found in Bereshith Rabbah.[386]

But I wonder about their words for this is the customary way for Scripture to relate the life of a father, his begetting a son, and his death, and afterwards to begin the narration of the son in all generations. This is the usual manner of Scripture. Noah himself lived yet in the days of Abraham,[387] and his son Shem lived thoughout Abraham's life span.[388] Now it is possible that the Rabbis came to conclusion of this Midrash because with respect to Terah, Scripture departed from the format of the entire chapter. Regarding Shem and his descendants, Scripture did not mention their death at all, nor did it total the sum of their years. But here with Terah it again follows the first order it used concerning the longevity of the people from Adam to Noah[389] and totals up all the days of Terah and mentions his death. In addition, it mentions the place of death as having been in Haran, the same place it had mentioned concerning Abraham, [i.e., that he had gone there, in Verse 31]. That is why the Rabbis expounded that all this was to make it easily apparent that Abraham was there with Terah when he died. Moreover, because Scripture had already begun the subject of Abraham and told how he had gone forth with his father *from Ur of the Chaldees to go into the land of Canaan,*[390] the Rabbis found it difficult to understand why Scripture did not systematically arrange Terah's life and death, and write it chronologically. [That is why they made the aforementioned interpretation.]

And as for that which the Rabbis also said in Bereshith Rabbah[386] – "First you interpret[390] that the wicked, even while alive, are called dead" – this too I find surprising, for the Sages[391]

(385) "Moreover." Not in our text of Rashi. (386) 39:7. (387) Noah lived 350 years after the flood (9:28), and the total number of years of all ten generations from Noah to Abraham was less than 300 years. Thus Noah was still alive in the time of Abraham. (388) Shem lived 500 years after the flood (11:11). See also Baba Bathra 121 b: *"Jacob saw Shem."* (389) Above, 5:5-31. (390) Verse 31 here. (391) Bereshith Rabbah 34:4; 38:18.

have already deduced from the verse,[392] "*And thou shalt come to thy fathers in peace.* [His father was an idolater, and yet G-d informed Abraham that after death he would go to him! Clearly the verse teaches you] that He announced to Abraham that his father would have a portion in the World to Come." Perhaps the intent of the Rabbis was that Terah repented at the time of death, but he lived all his days in wickedness and therefore was called "dead." In the words of Rashi:[392] "Scripture teaches you that Terah did repentance at the time of death." Perhaps it may be that our Sages, of blessed memory, say[393] that Terah has a portion in the World to Come by virtue of his son. And that was the announcement, for Abraham did not know it until he was informed of it at the time G-d told him, *And thou shalt come to thy fathers in peace.*[392] And so I found in a Midrash:[394] "All kinds of wood were valid for use in the altar fire save only the wood of the olive and the vine,[395] for since oil and wine were offered upon the altar, the fruits save the trees. And so we find in the case of Abraham that he saved Terah, as it is said, *And thou shalt come to thy fathers in peace.*"[392]

(392) Genesis 15:15. (393) Sanhedrin 104 a. (394) Possibly Ramban refers to Vayikra Rabbah at the beginning of Chapter 7. (395) Tamid 2:3. One of the reasons stated for this law is that it maintains the cultivation of *Eretz Yisrael.*

Lech Lecha

12 1. AND THE ETERNAL SAID UNTO ABRAHAM 'LECH LECHA' (GET THEE OUT). This means, "For your own benefit and for your own good. And there I will make of you a great nation whilst here you will not merit the privilege of having children." Thus the language of Rashi.

Now there is no need for it[1] for such is the normal expression of the Hebrew language as in the verses: *The rain is over and gone 'lo';*[2] *I will get 'li' unto the great men;*[3] *Rise up, and get 'lachem' over the brook Zered;*[4] and many similar examples. Our Rabbis, however, have made a Midrash —(a homiletical interpretation)— concerning the verses [addressed to Moses] which state, *And thou shalt make 'lecha' an ark of wood,*[5] and *Make 'lecha' two trumpets of silver,*[6] since it was not his work and it would have been proper for these verses to be stated in the same way as that concerning the tabernacle, i.e., *And thou shalt make the tabernacle.*[7]

(1) Ramban's intent is that it is unnecessary to explain the word *lecha* (literally, "to you") as meaning "for your own benefit" for it is merely the idiomatic usage of the Hebrew language, as explained further in the text. (2) Song of Songs 2:11. Literally, "gone to itself." (3) Jeremiah 5:5. Literally, "get to me." (4) Deuteronomy 2:13. Literally, "and get to you." (5) Deuteronomy 10:1. Literally, "make to thee." The Midrash of the Rabbis is as follows: "Here the verse states, *And 'thou' shalt make an ark,* meaning Moses, but in Exodus (25:10) it states, *And 'they' shall make an ark!* This teaches us that the people of a community are commanded to do the work of a Torah-scholar who resides in their midst." (Yoma 72 b.) (6) Numbers 10:2. Literally, "make to thee." The Rabbis commented: "As though it were possible, I would prefer it to be from that which is thine to that which is theirs." (Yoma 3 b.) (7) Exodus 26:1.

OUT OF THY COUNTRY, AND FROM THY BIRTHPLACE. Rashi wrote,[8] "But had he not already departed from there together with his father and reached as far as Haran?[9] But thus, in effect, did the Holy One, blessed be He, say to him, 'Go still further away from thy father's house.' "

And Rabbi Abraham ibn Ezra explained the verse as follows: "And G-d had already said to Abram, 'Get thee out of thy country,' since this command came to him when he was still in Ur of the Chaldees, and there He commanded him to leave his country, his birthplace and his father's house, in which he was."

But this is not correct, for if so, it would follow that Abram was the central figure in the journey from his father's house by command of G-d, while Terah his father voluntarily went with him. Yet Scripture says, *And Terah took Abram his son,*[9] which teaches us that Abram followed his father and that it was by his counsel that Abram went forth from Ur of the Chaldees to go to the land of Canaan! Furthermore, [according to Ibn Ezra, who says that the above command came to Abram when he was still in Ur of the Chaldees], the verse stating, *And I took your father Abraham from beyond the river and led him throughout all the land of Canaan,*[10] should have stated, "And I took your father from Ur of the Chaldees and led him throughout all the land of Canaan," for it was from there that he was taken, and it was there that he was given this command. In addition, the following difficulty may be put to Rashi and Ibn Ezra: when Abraham commanded Eliezer to get a wife for his son, he said to him, '*But thou shalt go unto my country and to my birthplace,*'[11] and he went to *Aram-naharaim, to the city of Nahor.*[12] If so, that is his "country" and his "birthplace!" And there, Scripture further says [when Eliezer recounts Abraham's charge to him], *But thou shalt go unto my father's house and to my family,*[13] thus clearly

(8) In Verse 2 here. (9) Above, 11:31. (10) Joshua 24:3. (11) Genesis 24:4. The word *moladeti,* generally translated "my kindred," connotes, according to Ramban, both "my birthplace" and "my family." This is made clear further on in the text. (12) *Ibid.,* Verse 10. Aram-naharaim is Mesopotamia. See Ramban above, 11:28. (13) *Ibid.,* Verse 38.

indicating that there (in Mesopotamia) were his father's house and his family which is "his kindred." This is not as Rabbi Abraham ibn Ezra erred in interpreting, "*Unto my country,*[11] Haran; *and to my birthplace,* Ur of the Chaldees." Now since Ibn Ezra says here that in Ur of the Chaldees it was said to Abraham, *Get thee out of thy country, and from thy kindred, and from thy father's house,* Abraham would thus have many countries![14] But the essential principle you already know from what we have written in the preceding *Seder,*[15] namely, that Haran is Abraham's country, and there is his birthplace, it having always been his father's country, and there Abraham was commanded to leave them. In Bereshith Rabbah,[16] the Rabbis similarly say "*Lech lecha:* one departure from Aram-naharaim, and one from Aram-nahor."

The reason for mentioning *out of thy country, and from thy birthplace, and from thy father's house* is that it is difficult for a person to leave the country wherein he dwells, where he has his friends and companions. This is true all the more if this be his native land, and all the more if his whole family is there. Hence it became necessary to say to Abraham that he leave all for the sake of his love of the Holy One, blessed be He.

UNTO THE LAND THAT I WILL SHOW THEE. He wandered and went about *from nation to nation, from kingdom to another people,*[17] until he came to the land of Canaan, where He said to him, *Unto thy seed will I give this land.*[18] Then the promise, *Unto the land that I will show thee,* was fulfilled, and Abraham tarried and settled there. The verse which states, *And they went forth to*

(14) Ramban points out the following contradiction in Ibn Ezra's interpretation: Here in our verse he says that the command was given to Abraham in Ur of the Chaldees. Accordingly, Ur of the Chaldees is Abraham's "country" for the verse says, *from thy country.* And further (Chapter 24, Verse 4) Ibn Ezra interprets *my country* as meaning "Haran," which is Mesopotamia! Thus Ibn Ezra has "many countries" assigned to Abraham. (15) Above, 11:28. (16) 39:8. The Rabbis here interpret the double expression of the verse as signifying two departures which Abraham is to make: one from Mesopotamia generally, and one from his city in particular. (17) Psalms 105:13. (18) Verse 7 here.

go into the land of Canaan,[19] means that he was not heading for Canaan for the purpose of settling there since he did not as yet know that he had been commanded concerning this land. Rather, the righteous one[20] set his goal towards the land of Canaan for that was his intention as well as that of his father when they originally set forth from Ur of the Chaldees. This is the reason why Abraham later said, *And it came to pass, when G-d caused me to wander from my father's house:*[21] he was indeed *gone astray like a lost sheep.*[22]

It is possible to say that Abraham knew from the first that the land of Canaan was "the inheritance of the Eternal," destined that His special Providence be bestowed upon it, and he believed that the Divine promise, *Unto the land that I will show thee*, alluded to the land of Canaan either in its entirety or to one of all those lands [which together comprise Canaan]. He set his direction towards the land of Canaan generally for [he was certain that] there was the land which He would indeed show him.

2. AND BE THOU A BLESSING. You will be the blessing by whom people will be blessed, saying, "G-d make thee as Abraham." To this He added that *all families of the earth*[23] will cite him in blessing, not just the people of his country alone. It may be that the expression, *And in thee shall all the families of the earth be blessed,*[23] means that they will all be blessed on his account.

Now this portion of Scripture is not completely elucidated. What reason was there that the Holy One, blessed be He, should say to Abraham, "Leave your country, and I will do you good in a completely unprecedented measure," without first stating that Abraham worshipped G-d or that he was *a righteous man,* [and] *perfect?*[24] Or it should state as a reason for his leaving the country that the very journey to another land constituted an act

(19) Verse 5. (20) Abraham. (21) Further, 20:13. (22) Psalms 119:176. (23) Verse 3 here. (24) Above, 6:9. As was the case with Noah.

of seeking *the nearness of G-d.*[25] The custom of Scripture is to state, "*Walk before Me,*[26] and hearken to My voice, and I will do good unto you," as is the case with David[27] and Solomon,[28] as well as throughout the Torah: *If ye walk in My statute;*[29] *And it shall come to pass, if thou shalt hearken diligently unto the voice of the Eternal thy G-d.*[30] And in the case of Isaac, it says, *For My servant Abraham's sake.*[31] But there is no reason for G-d to promise [Abraham a reward merely] for his leaving the country.

However, the reason [for G-d's promising Abraham this reward] is that the people of Ur of the Chaldees did him much evil on account of his belief in the Holy One, blessed be He, and he fled from them to go to the land of Canaan, tarrying for a time at Haran, whereupon the Eternal told him to leave these places as well and to fulfill his original intention that his worship be dedicated to Him alone and that he call upon people [for the worhip of] the Name of the Eternal in the Chosen Land. There He would make his name great, and these nations would bless themselves by him, not as they treated him in Ur of the Chaldees, where they abused and cursed him, put him in prison or in the fiery furnace. He further told Abraham that He will bless those who bless him, and if some individual will curse him, he will be cursed in turn.

This then is the meaning of this portion of Scripture. The Torah, however, did not want to deal at length with the opinions of idol worshippers and explain the matter between him and the Chaldeans in the subject of faith, just as it dealt briefly with the matter of the generation of Enosh[32] and their thesis concerning the idol-worship which they instituted.

6. AND ABRAM PASSED THROUGH THE LAND. I will tell you a principle by which you will understand all the coming

(25) Psalms 73:28. This may indeed be an illuminating personal remark shedding light on Ramban's journey, towards the end of his life, to the Land of Israel; the very journey constituted to him a religious experience of "seeking the nearness of G-d." (26) Genesis 17:1. (27) See I Kings 2:4. (28) *Ibid.*, 3:13-14. (29) Leviticus 26:3. (30) Deuteronomy 28:1. (31) Genesis 26:24. (32) Above, 4:26. See also above in *Seder Noach*, Note 280.

portions of Scripture concerning Abraham, Isaac, and Jacob. It is indeed a great matter which our Rabbis mentioned briefly, saying: [33] "Whatever has happened to the patriarchs is a sign to the children." It is for this reason that the verses narrate at great length the account of the journeys of the patriarchs, the digging of the wells, and other events. Now someone may consider them unnecessary and of no useful purpose, but in truth they all serve as a lesson for the future: when an event happens to any one of the three patriarchs, that which is decreed to happen to his children can be understood.

Concerning all decisions of "the guardians [angels]," [34] know that when they proceed from a potential decree to a symbolic act, the decree will in any case be effected. It is for this reason that the prophets often perform some act in conjunction with the prophecies, just as Jeremiah commanded Baruch his disciple, *And it shall be, when thou hast made an end of reading this book, that thou shalt bind a stone to it, and cast it into the midst of the Euphrates, and thou shalt say: Thus shall Babylon sink.* [35] Likewise is the matter of Elisha when he put his arm on the bow [held by Joash, King of Israel]: *And Elisha said, Shoot. And he shot. And he said, The Eternal's arrow of victory, even the arrow of victory against Aram.* [36] And it is further stated there, *And the man of G-d was wroth with him, and said, Thou shouldst have smitten five or six times; then hadst thou smitten Aram till thou hadst consumed it whereas now thou shalt smite Aram but thrice.* [37] It is for this reason that the Holy One, blessed be He, caused Abraham to take possession of the Land and symbolically did to him all that was destined to happen in the future to his children. Understand this principle. Now, with the help of G-d, I will begin to explain in detail the subject matter of the verses.

And Abram passed through the land unto the place of Shechem. This is the city of Shechem for such was the name of this place, [38]

(33) Tanchuma *Lech Lecha,* 9. (34) Daniel 4:14. (35) Jeremiah 51:63-64. (36) II Kings 13:17. (37) *Ibid.*, Verse 19. (38) Ramban differs with Ibn Ezra's comment that the name Shechem was non-existent in the days of Abraham but is used here because Moses called it by the name by which it was known in his time.

and Shechem the son of Hamor [39] was called by the name of his city. Now Rashi wrote, "He entered it *unto the place of Shechem* in order to pray on behalf of Jacob's sons when they would come grieved from the field." [40] This is correct. And I add that Abraham took possession of this place at the very beginning, even before the land was given to him. [41] It was thus hinted to him that his children would first conquer this place [42] before they would merit it and before the guilt of the dwellers of the land was full [43] to warrant their exile therefrom. It is for this reason that the verse here states, *And the Canaanite was then in the land.* [44] And when the Holy One, blessed be He, gave him the land by His Word, Abraham journeyed from there and pitched his tent between Beth-el and Ai for this was the place that Joshua captured first. [45]

It is possible that Scripture mentions, *And the Canaanite was then in the land*, to teach us concerning the substance of this chapter, i.e., to state that Abram came into the land of Canaan, but G-d did not show him the land He had promised him. He passed to the place of Shechem while the Canaanite, *that bitter and impetuous nation,* [46] was yet in the land, and Abram feared him. Therefore he did not build an altar to G-d. But when he came to the vicinity of Shechem at the oak of Moreh, G-d appeared to him and gave him the land, and as a result his fear departed from him for he was already assured in *the land that I will show thee*, and then he built an altar to G-d in order to worship Him openly.

Now *eilon Moreh* (the oak of Moreh) is in the vicinity of Shechem and is also called *eilonei Moreh*, as it is written *over against Gilgal, beside 'eilonei Moreh.'* [47] There in Shechem, near the Jordan, are Mount Gerizim and Mount Ebal, where the Israelites arrived at the beginning of their entrance into the land. [48]

(39) Genesis 34:2. (40) *Ibid.*, 34:7. In our text of Rashi: "when they would come to fight against Shechem." (41) As told later in Verse 7. His taking possession of Shechem is stated in the preceding Verse 6. (42) Reference is to the capturing of the city by the sons of Jacob. See further, 34:25. (43) Further, 15:16. (44) He took possession of this place even though the Canaanite was yet in the land. (Tur.) (45) In battle. (Joshua 8:1-24.) The capture of Jericho earlier was effected by a miracle. (46) Habakkuk 1:6. (47) Deuteronomy 11:30. (48) Sotah 36 a: "On the day Israel crossed the Jordan, they came to Mount Gerizim and Mount Ebal."

Eilonei Mamre, [49] however, is a place in the land of Hebron, [50] far from the Jordan.

Know that wherever Scripture states, *eilonei Mamre,* the name Mamre is on account of an Amorite by that name to whom the place belonged, just as it says, *And he dwelt at the oaks of Mamre the Amorite, brother of Eshkol and brother of Aner,* [51] and wherever it says, *eilon moreh* or *eilonei moreh,* [52] the places were so called on account of a man by the name of Moreh, but he was a Canaanite from *the land of the Canaanites, who abide in the plains.* [53] When Scripture mentions Mamre alone, it means the name of a city, just as it is said: *And Jacob came unto Isaac his father unto Mamre, the city of Arba, which is Hebron;* [54] *Before Mamre which is Hebron.* [55] The man to whom the oaks belonged was called after the name of the city. A similar case is that of Shechem the son of Hamor, who was called Shechem after the name of the city Shechem.

In Bereshith Rabbah [56] it is said, "In the opinion of Rabbi Yehudah, Mamre is the name of a place, and in the opinion of Rabbi Nechemyah, it is the name of a person."

The sense of the expression, *And there he built an altar unto the Eternal, who appeared unto him,* [57] is that he gave praise to the *Glorious Name* [58] and offered unto Him a sacrifice of thanksgiving for His having appeared to him. Until now G-d had not appeared to him neither in a *mar'eh* nor in a *machzeh.* [59] Rather, the command, *Get thee out of thy country,* was said to him in a nocturnal dream or through *Ruach Hakodesh.* [60] It is possible that the expression, *Who appeared unto him,* alludes to the mystery of the sacrifice. The one enlightened [in the mysteries of the Torah] will understand.

(49) "The oaks of Mamre." (Genesis, 18:1.) (50) As is clearly stated: *Mamre... the city of Arba which is Hebron. (Ibid.,* 35:27.) (51) *Ibid.,* 14:13. (52) Deuteronomy 11:30. (53) *Ibid.* The end of this verse reads: *beside the oaks of Moreh.* From this Ramban derives the fact that Moreh was a Canaanite, unlike Mamre who was an Amorite. (54) Genesis 35:27. (55) *Ibid.,* 23:19. (56) 42:14. (57) Verse 7 here. (58) Deuteronomy 28:58. (59) *Mar'eh* and *Machzeh* are terms for different degrees of prophetic vision. See Ramban further, 15:1. See also Moreh Nebuchim, II, 41-5, for full discussion of these terms and other prophetic experiences. (60) Literally, "The Holy Spirit." See *ibid.,* Chapter 45, beginning: "second degree of prophecy."

8. AND HE CALLED UPON THE NAME OF THE ETERNAL. Onkelos explained it as meaning that he prayed there, just as in the verse, *I called upon Thy name, O Eternal, out of the lowest dungeon.*[61]

The correct interpretation is that Abraham loudly proclaimed the name of the Eternal there before the altar, informing people of Him and of His Divine essence. In Ur of the Chaldees he taught people but they refused to listen. Now, however, that he had come to the land concerning which he had been promised, *And I will bless them that bless thee,*[62] he became accustomed to teach and to proclaim the Deity. Scripture likewise tells of Isaac – when he went to the valley of Gerar where he was promised, *Fear not, for I am with thee*[63] – that he built an altar there *and invoked the name of the Eternal*[64] since he had come to a new place where they had not heard of His fame or seen His glory, and he proclaimed His glory among these nations.[65] Now a similar statement is not made concerning Jacob, [i.e., that he proclaimed the name of the Eternal before the peoples of the land of Canaan], for since he begot many children –all of whom were worshippers of G-d – and he had a great community, which was called "the congregation of Israel,"[66] it was through them that the Faith was proclaimed and became known to all people. Besides, the Faith had been proclaimed throughout the entire land of Canaan since the days of his ancestors. In Bereshith Rabbah[67] the Rabbis similarly say, "*And he called upon the name of the Eternal.* This teaches us that he caused the name of the Holy One, blessed be He, to be in the mouth of all people."

9. TOWARDS THE SOUTH. Rabbeinu Shlomo [Rashi] wrote, "To go to the southern part of the land of Israel, which is in the territory of the sons of Judah who took their portion in the south of the land of Israel." This was also to happen to Abraham's offspring in the future, as it is said, *Judah shall go up*[68] first.

(61) Lamentations 3:55. (62) Verse 3 here. (63) Further, 26:24. (64) *Ibid.*, Verse 25. (65) See Isaiah 66:19. (66) Exodus 12:3, *et al.* (67) 39:24. (68) Judges 1:2.

10. AND THERE WAS A FAMINE IN THE LAND. Now Abraham went down to Egypt on account of the famine to dwell there in order to keep himself alive in the days of the drought, but the Egyptians oppressed him for no reason [and attempted] to take his wife. The Holy One, blessed be He, avenged their cause with great plagues, and brought him forth from there *with cattle, with silver, and with gold,* [69] and Pharaoh even commanded his men to escort them from the land. [70] He thereby alluded to Abraham that his children would go down to Egypt on account of the famine to dwell there in the land, and the Egyptians would do them evil and take the women [71] from them, just as Pharaoh said, *And every daughter ye shall save alive,* [72] but the Holy One, blessed be He, would avenge their cause with great plagues until He would bring them forth with silver and gold, sheep and oxen, very rich in cattle, with the Egyptians pressuring to send them out of the land. [73] Nothing was lacking in all the events that happened to the patriarch that would not occur to the children.

The Rabbis have explained this subject in Bereshith Rabbah: [74] "Rabbi Pinchas said in the name of Rabbi Oshaya that the Holy One, blessed be He, said to Abraham, 'Go forth and tread out a path for your children!' Thus you find that whatever is written concerning Abraham is also written concerning his children. In connection with Abraham it is written, *And there was a famine in the land;* in connection with Israel, it is written *For these two years hath the famine been in the land.*" [75]

Know that Abraham our father unintentionally committed a great sin by bringing his righteous wife to a stumbling-block of sin on account of his fear for his life. He should have trusted that G-d would save him and his wife and all his belongings for G-d surely has the power to help and to save. His leaving the Land, concerning which he had been commanded from the beginning, on account of the famine, was also a sin he committed, for in famine G-d would redeem him from death. [76] It was because of this deed

(69) Genesis 13:2. (70) Verse 20 here. (71) Shemoth Rabbah 1:22. See also following note. (72) Exodus 1:22. They were to be saved alive for unchaste purposes. (73) *Ibid.,* 12:33. (74) 40:8. (75) Genesis 45:6. (76) See Job 5:20.

that the exile in the land of Egypt at the hand of Pharaoh was decreed for his children.[77] In the place of justice, there is wickedness[78] and sin.

11. BEHOLD NOW, I KNOW, ETC. 13. SAY, I PRAY, THOU ART MY SISTER. I do not know why Abraham was more fearful for her now than before. And if we say, as Rashi explains, that it was because the Egyptians were black and repulsive, now, to Abimelech, king of the Philistines, he also said so,[79] he as well as Isaac,[80] who lived in that land by command of G-d.[81] Perhaps the Canaanites in that generation were steeped in idolatry but restrained from unchastity more than the Egyptians and the Philistines. But this is not correct. It is possible that Abraham and Sarah had no fear until they came into a royal city for it was their custom to bring the king a very beautiful woman and to slay her husband through some charge they would contrive against him.

It appears to me correct that such was their procedure from the time they left Haran. At every place he would say, "She is my sister," for so Abraham said, *And it came to pass, when G-d caused me to wander from my father's house,* etc.[82] Scripture, however, mentions it only concerning those places where something happened to them on account of it. Thus Abraham now alerted Sarah as he had charged her from the beginning. Isaac, on the other hand, was not afraid in his country and in his city. Only when he came to the land of the Philistines did he adopt his father's way.

He [Abraham] said, *That it may be well with me for thy sake, and that my soul live because of thee*, meaning "as long as we are strangers in this land, until the famine will pass," for Abraham came to live in the land of Egypt on account of the famine. When the famine passes, he would return to the land concerning which he had been commanded and which G-d had given to him and his

(77) See my Hebrew commentary, pp. 79-80, for sources and differing opinions on the view of Ramban expressed in this paragraph. (78) See Ecclesiastes 3:16. (79) Genesis 20:2. (80) *Ibid.*, 26:7. (81) *Ibid.*, Verse 3. (82) *Ibid.*, 20:13.

children. He thus thought that they [he and his wife] would live through the famine and that relief and succor will come to them from G-d enabling them to return, or that it may be possible for them to flee to the land of Canaan when they [83] will give them up.

Now Rashi wrote, " *'Hinei na' (Behold now), I know.* A Midrash Agada: [84] Until now he had not perceived her beauty on account of her [85] modesty. Now, however, [he became cognizant of it] through an event. [86] Another interpretation is that because of the exertion of travelling a person usually becomes uncomely, but she [Sarah] has retained her beauty. Still the plain sense of the text is this: 'Behold, now the time has come to be anxious because of your beauty. I have long known that you are a woman of beautiful appearance, but now we are travelling among black people, brethren of the Ethiopians, who have never been accustomed to see a beautiful woman.' A similar example [where the Hebrew word *na* does not denote a request, as it usually does, but means "now"] is found in the verse, *Behold 'na' (now), my lords, turn aside, I pray you.*" [87] All this is the language of the Rabbi [Rashi].

This Midrash concerning the modesty between Abraham and Sarah is traditional and it has been adjoined to the verse, but there is no need for all these matters. The word *na* [*hinei na – behold now*] does not indicate only a newly arisen matter; it may be used with reference to anything which is presently in existence for it is a statement alluding to the present state of things. *Behold now I know* – from then until now – *that thou art a woman of beautiful appearance.* Of similar meaning is the verse, *Behold 'na' (now), the Eternal hath restrained me from having children,* [88] meaning from my youth until this day. Likewise is the verse,

(83) "They" are the Egyptians. They will no longer guard them for they will consider them permanent settlers in the land. Then they (Abraham and Sarah) will be able to flee the country and return to the land of Canaan. (84) A Midrash by that name. See Buber's edition of this Midrash, p. 27. (85) In our text of Rashi: "on account of the modesty of both of them." The Midrash Agada ascribes the modesty to Abraham. (86) Wading through a stream, he saw the reflection of her beauty in the water. (Midrash Agada.) (87) Genesis 19:2. The Hebrew reads, *hinei na adonai suru na.* Now since the request is covered by the second *na (suru na – turn aside, I pray you),* the first *na* (at the beginning of the expression) can no longer mean a request; rather it means "now." (88) Genesis 16:2.

Behold 'na' (now), I have two daughters,[89] for they were not born to him now. All [verses containing this expression] are to be interpreted in like manner.

It would seem from the simple meaning of the verses that Sarah did not obligate herself to say so, [i.e., that she is Abraham's sister], but when the Egyptians, who were wicked and sinners exceedingly,[90] saw her *and they praised her to Pharaoh,*[91] she was taken to his house. They did not ask them at all whether she is his wife or his sister, and she remained silent and did not tell them that she is his wife. It was Abraham himself who told them that she is his sister, and therefore they did well by him for her sake.[92] This is the intent of the verse quoting Pharaoh, which says, *What is this that thou hadst done unto me? Why didst thou not tell me that she was thy wife?*[93] He [Pharaoh] accused him for when he saw the princes of Pharaoh taking her, he should have told Pharaoh that she is his wife. Again, he accused him for saying afterwards to the princes and the household of Pharaoh that she is his sister.[94] But he did not at all accuse the woman for it is not proper that she contradict her husband, the suitable thing being for her to remain silent.

15. AND THE PRINCES OF PHARAOH SAW HER. The purport[95] thereof is that when the Egyptians saw her they said, "This one is worthy of the great princes," and so they brought her before them. But they were also afraid of touching her for due to her great beauty, they knew that the king would desire her exceedingly. "*And they praised her* among themselves saying, 'This one is worthy of the king.' " Thus the language of Rashi.

This is in accordance with the opinion of Onkelos who says, "And they praised her *for* Pharaoh."[96] Or it may be that they praised her to the king himself, and he sent for her and took her.

(89) *Ibid.*, 19:8. (90) *Ibid.*, 13:13. (91) Verse 15 here. (92) Verse 16. (93) Verse 18. (94) Verse 19. (95) Ramban is aiming to answer the following question: In the preceding verse it says, *And the Egyptians saw the woman.* Why does it say here again, *And the princes of Pharaoh saw her?* (96) Meaning that they praised her among themselves by saying that she is suitable *for* Pharaoh.

17. BECAUSE OF SARAI ABRAM'S WIFE. This means that because of the wrong done to Sarah, as well as to Abraham, and the merit of both of them, these great plagues came upon Pharaoh and his house.

18. AND PHARAOH CALLED ABRAM. It is possible that when the plagues suddenly came upon him and his house at the very time Sarah was taken to his house, he thought to himself, *What is this that G-d hath done unto us?* [97] And so he asked her, and she told him that she is Abraham's wife. For this reason he called Abraham and accused him. Or it may be, as our Rabbis say, [98] that Pharaoh was smitten with a certain skin disease which is aggravated by intimacy with a woman. Therefore he suspected that perhaps she is Abraham's wife, and so he said to him with uncertainty, *What is this that thou hast done unto me*?, in order to draw the truth from him. Were she his sister, he would say, "Indeed, she is my sister." And Pharaoh further said to him, *Now therefore behold thy wife, take her, and go thy way.* [94] He said this in order to see what he would say, and now he would answer his reproof. But Abraham remained silent and did not answer him a word out of his great fear. Then Pharaoh understood that she is his wife as he had suspected, and then Pharaoh commanded his men to send him away.

19. SO THAT I TOOK HER TO BE MY WIFE. The meaning thereof is that it was Pharaoh's intention that she be his regal wife, not just his concubine. Pharaoh mentioned this to Abraham so that he should confess to him if she is his sister, as I have explained.

13 1. HE, AND HIS WIFE, AND ALL THAT HE HAD. The purport thereof is to let us know that they did not rob him of any of all the great gifts they gave him on account of Sarah who was to be for the king. They did not say, "You have tricked us, and the gift was given by mistake." This was a miraculous event.

(97) Genesis 42:28. (98) Bereshith Rabbah 41:2. It is also mentioned in Rashi.

7. AND THERE WAS A QUARREL. Rashi wrote, "Because Lot's shepherds grazed their cattle in other people's fields, Abram's shepherds rebuked them for this act of robbery, but they replied, 'The land has been given to Abram, and he has no [son as an] heir, and so Lot will be his heir. Hence this is not robbery.' Scripture however states, *And the Canaanite and the Perrizite abode then in the land*, so that Abram was not yet the legitimate owner." This is a Midrash of our Rabbis.[99]

But I wonder: The gift of the Land declared to Abram was for *his* children, as it is said above, *Unto thy seed will I give this land,*[100] so how can Lot inherit it? Perhaps the shepherds heard of the gift and they mistook its meaning, for Scripture states that in the meantime, the land belonged neither to Abram nor to Lot. Accordingly, the verse stating at the outset, *for their possessions were great,*[101] intended to say that because of their extensive possessions, the land could not support them, and Lot's shepherds therefore found it necessary to bring their cattle into fields that had owners. This was the cause of the quarrel.

By way of the plain meaning of Scripture the quarrel concerned the pasture as the land could not support them both. When Abram's cattle were grazing in the pasture, Lot's shepherds would come into their territory and graze their cattle there. Now Abram and Lot were both strangers and sojourners in the land. Abram, therefore, feared that the Canaanite and the Perrizite, who inhabit the land, might hear of the abundance of their cattle, [whose great number was made apparent when Lot's shepherds encroached on Abram's land, thereby combining the flocks], and drive them out of the land or slay them by sword and take their cattle and wealth since the mastery of the land belonged to them, not to Abram. This is the purport of the verse, *And the Canaanite and the Perrizite*. Scripture thus mentioned that there were many peoples dwelling in that land, they and their cattle being innumerable, and the land could not support them and Abram and Lot.

From the word *oz (then)* – [*And the Canaanite and the Perrizite abode 'then' in the land*] – it appears to me that the nations dwelling

(99) Bereshith Rabbah 41:6. (100) Above, 12:7. (101) Verse 6 here.

in the land at that time were those who live in tents and have cattle, some of them converging on one district and grazing there for a year or two and then journeying from there to another district in which they had not previously pastured. And so they continued to do, as is customary among "the children of the east."[102] The Canaanite and the Perrizite were thus "then" in the land of the south, and in the following years the Jebusite and the Amorite would come there.

10. AS THE GARDEN OF THE ETERNAL, LIKE THE LAND OF EGYPT. The verse states that the whole land of the Plain was adequately irrigated from the Jordan by working with the foot, just as was done with the garden of G-d, concerning which it is stated, *And a river went out of Eden to water the garden,*[103] and as is the way in the land of Egypt, concerning which it is stated, *And thou didst water it with thy foot.*[104] The verse mentions both places: it says that the land of the Plain was as adequately irrigated as the garden of the Eternal, which is the most perfect place on this earth, and it also mentions, *like the land of Egypt*, a place well known for pasture.

Our Rabbis have said,[105] "*As the garden of the Eternal* for trees; *Like the land of Egypt* – for herbs." Their intent was to explain that there were large rivers in the Plain, which watered the trees of the gardens, as was the case in the garden of G-d, and that there were also ponds in it, as in the land of Egypt, from which vegetable gardens were watered. Lot chose this part, for a land which is so irrigated is unlikely to suffer from a drought and is good for pasture.

12. ABRAM DWELT IN THE LAND OF CANAAN. The meaning thereof is that he dwelt in the remainder of the entire land of Canaan; he did not stay in one place but abode in the entire land of Canaan while Lot settled in one place thereof, namely, the cities of the Plain, for the cities of the Plain are part of the land of Canaan.

(102) See Judges 6:3. (103) Above, 2:10. (104) Deuteronomy 11:10. (105) Sifre *Ekev,* 38. The Sifre is a Tannaitic Midrash on the book of Numbers and the book of Deuteronomy.

The meaning of [the plural "cities" in the expression, *and Lot dwelt in*] *the cities of the Plain,* is that he dwelt for a time in this city and a time in the other on account of his many cattle. This is the reason that the verse says, *So Lot chose him all the plain of the Jordan;* [106] he made a condition with Abram that he [Abram] should not come into the entire Plain.

13. NOW THE MEN OF SODOM WERE WICKED AND SINNERS. The purport thereof, as Rashi wrote, is that Scripture accuses Lot for not restraining himself from dwelling with them and also speaks of the merit of the righteous one [Abraham] whose lot did not fall in a place of wickedness *for the rod of wickedness shall not rest upon the lot of the righteous.* [107] And all the cities of the Plain *were wicked and sinners against the Eternal exceedingly.* This was why they alone were overthrown even though all the Canaanites were people of great abominations, for so it is written.[108]

17. ARISE, WALK THROUGH THE LAND IN THE LENGTH AND IN THE BREADTH OF IT. It is possible that this is a matter of option, depending on his will.[109] The Eternal thus told Abraham, "Go wherever you wish to go in the land for I will be with you and guard you from the evil of the nations, *for unto thee will I give it,* that is to say, the land will be yours." And if it be a command that Abraham should traverse the length and breadth of the land in order to take possession of his gift, as I have explained, [110] he was not commanded to do this immediately. He did so ultimately for he was now in the east, and afterwards he went to the land of the Philistines which is in the west, and thus he fulfilled the command during his lifetime.

The meaning of the expression, *to thee... and to thy children,*[111] is that you are to take possession of the gift now, in order to transmit it to your children, even as our Rabbis have said: [112] "The land of Israel is an inheritance to the people of Israel from their patriarchs."

(106) Verse 11 here. (107) Psalms 125:3. (108) Leviticus 18:3. (109) It is not a command that he go through the entire land, rather it is a promise that he need not fear whenever and wherever he will go. (110) Above, 12:6. (111) Verse 15 here. (112) Baba Bathra 119 b.

By way of the plain meaning of Scripture, it is possible that the meaning of the verse is that Abraham was to be a ruler over the land and *a prince of G-d* in its midst, [113] wherever he will go in this land.

14 1. AND IT CAME TO PASS IN THE DAYS OF AMRAPHEL KING OF SHINAR. This event happened to Abraham in order to teach us that four kingdoms will arise to rule the world. In the end, his [Abraham's] children will prevail over them, and they will all fall into their hands. Then they will return all their captives and their wealth. The first one mentioned here is the king of Babylon [114] for so it was to be in the future, as it is written, *Thou art the head of gold.* [115] Perhaps Ellasar, mentioned here second, is the name of a city in Media or Persia, [116] and Elam, mentioned third, is the city in which the first Greek king – Alexander – was crowned. From there his kingdom spread after he was victorious over Darius, [king of the Persians]. Our Rabbis have already mentioned this matter: [117] "Rabbi Yosei said, 'For six years the Greeks ruled in Elam, and after that their kingdom spread over the entire world.' " The *king of Goïim,* [118] [the last of the four kings mentioned here], who ruled over various nations that had made him their head and leader, is an allusion to the king of Rome who ruled over a city comprised of many peoples: Kittim, Edom, and the rest of the nations. Thus the Rabbis said in Bereshith Rabbah, [119] "Rabbi Avin said, 'Just as Abraham's grief began with four kingdoms, so will it end for his descendants only with four kingdoms.' " And it further says there: [120] *"And it came to pass in the days of Amraphel king of Shinar* – this is Babylon; *Arioch king of Ellasar* – this is Media; *Chedorlaomer king of Elam* – this is Greece; *And Tidal king of Goïim*– this is that kingdom (Rome) which writes out a levy [and collects assessment] from all nations of the world."

(113) See Genesis 23:6. (114) Shinar is Babylon. See Onkelos. (115) Daniel 2:38. This was said by Daniel to Nebuchadnezzar, king of Babylon, when interpreting the king's dream of the four kingdoms that will rule the world. (116) Since Media and Persia ruled over Babylon. (117) Abodah Zarah 10 a. (118) Rashi explains *Goïim* as the name of a place. Ramban explains it as meaning "nations," and it is hence an allusion to Rome, whose kings ruled over many nations. (119) 42:2. (120) 42:4.

2. AND THE KING OF BELA. The reason [why Scripture does not mention his name as it does with the kings of Sodom, *et al*], is that he ruled over a small city with few men in it and he had no generally recognized reputation.

6. 'EIL PARAN.' It is translated in the Targum as "Plain of Paran." But I say that the word *eil* does not signify a plain. Rather, the lowland of Paran was called *Eil*, that of Mamre was named *Eilonei*, that of the Jordan was called *Kikar*, and that of Shittim was *Abel*. All these are translated in the Targum as *meishra* (plain), but each really had its own particular name. Thus the language of Rashi.

But if it were so,[121] Onkelos would have mentioned them in his Targum by their name – i.e., "*Eila* of Paran," "*Eilonei* of Mamre," – as is his custom with names. Besides, who told him[122] whether these many places were all plains or high mountains [if *Eil, Eilonei* and *Kikar* were but proper names of these places]? Again, Mamre is the name of a person – as it is written, *brother of Eshcol, and brother of Aner, and they were confederate with Abram*[123] – and that place was his, just as it says, *'Eilonei' Mamre the Amorite*,[124] as I have explained.[125] Rather, *Eil paran* means a place of terebinths, as it is said, *For they shall be ashamed 'me'eilim' (of the terebinths) which ye have desired;*[126] *eilonei* is a place of oaks, as it is said, *As a terebinth, 'veka'alon' (and as an oak)*[127] *Of the 'alonim' (oaks) of Bashan.*[128] It was customary among them that these terebinths and oaks be planted in the plains before the cities which serve them as "an open land." And so did Onkelos translate *alon bachuth*[129] as

(121) That *Eil, Eilonei* and *Kikar* are the proper names of these places. (122) "Him" refers both to Rashi and Onkelos. (123) Verse 13 here. (124) *Ibid.* Ramban's intent is to argue that since Mamre is the name of an individual, the word *Eilonei* could not be a proper name since two names cannot be in the constructive state. (125) Above, 12:6. (126) Isaiah 1:29. (127) *Ibid.*, 6:13. (128) Ezekiel 27:6. (129) Genesis 35:8. *And Deborah Rebekah's nurse died, and she was buried below Beth-el under the 'alon' and he called its name 'Alon Bachuth.'*

"the plain of Bechuta." There the word *alon* is surely not a proper noun of the location [130] but only the name of the species of tree planted there, as is made explicit [in the same verse: *and she was buried*] ...*under the 'alon.'* [129] Onkelos' intent, however, is to convey the sense of the expression and not to merely translate the words.

Now the Targum Yerushalmi says with respect to both *eil Paran* and *eilonei Mamre* that they mean the plain of Paran and Mamre as Onkelos said, but in the case of *alon bachuth,* [129] he [Targum Yerushalmi] says it is the nut-tree of Bachut for he considers *alon bachuth* to be the name of a tree and not a place. [130] Onkelos, however, thought that *alon bachuth* is the name of a place, so called because there were many oak trees there, just as *Eilonei Mamre* [is the name of a place]. It is for that reason that Scripture there uses the word *ha'alon.* [131] Thus according to Onkelos they are all [132] descriptive nouns.

(130) As opposed to Rashi who says that the name of the place was Alon. (131) *And she was buried below Beth-el under 'ha'alon' (the oak).* See Note 129 above. Ramban's intent is to say that since the word *alon* appears there with the definite article, (namely, *ha-alon*), it could not be a proper noun since the definite article is never attached to a proper noun. Hence in the end of the verse, which reads, *And he called its name 'alon bachuth,'* the word *alon* is also not a name designating a particular tree but a descriptive noun referring to a place containing many oaks. Hence Onkelos translates *alon Bachuth* as "the plain of Bechuta." According to Targum Yerushalmi, who takes *alon bachuth* to be the name of a particular kind of tree, the verse should have read, "And she was buried below Beth-el under *alon,*" not *ha-alon.* (132) *Eil Paran, Eilonei Mamre and alon bachuth.* Hence in all these cases Onkelos translated "the plain of Paran... Mamre... Bechuta" as meaning a plain containing oak trees. Onkelos does this in keeping with his general method of conveying the intent of the verse rather than its strict translation since *eil, eilonei* and *alon,* strictly speaking, mean particular kinds of trees. Onkelos however felt free to say *"the plain* of Paran... Mamre... Bachuth" for his intent is but to convey the general meaning. Ramban continues to point that out in *kikar hayarden,* (13:11), where Onkelos said, "the plain of the Jordan," that is indeed the exact translation of the word *kikar.*

But *kikar hayarden*[133] is indeed the actual word for a plain, for *kikar* in the Sacred Language is the name for the place where the natural streams of rivers overflow. It is for this reason that the messenger who came to rescue Lot said, *Stay not in all 'hakikar' (the plain; escape to the mountain.*[134] Of similar usage are the expressions, *Kar nirchav (wide pasture);*[135] *'Karim' (the meadows) are clothed with flocks; the valleys also are covered over with corn.*[136] Sometimes Scripture doubles the first letter of the word *kar* (meadow), making it *kikar*, and at other times Scripture discards the double form, as in, *bath ayin (the apple of the eye).*[137] There are many other such cases.

Swift couriers are also called by this name *kar*, as in *'lakari velaratzim;'*[138] *The captains over hundreds and 'hakari.'*[139] The word *bakirkaroth*[140] is also of the same root. It is the name for speedy camels such as "the flying camel" mentioned in the Talmud.[141] The word *mecharkar,*[142] containing the double use of *kar*, is a derivative of this word.

Abel Hashittim,[143] and also *Abel Mecholah,*[144] they[145] translated to mean the plain of Shittim and Mecholah. It is [called *Abel*, which in Hebrew means "mourning"], because it is a desolate place, without plantings or structures for the word *abel* is, to them, an expression of destruction and waste, as in the verses: *'Vaya'avel' (And He made to mourn) the rampart and the wall;*[146] *The new wine 'aval' (faileth), the vine fadeth.*[147]

7. TO EIN MISHPAT, WHICH IS KADESH. It is named [Ein Mishpat, meaning, "the Well of Judgment"] on account of a future

(133) Above, 13:10. (134) Further, 19:17. (135) Isaiah 30:23. (136) Psalms 65:14. (137) *Ibid.*, 17:8. The double letter form of the word would be *babath ayin*, with a double *beth.* (138) II Kings 11:4. It is usually translated: *of the Carites and of the guard.* According to Ramban its meaning is: *of the couriers and the dispatchers.* (139) *Ibid.*, Verse 19. Here too the usual translation is: *the Carites.* According to Ramban it means: *the couriers.* (140) Isaiah 66:20. (141) Makkoth 5 a. (142) II Samuel 6:14. *And David 'mecharkar' (danced) before the Eternal with all his strength.* (143) Numbers 33:49. (144) Judges 7:22. (145) Onkelos and Jonathan (146) Lamentations 2:8. (147) Isaiah 24:7.

event, for Moses and Aaron will be judged because of what will occur at that fountain.[148] Thus the words of Rashi based upon an *Agadah.*[149]

But I do not understand this for this Kadesh [mentioned here] is Kadesh-barnea which is in *El-paran which is by the desert,*[150] and it is from there that the spies were sent by Moses in the second year following the Exodus from Egypt, as it is said, *Unto the wilderness of Paran, to Kadesh.*[151] And it is further written, *And we came to Kadesh-barnea... and ye said, Let us send men before us,*[152] and there Israel *abode many days.*[153] But the Kadesh where the judgment of the righteous ones[154] took place is in the wilderness of Zin, which they entered in the fortieth year following the Exodus, as it is said, *And the children of Israel, even the whole congregation, came into the wilderness of Zin in the first month, and the people abode in Kadesh,*[155] and finish the chapter.[156] Perhaps the Midrash [mentioned above] alludes only to the name, meaning that a place bearing this name Kadesh will become "the Well of Judgment."

Now Onkelos said, "the plain of *pilug dina,*" but I do not know what this means. Perhaps the word *pilug* is derived from [the Hebrew word used in the following verses]: *'Plagim' (Streams)* and watercourses;[157] *Who 'pilag' (hath cleft) a channel for the waterflood.*[158] Similarly, in the language of the Sages we find,[159] "*Pilgo* (The openness) of the sea." The verse thus states that on that plain there will flow "a fountain of judgment" entering the depth of the case, as this was a fitting plain destined for kings who would sit there to judge all the peoples of these lands.

THE COUNTRY OF THE AMALEKITES. Rashi comments: "Amalek, it is true, was not yet born, but it is so named here because of the name it would bear in the future."

(148) See Numbers 20:7-13. (149) Tanchumah *Chukath,* 11. So also in Targum Jonathan here. (150) As mentioned here in Verse 6. (151) Numbers 13:26. (152) Deuteronomy 1:19, 22. (153) *Ibid.,* Verse 46. (154) Moses and Aaron. (155) Numbers 20:1. (156) A charge by the author to finish the chapter containing the account of the smiting of the rock by Moses to bring forth water and his consequent punishment. (157) Isaiah 30:25. (158) Job 38:25. (159) Esther Rabbah, 5.

Now I do not know whether Rashi's intent is to say that Moshe Rabbeinu called the place by the name it was referred to in his time, but if this be the case, there is no reference to future events involved. Or [if Rashi's intent is that the nations of Abraham's era called it by that name] what is being foretold by the nations' prophetic naming of this place?

But the language of Bereshith Rabbah [160] is as follows: "Amalek was not yet born and yet you say, 'All the country of the Amalekites!' However, the Torah *declares the end from the beginning.*" [161] This method of *d'rash* [162] of the Sages is found in many places. Concerning the rivers of the garden of Eden they also made a similar statement. [163] The intent of the Rabbis is to say that from the time the rivers came forth it was already declared that a particular river go towards a land which is destined to be called Assyria. [164]

The correct interpretation concerning "the country of the Amalekites" mentioned here is that there was in ancient times some honorable person of the sons of the Horites, the inhabitants of the land, [165] by the name of Amalek, who ruled over this place. Eliphaz, Esau's firstborn, named his son after this man. [166] Perhaps this Amalek mentioned here was of the family of Timna, his mother, [166] and he also ruled in that place and was chieftain over them.

10. 'BE'EROTH BE'EROTH CHEIMAR' (FULL OF SLIME PITS). There were many pits there since they removed earth to be used as clay for building purposes. The Midrashic explanation is that the clay was closely kneaded together in them, [that is, it was very sticky], but a miracle happened to the king of Sodom and he

(160) 42:11. (161) Isaiah 46:10. (162) Homiletical interpretation of Scripture. (163) "*That* [river] *is the one which surrounds the whole land of Havilah.* (Genesis 2:11). Havilah was not yet in existence, and yet the verse says, *the whole land of Havilah!* However, the Torah *declares the end from the beginning.*" (Bereshith Rabbah 16:2.) (164) Reference here is to the third river, namely, the Tigris. (Above, 2:14.) (165) See further, 36:20. (166) *Ibid.*, Verse 12.

escaped from there. This miracle occurred because there were some among the nations who did not believe that Abram had been delivered from the fiery furnace, but as soon as this one escaped from the slime, in retrospect they believed in Abram. Thus the language of Rashi.

There is no doubt that the meaning of *be'eroth cheimar* is "pits containing mud and slime," even as it is written, *And in the pit there was no water, but mire, and Jeremiah sank in the mire,* [167] and it is further written, *He brought me up out of the tumultuous pit, out of the miry clay.* [168] And it is possible that the king of Sodom went out from there naturally, without a miracle.

And I wonder concerning the above Midrashic explanation, for those nations that did not believe that the Holy One, blessed be He, had performed a miracle for Abraham would not have their faith in the Holy One, blessed be He, augmented by witnessing the miracle which befell the king of Sodom. The king of Sodom was an idol worshipper, and his miracle would either strengthen the hands of the idol worshippers or it would cause them to believe that all miracles are done by witchcraft or are due to some remotely possible chance. His miracle would thus cast doubt into the hearts of those who believed in Abraham's miracle! Perhaps [the Rabbis who authored this Midrashic explanation] will interpret the verse, *And the king of Sodom went out to meet him,* [169] as implying that "he went out" from the pit when Abraham passed by for it was in honor of Abraham that a miracle was done to him so that he could go forth to meet him in order to honor and bless Abraham.

And it is possible that Abraham, upon his return, looked into that pit for he wanted to save the kings and return their wealth to them, and then the miracle happened on his account. Now if a miracle was done to the king of Sodom in honor of Abraham, the nations could now believe all the more that a miracle would be done to Abraham himself in order to rescue him from death.

(167) Jeremiah 38:6. (168) Psalms 40:3. (169) Verse 17 here.

We must further say that the king of Gomorrah had already died[170] when Abraham passed him by or that he had fallen into another pit, as the word "there"[171] refers to "the vale."

15. AND HE DIVIDED HIMSELF, BY NIGHT. Rashi wrote: "In accordance with the plain sense of the verse it means [that they divided into groups] as is the manner of those who pursue their enemies when they flee in different directions. *By night* means that even after it became dark, they did not cease pursuing them."

The correct interpretation is that he pursued the enemies to Dan during the daytime with his entire army. When it became dark and he was not able to see by which road they fled, he divided his people and servants into two or three groups, taking one part with him, and they pursued them on all roads, smiting them as far as *Hobah, which is on the left hand of Damascus.* Then he returned from pursuing them. The order of the words [in the verse are thus interpreted as follows] : "And he divided himself, he and his servants, by night."

AND HE PURSUED THEM UNTO HOBAH, WHICH IS ON THE LEFT HAND OF DAMASCUS. It is known that there is a great distance from the oaks of Mamre in Hebron in the land of Judah, to Damascus, which is outside the Land. If so, he pursued them for many days until he forced them to leave the land for they were returning to Babylon, their country. Or possibly there occurred here a great miracle, just as our Rabbis expounded from the verse, *The way with his foot he treadeth not.*[172]

18. AND MELCHIZEDEK KING OF SALEM. This is Jerusalem, just as it is said, *In Salem is set His tabernacle.*[173] In the days of Joshua, its king was also called Adoni-zedek.[174] Since time

(170) Hence he did not come out from the pit. (171) *And they fell 'there.'* The word "there" does not refer to the pit, in which case it would then imply that all five kings fell into one pit. Rather it refers to *'the vale' of Siddim.* Thus the king of Gomorrah fell into a different pit, near which Abraham did not pass. (172) Isaiah 41:3. This is interpreted in Bereshith Rabbah (43:7) as referring to Abraham and asserting that he took such long steps that he traveled a mile without setting foot on the ground. (173) Psalms 76:3. (174) Joshua 10:1.

immemorial the nations knew that this place, which was the choicest of all places, is in the center of the inhabited region. Or perhaps they knew of its superiority by tradition, i.e., that it is exactly opposite the Heavenly Sanctuary, where the Divine Glory of the Holy One, blessed be He, who is called *Tzedek (Righteousness)* abides.[175]

In Bereshith Rabbah[176] [we find that Jerusalem is called *Tzedek* because] "this place makes its inhabitants righteous. *And Melchizedek* means 'the lord of Zedek.'[177] Jerusalem is called *Tzedek*, as it is said, *'Tzedek' (Righteousness) lodged in it.*"[178]

AND HE WAS PRIEST OF G-D THE MOST HIGH. This is stated in order to inform us that Abraham would not give a tithe to the priest of other gods, but since he knew that *he was a priest of G-d the Most High*, he gave him the tithe as an honor to G-d. He alluded to Abraham through this episode that the House of G-d will be there, and there his descendants will bring the tithe and the Heave-offering,[179] and there they will bless the Eternal.

Now according to the opinion of our Rabbis[180] who say that Melchizedek was Shem, the son of Noah, we must say that he left his country in the east[181] and came to Jerusalem to worship the Eternal. He became the people's priest of G-d the Most High since he was the honored one among their father's brothers,[182] as Jerusalem was ever in the boundary of the Canaanites.

Now Rashi wrote above, "*And the Canaanite was then in the land.*[183] They were gradually conquering the land of Israel from the descendants of Shem, the ancestor of Abraham, for it had fallen to the share of Shem when Noah apportioned the earth among his sons, as it is said, *And Melchizedek king of Salem.*"

(175) This explains why the early inhabitants of Jerusalem called their king *Malki tzedek*, literally, "My king is righteousness." (176) 43:6. (177) The Midrash is thus teaching that his name was not "Tzedek" but that he was the lord of a place called Zedek. (178) Isaiah 1:21. (179) Malachi 3:8. (180) Nedarim 32 b. (181) See above, 10:30. (182) That is, of the three sons of Noah – Shem, Ham and Japheth – Shem was the most honored. Now since according to the Rabbis, Melchizedek is none other than Shem, the Canaanites who were then in possession of Jerusalem recognized in Shem their father Ham's most honored brother and therefore appointed him "priest of G-d the Most High." (183) Above, 12:6.

This is not correct because *the boundary of the Canaanite was from Sidon,* [184] which includes all of the land of Israel. The boundary of the children of Shem, on the other hand, was to the east of Mesha, [185] far from the land of Israel. But if Noah apportioned the countries among his sons and gave Shem the land of Israel, it would be similar to the case of a person who apportions his goods by word of mouth. [186] Meanwhile, the children of Canaan, [who were the descendants of Ham], settled there until the time came when G-d caused the seed of His friend Abraham [187] to inherit it, as I have already mentioned. [188]

AND HE WAS PRIEST OF G-D THE MOST HIGH. Since there were, among all nations, priests serving the angels called *eilim* (the mighty ones) – even as it is said, *Who is like unto Thee 'ba'eilim' (among the mighty)* [189] – the Holy One, blessed be He, is called *G-d the Most High*, the purport thereof being "the Mighty One, Who is Supreme over all," as in the verse, *It is 'ba'eil' (the power of) my hand.* [190] Now Melchizedek did not mention the Eternal, whereas Abraham said, *the Eternal, G-d of the Most High.* [191]

19. KONEI (POSSESSOR) OF HEAVEN AND EARTH. Rashi wrote: "*Konei* is similar to *osei* (maker); [192] through His having made them He acquired them as His possession."

But these are really two different interpretations. [193] Perhaps it is indeed the case that the word *kinyan* (acquisition) is also used in the case of *asiyah* (making). Thus you find, *For Thou 'kanita' (hast made) my reins,* [194] repeating the thought [expressed in the second half of the verse], *Thou hast knit me together in my mother's*

(184) *Ibid.*, 10:19. (185) *Ibid.*, Verse 30. (186) Baba Bathra 156 a. That the land of Israel should belong to the descendants of Shem would thus be a special oral provision by Noah since all their other lands were to the east of Mesha, far from the land of Israel. (187) Isaiah 41:8. *The seed of Abraham My friend.* (188) Above, 12:6. (189) Exodus 15:11. (190) Genesis 31:29. (191) Verse 22 here. (192) In our text of Rashi, *'Osei' (Maker) of heaven and earth.* Psalms 134:3. (193) From Rashi it would appear that *osei* and *kinyan* – making and acquiring – constitute but one interpretation when in fact they are two: *konei* is similar to *osei,* and *konei* is like *kinyan* (acquisition). (194) Pslams 139:13.

womb.[195] A similar case is the verse, *Is He not 'konecha' thy father? Hath He not made thee, and established thee?*[196] Thus the Sacred Language uses *kinyan* in the case of "making." Conversely, *And the souls which 'asu'* [literally, *they made*] *in Haran,*[197] means "they *acquired.*" *And of that which was our father's 'asah' (hath he made)*[198] – [here too it means "hath he *acquired.*"]

That which Rashi says further – "He acquired them as His possession," is correct, for whatever belongs to a person is called *kinyano* (his acquisition). Sheep are called *mikneh* because they constitute the main wealth of a person. In the language of the Sages: "He who picks up a find for his friend, his friend *kanah* [has taken title to it];"[199] "watching gives *'keniya'* (the right of possession) in ownerless property;"[200] "a man's yard *koneh* (obtains title) for him without his knowledge."[201] Similarly, the Sages, in all places, use the expression of *kinyan* for taking possession, meaning that it is his. This was the intention of Onkelos when he translated *konei (of heaven and earth) as d'kinyanei,* [meaning *"Whose possessions* are heaven and earth"], and he did not say *kanah* (who acquired).

20. AND HE GAVE HIM A TENTH OF ALL. Abraham did not wish to take for himself *from a thread even to a sandal tie.*[202] But the part of the Most High he set aside in order to give it to the priest. Now the king of Sodom went out to meet Abraham at the vale of Shaveh[203] in his honor, and he accompanied him to the city of Salem where Melchizedek brought out bread and wine for the people

(195) Ramban's point is that since the second half of the verse clearly speaks of the making of man, the first half of the verse which uses the word *kanita* must also refer to "making," rather than "acquiring." (196) Deuteronomy 32:6. Here too the word *konecha* is used together with *asiyah,* indicating that they have a similar connotation. (197) Above, 12:5. (198) Further, 31:1. (199) Baba Metziah 10 a. Here the word *konah* does not mean that he acquired it from the other since he never picked it up for himself. Instead, it means taking title to it. (200) *Ibid.,* 118 a. Here too *konah* does not mean that he acquired it from another person but that he took title to it. (201) *Ibid.,* 11 a. This too is a similar case. (202) Verse 23 here. (203) Above, Verse 17.

that followed him. The king of Sodom did not ask anything of Abraham, but when he saw his generosity and righteousness in giving the tithe to the priest, then he also asked for the souls [204] by way of charity. Abraham, trusting that his G-d will give him riches, possessions and honor, did not wish to take anything from him, and so he returned all the wealth of Sodom which belonged to him, and all the wealth of Gomorrah for it to be returned to its owners. The king of Sodom had asked above all for the souls,[204] but Abraham's consideration above all was that they should not say that they made Abram rich.[202] Now the other places mentioned [205] had been destroyed by the enemy in battle; only the wealth of Sodom and Gomorrah, among the cities of the five kings, fell into the hands of the enemy because since their kings were lost in the slime pits, their cities remained defenseless.[206]

It is possible[207] that [the plunder from the other three cities is alluded to] in the words of Abraham: "*If from a thread even to a sandal tie* [202] will remain with me of all the wealth that has come to me from all of you;[208] *and if I take anything that is thine* [202] of your wealth which you, the king of Sodom, gave me."

22. I HAVE LIFTED UP MINE HAND TO THE ETERNAL. This is an expression signifying an oath: "I lift up my hand to G-d Most High."[209] Similarly, the verse, *By myself have I sworn,*[210] means "By Myself do I swear." Thus the language of Rashi.

I have found a similar text in the Sifre:[211] "We find in the case of all the righteous that they bring their inclination under oath in order

(204) The prisoners. Verse 21 here. (205) Admah, Zeboim and Bela. Verse 2. (206) Hence the four kings were able to plunder Sodom and Gomorrah, and when Abraham recaptured it from them he restored it to its original owners. The other three cities (see preceding note) defended themselves and were completely destroyed in battle. (207) Ramban is now suggesting that the four kings had taken plunder from the other three cities as well and that is alluded to in the verse, as will be explained. (208) "From all of you," i.e., from all the five cities. (209) Besides explaining that this is an expression signifying an oath, Rashi also states that even though the verse uses a past tense *harimothi*, the sense is that of the present tense: "I lift up my hand." (210) Further, 22: 16. Here too the verse uses a past tense, but its meaning is that of the present tense. (211) *Vaethchanan* 33.

not to do evil. In the case of Abraham, he says, *I have lifted up mine hand to the Eternal.*" It is thus similar to the verse, *And he lifted up his right hand and his left hand unto heaven, and swore by Him that liveth forever.* [212]

But Onkelos said, "I have lifted my hand in prayer before the Eternal." The intent of Abraham's words according to Onkelos is: "I have prayed to G-d, with my hands spread forth toward heaven, [213] if I take anything that is thine." That is to say, "*G-d do so to me, and more also,* [214] if I take, etc."

The correct interpretation appears to me to be that Abraham said, "I have lifted my hand to G-d to make those things Sacred and Devoted [215] to Him, were I to take from that which is thine." Declaring things to be sacred to Him is called in Hebrew "lifting of a hand," just as in the verses: *Every one that did lift up a heave offering of silver and copper;* [216] *and every man that offered a wave offering of gold unto the Eternal.* [217] This Abraham said because having given a tenth of it to the priest, he declared that whatever he takes from the king of Sodom would be a heave offering to G-d, from which he would derive no benefit.

In Bereshith Rabbah [218] it is similarly said, "Abraham made it a heave offering, even as it is said, *And ye shall heave a heave offering of it for the Eternal.*" [219]

15 1. THE WORD OF THE ETERNAL CAME UNTO ABRAM IN A VISION. Abraham now merited that the word of G-d should come to him in a daytime vision for at first his prophecy came to him in nocturnal visions. The meaning of the word *bemachzeh* (in a vision) is as in the meaning of the verse, *And all the people saw the thunderings,* [220] and the secret thereof is known to those who are learned in the mysteries of the Torah.

(212) Daniel 12:7. (213) See 1 Kings 8:22. (214) *Ibid.,* 2:23. (215) See Leviticus 27:28. (216) Exodus 35:24. (217) *Ibid.,* Verse 22. (218) 43:12. (219) Numbers 18:26. (220) Exodus 20:18.

FEAR NOT ABRAM. Abraham feared two things: that the four kings – either they or their successors – might increase their forces against him and he would go down into the battle and perish, or that his day shall come to die without child. [To remove these two fears from Abraham, the Eternal] promised him that He will be his shield against them, and that his reward for walking with G-d shall be very great.

2. AND ABRAM SAID, O LORD ETERNAL, WHAT WILT THOU GIVE ME? "Behold, Thou hast saved me from the kings, but Thou hast not assured me against extinction. Thou hast only said that Thou wilt give me great reward, but what can my reward be without children?"

Now it had not occurred to Abraham that this great reward would be in the World to Come for there is no necessity for such a promise; every servant of G-d will find life in the hereafter before him. But in this world *there are righteous men, unto whom it happened according to the work of the wicked.* [221] It is for this reason that the righteous have need of assurance. Moreover, *very great* [222] implies that he will merit both worlds [223] with all the best therein without any punishment whatever as befits the really righteous people. Moreover, an assurance is given for that which a person fears. [Hence, he needed no assurance concerning the hereafter. But he feared being childless; therefore G-d] rejoined and explained that His assurance included that he should not fear this either,as He will make his children *as the stars of heaven for multitude.* [224]

You may ask: Has it not been told to Abraham already, *For all the land which thou seest, to thee will I give it, and to thy seed forever. And I will make thy seed as the dust of the earth,* [225] and so, how could Abraham now say, *Since I go childless...lo, my household slave will be mine heir?* [226] And why did he not believe in the first prophecy, as he would believe in this [second one which G-d will

(221) Ecclesiastes 8:14. (222) *Thy reward shall be 'very great.'* (223) "Both worlds," literally "two tables," a Rabbinic figure of speech (Berachoth 5 b) signifying access to the best of this world and also of the hereafter. (224) Deuteronomy 1:10. (225) Above, 13:15-16. (226) Verses 2-3 here.

now relate to him?] The answer is that the righteous ones have no trust in themselves, fearing they might have sinned in error. Thus it is written *At one instant I may speak concerning a nation, and concerning a kingdom, to build and plant it; but if that nation turn and do evil before Me, then I repent of the good.*[227] Now when Abraham saw himself advanced in years and the first prophecy concerning him had not yet been fulfilled, he thought that his sins had withheld that good from him.[228] And perhaps he now feared that he would be punished for the people that he killed in the war, as our Rabbis have said.[229] They have expressed a similar thought in Bereshith Rabbah:[230] "*Then Jacob was greatly afraid and was distressed.*[231] From this we derive the principle that there is no assurance for the righteous ones in this world, etc."

WHAT WILT THOU GIVE ME, SINCE I 'HOLECH' (GO) CHILDLESS? They[232] have explained the word *holech* as meaning "I die childless," even as is the meaning of that word in the verse, *For man is 'holech' (going) to his eternal home.*[233]

The correct interpretation appears to me to be that at first he [Abraham] complained: "What can my reward be since I have no children and I go as a vagrant and vagabond alone in a strange land, *like a tamarisk in the desert,*[234] *no one going out, and no one coming in*[235] in my house except Eliezer, a stranger that I brought to me from Damascus, not from my family, and not from my country." Then Abraham said, "*Behold, to me Thou hast given no seed*[236] as Thou hast promised me, and lo my household slave, the one mentioned, will be mine heir, as I am old without child, and my time will come to die childless. I am thus punished, having lost the reward which Thou hast promised me at first."

(227) Jeremiah 18:7-10, with some changes. (228) See *ibid.*, 5:25. (229) Bereshith Rabbah 44:5. (230) *Ibid.*, 76:2. (231) Genesis 32:8. (232) Jonathan and R'dak. Jonathan translates: "For I pass from the world." R'dak expressly says that Abraham feared that he might "die" childless. (233) Ecclesiastes 12:5. Now just as *holech* here refers to death, so in the words of Abraham it has the same connotation. (234) Jeremiah 17:6. (235) Joshua 6:1. (236) Verse 3 here.

4. AND, BEHOLD, THE WORD OF THE ETERNAL CAME UNTO HIM, SAYING: THIS MAN SHALL NOT BE THINE HEIR. Since Abraham had his son who would be his heir after his old age, the Eternal assured him only concerning the inheritance, [237] i.e., that he should not worry, and his seed will inherit it.

The meaning of the expression, *And, behold, the word of the Eternal came unto him*, is that while Abraham was still saying, *And, lo, my household slave will be mine heir,* the word of G-d suddenly came to him, saying *This man shall not be thine heir.*

5. AND HE BROUGHT HIM FORTH OUTSIDE. According to the simple interpretation of Scripture it means that He brought him forth from his tent into the open so that he could see the stars. And according to the Midrash its explanation is as follows: G-d said to him, "Leave your astrological speculations, for you have seen by the constellations that you are not destined to raise a son. "Abram" indeed may not have a son, but "Abraham" will have a son; "Sarai" will not bear a child, but "Sarah" will bear a child. Thus the language of Rashi.

But 'Abram' did have Ishmael! [238]

The meaning of the Midrash, however, is that Abram sought a son who would qualify to become his heir, [which excluded Ishmael, who would not inherit him], even as he said, *And, lo, my household slave will be mine heir.* [236] The Holy One, blessed be He, then said to him, "This man shall not be thine heir, but one born of thine own body shall be thine heir, [239] and leave your astrological speculations. 'Abram' will not have a son as his heir, but 'Abraham' will have a son as his heir."

(237) Ramban here suggests that Abraham's faith in the first promise (see above, Note 223) remained unshaken. However, as he grew older, he feared that if his son will be born near the time of his death, Eliezer will do with the child as he pleases, and he instead will become his heir. On this matter of inheritance G-d now assured Abraham that he should not worry for his seed will inherit him. (Tur.) (238) Further, 16:15. How then could the Midrash say, " 'Abram' indeed may not have a son?" (239) Verse 4 here.

It is also possible that the astrological speculation concerned the pair together, namely, the "Abram and Sarai" as a pair will not beget children, and the Eternal now assured him that "Abraham and Sarah" will beget children. In my opinion, however, [the Divine assurance now given to Abraham did not mention Sarah, rather], her name is an addition on the part of the Midrash, meaning that such indeed was the case also with Sarah.[240] The Holy One, blessed be He, however, did not assure him concerning Sarah at the present time. Even at the time of the prophecy concerning the circumcision, Abraham was still in doubt whether "Sarah" would bear a child.[241]

6. AND HE BELIEVED IN THE ETERNAL; AND HE ACCOUNTED IT TO HIM FOR RIGHTEOUSNESS. Rashi's explanation is: The Holy One, blessed be He, accounted it to Abraham for righteousness and merit because of the faith with which he had trusted in Him.

But I do not understand the nature of this merit. Why should he not believe in the G-d of truth, and he himself is the prophet, and *G-d is not a man, that He should lie?*[242] Furthermore, he who believed [and on the basis of this belief was ready] to sacrifice his only son, the beloved one, and withstood the rest of the trials, how could he not believe a good tiding?

The correct interpretation appears to me to be that the verse is stating that Abraham believed in G-d and he considered it due to the righteousness of the Holy One, blessed be He, that He would give him a child under all circumstances, and not because of Abram's state of righteousness and his reward, even though He told him, *Your reward shall be very great.*[243] Thus from now on he would no longer have to fear that sin might prevent the fulfillment of the promise. Now although in the case of the first prophecy[244] Abraham had thought that the promise was conditional upon the recompense for his deeds, yet now since He promised him that he should have no fear on account of sin and that He will give him a child, he believed

(240) That "Sarai" will not bear a child, but "Sarah" will. (241) See further, 17:17. (242) Numbers 23:29. (243) Above, Verse 1. (244) See above, Note 223, and Ramban to Verse 2.

that *the thing is established by G-d,* [245] *truth He will not turn from it.* [246] For since this is a matter of the righteousness of G-d, it has no break in continuity, even as it is written, *By Myself have I sworn, saith the Eternal, the word is gone forth from My mouth in righteousness, and shall not come back.* [247]

It may be that the verse is stating that Abraham believed that he would have a child as an heir under all circumstances, but the Holy One, blessed be He, accounted to him that this promise He had assured him would in addition be as righteousness [248] since in His righteousness G-d did so, just as it says, *G-d thought it for good.* [249] A similar case is the verse regarding Phinehas: *And that was accounted unto him for righteousness,* [250] meaning that the trust he [Phinehas] has in G-d when committing that particular deed [251] was accounted as righteousness unto all generations since G-d will forever keep His righteousness and kindness for every generation on account of [Phinehas' deed, and this recompense transcends any strictly merited reward]. This is similar to that which is stated, *Forever will I keep for him My mercy.* [252]

7. I AM THE ETERNAL WHO BROUGHT THEE OUT OF UR OF THE CHALDEES, TO GIVE THEE THIS LAND TO INHERIT IT. I have already explained this verse [253] as stating: "From the time I brought you out of Ur of the Chaldees and performed a miracle for you [which saved your life], it was the Will before Me to give you this land." But at this present moment He did not decree giving it to Abraham, rather he said that He had brought him out of Ur of the Chaldees with the intention of giving it to him. It was for this reason that Abraham feared lest a condition of good deeds be attached to the inheritance of the land even though He already had told him

(245) Further, 41:21. (246) Psalms 132:11. (247) Isaiah 45:23. "Saith the Eternal" is here an addition based upon Genesis 22:16. (248) Ramban is now suggesting that Abraham did consider his having a child as being a reward for his deeds, but the Holy One, blessed be He, accounted it to him as an act of righteousness in order not to diminish his future reward for his good deeds. (249) Further, 50:20. (250) Psalms 106:31. (251) See Numbers 25:7-8. (252) Psalms 89:29. (253) Above, 11:28.

twice, *Unto thy seed will I give this land,* [254] since He did not decree the gift of the land now as He did decree to give him a child. Therefore, Abraham said, *Whereby shall I know that I shall inherit it?* [255] This is not similar to the question of Hezekiah, *What shall be the sign that the Eternal will heal me?* [256] The Holy One, blessed be He, also did not act with Abraham as He did with the other signs by showing him a sign or wonder in some miraculous matter. [257] But Abraham desired to have definite knowledge that he would inherit the land and that neither his sin nor that of his seed would withhold it from them. Or perhaps the Canaanites might repent, in which case the following verse might apply to them: *At one instant I may speak concerning a nation, and concerning a kingdom, to pluck up and to break down and destroy it; but if that nation turn from their evil... I repent of the evil that I thought to do unto it.* [258] And then the Holy One, blessed be He, made a covenant with him that he will inherit the land under all circumstances.

9. A HEIFER 'MESHULESHETH' AND A SHE-GOAT 'MESHULESHETH.' Rabbi Abraham ibn Ezra explained the word *meshulesheth* as meaning three years old. But Onkelos said "three." [259] This is indeed correct since a three-year old cow is no longer called *eglah* (heifer), just as we have learned in a Mishnah: [260] "But the Sages say that an *eglah* (heifer) is two years old; a *parah* (cow) is three years old."

The allusion here is to the three sacrifices [261] which his seed will bring from them before Him: the Whole-offering, the Sin-offering and the Peace-offering. And as for the Guilt-offering, that is like the Sin-offering, [262] the difference between them being merely in the name.

(254) *Ibid.*, 12:7; 13:15. (255) Verse 8. Meaning: "How shall I know that this gift of the land will be an enduring one, unaffected by my sins?" This interpretation is clearly stated by Ramban further on in the text. (256) II Kings 20:8. (257) Instead, He made a covenant with him to inherit the land by all means.(Tur.) (258) Jeremiah 18:7-8. (259) "Three heifers and three she-goats." (Onkelos.) (260) Parah 1:1. And here when the verse says *eglah* (heifer) it cannot therefore refer to a three-year old, as Ibn Ezra says. (261) The heifer, the she-goat and the ram. (262) Leviticus 7:7.

It is possible that the meaning of the word *meshulesheth* is that he bring the three of them consecutively, each kind remaining separate. A similar use of this word is found in the verse, *For they were in 'meshulashoth' (three) stories,* [263] meaning that there were upper, middle and lower chambers.

10. AND HE DIVIDED THEM IN THE MIDST. This he did in order that He make the covenant with him, to pass between these parts.

He thereby alluded to Abraham that all sacrifices of cattle and fowl will be from these species since the *gozeil* (young pigeon) mentioned here [264] is identical with the *ben yonah* (young pigeon) mentioned in the Book of Leviticus. [265] Here it is called *gozeil* to indicate that only the young of this specie are fit for sacrifices. Now even though all young fowl are called *gozlim*— as it is said, *As an eagle that stirreth up her nest, hovereth over 'gozalav' (his young ones)* [266] – Abraham understood on his own that the command of the Eternal applied to the kind which was to be selected [by the Torah, namely, young pigeons]. It may be that Abraham followed his own will in offering a young pigeon, and Scripture selected forever the specie which the patriarch had offered.

Thus did Abraham know that the sacrifices would be of these species and that all of them would be divided into parts: the Whole-offering into its pieces, [267] the Peace-offering into the breast, shoulder and fats, [268] and the Sin-offering and the Guilt-offering into their fats. [269]

BUT THE BIRD HE DID NOT SPLIT. He placed the turtle-dove [264] and the young pigeon opposite each other for they too were in the covenant, but Abraham did not split them in the middle since concerning all fowl offered on the altar it says, *He shall not separate it.* [270] In Bereshith Rabbah the Sages said, [271] "The Holy One, blessed be He, indicated to him that in a bird

(263) Ezekiel 42:6. (264) In Verse 9 above. (265) 1:14. (266) Deuteronomy 32:11. (267) Leviticus 1:12. (268) *Ibid.*, 7:30-32 (269) *Ibid.*, 4:31; 7:2-5. (270) *Ibid.*, 1:17. (271) 44:14.

Whole-offering, the ministering-priest severs both the gullet and the windpipe, but in a bird Sin-offering he does not sever" [the head from the body, as he must cut one and not both of the organs].[272]

11. AND THE BIRDS OF PREY CAME DOWN UPON THE CARCASSES. [They came down] to eat them, as is the nature of birds.

AND ABRAM DROVE THEM AWAY. It was thus alluded to Abraham that the nations would come to abolish the sacrifices, but the children of Abraham would drive them away.

12. AND LO, A DREAD, EVEN A GREAT DARKNESS FELL UPON HIM. The Rabbis in the Midrash have interpreted this fourfold [273] expression to be an allusion to the servitude of the four exiles, [274] for the prophet [275] Abraham found his soul overtaken by "a dread," followed by "darkness," which in turn became "a great darkness," and then he felt as if an overwhelmingly heavy load "fell" upon him. Thus the Rabbis have said: [276] "*A dread*, this is Babylon. *Darkness*, this is Media that darkened the eyes of Israel with fasting [277] and affliction. *Great*, this is the kingdom of Antiochus. [278] *Fell upon him,* this is Edom. [279]

This experience came to Abraham because when the Holy One, blessed be He, made a covenant with him to give the land to his children as an everlasting possession, He said to him, by way of a

(272) See Rashi, Leviticus 1:15 and 5:8. The principle is derived from the following textual inference: Since Abraham was asked to bring both "a turtle-dove and a young pigeon," why does Scripture conclude by saying, *And the bird* [*hatzipor* – singular] *he did not split?* This is to indicate that of the two kinds of sacrifices to be brought from fowl, namely, the Sin-offering and the Whole-offering, only one would be subject to the injunction not to separate it, and Scripture later specifies that this is the bird Sin-offering. (Leviticus 5:8.) (273) "A dread," "a great," "darkness," "fell." (274) Mentioned further in the text. (275) See Ramban further, Verse 17, as to the nature of the prophetic vision. (276) Bereshith Rabbah 44:20. (277) A reference to the fasting in the time of Mordecai and Esther. (Esther 4:16.) (278) By prohibiting the practice of the commandments of the Torah, the Greeks caused "a great" darkness to descend upon the descendants of Abraham. (279) Edom being a synonym for Rome.

residuary of His gift, that during the four exiles the nations will subjugate his children and rule in their land, subject to the condition that they sin before Him. Following this general allusion, He then informed him explicitly concerning another exile into which they will first go, namely, the Egyptian exile with which he had already been punished, as I have explained.[280]

13. THAT THY SEED SHALL BE A STRANGER. This is a verse that is to be transposed, its purport being that "thy seed shall be a stranger for four hundred years in a land that is not theirs, and they shall enslave them, and they shall afflict them." He has thus not specified the length of the period of servitude and affliction.

There are many cases in Scripture where verses must be transposed if they are to be interpreted properly. Thus: *There came unto me the Hebrew servant, who thou hast brought unto us, to mock me;*[281] *And all countries came into Egypt to buy corn to Joseph;*[282] *For whosoever eateth leavened bread, that soul shall be cut off from Israel, from the first day until the seventh day;*[283] *In that day a man shall cast away his idols of silver, and his idols of gold, which they made for themselves to worship, to the moles and to the bats;*[284] *Come, and hearken, and I will declare, all ye that fear G-d, what He hath done for my soul;*[285] *They cry unto Me, My G-d we Israel know Thee;*[286] *And they shall be Mine, saith the Eternal of hosts, in the day that I do make, even Mine own treasure, and I will spare them.*[287] There are many other such verses.

The sense of the verse is: "Even though I tell you that I have given this land to your children, you should surely know that before I give

(280) Above, 12:10. (281) Further, 39:17. The meaning being: "There came unto me to mock me the Hebrew servant...." (282) *Ibid.*, 41:57. The meaning being: "And all countries came into Egypt to Joseph...." (283) Exodus 12:15. The meaning being: "For whosoever eateth leavened bread, from the first day until the seventh day, that soul...." (284) Isaiah 2:20. The meaning being: "In that day a man shall cast away to the moles and to the bats his idols...." (285) Psalms 66:16. The meaning being: "All ye that fear G-d, come...." (286) Hosea 8:2. The meaning being: "Unto Me crieth Israel, 'My G-d, we know Thee.'" (287) Malachi 3:17. The meaning being: "And they shall be Mine treasure, saith the Eternal...."

it to them they shall be strangers for four hundred years in a land not belonging to them, and they shall also enslave them and afflict them."

Rabbi Abraham ibn Ezra said [that the verse should be interpreted as follows]: "You should surely know that your children shall be strangers in servitude and affliction until the end of a four hundred year period commencing from this day of the covenant." If so, G-d informed Abraham of the time of the redemption, but He did not inform him of the exact length of the exile. This too is correct.

14. 'VEGAM' (AND ALSO) THAT NATION THAT MADE SLAVES OF THEM WILL I JUDGE. The words, *And also,* include the kingdoms of the four exiles which will be judged for having enslaved Israel. Thus the language of Rashi.

By way of the simple meaning of Scripture, the verse is stating: "Just as I decreed exile and affliction for your children on account of sin,[288] so will I bring judgment upon the nation that will enslave them for the violence they will do to them."

The correct meaning of the word *vegam* appears to me to be as follows: Even though I have decreed that your children be strangers in a land not their own, and they shall enslave them and afflict them, I will nevertheless judge the nation that will enslave them for what they will do to them, and they will not be exonerated for having done My decree." The reason for this is as Scripture states: *I am jealous for Jerusalem and for Zion with a great jealousy; and I am very sore displeased with the nations that are at ease; for I was but a little displeased, and they helped for evil.*[289] And it says again, *I was wroth with My people, I profaned Mine inheritance, and gave them into thy hand; thou didst show them no mercy; upon the aged hast thou very heavily laid the yoke.*[290] Such was the case with the Egyptians who increased the evil. They threw the children of the Israelites into the river, embittered their lives,[291] and they intended to eradicate their name from memory. This is the meaning of the expression *will I judge,* i.e., "I will bring them to judgment to

(288) See Ramban above, 12:10. (289) Zechariah 1:14-15. (290) Isaiah 47:6. (291) Exodus 1:14.

determine whether they did as was decreed upon them or if they increased the evil inflicted upon them." It is this principle which Jethro stated: *For it is the thing wherein they acted presumptuously* [that caused the punishment to come] *upon them.* [292] It was their presumptuousness that brought upon the Egyptians the great punishment which utterly destroyed them. And this principle is also expressed in the verse: *for thou knewest that they dealt proudly against them.* [293]

Now the Rabbi [294] stated the reason [for the punishment of the Egyptians – a punishment meted out even though it had been decreed that they were to enslave the Israelites]– in the Book of Knowledge: [295] "It had not been decreed on any particular [Egyptian that *he* was to afflict the Israelites], and if any one of all those who perpetrated evil against Israel had not wanted to do it, he had the liberty to do so since the decree was not directed at any specific person." [296]

But to me the Rabbi's words are not reconciled with the facts. Even if the Holy One, blessed be He, were to decree that any individual among all the nations should do them [the Israelites] evil in such-and-such a manner, and this specific individual fulfilled His decree with alacrity, he has the merit of fulfilling a Divine commandment. What sense is there in the Rabbi's words? If a king were to command that the inhabitants of a certain country do a particular deed, he who is slack and throws the matter upon others offends and sins against himself, while he who does it wins the king's favor. And this is all the more since Scripture states, *And also that nation that made slaves of them,* which clearly implies that the entire Egyptian nation was to enslave them, and they came to Egypt of their own free will! Instead, the reason [for the punishment of the Egyptians] is as I have written above.

(292) *Ibid.*, 18:11. (293) Nehemiah 9:10. (294) Rabbi Moshe ben Maimon (Rambam). See *Seder Bereshith*, Note 139. (295) Mishneh Torah, Mada, Hilchoth Teshuvah, end of Chapter 6. (296) Hence the individual Egyptian was properly punished since each one could, by exercise of his free choice, have not been a party to the suffering caused to the Israelites. Ramban's position as explained in the text is shared by Rabbi Abraham ben David (Rabad), Rambam's chief critic. (*Ibid.*)

Our Rabbis already mentioned this matter when they said in Shmoth Rabbah:[297] "This may be likened to a lord who told his son that he should work for a certain person who should not cause him any suffering. So he went and worked for him. Now even though he worked for him without recompense, the master did not cease causing him suffering. When the lord finally was reconciled with his son, he decreed death to those who caused his son suffering. Similarly, the Holy One, blessed be He, decreed that Israel be in servitude in Egypt. But the Egyptians overwhelmed them and enslaved them by force. "Said the Holy One, blessed be He: 'You should have used them as servants who would do your needs. *I was but a little displeased, and they helped for evil.*'"[298] Thus far [is the quote from the Midrash Shmoth Rabbah].

Now it is clear that throwing Hebrew children into the river was not included in the decree, *And they shall enslave them, and afflict them,* for this would result in their complete destruction. Similarly, that which the Egyptians said at first, *Come, let us deal wisely with them lest they multiply*[299] is not part of servitude or affliction. Besides, they themselves increased the degree of affliction, as Scripture testifies, *And they made their lives bitter with hard service,* etc.[300] It is this which Scripture states in the following verse: *And he saw our affliction, and our toil, and our oppression.*[301]

Know and understand that a person who, on the New Year, has been inscribed and sealed for a violent death,[302] the bandits who kill him will not be guiltless because they fulfilled that which had been decreed against him. *That wicked man shall die in his iniquity,*[303] but his blood will be sought from the murderer. However, when a decree issues from the mouth of a prophet, there are different laws

(297) 30:15. (298) Zechariah 1:15. (299) Exodus 1:10. (300) *Ibid.,* Verse 14. (301) Deuteronomy 26:7. (302) During the coming year. The significance of the words "and sealed" is as follows: According to the Talmud (Rosh Hashanah 16 b), only the completely wicked people are inscribed "and sealed" immediately on Rosh Hashanah for death. The fate of the average person is not "sealed" until the Day of Atonement. Yet, continues Ramban, no one has a right to kill that person even though death was already decreed for him on the New Year, which would indicate that he was a completely wicked person. (303) Ezekiel 3:18.

concerning one who fulfills it. If he heard it and he wishes to fulfill the Will of his Creator as decreed, there is no sin upon him for doing so. On the contrary, it is accounted to him as a merit, just as it is said concerning King Jehu: *Because thou hast done well in executing that which is right in Mine eyes, and hast done unto the house of Ahab according to all that was in My heart, thy sons of the fourth generation shall sit on the throne of Israel.* [304] However, if he heard the command and killed him out of his personal hatred or in order to take his wealth, he is subject to punishment for his intention was to sin, and it is accounted to him as a transgression. Scripture so states with respect to Sennacherib, [king of Assyria]: *O Asshur the rod of Mine anger... I do send him against an ungodly nation, and against the people of My wrath do I give him a charge.* [305] And Scripture continues: *but not so doth he mean, neither doth his heart think so, but it is in his heart to destroy.* [306] This is why he was punished in the end, just as it is said, *Wherefore it shall come to pass, that when the Eternal hath performed his whole work... I will punish the fruit of the arrogant heart of the king of Assyria, and the glory of his haughty looks, etc.* [307] Again it says concerning Sennacherib: *Israel is a scattered sheep, the lions have driven him away; first the king of Assyria hath devoured him, and last this Nebuchadrezzar king of Babylon. ...Therefore thus said the Eternal... Behold, I will punish the king of Babylon and his land, as I have punished the king of Assyria.* [308] This is proof that the king of Assyria was punished because of the evil he did to Israel. Now Nebuchadrezzar heard that the prophets unanimously called upon him to destroy Jerusalem, and he and all his people were commanded to do this by word of the prophet, as it is written, *Behold, I will send and take all the families of the north, saith the Eternal, and I will send unto Nebuchadrezzar the king of Babylon, My servant, and will bring them against this land, and against the inhabitants thereof... and I will utterly destroy them.* [309] And it is further written, *Behold I will give this city into the hand of the Chaldeans, and into the hand of Nebuchadrezzar king of Babylon... and they shall set the city on fire.* [310] Concerning

(304) II Kings 10:30. (305) Isaiah 10:5-6. (306) *Ibid.*, Verse 7. (307) *Ibid.*, Verse 12. (308) Jeremiah 50:17-18. (309) *Ibid.*, 25:9. (310) *Ibid.*, 32:28-29.

the Sanctuary itself, the prophet said, *I will make this house like Shiloh.* [311] The Chaldeans knew that it was the command of G-d, as Nebuzaradan [captain of the guard of the King of Babylon] said to Jeremiah, *The Eternal thy G-d pronounced this evil upon this place; and the Eternal hath brought it, and done according as He spoke, because ye have sinned against the Eternal.* [312] Yet despite this, the Chaldeans were all punished in the end. This was because of two reasons. First, Nebuchadrezzar also intended to destroy the entire land in order to increase his authority, as it is written concerning him: *And I will cause the arrogancy of the proud to cease, and will lay low the haughtiness of the tyrants;* [313] and again it is written: *And thou hast said in thy heart, I will ascend into heaven... I will ascend above the heights of the clouds; I will be like the Most High.* [314] Concerning his nation it is written, *Thou sayest in thy heart: I am, and there is none else beside me.* [315] Habakkuk the prophet said concerning him, *Woe to him that gaineth evil gains for his house, that he may set his nest on high,* etc. [316] Thus Nebuchadrezzar's punishment is as that of Sennacherib. It is for this reason that Scripture says, *Therefore thus saith the Eternal... Behold, I will punish the king of Babylon and his land, as I have punished the king of Assyria.* [317] And there was yet another reason for punishment in the case of the king of Babylon, i.e., for his having added to the decree and having exceedingly perpetrated evil against Israel, as it is said concerning him, *I was wroth with My people, I profaned Mine inheritance, and gave them into thy hand; thou didst show no mercy, upon the aged hast thou very heavily laid thy yoke.* [318] Therefore did a twofold punishment come upon him: his people were utterly destroyed, there remaining of Babylon no *name and remnant, offshoot and offspring,* [319] and his city was destroyed forever, as it is said, *And Babylon, the glory of kingdoms, the beauty of the Chaldeans' pride, shall be as when G-d overthrew Sodom and Gomorrah. It shall never be inhabited, neither shall it be dwelled in from generation to generation... But wild-cats shall lie there... and*

(311) *Ibid.*, 26:6. Shiloh was destroyed by the Philistines. (I Samuel 4.) (312) *Ibid.*, 40:2-3. (313) Isaiah 13:11. (314) *Ibid.*, 14:13-14. (315) *Ibid.*, 47:8. (316) Habakkuk 2:9. (317) Jeremiah 50:18. (318) Isaiah 47:6. (319) *Ibid.*, 14:22.

satyrs shall dance there.[320] Scripture further states concerning him, *For it is the vengeance of the Eternal, the vengeance of His temple,*[321] and it is written, *'The violence done to me and to my flesh be upon Babylon,' shall the inhabitants of Zion say; and 'My blood be upon the inhabitants of Chaldaea,' shall Jerusalem say. Therefore thus saith the Eternal: Behold, I will plead thy cause, and take vengeance for thee.*[322] There are many verses like these.

15. AND THOU SHALT COME TO THY FATHERS IN PEACE. And thou shalt not behold at this. Thus the language of Rashi.

This is not correct according to Rashi's own interpretation, namely, that the decree, *thy seed shall be a stranger in a land not their own,*[323] took effect as soon as Abraham had a child. Thus, soon after Isaac was born it states, *And Abraham sojourned ('vayagar') in the land of the Philistines;*[324] *And Isaac sojourned in Gerar.*[325] Now if so, Abraham was also included in the decree! But the meaning of the verse, *And thou shalt come to thy fathers in peace,* is that "no punishment will come to you from Me even though I decree on your children punishments of servitude and affliction."

16. AND IN THE FOURTH GENERATION THEY SHALL COME BACK HITHER. After they are exiled into Egypt, they will be there for three generations. And thus it happened; Jacob was exiled into Egypt. Go and reckon his generations: Judah, Peretz, Chetzron, and Caleb the son of Chetzron was amongst those who entered the Land. Thus the language of Rashi. But this is not correct at all.[326]

(320) *Ibid.*, 13:19-21. (321) Jeremiah 51:11. (322) *Ibid.*, 51:35-6. (323) Above, Verse 13. (324) Further, 21:34. The word *vayagar* has the same root letters as *geir* (stranger), thus suggesting that Abraham lived as a "stranger" in a land which was not his own. (325) *Ibid.*, 26:6. The verse however states, *vayeshev* (and he "dwelled"), and not *vayagar*. In Rashi a different verse is quoted: *Sojourn ('gur') in this land. (Ibid.,* Verse 3.) Now *gur* has the same root as *vayagar*. (See preceding note.) (326) Since Chetzron was among those who went down to Egypt (further, 46:12), they were in Egypt for only two generations. And if "the dwelling in a strange land" is to be reckoned as beginning with Abraham, there are seven generations from Abraham to Caleb: Abraham, Isaac, Jacob, Judah, Peretz, Chetzron and Caleb. (Tur.)

The correct interpretation appears to be that *the fourth generation* refers to the Amorite whose sin will then become full,[327] for from the day of the decree He prolonged the time of the Amorite, as He visits iniquity upon the third and fourth generation. Had the Amorites repented of their iniquities He would not have utterly destroyed them. Rather, they would have been a levy of bondservants, or they might have gone elsewhere.

THE INIQUITY OF THE AMORITE. He mentioned the strongest among them,[328] *Whose height was like the height of the cedars.*[329] The Israelites would not be able to overpower him until his measure of sin was full and his own iniquities will ensnare him.[330] Moreover the Amorite was the first one to be captured by them, and it was his land which they inherited first.[331]

17. AND BEHOLD, A SMOKING FURNACE, AND A FLAMING TORCH. It appeared to Abraham as if the furnace was all smoke and in its midst a flaming torch was burning, similar to *a great smoke, with a fire flashing up.*[332] The "smoke" mentioned here is *the cloud, and thick darkness* mentioned at the giving of the Torah,[333] and "the flaming torch" in its midst is "the fire" mentioned there: *And thou didst hear His words out of the midst of the fire;*[334] and it is further written: *And the appearance of the glory of the Eternal was like devouring fire,* etc.[335] Thus the Divine Glory passed between the parts of the sacrifices, and this is the covenant which He made with Abraham forever. This is the meaning of the verse, *the Eternal made a covenant with Abraham,*[336] as the Holy One, blessed be He, Himself carried through "the covenant of between the parts." The student versed in the mysteries of the Torah will understand.

(327) Thus enabling Israel to return and take the land from him. (Tur.) (328) Or else He should have mentioned "the Canaanites," whose name the land carried. The Amorites are specifically singled out for their height by the prophet Amos, mentioned further on. (329) Amos 2:9. The verse begins: *Yet I destroyed the Amorite, whose height....* (330) See Proverbs 5:22. (331) The land of Sichon, king of the Amorites, was later the first to be captured by the Israelites. Hence his name is singled out here in the verse. (332) Seen by the prophet Ezekiel (1:4). In the actual verse the word "cloud" appears instead of the word "smoke." (333) Deuteronomy 4:11. (334) *Ibid.*, Verse 36. (335) Exodus 24:17. (336) Verse 18.

18. IN THAT DAY THE ETERNAL MADE A COVENANT WITH ABRAM, SAYING. Now the Holy One, blessed be He, promised Abraham the gift of the land many times, and all of the promises served a purpose. When he originally arrived in the land, He said to him, *Unto thy seed will I give this land,* [337] but He did not clarify the extent of His gift, for included in this promise is only the land where he walked, *unto the place of Shechem unto the oak of Moreh.* [338] Afterwards, when his merits increased while in the Land, He bestowed upon him the additional promise: *Lift up now thine eyes, and look from the place where thou art, northward and southward, and eastward and westward,* [339] meaning that He will give him all those lands in their totality, for the meaning of the expression, *which thou seest,* [340] is not literally "with your eyes" for the sight of a person does not extend far. Rather, it means that He will give him [land which lies in] every direction in which he looks. It may be that He miraculously showed him all the land of Israel, as was the case with Moshe Rabbeinu. [341] He further added in this second blessing: *and to thy seed forever,* [340] and that his seed will increase *as the dust of the earth.* [342] At the third time, He clarified to him the boundaries of the land, mentioning all the ten nations [who presently inhabited it], [343] and in addition He made a covenant with him that sin would not cause [the annulment of the gift]. When He commanded him concerning circumcision, He told him, *for a possession forever,* [344] that is to say, if they will be exiled from it they will again return and inherit it. [345] He also added at that time, *And I will be their G-d,* [346] meaning that He in His Glory will lead them, and they shall not be under the rule of a star or constellation or any power of the powers above, as will yet be explained in the Torah. [346]

(337) Above, 12:7. (338) *Ibid.*, Verse 6. (339) *Ibid.*, 13:14. (340) *Ibid.*, Verse 15. (341) Deuteronomy 34:1-3. (342) Above, 13:16. (343) Here, Verses 19-21. (344) Further, 17:8. (345) The promise, *And to thy seed forever* (13:15), does not imply that if they will be exiled from the land they will return and re-inherit it. It assures legal title but not necessarily actual possession. However, the expression, *for 'a possession' forever*, does indicate that it is to be their land forever. Hence even if they are exiled they will return and possess it. (346) See Ramban to Leviticus 18:25.

Now at the time of the first gift, Scripture states, *Unto thy seed will I give,* [337] the verb being in a future tense, and similarly in the second time, [347] because until then He had not given him the entire land, and therefore, He said to him, *will I give it.* [337] But at the third time, during the covenant, He said, *Unto thy seed have I given,* [348] meaning that He will make the covenant for the gift that He had already given him. Similarly, at the time of the circumcision, when He said, *for a possession forever,* [344] He said to him, *And I will give unto thee,* [344] in the future tense. [349]

Rashi wrote: *Unto thy seed have I given.* [348] The word of the Supreme One is as if it were already accomplished. — But there is no need for this explanation in this passage. [350]

16 2. AND ABRAM HEARKENED TO THE VOICE OF SARAI. Scripture does not state, "And he did so." Rather it says that he hearkened to the voice of Sarai, thus indicating that even though Abram was very desirous of having children, he did not do so without permission of Sarai. Even now it was not his intention to build up a family from Hagar, and that his children be from her. His intent was merely to do Sarai's will so that she may build a family from Hagar for she will find satisfaction in her handmaid's children, or that by the merit of this act she will become worthy to have children, as our Rabbis have said. [351]

Scripture further says, *And Sarai took,* [352] to inform us that Abram did not hurry the matter until Sarai took Hagar and gave her to him. Again, Scripture mentions *Sarai Abram's wife... to Abram her husband,* [352] to allude that Sarah did not despair of Abraham and that she did not render herself distant from him as she was his wife and he her husband, but she wanted that Hagar also be his wife. This is why the verse states, *And she gave her to Abram her husband to be his wife,* [352] meaning that she was not to be as a concubine but

(347) *To thee will I give it.* (Above, 13:15). (348) In Verse 18 here. (349) Since, as explained above, this promises that if they will be exiled from the land, they will return and inherit it, the future tense refers to this future return to and repossession of the land. (350) Instead, the explanation is as set forth above. (351) Bereshith Rabbah 71:7. (352) Verse 3 here.

as a woman married to him. All this reflects the ethical conduct of Sarah and her respect towards her husband.

3. AT THE END OF TEN YEARS. This is the established period for a woman who has lived with her husband for ten years without having given birth to children, after which he is bound to take another.

AFTER ABRAM DWELLED IN THE LAND OF CANAAN. This tells us that the period he dwelled outside of the Land is not to be included in the count of those ten years since he was not told *And I will make of thee a great nation*[353] until after he had come to the land of Israel. Thus the language of Rashi.

This reason is not proper since it is a clear-cut halachic decision that the time spent living outside the Land is not to be included in the ten year period for any person in the world.[354] The Mishnah[355] containing this principle applies to all men. And if it were as Rashi stated it, i.e., on account of this promise made to Abram, then for other people [the years they dwelled outside the land of Israel] should be included in the ten years period![356] Some Talmudic commentators[357] have already made another mistake concerning this rule, stating that the law does not require a person who dwells outside the Land to divorce a woman with whom he has lived for ten years without her giving birth, nor does the law require him to marry

(353) Above, 12:2. (354) Why then did Rashi add, "since the promise, *And I will make of thee a great nation,* was made to Abraham after he had come to the Land of Israel?" This language would make it appear that only in Abraham's case was the time spent living outside the Land excluded from the ten year period, when it really applies to everyone. (355) Yebamoth 64 a. The Mishnah is the collection of teachings by the Tannaim, compiled by Rabbi Yehuda Hanasi. (356) But the law is not so. The years that husband and wife have lived together outside the Land of Israel are not included in the ten years total for anyone, and they begin to count the years after they arrive in the Land. (357) The forthcoming opinion which Ramban refutes is mentioned in Rabbeinu Asher, Yebamoth, Chapter 6, par. 12, in the name of "some scholars who wish to say." Rabbeinu Asher also refutes their opinion.

another woman.[358] But the matter is not so. Rather, the intent [of the law which excludes the period one dwells outside the land of Israel from the ten year total] is that if a man lived with his wife for five or ten years outside the Land and then they came to the land of Israel, we give them a period of ten years from the time they came to the Land, for perhaps due to the merit of the Land they will build up a family. And thus did Abraham and Sarah our mother do from the time they came there.

6. AND SARAI DEALT HARSHLY WITH HER, AND SHE FLED FROM BEFORE HER FACE. Our mother did transgress by this affliction, and Abraham also by his permitting her to do so. And so, G-d heard her [Hagar's] affliction and gave her a son who would be *a wild-ass of a man,*[359] to afflict the seed of Abraham and Sarah with all kinds of affliction.

9. RETURN TO THY MISTRESS, AND SUBMIT THYSELF UNDER HER HANDS. The angel commanded her to return and accept upon herself the authority of her mistress. This implies that she will not go out free from her, as Sarah's children will ever rule over her children.

11. AND THOU SHALT CALL HIS NAME ISHMAEL. The angel informed Hagar that his name will be Ishmael – just as in the verse, *Behold, a son shall be born unto the house of David Josiah by name*[360] – and he told her that she should so call him, and thus remember that G-d heard her affliction.[361] Now Abraham either called him by this name on his own,[362] with the intent that G-d hear him and answer him, or the Holy Spirit rested upon him, as Rashi has

(358) Their reasoning being that childlessness may be a form of punishment for living outside the Land. Therefore he need not divorce her. This opinion, however, is refuted, for the law applies everywhere. Only in a case where, after having lived together outside the Land of Israel, husband and wife then move to the Land, the years they lived outside the Land are not included in the ten year period. (359) Verse 12 here. (360) I Kings 13:2. (361) The name *Ishmael* (G-d heareth) is, as the angel explained to Hagar, "because the Eternal hath heard thy affliction." (Verse 11.) (362) Verse 15: *And Abraham called the name of his son, whom Hagar bore, Ishmael.*

it, and he called him Ishmael because G-d had heard his mother's affliction, as the angel had said.

The correct interpretation appears to me to be that the angel commanded Hagar that she call him so, but she, being a concubine,[363] was afraid to give a name to her master's son, so she revealed the matter to him, and Abram fulfilled the word of G-d. Scripture, however, did not need to delve at length into this matter.

12. 'PERE ADAM.' Rashi comments: "One who loves the deserts[364] [and] to hunt wild animals, as it is written, *And he dwelt in the wilderness and became an archer.*[365] *His hand shall be against every man.* This means that he will be a highway man. *And every man's hand against him.* Everyone will hate him and attack him."

The correct interpretation is that *pere adam* is a construct form, meaning that he will be a wild-ass man accustomed to the wilderness, going forth to his work, seeking for food, devouring all and being devoured by all. The subject pertains to his children who will increase, and they will have wars with all the nations.

Rabbi Abraham ibn Ezra said: "*His hand shall be against every man* in that he will be victorious at first over all nations, and afterwards, *every man's hand shall be against him,* meaning that he will be vanquished in the end. *And in the face of all his brethren,* who are the sons of Keturah,[366] *he should dwell,* meaning that Ishmael's children will outnumber those of Keturah."

17 1. 'E-IL SHA-DAI.' These are two distinct Divine names, each one descriptive in itself.[367] Now the meaning of the word *eil* is "mighty", derived from the expression, *Eilei Moab* (the mighty ones of Moab).[368] The meaning of *Sha–dai*, according to Rashi, is "He

(363) Verse 3 above is no proof to the contrary, as it may express only Sarai's desire. (364) The word *pere* is thus, according to Rashi, synonymous with "desert," as it says *peraim bamidbar* (Job 24:5). *Pere adam* is thus: "a man who loves the desert." (Mizrachi.) (365) Further, 21:20. (366) Further, 25:1-4. (367) And not as Abraham ibn Ezra has it, i.e., that they both constitute one descriptive noun: "a G-d who is almighty" and "an almighty G-d." (368) Exodus 15:15.

whose G-dship suffices for every creature." In the book Moreh Nebuchim[369] the Rabbi[294] explained that the name *Sha–dai* signifies "he who is sufficient." That is to say, He does not require the existence of what He created or the conservation of any other being; rather, His existence is self-sufficient. Rabbi Abraham ibn Ezra explained in the name of the Nagid[370] that the name is from the root *shodeid*, meaning "victor and prevailer over the hosts of heaven." This is the correct interpretation, for the name *Sha–dai* represents the attribute of power which conducts the world, concerning which the Sages have said that it is "the attribute of Justice of the world below."[371]

The reason for mentioning this Divine Name now is that with it are done the hidden miracles[372] for the righteous, *to deliver their soul from death, and to keep them alive in famine,*[373] as well as to redeem them in war from the power of the sword,[374] just as all the miracles done to Abraham and to the other patriarchs, and as all the blessings and curses mentioned in the Torah in the section *Im Bechukothai*[375] and in the section *Vehaya Ki Thavo.*[376] These blessings and curses are all miracles for it is not in nature that the rains should come in their due season[377] when we worship G-d, nor are the skies to be like iron[378] if we plant our fields in the seventh year, and similarly all promises in the Torah. Rather, they are all miracles by which the disposition of natural law is overpowered, except that no change from the natural order of the world is noticeable, as was the case with the miracles done through Mosheh Rabbeinu with the ten plagues, the dividing of the Sea, the Manna, the well, and their like, for these are miracles which openly changed

(369) I, 63 (toward the end). (370) Shmuel Hanagid. In our text of Ibn Ezra, it appears anonymously as "And many explain." (371) Bereshith Rabbah 35:4. (372) All miracles which a man can deny, saying that they are part of the natural order, are called "hidden," while those that cannot be denied but are clearly the intervention of the power of G-d are called "open." (Ma'or Veshamesh.) This concept is a major foundation in Ramban's thinking. It will appear in many other places in a more developed manner. See e.g., further, 46:15; Exodus 6:2; Leviticus 26:11. (373) Psalms 33:19. (374) See Job 5:20. (375) Leviticus 26:3-46. (376) Deuteronomy 28:1-69. (377) Leviticus 26:4. (378) *Ibid.*, Verse 19.

nature, and they were done with the Tetragrammaton which He told to him. It is for this reason that He now told Abraham our father that He is the Almighty, the Victor Who will prevail over his constellation of birth so that he will have a son, and thus there will be a covenant between Him and his seed forever, meaning *that the portion of the Eternal is His people,*[379] and that He will lead them at His own will, as they will not be under the rule of a star or constellation.

Know and consider that our father Abraham did not mention the Tetragrammaton [Eternal] in any of his utterances except in combination with the Divine Name written [G-d],[380] or in combination with *E-il Elyon* [G-d Most High],[381] but he did mention in his affairs the name *Elokim* [G-d]. Thus he will say, *The Eternal, the G-d of heaven.*[382] He said, however, *the Eternal seeth,*[383] because it refers to the place of the future Sanctuary. Jacob, on the other hand, always mentioned *E-il Sha-dai* [G-d Almighty],[384] which Moses our teacher never mentions. If you will be worthy you will understand this entire matter from that which the Rabbis said in Tractate Yebamoth:[385] "All prophets contemplated Deity through an unlucid speculum," which is why Isaiah said, *And I saw G-d,*[386] [i.e., the Divine Name written *Aleph Dalet*]. "But Moses contemplated Deity through a lucid speculum." This is why He said, *For a man shall not see Me and live,*[387] whereas Isaiah's verse, *and I saw G-d,*[386] is written with the *Aleph Dalet*. I will mention this theme again in *Parshath Va'eira*[388] if G-d will look upon my grief.[389]

(379) Deuteronomy 32:9. (380) Such as in 15:2 above. (381) *Ibid.*, 14:22. (382) Further, 24:3. (383) *Ibid.*, 22:14. In this case Abraham used the Tetragrammaton (Eternal) by itself. This would contradict the principle stated by Ramban above that Abraham never used this Divine Name except in some combination with another Name. Ramban answers that since the reference there is to the Sanctuary which was destined to be built on that mountain in the future and where the sacrifices were to be brought, the Tetragrammaton is the proper name to be used, as will be explained in the beginning of the book of Leviticus when sacrifices are discussed. (384) *Ibid.*, 43:14; 48:3. (385) 49 b. (386) Isaiah 6:1. (387) Exodus 33:20. (388) *Ibid.*, 6:2. (389) A personal reference of Ramban to the difficult times in his life when he was engaged in the writing of this work.

WALK BEFORE ME. i.e., by following the path which I will show you. [This command is similar in] meaning to the verse, *After the Eternal G-d shall ye walk, and Him shall ye fear,* [390] except that with respect to a general command to follow His way which precedes His specific instructions, He says, *Walk before Me*, while with respect to a command which follows the specific command, He says, *After the Eternal ye shall walk.* [391] The purport of both commands is to walk after G-d, fear Him alone and do whatever He commands.

AND BE THOU WHOLE-HEARTED. This is an additional commandment in this matter, similar in meaning to the verse, *Thou shalt be whole-hearted with the Eternal thy G-d,* [392] which follows G-d's admonition: *There shall not be found among you any one that ... useth divination, a soothsayer, or an enchanter, or sorcerer,* etc. [393] The purport of both verses is that one should believe in his heart that the Holy One, blessed be He, alone is the Omnipotent from beginning to end. It is He who has the power to do and to undo, and therefore he should not listen to the soothsayers and diviners or to the enchanters and the sorcerers. He shall in no way believe that their words shall be fulfilled, but he should decree in his heart that everything is in the hand of the Supreme One, who is G-d, G-d Almighty, Who doeth a person good, which was not predestined by his constellation, and bringeth evil upon him despite a constellation that was good and auspicious. In accordance with the manner in which a man walks before Him, *He frustrateth the tokens of the impostors, and maketh diviners mad.* [394] It is this which the Sages had in mind when they said: "[G-d said to Abraham], 'Go forth from your astrological speculations, etc.' " [395]

Now Rashi explained: "*And be thou whole-hearted.* Be whole-hearted in all the trials I impose upon you." And Rabbi

(390) Deuteronomy 13:5. (391) Here Abraham had not yet specifically been commanded what to do, for the command concerning circumcision was later revealed to him. Hence G-d says to him, *Walk 'before' Me,* meaning "follow the commandment which I will give to you." But in the verse from Deuteronomy, where the commandments have already been annunciated, the verse properly says, *'After' the Eternal ye shall walk.* (392) *Ibid.*, 18:13. (393) *Ibid.*, Verse 10. (394) Isaiah 44:25. (395) See above, 15:5.

Abraham ibn Ezra said that the verse means that he should not seek the reason for the commandment of circumcision, it being similar in meaning to the verse: *Let my heart be undivided in Thy statutes, in order that I may not be put to shame.* [396] The correct interpretation is as I have explained.

3. AND ABRAM FELL ON HIS FACE. The purpose of this expression was to direct his mind towards the prophecy. When the prophecy concerning the commandment of circumcision was completed, Abraham rose and stood. When the word from heaven came to him a second time, saying to him, *As for Sarai thy wife*, etc.,[397] he once again fell on his face to direct his mind towards the prophecy, and he also prayed concerning Ishmael.[398] in line with the verses: *And they fell upon their faces, and said, O G-d, the G-d of the spirits*, etc.;[399] *That I may consume them in a moment. And they fell upon their faces.* [400]

4. BEHOLD, MY COVENANT IS WITH THEE, AND THOU SHALT BE THE FATHER OF A MULTITUDE OF NATIONS. This refers to the covenant of the circumcision, as He will explain, "This is the sign of the Covenant, [401] and after the covenant you will be the father of a multitude of nations."

Blessed be the Lord! By Him alone are actions weighed, for He preceded and commanded Abraham to enter into His covenant to be circumcised before Sarah became pregnant so that his seed would be holy.

6. AND I WILL MAKE NATIONS OF THEE. The language of Rashi: "Israel and Edom are referred to here, for Ishmael was already born to him, and He could not therefore have been making any announcement concerning him."

But in my opinion it is not correct that He should inform him of Esau at the time of the covenant of circumcision since Esau does not

(396) Psalms 119:80. (397) Further, Verse 15. (398) Verse 18 here. (399) Numbers 16:22. (400) *Ibid.*, Verses 21-22. (401) In Verse 10: *This is my covenant.*

observe circumcision and has not been commanded thereon, as the Sages expounded in Tractate Sanhedrin:[402] *"For in Isaac shall seed be called to thee,*[403] but not all of Isaac."[404] Instead, [the proper interpretation is that] Israel alone is called "nations" and "peoples," as in the verses: *Yea, He loveth the peoples;*[405] *They shall call peoples unto the mountains;*[406] *After thee, Benjamin, among the peoples.*[407] Even after the birth of all the tribes, He said: *A nation and a company of nations shall be of thee;*[408] *And I will make of thee a company of peoples.*[409]

9. 'VE'ATAH' (AND AS FOR THEE), THOU SHALT KEEP MY COVENANT. Rashi commented, "The *vav* of *ve'atah* connects the verse with the preceding matter [in Verse 4]: '*As for Me behold My covenant is with thee*, and as for thee, thou shalt be careful to keep it.' And what constitutes this 'keeping' of it? *This is My covenant, which you shall keep, between Me and you* – this applies to those who were then alive; *and thy seed after thee*[410] – this applies to those who are yet to be born." The Rabbi is correct in his interpretation of the plain meaning of the verse.

Now they[411] have said concerning the reason for the commandment of circumcision that He has thereby placed a reminder in the organ of lust, which is the source of much trouble and sin, in order that it should not be used excepting where it is commandatory and permissible.

By way of truth,[412] the meaning of the verse, *Behold, My covenant is with thee,*[413] is similar in meaning to the verses: *Behold, I am with thee;*[414] *And He said, Certainly, I will be with thee;*[415] *The Eternal our G-d be with us.*[416] He is thus saying that the covenant will be with him, and therefore he will be fruitful and

(402) 59 b. (403) Further, 21:12. (404) Not *all* of the children of Isaac, namely Jacob and Esau, but only "in" Isaac, meaning only one, Jacob. (405) Deuteronomy 33:3. (406) *Ibid.*, Verse 19. (407) Judges 5:14. (408) Further, 35:11. (409) *Ibid.*, 48:4. (410) Verse 10 here. (411) This reason is found in the Commentary of R'dak. See also Moreh Nebuchim (III, 49), where other reasons are given. (412) A reference to the mystic teachings of the Torah. See *Seder Bereshith*, Note 63. (413) Verse 4 here. (414) Further, 28:15. (415) Exodus 3:12. (416) I Kings 8:57.

multiply. After that He commanded that Abraham keep this covenant, and the circumcision will be as a sign of the covenant. Thus it is that this "sign" is as "the sign" of the Sabbath,[417] and therefore circumcision sets aside the Sabbath. Understand this.

14. AND THE UNCIRCUMCISED MALE. Here Scripture teaches you that this circumcision must be at the location where the distinction between male and female is evident. Thus the words of Rashi. Our Rabbis have likewise mentioned other reasons.[418]

Rabbi Abraham ibn Ezra said:[419] *"his foreskin,*[420] which is known, for it is in the genital organ. But not so are the expressions: *uncircumcised in the heart;*[421] *uncircumcised lips;*[422] *their ear is uncircumcised.*[423] All of these latter are in a construct state.[424]

In my opinion the matter is clearly explained in Scripture. It does not say, "And ye shall circumcise your foreskin," thus leaving the meaning in doubt, nor does it say, "the foreskin of your flesh," just as it says *the foreskin of your heart,*[425] and "the foreskin of your lips."[426] But instead it says, *And ye shall circumcise the flesh of your foreskin,*[427] meaning that you are to cut off the flesh which is your foreskin, namely, your flesh which obstructs, and there is no flesh in the body which obstructs and covers a limb [as is the case with the genital organ], where one can cut the flesh and remain without the foreskin, other than the "flesh that covers the corona," which the Sages mentioned.[428] The word "flesh" in the expression, *uncircumcised in flesh,*[429] is a euphemism for the genital organ, just as in the verses *great of flesh,*[430] and *an issue of his flesh.*[431]

(417) Concerning the Sabbath, it is also written: *It is a sign forever.* (Exodus 31:17.) (418) Shabbath 108 a. (419) In his commentary to Leviticus 12:3. (420) Leviticus 12:3. (421) Jeremiah 9:25. (422) Exodus 6:12. (423) Jeremiah 6:10. (424) But when the word *orlah* is not used in the construct state (as in Leviticus 12:3) it refers to the genital organ. (425) Deuteronomy 10:16. (426) I did not find this exact quote. Perhaps reference is to Exodus 6:12, mentioned above. (427) Verse 11 here. (428) Shabbath 137 a. In our text of the Mishnah there: "flesh that covers 'the greater part' of the corona." Ramban's version is similar to that of the Talmud Munich Ms. (See Dikduke Sofrim, *ibid.*) (429) Ezekiel 44:9. (430) *Ibid.*, 16:26. (431) Leviticus 14:2. The word "flesh" in these two verses refers to the genital organ.

17. 'VAYITZCHAK' (AND HE LAUGHED). Onkelos translated: "and he rejoiced." This is correct since the word *tzachak* can be used intermittently for sporting or rejoicing, just as in the verses: *'Mesacheketh' (Sporting) in His habitable earth,*[432] *'mesachkim' (rejoiced) before the Eternal.*[433]

In my opinion the intent of this expression is to convey the thought that whoever sees a favorable unusual event in one's life rejoices to the point where "his mouth is filled with laughter."[434] It is this thought which Sarah expressed: *G-d hath made laughter for me; everyone that heareth will laugh on account of me,*[435] just as in the verse, *Then was our mouth filled with laughter, and our tongue with singing.*[434] And this is what Abraham did. When this good tiding was related to him, he rejoiced and his mouth was filled with laughter, *and he said in his heart* that this is an occasion for rejoicing as it is a very wonderful matter. *Shall a child be born unto him that is a hundred years old? and shall Sarah, that is ninety years old, bear?* And will this matter not give cause for rejoicing and happiness? Only, Scripture speaks summarily of his wonderment, as it is connected with the word *vayitzchak.* A similar case is the expression, *Have I even here seen,*[436] which is connected with the beginning of the verse: *for she* [Hagar] *said, "Have I even here seen* G-d, revealing to me that He saw in my affliction, and shall I not call Him *E-il-ro'i* [the G-d who seeth me]?" Another such example is the expression, *Did I reveal Myself unto the house of thy father,*[437] which is connected with the following verse, *Why do you kick at My sacrifice and at Mine offering,*[438] thus stating, "Have I chosen you so that you kick at My sacrifice and Mine offering? Why then do you do so?"

It may be that the question, *Shall a child be born to him that is a hundred years old?* is an expression of amazement, not one of impossibility, just as in the verse, *Wilt thou judge the bloody city,*[439] which means, "Do you want to judge her and cause her to know all her abominations?" A similar case is the verse, *Wilt thou set thine eyes upon it? it is gone.*[440] Likewise is the verse, *Hast thou*

(432) Proverbs 8:31. (433) II Samuel 6:5. (434) Psalms 126:2. (435) Further, 21:6. (436) Above, 16:13. (437) I Samuel 2:27. (438) *Ibid.*, Verse 29. (439) Ezekiel 22:2. (440) Proverbs 23:5.

eaten of the tree, whereof I commanded thee that thou shouldst not eat?[441] That is to say, "Has the thought occurred to you to eat of the tree?" This verse likewise is saying, "Has the thought occurred to anyone that a child be born to him that is a hundred years old, and that Sarah, who is ninety years, shall bear?" After that Abraham said to Him that he wishes this miracle be with the life of Ishmael.[442]

SHALL A CHILD BE BORN TO HIM THAT IS A HUNDRED YEARS OLD? There is no wonder that a person who is a hundred years old should beget children, for men beget as long as they have vigor even if they be ninety years old or a hundred years old, even in these generations. All the more in the days of Abraham, who had not yet lived two thirds of his life.[443] Moreover, forty years after this, he begot many children from Keturah.[444] But Abraham's saying, *Shall a child be born to him that is a hundred years old,* expressed this thought: Since he did not beget a child from this woman while he was young, how could he beget from her after he was a hundred and she ninety? He knew that her womanly periods had ceased. Therefore Abraham did not say so originally when he was told, *And I will make nations of thee,*[445] but only when he was told that he would beget a child from Sarah.

Now He commanded him, *And thou shalt call his name Isaac,*[446] on account of the rejoicing done by Abraham, which is proof that it was out of faith and joy [that Abraham said, *Shall a child be born,* etc.][447] And after Abraham called him so, as G-d had commanded him, Sarah said, "Is he not rightly named Isaac? For *G-d hath made laughter* for me."[448]

(441) Above, 3:11. (442) Verse 18 here. (443) Since Abraham lived 175 years (25:7) and was now only 100, he had not yet passed two-thirds of his life-span. So it is no wonder that he was yet in his vigor. (444) Further 25:1-2. "Forty years later." Isaac was wed at the age of forty (25:20), and Abraham married Keturah after Isaac's marriage (25:1). There was thus an interval of at least forty years between the time Abraham begot Isaac and when he begot children from Keturah. (445) Above, Verse 6. (446) Verse 19 here. (447) As explained above. Had it been said out of a sense of derision, G-d would not have told him to call his son by a name which would commemorate his lack of faith. (Bachya.) (448) Further, 21:6.

18. 'LU' (O) THAT ISHMAEL MIGHT LIVE BEFORE THEE. The meaning of this word *lu* everywhere is as the word *im* (if), and it is also found combined in the word *lulei*, which means "if not." [The Hebrew word *lulei*, ordinarily written with a *yud* at the end] is sometimes written with an *aleph* at the end.[449] It is also combined into the form of *ilu*, as in the verses: *'Ve'ilu' (But if) we had been sold for bondmen and bondwomen;*[450] *'Ve'ilu' (And if) a thousand years twice told.*[451] The purport of this word *ilu* is "even if," and its meaning is as if it said, "if if," the double use of the word being for the purpose of emphasis, as in the expressions: *Is it only through Moses alone;*[452] *Was it because there were no graves;*[453] and other similar cases. Abraham thus said: "If Ishmael live before Thee, I will be pleased with this blessing with which Thou hast blessed me, namely, with seed from Sarah." For since He promised him at first, *One born of your own body is to be your heir,*[454] and the heir was to be one person, he [Abraham] had thought that this referred to Ishmael. But now that he was told that he will beget a child from Sarah and he understood that this child was to be the heir, he feared lest Ishmael die. Therefore, he said this: [*O that Ishmael might live before Thee*].

Live before Thee. Rashi explained: "Live in reverence of Thee, similar in meaning to *Walk before Me,*[455] which Onkelos renders, 'Worship Me.' " But this is not correct, since He said, *And as for Ishmael, I have heard thee.*[456] Instead, its meaning is that he live and his seed will always exist.

19. 'AVAL' SARAH THY WIFE. This is like the verse, *"Aval" she has no son,*[457] the word *aval* meaning "only." He thus said: "Only

(449) See Hebrew text of Scripture, *ibid.*, 43:10. (450) Esther 7:4. (451) Ecclesiastes 6:6. (452) Numbers 12:2. The words "only" and "alone" (*harak; ach*) are redundant and used for emphasis. (453) Exodus 14:11. The Hebrew words *hamibli ein* are both negatives. Again the redundancy is for special emphasis. (454) Above, 15:4. (455) Verse 1 here. (456) Verse 20 here. If the sense of Abraham's prayer is, as Rashi explained, that Ishmael live in reverence of G-d, how could G-d assure him of that, since, as the Sages express it, "Everything is by hand of Heaven except the fear of Heaven," (Berachoth 33 b) which is in the hands of man to be determined by his free choice. (Mizrachi.) (457) II Kings 4:14.

the son of whom I informed you, your wife Sarah will give birth to, and with him will I establish My covenant forever and with his seed after him; and Ishmael I will bless by making his children numerous, but this will not be because of My covenant with him."

22. AND G-D WENT UP FROM ABRAHAM. This is an expression of respect towards G-d,[458] and we learn from it that the righteous are the Chariot of the Holy One, blessed be He. Thus the language of Rashi. But the saying of the Sages in the Bereshith Rabbah[459] is: "It is the patriarchs[460] that constitute the Chariot." This is an allusion to that which is written: *Thou wilt give truth to Jacob, kindness to Abraham;*[461] *And the Fear of Isaac had been on my side.*[462] The student learned [in the mysteries of the Torah] will understand.

26. IN THE SELFSAME DAY WAS ABRAHAM CIRCUMCISED. Rashi wrote: "*In the selfsame day* when Abraham completed his ninety-ninth year and Ishmael his thirteenth, they were circumcised."

But what reason is there to mention this? Moreover, there is already general agreement with the words of Rabbi Eliezer[463] who said that in the month of Tishri the world was created, and in Tishri the patriarchs were born, with the exception of Isaac who was born on Passover. Now Scripture says that the birth of Isaac will be *at this time in the next year,*[464] and Rashi himself wrote further on in *Seder Vayeira*[465] that the tidings were given on Passover. Consequently, Isaac was born on the next Passover![466]

Instead, the expression, *In the selfsame day,* means that on the very day he was charged with this commandment, he and the men of

(458) Since the *Shechinah* was standing *beside* Abraham, why then is it written, *And He went up*, suggesting that G-d had been *above* him? It is out of respect to G-d that this is so written. (Gur Aryeh.) (459) 47:8. (460) But not the other righteous. (461) Micah 7:20. (462) Further, 31:42. (463) Rosh Hashanah 12 a; also *ibid.*, 27 a. See also *Seder Noach*, Note 148, for fuller discussion of this point. (464) Verse 21 here. (465) Further, 18:10. (466) How then could Rashi say that on this selfsame day Abraham completed his ninety-ninth year, thus making Passover his birthday, when the consensus of opinion is, as Rabbi Eliezer says, that the patriarchs were born in Tishri?

his house – three hundred and eighteen[467] – and all those purchased with his money were circumcised. Scripture thus tells of Abraham's distinction with respect to the fear of G-d, as well as that of all the men of his house, i.e., that they were all zealous, fulfilling their religious duty as promptly as possible.

Now the meaning of the phrase, *was Abraham circumcised and Ishmael his son*, is not that Abraham was circumcised first. Instead, it was Ishmael who was circumcised first, and then all the men of Abraham's house, for it is so written: *And Abraham took Ishmael his son, and all that were born in his house,*[468] and after that it says, *And Abraham was ninety years and nine when he was circumcised.*[469] The reason for this was that Abraham was zealous concerning the commandment to circumcise them first, either doing it himself or perhaps inviting many circumcisers whom he supervised, and then he circumcised himself. Had he performed his circumcision first, he would have been sick or in danger on account of his advanced age, and he would then not have been in a position to concern himself with their circumcision.

(467) Above, 14:14. (468) Verse 23 here. (469) Verse 24 here.

Vayeira

18 1. AND HE APPEARED TO HIM. Rashi comments: "To visit the sick man. Said Rabbi Chama the son of Chanina, 'It was the third day after his circumcision, and the Holy One, blessed be He, came and inquired after him.'[1] *And, lo, three men:*[2] angels who came to him in the form of men. *Three*: one to announce to Sarah that she would bear a son, one to heal Abraham, and one to overthrow Sodom. Raphael who healed Abraham went from there to rescue Lot" for these do not constitute two commissions.[3] This is because the second mission was in another place, and he was commanded thereon after [he had completed his first mission].[4] Perhaps it is because the two missions had rescue as their common goal.[5] "*And they did eat:*[6] they appeared to be eating."

In the book Moreh Nebuchim[7] it is said that this portion of Scripture consists of a general statement followed by a detailed description. Thus Scripture first says that the Eternal appeared to Abraham in the form of prophetic visions, and then explains in

(1) "After him." In our text of Rashi: "after the state of his health." (2) Verse 2 here. (3) "One angel does not carry out two commissions." (Bereshith Rabbah 50:2 and mentioned in Rashi here.) But, continues Ramban, these two missions given to the angel Raphael—healing Abraham and rescuing Lot from Sodom—do not violate the principle. See text. (4) It is as if he was sent on a new mission in another place after he had completed his mission in a different place. For it is clear that the principle of one angel not carrying out two commissions applies only to two simultaneous commissions, as explained in Mizrachi's commentary on Rashi. (5) Since healing and rescue are missions with a common purpose, one angel could be charged with both missions. (6) Verse 8 here. (7) Ibn Tibbon's translation, II, 42: in Al Charizi, Chapter 43.

what manner this vision took place, namely, that he [Abraham] lifted up his eyes in the vision, *and lo, three men stood by him,*[2] *and he said, if now I have found favor in thy eyes.*[8] This is the account of what he said in the prophetic vision to one of them, namely, their chief.

Now if in the vision there appeared to Abraham only men partaking of food, how then does Scripture say, *And the Eternal appeared to him,* as G-d did not appear to him in vision or in thought?[9] Such is not found with respect to all the prophecies. And according to his[10] words, Sarah did not knead cakes, nor did Abraham prepare a bullock, and also, Sarah did not laugh. It was all a vision! If so, this dream came *through a multitude of business,*[11] like dreams of falsehood, for what is the purpose of showing him all this![12] Similarly did the author of the Moreh Nebuchim say[7] in the case of the verse, *And a man wrestled with him,*[13] that it was all a prophetic vision. But if this be the case, I do not know why Jacob limped on his thigh when he awoke! And why did Jacob say, *For I have seen an angel face to face, and my life is preserved?*[14] The prophets did not fear that they might die on account of having experienced prophetic visions. Jacob, moreover, had already seen a greater and more distinguished vision than this since many times, in prophetic visions, he had also seen the Revered Divinity.[15] Now according to this author's opinion, he will find it necessary for the sake of consistency to say similarly in the affair of Lot that the angels did not come to his house, nor did he bake for them *unleavened bread and they did eat.*[16] Rather, it was all a vision! But if Lot could ascend to the height of a prophetic vision, how did the wicked and sinful people of Sodom become prophets? Who told them that men had come into Lot's

(8) Verse 3 here. (9) In other words, why does Scripture begin the chapter with the statement, *And the Eternal appeared to him,* when in the detailed account of the vision it is explained that he saw only angels? (10) The author of the Moreh Nebuchim. (11) See Ecclesiastes 5:2. (12) Since the vision concerning the preparation and the eating of the meal were not relevant to the prophecy of the birth of Isaac. (13) Further, 32:25. The reference deals with Jacob wrestling with the angel. (14) *Ibid.,* Verse 31. (15) *Ibid.,* 28:13. (16) *Ibid.,* 19:3.

house? And if all these [i.e., the actions of the inhabitants of Sodom], were part of prophetic visions, then it follows that the account related in the verses, *And the angels hastened Lot, saying: Arise take thy wife. ...And he said, Escape for thy life... See, I have accepted thee,*[17] as well as the entire chapter is but a vision, and if so, Lot could have remained in Sodom! But the author of the Moreh Nebuchim thinks that the events took place of themselves, but the conversations relating to all matters were in a vision! But such words contradict Scripture. It is forbidden to listen to them, all the more to believe in them!

In truth,[18] wherever Scripture mentions an angel being seen or heard speaking it is in a vision or in a dream for the human senses cannot perceive the angels. But these are not visions of prophecy since he who attains the vision of an angel or the hearing of his speech is not yet a prophet. For the matter is not as the Rabbi[19] pronounced,[20] i.e., that every prophet, Moses our teacher excepted, received his prophecy through the medium of an angel. The Sages have already said[21] concerning Daniel: "They[22] were greater than he for they were prophets and he was not a prophet." His book, likewise, was not grouped together[23] with the books of the prophets since his affair was with the angel Gabriel, even though he appeared to him and spoke with him when he was awake, as it is said in the vision concerning the second Temple: *Yea, while I was speaking in prayer, the man Gabriel,*etc.[24] The vision concerning the ultimate redemption[25] also occurred when

(17) *Ibid.*, Verses 17-21. (18) Ramban partially agrees with Rambam's position. He says that wherever seeing or hearing an angel is mentioned in Scripture, it refers to a vision since the human senses can not perceive an angel. However, wherever Scripture ascribes human appearances to the angels, as in the case of Abraham, then their presence is sensually perceived. Other differences of opinion between Ramban and Rambam regarding prophecy are mentioned further on in the text. (19) Rabbi Moshe ben Maimon (Maimonides). See *Seder Bereshith,* Note 139. (20) Moreh Nebuchim, II, 41. (21) Megillah 3 a. (22) Haggai, Zechariah and Malachi—three prophets who lived at the beginning of the second Temple. (23) The Men of the Great Assembly redacted the books of the Bible. See Baba Bathra 15 a. They placed the book of Daniel in the section of the Writings. (*Ibid.*, 14 b). (24) Daniel 9:1. (25) From the beginning of Chapter 10 there.

Daniel was awake as he walked with his friends beside the Tigris River.[26] Hagar the Egyptian[27] is not included in the group of prophetesses.[28] It is also clear that hers was not a case of the *bath kol* (prophetic echo),[29] as the Rabbi[19] would have it. Scripture, furthermore, sets apart the prophecy of Moses our teacher from that of the patriarchs, as it is said, *And I appeared unto Abraham, unto Isaac, and unto Jacob, by* [the name of] *G-d Almighty*,[30] this name being one of the sacred names for the Creator, and not a designation for an angel. Our Rabbis also taught concerning the difference in the degree of prophecy between Moses and the other prophets, and they said:[31] "What is the difference between Moses and all the prophets? The Rabbis say that all prophets saw through unclear vision. It is to this matter that Scripture refers in saying, *And I have multiplied visions, and by the ministry of the prophets have I used similitudes.*[32] Moses saw through a clear vision. It is to this matter that Scripture refers in saying, *And the similitudes of the Eternal doth he behold*,"[33] as is explained in Vayikra Rabbah[31] and other places. But in no place did the Sages attribute the prophecy of the prophets to an angel.

Do not expose yourself to argument by quoting the verse, *I also am a prophet as thou art; and an angel spoke unto me by the word of the Eternal, saying*,[34] since its meaning is as follows: "I

(26) *Ibid.*, 10:4. As for his friends, see *ibid.*, Verse 7. Tradition specifies that these were Haggai, Zechariah and Malachi. (Megillah 3 a.) (27) She was not a prophetess even though angels appeared to her. (Above, 16: 7.) Ramban thus differs with Rambam, who had said that all prophets received the prophecy through the medium of an angel. Rambam's position is defended as follows: Rambam's intent was not that whenever an angel is seen it is an instance of prophecy. Rather his intent was that whenever prophecy comes to any of the prophets it comes through an angel. However, it is possible that an angel may appear for the purpose of conveying information to one who is not a prophet. This was the case with Daniel and Hagar. (28) In Megillah 14 a, the Rabbis list seven prophetesses who arose in Israel: Sarah, Miriam, Deborah, Hannah, Abigail, Huldah and Esther. Hagar however was not listed among them. See Note 103 further. (29) Guide of the Perplexed, II, 42. See Friedlander's note on *bath kol*, p. 199, n.2. (30) Exodus 6:3. (31) Vayikra Rabbah 1:14. (32) Hosea 12:11. (33) Numbers 12:8. (34) I Kings 13:18. From this you might argue that the prophets themselves attributed their prophecy to an angel. This is not correct, as is explained in the text.

also am a prophet as thou art, and I know that the angel who spoke to me was by word of G-d, this being one of the degrees of prophecy, as the man of G-d said, *For so was it charged me by the word of the Eternal,*[35] and he further said, *For it was said to me by the word of the Eternal.*[36]

Our Rabbis have further stated[37] in the matter of Balaam, who said, *Now, therefore, if it displease thee, I will get me back,*[38] [that is as if Balaam commented]: "I did not go [with the messengers of Balak] until the Holy One, blessed be He, told me, *Rise up, go with them,*[39] and you [i.e., an angel], tell me that I should return. Such is His conduct! Did He not tell Abraham to sacrifice his son, after which the angel of the Eternal called to Abraham, *And he said, Lay not thy hand upon the lad.*[40] He is accustomed to saying something and to have an angel revoke it, etc." Thus the Sages were prompted to say that the prophecy comprising the first charge where G-d is mentioned is not like the second charge of which it is said that it was through an angel, only this was not unusual, for it is customary with the prophets that He would command by a prophecy and revoke the command through an angel since the prophet knew that the revocation was the word of G-d.

In the beginning of Vayikra Rabbah[41] the Sages have said: "*And He called to Moses,*[42] unlike Abraham. Concerning Abraham it is written, *And the angel of the Eternal called unto Abraham a second time out of heaven.*[43] The angel called, and G-d spoke the word, but here with respect to Moses, the Holy One, blessed be He, said, 'It is I Who called, and it is I Who spoke the word.' " That is to say, Abraham did not attain prophecy until he prepared his soul first to perceive an angel, and from that degree he ascended to attain the word of prophecy, but Moses was prepared for prophecy at all times.

(35) *Ibid.*, Verse 9. (36) *Ibid.*, Verse 17. (37) Bamidbar Rabbah 20:13. (38) Numbers 22:34. (39) *Ibid.*, 22:20. (40) Further, 22:12. (41) 1:9. (42) Leviticus 1:1. (43) Further, 22:15.

Thus the Sages were prompted to inform us everywhere that seeing an angel is not prophecy, and those who see angels and speak with them are not included among the prophets, as I have mentioned concerning Daniel. Rather, this is only a vision called "opening of eyes," as in the verse: *And the Eternal opened the eyes of Balaam, and he saw the angel of the Eternal;*[44] similarly: *And Elisha prayed, and said, O Eternal, I pray thee, open his eyes, that he may see.*[45] But where Scripture mentions the angels as men, as is the case in this portion, and the portion concerning Lot – likewise, *And a man wrestled with him,*[13] *And a certain man found him,*[46] in the opinion of our Rabbis[47] – in all these cases there was a special glory created in the angels, called among those who know the mysteries of the Torah "a garment," perceptible to the human vision of such pure persons as the pious and the disciples of the prophets, and I cannot explain any further. And in those places in Scripture where you find the sight of G-d and the speech of an angel, or the sight of an angel and the speech of G-d, as is written concerning Moses at the outset of his prophecy,[48] and in the words of Zechariah,[49] I will yet disclose words of the living G-d in allusions.

Concerning on the matter of the verse, *And they did eat,*[6] the Sages have said:[50] "One course after the other disappeared."[51] The matter of "disappearance" you will understand from the account about Manoah,[52] if you will be worthy to attain it.

Now here is the interpretation of this portion of Scripture. After it says that *In the selfsame day was Abraham circumcised,*[53] Scripture says that G-d appeared to him while he was sick from the circumcision as he was sitting and cooling himself in his tent door on account of the heat of the day which weakened him.

(44) Numbers 22:31. (45) II Kings 6:17. (46) Further, 37:15. (47) According to the Sages the man who wrestled with Jacob was the angel of Esau (Bereshith Rabbah 77:2), and the man who found Joseph was the angel Gabriel (Tanchuma Vayeshev 2). (48) Exodus 3:2. (49) Zechariah 1:14, etc. (50) Bereshith Rabbah 48:16. (51) That is, the angels really did not eat. Rather as soon as a dish of food was brought, it was consumed by fire. (52) Judges 13:19. (53) Above, 17:26.

Scripture mentions this in order to inform us that Abraham had no intention for prophecy. He had neither fallen on his face nor prayed, yet this vision did come to him.

IN THE OAKS OF MAMRE. This is to inform us of the place wherein he was circumcised.

Now this revelation of the *Shechinah* (the Divine Presence) came to Abraham as a mark of distinction and honor, even as it is said in connection with the dedication of the Tabernacle, *And they* [Moses and Aaron] *came out, and blessed the people, and the glory of the Eternal appeared unto all the people,*[54] as it was on account of their effort in fulfilling the commandment of building the Tabernacle that they merited seeing the *Shechinah.* Now the revelation of the *Shechinah* here and there was not at all for the purpose of charging them with some commandment or to impart some communication. Instead, it was a reward for the commandment which had already been performed, and it informed them that their deeds have G-d's approval, even as it says, *As for me, I shall behold Thy face in righteousness; I shall be satisfied, when I awake, with Thy likeness.*[55] Similarly, in connection with Jacob, Scripture says, *And the angels of G-d met him,*[56] and yet we find no communication there, nor is any new matter conveyed. Instead, the verse only informs us that he merited seeing angels of the Supreme One, and thus he knew that his deeds had His approval. And so it was with Abraham: the seeing of the *Shechinah* (the Divine Presence) was both merit [for his having performed the commandment of circumcision] and assurance of G-d's approval.

Similarly did the Sages say[57] of those who passed through the Red Sea and said, *This is my G-d, and I will glorify Him:*[58] "A handmaid saw at the sea what Ezekiel the prophet never saw." This they merited at the time of the great miracle because *they believed in the Eternal, and in Moses his servant.*[59]

(54) Leviticus 9:23. (55) Psalms 17:15. (56) Further, 32:2. (57) Mechilta Shirah 3. (58) Exodus 15:2. (59) *Ibid.*, 14:31.

At times the appearance of the *Shechinah* comes in a moment of anger, as mentioned in the verse: *And the whole congregation bade stone them with stones, when the glory of the Eternal appeared in the tent of meeting unto all the children of Israel.*[60] That was for the protection of His righteous servants and their honor.

Now do not be concerned about the interruption of the portion[61] since the subject is after all connected. It is for this reason that the verse says, *And He appeared to him,* and it does not say, "And the Eternal appeared to Abraham." But in this present chapter Scripture wishes to give an account of the honor that was bestowed upon him [Abraham] at the time he performed the circumcision, and it tells that the *Shechinah* appeared to him and sent him His angels to inform his wife [that she would give birth to a son], and also to save his relative Lot on his account. Abraham had already been informed by the *Shechinah* concerning the birth of a son,[62] and Sarah was now informed by word of the angel who spoke with Abraham in order that Sarah should hear, even as it says, *And Sarah heard.*[63]

This is the intent of the Sages' saying,[64] "G-d came to visit the sick man," meaning that it was not for the purpose of some utterance but as a mark of honor to him.

They have also said,[65] "*An altar of earth thou shalt make unto Me.*[66] Now if any person just built an altar to My name, he is assured that I will appear unto him and bless him.[67] All the more is such assurance given to Abraham who circumcised himself for My name."

(60) Numbers 14:10. (61) Since, as Ramban explains, the appearance of the Eternal to Abraham was in the merit of his having fulfilled the commandment of circumcision, one might ask: Why then are these two events presented in two different sections rather than in one consecutive chapter? It is to this point that Ramban now addresses himself. "Now do not be concerned, etc.," for the events are after all connected. (62) Above, 17:19. (63) Verse 10 here. (64) Baba Metziah 86 b. Also quoted in Rashi above. (65) Bereshith Rabbah 48:4. (66) Exodus 20:24. (67) As Scripture concludes: *I will come unto thee and bless thee.* (Exodus 20:25.)

It is possible that the Sages may have further intended to say [by their remark, "He came to visit the sick man,"] that the vision of the *Shechinah* was a cure for his sickness on account of the circumcision, for so it should be, as it is written, *In the light of the King's countenance is life.*[68]

2. STOOD OVER HIM. The purport thereof is that they were standing opposite Abraham and looking at him, the expression being similar to: *that stood over the reapers;*[69] *the chief officers that stood over the work.*[70] And due to the fact that he [Abraham] was sitting and they were standing and looking at him, the verse says, "over him." This is also the meaning of the expression, *And he saw, and ran to meet them*, for as he saw them standing opposite him and not continuing their journey, he ran to meet them in order to bring them to his house.

The sense of the expression, *From the tent door*, is that Abraham was still sitting there after the vision of the *Shechinah* had departed from him.

It is possible that the expression "over him" refers to the tent, i.e., that they were near it on the side which was not opposite the door, and there they stood and did not approach Abraham, just as in the verse, *encamping 'al' (on) the sea.*[71]

3. 'ADONAY,' IF NOW I HAVE FOUND FAVOR IN THY EYES. We find the word *Adonay* here in the books marked with a *kamatz.*[72] Thus it must be that he called them by the name of their Master, i.e., with the *Aleph Dalet,*[73] as he recognized them

(68) Proverbs 16:15. (69) Ruth 2:6. (70) I Kings 5:30. (71) Exodus 14:9. Meaning "encamping alongside the sea." Here too *alav* means "standing alongside him." (72) A word whose end is voweled with a *kamatz* stands by itself and is not in construct form. This is not the case with a word whose end is voweled with a *patach.* Thus, *Ado-noy* voweled with a *kamatz,* must have reference only to G-d, but *Adonay* voweled with a *patach,* has a "profane" sense and does not refer to G-d. Ramban continues: Since we find the word in this verse written in the books with a *kamatz,* and Abraham was speaking to the angels, it must be because he referred to them by the name of their Master. (73) *Ado-noy.*

to be angels of the Supreme One, even as they are called *elohim* and *eilim*.[74] For this reason he bowed down to the earth to them.

PASS NOT AWAY, I PRAY THEE, FROM THY SERVANT. Abraham spoke to each one of the angels, as is the way of the whole Torah: *Ye shall keep all My statutes... and do them;*[75] *The nakedness of thy father, and the nakedness of thy mother, shalt thou not uncover;*[76] *And when ye reap the harvest of your land, thou shalt not wholly reap the corner of thy field;*[77] *And from thence ye will seek the Eternal thy G-d, and thou shalt find Him, if thou search after Him with all thy heart and with all thy soul.*[78] The greater part of the *Mishneh Torah*[79] is written in this manner. A counter-example to the above is the verse: *Behold, I set before you this day a blessing and a curse.*[80]

Now our Rabbis have said,[81] "Abraham spoke to the chief of the angels."[82] It is also possible that he said to the chief, "*Pass not away, I pray thee*, [in the singular sense], and thou and thy companions who will remain with thee wash your feet," [the verb "wash" being in the plural form].

The correct interpretation appears to me to be that he called them all "lords," and he turned to each individual, saying to the first one: *If now I have found favor in thy eyes, pass not away*, and to the second one he said the same, and the same to the third one. He begged each one individually: *If now I have found favor in thy eyes, pass not away, and, let now a little water be fetched, and* all of ye *wash your feet.*[83] This was by way of ethical conduct and respect out of his great desire to show kindness towards them. Now he recognized them as transients who did not have the desire

(74) See Ramban, Exodus 20:3 and Leviticus 18:27. (75) Leviticus 20:22. According to the author of Kesef Mezukak, the verse here should be [*ibid.* 18:5]: *Ye shall keep My statutes, and Mine ordinances, which if a man do....* Here, as in the succeeding examples, the verse begins with a plural and ends with a singular because the Torah speaks to each person. (76) *Ibid.*, 18:7. (77) *Ibid.*, 19:9. (78) Deuteronomy 4:29. (79) The book of Deuteronomy. See *ibid.*, 17:18, for origin of the expression. (80) *Ibid.*, 11:26. Here He speaks to the whole congregation as a unit and not to each person individually. (81) Bereshith Rabbah 48:9. (82) According to this opinion, the word *Adonay* does not refer to G-d. (83) Verse 4 here.

to lodge there. This is why he asked of them only that a little water be fetched to wash their feet a little from the heat, to give *cold waters to a faint soul,*[84] and that they recline under the tree in the cool of the day without coming into the tent and the tabernacle.

5. FORASMUCH AS YE PASSED BY. Since your path crossed near me, it is not proper that you should not rest a little with me.

So do, as thou hast said. This is an ethical expression indicating that a morsel of bread will be sufficient.[85] Thus the language of Rabbi Abraham ibn Ezra.

It may be that the verse is stating, "So shalt thou do to us, that we recline under the tree and pass immediately as we are messengers, and therefore do not detain us by making us come into the tent or lodge with you."

6. MEAL, FINE FLOUR. The fine flour for the cakes; the meal for the dough used by cooks to place over the pot to absorb the scum. Thus the words of Rashi. And so it is found in Bereshith Rabbah.[86] Now there the Sages explained that there were three measures of meal and three measures of fine flour for each one of the guests. But we do not know why he served so much bread for three men. Perhaps he was aware of how the food disappeared successively,[87] and it was as if he was offering more Burnt-offerings upon the altar, or perhaps because in their honor chiefs of his house dined with them.

By way of the simple meaning [of Scripture, the verse is to be interpreted as follows: *Make ready quickly three measures of meal* to make of them *fine flour.* Thus from the entire three measures of meal, they extracted a bit of fine flour.

(84) Proverbs 25:25. (85) Since it should have stated, "*We* will do as thou hast said," and instead it says, "So *thou* do, as thou hast said," Abraham ibn Ezra takes it to mean "So do, as thou hast spoken: *And I will take a morsel of bread,* and do not trouble thyself for more." (86) 48:13, with changes. (87) See above, Note 51.

7. AND ABRAHAM RAN UNTO THE HERD. The purport thereof is to tell us of his great desire to bestow kindness. This great man had three hundred and eighteen men[88] in his house, each one a swordsman, and he was very old and weakened by his circumcision, yet he went personally to Sarah's tent to urge her in the making of the bread, and afterwards he ran to the place of the herd to chose *a calf, tender and good*, to prepare for his guests, and he did not have all these done by means of one of his servants who stood ready to serve him.

10. I WILL CERTAINLY RETURN UNTO THEE WHEN THE SEASON COMETH AROUND. Rashi comments, "The angel was not announcing that he would return to him, but he was speaking to him as G-d's agent, [meaning that G-d would return]. This is similar to the verse: *And the angel of the Eternal said to her [Hagar], I will multiply thy seed exceedingly.*[89] But he [the angel] has no power to multiply, and he was therefore speaking as G-d's agent. So also here, he spoke as G-d's agent."

Now the Rabbi[90] found it necessary to say so because the Holy One, blessed be He, told Abraham here, *At the set time I will return unto thee.*[91] However, whether it be a reference to the angel or to the Holy One, blessed be He, we do not find it recorded that at the set time He returned. Perhaps a reference to this return is included in the expression, *And the Eternal remembered Sarah, as He had said, and the Eternal did unto Sarah as He had spoken.*[92]

Rabbi Abraham ibn Ezra said that the verse beginning, *And the Eternal said to Abraham,*[93] means that the angel said it in the name of Him Who sent him, and he did return at the set time which he had told him, even though it is not written in Scripture.

(88) Above, 14:14. (89) *Ibid.*, 16:10. (90) Rashi. See *Seder Bereshith,* Note 139. (91) Verse 14 here. The words of the angel, in Verse 10 here, *I will certainly return unto thee.* (92) Further, 21:1. (93) Verse 14 here. It ends with the promise: *At the same time I will return unto thee.*

The correct interpretation appears to me to be that [the expression, *shov ashuv (I will certainly return)*], is akin to the phrase, *liteshuvath hashanah (at the return of the year).*[94] The verse is thus stating: "I will surely bring back to thee a time as this time, that you will be alive and Sarah your wife will have a son." This is similar to what was said to Abraham, *At this set time in the next year.*[95] The word *ashuv* will then be like, *'Veshav' (And) the Eternal your G-d (will bring back) thy captivity and have compassion upon thee and will return and gather thee.*[96]

11. 'BA'IM BAYAMIM' (ADVANCED IN DAYS). In his youthful days a man is called "standing in days," and they are referred to as "his days" because they belong to him, just as in verse *The number of thy days will I fulfill.*[97] But when he gets old and has lived longer than most people of his generation, it is said of him that he is *ba bayamim*, [literally, "came into days"], because it is as if he came into another land, travelling from and arriving in a city each and every day.

IT HAD CEASED TO BE WITH SARAH AFTER THE MANNER OF WOMEN. This is the time of pregnancy, for after menstruation has ceased due to old age, a woman will not become pregnant.

13. I BEING OLD. This is the explanation of Sarah's words, *after I am waxed old.*[98] And G-d's words [that Sarah had said, "I being *old*"], were true, but for the sake of peace He did not reveal what she also said, namely, *My lord being old also,*[98] for [if He were quoting Sarah], He should have said, "I and my lord are old," as Sarah had laughed concerning both of them.

(94) II Samuel 11:1. (95) Above, 17:21. (96) Deuteronomy 30:3. Ramban's intent is as follows: The word *ve'shov* there means "and He will bring back." Here too the word *ashuv* means "I will bring back a time, like the present, in which you will be alive, and in which time, in addition to your being alive, Sarah will have a son." (97) Exodus 23:26. (98) Verse 12 here.

14. IS ANYTHING TOO HARD ('HAYIPALEI') FOR THE ETERNAL? Is anything too hard and improbable for G-d to cause to happen? This expression is similar to the verse, *For all things come of Thee, and of Thine own have we given Thee.*[99] Likewise, *Out of Asher his fat bread,*[100] meaning "Out of Asher will come fat bread."

Onkelos translated: "Is anything hidden?" He interpreted it as similar to the expression, *If there arise a matter hidden ('yipalei') for thee in judgment.*[101] If so, there is a hidden secret here.

Rashi's language: "*Hayipalei*, is anything apart and hidden from Me that I cannot do as I would wish?" Rashi has thus grafted together in [the word *hayipalei*] two separate concepts.[102]

15. AND SARAH DENIED, SAYING. I wonder about the righteous prophetess:[103] How did she deny that which G-d had said to the prophet,[104] and also, why did she not believe in the words of G-d's angels?

The answer appears to me to be that these angels who appeared as men came to Abraham, and he, in his wisdom, recognized them. They announced to him, "*I will certainly return unto thee,*[105] and Sarah shall have a son." *And Sarah heard it*, but she did not know that they were angels of the Supreme One, as was the case with the wife of Manoah.[106] It is even possible that she did not see them at all. Therefore she laughed within herself in derision, just [as the word "laugh" is used in the verse]: *He that sitteth in heaven laugheth, the Eternal hath them in derision.*[107] For joyous laughter is [expressed in Hebrew as originating] in the mouth – *Then was our mouth filled with laughter*[108] – but laughter

(99) I Chronicles 29:14. Here the word "come" is not found in the Hebrew but is added to complete the thought. Likewise, Ramban suggests, in our own verse here, the expression "to cause to happen" is to be added: "Is anything too hard for G-d to cause to happen?" (100) Further, 49:20. (101) Deuteronomy 17:8. (102) Hidden and apart. (103) See above, Note 28, that Sarah was regarded as a prophetess. (104) Abraham. In Megillah 14 a, Rashi quotes the Hilchoth Gedoloth listing the forty-eight prophets who arose in Israel, and the three patriarchs are listed among them. (105) Verse 10 here. (106) Judges 13:6. (107) Psalms 2:4. (108) *Ibid.*, 126:2.

originating in the heart is not spoken of as joyous. Now the Holy One, blessed be He, accused her before Abraham as to why the matter appeared to her to be impossible. It was fitting for her to believe, or she should have said, "Amen, G-d do so!" Now Abraham said to her, "Why did you laugh? Is anything too hard for the Eternal?" He did not explain to her that G-d had revealed her secret to him. And she, because of Abraham's fear of G-d, denied it for she thought that Abraham had said so through recognition of the expressions on her face or because she had kept quiet and gave no expression of praise and thanksgiving or joy. And he said to her, *Nay, but thou didst laugh.* Then she understood that it was told to him in a prophecy, and so she remained quiet and did not answer a word.

It is proper that we also say that Abraham had not revealed to her what had originally been told to him: *Indeed, Sarah, thy wife shall bear thee a son.*[109] Perhaps he waited until G-d would send her the announcement on the following day for he knew *that the Eternal G-d will do nothing, but He revealed His counsel unto His servants the prophets.*[110] It may be that due to his great diligence in fulfilling commandments, he was occupied with his circumcision and the circumcision of the many people in his house. Afterward, on account of his weakness, he sat at the doorway of the tent, and the angels came before he had told her anything.

17. AND THE ETERNAL SAID. I.e., to the host of heaven standing by Him,[111] or to the angel messengers.

It is possible that the word *amar* (He said) refers to thought, meaning that He thought He should not keep it hidden from Abraham on account of these reasons. Similarly: *I 'said,' in the noontide of my days I shall go;*[112] *And he 'said' to slay David.*[113] Likewise all expressions of speaking within the heart refer to thought.[114]

(109) Above, 17:19. (110) Amos 3:7. (111) See I Kings 22:19. (112) Isaiah 38:10. The word "said" here means "thought." (113) II Samuel 21:16. Here too the word "said" means "thought." (114) E.g., *And Esau said in his heart,* further, 27:41. See Ramban there.

18. AND ABRAHAM SHALL SURELY BECOME. A Midrash Agadah comments: *The memory of the righteous shall be for a blessing.*[115] Since He mentioned Abraham, He blessed him. The simple meaning of the verse though is, "Shall I conceal it from him since he is so beloved by Me to become a mighty nation?" Thus the language of Rashi.

The correct interpretation is that G-d, blessed be He, spoke of the honor of Abraham, saying: "Behold, he is destined to become a great and mighty nation, and his memory will be a blessing among his seed and all nations of the earth. Therefore, I shall not conceal it from him for the future generations will say, "How could He hide it from him?' or, 'How could the righteous one[116] be so callous about his close neighbors and have no mercy on them, not praying at all in their behalf, and that which was known to him, [i.e., that the cities will be destroyed], was good and pleasing!' For I know that he recognizes and is cognizant that I the Eternal *loveth righteousness and justice,*[117] that is to say, that I do justice only with righteousness, and therefore *he will command his children and his household after him*[118] to follow in his path. Now if it is possible in keeping with righteousness and justice to free the cities from destruction, he will pray before Me to let them go, and it will be well and good. And if they are completely guilty, he too will want their judgment. Therefore, it is proper that he enter *in the council of G-d.*"[119]

19. FOR I HAVE KNOWN HIM ('YEDATIV'), TO THE END ('LEMA'AN') THAT HE MAY COMMAND HIS CHILDREN. Rashi comments: "*For I have known him*, as the Targum takes it, is an expression denoting affection, just as *A kinsman ('moda') of her husband's;*[120] *And I know thee.*[121] Still the main connotation of all these expressions is that of knowing, for he who holds a person in affection and draws him to himself knows him well and is

(115) Proverbs 10:7. (116) Abraham. (117) Psalms 33:5. (118) Verse 19 here. (119) Jeremiah 23:18. (120) Ruth 2:1. (121) Exodus 33:17.

familiar with him. But if you explain it as the Targum does – i.e., "I know that he will command his children" – then the word *lema'an* (to the end) does not fit into the sense." [122]

It is possible that the word *yedativ* means "I have raised him and elevated him so that he shall command his children after him to do that which is right before Me, and therefore I will make him a great and mighty nation so that he should serve Me. In a similar sense are the verses: *I know thee ('yedaticha') by name;* [123] *What is man, that Thou knowest him?* [124] Or the verse may be stating, I know that he will command, [125] and in a similar sense is the verse, *So that thine ox and thine ass may have rest (lema'an yanuach),* [126] meaning that he may have rest.

The correct interpretation appears to me to be that the word *yedativ* literally means "knowing." He is thus alluding that G-d's knowledge, which is synonymous with His Providence in the lower world, is to guard the species, and even the children of men are subject despite it to the circumstantial evil occurrences until the time of their visitation comes. But as regards His pious, He directs His Providence to know each one individually so that His watch constantly attaches to him, His knowledge and remembrance of him never departs, as it says: *He withdraweth not His eyes from the righteous.* [127] There are many verses on this theme, as it is written, *Behold, the eye of the Eternal is toward them that fear Him,* [128] and other verses besides.

(122) Our Rashi has a different text. See notes in my Hebrew commentary, p. 110. See also Note 125 further. (123) Exodus 33:12. The sense would thus be: "I have made thee great in name." (124) Psalms 144:3. The sense here then would be: "What is man before Thee that Thou hast given him greatness?" (125) Ramban thus differs with Rashi, who said that if you take the sense of the verse to be, "I know of him that he will command," then the word *lema'an* does not fit the context. Ramban proceeds to show from Exodus 23:12 that the words *lema'an yanuach* mean *she'yanuach* (that he may rest); here likewise, *lema'an asher yetzaveh* means *she'yetzaveh* (that he will command). Thus, the word *lema'an* is seen to fit into the context. (126) Exodus 23:12. See Note above. (127) Job 36:7. (128) Psalms 33:18. See Moreh Nebuchim III, 51, where Rambam's theory on Divine Providence is seen to be similar to that which Ramban expresses here.

20. AND THE ETERNAL SAID, THE CRY OF SODOM AND GOMORRAH. Rashi comments: *"And the Eternal said* to Abraham, thus doing what He had said, i.e., that He would not conceal the matter from him,"

And Rabbi Abraham ibn Ezra said that the verse, *And the men turned from there,*[129] was inserted in the middle of the account[130] in order to let us know that at the time the angels arrived in Sodom, then G-d said to Abraham: *The cry of Sodom and Gomorrah is great.*

The opinion of all commentators is likewise that G-d was speaking with Abraham. Now according to this, the correct interpretation of the verse, *And the men turned from there,*[129] is that when G-d said to Abraham after the men journeyed from him, *The cry of Sodom and Gomorrah is great,* Abraham stood in prayer and supplication before Him to forgive them and to give him permission to speak. And he prolonged his prayer until the men came to Sodom, and then Abraham drew near and said, *Wilt Thou also sweep away the righteous with the wicked?*[131] Or the explanation may be that Scripture itself returns to clarify the expression, *Abraham stood yet before the Eternal,*[132] as meaning that Abraham drew near and said, *Wilt Thou also sweep away the righteous with the wicked?* Thus he prolonged his supplication before Him, saying each time, "Let not the anger of the Eternal blaze,"[133] and directing the intent of his mind each time towards prophecy until he heard an answer to his words direct from the Holy One, blessed be He. They continued in this manner the entire day [until, as the verse says], *the Eternal finished speaking with Abraham,*[134] and the two angels came to Sodom.

(129) Verse 22 here. (130) According to Ibn Ezra, Verse 22, which states, *And the men turned from there and went toward Sodom, and Abraham stood yet before the Eternal,* actually took place before our present verse for it was after the angels had walked toward Sodom that G-d said to Abraham, *The cry of Sodom and Gomorrah...* However, Verse 22 was entered later in the account in order to let us know the time of G-d's word to Abraham – *the cry of Sodom and Gomorrah,* etc. – was when they came to Sodom. (131) Verse 23 here. (132) Verse 22 here. According to this interpretation, Abraham did not pray before he began saying, *Wilt Thou also sweep away.* (133) See Exodus 32:22. (134) Verse 33 here.

THE CRY OF SODOM AND GOMORRAH. This is the cry of the oppressed, crying out and begging for help from the arm of their wickedness. It would have been proper for Scripture to say, "*The cry of Sodom and Gomorrah* I heard *because it is great*," or "The cry of Sodom and Gomorrah is great and their sin is very heavy." But the purport of the verse is to state that "I will go down and see the cry of Sodom and Gomorrah and their sin which have become very great. If they have all sinned, I will bring the law to bear down on them, and if not, I will know who are the sinners."

Concerning the matter of "going down and seeing," Rashi said by way of *derash:* [135] "This teaches that judges are not to give decisions in cases involving capital punishment except after having carefully looked into the matter."

According to the simple meaning of Scripture, the explanation is as follows: Since the Holy One, blessed be He, wished to reveal to Abraham the matter of Sodom and to inform him that there was none among them who did good, He said to him "Because it is great, the cry of Sodom and Gomorrah will I go down to see, meaning I have come to judge. If they have sinned, I will make an end of them, and if not, I shall know what I shall do to them: *Then will I visit their transgression with the rod, and their iniquity with strokes.*" [136] He thus informed him that their judgment was not yet complete for now He will visit their sin and judge them. This is like the verse: *The Eternal looketh from heaven upon the children of men, to see if there were any man of understanding, that did seek after G-d. They are all corrupt; they are together become impure.* [137]

Now Rabbi Abraham ibn Ezra said concerning this [138] ["going down and seeing"] a mystery [i.e., a mysterious explanation], pleasing himself with foreign offspring. [139] I shall now intimate to

(135) The homiletical interpretation of Scripture. (136) Psalms 89:33. (137) *Ibid.*, 14:2-3. (138) Ibn Ezra's comment is found in Verse 21 here. (139) See Isaiah 2:6. Ramban says that "the mystery" suggested here by Ibn Ezra as an explanation of the verse comes to him from the philosophers who please themselves with theories which are "the offspring of aliens." Ibn Ezra's "mystery" explanation is that G-d's knowledge of earthly matters is general, rather than detailed. Ramban rejects this concept as "foreign" to the Torah.

you the opinion of those who received the truth. Our Rabbis have expositited[140] from the verse, *For behold, the Eternal cometh forth out of His place, and will come down, and tread upon the high places of the earth:*[141] "He cometh forth and goeth from attribute to attribute; He cometh forth from the attribute of mercy, and goeth to the attribute of justice." We interpret this matter similarly. *And the Eternal said* in His heart, *"The cry of Sodom and Gomorrah, because it is great, I will go down* from the attribute of mercy to the attribute of justice, *and I will see* in mercy *if they have done according to the cry of it which is come unto Me* through the attribute of justice, and if so, *punishment; and if not, I will know* and I will show mercy," just as in the verse, *And G-d knew.*[142] Now after Scripture tells of the knowledge of the Most High, it returns to the first matter and relates the story of how the men who glanced towards Sodom with the intention of going there and whom Abraham sent away arrived there. And Abraham, from the moment they left him until they arrived there, still stood before the Eternal for He called him and told him that the angels were those messengers who would destroy the place, as He had said. It was not necessary for Scripture to explain when Abraham stood before Him for from the moment He said, *Shall I conceal it from Abraham,*[143] it is known that He told him.

23. AND ABRAHAM DREW NEAR AND SAID, WILT THOU ALSO SWEEP AWAY THE RIGHTEOUS WITH THE WICKED? The anger[144] of the Holy One, blessed be He, is His attribute of justice. Now Abraham thought that this would sweep away the righteous with the wicked, not knowing of G-d's thoughts in which He thought of them with His mercies, as I have explained.[145]

(140) Yerushalmi Ta'anith II, 1. (141) Micah 1:3. (142) Exodus 2:25. He knew of the suffering of the children of Israel and directed His mercy upon them. Here, likewise, Ramban teaches that the word *eida'ah* (I will know) bespeaks Divine mercy. (143) Verse 17 here. (144) Ramban understood the verse as Onkelos rendered it, namely, that the word *ha'aph* does not mean "shall also", but it means "the anger." The verse reads: "shall the anger of G-d sweep away." See Rashi. (145) At the end of Verse 20 here.

Therefore, Abraham said that it is proper and good that He should forgive the entire place because of the fifty righteous inhabitants, but it is inconceivable even according to the Divine attribute of Justice *to slay the righteous with the wicked,*[146] for if so *the righteous will be as the wicked,* and they will say, *It is vain to serve G-d.*[147] And all the more is this inconceivable according to the Divine attribute of Mercy since He is *the Judge of all the earth,*[144] and He does justice,[148] even as it is said, *And the Eternal of hosts is exalted through justice,*[149] and we say in our prayers, "The King of judgment."[150] This is the significance of the double use of the expression, *It is unworthy of Thee.*[151] And the Holy One, blessed be He, conceded that He would forgive the entire place for the sake of the fifty righteous, for He will conduct Himself towards them with the attribute of Mercy.

What informs you of all this[152] is the fact *vayomer hashem* (And the Eternal said)[153] is written with the Tetragrammaton, and all references by Abraham to the Divine Name are written *Ado-noy.*[154] This has now been clarified.

24. FIFTY RIGHTEOUS. Rashi wrote: "Ten righteous men for each city. *Wilt thou destroy on account of the five.*[155] Nine for each city, and You, the All-Righteous One of the Universe, will be counted with them [to make up the original number of ten]. *Perhaps there shall be found there forty.*[156] Then let four cities be saved. So, too, thirty will save three of them, twenty will save two of them, and ten will save one of them. And he did not plead for less than ten since in the generation of the flood there were eight

(146) Verse 25 here. (147) Malachi 3:14. (148) With righteousness. (Tur quoting and interpreting Ramban.) (149) Isaiah 5:16. (150) Literally, "the king, the Justice," implying that the King is Justice. (See my Hebrew commentary, p. 112.) This prayer is said on the ten days from Rosh Hashanah to Yom Kippur. (Berachoth 12 b.) (151) In Verse 24 here. One for the attribute of justice, and one for mercy, as explained above. (152) That Abraham thought that they would be judged only by Divine justice, and G-d told him that they would be judged with Divine mercy. (153) Verse 26 here. (154) The Tetragrammaton signifies Divine mercy, while the Name beginning with *Aleph Dalet* signifies Divine justice. (155) Verse 28 here. (156) Verse 29 here.

righteous people,[157] and they could not save their generation. For nine, in association with G-d, he had already pleaded but found no acceptance." All these are the words of the Rabbi, of blessed memory.

But I wonder: If so, what is this prayer and supplication which he pleads each and every time, saying, *oh let not the Lord be angry;*[158] *Behold, now, I have taken upon me to speak?*[159] It is proper that forty should save four cities, and thirty and twenty should save in proportion, just as fifty would save five! Similarly, concerning that which Rashi said, "for nine in association with G-d he had already pleaded but found no acceptance," it may be asked: When he pleaded about forty-five, [i.e., to save all five cities by having nine righteous men for each city] in association [with G-d to make up ten], and he did not find forty-five, but perhaps he might have found there nine![160] Now it would seem that the intention of the Rabbi[161] is that many righteous people can effect a proportionately greater salvation than a few righteous people can, just as the Sages have said:[162] "A few who fulfill the commandments of the Torah cannot compare with the many who fulfill the commandments of the Torah." And thus,[163] the Holy One, blessed be He, having conceded that forty-five righteous men in association with the All-Righteous One of the Universe would save all the five cities just as if there were the entire fifty, it follows that if forty could save four cities — in association with the Righteous One, praised be He — they would also save with even thirty and twenty, since He already conceded this association. [Thus, thirty-six would save four, twenty-seven three, eighteen two, and nine one]. And in case you say that He conceded only

(157) Noah, his three sons, and their wives. (Rashi.) (158) Verse 30 here. (159) Verse 31 here. (160) Why then did Abraham not plead for nine men who, in association with G-d, would be ten, and thus save one city, for the principle of using G-d as a tenth was not declared invalid; rather, it was previously inapplicable since there were not forty-five righteous inhabitants. (161) Rashi. (162) Sifra, Leviticus 26:8. The wording of the quotations used here is that of Rashi in his commentary to the Torah. (*Ibid.*) (163) "And thus." The Tur quoting Ramban writes, "Perhaps."

the case of forty-five because they are many, and perhaps He might not concede the principle of association with the few, as we have said, the refutation is that it is proper for the righteousness of G-d to associate even with the few and save [as many of the cities as possible] since He had conceded the principle of association, for He would not distinguish between the many and the few.[164] This is the opinion of the Rabbi.[161]

But the way of the simple meaning of the verses is smooth.[165] First Abraham said fifty in order to give a perfect number of ten for each city, and then he decreased the number as much as possible, and each time he thought to save all five cities. And I do not know who brought the Rabbi[161] to that which he said.

26. WITHIN THE CITY. Rabbi Abraham ibn Ezra explained that [these men for whose sake the cities were to be saved] fear G-d publicly. In a similar sense is the verse: *Run ye to and fro through the streets of Jerusalem.*[166]

The correct interpretation appears to me to be that Abraham said, *within the city,* meaning that even if they are strangers therein, it is fitting that they save it. He said this on account of Lot, and he thought that perhaps there are others there.

28. I WILL NOT DESTROY IT IF I FIND THERE. He assured him that He would not destroy it if that number of righteous men will be found there. And He did not tell him, "Know that there is not such a number there as you said," since their trial had not been completed, just as He said, *I will go down now, and see.*[167]

(164) In other words, having admitted the principle of association in the case of forty-five, there could not be any difference between a larger and smaller group of righteous men with respect to the principle of association. Hence Abraham did not have to ask for nine, for in association with G-d there would be ten, and one city would be saved. But without the principle of association there might be a difference between a larger and smaller group. Hence Abraham had to ask for forty, thirty, twenty and ten. All this is to satisfactorily explain the interpretation of Rashi. Ramban's own position is made clear further in the text. (165) See Proverbs 15:19. (166) Jeremiah 5:1. *If ye can find a man, if there be any that doeth justly.* (167) Verse 21 here.

Now Abraham did not know what would be done to them. Therefore, he rose early in the morning and looked towards Sodom,[168] and upon seeing that they were destroyed, he knew that the required number of righteous men had not been there.

19 2. BEHOLD NOW, MY LORDS. Rashi comments: "Behold now you are my lords since you have passed by me" The correct interpretation is that it is an expression of pleadings: "My lords, behold now your servant's house; turn aside, I pray you, to me" The word *suru* (turn aside) is as in the expressions: *Turn aside ('surah'), sit down here;*[169] *Turn in ('surah'), my lord, turn in to me; fear not.*[170]

AND YE SHALL RISE UP EARLY, AND GO ON YOUR WAY. The purport of that was to tell them that they should not tarry in the city after the morning for Lot knew the nature of the men of the city and of their wickedness, but he thought, *In the morning light they do it.*[171] It may be that he saw them as transients who would not tarry in the city, and so he said, *And ye shall rise up early and go on your way* if you desire.

3. AND HE URGED THEM GREATLY. His urging them was meritorious on the part of Lot, and he indeed had a sincere desire to welcome wayfarers. They, however, at first refused in order to increase his merit, and therefore they finally listened to him; but originally they did not want to come into his house as he was not a perfectly righteous man. But our Rabbis have said [in order to explain their original refusal]:[172] "One may decline an offer from an inferior person, but not from a superior person."[173] If so, their declining his offer at first was merely an act of ethical conduct.

(168) Further, 19:27-28. (169) Ruth 4:1. (170) Judges 4:18. (171) Micah 2:1. But at night they would not know of them. (Tur.) (172) Baba Metzia 87 a. (173) Hence, to Abraham the angels immediately said, *So do, as thou hast said,* (above, 18:5), but with Lot, they at first declined.

5. AND WE SHALL KNOW THEM. Their intention was to stop people from coming among them, as our Rabbis have said,[174] for they thought that because of the excellence of their land, which was *as the garden of the Eternal,*[175] many will come there, and they despised charity. Lot, however, came to them with his riches and wealth [and was given permission to live in Sodom because] he either asked permission of them, or that they accepted him in honor of Abraham.

Now Scripture testifies that this was the intent of the people of Sodom, as it is said, *Behold, this was the iniquity of thy sister Sodom: pride, fullness of bread, and careless ease was in her and in her daughters; neither did she strengthen the hand of the poor and needy.*[176] The verse stating, *And the men of Sodom were wicked and sinners against the Eternal exceedingly,*[177] really means that they continued provoking and rebelling against Him with their ease and the oppression of the poor. It is this thought which Scripture expresses by saying, *And they were haughty, and committed abomination before Me; therefore I removed them when I saw it.*[178]

In the opinion of our Rabbis,[179] all evil practices[180] were rampant among them. Yet their fate was sealed because of this sin – i.e., they did not strengthen the hand of the poor and needy – since this sin represented their usual behavior more than any other. Besides, since all peoples act righteously towards their friends and their poor, there was none among all the nations who matched Sodom in cruelty.

Know that the judgment of Sodom was due to the superiority of the Land of Israel since Sodom is part of *the inheritance of the Eternal,*[181] and it does not suffer men of abominations. And just as it later vomited out a whole nation on account of their abominations,[182] so it now anticipated and saw that this entire

(174) Sanhedrin 109 a. (175) Above, 13:10. (176) Ezekiel 16:49. (177) Above, 13:13. This would seem to indicate that they sinned only against G-d but not against their fellow man. (178) Ezekiel 16:50. (179) Sanhedrin 109 a. (180) Such as blasphemy, bloodshed, etc. (*Ibid.*) (181) II Samuel 20:19. (182) See Leviticus 18:25.

people behaved worse than all nations towards Heaven and mankind. It thus laid waste heaven and earth for them, and the land was destroyed forever, never to be restored, since they became haughty on account of the goodness that was bestowed on them. The Holy One, blessed be He, thus made Sodom *a token against the rebellious children,*[183] that is, against the children of Israel who were destined to inherit it, even as He warned them: *The whole land thereof is brimstone, and salt, and a burning... like the overthrow of Sodom and Gomorrah, Admah and Zeboiim, which the Eternal overthrew in His anger, and in His wrath.*[184] For there have been among nations those who were evil and exceedingly sinful, and yet He did not do to them as He did to Sodom. However it was all on account of the superiority of this land for there is the *temple of the Eternal.*[185] I plan to explain this in *Seder Achrei Moth,*[186] if He Who taketh life and giveth life will sustain me in life.

8. LET ME, I PRAY YOU, BRING THEM OUT UNTO YOU. From the praise of this man Lot we have come to his disgrace: he made every effort on behalf of his guests in order to save them because they came under the shadow of his roof, but he is ready to appease the men of the city by abandoning his daughters to prostitution! This bespeaks nothing but an evil heart for it shows that the matter of prostitution of women was not repugnant to him, and that in his opinion he would not be doing such great injustice to his daughters. It is for this reason that our Rabbis have said,[187] "It is the custom of the world that a man fights to the death for the honor of his daughters and his wife, to slay or to be slain, but this man hands over his daughters for dishonor. Said the Holy One, blessed be He, to him, 'It is for yourself that you keep them.' "[188]

Now Lot was fearful [for the welfare of the angels] as he thought that they were men, but when they smote the men of the

(183) Numbers 17:25. (184) Deuteronomy 29:22. (185) Jeremiah 7:4. (186) Leviticus 18:24. (187) Tanchuma Vayeira 12. (188) See further, Verses 30-36.

city with blindness and they said to him, *For we will destroy this place... and the Eternal hath sent us,*[189] then he recognized them and believed in doing whatever they commanded him.

Know and understand that the matter of the concubine of Gibeah,[190] even though it resembles this affair, does not attain the degree of evil of the inhabitants of Sodom. Those wicked ones of Gibeah had no intention of stopping people from coming among them. Rather, they were steeped in immorality and desired sexual relations with the wayfarer, and when he brought his concubine out to them, they were satisfied with her.[191] The old man [who had invited the wayfarer to his house] and who said to the men of Gibeah, *Behold, here is my daughter, a virgin, and his concubine; I will bring them out now... and do with them what seemeth good unto you,*[192] knew that they would not want his daughter and that they would not harm her. This was why they refused to listen to him. And when he finally turned his concubine alone outdoors to them, they ceased molesting him. Now the master of the house, as well as the guest, both wanted to save the man through his concubine, as a concubine does not have the status of a man's wife. Besides, she had already played the harlot against him.[193] In that breach, too, not all of the men of the city were involved as they were in Sodom, concerning which it is said, *Both young and old, all the people from every quarter,*[194] while of Gibeah it is said, *Behold, the men of the city, certain base fellows*[195] – only some of them, those who were the rulers and strong men of the city, even as the man said in relating the incident, *And the masters of Gibeah*[196] *rose against me.*[197] This was why the others did not protest against them. *Now the chiefs of all the people, of all the tribes of Israel*[198] wanted to erect a great guard in the matter of

(189) Verse 13 here. (190) Judges, Chapter 19. Ramban digresses here to explain the crime of Gibeah, which bears a certain resemblance to that of Sodom, and consequently explains also the civil war between the tribe of Benjamin and the rest of Israel. Thus Chapters 19 and 20 in the book of Judges are here explained by Ramban. (191) *Ibid.*, Verse 25. (192) *Ibid.*, Verse 24. (193) *Ibid.*, Verse 2. (194) Verse 4 here. (195) Judges 19:22. (196) "Masters of Gibeah." This is obviously the way Ramban understood the verse since the Hebrew had "*ba'alei* [rather than *anshei*] Gibeah." The J.P.S. translation, however, renders it: *And the men of Gibeah rose against me*. (197) Judges 20:5. (198) *Ibid.*, Verse 2.

immorality by slaying them, as it is said, *Now therefore deliver up the men, the base fellows that are in Gibeah, that we may put them to death.*[199] It is clear that according to the law of the Torah they were not guilty of the death-penalty as they had done no deed exclusive of the torture of the concubine – harlot. They did not intend her death, nor did she die at their hands for *they let her go at the approach of dawn,*[200] and she walked from them to her master's house and after that she died,[201] weakened perhaps by her numerous violations, and chilled while lying at the door until it was light, and there she died. But because the men of Gibeah had wanted to do a shameful deed just as the men of Sodom, the tribes saw fit "to make a fence unto the Torah" so that this should never again happen or be contemplated in Israel, even as they said, *And that we may put away evil from Israel.*[202] This judgment has its origin in the principle which our Rabbis have stated:[203] "The Court may administer stripes and the death penalty which are not authorized by the Torah. However, they may not do this [with the intent of instituting a law which] transgresses the words of the Torah but only for the purpose of erecting a fence around the Torah."[204] The tribe of Benjamin, however, did not consent to this[205] as they were not guilty of the death-penalty for violating the concubine. Perhaps the Benjamites were also provoked by the fact that the tribes did not communicate with them first and reached a consensus without asking for their opinion.

In my opinion, this [failure to consult Benjamin] caused Israel's punishment which resulted in their being routed at first since the war was done not in accordance with the law. The obligation of making "the fence"[206] lay upon the tribe of Benjamin, and not upon them, as it is the tribe itself that is obligated to judge its constituents.[207]

(199) *Ibid.*, Verse 13. (200) *Ibid.*, 19:25. (201) *Ibid.*, Verse 26. (202) *Ibid.*, 20:13. (203) Yebamoth 90 b. (204) That is, as a temporary measure which the times require, they may act accordingly. See Rashi Sanhedrin 46 a, that this is its meaning. (205) That the men of Gibeah, involved in the affair, should be put to death. (206) To punish the men of Gibeah as an extraordinary measure. (207) Deuteronomy 16:18. Sanhedrin 16 b: "It is commandatory upon the tribe to judge the people of the tribe."

Thus both parties were deserving of punishment. Benjamin sinned by not bothering to punish the wicked ones or even rebuke them. Israel sinned by making war not in accordance with the law, *and they asked not counsel at the mouth of the Eternal*[208] on this matter. Instead they questioned G-d and said, *Who shall go up for us first to battle against the children of Benjamin?*[209] They themselves had decided to do battle in any case. Similarly, they did not inquire concerning the outcome of the battle, "If Thou wilt give them into my hand," since they relied on their man-power which was exceedingly great as they were now more than ten times [as numerous as the Benjamites].[210] All they asked was, *Who shall go up for us first,*[209] this being like casting lots among them. Perhaps each tribe was saying, "I will not go up first," or each tribe was saying, "I will be first."[211] And the Holy One, blessed be He, answered in accordance with their question: *Judah first,*[209] meaning Judah is always first, *For He hath chosen Judah to be prince.*[212] This was why He did not say, "Judah shall go up," as in other places,[213] for He did not give them permission. However, He did not stop them, and neither did he tell them, *Go not up, neither fight,*[214] because of the merited punishment of the Benjamites. Thus did G-d walk with both of them by chance, leaving them to natural circumstances. Accordingly, the Benjamites, who were valiant men and whose cities were well fortified, destroyed the Israelites who had "made flesh their arm of strength."[215] But now the Benjamites compounded their merited punishment. It would have been sufficient for them to drive the Israelites away from Gibeah. Instead, they killed them, *seeking to destroy them by a perpetual hatred,*[216] and they slew the mighty number of twenty-two

(208) Joshua 9:14. (209) Judges 20:18. (210) The Israelites mustered four hundred thousand (*ibid.*, Verse 17) while the Benjamites numbered twenty-six thousand (*ibid.*, Verse 15). (211) A similar case occurred when the Israelites stood before the Red Sea. There is a difference of opinion among the Rabbis as to their attitude. According to one authority each tribe said, "I will not go into the sea first [to escape the Egyptians]," while another authority maintains that each tribe was saying, "I will go first." (212) I Chronicles 28:4. (213) As in Judges 1:2. (214) Deuteronomy 1:42. (215) See Jeremiah 17:5. (216) Ezekiel 25:15.

thousand of their people.[217] Now when the Israelites suffered such a great defeat they became aware of their error, namely, that they did battle with their brethren without receiving Divine permission and engaged in a battle which was not in accordance with the law of the Torah. Therefore, on the second day they asked, *shall I again draw nigh to battle against the children of Benjamin my brother?*[218] Now they mentioned the brotherhood among them, asking whether He forbids them to do battle. But now on the second day, G-d permitted them, saying, *Go up against him,*[218] as it was now permissible for them to avenge the spilled blood of their brethren.[219] However, they did not ask whether they will be victorious because they were still relying upon their superior numbers to bring victory under all circumstances. But since G-d had explained to them only that the battle was permissible to them, and since their first sin had not yet been atoned for, there fell among them also on the second day eighteen thousand.[220] On the third day they decreed a fast, and they fasted *and they wept... before the Eternal,*[221] and they offered burnt-offerings to atone for their sinful thoughts[222] through which they relied upon the strength of their arm. They also offered peace-offerings,[221] which were Thanksgiving peace-offerings, since they considered themselves as if they had all escaped from the sword of Benjamin. This indeed is the law of all who are delivered from danger: they are to bring a thanks-offering, just as it is said, *And let them offer the sacrifices of thanksgiving, and declare His works with singing,*[223] and it is further written, *And now shall my head be lifted up above mine enemies round about me; and I will offer in His tabernacle sacrifices with trumpet-sound; I will sing, yea, I will sing praises unto the Eternal.*[224]

(217) Judges 20:21. (218) *Ibid.*, Verse 23. (219) Spilled needlessly. All the Benjamites had to do on the first day of battle was to drive the Israelites from Gibeah, as explained above. Instead, they killed twenty-two thousand of them. Hence, on the second day, it became "permissible" for the Israelites to attempt to avenge their death. (220) Judges 20:25. (221) *Ibid.*, Verse 26. (222) *A Burnt-offering is brought only for sinful thought.* (Vayikra Rabbah 7:3.) (223) Psalms 107:22. (224) *Ibid.*, 27:6.

Now the number of dead among the Israelites during the two days was forty thousand, and in the end twenty-five thousand[225] of Benjamin's warriors fell, besides those that were put to the sword *from the whole city and all that they found.*[226] It is possible that among the men, women and children they totalled fifteen thousand additional casualties, thus making the punishment of the two groups equal.

And how significant are the words of our Rabbis[227] who said that the anger of G-d at that time was due to the idol of Micah![228] "Said the Holy One, blessed be He, 'Concerning My honor, which was violated by those guilty of death and those who raised their hand against the principle of religion, namely, the unity of G-d, you did not protest; but for the honor of a mortal you did protest, to an extent which exceeded the limits of justice!"

Therefore He confounded the counsel of the two groups and made their hearts stubborn, *and they remembered not the brotherly covenant.*[229] But after the affair they had regrets, just as it is said, *And the people came to Beth-el and sat there till evening before G-d, and lifted up their voice, and wept bitterly. And they said: O Eternal, G-d of Israel, why is this come to pass in Israel, that there should be today one tribe missing from Israel?*[230] For now they realized their mistakes and punishment.

We have thus incidentally explained a concealed matter which is not clear [with a cursory reading of the text], and we have mentioned the cause thereof.

9. AND THEY PRESSED HARD ('VAYIFTZERU') UPON THE MAN, EVEN LOT. I have found this word *vayiftzeru* only in connection with words of pleading. If so, we will explain its usage here as follows: the men of Sodom begged him [Lot] exceedingly to open the door for them, and when he refused to do so, they approached in order to break it. It may be that he stood in front

(225) Judges 20:35. (226) *Ibid.*, Verse 48. (227) Sanhedrin 103 b. (228) See Judges, Chapter 17. (229) Amos 1:9. (230) Judges 21:2-3.

of the door, not letting them come near him, and they begged him to turn aside as they did not want to harm him. This is the meaning of their saying, *Stand back,*[231] meaning "stand in another place."

12. SON-IN-LAW, AND THY SONS, AND THY DAUGHTERS. Rashi comments: "Whom else of your family have you in the city besides your wife and daughters who are at home with you? If you have additionally a son-in-law, or sons and daughters, take them out from this place." Now if so, they [the angels] spoke in the manner of ordinary people for Lot had no sons, only daughters.

Rabbi Abraham ibn Ezra explained: "*Son-in-law, and thy sons* – sons-in-law who are [as dear to you] as your sons."

It is possible that Lot had grown sons who were married, and he spoke with his sons-in-law first as he thought that his own sons would listen to him [and leave the place]. But as his sons-in-law laughed at him and their conversation continued, dawn appeared, and the angels only permitted him to take those who were at hand. Thus the merit of Lot could have saved his sons and daughters and sons-in-law, not as Abraham had thought that He would make the righteous perish with the wicked.[232] It is clear that the angels were acquainted with the knowledge of the Most High on this matter since the city of Zoar was also saved by his prayer.[233]

It is possible that [the salvation of Lot's family was not on account of his merit but] was in honor of his hospitality for it is the ethical way of messengers to save their host and all that belong to him, just as the messengers of Joshua also saved all the families

(231) In the beginning of this verse. (232) Above, 18:25. (233) This is unlike the opinion of R'dak, who maintains that an angel who carries out a Divine mission also has the right to add or detract somewhat from the charge given to him. His proof is the fact that the angel here granted the sudden request of Lot to save the city of Zoar, (Verses 20-21). Ramban, however, is of the opinion that the angels were acquainted with the knowledge of the Most High and knew that He granted Lot's request; they could thus assure Lot that the city of Zoar would be saved.

of their hostess.[234] And in Bereshith Rabbah[235] it is said, "Because Lot honored the angel by offering him hospitality, he in turn befriended Lot."[236]

16. AND THE MEN LAID HOLD UPON HIS HAND. Rabbi Abraham ibn Ezra said that the word *vayachziku (and they laid hold upon)* clearly shows that Lot was afraid and had no strength to flee. The correct interpretation of the word is that it is like the verse, *'Vatechezak' (And) the Egyptians (were urgent) upon the people, to send them out of the land in haste.*[237] Here likewise they were pulling them with strength to send them out in haste.

THE ETERNAL HAVING PITY UPON HIM. Not for Lot's merit but only because of G-d's pity and His abundant mercies. It may be that the verse is saying that they seized him to take them out while G-d's pity was still upon him, lest the wrath go forth from G-d[238] and he perish.

17. LOOK NOT BEHIND THEE, NEITHER STAY IN ALL THE PLAIN. The purport of the verse is to state: "Do not stay in all the Plain and do not look behind you after you have been saved." For as long as Lot had not reached the mountain, disaster would not overtake the inhabitants of Sodom. It is for this reason that Lot said, *"And I cannot escape to the mountain, lest the evil overtake me*[239] when I am in the Plain since you will not extend the time for me more than a little, as you have said, *Haste thee, escape thither."*[240]

Rabbi Abraham ibn Ezra said, "*Look not behind thee*, i.e., 'thou and all who belong to thee.' And similarly is the verse, *Thou shalt not eat of it."*[241]

But what need is there for this interpretation? The punishment here was not because they would violate the warning of the angel

(234) Joshua 6:23. (235) 50:21. (236) And granted his request to save Zoar. (237) Exodus 12:33. (238) See Numbers 17:11. (239) Verse 19 here. (240) Verse 22 here. (241) Above, 2:17. This command, given to Adam, must have included Eve as well, for otherwise she would not have been punished. Similarly, the command given to Lot must have included his wife and all who belonged to him.

by looking at them. Instead, the angel merely warned them on his own that punishment would overtake them for such a glance, and he warned Lot because of his merit, and all who listened and took warning saved their lives.

Now as to the significance of the prohibition of looking, Rashi said: "You sinned with them but art saved through the merit of Abraham. You are not permitted[242] to see their doom."

There is yet another matter. Looking upon the atmosphere of a plague and all contagious diseases is very harmful, and they may cleave to him. Even the thought of them is harmful. Therefore, the leper is isolated and dwells alone.[243] Similarly, those who have been bitten by mad animals such as a mad dog and other animals besides, when they look into the water or any mirror, they behold in them the likeness of the offender, and as a result of this, they did just as the Rabbis have said in Tractate Yoma,[244] and as the students of nature have mentioned. It was for this reason that Lot's wife turned into a pillar of salt[245] for the plague entered her mind when she saw the brimstone and salt[246] which descended upon them from heaven, and it cleaved to her.

I am inclined to say that when G-d destroyed these cities the destroying angel *stood between the earth and heaven,*[247] appearing in a flame of fire, as did the destroying angel whom David saw.[247] Therefore, he prohibited them from looking.

In Pirkei d'Rabbi Eliezer[248] there is a similar text: "The angels said to them, 'Do not look behind you since the Divine Presence of the Holy One, blessed be He, has descended to rain brimstone and fire upon Sodom and Gomorrah.' The compassion of Edis, Lot's wife, welled up for her married daughters who were in Sodom,[249] and she looked behind her to see if they were

(242) "You are not permitted." In our Rashi the text reads, "It is not fitting that...." (243) Leviticus 13:40. (244) Yoma 84 a. See also Ramban, Numbers 21:9. (245) Verse 26 here. (246) Brimstone and salt. Here in the chapter, brimstone and *fire* are mentioned (Verse 24). Salt however is mentioned in Deuteronomy 29:22, in connection with the overthrow of Sodom. (247) I Chronicles 21:16. (248) Chapter 25. (249) Lot, according to Pirkei d'Rabbi Eliezer, had two married daughters in Sodom in addition to the two betrothed daughters who were yet in his house. See Verse 15.

following her. She thereupon saw the back of the Divine Presence, and she became a pillar of salt."

24. AND THE ETERNAL CAUSED TO RAIN UPON SODOM (AND UPON GOMORRAH BRIMSTONE AND FIRE FROM THE ETERNAL OF HEAVEN). Rashi wrote: "Wherever it is said, *And the Eternal* it means Him and His Celestial Court. *From the Eternal.* It is not written 'from Him,' [with the pronoun 'Him' replacing the noun 'Eternal' in the second part of the verse, for] this is the Scriptural way of speaking. For example, *Ye wives of Lamech,*[250] and he did not say 'my wives.' And David also said, *Take you the servants of your lord,*[251] and he did not say, 'my servants.' Ahaseurus also said, *Write ye... in the name of the king,*[252] and he did not say, 'in my name.' "

Now I wonder about the Rabbi[253] who wrote down conflicting opinions and made them alike for there is a division of opinion on this matter in Bereshith Rabbah.[254] And there is yet a third opinion: "Aba Chilfi, the son of Rabbi Simki, said in the name of Rabbi Yehudah the son of Rabbi Simon: '*And the Eternal caused to rain upon Sodom* — this refers to the angel Gabriel. *From the Eternal out of heaven* — this refers to the Holy One, blessed be He.' Rabbi Eleazar said, 'Wherever it says, *And the Eternal*, it means Him and His Celestial Court.' Rabbi Yitzchak said, 'We find in the Torah, Prophets, and Writings, that a person mentions his name twice. In the Torah, *And Lamech said to his wives,*[250] etc.' " Thus there are three conflicting opinions here. Rabbi Yehudah the son of Rabbi Simon ascribes the first Divine Name mentioned in the verse as referring to Gabriel as he was the messenger sent to destroy the city, it being a case of the deputy being referred to by the name of Him Who sent him. And Rabbi Eleazar said that He and His Celestial Court agreed on the judgment, and it was from Him that the brimstone and fire came. And Rabbi Yitzchak said that it is the Scriptural way of speaking.

Now if you will understand what I have written above,[255] you

(250) Above, 4:23. (251) I Kings 1:33. (252) Esther 8:8. (253) Rashi. See *Seder Bereshith*, Note 139. (254) 51:50. (255) 11:2, at the end.

will know the intent of the Sages' expression, "He and His Celestial Court," and then the plain meaning of the verse will be clear to you. In a similar manner is the verse, *That they may keep the way of the Eternal... to the end that the Eternal may bring...*[256] He did not say, "that they may keep My way... to the end that I may bring." Likewise: *Because the cry concerning them is great before the face of the Eternal, and the Eternal hath sent us.*[257] And similarly: *And it came to pass, when G-d destroyed... that G-d remembered.*[258]

26. AND HIS WIFE LOOKED BACK FROM BEHIND HIM. From behind Lot, who was following them, acting as the rearguard for all his household, who were hurrying to be saved.

29. AND G-D REMEMBERED ABRAHAM, AND SENT LOT OUT FROM THE CATASTROPHE. The purport of this verse is that Lot had shown kindness towards the righteous one[259] by going with him and roaming here and there, following him wherever he went. This is the intent of the verse, *And Lot went with him,*[260] meaning that he went at Abraham's command. Therefore he had the merit to be saved on account of Abraham's meritoriousness as it was on account of him that he lived in Sodom, and were it not for Abraham he would have still been in Haran with his family. Now it is inconceivable that some evil should overtake him [Lot] because of Abraham who had left his country at his Creator's command. This was also the reason why Abraham endangered himself by pursuing the kings on account of him.[261]

30. FOR HE FEARED TO DWELL IN ZOAR. Rashi wrote, "Because it was near to Sodom."

This is not so.[262] Rather, since it was one of the places upon

(256) Above, 18:19. (257) Above, Verse 13. (258) Further, Verse 29. (259) Abraham. (260) Above, 12:4. (261) *Ibid.*, 14:14. (262) For since the angel had assured Lot, *See, I have accepted thee concerning this thing also, that I will not overthrow the city* [Zoar], (Verse 21), Zoar would no longer be in danger of destruction even though it was near Sodom. (Mizrachi.)

which destruction had originally been decreed and it was only by Lot's supplication that the angel exempted it because Lot could not make his escape to the mountain on that day,[263] Lot now thought that the angel would no longer extend his request, for he now had sufficient time to make the escape to the mountain.[264] This was why his daughter said, *And there is not a man in the earth,*[265] for she thought that with her father's departure from Zoar the city was destroyed.

31. AND THE FIRST-BORN SAID. Rabbi Abraham ibn Ezra said, "It is possible that Lot had another wife[266] who died before."

But there is no need for this; *the first-born* is just in contrast to *the younger.* In fraternal relations the one who is older is called "first-born," and all those younger than he are called "the younger ones."

Thus the first fruits of the year are called *bikurim;*[267] likewise, *the first-born of the poor,*[268] meaning the most destitute, the poor of the poor. Likewise, *With the loss of his first-born shall he lay the foundation thereof, and with the loss of his younger shall he set up the gates of it.*[269] Onkelos also here translated, *rabtha.*[270]

32. THAT WE MAY KEEP ALIVE SEED FROM OUR FATHER. The intent is perhaps that they said: "Let us do what we can, so that G-d should have mercy, and we shall give birth to a boy and a girl from whom the world shall be sustained, for *the*

(263) Verse 19 here. (264) This was why he *feared to dwell in Zoar.* (265) Verse 31 here. (266) Since Scripture mentions that Lot had married daughters (Verse 14), these two mentioned here must surely have been younger ones as it was customary for the older ones to marry before the younger ones. (See further, 29:26.) If so, how does Scripture call one of the single daughters *the first-born*? It must therefore be, concluded Ibn Ezra, that the ones mentioned above were from another wife who had died. Ramban, however, differs with this suggestion, as explained below in the text. (267) *Bikurim* has as its root the word *b'chor* (the first born). Here also the first fruits are relative to this year's crop. (268) Isaiah 14:30. (269) Joshua 6:26. (270) "The older." And he did not translate, as elsewhere, *buchra* (the first-born).

world will be built with kindness,[271] and it is not in vain that G-d has saved us." Now they were modest and did not want to tell their father to marry them, as a Noachide[272] is permitted to take his daughter.[273] It may be that the matter was extremely repulsive in the eyes of the people of those generations and was never done. Our Rabbis,[274] in Agadic expositions, likewise discredit Lot very much.

20 2. AND ABRAHAM SAID OF SARAH HIS WIFE, SHE IS MY SISTER. This was not like what happened in Egypt. There, when they entered the land, it is said that the Egyptians saw that the woman was beautiful, and they praised her to the lords and to Pharaoh,[275] as they were an immoral people but this king was perfect and upright, and his people were likewise good. However Abraham suspected them, and he told everyone that she was his sister.

AND ABIMELECH, KING OF GERAR, SENT AND TOOK SARAH. It is wondrous that Sarah, after being worn with age, was extremely beautiful, fit to be taken by kings. When she was taken to Pharaoh, though she was sixty-five[276] years old, it is possible that she still had her beautiful appearance, but after being worn with age and the manner of women had ceased with her, that is a wonder! Perhaps her youthfulness returned to her when the angel brought her the tidings, as our Rabbis have said.[277]

12. AND YET SHE IS MY SISTER, THE DAUGHTER OF MY FATHER. I know not the sense of this apology. Even if it were true that she was his sister and his wife, nevertheless when they

(271) Psalms 89:3. (272) See *Seder Bereshith,* Note 288. (273) Sanhedrin 58 b. (274) Bereshith Rabbah 51:11-12. (275) Above, 12:14-15. (276) According to the Seder Olam, the famine occurred in Egypt in the year in which Abraham left Haran, and that is when Abraham went there (Chapter 1). Now Scripture states that when he left Haran, Abraham was seventy-five years old (12:4); Sarah who was ten years younger (17:17) was thus sixty-five. (277) Baba Metzia 87 a: "Her skin became smooth, and the wrinkles straightened, and beauty returned to its form."

wanted to take her as a wife and he told them, *She is my sister,*[278] in order to lead them astray, he already committed a sin towards them by bringing upon them a *great sin,*[279] and it no longer mattered at all whether the thing was true or false!

Perhaps it was because Abimelech said, *What sawest thou, that thou hast done this thing?*[280] meaning "What sin or wickedness have you seen in me that caused you to do this out of fear? I have never attempted to take women away from their husbands." Then Abraham answered: "I did not know you, but I thought, perhaps *the fear of G-d is not in this place,*[281] for in most places in the world there is no fear of G-d. Therefore, from the time I left my country and aimlessly wandered among the nations not knowing to which place we would come, I made this condition with her that she say thus in all places. For the matter is true, and I thought that by doing this, human life would be saved. I did not begin this practice upon entering your country for I did not see that you had committed any sin." *And yet she is my sister, the daughter of my father.* This expression represents a different argument. Abraham said: "According to my custom, I said so for it is true, and I further thought that in case they will want her they will ask me if she is also my wife. Since your servants took her and they did not ask me any questions, I said, 'The fear of G-d is also not in this place' and I remained quiet."

It is possible that he established this condition with her when they came to Egypt even though he said that he did it *when G-d caused me to wander from my father's house.*[282] It may be that he again warned her there in Egypt at the time of the event, as I have explained.[283]

Rabbi Abraham ibn Ezra's opinion is that all these words were to put off Abimelech.

16. BEHOLD, I HAVE GIVEN THY BROTHER A THOUSAND PIECES OF SILVER. The sheep, the cattle and the servants which he gave him were worth a thousand pieces of silver. He thus said

(278) Verse 2 here. (279) Verse 9 here. (280) Verse 10 here. (281) Verse 11 here. (282) Verse 13 here. (283) Above, 12:11.

to Sarah: "Behold, I have given much money to your brother. Now the money will serve you as a cause for the covering of the eyes of all those who look at your beauty,[284] closing their eyes, and those of their leaders, the seers,[285] to prevent them looking at you and at all that belongs to you, even your manservants and maidservants. Thus your being taken forcibly to my house was for your benefit as they will fear you and cover their eyes to avoid looking at you, saying: 'The king had to redeem himself for having stretched forth his hand to the prophet's wife.' "

The verse thus tells that Abimelech mollified Abraham with money, and Sarah with words, so that he should not be punished on account of either of them. The verse states in conclusion, *venochachath,*[286] as Sarah did not accept his apology, *for with all this,*[287] she yet continued arguing with him, saying that she would not forgive him. The verse thus speaks in her praise. Abraham, however, was appeased, and he prayed for the king. The word *venochachath* is similar in usage to these verses: *And with Israel 'yithvakach' (He has an argument);*[288] *But my ways 'ochiach' (will I argue) before Him;*[289] *There the upright 'nochach' (might reason) with Him.*[290]

It is possible that the expression, *a thousand pieces of silver to thy brother*, means thousands of pieces of silver, much wealth, *according to the bounty of the king.*[291] Similarly, *The smallest shall become a thousand,*[292] [means that the smallest will become] a great people. Similarly: *Restore, I pray you, to them even this day, their fields, their vineyards, their oliveyards, and their houses, also the hundred pieces of silver, and the corn, the wine, and oil, that ye exact of them*[293] – [here too *the hundred pieces of silver* refer to] many hundreds, a great deal of money.

(284) "Had I given the money to you, people might say it was a harlot's hire. But now that I have given it to your brother, people will say that I had to redeem myself against my will, and this will thus enable you to speak freely in your defense." (Bachya.) (285) See Isaiah 29:10, *And your heads, the seers hath He covered.* (286) According to Ramban, as is clear from the text further on, the translation of this word is, "and she continued to protest." (287) The money he gave to Abraham and the words of apology he offered her. (288) Micah 6:2. (289) Job 13:15. (290) *Ibid.*, 23:7. (291) Esther 1:7. (292) Isaiah 60:22. (293) Nehemiah 5:11.

17. 'VAYEILEIDU' (AND THEY BORE CHILDREN). If this is understood literally as referring to *his wife, and his maidservants* and stating that the Eternal had restrained their wombs, it is astonishing! For it appears that on the first night that Sarah was taken to Abimelech's house, and he had not even approached her,[294] G-d immediately came to him in the dream, and in the morning he rose early and called his servants and also Abraham.[295] When then did they experience this restraining of the womb? Perhaps it so happened that they were in their due time, experiencing the pangs of childbirth, unable to be relieved by giving birth. Perhaps, also, Abraham delayed his prayer for many days. But according to this interpretation, the nature of Abimelech's healing as well as his sickness have not been explained in Scripture.

Now Rashi comments: "*Vayeileidu* – and they were relieved,[296] their channels were opened, and they brought forth their wastes. This was the *leidah* (bringing forth) as it referred to them. *All the wombs* means every opening of the body."

But this is not correct. Even if we were to say concerning the word *vayeileidu* that it means "bringing forth" – as we do indeed find the word *leidah* used in many contexts, such as: *Yea, he conceiveth mischief 'veyolad' (and bringeth forth) falsehood;*[297] *Before the decree 'ledeth' (bring forth);*[298] *for thou knowest not what a day 'yolad' (may bring forth),*[299] meaning what the days will bring forth and originate – but the word *rechem* (womb) never refers to any other openings. This is not contradicted by the verse, *Or, who shut up the sea with doors, when it broke forth, and issued out of the womb,*[300] for this is merely a figure of speech,[301] similar to "the belly of the earth."[302]

(294) Verse 4 here. (295) Verses 8-9 here. (296) In our Rashi: "Explain it as the Targum does, 'and they were relieved.'" (297) Psalms 7:15. (298) Zephaniah 2:2. (299) Proverbs 27:1. (300) Job 38:8. (301) Meaning when the sea broke from the abyss, where it was formed as a child in his mother's womb. (Ramban in his commentary to Job, *ibid.*,) (302) See Jonah 2:3, *the belly of the netherworld.*

Now Onkelos' opinion is not like that of the Rabbi[303] for even if he translated, "and they were relieved," yet the word *rechem* (womb) he renders literally as "the opening for giving birth to a child." However, [the reason why Onkelos translated it, "and they were relieved," and not "and they gave birth," is that] he wanted to include Abimelech also in the word *vayeileidu.*

In Bereshith Rabbah[304] it is said: *"For the Eternal had fast closed up ('atzor atzar'),*[305] i.e., closed up the mouth, closed up the neck, closed up the eye, closed up the ear, closed up above,[306] and closed up below." Now the Rabbis derived this exposition from the double usage of the expression, *atzor atzar,* but they did not explain the expression, *every* womb, as meaning every opening of the body.

The correct interpretation appears to me to be that from the day Sarah was taken to Abimelech's house, Abimelech was stricken in his limbs and was unable to fulfill his needs. This is [what the verse alludes to when it says], *Therefore I did not suffer thee to touch her,*[307] as "touching" or "approaching" women are euphemisms for sexual intercourse, as in the verse, *Draw not near a woman;*[308] *And I came unto the prophetess.*[309] And He restrained the wombs of his wife and his maidservants who were pregnant so they could not give birth. "Restraining a womb" means that the woman could not conceive, even as it says, *And the Eternal had closed up her womb.*[310] But "restraining the womb" denotes inability to give birth, similar in usage to the verse, *He hath hedged me about, that I cannot go forth.*[311]

Sarah stayed in Abimelech's house many days, and Abimelech did not repent his way as he did not understand his transgression until G-d came to him in a dream and informed him of it. Now Scripture does not explain Abimelech's sickness explicitly but mentions it only by hint in an ethical manner and out of respect for Sarah. After Abraham's prayer, Abimelech and his wife and his maidservants were healed, and the women gave birth.

(303) Rashi. (304) 52:14. (305) Verse 18 here. (306) "Above... below," a reference to urination, the minor function of the body, and defecation, the major function. (307) Verse 6 here. (308) Exodus 19:15. (309) Isaiah 8:3. (310) I Samuel 1:5. (311) Lamentations 3:7.

21 1. AND THE ETERNAL 'PAKAD' (VISITED) SARAH AS HE HAD SAID. That is, by granting her pregnancy. *And the Eternal did unto Sarah as He had spoken* by granting her the birth of a son. Thus the words of Rashi.

But the word *pekidah* is only an expression of remembrance and attention to the one who is remembered, such as: *G-d will surely remember ('pakod yiphkod') you;*[312] *I have surely remembered you;*[313] *And Samson remembered his wife by* [bringing her] *a kid.*[314] Here, too, the sense of the verse is that the Eternal remembered Sarah, and He did to her as He had spoken. This expression is also found in connection with all barren women who later give birth. Thus, in the case of Rachel: *And G-d remembered Rachel;*[315] and in the case of Hannah: *And G-d remembered her.*[316] Similarly, the Rabbis said,[317] "Biblical verses which mention *pikdonoth* are equivalent to verses which mention Divine remembrances."[318]

7. 'MI' (WHO) WOULD HAVE SAID UNTO ABRAHAM. The word *mi* is used as an exclamation of praise and distinction. The sense of the verse is thus: "See Whom it is and to what extent He keeps His promise. He promises and performs!" Thus the language of Rashi.

But we do not find the word *mi* used in this way in expressions of distinction and honor. Instead, we find it used only in a derogatory sense: *'Mi' (Who is) Abimelech, and 'mi' (who is)* Shechem?[319] *'Mi' (Who is) the son of Jesse?*[320]

The correct interpretation appears to me to be that Sarah said, *"G-d hath made laughter for me; and every one that heareth will*

(312) Further, 50:25. (313) Exodus 3:16. (314) Judges 15:1. (315) Further, 30:22. (316) I Samuel 1:19. (317) Rosh Hashanah 32 b. (318) In the Additional Service of the New Year day, ten Biblical verses which speak of Divine remembrance are recited. A verse mentioning *pikadon* is treated as one mentioning remembrance. Thus, Ramban proves that the word *pakad* in the verse here can mean "remembered," and not as Rashi explained it as meaning "granting pregnancy." (319) Judges 9:28. (320) I Samuel 25:10.

laugh on account of me,[321] filling his mouth with song and laughter for the wonder that has been done to me, for who among the hearers would have previously said to Abraham that Sarah will suckle children? There is not a person in the world who would have told him this, even merely to console him, for the possibility would never have occurred to anyone." Onkelos' rendition is close to this interpretation: "How faithful is He who spoke to Abraham! He has fulfilled His word that Sarah will suckle children." That is to say, "Everyone that heareth will laugh on account of me" for there is no person who would have maintained his credulity even in the eyes of Abraham if he were to have told him this wonder.

9. 'METZACHEIK' (MAKING SPORT). This refers to worshipping idols, murder and sexual immorality. He [Ishmael] quarrelled with Isaac about inheritance, saying, "I am the first-born and will take a double portion."[322] They then went into the field, and Ishmael took his bow and shot arrows at Isaac, just as you say, *As a madman who casteth firebrands, arrows and death, so is the man who deceiveth his neighbor, and saith, Am I not in sport?*[323] It is from Sarah's complaint to Abraham – *for the son of this bondwoman shall not be heir,* etc.[324] – that you learn [that they were quarrelling about the inheritance]. All this is Rashi's language.

Here too,[325] the Rabbi[303] writes all the different opinions, [mentioned in the following]: "We have been taught:[326] Rabbi Shimon the son of Eleazar said, 'There are four interpretations of Rabbi Akiba which I interpret differently, and my interpretation seems more acceptable than his. Rabbi Akiba interpreted: "*And Sarah saw the son of Hagar the Egyptian, whom she had borne unto Abraham, making sport. Making sport* is but a designation for idolatry, etc." But I say Heaven forbid that such be in the house of the righteous one! Is it possible that he, of whom it was

(321) Verse 6 here. (322) Deuteronomy 21:17. (323) Proverbs 26:18-19. (324) Verse 10 here. (325) See above, 19:24, where Ramban criticizes Rashi in a similar manner. Hence the word "too." (326) Tosefta Sotah 6:6. A part thereof is mentioned in Rosh Hashanah 18 b.

written, *For I have known him, to the end that he may command his children and his household*, etc.,[327] will have in his household idolatry, sexual immorality, and murder? *Making sport* mentioned here is but a designation for the inheritance. When Isaac was born and everyone rejoiced, Ishmael said to them, "Fools, I am the first-born, and I take a double portion." From the complaint of our mother Sarah to Abraham you learn [that *making sport* refers to the inheritance]. And my interpretation seems more acceptable than that of Rabbi Akiba.' "

The expression of the Rabbi,[303] "that Ishmael quarrelled with Isaac about the inheritance," also does not appear correct for if so, this must have happened much later when Isaac was grown up, and Ishmael would then have been too big for his mother to carry him on her shoulder.[328] Our Rabbis have also said[329] that Ishmael was seventeen years old [at the time he left his father's house]. If so, this happened at the time when Isaac was weaned,[330] [and Isaac was thus too young for Ishmael to quarrel with him about the inheritance].

Rabbi Abraham ibn Ezra said in line with the literal interpretation of Scripture that *metzachek* means "playing," as is normal for every boy, and she was jealous of him because he was bigger than her son.

The correct interpretation appears to me to be that this event took place *on the day that Isaac was weaned*,[331] and Sarah saw Ishmael mocking Isaac or the great feast. It is for this reason that the verse says, *And Sarah saw the son of Hagar the Egyptian* – rather than Ishmael – *making sport*. Similarly, she said, *Cast out this bondwoman and her son*,[324] for she said: "The slave who

(327) Above, 18:19. (328) See Verse 14 here. (329) Yalkut Shimoni Genesis, 95: "Ishmael was seventeen years old when he left his father's house." Isaac was then three years of age (see Note 330). See also the note in my Hebrew commentary, p. 123. (330) At the time of Isaac's birth, Ishmael was fourteen years old. (He was thirteen at his circumcision (17:25), and a year later Isaac was born.) Now since Ishmael was seventeen when he left his father's house, Isaac was three years old at the time, at which age he was weaned (Verse 8). (331) Verse 8 here.

mocks his master is deserving of death or stripes, but I want only that you cast him out from before me, and that he should in no way inherit your belongings together with my son, who is the son of the mistress." She also told Abraham to cast out his mother, as the boy was unable to leave her for he would die if he were to leave his mother.[332]

11. AND THE THING WAS VERY GRIEVOUS IN ABRAHAM'S SIGHT ON ACCOUNT OF HIS SON. That is, for he had taken to degenerate ways. The plain meaning, however, is that he was grieved because she had told him to send him away. Thus the language of Rashi.

The correct interpretation appears to me to be that Scripture is speaking in honor of Abraham, saying that the reason why the matter was very displeasing to him was not due to a craving for his concubine and his desire for her. Therefore, if she had told him to cast out only the maidservant, he would have done her will. But it was on account of his son that he was very much incensed and did not want to listen to her. But the Holy One, blessed be He, told him that he should not resent it at all, neither for the son nor for the maidservant, and that he should listen to Sarah's bidding for it is through Isaac alone that his name will be carried on, while Ishmael will not be referred to as his offspring. Now because Abraham feared lest an accident happen to Ishmael upon his sending him away, He told him that He will make a nation of him and He will bless him since he is indeed his son.

14. AND THE CHILD, AND HE SENT HER AWAY. This is to be understood in connection with the above: *And he gave to Hagar* [the bread and bottle of water]... *and the child*, for he gave her the child also to go with her wherever she will go.

15. AND SHE CAST THE CHILD. Thirst overtook him and he was unable to walk, and so his mother laid him under the tree, cast away and abandoned. It may be that the word *vatashleich*

(332) See further, 44:22.

(and she cast) is similar in sense to the verses: *And He cast them into another land;*[333] *Cast me not away from Thy presence,*[334] meaning "sending away."

Rabbi Abraham ibn Ezra said: "*And she cast* for she had taken him onto her lap when he was weakened by thirst, [and seeing that he was expiring from thirst, she cast him from her]."

Our Rabbis have said[335] that he was sick at the time he sent him away, and therefore he put the child on her shoulder. This is the sense of the word *vatashleich (and she cast)* him: [until that point she had carried him].

All this occurred to Abraham because he had been commanded to do whatever Sarah said, and she commanded that he send him away immediately, and it was at her command that he did not give them silver and gold, servants, and camels to bear them.

17. WHERE HE IS. He shall be judged according to his present deeds, and not according to those actions which he may do in the future. This was because the ministering angels laid charges, etc. Thus the words of Rashi quoting from the teachings of our Rabbis.[336]

The correct interpretation, in line with the simple meaning of Scripture, appears to me to be that the verse is stating that G-d heard the voice of the lad in the place in which he was. He informed her that she will not need to go from there to a fountain or well for in that very place he will quench his thirst immediately. He thus said to her, "*Arise, lift up the lad*[337] after you will have given him to drink, *for I will make him a great nation.*[337] Similarly, the word *sham (there)* in verses, *Where he sunk, there he fell down dead;*[338] *And where the slain are, there is she,*[339] alludes to the place.

(333) Deuteronomy 29:27. (334) Psalms 51:13. (335) Bereshith Rabbah 53:17. (336) *Ibid.*, 19. (337) Verse 18 here. (338) Judges 5:27. Meaning, " 'in the place' where he fell." (339) Job 39:30. Meaning "And 'in the place' where the slain are."

20. ROVEH KASHOTH (AN ARCHER). Since *kashoth* is an adjective, they[340] have said that *roveh* is one who shoots arrows, the word being derived from the expressions: *His archers compass me round about;*[341] *The archers have dealt bitterly with him,*[342] – and *kashoth* is one who makes arrows.

A more correct interpretation is that *roveh* is a shooter, and it can refer to one who shoots arrows or throws stones or other objects, even as it is said, *Behold this heap... which I have thrown up between me and thee.*[343] Therefore, the verse describes him further by saying that he was a shooter with the bow. In a similar sense is the verse, *And the shooters of arrows by the bow overtook him.*[344]

23. NOW THEREFORE SWEAR UNTO ME HERE BY G-D 'IM' (IF) YOU WILL BE FALSE TO ME. The word *im* always expresses doubt – do not think of it in any other way[345] – and it appears in most places in connection with an oath: *If you will be false to me;*[346] *And therefore I have sworn unto the house of Eli 'im' (if) the iniquity of Eli's house shall be expiated;*[347] *Once I have sworn by My holiness 'im' (if) I will be false unto David;*[348] *'im' (if) they should enter into My rest;*[349] *And he was wroth, and swore, saying, 'im' (if) one of these men will see.*[350]

The purport of this is that since oaths are given with imprecation, Abimelech is stating, "Swear to me, saying, *G-d do so*

(340) Ibn Ezra and R'dak. Their point is as follows: Since *kashoth* is an adjective, or more precisely, a *shem hatoar*, (a noun-adjective), as is also *roveh*, how could two adjectives appear without a noun? Therefore they said that the two words, *roveh kashoth*, are not in construct with one another, but they are interpreted as *roveh vekashoth* (a shooter of arrows and maker of bows) with the companion noun of each adjective being tacitly understood. Ramban's opinion, however, is that since *roveh* may mean either "a shooter of arrows" or "a thrower of stones," the word *kashoth* is used in order to explain that he was a shooter with the bow, meaning, a shooter of arrows and not a thrower of stones. (341) Job 16:13. (342) Further, 49:23. (343) *Ibid.*, 31:51. (344) I Samuel 31:3. (345) Ramban's intent is to differ with Rashi, who, in Leviticus 2:14, explains *im* to mean "that." See Ramban there, where he explains it in a manner consistent with his teaching here. (346) In the present verse. (347) I Samuel 3:14. (348) Psalms 89:36. (349) *Ibid.*, 95:11. (350) Deuteronomy 1:34-35.

to me, and more also[351] if you will be false to me." Likewise it is said, *Let there now be an oath between us.*[352] And in the matter of a Divine oath: *I have sworn by My holiness if I will be false to David;*[348] *if the iniquity of Eli's house shall be expiated,*[347] meaning "If that will be so, then My word is not true," and in similar cases, since it does not want to expressly state the condition.[353] Scripture modifies and shortens these expressions. A similar case of a shortened condition is the verse, *And Jabez called on the G-d of Israel, saying: Oh that Thou wouldest bless me indeed, and enlarge my border,* etc., *and that Thou wouldest work deliverance from evil that it may not pain me. And G-d granted him that which he requested.*[354] Here the entire condition[355] is missing. A similar example is the verse, *If they will see the land,*[356] referring back to the first verse, *As I live, and all shall be filled with the glory of the Eternal,*[357] and Scripture shortens the Divine oath.

The expression, *false to me*, is because Abimelech was a king, and Abraham dwelt in his land. [Thus, if Abraham were to do him evil, it would be an act of disloyalty towards him in his royal capacity], or it would be a betrayal of Abimelech's love for him, as he [Abimelech] was his trustworthy friend, honoring him and doing his will. For you see that Abraham found no fault with him except *the well of water, which Abimelech's servants had violently taken away,*[358] and the king said to him, *According to the kindness that I have done unto thee.*[359]

32. AND THEY RETURNED TO THE LAND OF THE PHILISTINES. The sense of the verse is that they returned to their city which was in the land of the Philistines for they lived in the land of the Philistines. However, they abode in Gerar,[360] which was the royal capital, while Abraham dwelled in Beer-sheba, which is in the land of the Philistines, in the valley of Gerar.[361]

(351) II Samuel 3:35. (352) Further, 26:28. (353) Namely, that "if that be so, My word is not true." (354) I Chronicles 4:10. (355) Namely, his vow of offering to G-d. (356) Numbers 14:23. (357) *Ibid.*, Verse 21. (358) Verse 25 here. (359) Verse 23 here. (360) Above, 20:1. (361) Further, 26:17.

33. AND HE CALLED THERE IN THE NAME OF THE ETERNAL, 'E-IL OLAM' (THE EVERLASTING G-D). Scripture explains that Abraham called by the name Eternal He Who in His might directs the time.

It may be that heaven and earth are here being called *olam* (world) [so that the sense of the verse is, "he called by the name Eternal the G-d of the world"], as is a customary expression in the words of our Rabbis. Thus Scripture informs us by this that Abraham called out and informed people of the secret of the leadership of the entire world, namely, that it is *in the name of the Eternal,* the Mighty One in strength, Supreme in power over all.

Now the Rabbi[362] said in the Moreh Nebuchim[363] that this alludes to the principle of the pre-existence of G-d since Abraham let it be known that G-d existed before the creation of time. Onkelos, however, said of the word *vayikra* (and he called), that it refers to prayer.

22 1. AND G-D TRIED ABRAHAM. The matter of "trial,"[364] in my opinion, is as follows: Since a man's deeds are at his absolute free command, to perform them or not to perform them at his will, on the part of one who is tried it is called "a trial." But on the part of the One, blessed be He, who tries the person, it is a command that the one being tested should bring forth the matter from the potential into actuality so that he may be rewarded for a good deed, not for a good thought alone.

Know further that *G-d trieth the righteous,*[365] for knowing that the righteous will do His will, He desires to make him even more upright, and so He commands him to undertake a test, but He does not try the wicked, who would not obey. Thus all trials in the Torah are for the good of the one who is being tried.

(362) Rambam. See *Seder Bereshith*, Note 139. (363) II, 13. See also III, 29. (364) See Rambam's discussion of this problem, *ibid.*, III, 24. (365) Psalms 11:5. See also Bereshith Rabbah 34:2. "The Holy One, blessed be He, trieth only the righteous."

2. TAKE NOW THY SON, THINE ONLY SON. Since Isaac was the son of the mistress and he alone was to be the one to carry his name, He called him Abraham's only son. The description was for the purpose of magnifying the command, thus saying: "Take now thy only son, the beloved one, Isaac, and bring him up before Me as a burnt-offering."

MORIAH. Rashi comments: "This is Jerusalem, and we find it in the book of Chronicles: *To build the house of the Eternal at Jerusalem on mount Moriah.*[366] Our Rabbis have explained that it is called *Moriah* (instruction) because from the Temple built there on that mountain, instruction came forth to Israel.[367] Onkelos translated it as "the land of Worship." This he derived on the basis of reference to the burning of incense, which contained *mor*[368] (myrrh) and other spices, [as part of the Divine Service]."

Now if so, [i.e., if this be the explanation of the name *Moriah*], the meaning of the verse will then be, "Go into the land which will be called *Moriah*." Or it may be that it was always called so on account of the future. In Bereshith Rabbah,[369] the Sages have said thus: "The Rabbis say, *Go into the land of Moriah* means into the land where incense will be offered on the altar of G-d, even as it is said, *I will get me to the mountain 'hamor' (of myrrh).*"[370] But the opinion of Onkelos, who said "the land of worship," does not appear to be based on the myrrh in the incense, as Rashi said, for the word "service" does not refer to one of the species used in one of the Divine Services. Besides, why did not Onkelos say, "to the land of the incense of spices?" Instead, Onkelos' intent is to say, "in the land in which they will worhip G-d."

Onkelos thus matched that which the Sages interpreted in Pirkei d'Rabbi Eliezer, where they said,[371] "The Holy One, blessed be

(366) II Chronicles 3:1. (367) The Chamber of Hewn Stone (*Lishchat hagazith*), the seat of the Great Sanhedrin, which was the highest court in Israel, was located in the Court of the Temple. See Deuteronomy 17:8-11. (368) Hence the name *Moriah*: the mountain on which *mor* (myrrh), as part of the incense, was to be burnt. Thus according to Rashi's understanding of Onkelos. Ramban will later differ with this interpretation in the meaning of Onkelos. (369) 55:9. (370) Song of Songs 4:6. (371) Chapter 31.

He, showed Abraham the altar with a finger. He said to him, 'This is the altar on which the first man sacrificed. This is the altar on which Cain and Abel sacrificed. This is the altar on which Noah and his sons sacrificed.' For it is said, *And Abraham built 'hamizbei'ach' (the altar) there,*[372] *mizbei'ach* (an altar) is not written here, rather, *hamizbei'ach (the* altar). This is the altar on which the predecessors have sacrificed." Thus far [is the interpretation of Pirkei d'Rabbi Eliezer]. And the name *Moriah* the Rabbis derived from the word *mora* (fear), for there the people feared G-d and worshipped Him.

The correct interpretation, in line with the plain meaning of Scripture, is that the name *Moriah* is like the expression, *To the mountain of myrrh, and to the hill of frankincense,*[370] for on that mountain [Moriah] are found *myrrh, aloes, and cinnamon,*[373] even as the Rabbis have said:[374] "Cinnamon grew in the Land of Israel, and goats and deers ate of it." Or it may be that it was so called in praise of the Land of Israel.[375]

Now here Scripture calls the name of the land, *the land of Moriah,* and there [in the book of Chronicles, mentioned above],[366] it appears that only the Temple mount was called mount Moriah. Perhaps, the city[376] was called by the name of that mountain which it contains, [and the name "land of Moriah" means] the land which contains the *Moriah*, but it was the mountain alone that was called *Moriah*. Now Abraham knew the land but did not know the mountain. Hence G-d told him to go to the land of *Moriah*, and He will there show him one of the mountains which is called by that name. He commanded him to offer up his son in that place for that is *the mountain which G-d hath desired for His abode,*[377] and He wanted the merit of the *Akeidah* (the Binding of Isaac) to be in the sacrifices forever, as Abraham said, *The Eternal seeth.*[378] Moreover, *for His*

(372) Verse 9 here. (373) Proverbs 7:17. (374) Yerushalmi Peah 7:3. (375) But myrrh, aloes and cinnamon actually do not grow on mount Moriah itself. It was, however, called by that name, in order to give praise to the land where these things grow. (376) "The City." The Tur, quoting Ramban, has "the land." (377) Psalms 68:17. (378) Verse 14 here.

righteousness' sake,[379] He increased the scope of the trial and wanted Abraham to do it after walking three days. Had Abraham been commanded to do so suddenly at his place, his deed would have been performed in haste and confusion, but since it was done after walking for days it was thus performed with reflection of mind and counsel. And so did the Rabbis say in Bereshith Rabbah:[380] "Rabbi Akiba said, 'G-d surely tried [Abraham with a clear-cut situation] so that people should not say that He confounded him and confused him and he did not know what to do.' "

3. AND HE CLEAVED THE WOOD FOR THE BURNT-OFFERING. This illustrates Abraham's zeal in performing a commandment for he thought that perhaps there would be no wood in that place, and so he carried it for three days. It may be that Abraham disqualified for use as an offering any wood in which a worm is found, as is the law of the Torah,[381] and so he took from his house sound wood for the burnt-offering. Hence it says, *And he cleaved the wood for the burnt-offering.*

4. AND HE SAW THE PLACE AFAR OFF. He saw a cloud attached to the mountain,[382] and through this was fulfilled the Divine assurance, *which I will tell thee of.*[383]

It is possible, in line with the simple meaning of Scripture, that the verse, *And he saw the place afar off,* means that he saw the land of *Moriah* for he knew that entire land [although he did not know the specific mountain].

9. AND THEY CAME TO THE PLACE WHICH G-D TOLD HIM OF – now,[384] "This is mount Moriah," for He told him, "Behold, this is the mountain of which I told you."

(379) Isaiah 42:21. (380) 55:5. (381) Midoth 2:5. (382) Bereshith Rabbah 56:2. (383) Verse 2 here. (384) As explained above, Abraham recognized the land of *Moriah* from a distance as he was acquainted with that whole land, and when he came near the mountain, G-d told him, "This is the place which I had designated to you." All this is in line with the plain meaning of Scripture, as Ramban mentioned above.

12. FOR NOW I KNOW THAT THOU ART A G-D FEARING MAN. At the beginning Abraham's fear of G-d was latent; it had not become actualized through such a great deed. But now it was known in actuality, and his merit was perfect, and his reward would be complete from the Eternal, the G-d of Israel.[385]

The doctrine of this chapter which teaches that G-d is the One who tries Abraham and commands him about the binding of Isaac, and it is the angel of G-d who restrains and promises him, will be explained in the verse, *The angel who hath redeemed me.*[386]

16. BECAUSE THOU HAST DONE THIS THING. In the beginning He promised him that he would increase his descendants as the stars of heaven[387] and the dust of the earth,[388] but now He gave him the additional assurance that *because thou hast done this* great deed, He swore by His Great Name [that He would increase his descendants *as the stars of heaven, and as the sand which is upon the seashore*],[389] and that his seed will possess the gate of its enemies.[389] Thus Abraham was assured that no sin whatever would cause the destruction of his descendants, nor would they fall into the hand of their enemies and not rise again. Thus this constitutes a perfect Divine assurance of the redemption which is destined to come to us.

20. BEHOLD, MILCAH, SHE ALSO HATH BORN CHILDREN. Since Milcah was the daughter of his brother Haran,[390] this was a tiding to Abraham that his older brother Nahor[391] had been visited with many children from the daughter of his dead brother Haran.[392]

Now from the text of Scripture it would appear that Abraham had no knowledge of any of them except on that day. If they were visited with children in their younger days, it would be impossible for them not to have been heard until this time for the

(385) See Ruth 2:12. (386) Further, 48:16. (387) Above, 15:5. (388) Above, 13:16. (389) Verse 17 here. (390) Above, 11:29. (391) *Ibid.*, Verse 28. (392) Abraham was older than Nahor for Scripture says, *Abram, Nahor, and Haran, (ibid.*, Verse 27). Since Nahor was older than Haran, Ramban refers to him as "the older" brother.

distance between Mesopotamia and the land of Canaan is not great. Now when Abraham left Haran he was seventy-five years old,[393] and Nahor was also elderly and his wife too was not young.[394] Indeed, we must say, G-d performed a miracle for them in that they were visited with children in their old age. This is the sense of the verse, *Milcah, she also*. In the words of our Rabbis, it is said[395] that Milcah was visited with children as was her sister Sarah.[396]

23. AND BETHUEL BEGOT REBEKAH. The verse does not mention Laban, even though he was older than Rebekah, for its intent is only to mention the eight children which Milcah bore to Nahor.[397] However, Rebekah is mentioned since the entire chapter is written to make known her genealogy.

Kemuel the father of Aram.[398] Aram is mentioned only in order to make known the identity of Kemuel as Aram was a more important man than his father. Perhaps, also, there was another Kemuel in their generation. Hence [Scripture identifies Kemuel by saying that] he was the father of Aram.

24. AND HIS CONCUBINE, WHOSE NAME WAS REUMAH. Scripture tells the entire tiding which they related to Abraham concerning his brother's children.

It is possible that this was written in order to make known the entire genealogy of Nahor, to establish that all of them were worthy to marry the children of Abraham, and it was with reference to all of them that Abraham said to Eliezer: *But thou shalt go unto my father's house and to my family.*[399]

(393) *Ibid.*, 12:4. (394) And if Nahor and his wife had had children many years ago, Abraham would have heard of it previously. (395) Yalkut Shimoni Numbers, 746. See the complete quote in my Hebrew commentary, p. 127. (396) Iscah, Milcah's sister (above, 11:29), is another name for Sarah. (Rashi, *ibid.*) (397) And Bethuel is already the eighth: Uz, Buz, Kemuel, Chesed, Hazo, Pildash, Jidlaph, Bethuel. Hence the verse does not intend to mention the children of Bethuel, namely, Laban. Rebekah, his daughter, however, was mentioned for the reason explained in the text. (398) Verse 21 here. (399) Further, 24:38.

Chayei Sarah

23 1. A HUNDRED AND TWENTY YEARS Rashi comments: "The reason the word 'years' is written at every term is that it informs you that each term must be interpreted by itself. At the age of one hundred she was as a woman of twenty as regards sin [for at the age of twenty she had not sinned since she had not reached the age when she was subject to punishment],[1] and at the age of twenty she was as beautiful as when she was seven." Rashi wrote similarly on the verse, *the years of Abraham's life.*[2]

However, this exegesis of his[3] is not correct. In the case of the verse, *the years of the life of Ishmael,*[4] it is stated exactly as in the verse, *the years of Abraham's life,*[2] whereas these years of Ishmael were not all equally good since Ishmael was wicked in his early years, and only in the end did he repent of his evil ways.[5] Furthermore, the repetition of the word "year" at every term would seem to indicate an intent to distinguish between them and, thus, should not be interpreted to imply equality. Rather, the use of the word *shanah* (year) and *shanim* (years) in this instance is the customary usage of the Hebrew language, while that which the Rabbis have said in Bereshith Rabbah,[6] "At the age of one

(1) The Heavenly Court does not punish one for sin before the age of twenty. The verse thus indicates that at the age of a hundred, Sarah never sinned, just as at the age of twenty she had never sinned. (2) Further, 25:7. (3) Ramban does not disagree with Rashi's interpretation as this is based on the Rabbis' comment in Bereshith Rabbah. However, Ramban does dispute which words in the Torah-text are the basis for their interpretation. Thus according to Ramban a similar interpretation would not follow in the verses concerning Abraham and Ishmael. (4) Further, 25:17. (5) See Ramban, *ibid.* (6) Bereshith Rabbah 58:1.

hundred she was as a woman of twenty as regards sin," is an interpretation which they derived only from the redundant expression, the *years of the life of Sarah,* which includes them all and equates them. The Rabbis would not make a similar interpretation of the verse concerning Abraham [since in his case Scripture does not conclude with a similar comprehensive expression].

2. AND ABRAHAM CAME. Rashi comments: "From Beer-sheba." Now this does not mean to imply that Abraham remained in Beer-sheba — as is indicated in the verse, *And Abraham abode at Beer-sheba,*[7] for how then would Sarah have been in Hebron? Rather, the intent is to state that Abraham had gone to Beer-sheba for the day for some purpose, and while there he heard of the death of Sarah and came from there to Hebron to mourn and weep for her. However, the expression of our Rabbis is,[8] *"And Abraham came* — from Mount Moriah." This is in accord with the Midrash which the Rabbi [Rashi] previously cited[9] which states that hearing of the Binding [in which her son had been made ready for sacrifice and had indeed almost been sacrificed] her soul flew from her and she died.

It would appear that the Divine command concerning the Binding was delivered to Abraham in Beer-sheba for there he dwelt and he returned thereto after the Binding, for so it is written at the outset: *And Abraham planted a tamarisk-tree in Beer-sheba and called there on the name of the Eternal, the Everlasting G-d.*[10] It further states, *And Abraham sojourned in the land of the Philistines many days.*[11] This refers to his dwelling in Beer-sheba, which is in the land of the Philistines, and it is there that he was commanded concerning the Binding. It is for this reason that he expended three days on the journey to Mount Moriah,[12] for the land of the Philistines is distant from Jerusalem. On the other hand, Hebron is in the mountains of Judah, as Scripture testifies,[13] and is therefore near to Jerusalem. Thus, when coming from the

(7) Above, 22:19. (8) Bereshith Rabbah 58:5. (9) In his commentary to Verse 2. (10) Above, 21:33. (11) *Ibid.*, Verse 34. (12) *Ibid.*, 22:4. (13) Joshua 20:7; 21:11.

Binding, he returned to Beer-sheba, as it is said, *So Abraham returned to his lads and they rose and went together to Beer-sheba.*[14] This teaches us that he tarried there and dwelled in Beer-sheba for a period of years. Now if this was the case, Sarah did not die during that period immediately following the Binding for it would not be that Abraham lived in Beer-sheba while Sarah dwelt in Hebron. And so it also appears since Isaac was born in Beer-sheba for it is previously written, *And Abraham journeyed from there towards the land of the south and abode between Kadesh and Shur and sojourned in Gerar,*[15] and Abimelech said to him, *Behold, my land is before thee; abide where it is good in thine eyes.*[16] There in that land Abraham settled in the city of Beer-sheba, for so it is written, *And it came to pass at that time that Abimelech and Phicol the captain of his host spoke unto Abraham, saying.*[17] Though it is not written there that they came to him from Gerar, [as it is written in the case of Isaac],[18] from which you might infer that Abraham lived in Gerar, this is not the case. Scripture clearly states that it was in Beer-sheba that they made the covenant.[19] Similarly, you will see that when Hagar was sent away from the house of Abraham *on the day that Isaac was weaned,*[20] she walked *in the desert of Beer-sheba,*[21] for it was there that they lived. However, after many days, he [Abraham] journeyed from the land of the Philistines and came to Hebron, and there the righteous woman Sarah passed away.

However, according to the Midrash [which states that Sarah died at the time of the Binding], we must say that Abraham and Sarah lived in Hebron at the time of the Binding, and there Abraham was commanded concerning it. The verse which states that *On the third day Abraham lifted up his eyes,*[12] poses this difficulty: Since Hebron is near Mount Moriah, which is in Jerusalem, why did he not arrive at the mountain until the third day? The answer is as follows: *The mountain which G-d had desired for His abode*[22] was

(14) Above, 22:19. (15) *Ibid.*, 20:1. (16) *Ibid.*, Verse 15. (17) *Ibid.*, 21:22. (18) Further, 26:26. (19) Above, 21:32. (20) *Ibid.*, Verse 8. (21) *Ibid.*, Verse 14. (22) Psalms 68:17. A reference to the fact that in the future the Temple of Jerusalem was to be built on that mountain. See Ramban, above, 22:2.

not revealed to him until the third day. Thus for two days he wandered in the environs of Jerusalem, and it was not yet the Divine Will to indicate the mountain to him. After the Binding, Abraham did not return to his place in Hebron. Rather, he went first to Beer-sheba, the place of his tamarisk-tree, to give thanks for the miracle that befell him. It was there that he heard of the death of Sarah, and he came to Hebron. The two apparently divergent opinions – namely, that Abraham came from Mount Moriah and that he came from Beer-sheba – are thus one [since, as explained, on his way from Mount Moriah he went to the tamarisk-tree which was in Beer-sheba, there to give thanks for the miracle]. Accordingly, the verse which states, *And Abraham abode at Beer-sheba,*[7] is intended to indicate that upon his return from the Binding he went to Beer-sheba, and from there he went to bury Sarah. After the internment he immediately returned to Beer-sheba and settled there for years. Scripture, however, concludes the subject of Beer-sheba all at once, and following that it tells of the burial, [which explains the lack of chronology in the verse, *And Abraham dwelt in Beer-sheba*]. It was there in Beer-sheba that Isaac married Rebekah, as it says, *For he dwelt in the land of the South,*[23] the locus of Beer-sheba. It is thus the opinion of all the commentators that Abraham was in another place, and it was from there that he came to the burial.

In my opinion, Sarah had a tent for herself and her attendants. And so it is written elsewhere *into Jacob's tent, and into Leah's tent, and into the tent of the two maid servants.*[24] Sarah thus died in her tent, and Abraham came into her tent with a group of his friends to bewail her. [This is a simple explanation of the expression, *and Abraham came*.] It may be that the word *vayavo (and he came)* indicates that Abraham was bestirred to make this eulogy, and he began to make it, for all who bestir themselves to begin doing a certain task are spoken of in Hebrew as "coming to it." This usage is quite common in the language of Sages, as we learn in Tractate Tamid:[25] "He came to the neck and left with it two ribs on either side.... He came to the left flank.... He came to

(23) Further, 24:62. (24) *Ibid.*, 31:33. (25) Tamid, IV, 3.

the rump." And also (you have) their expression,[26] "I have not come to this principle." In Scripture, likewise, you find, *he came for his hire,*[27] meaning that he came for the purpose of this work and did it for his hire. However, it does not appear to me feasible that Abraham came from another city to Hebron.If that were the case, Scripture would have mentioned that place and would have expressly written: "and Abraham heard, and he came from such and such a place."

4. I AM A STRANGER AND SOJOURNER WITH YOU. It was customary for them to have separate burial grounds for each family and one burial ground for the internment of all strangers. Now Abraham said to the children of Heth: "I am a stranger from another land and have not inherited a burial ground in this land from my ancestors. Now I am a sojourner with you since I have desired to dwell in this land. Therefore give me a burying-place for an everlasting possession just as one of you." However, since Abraham used the word "*t'nu* (give), [which has the same root as *matanah*," (gift)], they suspected that he desired it from them as a gift. They therefore answered him: "You are not regarded by us as a stranger or sojourner. Rather, you are a king. G-d has made you king over us, and we and our land are subservient to you. Take any burial ground you desire, and bury your dead there. It shall be unto you a possession of a burial-place forever since no one of us shall withhold it from you."

8. IF IT BE YOUR MIND TO BURY MY DEAD FROM BEFORE ME. The intent thereof is: "I will not bury my dead in another burial ground. However if it be your desire that I bury my dead, entreat for me to Ephron who has a cave at the end of his field, which is not used as his family burial-place but as a field." The meaning of the word *milphanai,* (from before me), is that if you will not do so I will entomb her in a casket. It may be that it means "my dead wife who is before me, and as an obligation I must hurry to bury her." The reason Abraham requested, *and entreat for me*, is that Ephron was a rich and distinguished person,

(26) Bechoroth 20 a. (27) Exodus 22:14.

as is indicated by his saying, *What is that between me and thee?*[28] It would therefore not be to his honor to sell his ancestral inheritance, as was the case with Naboth of Jezreel.[29] It was for this reason that Abraham did not go to Ephron to offer him an inflated price for the field, but instead he asked of the people of the city to entreat to him [Ephron] on his behalf in an honorable way.

9. THAT HE MAY GIVE ME. The intent of this is "that he may give it to me in such a way that I will consider it as a gift (even) if I will buy it from him for its full value." It is for this reason that Abraham did not mention the word "selling." A similar usage is found in the verse, *Thou shalt sell me food for money, that I may eat; and give me water for money, that I may drink,*[30] meaning "for the water which is usually given as a gift I will give money." It may be that such is the ordinary usage of the language to mention "giving" when describing sales transactions.

THE CAVE OF MACHPELAH. Rashi comments: "It had a lower and an upper cave. Another explanation [of why it was called Machpelah – the root of which is *keiphel* (double)] – is that it was 'doubled' on account of the four couples who were buried there: Adam and Eve, Abraham and Sarah, Isaac and Rebekah, Jacob and Leah". But this is incorrect since Scripture states, *the field of Ephron which was in Machpelah.*[31] Thus we see that it is the name of the place in which the field was located, and there is no need to search for a reason for the names of places.

In Bereshith Rabbah, the Sages have said:[32] "The Holy One, blessed be He, bent double the stature of the first man and He buried him there." In their opinion, this entire place was always called Machpelah though the people did not know the reason for it for Ephron sold him everything for the price of the field unaware that there was a grave in it. Abraham, on the other hand, desired

(28) Verse 15: *Land worth four hundred shekels of silver – what is that between me and thee?* (29) I Kings, Chapter 28. (30) Deuteronomy 2:28. (31) Verse 17 here. (32) 55:10.

only that he should sell him the cave which was in the end of the field, and the field might be retained by Ephron. But Ephron by way of good conduct or trickery, [possibly hoping to receive a higher price for the larger transaction], said that he would give him the field and the cave which was in it since it would be unbecoming for such an honorable person to own the cave as a possession for a burial-place while the field belonged to another. Abraham rejoiced at this suggestion, and he purchased it in its entirety for the price that Ephron mentioned.

11. IN THE PRESENCE OF THE SONS OF MY PEOPLE. The intent thereof is to state: "Behold, all the people are present, and they are knowledgeable witnesses to the sale. Therefore do not fear denial or retraction, and so *bury thy dead* from now on, for it is yours and I cannot retract." But Abraham did not do so for even after he paid its full value in silver he first took symbolic legal possession of the field and the cave. He established them as his possession in the presence of the people of the city, *and all those who came in at the gate of the city,*[33] the merchants and the residents who happened to be there, and after that he buried her.

13. 'LU' (IF) THOU WILT HEAR ME. This is equivalent to saying, "If you, if you will hear me," and the purport thereof is like, "if you, if you would hear me," the redundancy being for the purpose of emphasizing the matter. Similar cases are found in these verses: *Turn in, my lord, turn in to me;*[34] *Art thou any better, better than Balak?*[35] *And to speak against him, saying;*[36] *And as for me, whither shall I go?;*[37] *And I turned myself;*[38] *And I saw myself;*[39] *Seeing all the congregation are all holy.*[40] All these are examples of expressions of synonimity. In my opinion, this is also the case in the verse, *If from a thread even to a sandal tie, if I take (anything that is thine),*[41] which is equivalent to saying, "If, from a thread even to a sandal tie, I take anything that is yours."

(33) Verse 18 here. (34) Judges 4:18. (35) *Ibid.*, 11:25. (36) II Chronicles 32:17. (37) Further, 37:30. (38) Ecclesiastes 2:12. (39) *Ibid.*, Verse 13. (40) Numbers 16:3. (41) Above, 14:23. Here too, there is a redundant "if."

It may be that [in the verse here before us the meaning is], "If you are as you have said." that is, if you are speaking what is in your heart concerning the matter, and if you will listen to me and consummate the sale. A similar usage of a missing word is found in the verse, *And their brethren said unto them, What are ye?*[42] [which means, "What are you saying?"] In my opinion, a similar case of such usage is the verse, *Wherefore am I?*[43] [meaning, "Wherefore am I in the world?"] Perhaps this is the opinion of Onkelos who translated here, "if you will do me a favor," meaning, "if you will do my will as you have said."

15. LAND OF FOUR HUNDRED SHEKELS OF SILVER. According to Onkelos' opinion, the intent of this is that the land was so worth, [since he translated, "land *worth* four hundred shekels of silver."]

Perhaps it was Ephron's intent to say that the price of the land was so fixed in that place for it was customary in most lands that the price of a field be fixed in accordance with its dimensions. In the words of our Rabbis,[44] however, Ephron set an exorbitant arbitrary price, and Abraham, out of the willingness of his heart, listened and *did according to his will, and magnified himself.*[45] If we follow the simple interpretation of Scripture, *land of four hundred shekels of silver* means that either Ephron bought it for that price, or it was so purchased by his forefathers.

19. AND AFTER THIS, ABRAHAM BURIED SARAH HIS WIFE IN THE CAVE OF THE FIELD OF MACHPELAH BEFORE MAMRE – THE SAME IS HEBRON – IN THE LAND OF CANAAN. The reason why Scripture reverts to clarify the field, the place and the land is that the whole section mentioned the sons of Heth and Ephron the Hittite. Therefore Scripture mentions at the conclusion that the field was in the land of Canaan which is the land of Israel. And so it said at the beginning of the section: *in Kiryath arba – the same is Hebron – in the land of Canaan.*[46] All

(42) Judges 18:8. (43) Further, 25:2. See also Ramban there. (44) Bereshith Rabbah 58:9. (45) Daniel 8:4. A reference to the Midrash (*ibid.*) which says that Abraham gave Ephron shekels of large size. (46) Above, Verse 2.

this is to explain that the righteous woman died in the land of Israel, and there she was interred, as the Hittites were of the families of Canaan.[47]

In my opinion, the reason for the verses is only to mention that this was the land of Canaan, not the land of the Philistines. Having said, *And Abraham sojourned in the land of the Philistines many days,*[48] and since all his habitats were in that land – in Gerar,[49] and the valley of Gerar,[50] and Beer-sheba,[51] and from there to Hebron and back – Scripture therefore mentioned that Hebron is in the land of *the Canaanite who dwelt in that hill country,*[52] not in the land of the Philistines, which is mentioned in connection with Abraham. And in the end Scripture added a phrase to inform us that the cave was in *the field of Machpelah before Mamre,* for this was the name by which it was known.

This section was written to inform us of G-d's kindnesses to Abraham, i.e., that in the land in which he came to live he was regarded as *a prince of G-d,*[53] and each individual as well as all the people called him "my lord" although he did not tell them that he was a prince and a great man. Also, in his lifetime G-d fulfilled His promise to him: *And I will make thy name great, and thou shalt be a blessing.*[54] Moreover, his wife died and was buried *in the inheritance of the Eternal.*[55] Further, Scripture wanted to inform us of the place of the burial of the patriarchs since we are obligated to honor the burial place of our holy ancestors. Our Rabbis said[56] that this also was one of the trials of Abraham: he desired a place to bury Sarah but did not find it until he purchased it, [despite G-d's promise that the entire land would be given to him].

I do not know a reason for the words of Rabbi Abraham ibn Ezra, who says that the purpose of this section is to let us know the superiority of the land of Israel as regards the living and the dead, and also to fulfill the word of G-d which promised him that

(47) *Ibid.,* 10:15. (48) *Ibid.,* 21:34. (49) *Ibid.,* 20:1. (50) Further, 26:17-18. (51) Above, 22:19. (52) Numbers 14:45. (53) Above, Verse 6. (54) *Ibid.,* 12:2. (55) I Samuel 26:19. A reference to the land of Israel. (56) Sanhedrin 111 a.

the land would be an inheritance of his. But what superiority of the land was thus demonstrated? Abraham would not have carried her to another land to bury her, and the word of G-d to Abraham applied to the whole land, and that was fulfilled only with his seed.

24 1. AND ABRAHAM WAS OLD, WELL STRICKEN IN AGE. Scripture reiterates [Abraham's old age although it has already mentioned it][57] in order to inform us of the reason that he adjured his servant. Thus Scripture says that because Abraham saw himself to be very old and he thought that if he will send the servant to the land of his origin, perhaps before the messenger would return, he will have gone *to his long home,*[58] he therefore adjured his servant – whose counsel Isaac would follow since *he ruled over all that he had*[59] – that he should not take for him a wife from the daughters of Canaan.

In Bereshith Rabbah,[60] the Rabbis said: "Here[61] it was old age combined with vitality; further on[62] it was old age without vitality." By this the Rabbis wanted to explain that *ba'im* [literally: "coming" in days – mentioned above][57] – means the beginning of the days of old age, as the word *ba'im* indicates the present, just as, *'Haba'im' (those that come) in at these gates.*[63] But here it says that he was very old for already he was *ba bayamim* [literally: "he had come in days" – past tense], just as: *Thy brother 'ba' (came) with subtlety.*[64]

AND THE ETERNAL HAD BLESSED ABRAHAM IN ALL THINGS. I.e., with riches, possessions, honor, longevity and children, which are all the treasures of man. Scripture mentions this in order to say that Abraham was perfect in every detail, lacking in no respect save seeing his son have children who would inherit his superior position and his honor. This was why he desired it.

(57) Above, 18:11. (58) Ecclesiastes 12:5. (59) Verse 2 here. (60) 48:19. (61) That is, above, 18:11, where Scripture says, *Now Abraham and Sarah were old.* (62) That is, in the verse before us. (63) Jeremiah 7:2. (64) Further, 27:35.

Now our Rabbis have a wonderful insight into this verse. They said:[65] *"And the Eternal had blessed Abraham 'bakol' (in all things).* Rabbi Meir said that Abraham was blessed in that he did not have a daughter. Rabbi Yehudah said that he did have a daughter. *Acheirim*[66] say that he did have a daughter and her name was *Bakol."*[67] Rabbi Meir thus explained that Abraham did not have a daughter. This was a blessing for Abraham for he could not have married her except to the cursed sons of Canaan. If he were to send her to his country, she would also worship the idols as they did because a woman is subject to the authority of her husband. Indeed, Abraham did not want his worthy children from his wife Sarah to go outside the Land, and surely not that they worship the idols. Rabbi Yehudah, however, explained that Abraham did have a daughter since the Merciful One did not even cause him to lack a daughter, and that was the blessing implied by the expression, *in all things,* for he had everything that people desire, completely without exception. Then came *Acheirim* and mentioned the name of the daughter. Now truthfully, the intent of *Acheirim* and their controversy with Rabbi Yehudah were not merely to inform us of the name of this daughter. Far it be from them to expend the great and generalized blessing of Abraham on this matter, i.e., that Scripture is saying that G-d blessed him with one daughter with that name. However, *Acheirim* established a new interpretation on this verse, a very profound matter, and they explained with it one of the secrets of the Torah. Thus they said that the word *bakol* hints at a great matter, namely, that the Holy One, blessed be He, has an attribute called *Kol* (All), so called because it is the foundation of everything. It is with reference to this attribute that it says, *I am the Eternal that maketh 'Kol' (all).*[68] And this is also what Scripture says, *And the profit of the*

(65) Baba Bathra 16 b. (66) Literally "other ones," other Rabbis besides those mentioned. Rabbi Meir is sometimes called by this name. Here, however, it could not refer to him since his opinion has already been stated. *Acheirim* here refers to anonymous authorities or to the opinion of Rabbi Meir's master, Elisha ben Abuyah, who was also known as Acheir. See Chagigah 15 a. (67) The profounder meaning of this saying will be explained further in the text. (68) Isaiah 44:24.

earth is 'bakol' (in all),[69] that is to say, the profit of the earth and the abundant goodness that is bestowed upon all that come into the world is on account of this attribute *Kol*. It is the eighth attribute of the thirteen attributes.[70] And there is another attribute called *bath* [literally "daughter"] that emanates from it, and with it He moves everything. This is "the Court of the Holy One, blessed be He," that is hinted at in the word, *Vahashem (And the Eternal)*, in all places. It is called *kalah* (bride) in the book of The Song of Songs because it is comprised of *hakol* (the All), and it is this attribute which the Sages have surnamed *Knesseth Yisrael* (the assembly of Israel) in many places because it is the gathering of *hakol* (the All). It was this attribute which was to Abraham as a *bath* because he was the man of kindness, and he conducted himself in accordance with it. This was why *Acheirim* said that this blessing with which Abraham had been blessed in all things does not allude either to his having begotten a daughter from his wife Sarah, as Rabbi Yehudah said, or not, as Rabbi Meir claimed, but instead it hints at a great matter, i.e., that he was blessed with an attribute called *bath* which is contained in the attribute *Kol*, and is therefore also called *Kol*, being analogous to the expression, *For My name is in him*.[71] Thus Abraham was blessed in heaven and on earth. This is why he said, *By the Eternal, the G-d of heaven and the G-d of the earth*.[72]

This matter is to be found hinted at in the traditions of our Rabbis in many places. Thus they said in the Midrash Chazita:[73] "Rabbi Shimon ben Yochai asked Rabbi Eliezer the son of Rabbi Yosi, 'Have you possibly heard from your father of the meaning of the verse, *The crown wherewith his mother hath crowned him?*'[74] He said to him, 'Yes.' He asked, 'How?' He replied, 'It is like a king who had an only daughter whom he loved very much, and he would call her "my daughter." This did not completely express his

(69) Ecclesiastes 5:8. (70) See Ramban Exodus 34:6. (71) Exodus 23:21. (72) Verse 3 here. (73) Another name for the Midrash Rabbah on the Song of Songs. The name Chazita is derived from the first word in the verse with which this Midrash opens. *'Chazita' (Seest thou) a man diligent in his business? he shall stand before kings.* (Proverbs 22:29.) The Midrash quoted is found *ibid.*, 3:21. (74) Song of Songs 3:11.

love for her until he called her "my sister." Still he was not satisfied until he called her "my mother." In the same way, the Holy One, blessed be He, loved Israel in the beginning and called them "My daughter." It is this which Scripture says, *Hearken, O daughter, and consider.*[75] This did not completely express His love for them until He called them "My sister," as it is said, *Open to me, my sister, my love.*[76] Still He was not satisfied until He called them "My mother," as it is said, *Attend unto Me, O My people, 'ule'umi' (O My nation).*[77] The word is written *le'imi* (O My mother).' Then Rabbi Shimon ben Yochai arose and kissed him on his head, and he said to him, 'Had I come to listen to this word of yours it would have been sufficient.'..."

Now, had the commentator who prides himself on his knowledge of the Torah's secrets[78] known this, his lips would be dumb and not deride the words of our Rabbis. Therefore, I have written this in order to silence those who speak arrogantly against the righteous one.[79]

3. AND I WILL MAKE THEE SWEAR BY THE ETERNAL. It would have been proper for Abraham to command his son Isaac that he should not take a wife from the daughters of Canaan. But since it was his wish to dispatch someone during his lifetime to his country and his family, and he made the servant swear to do so whether in his lifetime or after his death, therefore Abraham found it necessary in any case to make the servant swear to go there. In addition he found it necessary to say to him, "I command you that you should not take a woman for my son of the daughters of Canaan. Instead you are to go to my country and take for him a wife from my father's house." Now having required the servant to swear to this, he no longer found it necessary to command Isaac at all for he knew that he would not transgress his father's wish or

(75) Psalms 45:11. (76) Song of Songs 5:2. (77) Isaiah 51:4. (78) Reference here is to Ibn Ezra who often prides himself on knowing the secrets of the Torah but who, in the case of this Midrash concerning Abraham's having a daughter by the name of *Bakol*, criticizes the interpretation by commenting that if that were the case, the word *bakol* should have had an additional letter *beth* preceding it and meaning "and G-d blessed Abraham 'with' *bakol*." (79) See Psalms 31:19.

the oath which he made his servant swear, as the matter was indeed known to Isaac.

It is also possible that the servant Eliezer was the administrator of his possessions, and Abraham commanded him to marry off Isaac in accordance with his will and cause him to inherit his estate on this condition, [namely, that he marry in accordance with his father's wish]. This is the significance of the expression, *that ruled over all that he had.*[80]

THE G-D OF THE HEAVEN, AND THE G-D OF THE LAND.[81] The Holy One, blessed be He, is called the G-d of the Land of Israel, as it is written, *They know not the manner of the G-d of the land,*[82] and it is further written, *And they spoke of the G-d of Jerusalem, as of the gods of the people of the earth.*[83] There is a secret in this matter which I will yet explain[84] with the help of G-d. However [in Verse 7], further on where it says, *Who took me from my father's house,* it does not say "the G-d of the land" because he [Abraham] was then in Haran or Ur of the Chaldees. So also the Rabbis have said:[85] "He who lives outside the land of Israel is as if he had no G-d, as it said, *For they have driven me out this day that I should not cleave unto the inheritance of the Eternal, saying, Go, serve other gods.*[86]

5. PERADVENTURE THE WOMAN WILL NOT BE WILLING. The meaning [of the definite article in the word *ha'ishah*] is that it refers to "the woman to whom I will speak of all the women there", or it may mean the woman who is fit for Isaac.

7. FROM MY FATHER'S HOUSE, 'UMEI'ERETZ MOLAD'TI' (AND FROM THE LAND OF MY NATIVITY). Rashi comments: "*From my father's house* – from Haran. *And from the land of my*

(80) Verse 2 here. (81) "Of the land." From Ramban's commentary it becomes obvious that he understood the word *ha'aretz* (the land) to mean "the land of Israel." (82) II Kings 17:26. (83) II Chronicles 32:19. (84) See further, 26:5, and Leviticus 18:25. (85) Ketuboth 110 b. (86) I Samuel 26:19. But who said to David, *Go serve other gods?* However this verse teaches you that he who lives outside of the land of Israel is considered as if he worshipped idols. (Ibid.)

nativity – from Ur of the Chaldees." If this is so, the expression, *Unto my country and to 'molad'ti' thou shalt go,*[87] must also refer to Ur of the Chaldees. But Heaven forbid that the sacred seed should mix with the sons of Ham,[88] the sinful one![89] Even if one would say that Abraham had some family there from the seed of Shem, the fact is however that the servant went to Haran as his master said! Now perhaps the Rabbi [Rashi] thinks that *eretz molad'to*[87](the land of his birth) was Ur of the Chaldees, but *molad'ti*[87] means "my family," and *my country*[87] means the land wherein he lived. But all these are futile words since here, in the verse before us, he said, *And thou shalt take a wife for my son from there,* [and according to Rashi, who explained *ume'eretz molad'ti,* mentioned in this verse, as meaning Ur of the Chaldees, it would follow that Abraham commanded Eliezer to go there to get a wife from the children of Ham] ! Moreover, Abraham stayed in the land of Canaan for a longer period than he did in Haran, and so why should Haran be called his country simply because he lived there for some time? Instead, the meaning of the expression, *unto my country and to 'molad'ti',*[87] is "unto my country in which I was born," [namely, Haran in Mesopotamia], for there he stayed and from there his ancestors came, as was already explained.[90] In Bereshith Rabbah we find:[91] *"From my father's house* – this is the house of his father. *And from the land of my birth* – this is the environs [of his father's house]."

It is possible that *unto my country and unto 'molad'ti'* means "Unto my country and unto my family," for he did not want a wife to be taken for Isaac even from the people of his country but only from his family. Similarly in the verse, *And thou shalt take a wife for my son from there,* [the word *misham* (from there)] alludes to the expression, *from my father's house,* mentioned at the beginning of the verse. And so did the servant say when quoting Abraham, *And thou shalt take a wife for my son of my family, and of my father's house,*[92] and again he said, quoting his

(87) Verse 4 here. (88) The Chaldees and the entire land of Shinar belonged to the sons of Ham. See Ramban, above, 11:28. (89) Above, 9:22-24. (90) See Ramban above, 11:28 and 12:1. (91) 59:13. (92) Further, Verse 40.

master. *Then shalt thou be clear from my oath when thou comest to my family.*[93] These words were said by the servant to honor them so that they would listen to him.

AND WHO SPOKE 'LI' (UNTO ME). Rashi comments: "The word *li* means 'in my interest,' just as in the verse, *which He spoke 'alai' (concerning me).*[94] In the same way, in every case where *li* and *lo* and *lahem* follow the word *dibur* (speaking), they are to be explained in the sense of *al* (concerning). For proper usage of the verb *dibur* [in the sense of speaking to a person, the pronouns *li* and *lo* and *lahem* are not appropriate, and] only *eilai* and *eilav* and *aleihem* are appropriate, and their renderings in the Targum are *imi* and *imei* and *imhon*. In the case of the word *amirah*, however, the expressions *li* and *lo* and *lahem* are appropriate."

In the section of *Vayeitzei Yaakov*, Rashi brought [proof of his above mentioned principle which states that *li* or *lecha*, etc., following the word *dibur*, must be explained in the sense of *al* (concerning)] from that which is written there, *that which 'dibarti' (I have spoken) 'lach,'*[95] [which must be interpreted to mean "in thy interest and concerning thee"] since He had never spoken to Jacob before this occasion.

But this difference is not valid for we find: *And now go, lead the people unto the place of which 'dibarti' (I have spoken) 'lach';*[96] *And the Chaldeans spoke to the king in Aramaic;*[97] *And thou shalt drive them out, and make them to perish quickly, as the Eternal hath spoken unto thee.*[98] Similarly the verb *amirah* is used with both *li* and *eilai: And they shall say 'li' (to me), What is His name? What shall I say 'aleihem' (to them)?*[99] And as for [the verse which Rashi mentioned as his proof], *that which 'dibarti' (I have spoken) 'lach,'*[95] [which must mean, as Rashi said, "concerning thee," since He had never spoken to Jacob before this

(93) *Ibid.*, Verse 41. (94) I Kings 2:4. (95) Further, 28:15. (96) Exodus 32:34. Here the word *dibur* is found in connection with *lach*, and yet it means "to you," and not "concerning you," as Rashi claimed. (97) Daniel 2:4. This too is a case similar to the above. (98) Deuteronomy 9:3. This too is similar to the above. (99) Exodus 3:13.

occasion], its interpretation is as follows: "that which I have said to you now that I will give the land to you and to your seed, and I will bless you." [Thus the word *lach* (to you) follows the understood verb "give" and is not related to *dibarti.*]

8. THEN THOU SHALT BE CLEAR FROM THIS MY OATH. Abraham did not permit him to take a wife for Isaac from the daughters of Canaan, but he would be free [from the oath if Isaac were to do it on his own] *and the Eternal do that which is good in His sight.*[100]

But Rashi wrote, "And take a wife for him from the daughters of Aner, Eshkol or Mamre." Now if they were Canaanites, far be it from him! And in truth they were of the seed of Canaan for Scripture says, *Mamre the Amorite, brother of Eshkol, and brother of Aner.*[101] And in Bereshith Rabbah, the Rabbis have said:[102] *"That thou shalt not take a wife,* etc.[103] He warned him against the daughters of Canaan, Aner, Eshkol, and Mamre." For it was with reference to Aner, Eshkol, and Mamre that Abraham said, *Among whom I dwell,*[103] since he did not dwell among all the Canaanites as they were many nations. But he warned him against these his confederates, and all the more against the others. But the verse, *Then thou shalt be clear from this my oath,* means that the servant would be free from the oath if Isaac would want to do it on his own, and Abraham relied on his knowledge that his righteous son Isaac would listen to his father and that he would beware of them and go instead to Ishmael or to Lot and the other nations.

It is possible that *from this my oath* is a hint to that which he said, *And thou shalt take a wife unto my son from there,*[104] since perhaps the oath was for everything, [meaning that the oath covered two points: a) that he should not take for him a wife from the daughters of Canaan, and b) that he should go to his family. In case they refused, he would be free from the second

(100) II Samuel 10:12. (101) Above, 14:13. (102) 59:11. (103) Verse 3 here. (104) Verse 7 here.

oath, while the first oath would always remain in effect]. Accordingly, *then thou shalt be clear from this my oath* does not allude to that which Abraham told him, *Thou shalt not take a wife unto my son of the daughters of the Canaanites,*[103] [since he never freed him from this oath]. This explains the word *zoth (this)* – *[thou shalt be clear from 'this' my oath* – implying there was another oath from which he was not freed]. Therefore, the servant said, *That I may turn to the right hand, or to the left,*[105] and he did not say, "I would return [to the land of Canaan," since he was not freed from the oath not to take a wife from the daughters of Canaan].

10. AND ALL THE GOODS OF HIS MASTER BEING IN HIS HAND. Rashi comments: "This refers to a deed of gift of all his possessions which he wrote in favor of Isaac so that they would be eager to send him their daughter." And so it is also stated in Bereshith Rabbah,[106] "He carried with him a disposition of property."

According to this opinion, the verse stating, *And Abraham gave all that he had unto Isaac,*[107] means that he caused him to take possession of the belonging at the time of his death so that the other children would not contest his ownership, just as it is said, *And he sent them away from Isaac his son, while he yet lived.*[108] If so, the word "taking" applies also to the first part of the verse, *And the servant 'took' ten camels, and departed, and all the goods of his master he took in his hand.* Perhaps [the words of the verse are to be transposed as follows]: "And the servant took ten camels and all the goods of his master in his hand, and departed."

Others[109] explain the sense of the verse as meaning that immediately upon being sworn, the servant himself went and took many camels from his master's camels because all his master's goods were in his hand, he being the officer and captain over all and authorized to take from him whatever he desired, just as the verse says, *that ruled over all that he had.*[80]

(105) Further, Verse 49. (106) 59:15. (107) Further, 25:5. (108) *Ibid.*, Verse 6. (109) This interpretation is found in the commentary of Chizkuni.

The correct interpretation appears to me to be that the meaning of this verse is similar to that of the verse concerning Hazael, general of Aram, *And Hazael went to meet him* [Elisha the prophet], *and took a present with him, and every good thing of Damascus, forty camels' burden,*[110] [which means "and 'of' every good thing of Damascus]." Here too Scripture states that he took in his hand of all his master's goods ten camels' burden. The sense of the verse concerning Hazael is that the camels carried all that was good and excellent among those species of fruits and precious things that were found in Damascus or in his master's house, and in addition they carried a present with them. In a similar sense is the verse, *ten asses laden with the good of Egypt,*[111] [which means laden with the good and excellent fruits of Egypt]. The verses, however, shorten expressions when the subjects are understood.

14. HER THOU HAST APPOINTED FOR THY SERVANT, EVEN FOR ISAAC. Rashi comments: "She is fit for him since she is charitable and worthy of admission into the house of Abraham. *And thereby shall I know* – this is a petition: 'Let me know through her *that Thou hast shown kindness unto my master.*" If so, Eliezer is saying, "I know for certain that You have appointed her for Your servant Isaac." But in that case [his petition, which still indicates a doubt as to whether she was the appointed one,] does not connect well.

Its interpretation however is as follows: "Make it happen to me this day that the girl to whom I will speak be the one that You have appointed for Your servant Isaac, and with this, show kindness to my master Abraham for with this I will know that You have shown kindness to him if she be of his family and of good mind and of beautiful appearance." And so he said [when recounting the events of the day]: *And let it come to pass, that the maiden,* etc., *let the same be the woman whom the Eternal hath appointed.*[112]

(110) II Kings 8:9. (111) Further, 45:23. (112) Further, Verses 43-44.

15. WHO WAS BORN TO BETHUEL THE SON OF MILCAH THE WIFE OF NAHOR, ABRAHAM'S BROTHER. Because Nahor also had children from his concubine Reumah,[113] they always described the lineage of Bethuel by saying that he was the son of Milcah who was the mistress of the household. And because the girl mentioned her father's mother first, as it says, *I am the daughter of Bethuel the son of Milcah*[114] – for such was customary among the girls, analogous to the verse, *And she told her mother's house*[115] – therefore Scripture mentions in the verse before us that he [Bethuel] was *the son of Milcah, the wife of Nahor.* But the servant later said, *And she said, The daughter of Bethuel Nahor's son,*[116] for he corrected the matter as is ethically proper. However, he did say, *whom Milcah bore unto him,*[116] in order to state that Bethuel was the son of the mistress and not the concubine.

17. AND THE SERVANT RAN TO MEET HER. Rashi comments: "Because he saw that the waters rose in the well when she approached it." In Bereshith Rabbah the Rabbis said,[117] "*And she filled her pitcher, and came up.*[118] All the women went down and filled their pitchers from the well. But this one, as the waters saw her they immediately rose. The Holy One, blessed be He, said to her, 'You are a sign of blessing to your children.' "[119]

It would appear that the Rabbis derived this interpretation upon observing the language, *And she filled her pitcher, and came up,*[118] for it does not say, "and she drew water and filled [the pitcher]." Now this miracle happened to her only the first time for afterwards it is written, *and she drew.*[120] The servant, when recounting the day's events to them, said: *And she went down unto the well, and drew water.*[121] That was because he thought that perhaps they would not believe in the miracle.

(113) Above, 22:24. (114) Further, Verse 25. (115) Verse 28 here. (116) Verse 47 here. (117) 60:6. (118) Verse 16 here. (119) When Israel wandered in the desert, the waters in the well would rise as soon as they approached it. See Numbers 21:17 and Midrash Rabbah, *ibid.* (120) Verse 20 here. (121) Verse 45 here.

22. AND THE MAN TOOK A GOLDEN RING... AND TWO BRACELETS UPON HER HANDS. This verse omits the deed for it should have said: "And the man took a golden ring and put it upon her nose[122] and two bracelets upon her hands." Therefore I say that the interpretation of the verse is as follows: And the man took a golden ring and two bracelets which would be upon her hands, and he said to her, *Whose daughter art thou?*[123] And after she had told him, *I am the daughter of Bethuel,*[124] he put the ring upon her nose and the bracelets upon her hands, as he told them.[125] Here, however, Scripture omits the actual giving, and similarly in many places.

32. AND THE MAN CAME INTO THE HOUSE. Eliezer is the man who entered the house. *And he ungirded the camels* – this refers to Laban who acted ethically towards his guests, unharnessed their camels and gave them straw and fodder, and he also gave water to wash the feet of Eliezer *and the feet of the men that were with him.* It must refer to Laban for it would be unlikely that it was Eliezer who gave water to wash his own feet and those of his men. A similar case is the verse, *And there passed by Midianites, merchantmen, and they drew and lifted up Joseph out of the pit.*[126] The words, *and they drew,* refer back to the brothers of Joseph mentioned in the preceding verse, and not to the Midianites. And so in the verse, *Then said Ziba unto the king* [David]: *According to all that my lord the king commandeth his servant, so shall thy servant do; but Mephibosheth eateth at my table as one of the king's sons.*[127] [The concluding words, *but Mephibosheth eateth*], are the words of David and not Ziba. There are many such verses.

(122) So it says in Verse 47 here. (123) Verse 23 here. (124) Verse 24 here. (125) In Verse 47 here. He first asked her who she was, and then he gave her the presents. This interpretation differs from Rashi (in Verse 23) who says that after he had given her the presents, he asked her whose daughter she was, for he was confident that, on account of Abraham's merit, G-d would make his journey successful. Later, however, in Verse 47, when he recounted the story, he changed the sequence of the two events so that they should not sense the inconsistency and say, "How could you give her anything when you did not know who she was?" (126) Further, 37:28. (127) II Samuel 9:11.

Now the purport of the expression, *and he ungirded the camels*, is that he unloosened the bands on their necks, as it was customary to lead them knotted, or perhaps they travelled with saddles girded upon them, just as is expressed in the verses: *Let not him that girdeth on his armor boast himself as he that putteth it off,*[128] *Loose thyself from the band of thy neck.*[129]

Now Rashi wrote, "He removed their muzzles for he had closed their mouths so that they might not graze in other peoples' fields." And in the words of Bereshith Rabbah,[130] "He removed their muzzles. Rabbi Huna and Rabbi Yirmiyah asked Rabbi Chiya the son of Rabbi Aba, 'Were not the camels of our father Abraham like the ass of Rabbi Pinchas ben Ya'ir,[131] etc.?' " This question is intended to contradict [the interpretation which maintains that the ungirding refers to] the removing of the muzzles for it is impossible that the piety in the house of Rabbi Pinchas been Ya'ir should have been greater than that in the house of our father Abraham, and just as the ass of Rabbi Pinchas ben Ya'ir did not have to be guarded against eating things which its master was forbidden to feet it, all the more so were the camels of our father Abraham. There was thus no need to muzzle them for *no injustice befalleth the righteous.*[132]

45. BEHOLD, REBEKAH CAME FORTH WITH HER PITCHER ON HER SHOULDER. This indicates that while he was in her house he heard her name, or perhaps she told him her name at the beginning even though it is not mentioned in Scripture.

61. AND REBEKAH AROSE, AND HER MAIDS. Scripture relates that after they gave permission for Rebekah and her nurse to go, as well as for Abraham's servant and his men, Rebekah rose and called her maids. *And they rode upon the camels, and followed the man* because he led them on the way.

(128) I Kings 20:11. (129) Isaiah 52:2. (130) 60:1. (131) A Sage of the Tannaitic period. He was a son-in-law of Rabbi Shimon ben Yochai. He was celebrated for his great piety; even his ass refused to eat untithed corn. (132) Proverbs 12:21.

AND THE SERVANT TOOK REBEKAH, AND WENT HIS WAY. The purpose of this is to tell of his zealousness for after having left the city with all the women following him, the servant took Rebekah to him and did not part from her in order to guard her against any mishap along the way. And Rabbi Abraham ibn Ezra said that it means that he walked with Rebekah and never felt the weariness of the journey until Isaac came and met him.

62. AND ISAAC 'BA MIBO' (HAD JUST COME) FROM THE WELL LAHAI-ROI. Scripture states that Isaac had just now come from the well Lahai-roi, having returned from the well of Lahai-roi to which he had previously come. Had the verse stated, "*Ba* (he came) from the well of Lahai," it would have appeared as if he lived there. Therefore, it was necessary to explain *ba mibo* as meaning that he returned to his city from the temporary visit that he had made to the well of Lahai-roi, for *he abode in the south country* and he was returning to his city.

It is possible that since the word *mibo* is an infinitive, it indicates that Isaac constantly went to that place since it was a place of prayer for him because of the revelation of the angel there,[133] and he *abode in the south country* near there. And so did Onkelos translate it, "He came from his coming," [thus indicating that he was in the habit of so doing].

In Onkelos' opinion this was Beer-sheba for he translated both *between Kadesh and Shur*[134] and *between Kadesh and Bered*[135] as "Rekem and Chagra."[136] If so, that place – the place of the tamarisk-tree of Abraham[137] – was suitable for prayer. Now Isaac came from that well while he was on his way to another city which was on the same road as his city, and he went out towards eventide to converse in the field with his companions and friends who were there. He met the servant and Rebekah, whereupon they all walked together to the city, *and Isaac brought her into his mother Sarah's tent.*[138]

(133) See above, 16:14. (134) Above, 20:1. (135) *Ibid.*, 16:14. (136) Thus it is obvious that Shur and Bered are synonymous. Now Shur is in Gerar (above, 20:1), and Beer-sheba is in the land of the Philistines near Gerar (see Ramban, above, 21:32). The well of Lahai-roi, which is between Kadesh and Bered (above, 16:14), is thus near Beer-sheba. (137) Above, 21:33. (138) Verse 67 here.

64. AND SHE SAW ISAAC. Rashi comments: "She saw his lordly appearance and felt abashed[139] of him." And Rabbi Abraham ibn Ezra explained that the latter verse, [namely, Verse 65, *And she said unto the servant, What man is this*], preceded Verse 64. Thus the expression, *And she said unto the servant,* means "And she had already said to the servant." In Ibn Ezra's opinion there are many such verses in the Torah.

This is truly so, but here it is not correct, for in this case you would have to mix the verses and transpose their parts as follows: *And Rebekah lifted up her eyes, and she saw Isaac* [Verse 64] – *and she said unto the servant: What man is this that walketh in the field to meet us? And the servant said: It is my master* [Verse 65] – *and she alighted from the camel* [Verse 64] – *and she took her veil, and covered herself* [Verse 65].

In my opinion [we need not mix the verses, but the sense thereof is as follows]: When Rebekah saw a man walking in the field towards her, hastening on the road and walking in the field towards them, she knew that he had come to see them and greet them or to bring them into his house for lodging, and so she did as was ethically proper for women, and she stood modestly.

AND SHE ALIGHTED ('VATIPOL') FROM THE CAMEL. Rashi comments: "She let herself slide towards the ground, as the Targum renders it, 'She inclined herself [towards the earth but did not actually reach the ground]. Similarly, *Let down thy pitcher* [140] was translated by Onkelos to mean 'incline.' *And He bowed down the heavens*[141] – the Targum translates: 'and He bent.' A similar case is the verse, *Though he fall, he shall not be utterly cast down,*[142] which means though he bends himself towards the earth, yet he shall not touch the ground."

But Onkelos' opinion is not that she let herself slide off the camel to the earth, for if so, she actually fell off the camel and did not just incline herself. Similarly, all expressions of "inclining"

(139) "Abashed." In our Rashi: "and she gazed at him in astonishment." (140) Above, Verse 14. (141) Psalms 18:10. (142) *Ibid.*, 37:24.

merely mean a bending towards one side. Onkelos' opinion, however, is that on the camel upon which she was riding she bent herself towards one side in order to turn her face away from him. A similar case, in my opinion, is the verse: *And when Naaman saw one running after him, 'vayipol' from upon the chariot to meet him, and said, Is all well?*[143] The word *vayipol* here only means that he bent himself in the chariot towards the runner who was on the ground to ask of him whether all is well. And so indeed it is said there, *When the man turned back from his chariot to meet thee.*[144] It is possible that as far as Onkelos is concerned, the expression, *from on the camel,* is like "on the camel," [the letter *mem* in the word *mei'al (from* on) being redundant]. A similar case is the verse, *For great 'mei'al' the heavens is Thy mercy,*[145] [which means "for great on the heavens is Thy mercy," and not "from on the heavens"]. A redundant letter *mem* like this is also found in these verses: *There shall be no more 'misham' an infant of days, nor an old man,*[146] [which means "there shall be no more *there,*" and not "from there"]; *Ye waters that are 'mei'al' the heavens,*[147] [which means "ye waters that are on the heavens," and not "from on the heavens"].

In line with the plain meaning [of Scripture, however, the letter *mem* in the word *mei'al* is not redundant, but instead] it is like the *mem* in the verse, *And, behold, there came many people 'miderech' (from a way) round-about.*[148] [And thus in the verse before us, *mei'al hagamal* would mean that she alighted "from on the camel."] There are many similar verses.

67. AND ISAAC BROUGHT HER INTO HIS MOTHER SARAH'S TENT. The construct is missing here [for the noun *ohel* (tent) appears with the definite article, and in this form it cannot be used in construct with "his mother Sarah." The verse then should be understood as if it were written, "and Isaac brought her into the tent which was the tent of his mother Sarah."] There are many cases like this.

(143) II Kings 5:21. (144) *Ibid.*, Verse 26. (145) Psalms 108:5. (146) Isaiah 65:20. (147) Psalms 148:4. (148) II Samuel 13:34.

The purport of the verse is to tell of the honor that Isaac bestowed upon his mother for from the time that Sarah died they did not take down her tent because they said, "Let not another woman come into the tent of the honorable mistress." But when he saw Rebekah he brought her into that tent in her honor and there he took her as his wife. This is the meaning of the words, *and he loved her, and he was comforted,* indicating that he was deeply grieved for his mother, finding no comforter until he was comforted by his wife through his love for her. Otherwise, what reason is there for Scripture to mention a man's love for his wife?

But Onkelos explained: *And Isaac brought her into the tent* and, behold, she was like *Sarah his mother*. It is for this reason that Scripture mentions the love he had for her because it was on account of her righteousness and the aptness of her deeds that he loved her and was comforted by her. And so the Rabbis mentioned in Bereshith Rabbah,[149] "Before Sarah died there was a blessing of miraculous increase in the dough. [After her death it stopped, and when Rebekah came the blessing reappeared."]

25 3. ASSHURIM, AND LETUSHIM, AND LEUMMIM. Rashi comments: "These were the names of clan chieftains. But I cannot reconcile Onkelos' translation with the language of the text."[150]

It appears to me that Onkelos was of the opinion that *Asshurim* means camps, companies that travel the roads from city to city, just as it says, *a company of Ishmaelites.*[151] Onkelos thus considered *Asshurim* as being derived from the expressions, *To His steps ('ba'ashuro') hath my foot held fast;*[152] *His steps ('ashurav') do not slide.*[153] And Onkelos' opinion of *Letushim* is that they are the ones who dwell in tents that are scattered over the face of the earth, resting today in one place and tomorrow in another, for

(149) 60:15. (150) Onkelos translates *Asshurim* as meaning "camps," *Letushim* as "owners of tents who spread about in all directions," and *Leumim* as "islands" or "sea-districts." Upon this Rashi comments that he cannot make Onkelos' translation fit in exactly with the words of the text. Ramban now proceeds to explain Onkelos' understanding on the verse and also the reason why he was forced to make this translation. (151) Further, 37:25. (152) Job 23:11. (153) Psalms 37:31.

the letter *lamed* and *nun* interchange in many places, [thus *Letushim* would be like *Netushim* (scattered ones)] just like *lishchah* and *nishchah,*[154] [both of which mean "chamber"]; *And on that day men were appointed over 'haneshachoth' (the chambers).*[155] From this root is derived the expression, *a sword 'netushah,'*[156] which is the same as *letushah* (sharpened). And of the word *Le'ummim* Onkelos said *ulenagvon,* [which is Aramaic for the Hebrew word] *iyim* (islands).[157]

Onkelos was stirred to this translation by the word *hayu* [*and the children of Dedan 'hayu' (were) Asshurim, and Letushim, and Leummim*], when it would have been proper to express it similarly to the verse, *And Mitzraim begot Ludim, and Ananim, and Lehabim, and Naphtihim.*[158]

And in Bereshith Rabbah we find:[159] "Rabbi Shmuel the son of Rav Nachman said that even though we translate these names and say, 'Merchants, flaming ones, and heads of peoples,' all of them were heads of peoples." The matter is as I have explained. The translators rendered *Asshurim* as "merchants, those who walk the road." From the word *Letushim* (sharp, shiny) they derived "men of wickedness," *their faces are faces of flame,*[160] burning as torches, from the roots: to *sharpen (liltosh) his plowshare, and his coulter;*[161] *He sharpened (yiltosh) his eyes upon me.*[162] But Rabbi Shmuel the son of Rav Nachman said that even though they are accustomed to thus translate these names, they are still only the proper names of the heads of people, there being no descriptive name among them at all. And such is the case.

6. BUT UNTO THE SONS OF THE CONCUBINES, THAT ABRAHAM HAD. By way of the plain meaning of Scripture, since it was said to Abraham, *For in Isaac shall seed be called to thee,*[163] and in no other seed, all his consorts were concubines to him, not as wives since their children would not be among his

(154) Nehemiah 13:7. (155) *Ibid.,* 12:44. (156) Isaiah 21:15. (157) See Isaiah 41:1 and Targum. (158) Above, 10:13. (159) 61:4. (160) Isaiah 13:8. (161) I Samuel 13:20. (162) Job 16:9. (163) Above, 21:12.

heirs. Thus, Hagar, Sarah's handmaid, was his concubine. However, Keturah he took unto himself as a wife for if she whom he took as a concubine had been a handmaid in his house, Scripture would not have said, *And Abraham took a wife, and her name was Keturah.*[164] She is called "concubine" in Scripture – it is written in Chronicles, *And the sons of Keturah, Abraham's concubine*[165] – only for the reason that I have explained, [namely, that it had been said to Abraham, *For in Isaac shall seed be called to thee*]. Thus we note that Abraham took unto himself a wife from the daughters of Canaan! And should you say that she was an Egyptian or from the land of the Philistines, we may yet question why he did not send to his country and to his kindred as he did in the case of his son. But the answer is that he guarded only the seed of Isaac since it was concerning him that the Covenant was made. Furthermore, Scripture does not say, "And Abraham took a wife by the name of Keturah, the daughter of a certain Hivite or Philistine or Egyptian from a certain land," as it says concerning Esau's wives[166] and similar cases. Rather, Scripture mentions only Keturah's name because she was a Canaanite, and therefore it cut short her genealogy. Scripture does so in many places where it is not concerned with the genealogy.

Perhaps Keturah was called "concubine" because she was a handmaid who was descended from a family of slaves. And if she was a handmaid in his [Abraham's] household and he had connection with her, Scripture would not mention her genealogy since even among the matriarchs, such as Zilpah and Bilhah, it mentions only their names.

Now Rashi wrote, "Wives are those whom a man marries with a marriage-contract; concubines have no marriage-contract, as it says in reference to the wives and concubines of David, in Tractate Sanhedrin."[167] But the matter is not so. A woman is called a concubine only when there is no betrothal, for a marriage-contract is only a Rabbinic ordinance. And the correct text in Tractate Sanhedrin is: "A concubine has no marriage-contract or betrothal." However, it is possible that the sons of Noah[168] too when they

(164) Verse 1 here. (165) I Chronicles 1:32. (166) Further, 26:34 and 28:9. (167) 21 a. (168) See *Seder Bereshith,* Note 222.

married wives, as is their law, by intercourse, were accustomed to write them a marriage-contract which granted *dowry and gift.*[169] However, for one who wished to be a concubine to them, whom he could send away when he pleased and whose children would not be among his heirs, he would not write anything. But according to the opinion of our Rabbis that Keturah is Hagar,[170] she was certainly a concubine [since it clearly says that Hagar was Sarah's handmaid].[171]

8. OLD AND FULL OF YEARS. He witnessed the fulfillment of all the desires of his heart and was sated with all good things. In a similar sense is [the verse written in connection with Isaac's life], *and full of days,*[172] which means that his soul was sated with days, and he had no desire that the future days should bring something new. This is as it is said of David: *And he died in a good old age, full of days, riches and honor.*[173] This is a story of *the mercies of the Eternal*[174] towards the righteous ones, and of their attribute of goodness by virtue of which they do not desire luxuries, just as it is said of them, *Thou hast given him his heart's desire,*[175] and not as it is said of other people, *He that loveth money shall not be satisfied with money,*[176] and as the Rabbis have commented thereon:[177] "No man leaves the world having amassed half of his desires. If he has a hundred, he desires two hundred. If he succeeds in acquiring two hundred, he desires to make of it four hundred, as it is said, *He that loveth money shall not be satisfied with money.*"[176] In Bereshith Rabbah the Rabbis have said:[178] "The Holy One, blessed be He, shows the righteous in this world the reward He is destined to give them in the Coming World, and their souls become full and they fall asleep."[179] The Sages were stirred by this and they explained the verse which says, *and full of years*, with this vision [of the reward that G-d shows the righteous before they die].

(169) Further, 34:12. (170) Bereshith Rabbah 61:4. (171) Above, 16:1. (172) Further, 35:29. (173) I Chronicles 29:28. (174) Isaiah 63:7. (175) Psalms 21:3. (176) Ecclesiastes 5:9. (177) Koheleth Rabbah 1:34. (178) 62:3. (179) I.e., they die without pain.

9. AND HIS SONS ISAAC AND ISHMAEL BURIED HIM. In the language of Bereshith Rabbah,[180] "Here the son of the handmaid bestowed respect upon the son of the mistress" [since he yielded precedence to Isaac].

11. AND ISAAC DWELLED BY THE WELL LAHAI-ROI. I.e., near that place, or perhaps because it was not a city,[181] Scripture says that he pitched his tent near the well.

17. AND THESE ARE THE YEARS OF THE LIFE OF ISHMAEL. It appears plausible in line with the simple explanation that Scripture relates, in the case of the sons of the righteous, their generations and the number of their years in order to inform us that the seed of the righteous shall be blessed.[182] However, it did not relate the number of Esau's years for he outlived Jacob,[183] and the narrative was concluded with the death of Jacob. Hence, Scripture did not want to return to the life of Esau since it had already mentioned his generations in their appropriate place.[184]

In the Midrash of our Rabbis[185] there are many reasons for the Scriptural account of Ishmael's years. The correct one among them is that he was righteous, a man of repentance, and Scripture tells of him as it does with all righteous people.

AND HE EXPIRED ('VAYIGVA'). Rashi comments: "This expression — 'expiring' — is only mentioned in the case of righteous people." But in the Gemara[186] the Rabbis objected, "But it says 'expiring' with reference to the generation of the flood: *And all flesh expired that moved upon the earth,* etc., *and*

(180) 62:6. (181) See above, 16:14, for the origin of the name "the well of Lahai-roi," and there it expressly says that it was *by a fountain of water in the wilderness.* It was thus not a city. (182) See Psalms 112:2. (183) See my Hebrew commentary, p. 42, Note 90. (184) Further, Chapter 36. (185) Megillah 17 a; Bereshith Rabbah 62:8. (186) Baba Bathra 16 b. The *Gemara* (teaching) constitutes the collected discussions of the *Amoraim,* centering around the *Mishnah.* The Mishnah and Gemara combined are known as the Talmud.

every man;[187] *Every thing that is in the earth shall expire."*[188] And the Gemara answers: "We were referring to [those places where it mentions both] 'expiring' and 'gathering,' " [as it says in the case of Abraham and in the present verse concerning Ishmael].

The intent of the Rabbis is that the expression "expiring" indicates death without prolonged sickness and without pains. This death is merited only by the righteous people, [and concerning their death both "expiring" and "gathering" are mentioned]. But the men of the generation of the flood, who were *overthrown as in a moment, and no hands fell upon* them,[189] as also those who died in the desert – with them Scripture therefore mentions only "expiring": *when our brethren expired.*[190] And so is the sense of the verse, *And that man expired not alone in his iniquity,*[191] meaning that his iniquity did not cause him instant death. But when Scripture so mentions the term "expiring" in reference to death together with the word *vayei'aseph* (and he was gathered [unto his people]) or *vayamoth* (and he died), it hints to the death of the righteous ones.

In the words of Bereshith Rabbah,[192] *"And Abraham expired, and died,*[193] Rabbi Yehudah the son of Rabbi Ilai said, 'The early pious men used to suffer with intestinal disease for about ten or twenty days before death, thus establishing the principle that illness cleanses from sin.' Rabbi Yehudah said, 'All who are said to have expired died of intestinal disease.' " There in Bereshith Rabbah the Rabbis also said,[194] *"Everything that is in the earth 'yigva'*[188] – will shrivel."

It would appear that to the Rabbis, the word *gviyah* (expiring) was analogous to *Their flesh shall consume while they stand upon their feet.*[195] So also is the opinion of Onkelos who translated here *ve'isnagid*, meaning "fainting," similar to the expressions: "*isnagid* (he became faint) and sighed";[196] "You might think he

(187) Above, 7:21. (188) *Ibid.*, 6:17. (189) Lamentations 4:6. (190) Numbers 20:3. (191) Joshua 22:20. (192) 62:2. (193) Verse 8 here. (194) 31:15. (195) Zechariah 14:12. (196) Sanhedrin 39 a.

may pay as a fine five *negidim* (emaciated) oxen."[197] It is so said in the case of the flood, as Scripture states, *And He blotted out every being.*[198] And in the case of Ishmael it is stated in the verse before us: *And he expired and died,* as a man who is powerless and dies, and this is the measure[199] meted out to righteous people.[200]

(197) Baba Kamma 67 b. In case of a thief who makes restitution for stolen oxen. See Exodus 21:37. Now "you might think that if he stole an ox worth one hundred (weights in gold or silver) he may pay as a fine five oxen emaciated ('and in near-dying condition' - Rashi). It is for this reason that Scripture says (*he shall pay five oxen) 'tachtav'* " – in its place. In other words each one of the five oxen must be equal in value to the stolen ox, "for otherwise he might pay him back five emaciated oxen which together will not equal even the value of the one stolen" (Meiri, Baba Kamma *ibid.*). (198) Above 7:23. Ramban's intent here is to be understood in the light of what he has written above on that verse: "*And He blotted out every living substance...*" After having said, *And all flesh perished ('vayigva'),* and having said, *whatever was in the dry land, died,* Scripture continues to say,"*And He blotted out,* meaning etc."(see above p. 112). Here in discussing the meaning of the word *gviyah,* Ramban brings proof to his theory that *gviyah* in itself does not mean death but fainting, emaciation, etc. For it is on this basis that we can understand why after having said *'vayigva' all flesh* Scripture continued to inform us further that it died and was blotted out, since these facts are not included in the term of *gviyah.* (199) "A measure." In the Lisbon edition of Ramban: "the death." (200) For since in the present verse concerning Ishmael it says both "expired" and "died" the reference must be to the death of a righteous person, as explained in the text above. "It is based upon this (double expression) that the Sages of blessed memory have said that Ishmael repented of his evil ways" (Bachya, p. 219 in my edition).

Toldoth

19. AND THESE ARE THE GENERATIONS OF ISAAC, ABRAHAM'S SON. Scripture says this of Esau and Jacob,[1] Isaac's sons who are mentioned further on. Scripture further mentions the circumstances of their birth.[2]

ABRAHAM BEGOT ISAAC. Rashi comments: "Since it was written, *Isaac, Abraham's son,* it became necessary for Scripture to say, *Abraham begot Isaac,* since the scoffers of the generation[3] were saying, 'It was from Abimelech that Sarah became pregnant.' Therefore the Holy One, blessed be He, formed Isaac's facial features similar to those of Abraham so that all should say,[4] *Abraham begot Isaac.*"

Rabbi Abraham ibn Ezra further says that the meaning of the word *holid* (begot) is "bring up and raise," as is the expression, *'Yuldu' (were raised) upon Joseph's knees,*[5] even as it says, *And he sent them away from Isaac his son.*[6]

(1) Ramban's intent is to teach us that the word *toldoth* is not to be understood in the broad sense of "generations" but in the more specific sense of "children." Thus the verse reads, *And these are the children of Isaac,* namely, Esau and Jacob mentioned further on. Compare Ramban at beginning of *Seder Noach.* (2) Thus, in order to explain fully the story of Jacob and Esau, Scripture begins with an account of their genealogy. (3) Those who did not believe in the Divine Providence that guided Abraham's destiny. (4) "Say." In our text of Rashi: "testify." (5) Further, 50:23. The word *yuldu* there could not mean "were born," for it would then mean that Joseph's great grandchildren were actually born upon his knees. It must mean "raised." Similarly, it means here, "Abraham *raised* Isaac." (6) Above, 25:6, referring to the other children that Abraham sent away. Thus it is clear that only Isaac was raised by Abraham.

In my opinion the correct reason [that Scripture states here, *Abraham begot Isaac*], is that it now reverts and begins the genealogy with the founding father, in consonance with Scriptural custom, which is to revert to the head of the ancestry when dealing with people of distinction.[7] Similarly, it is written in the book of Chronicles, *The sons of Shem: Elam and Asshur, and Arpachshad, and Lud, and Aram, and Uz, and Hul, and Gether, and Meshech. And Arpachshad begot Shelah, and Shelah begot Eber.*[8] After Scripture concluded this listing, it began again by saying, *Shem, Arpachshad, Shelah,*[9] until, *Abram, the same is Abraham.*[10] So also in the genealogy of Benjamin in the book of Chronicles, Scripture reverts to previous generations and begins, *And Ner begot Kish, and Kish begot Saul.*[11] Here also [the Torah reverts to the founding father and says], *Abraham begot Isaac,* and Isaac begot Jacob, as Scripture will soon mention.

It is necessary that Scripture return to relate this[12] since it said, *And these are the generations of Ishmael, Abraham's son.*[13] Now, had it only said, *And these are the generations of Isaac, Abraham's son,* it would appear that Scripture equated Ishmael and Isaac with respect to genealogy and distinction, all the more so since it mentioned the firstborn first.[14] Furthermore it would have been

(7) The Hebrew *anshei hama'alah*, which literally means "men of elevation," refers to spiritual or political distinction. (8) I Chronicles 1:17-18. (9) *Ibid.*, Verse 24. This is explained by the fact that Shem is the head of Abraham's ancestry. Hence Scripture reverts to him in tracing the generations. (10) *Ibid.*, Verse 27. (11) *Ibid.*, 9:39. Saul was king of Israel. Hence Scripture reverts to his founding ancestor. (12) "This" refers to the statement, *Abraham begot Isaac.* For the purpose of indicating Jacob's distinction it would have been sufficient to mention, *And these are the generations of Isaac, Abraham's son.* Merely mentioning Abraham in this connection would have satisfied the Scriptural principle of reverting to the founding father in the case of "people of distinction." Why then did the Torah continue, *Abraham begot Isaac?* Ramban proceeds to resolve this difficulty in accordance with Scriptural textual principles as opposed to Rashi, quoted above, who resorted to an Aggadic explanation: "Since the scoffers of the generation were saying etc." (13) Above, 25:12. (14) Thus, Ishmael, the firstborn son of Abraham, would seem to be more significant than Isaac since he was referred to in exactly the same manner as Isaac and additionally he was mentioned first. Hence it became necessary to augment Isaac's distinction by saying, *Abraham begot Isaac.*

fitting that it begin with Abraham[15] and say, "These are the generations of Abraham." But Scripture did not wish to do this in order to avoid listing Ishmael and the children of Keturah.[16] It is for this reason that Scripture returns and completes the verse by stating, *Abraham begot Isaac,* as if to say that it is he [Isaac] alone who is Abraham's offspring. It is considered as if he [Abraham] did not beget anyone else, just as it says, *For in Isaac shall seed be called to thee.*[17] It is for this reason that it also says above, *And these are the generations of Ishmael, Abraham's son, whom Hagar the Egyptian, Sarah's handmaid, bore unto Abraham:*[13] the phrase, *whom Hagar*, etc., is for the honor of Isaac, as if to say that the genealogy of these generations is not traceable to Abraham, rather they are the children of the handmaid, even as it says, *And also of the son of the bondwoman will I make a nation.*[18] Scripture does also similarly in the book of Chronicles. At first it states: *The sons of Abraham; Isaac and Ishmael. These are their generations: the first born of Ishmael, Nebaioth.*[19] Then it mentions, *And the sons of Keturah, Abraham's concubine: she bore Zimran.*[20] Now it would have been logical to follow this by saying, "the sons of Isaac," but instead it reverts and begins: *And Abraham begot Isaac. The sons of Isaac: Esau, and Israel.*[21]

22. AND SHE SAID: IF IT BE SO, 'LAMAH ZEH ANOCHI?' "If the pain of pregnancy is so great, *lamah zeh anochi* (why did I) pray for and aspire to pregnancy?" Thus Rashi. But it is not correct.[22] Rabbi Abraham ibn Ezra says that she asked the women if they had experienced such pains, and they said, "No," whereupon she said, "If the matter and custom of pregnancy be as they said, *lamah zeh anochi*, why am I beset with an unusual

(15) In other words, instead of saying, *And these are the generations of Isaac,* it would have been proper that Scripture begin with Abraham, but Scripture had to avoid this for reasons explained further on in the text. (16) Above, 25:1-4. (17) *Ibid.*, 21:12. (18) *Ibid.*, Verse 13. (19) I Chronicles 1:28-29. (20) *Ibid.*, Verse 32. (21) *Ibid.*, Verse 32. The repetition, *And Abraham begot Isaac,* is necessary lest we equate "the sons of Ishmael" with "the sons of Isaac." (22) For the word *anochi* (I), according to Rashi, implies "I prayed for pregnancy." And this, comments Ramban, is not correct. (Gur Aryeh.)

pregnancy?" Now according to this exposition, the verse is missing and not complete.[23]

The correct interpretation in my opinion is that she said, "If it shall be so with me, *lamah zeh anochi,* [why am I in the world]? Would that I did not exist, that I should die or never have come into existence."[24] This is similar to the verse, *I should have been as though I had not been.*[25]

AND SHE WENT 'LIDROSH' (TO INQUIRE) OF THE ETERNAL. Rashi comments: "To tell[26] what her outcome will be." Now I have not discovered the word *drishah* [*lidrosh,* to inquire] in relation to G-d except in the context of prayer, as in the verses: *I sought ('darashti') the Eternal and He answered me;*[27] *seek ye Me, ('dirshuni') and live;*[28] *As I live, saith G-d the Eternal, I will not be inquired of ('edareish') by you.*[29]

23. TWO NATIONS ARE IN THY WOMB. The intent of this is that He informed her that she should not fear, for the reason that the struggle in her womb is that she is pregnant with twins, this being the customary way among women who are pregnant with twins.

It is possible that He is also saying that since they are destined to be two peoples, hating and warring with each other, at the very beginning of their creation they initiated a quarrel, thus intimating at the situation which will ultimately exist between them. But He assured her that now they will rest, and she will find rest and quiet for herself.

28. BECAUSE THERE WAS VENISON IN HIS MOUTH. The commentators[30] explained it as meaning either that he [Esau] gave venison into Isaac's mouth, or that he brought Isaac venison.

(23) Her inquiring of other women as to their experiences with pregnancy is not even mentioned explicitly although it is central to the thought expressed in the verse, according to Ibn Ezra. (24) The J. P. S. translation, *If it be so, wherefore do I live?*, follows Ramban's interpretation. (25) Job 10:19. (26) "To tell." Our text of Rashi reads: "that He should tell her." (27) Psalms 34:4. (28) Amos 5:4. (29) Ezekiel 20:3. See Ramban on Exodus 18:15. (30) Ibn Ezra and R'dak.

The act of giving or bringing is thus missing from the verse. Similarly: *The set time which Samuel;*[31] *But the Lord* – presented or made – *me as a mighty warrior.*[32]

It is possible to explain that *Isaac loved Esau* because there was always venison in the mouth of Isaac. All day he would desire to eat the venison, and it was always in his mouth. He would not eat anything else, and Esau was the one who brought it to him, as Scripture said, *A cunning hunter.*[33]

In my opinion the correct interpretation is that it is a metaphor which tells us that Esau, in the mouth of his father, was a hunter,[34] as a person is surnamed by his constant occupation. Similarly, *Thy habitation is in the midst of deceit;*[35] likewise, *But I am all prayer.*[36] And so they said in Bereshith Rabbah,[37] "Good meat for his mouth, good drink for his mouth."[38]

30. OF THIS RED, RED POTTAGE. The dish was either reddened by the lentils which were red, or it had been compounded with some red substance, and Esau, not knowing what it was, called it *edom* (red). *Therefore was his name called Edom* since they mocked at him for having sold an honorable birthright for a small dish. *For the drunkard and the glutton shall come to poverty.*[39]

31. SELL ME THIS DAY ('KAYOM') THY BIRTHRIGHT. "I.e., as this day.[40] Just as this day is certain, so make me a binding sale." This is Rashi's language.

(31) I Samuel 13:5. Here the word "appointed" is missing, the meaning of the verse being "at the set time which Samuel had appointed." (32) Jeremiah 20:11. (33) Above, Verse 27. (34) Instead of calling him by his name, Isaac would call him "hunter." (35) Jeremiah 9:5. Meaning "in the midst *of people* of deceit." But the verse refers to the people by their constant practice. (36) Psalms 109:40. Meaning, "But I am *a man* of constant prayer." (37) Bereshith Rabbah 63:15. (38) If he would find good meat or drink, he would bring it to his father. This Midrash thus indicates that Esau was constantly engaged in bringing food and drink to his father. Hence Isaac came to call him "hunter" because of his steady preoccupation with bringing him food. (39) Proverbs 23:21. Esau was thus mocked that because of his gluttony he would be reduced to poverty. (40) "As this day." Our text of Rashi reads: "*Ketargumo* (Explain it as the Targum rendered it), 'as this day.' " Rashi now proceeds to interpret the Targum to mean, "just as this day is certain, etc."

The literal meaning of the word *kayom* is "at this time," just as: *But stand thou still at this time ('kayom'), that I may cause thee to hear the word of G-d;*[41] *At this time ('kayom') you shall find him;*[42] *Let the fat be made to smoke at this time ('kayom');*[43] *But unto us belongeth confusion of face, as at this day ('kayom').*[44]

It would appear from the opinion of Onkelos[45] that because the sale of the birthright was to take effect after the death of his father Isaac, he [Jacob] said, "Sell me the birthright, with the sale to take effect on whatever day [our father's death] may occur."[46] This is a typical usage of *lahein* in the Aramaic language: "Wherever (*lahein*) are you going?"[47] This means, "To what place are you going?" This is derived from the expression, "Whatever (*hein*) you let me know."[48] Similarly in Bereshith Rabbah, *Parshath Vayishlach,*[49] "Wherever (*velahein*) are they going?"[50] is derived from the expression, "Whatever (*hein*) is broken."[49] This is their[51] customary usage of language in many places. And in the book of Daniel this form appears with a *patach*[52] under the letter *lamed*, similar in meaning to the word *ilahin* (which): *Which 'lohin' the angels whose dwelling is not with flesh;*[53] *whatever*[54] *('lohin'), O king, let my counsel be acceptable unto thee.*[55] Now Onkelos

(41) I Samuel 9:27. (42) *Ibid.*, Verse 13. (43) *Ibid.*, 2:16. (44) Daniel 9:7. (45) Since Onkelos, the author of the Targum, added the word *dilhein*, it would appear from this, etc. (46) Ramban's intent is as follows: Since Esau would not possess the birthright until after Isaac's death —(see Ramban further, Verse 34, that the birthright carried with it no distinction except after the passing of the father)— if he were to attempt to sell it effective immediately, the sale would not be valid. But in this way, having stipulated "whenever that may be," even though the death of Isaac and the subsequent acquisition of the birthright by Esau have not yet occurred, the sale by Esau is nevertheless valid since Jacob stipulated "whenever that may be." See my Hebrew commentary, p. 145. (47) Yerushalmi Berachoth II, 8: *lahein yeizil lei.* (48) Yalkut Shimoni Ezra 10:3. (49) Bereshith Rabbah 78:1. (50) Our Bereshith Rabbah reads: *ule'an atun azlin.* See, however, Theodore's edition of this Midrash, p. 906, where he quotes from manuscript, *velahein*, as Ramban has it. (51) Those conversing or writing in the Aramaic language. (52) That is our *kametz.* (53) Daniel 2:11. (54) "Whatever, you do, O king...." (55) *Ibid.*, 4:24.

translated the Hebrew word *zulathi* as *ilahin*[56] its meaning being as the two words, *ila hin.*

Now in carefully edited texts of Onkelos I found the reading, *kayom dilhei.* This conforms with my interpretation, for *hei* in their language[57] means "which," as it is said in the Talmud: "Which (*hei*) Rabbi Meir?"[58] "Which (*hei*) Rabbi Yehudah?"[59] and others.

It is possible that Onkelos understood the word *kayom* (as the day) as if it were *bayom* (on the day). The verse would then be stating, "Sell the birthright to me on the day it will come into your possession." We find such usage of the letter *kaf* elsewhere: *As ('Ka'asher') they go, I will spread My net upon them,*[60] meaning *ba'asher* (wherever they go) rather than "whenever they go." Similarly, *And for the blood ('kidmei') of thy children that thou didst give unto them;*[61] *For I have spread you abroad as the four ('ke'arba') winds of the heavens.*[62]

And some scholars say[63] that the price for the birthright was not the pottage at all. Rather, Scripture tells that when Esau, being faint, desired to eat, Jacob said to him, "Sell me your birthright for money and then eat," and Esau, in his haste for food, answered him, "What is this birthright to me? It is sold to you." He then swore to him upon it, and they sat down to eat and drink. Scripture however did not reveal the price. I do not agree with this interpretation.

(56) Deuteronomy 1:36. *Zulathi Caleb* (excepting Caleb) is translated by Onkelos as *elahin Caleb.* To the Aramaic root *lahin* which appears in the book of Daniel – (see my Hebrew text, p. 145 line 2 from bottom, covering Notes 53 and 55 here) – Onkelos added the letters *aleph* and *yod,* thus making it *elahin.* The intent of Ramban is to indicate that it should not surprise us that Onkelos added a *dalet* in the text before us, thus making it *dilhein,* for just as the original word *hen* was augmented to become *lahein* so he further expanded it to read *dilhein.* (Aboab.) (57) Aramaic. (58) Baba Kamma 99 b. (59) Baba Bathra 141 a. (60) Hosea 7:12. (61) Ezekiel 16:36. *Ve'kidmei* is to be interpreted as *ubidmei* (and *in* the blood). (62) Zechariah 2:10. *Ke'arba* is here to be interpreted as *be'arba (in* the four). (63) Quoted by R'dak in his commentary in the name of his father. It is mentioned in Pesikta Zutrata, and a reference to it is also found in Bamidbar Rabbah 6:2.

33. SWEAR TO ME THIS DAY. When Esau said, "What is this birthright to me? I do not desire it," Jacob said to him, "Swear to me that you will not desire it, nor will you inherit it forever." Thereupon he swore to him, and following that he sold it to him, and Jacob gave him the purchase price[64] or the pottage he desired.

It is possible that Esau said, "What is this birthright to me? It is sold to you," and Jacob said, "Swear to me that you will never complain about the sale." And when Scripture says that first he swore to him and then he sold it to him, its intent is as if it said that he sold it to him first and then swore to him.

34. SO ESAU DESPISED HIS BIRTHRIGHT. *Who so despiseth the word shall suffer thereby.*[65] But, indeed, Scripture has already explained the reason that Esau consented to the sale. This was because he was in mortal danger from his hunting animals, and it was likely that he would die while his father was alive, and the birthright carried with it no distinction except after the passing of the father. So of what benefit was the birthright to him? This then is what Scripture says: *And he did eat and drink, and he rose and went, and he despised,* for, after having eaten and drunk, he returned to his hunt in the field which was the cause of the despising of the birthright. *For there is no desire in fools*[66] except to eat and drink and to fulfill their momentary desire, not giving a care for tomorrow.

Now Rabbi Abraham ibn Ezra has erred here exceedingly by saying that Esau despised the birthright because he saw his father destitute of wealth. Now, [continues Ibn Ezra,] many wonder about Isaac's poverty since Abraham left him with great wealth. But have they never seen a person who was wealthy in his younger

(64) That is, the money. This is in accordance with the opinion stated above. Although Ramban does not agree with it, he nevertheless mentions it as an alternate interpretation of the verse. (65) Proverbs 13:13. Ramban's intent in quoting this verse is to explain why it was necessary for the verse before us to say, *So Esau 'despised,'* since, as is clearly indicated in Scripture later on, Esau regretted his action and complained that *he* [Jacob] *took my birthright.* (Further, 28:36.) Scripture therefore justifies what befell Esau later on by saying here, *So Esau 'despised' the birthright,* and he who despises the word shall suffer thereby. (66) Ecclesiastes 5:3.

years and became poor in his old age? An indication that Isaac was indeed poor is the fact that Isaac loved Esau because of his venison. Furthermore, had there been abundant food in his father's house and he [Esau] "the honorable one in his sight,"[67] he would not have sold his birthright for pottage. Also, if his father ate savory meat every day, what reason was there for him to say to Esau, "Bring me some venison?"[68] Why did Jacob not have costly garments as Esau had?[69] Why did his mother not give Jacob some silver and gold for his journey when he fled to Haran so that he had to say, *And He will give me bread to eat, and a garment to put on?*[70] Why did she not send him some money – since she loved him – so that he was required to tend Laban's flock?[71] The verse which states, *Thus the man grew*[72] [in wealth], must refer to the period before he became old. Now ignorant people think that wealth is a great distinction for the righteous. Let Elijah prove the contrary.[73] These ignorant people further ask, "Why did G-d cause Isaac to lack wealth?" Perhaps they could also inform us why He caused Isaac's vision to be diminished? And let them not dismiss me with a reply based upon a *d'rash*[74] for there is indeed a secret[75] in the matter, and we must not probe since the thoughts of G-d are deep and no man has the power to understand them. All these are Abraham ibn Ezra's words.

Now I wonder who has blinded Abraham ibn Ezra's reasoning in this matter, causing him to say that Abraham left Isaac great wealth, and he lost it just prior to this event, [that is, the sale of the birthright], and for this reason, Esau despised the birthright, for this matter of the sale of the birthright took place when Jacob and Esau were still young, before Esau married, as Scripture tells,[76] and after the sale of the birthright, Isaac again became

(67) See Isaiah 43:4. (68) See further, 27: 3-4. (69) See *ibid.*, Verse 15. (70) *Ibid.*, 28:20. (71) All these questions indicate that Isaac was indeed poor. (72) Further, 26:13. (73) See I Kings 17:6, where Elijah's poverty is depicted. (74) The *D'rash* (Aggadic) answer is that Isaac's eyes became dim as a result of Esau's wives offering incense to the idols. See Rashi further, 27:1, where this is one of several reasons mentioned. (75) Interpreters of Ibn Ezra suggest that " the secret" referred to here is the fact that Isaac was a son of Abraham's old age, and it was for this reason that his eyesight was weak. (76) *And Esau was forty years old when he took to wife.* (26:34).

wealthy in the land of the Philistines *until he became very great... and the Philistines were jealous of him.*[77] Following that, [according to Ibn Ezra, we must say that Isaac] again became poor, and he desired the venison of his son Esau and the savory meats. All this is laughable. Furthermore, the verse says, *And it came to pass after the death of Abraham, that G-d blessed his son Isaac.*[78] Now the blessing refers to increase of wealth, possessions and honor, but where was His blessing if he lost the wealth of his father and became impoverished? Afterwards it says, *And I will be with Thee, and I will bless thee,*[79] [but according to Ibn Ezra you will have to say that Isaac] became rich and then poor! And if it be true that in matters of wealth, *There are righteous men unto whom it happeneth according to the work of the wicked,*[80] this does not apply to those righteous men who have been expressly blessed by the Holy One, blessed be He, since *the blessing of the Eternal maketh rich, and no sorrow is added thereto.*[81] Rather, the patriarchs all were as kings before whom kings of the nations came and with whom they made covenants. Now it is written concerning Isaac and Abimelech, *And they swore one to another.*[82] But if Isaac had suffered bad fortune and lost his father's wealth, how did [Abimelech, King of the Philistines, and Phichol, the head of his army], say, *we saw plainly that the Eternal was with thee,*[83] when he was already in financial difficulty? Rather, Esau's disdain of the birthright was due to his brutal nature.

It is possible that the law of double portion to which the firstborn is entitled according to the statutes of the Torah[84] was not in effect in ancient times.[85] [At that time the birthright] was only a matter of inheriting the pre-eminence of the father and his authority so that he [the firstborn] would receive honor and distinction in relation to his younger brother. It is for this reason that Esau said to Isaac, *I am thy son, thy firstborn,*[86] meaning to

(77) Further, 26:13-14. (78) Above, 25:11. (79) Further, 26:3. (80) Ecclesiastes 8:14. (81) Proverbs 10:22. (82) Further, 26:31. (83) *Ibid.*, Verse 28. (84) Deuteronomy 21:17. (85) That is, in the time of the patriarchs. (86) Further, 27:32.

say that he is the firstborn who deserves to be blessed. Similarly, [Joseph said to his father, Jacob], *For this is the firstborn; put thy hand upon his head,*[87] thereby meaning that Jacob should give him precedence in the blessing. Perhaps the firstborn also took slightly more of the inheritance since the law of double portion is an innovation of the statutes of the Torah.[88] And as for the venison in his mouth which Isaac desired so strongly, this is in keeping with the custom of princes and kings. They prefer venison above all food, and out of fear, all nations bring them gifts of venison. Esau flattered his father by bringing him all the venison so that he may always eat of it to his heart's content,[89] and the love of a father for his firstborn is easily understood.

As for Isaac's saying that he would bless Esau after he had prepared the savory meats for him, that was not a reward or a recompense for the food. Instead, he wanted to derive some benefit from him so that his very soul would be bound up in his at the time that he brought him the food so that he would then bless him with a complete desire and a perfect will. Perhaps Isaac discerned in himself that following the meal his soul would be delighted and joyous, and then the *Ruach Hakodesh*[90] would come upon him, [as was the case with Elisha the prophet, who said], *'But now bring me a minstrel. And it came to pass, when the minstrel played, that the hand of the Eternal came upon him.*[91]

And as for not giving wealth to Jacob, that was [not due to Isaac's poverty but rather] because Jacob was fleeing for his life. He left the country alone without his brother's knowledge, and had he been given along wealth, servants and camels, they would have increased his enemies' jealousy and resulted in their

(87) *Ibid.*, 48:18. (88) Thus even in ancient times it was customary that the firstborn inherit more than one share. However, the Torah established his portion to be two shares. This interpretation differs from Ramban's original thesis that the firstborn originally had no preference whatever in inheritance, and that the Torah instituted this law. (89) Ramban thus explains Isaac's desire for venison without postulating Isaac's poverty as Ibn Ezra did. (90) "The holy spirit." The expression refers to a degree of prophecy. See Moreh Nebuchim, II, 45 (2). (91) II Kings 3:15.

ambushing him and killing him. Our Rabbis do indeed say that Jacob was robbed [at the outset of his journey[92] of whatever possessions he had].

And who has told Rabbi Abraham ibn Ezra that Jacob had no costly garments, *fine linen and silk and embroidered robes?*[93] Rather, Scripture states that when going to the field to hunt, Esau would change his garments for his hunting clothes, and due to the fact that [because of his dim eyesight], Isaac always touched his son and his clothes with his hands, Rebekah clothed Jacob with them lest he recognize him by his clothes. You see that this is precisely what Isaac did: *And he smelled the odor of his garments*[94] because he had put them among calamus and cinnamon, even as it is written, *Myrrh and aloes, and cassia are all thy garments.*[95] The spices grew in the Land of Israel, and it is for this reason that Isaac said, *The odor of my son is as the odor of a field.*[94] Because he was a man of the field[96] his garments had the odor of the field or that of the blossoms of the trees, just as our Rabbis explained it: *As the odor of a field*[94] of apples.[97]

And as for the question raised above concerning the quality of Isaac's lack of vision, it is a question raised by the ignorant, for if[98] it was brought about especially by G-d, it was in order that Isaac bless Jacob, this being the purport of the verse, *And it came to pass, that when Isaac was old, and his eyes were dim, he called Esau.*[99] And in line with the natural meaning of Scripture, this was but a manifestation of old age, the explanation of the verse being as follows: *And it came to pass, that when Isaac was old, and his eyes were dim* in his old age, *he called Esau.* Now of Jacob himself it is said later on, *Now the eyes of Israel were dim for age, so that he could not see.*[100] Of Achiyah the Shilonite it is also written, *Now Achiyah could not see; for his eyes were set by*

(92) Bereshith Rabbah 68:2. Thus another difficulty tending to favor Ibn Ezra's thesis that Isaac was poverty stricken is resolved. (93) Ezekiel 16:13. (94) Further, 27:27. (95) Psalms 45:9. (96) See above, Verse 27. (97) Taanith 29 b. (98) Further in the text Ramban suggests that Isaac's dim vision was a natural result of his old age. Hence he writes here: "*If* it was brought about." (99) Further, 27:1. (100) *Ibid.*, 48:10.

reason of his age,[101] and concerning Moses our teacher it is related with wonder that *his eye was not dim.*[102]

26 1. BESIDE THE FIRST FAMINE THAT WAS IN THE DAYS OF ABRAHAM. Perhaps[103] there was no famine in the world until the days of Abraham. This is why Scripture counts from it, for otherwise, what need is there to mention it? In my opinion the correct reason why Scripture mentions it is to tell us that people remembered the first famine, mentioning that on account of it Abraham went down to Egypt and there G-d did him great honor. It was for this reason that Isaac wanted to go in his father's footsteps by descending into Egypt until it was said to him, *Go not down into Egypt.*[104] The reason for the prohibition has been stated by our Rabbis: "You [Isaac] are a perfect burnt-offering and residence outside of the Land of Israel does not befit you."[105]

In my opinion, there is also included in this subject a reference to the future. Abraham's exile into Egypt on account of the famine is an allusion to the exile of his children there.[106] His going to Abimelech[107] however was not an exile for he resided there of his own volition. But Isaac's going [to the land of Abimelech, as recorded here in this verse, *And Isaac went unto Abimelech*] on account of the famine, does allude to an exile since he left his place against his will and went to another land. Now Isaac's exile was from his own place to the land of the Philistines, which was the land in which his father had resided. This alludes to the Babylonian Exile, which took place in the land in which their ancestors had resided, namely, Ur of the Chaldees.[108]

(101) I Kings 14:4. (102) Deuteronomy 34:7. (103) "Perhaps." Since in Bereshith Rabbah 25:3, it is stated that there were ten famines in the world, the first one having been in the days of Adam, Ramban writes, "Perhaps," meaning that a famine of such magnitude had never occurred before the days of Abraham, and this explains why Scripture uses it as a reference point. (104) Verse 2 here. (105) Quoted by Rashi in this form. The source is in Bereshith Rabbah. (106) See Ramban above, 12:10, for complete exposition of this subject. (107) Chapter 20. (108) In view of the fact that Ramban, at the end of *Seder Noach* (11:28), states his opinion at length that Abraham's birthplace was not Ur of the Chaldees, it is necessary to say that the author's reference here is to the time when Terah, his father, took him there, and while being there his life was saved by a miracle. See Ramban there at the end of Verse 28.

Know further that this Babylonian Exile mentioned is mirrored in the events which befell Isaac in that they did not take his wife[109] in the land of the Philistines. Rather, his lot there was only exile and fear. At the beginning Abimelech said, *He that toucheth this man or his wife shall surely be put to death.*[110] Later he regretted it and said, *Go from us.*[111] Afterwards, he returned and made a covenant with Isaac[112] Similarly, in the Babylonian Exile, they were exiled there *because of the burning heat of famine,*[113] and while there, they were neither subjugated, nor were they treated harshly. On the contrary, their leaders were princes in the government. Later on, they said, *Whosoever there is among you of all His people – his G-d be with him – let him go up,*[114] even alerting the princes and governors beyond the River[115] to help them. Later on, they ceased work [on the House of G-d in Jerusalem], and it ceased "for a season and a time."[116] Later, they again changed their policy and gave permission for the construction of the House of G-d, saying, *That they may offer sacrifices of sweet savor unto the G-d of heaven, and pray for the life of the king and his sons.*[117]

TO ABIMELECH, KING OF THE PHILISTINES. It is not known whether this is the same Abimelech who lived in the days of Abraham[107] or whether every Philistine king was so called, for in the time of David he was also called Abimelech.[118] Onkelos, however, is of the opinion that the Abimelech with whom Isaac dealt was a son [of the one mentioned in the account of Abraham].[119]

(109) As they did to Abraham in Egypt. (12:15). (110) Further, Verse 11. (111) Verse 16 here. (112) Verses 25-31 here. (113) Lamentations 5:10. (114) Ezra 1:3. (115) Euphrates. The term "beyond the River" here applies to the region beyond the River westward from the standpoint of those in Babylonia or Persia. (116) See Ezra 4:24 and Daniel 7:12. (117) Ezra 6:10. (118) Psalms 34:1. (119) Ramban refers to Onkelos' translation of Verse 28, *Let there be now an oath between us, and thee,* which Onkelos translates as follows: "Let there be now an oath *which was between our fathers* between us and thee." Thus Onkelos states that the present Abimelech was a son of the one who lived in the days of Isaac's father.

The reason that Isaac went to Abimelech was that he intended to go down to Egypt, so he went to Abimelech, his father's confederate, in the hope that perhaps he would deal kindly with him in the days of the famine, thus making it unnecessary for him to go down to Egypt. Now Abimelech, on account of his covenant with Abraham, did not harm him or his family at all. However, *the men of the place*[120] asked Isaac, in mere quest, concerning his wife, and he said, *She is my sister.*[120] Even so, neither the king nor any of his men touched her for they remembered the affair of Abraham.[107] Hence Abimelech said, *One of the people might lightly have lain,*[121] meaning to say, "I Abimelech did not touch her, and I was careful concerning her, but one of the men of the land might easily have stumbled, and then you would have made us incur guilt, as we sinned in the matter of your father."

2. DWELL IN THE LAND WHICH I SHALL TELL THEE OF. It is incomprehensible that G-d should tell Isaac at one time, *Dwell in the land which I shall tell thee of*, [and in the following verse continue], *Sojourn in this land,*[122] [and in both cases be referring to the same land]. Instead, its explanation is as follows: "*Go not down into Egypt*, and dwell all your days in the land which I shall tell you from time to time. At the bidding of G-d you should move, and at the bidding of G-d you should encamp,[123] and right now, *sojourn in this land,* the land of the Philistines, *for unto thee and unto thy seed I will give it,* even as it is written, *Counted to the Canaanites are the five lords of the Philistines.*"[124]

It is possible that [the event referred to in the beginning of the verse], *And the Lord appeared unto him, and said ... dwell in the land which I shall tell thee of,* happened earlier so that before Isaac left his place it was said to him, "*Go not down into Egypt; dwell in the land which I shall tell thee of* when you will be there. Now dwell in this land, the land of Canaan, which will comprise many peoples and many lands, for I now command that you should not leave it forever for all these lands will I give to thy seed." Following this command, Isaac journeyed from his place because of the famine to go into all the lands of Canaan, to dwell

(120) Verse 7 here. (121) Verse 10 here. (122) Verse 3 here. (123) See Numbers 9:18. (124) Joshua 13:3.

in the land which He would tell him. And when he came to Gerar, He said to him, "Dwell here." It was not necessary however for Scripture to detail this for it is known that Isaac would not transgress the command of G-d.[125] A similar case of interpretation appears in the verse, *Upon one of the mountains which I will tell thee of,*[126] as I mentioned there.

3. AND I WILL FULFILL THE OATH WHICH I SWORE UNTO ABRAHAM THY FATHER. There is no need for the Holy One, blessed be He, to assure Isaac that He will not violate the oath which He swore to his father, *for He is not a man, that He should repent.*[127] Abraham had no other seed upon whom a covenant had been established with G-d except Isaac. The oath, moreover, was not given on condition. In the case of Jacob,[128] it was necessary that he be given such assurance on account of his brother Esau. He was thus saying that in him [Jacob] and his seed will the covenant be fulfilled, not in Esau. [But in the case of Isaac, why was it necessary that he be given such a promise?]

It would appear then that this expression, *Vehakimothi eth hashevuah,* is itself an oath.[129] It is for this reason that the Torah always says, *The land which I swore unto Abraham, unto Isaac, and unto Jacob;*[130] *Remember Abraham, Isaac, and Israel, Thy servants, to whom Thou didst swear by Thine own self.*[131] For we find no source for an oath having been given to Isaac except this verse.

Now it was the desire of the Holy One, blessed be He, to swear to each one of the patriarchs to let it be known that each one was

(125) Therefore, when Scripture wrote that Isaac was given the charge, *Dwell in the land which I shall tell thee of,* he left his place and went searching within the land of Canaan for a new home. When he finally reached Gerar he was told, *Sojourn in this land.* Thus Ramban explains that there was a lapse of time between Verses 2 and 3. The original difficulty which Ramban mentions at the beginning of his comments on this verse is thus removed. (126) Above, 22:2. (127) I Samuel 15:29. (128) Further, 35:12. *And the land which I gave to Abraham and Isaac, to thee will I give it.* (129) It is thus to be translated, *And I will 'establish' the oath.* This is now found in most English translations. (130) Deuteronomy 34:4. (131) Exodus 32:13.

worthy of the covenant being made with him alone, and that the merit of each one stands before Him together with their seed. Even though the previous one suffices, it is an additional merit and honor to them.[132] It is for this reason He said, *Then will I remember My covenant with Jacob, and also My covenant with Isaac, and also My covenant with Abraham will I remember; and I will remember the land,*[133] since all of them had the distinction of G-d having made a covenant with them.

It is possible that He promised something additional to Isaac through this oath, namely, that He will fulfill in him himself, the oath He had sworn to Abraham his father, i.e., that he [Isaac] will be a blessing among the nations, even as He said to Abraham his father, *And all the nations of the earth shall bless themselves with thy seed.*[134] The explanation of the verse before us will thus be: "*And I will fulfill* in thee *the oath which I swore unto Abraham thy father* since you will be a blessing among the nations." Similarly, He also says in the case of Jacob, *And in thee and in thy seed shall all of the families of the earth be blessed.*[135]

5. AND HE KEPT MY CHARGE. Rashi comments: "*As a reward that Abraham hearkened to My voice* when I tested him. *And he kept My charge* – these are the precautionary decrees instituted by the Sages, which are intended to make us avoid the violation of Biblical laws, such as Second Degrees of forbidden marriages and certain prohibited acts on the Sabbath. *My commandments* – these are precepts which, had they not been written in the Torah, were requisite to have been written, such as robbery and murder. *My statutes* – these are matters against which the evil inclination and the heathen nations argue, such as the prohibitions against eating the swine and the wearing of garments woven of wool and linen, there being no apparent rationale for them except that they are decrees of the King imposed on His subjects. *And My laws* – the plural is intended to include, [besides the Written Law], the Oral Law as well as those rules given to Moses from Sinai." [Thus far the words of Rashi.]

(132) That is, their descendants. (133) Leviticus 26:42. (134) Above, 22:18. (135) Further, 28:14.

Now if so, all this interpretation is posited on the opinion that Abraham fulfilled and observed the Torah before it was given on Sinai. This is indeed what the Sages of the Midrash said in connection with the verse, *And Joseph gave them 'agaloth' (wagons),*[136] thereby indicating to his father that when he left him they were studying the section dealing with *Eglah Arufah.*[137] Thus Joseph occupied himself with Torah just as his fathers did. Though the Torah had not yet been given, it is still written of Abraham, *And he kept My charge, My commandments, My statutes, and My laws.*[138] There the Sages also said[139] that Abraham observed the details of the Torah, which he taught to his children, etc.[140]

The question presents itself: If it be the case [that the laws of the Torah were observed by our ancestors before the Torah was given on Sinai], how did Jacob erect a pillar[141] and marry two sisters in their lifetime,[142] and, in the opinion of our Rabbis, four sisters.[143] Also, Amram [Moses' father] married his aunt,[144] and Moses our teacher erected twelve pillars.[145] How then was it possible that they should be permissive in matters of Torah which Abraham their ancestor had prohibited on himself, and for which G-d appointed him reward, when he [Abraham] was wont *to command his children and his household after him*[146] to walk in His ways? In the case of Jacob the Sages taught that he observed the Sabbath and established borders for Sabbath distances.[147] In

(136) *Ibid.*, 45:21. The word *agaloth* (wagons) may also mean "heifers," thus suggesting that as a mark of identification to his father, Joseph gave his brothers a reference to the law of the Heifer (Deuteronomy 21:6) which he studied with his father just before he became separated from him. The Midrash referred to is in Bereshith Rabbah 95:2. (137) See Deuteronomy 21:1-9. (138) Thus far the Midrash in Bereshith Rabbah, 95:2. (139) Bereshith Rabbah, *ibid.* (140) To his children, as it is said, *For I know him that he will command his children and his household after him,* etc. (Above, 18:19.) Bereshith Rabbah, *ibid.* (141) Further, 28:18. This is forbidden in Deuteronomy 16:22. (142) Forbidden in Leviticus 18:18. (143) According to Bereshith Rabbah 74:11, Bilhah and Zilpah were also daughters of Laban. Thus Jacob married four sisters: Leah, Rachel, Bilhah and Zilpah. (144) Exodus 6:20. (145) *Ibid.*, 24:4. (146) Above, 18:19. (147) Bereshith Rabbah 79:7.

this matter of the Sabbath it is possible though that Jacob observed it because it is equal in importance to the entire Torah since it testifies to the act of Creation.

Perhaps then we should say that *My charge* refers to the Second Degree of marriages which were forbidden to the Sons of Noah;[148] *My commandments* applies to robbery and murder; *My statutes* refers to the laws against eating a limb torn off from a live animal, as well as breeding mixed kinds of cattle or grafting together different species of trees; and *My laws* refer to civil statutes and the prohibitions against idol worship. The Sons of Noah were commanded concerning all of these matters, and Abraham observed and fulfilled the Will of his Creator, observing even the details and the strictures of their commandments, even as the Sages mentioned: "The tractate of idolatry of our father Abraham contained four hundred chapters."[149] They further expounded [on the verse referring to Isaac, which says], *And he found in that year a hundredfold,*[150] that he measured the produce for the purpose of tithing,[151] since the patriarchs were *the generous ones of the peoples,*[152] giving tithes to the poor or the priests of G-d, such as Shem and Eber and their disciples, just as it is said, *And he was a priest of the most high G-d.*[153]

Now it appears to me from a study of the opinions of our Rabbis that Abraham our father learned the entire Torah by *Ruach Hakodesh*[154] and occupied himself with its study and the reason for its commandments and its secrets, and he observed it in its entirety as "one who is not commanded but nevertheless observes it."[155] Furthermore, his observance of the Torah applied only in

(148) See *Seder Bereshith*, Note 222, and *Seder Vayishlach*, Note 148. (149) Abodah Zarah 14 b. (150) Further, Verse 12. (151) Bereshith Rabbah 64:6. (152) Psalms 47:10. (153) Above, 14:18. Reference is to Melchizedek, whom tradition identifies as Shem, the son of Noah. See Ramban, *ibid.* (154) See Note 90. (155) The concept of "one who is not commanded but observes" is found in the Talmud (Kiddushin 31 a). His reward is less than that of "one who *is* commanded and observes." (*Ibid.*) The reason for it, as explained in Tosafoth, is that he who is commanded to do a certain *mitzvah* (commandment) is under tension lest he might not properly fulfill it, while he who is not commanded therein has no responsibility in the matter and may leave it at his will. Consequently, his reward is less.

the Land of Israel, whereas Jacob married two sisters only when outside the Land, [156] and similarly with Amram who married his aunt. For the Commandments are *the ordinance of the G-d of the land,* [157] even though we have been charged with personal duties in all places. Our Rabbis have already alluded to this secret, and I will yet call your attention to it with the help of G-d. [158] And the matter of the erection of the pillar [by Jacob and Moses referred to above] was a commandment that was innovated at a certain time, as the Sages expounded from the verse, "*Neither shalt thou set up a pillar which the Eternal thy G-d hateth,* [159] He hated it although it was pleasing to Him in the days of the ancestors." [160] And with respect to Joseph concerning whom the Sages expounded that he observed the Sabbath even in Egypt, [161] it was because it is equal in importance to all the commandments, constituting, as it does, a testimony to *Creatio ex nihilo.* [162] Therefore Joseph would do so in order to teach his children faith in the Creation of the world, to remove from their hearts the false doctrine of idolatry and the opinion of the Egyptians. This then is the intent [of the Sages when speaking of the patriarchs and their children observing the Torah].

In accordance with the literal meaning of Scripture, you may say that *My charge* means faith in the Deity, implying that Abraham believed in the unique Divine Name and kept vigilant guard over it in his heart, differing thereby with the worshippers of idols, and calling by the name of the Eternal to bring many to His worship. *My commandments* refers to all that G-d commanded Abraham: *Go out of thy land,* [163] the bringing of his son as a burnt-offering, and the expulsion of the maid-servant and her son. [164] *My statutes* refers to walking in the paths of G-d by being

(156) See Leviticus 18:25 where Ramban extends the explanation further by saying that the reason Rachel died as they entered the Land of Israel (35:16-19) was that she was the sister whom Jacob married last. (157) II Kings 17:26. (158) See Ramban on Leviticus 18:25. (159) Deuteronomy 16:22. (160) *Ibid.*, Sifre. The reason for the change being that the Canaanites afterward had made it an ordinance of idol worship. (161) Bereshith Rabbah 92:4. (162) In Hebrew, *chiddush* (new), thus implying that G-d created a new world out of an absolute void. (163) Above, 12:1. (164) *Ibid.*, 21:12.

gracious and merciful, doing righteousness and judgment,[165] and commanding his children and his household concerning them.[166] *And My Laws* refers to the circumcision of Abraham himself and his sons and his servants, as well as all Commandments of the Sons of Noah[148] which constitute their Law.

7. AND HE SAID: SHE IS MY SISTER. They did not ask concerning the children for he would say, "They are my children from another woman."

14. AND HE HAD POSSESSIONS OF FLOCKS, AND POSSESSIONS OF HERDS, AND A GREAT HOUSEHOLD, meaning she-asses and camels, he-asses, and men-servants and handmaids. Now Scripture mentions these but not silver and gold, as it says concerning Abraham,[167] because the wealth which he amassed in the land of the Philistines consisted of flocks and a great household.[168] *And the Philistines were jealous of him* in this matter. This is the meaning of that which Abimelech says to Isaac, *For thou art become much mightier than we.*[169] The king said to him, "I, too, who am the king do not have in my home such flocks and domestics as you, and it is a disgrace to us that your household is greater than that of the king."

17. IN THE VALLEY OF GERAR, far away from the city. *And* [Isaac] *digged again the wells of water, which they had digged in the days of Abraham his father,* and which the Philistines had stopped up before Isaac left Gerar, he once again dug. Thus the words of Rashi.

It would appear from Rashi's words, then, that the wells mentioned here [in Verse 18] are the same as those mentioned [above in Verse 15]: *For all the wells which his father's servants had digged in the days of Abraham his father the Philistines had*

(165) See Maimonides, "The Commandments," Vol. I, pp. 11-12 Soncino edit. Positive Commandment 8. (166) Above, 18:19. (167) *Ibid.*, 13:2. (168) Since these possessions which Isaac accumulated in the land of the Philistines were visible to all, the Philistines became jealous of him. Ramban thus explains the beginning and end of this verse as cause and effect. (169) Verse 16 here.

stopped them, and filled them with earth. But this is not so, for how would the Philistines give him permission when they had said, "These wells are a source of danger to us because of invaders."[170] Rather, the wells [mentioned in Verse 18] are different ones in another location since *the valley of Gerar* is the name of a place, or perhaps the valley extended from Gerar to another land, and when the Philistines, namely, the lords of Gerar—the principality of the king – became jealous of Isaac, they stopped the wells which were his by inheritance from his father in the boundary of the city of Gerar. The king then sent him away from his throne-city, and he went to another city. Possibly, this new place was not part of his kingdom even though it was in the land of the Philistines. There were other wells there which Abraham had dug when he lived there for many days[171] but which the Philistines stopped upon his death since Isaac did not dwell there. They did not do this out of hatred. But in the days of Abraham, [even after he had moved from there], they did not want to stop them out of respect to him, saying, "Perhaps he will return to dwell there." This was why Isaac returned and dug them in the valley. But the herdsmen of the valley quarrelled with him *saying, The water is ours,*[172] meaning, "The well is in the valley, and the waters ooze forth from that valley while those in the valley are diminished. Hence they are ours." It is for this reason that Scripture mentions, *And they found there a well of living water,*[173] stating that it was a source gushing forth living water which did not come from the valley as those who quarrelled with Isaac had previously claimed.

20. AND HE CALLED THE NAME OF THE WELL ESEK. Scripture gives a lengthy account of the matter of the wells when in the literal interpretation of the story there would seem to be no benefit nor any great honor to Isaac in that he and his father did the identical thing.[174] However, there is a hidden matter involved

(170) Quoted in Rashi, Verse 15 here. (171) Above, 21:34. (172) Verse 20 here. (173) Verse 19 here. (174) Both Isaac and Abraham dug wells in the land of the Philistines. They did not quarrel with Abraham, but they did quarrel with Isaac. Thus, in the literal meaning of the story, there "is no great honor to Isaac."

here since Scripture's purpose is to make known a future matter. *A well of living water* alludes to the House of G-d which the children of Isaac will build. This is why Scripture mentions *a well of living waters,* even as it says, *A fountain of living waters, the Eternal.* [175] He called the first well *Esek* (Contention), which is an allusion to the First House, [176] concerning which the nations contended with us and instigated quarrels and wars with us until they destroyed it. The second well he called *Sitnah* (Enmity), [177] a name harsher than the first. This alludes to the Second House, [178] which has indeed been referred to by this very name, *in the beginning of his reign, they wrote 'sitnah'* [179] *against the inhabitants of Judah and Jerusalem.* [180] And during its entire existence they [181] were a source of enmity unto us until they destroyed it and drove us from it into bitter exile. The third well he called *Rechovoth* (Spacious). This is a reference to the Future House, which will be speedily built in our days, and it will be done without quarrel and feud, and G-d will enlarge our borders, even as it says, *And if the Eternal thy G-d enlarge thy border, as He hath sworn,* etc., [182] which refers to the future. And concerning the Third House of the future it is written, *Broader* [183] *and winding about higher and higher.* [184] [The concluding statement in the present narrative, concerning the naming of the third well], *And we shall be fruitful in the land,* [185] signifies that all peoples will come to worship G-d *with one consent.* [186]

(175) Jeremiah 17:13. From the context of Ramban's language it would appear that he interprets the verse as if it said, *A fountain of living waters,* which is the house of *the Eternal.* (176) The First Sanctuary, which was built by Solomon and destroyed by the Babylonians. (177) Verse 21 here. (178) The Second Sanctuary, which was built by the Jews who returned from the Babylonian Captivity and which was destroyed by the Romans. (179) Hatred, accusation. Thus the same word *sitnah* appears in connection with the Second Sanctuary. (180) Ezra 4:6. (181) Our historic enemies during the period of the Second Temple, signified in the chapter here by the Philistines. (182) Deuteronomy 19:8. (183) In Hebrew *verachavah,* from the same root as the name of the third well, *Rechovoth.* The connection between the third well and the Third Temple of the future, concerning which Ezekiel prophesied, is thus established. (184) Ezekiel 41:7. (185) Verse 22 here. (186) Zephaniah 3:9.

24. FEAR NOT, FOR I AM WITH THEE. Since Abimelech drove him away because of the Philistines' jealousy of him, and since the herdsmen of Gerar quarrelled with him, Isaac feared lest they gather against him and smite him and his family. Therefore the Holy One, blessed be He, assured him that he should not fear them, and He blessed him. Then He prompted them so that the king went to Isaac with greater honor than that which he did to his father since he came with Phichol, the chief of his host, and also brought with him many of his friends.

29. IF THOU WILT DO US HURT, AS WE HAVE NOT TOUCHED THEE. The king is saying: "If you will do us hurt [and we could do nothing against you], just as we have not touched you because *thou art now the blessed of the Eternal* and we do not have it in our power to harm you, the time will yet change on account of the violence you will do against us and you will need to return to our land. Then we will requite you accordingly."

The meaning of the phrase, *We have not touched thee,* is: "We did not persuade our hearts concerning your wife, causing her to be touched by one of them." This is similar in expression to the verse, *He that toucheth this man or his wife.*[187]

"*We have done thee nothing but good*, guarding whatever you had, by our commanding the people to beware of you. *And we have sent thee away in peace* for even when we were jealous of you we took nothing of all the wealth you amassed with us, and we sent you away in peace with all you had." The reason for their being fearful of him could hardly have been the apprehension of the king of the Philistines lest Isaac come to war against him. Instead, it was because Abraham had promised them a covenant, "to him, to his son, and his son's son," [188] and now they thought, "Since we annulled our covenant with Isaac and sent him away from us, he too will annul his covenant with us, and his children will drive our children from the land." This was why they made a new covenant with him, excusing themselves by telling him that they did not annul the first covenant, since they have done him

(187) Verse 11 here. (188) Above, 21:23.

nothing but good. And this is the meaning of their saying, *Let there now be an oath between us:* [189] "We will now come with you in oath to express a ban upon whoever will transgress the covenant." This is similar in meaning to the verse, *That thou shouldst enter into the covenant of the Lord thy G-d, and into His oath.* [190]

It is possible that Abraham was very great and mighty in power, having in his household three hundred men [191] that drew sword, and also many confederates; *and he also that is valiant, whose heart is as the heart of a lion,* [192] and he chased after four powerful kings and subdued them.[193] When they saw Abraham's success which clearly was from G-d, the king of the Philistines was then fearful of him lest he conquer his kingdom, since this would be easier than the war against the four kings. Perhaps the king of the Philistines had also heard the matter of G-d having given the land to Abraham. Hence he made a covenant with him, making him swear *that thou wilt not deal falsely with me, nor with my son, nor with my son's son,*[188] it being considered an act of falsehood if Abraham were to rebel against the king, and considering it possible that Abraham might live until his grandson will rule, [he also mentioned *my sons's son*]. And as the fathers are, so are the sons. Isaac was as great as his father, and the king therefore feared lest Isaac war against him because he had driven him from his land.

32. AND ISAAC'S SERVANTS CAME AND TOLD HIM CONCERNING THE WELL WHICH THEY HAD DIGGED. This is the same well mentioned above in the verse, *And there Isaac's servants digged a well.* [194] They had begun to dig it, and Abimelech came to him during that period, and on the day of the making of the covenant, when Abimelech and his retinue had left, Isaac's servants brought him the tidings that they had found water.

It appears feasible to me that this is the same well which

(189) Verse 28 here. (190) Deuteronomy 29:11. (191) Above, 14:14. (192) II Samuel 17:10. The verse refers to David, but Ramban uses it also in connection with Abraham, since as pointed out he was also mighty in battle. (193) Above, 14:14-15. (194) Verse 25 here.

Abraham dug, in connection with which he gave Abimelech seven lambs as a witness [to his ownership of the well].[195] The Philistines, however, stopped it together with the other wells, whereupon Isaac dug it again and called it by the same name which his father had called it. It is for this reason that the name of the city is Beer-sheba: on account of the well (*be'er*) which both the father and the son called by that name *because there they swore both of them.*[196]

This well of theirs alludes to the Tabernacle at Shiloh, which the Philistines stopped when the Ark of G-d was taken captive by them.[197] And they redug it, indicating that the Philistines indeed returned the Ark together with the honorary gift to G-d.[198]

27 4. THAT MY SOUL MAY BLESS THEE. It was Isaac's intent to bless Esau that he merit the blessing of Abraham to inherit the land and to become the one with whom G-d would make the covenant since he was the firstborn.

It would appear that Rebekah never told Isaac of the prophecy which G-d had related to her, i.e., *And the elder shall serve the younger,*[199] else how would Isaac *transgress the commandment of the Eternal, seeing that it shall not prosper.*[200] Now at first she did not tell it to him due to ethical modesty, for the verse, *And she went to inquire of the Eternal,*[201] suggests that she went without Isaac's permission.[202] [Perhaps she did not tell him because] she said, "I need not relate a prophecy to a prophet for Isaac is greater than the one who told it to me."[203] And now she

(195) Above, 21:30. (196) *Ibid.*, Verse 31. The verse there refers to Abraham and Abimelech. Ramban uses it here only as an expression to indicate that both Abraham and Isaac called the same well by the same name and both had occasion to swear over it. The name of the city "Beer-sheba" thus derives its historical significance from both the first patriarch and his son. (197) I Samuel 4:11. (198) *Ibid.*, 6:11. (199) Above, 25:23. (200) Numbers 14:41. (201) Above, 25:22. (202) Hence due to ethical modesty she did not tell him of the prophecy for it would indicate a breach of wifely modesty for her to have gone without permission. (203) This is a reference to the tradition mentioned by Rashi (25:23), which says that the prophecy was told to Shem the son of Noah and he told it to Rebekah. Therefore Rebekah said: "There is no reason for me to tell Isaac since he is greater in prophecy than the one who told it to me."

did not want to tell him, "So was it said to me in the name of G-d before I gave birth," for she reasoned that because of his love for Esau he will not bless Jacob, but he will leave everything in the hands of Heaven. And she further knew that by this arrangement of hers, Jacob will be blessed from Isaac's mouth by an undivided heart and a willing mind. Perhaps these are causes induced by G-d so that Jacob would be blessed, and Esau as well with the blessing of the sword, *And by Him* alone *actions are weighed.* [204]

7. AND I WILL BLESS THEE BEFORE THE ETERNAL BEFORE MY DEATH. In this entire section, the expression, *before the Eternal,* is not mentioned except in this place. This is because his mother said to Jacob, "The blessing will be *before the Eternal* with the *Ruach Hakodesh,* [205] and if Esau your brother be blessed with it, it will remain with his children forever, and you will have no standing before him."

12. PERHAPS MY FATHER WILL FEEL ME. The reason that Isaac will feel him is not for the purpose of recognition. Instead, Jacob said, "Perhaps he will bring me near him to kiss me or to put his hand on my face in the manner of a father demonstrating affection for his son, and in feeling me he will discover that I am smooth."

Now I wonder why Jacob was not afraid of vocal recognition for all people are recognizable by their voice as our Rabbis have said, "How is a blind man permitted to live with his wife? And how are people permitted to live with their wives at nighttime? Only by vocal recognition." [206] Now if ordinary people have such power of recognition, what of Isaac, who was wise and expert in distinguishing between his sons? [207] He should truly have the power of recognition by voice. Perhaps the brothers had similar voices, and therefore the Sages said that the verse, *The voice is the voice of Jacob,* [208] refers not to Jacob's voice but to his words,

(204) I Samuel 2:3. (205) See above, Note 90. (206) Chullin 96 a. (207) As Scripture testifies (25:28), his love was centered on one. (208) Further, Verse 22.

i.e., that he speaks gentle language and mentions the Name of Heaven.[209] It may be that he altered his voice in order to speak as his brother did, for there are people who know how to do this.

15. ESAU HER ELDER SON, JACOB HER YOUNGER SON. The reason why Scripture mentions this is to accentuate the unusual action of the righteous one,[210] for parents customarily give recognition to the firstborn in blessing, honor, and gift,[211] but she, knowing of the righteousness of the younger and the wickedness of the elder, went to all this trouble to transfer the blessing and the honor from the elder to the younger. Similarly, it says further on, *And the words of Esau her elder son were told to Rebekah, and she sent and called Jacob her younger son.*[212]

21. COME NEAR, I PRAY THEE, THAT I MAY FEEL THEE. Rashi comments: "Isaac said to himself, 'It is not Esau's way to have the Name of Heaven so readily in his mouth.'" This interpretation is found in Bereshith Rabbah.[209]

But I wonder about this for Esau was not wicked in his father's eyes![213] Perhaps Isaac thought that since Esau is a man of the field and his heart is set on the hunt, he is not wont to mention the Name of Heaven for fear that he might mention it in some unclean place and without proper concentration. In the eyes of his father, this was considered a manifestation of his fear of Heaven. In line with the simple meaning of Scripture, this was because of vocal recognition.[214]

28. OF THE DEW OF HEAVEN. The blessing is not that G-d give him of the dew of heaven for the dew descends in all places. Now had he said that G-d give him an abundance of dew, or that

(209) Bereshith Rabbah 65:16. Due to the fact that the voices of the brothers were alike, it was necessary for the Sages to interpret the verse, *The voice is the voice of Jacob,* as referring to the kind of language Jacob used. (210) Rebekah. (211) See Ramban above, 25:34. (212) Further, Verse 42. (213) This being so, how could the mention of G-d be a distinguishing mark for Jacob? (214) Since the voice instilled doubt as to his identity, Isaac desired to feel him.

it come in its season, even as it says, *Then I will give your rains in their season,* [215] that would have constituted a blessing. Instead, its meaning is as follows: Since above he mentioned G-d's blessing, *As the odor of a field which the Eternal hath blessed,* [216] meaning "which G-d had blessed for my son" [217] – that is, since G-d blessed him in the field by giving him success there in his hunt and by guarding him from death or any mishap – he now says, *So G-d give thee,* [as an additional blessing], *of the dew of heaven, and of the fat places of the earth.* It is thus a blessing of addition and abundance. It may be that the expression, *And plenty ('verov') of corn and wine,* is written in the Torah with an extra *vav,* [which should not affect the meaning], with the sense of the verse being: "So G-d give thee of the dew of heaven and of the places of the earth, i.e., plenty of corn and wine."

In my opinion the correct interpretation is that G-d's gift is steady and there is never any interruption in it. Therefore he says, "*So G-d give thee* for the extent of your days upon your land *of the dew of heaven,* and give thee *of the fat places of the earth,*" meaning the fattest of all lands, even as it is written, *The beauty of all lands.* [218]

Now Rabbi Abraham ibn Ezra says that the prefix *mem* in the word *mital,* (of the dew) applies to itself and yet to another word, [namely, *mishmanei* (the fat places of the earth), which is then to be understood as] *umimishmanei ha'aretz* and from the fat places of the earth. [219]

To Esau, on the other hand, he gave a blessing which mentions neither through a gift of G-d nor with abundance. Rather he said, "For you too I have reserved a blessing after him: of the fat places of the earth and of the dew of heaven shall your dwelling be." [220]

(215) Leviticus 26:4. (216) Verse 27 here. (217) Ramban interprets the phrase, *which the Eternal hath blessed,* as referring back to the word *b'ni* (my son), thus making it "the field which G-d had blessed for my son." Isaac thus continues his blessing by saying, "Just as He has blessed the field for you, my son, may He also give you another blessing, namely, of the dew of the heavens." (218) Ezekiel 20:6. (219) According to Ibn Ezra, reference is thus to the fruits from the fat places of the earth. (220) Based on Verse 39 here.

That is "as long as you will dwell there," thereby alluding that he will ultimately be destroyed and lost, for only as long as he will live will his lot be good.

29. CURSED BE EVERY ONE THAT CURSETH THEE, AND BLESSED BE EVERY ONE THAT BLESSETH THEE. But in the case of Balaam it says, *Blessed be every one that blesseth thee, and cursed be every one that curseth thee.*[221] [The reason for this change in order is that] the righteous begin with affliction and ultimately attain tranquility, so that those who curse them precede those who bless them.[222] But the wicked experience tranquility first and their end is affliction. Hence Balaam mentioned the blessing before the curse. This is Rashi's language quoting Bereshith Rabbah.[223]

But if this be so, why did the Holy One, blessed be He, say to Abraham, *And I will bless them that bless thee, and curse him that curseth thee?*[224] This however is no difficulty since He concludes there, *And in thee shall all families of the earth be blessed.* Thus there is a blessing at the beginning and at the end. It may be, as we have explained it there, that He speaks in terms of both an individual and many,[225] suggesting that Abraham will be universally blessed, and the single person who will curse him will be cursed.[226]

32. WHO ART THOU? When Esau said to him, *Let my father arise,*[227] Isaac thought that it was Jacob, i.e., that because Jacob knew that he had eaten of Esau's venison and blessed Esau, he too

(221) Numbers 24:9. The question thus arises: Why did Isaac mention first the curse and then the blessing while Balaam did the opposite? (222) Therefore, Isaac, himself a righteous man, speaks first of those who afflict the righteous, and then mentions those who bless them. The opposite is true in the case of Balaam. (223) Bereshith Rabbah 66:5. (224) Above, 12:3. Now here in the case of the righteous, it still mentions the blessing first! (225) The blessing is expressed in plural form — *And I will bless 'those' who bless thee* — while the curse is expressed in singular form — *and curse 'him' that curseth thee.* (226) Hence He mentions the blessing first as there will be many who will bless Abraham. (227) Verse 31 here.

prepared savory meats so that he should bless him also. Therefore he asked, *Who art thou?*, in order to know the truth.[228]

33. AND ISAAC TREMBLED VERY EXCEEDINGLY, AND SAID, WHO THEN IS HE THAT HATH TAKEN VENISON AND BROUGHT IT TO ME, AND I HAVE EATEN OF ALL BEFORE THOU COMEST AND HAVE BLESSED HIM? YEA, AND HE SHALL BE BLESSED. It is not natural for a person who just trembled violently and complained, "Who was it that subtly made me bless him?" to conclude his complaint by immediately saying, *Yea, and he shall be blessed*! Rather, it would have been proper that he curse him! Moreover, Esau would then complain to his father, saying, "But why do you bless him now, my father?" And how would Esau believe his father that it was originally done through subtlety[229] when he saw that he was now blessing him willingly!

The correct interpretation appears to me to be that it is in the present tense.[230] Isaac is saying, "*Who then is he that hath hunted venison*, who could have beguiled me so that I should bless him and that he should remain blessed under all circumstances for I knew that he is a blessed one?" Or it may be that the expression, *Yea, and he shall be blessed*, means "against my will, since it is impossible for me to transfer the blessing from him." From the moment he blessed him, Isaac knew by *Ruach Hakodesh*[231] that his blessings indeed rested upon Jacob. This then is the reason for his violent trembling for he knew that his beloved son Esau had lost his blessing forever. This also is the explanation for his saying, *Thy brother came with subtlety,*[229] meaning that after he said, *Who then is he* etc. he realized that Jacob had been the one who came before him to receive the blessing for it would have been impossible for the blessing to rest on any but his offspring, [and, as mentioned above, Isaac knew by *Ruach Hakodesh* that the

(228) If Isaac did not think him to be Jacob, why should he ask, "Who art thou?" He himself had told Esau to make him savory food, and now he came and said, "Let my father arise." However, since Ramban explains that Isaac thought him to be Jacob, the question is understandable. (229) Verse 35 here. (230) The word *yihyeh,* generally understood as a future tense – *and he shall be blessed* – is here to be understood as a present tense, as explained below in the text. (231) See above, Note 90.

blessing had taken effect. Hence he was sure that it was Jacob who had come before him.]

37. AND ALL HIS BRETHREN HAVE I GIVEN HIM AS SERVANTS. This is not the blessing, *Be lord over thy brethren,* [232] for Isaac had already said, *Behold, I have made him thy lord.* [233] However, it is possible that Jacob be the lord and they not be his servants, just as the verse says, *For Judah 'gavar' above his brethren.* [234] But the source for his saying, *I have given to him as servants,* comes from his expression, *And let thy mother's sons bow down to thee,* [232] for this refers to the bowing of the servant to his masters, just as he says, *Let people serve thee,* [232] and then repeats, *And nations bow down to thee.* [232]

The meaning of the expression, *And all his brothers,* [235] is the same as that of *thy brothers* and *thy mother's sons.* [232] These he mentions in the plural in order to allude to all of Esau's offspring. And Rabbi Abraham ibn Ezra says that it refers to the children of Abraham's concubines. [236]

39. BEHOLD ('HINEI'), OF THE FAT PLACES OF THE EARTH SHALL BE THY DWELLING. The intent of the word *hinei* (behold) is: "Now I could give you of the fat places of the earth and of the dew of heaven, for of these there is sufficient [abundance] for both of you to have of the fat places of the earth and of the dew of heaven, but in the matter of lordship, that will be his, and you shall serve him." Isaac also did not give him *plenty of corn and wine* as he gave to his brother since he wanted to honor the one who had been blessed first above him. Later he said to Jacob, *And G-d Almighty give thee the blessing of Abraham... that thou mayest inherit the land of thy sojournings,* [237] meaning that he should have the plentifulness of the corn and wine in the land of Canaan, which was Abraham's gift, while Esau would have the dew and the fat places of the earth in another land.

(232) Verse 29 here. (233) In the beginning of the present verse. (234) I Chronicles 5:2. There the word *gavar* does not indicate a master and servant relationship. Similarly, the word *gvir* (lord) does not indicate such a relationship. (235) Jacob had only one brother. Why then does Isaac use the plural form, "his brothers?" (236) See above, 25:6. (237) Further, 28:4.

40. AND ON THY SWORD ('VE'AL CHARBECHA') YOU SHALL LIVE. The meaning of *ve'al charbecha* is as if it were written, *becharbecha (by* thy sword). A similar case is the verse, *For man does not live 'al halechem' (on bread) alone,*[238] which means *belechem* (by bread). Now the blessing is not that he live on the booty he takes from his enemies by the sword, for he has already given him of the fat places of the earth and of the dew of heaven by which he shall live. Instead, the purport of the blessing is that he survive his battles and be victorious, and not fall by the sword of an enemy. It is for this reason that immediately following this he said, *And thou shall serve thy brother,* meaning, "but you will not prevail over him. Instead, he will prevail over you."

AND IT SHALL COME TO PASS WHEN THOU SHALL BREAK LOOSE in thy suffering on account of Jacob's transgression,[239] THEN THOU SHALT SHAKE HIS YOKE FROM OFF THY NECK. This is an indication to Israel that they should not contend with the children of Esau too much in order to do them evil. This is what Scripture commanded: *Take ye good heed, contend not with them,* etc.[240] And so did our Rabbis[241] say: *"For Joab and all Israel remained there six months, until he had cut off every male in Edom.*[242] The Holy One, blessed be He, said to David, 'I said, *Contend not with them,* and you did contend. By your life, these six months will not accrue to you and your reign.' We know this was fulfilled since it is written, *And the days that David reigned over Israel were forty years,*[243] but in truth he reigned six more months, as it is written, *In Hebron he reigned over Judah seven years and six months."*[244] The Rabbis also said,[245] "The Holy One, blessed be He, said to David, 'Thy hands

(238) Deuteronomy 8:3. (239) Specifically, the transgression of the command, *Contend not with them,* as is explained further on. (240) Deuteronomy 2:4-5. referring to the children of Esau in the land of Se'ir. (241) Yerushalmi Rosh Hashanah, I, 1. (242) I Kings 11:16. (243) *Ibid.*, 2:11. (244) II Samuel 5:5. *And in Jerusalem he reigned thirty and three years* for a total of forty years and six months. Yet he is credited with only forty years. (245) Devarim Rabbah 1:15.

are sharp and pointed, and I seek to rule my world with them, etc.' "[246]

41. AND ESAU SAID IN HIS HEART. Rabbi Abraham ibn Ezra said, "It is possible that he revealed his secret to one of his friends." [247]

But this is not necessarily so for any decision which a person reaches after deliberation is referred to in Hebrew as "speaking with the heart," even when it also includes speech with the lips. A similar case is found in the verse, *And with a double heart do they speak,* [248] for the will is synonymous with the heart. *And all Israel were of one heart to make David king,* [249] meaning that they had all arrived at the same decision and were talking of it. Similarly, *And Jeroboam said in his heart.* [250] Similarly did Eliezer say, *And before I had finished speaking in my heart,* [251] whereas the prayer there was with his lips, as Scripture states, *And he said, O Eternal G-d of my lord Abraham.* [252] However it is possible that the expression, *before I had finished speaking in my heart,* means "before I had concluded the thought in my mind."

Now here the verse states that when the great hatred of Jacob permeated Esau's soul because of the blessing, he conceived the idea of murdering his brother, and with this he comforted himself from his depressed state. This explains the verse, *And the words of Esau were told to Rebekah.* [253] This is why she said to Jacob, *Thy brother Esau comforts himself to slay thee.* [254]

Now Rashi comments, "She was told, through *Ruach*

(246) The Midrash concludes: "Moses your teacher has already desired to confront them, and I told him, 'It is sufficient for you.' " (Deuteronomy 2:3). (247) If not, how did Rebekah become aware of the fact that Esau was planning to kill Jacob? (Verse 42 here). (248) Psalms 12:3. (249) I Chronicles 12:39. (250) I Kings 12:26. Further on it says, *And the king took counsel,* (Verse 28). Here also there was speech which Scripture had referred to as being said in his heart. (251) Above, 24:25. (252) *Ibid.,* Verse 12. (253) Verse 42 here. As Ramban explained, a decision in one's heart, even though coupled with speech, is still referred to in Hebrew as "the speech of heart." Therefore, the verse means that Esau decided upon a course of action, and he himself informed his mother of his decision. (254) Verse 42 here.

Hakodesh,[231] what Esau was thinking in his heart." And so it is found in Bereshith Rabbah.[255] If so, Esau's words and thoughts were only in his heart, just as in the verse, *I spoke with my own heart.*[256]

The reason that Esau said, *Let the days of mourning for my father be at hand then will I slay my brother* is because he would not bring grief to his father during his lifetime. Perhaps it was due to his fear lest his father curse him, and his blessing would then turn into a curse. Rebekah, [who nevertheless advised Jacob to flee], feared that perhaps the elderly one would die suddenly, and Esau would then kill Jacob, or perhaps he might find occasion to kill him even during Isaac's lifetime.

42. AND SHE SENT AND CALLED JACOB. The meaning thereof is that Jacob was in another place, not in the tent of his father and mother, since he was hiding from his brother Esau who was complaining about him, and he was ashamed or afraid of him.

HE DOTH COMFORT HIMSELF ('LECHA') TO SLAY THEE. "He comforts himself for the loss of the blessings by killing you." Thus the language of Rashi.

But the simple interpretation is that "he comforts himself with you."[257] Similar cases [of the letter *lamed* having the meaning of a *beth*] are found in the verses, *Thou hast chosen the son of Jesse,*[258] *And he took hold of him,*[259] and many similar cases.

Perhaps the interpretation is that "he is comforting himself concerning you," just as in the verses: *And the men of the place*

(255) Bereshith Rabbah 67:9. (256) Ecclesiastes 1:16. (257) According to Rashi, the comfort is for the blessings Esau lost. Thus the verse states that "his comfort for the loss he suffered is to slay thee." But according to Ramban the comfort is for his own personal sake, and the meaning of the word *lecha* (to you) is as if it were written *becha* (with you), and the thought of the verse is that "his comfort with you is to kill you." (258) I Samuel 20:7. The Hebrew: *l'ben Yishai* (to the son of Jesse). The verse thus means that "your choice lies with the son of Jesse." (259) II Samuel 15:5. The Hebrew *vehechezik lo* here means *vehechezik bo.*

asked him of his wife; [260] *And he fell on his face;* [261] *For the king had so commanded concerning him.* [262] Onkelos, however, translates it as *kemin lecha*, meaning, "he lies in wait for you." It would appear from his opinion that the meaning of the Hebrew expression, *mithnachem lecha*, is that "Esau effects the appearance of having been consoled about the matter of the blessings as if he no longer cares for them, but in truth he lies in wait for you and acts this way so that you should not be on guard." Now Onkelos translated according to the intent of the verse but not according to the language.

28 5. THE BROTHER OF REBEKAH, JACOB'S AND ESAU'S MOTHER. Because it stated [263] that Isaac commanded Jacob to get a wife from the daughters of Laban, his mother's brother, Scripture mentions that he was also the brother of Esau's mother. It would have been proper for Isaac to have commanded Esau likewise, but since he knew that the blessing of Abraham would apply only to Jacob and his seed, he did so only to Jacob. Now Scripture further mentions that Esau heard that his father had commanded Jacob not to take a wife from among the daughters of Canaan [264] and that he should go to his mother's brother Laban. He [Esau] heeded his father's will that one not take a wife from among the daughters of Canaan, but he did not act properly and take a wife from the daughters of Laban, despite his [Laban's] being his mother's brother. Scripture further mentions that he took her [265] *besides his former wives,* and he did not divorce the evil wives since he followed his heart's desire more than he followed the will of his father.

(260) Above, 26:7. The Hebrew word *le'ishto* in this verse does not mean "to his wife," but "concerning his wife." (261) I Samuel 20:41. The Hebrew word *le'apav* in this verse does not mean "to his face," but "on his face." (262) Esther 3:2. The word *lo* (to him) here means *alav* (concerning him). (263) It is obvious that Ramban has in mind the words of Rashi, whose comment upon the expression, *Jacob's and Esau's mother,* was, "I do not know what this intends to tell us." Ramban then proceeds to offer an explanation. (264) Verse 1 here. (265) Mahalath, the daughter of Ishmael. (Verse 9 here.)

Vayeitzei

12. AND BEHOLD A LADDER SET UP ON THE EARTH AND THE TOP OF IT REACHED TO HEAVEN; AND BEHOLD THE ANGELS OF G-D ASCENDING AND DESCENDING ON IT. In a prophetic dream, He showed Jacob that whatever is done on earth is effected by means of the angels, and everything is by decree given to them by the Supreme One. The angels of G-d, *whom the Eternal hath sent to walk to and fro through the earth,*[1] would not do anything minor or major until they return to present themselves before the Master of the whole earth, saying before Him, "We have traversed the earth,[2] and behold it dwells in peace, or is steeped in war and blood," and He commands them to return, to descend to the earth and fulfill His charge. And He further showed him [Jacob] that He, blessed be He, stands above the ladder, and promises Jacob with supreme assurance to inform him that he will not be under the power of the angels, but he will be *G-d's portion,*[3] and that He will be with him always, as He said, *And, behold, I am with thee, and will keep thee wherever thou goest*[4] for his [Jacob's] excellence is superior to that of the other righteous ones of whom it is said, *For He will give His angels charge over thee, to keep thee in all thy ways.*[5]

And in the opinion of Rabbi Eliezer the Great[6] this vision was akin to the one seen by Abram at the time of the covenant "between the parts"[7] for He also showed Jacob the dominion of

(1) Zechariah 1:10. (2) See *ibid.*, Verse 11. (3) Deuteronomy 32:9. (4) Verse 15 here. (5) Psalms 91:11. (6) Pirkei d'Rabbi Eliezer, 35. (7) Above, 15:9-18.

the Four Kingdoms,[8] their ascent and descent. This is the meaning of *angels of G-d* (mentioned here), just as it is said in the visions of Daniel: the prince of the kingdom of Greece,[9] and the prince of the kingdom of Persia.[10] And He promised him that He, exalted be He, will be with him wherever he will go among the nations, and He will guard him and rescue him from them. Thus the Rabbis have said:[6] "The Holy One, blessed be He, showed him the Four Kingdoms, their dominion and their destruction. He showed him the prince of the kingdom of Babylon ascending seventy rungs[11] and then descending the ladder. Then He showed him the prince of the kingdom of Media ascending one hundred and eighty rungs[12] and then descending. And then He showed him the prince of the kingdom of Edom ascending and not coming down. Jacob then said to the prince of Edom, *Yet thou shalt be brought down to the nether-world.*[13] The Holy One, blessed be He, said to [the prince of Edom], *Though thou make thy nest as high as the eagle,* etc."[14]

17. THIS IS NONE OTHER THAN THE HOUSE OF G-D, AND THIS IS THE GATE OF HEAVEN. This refers to the Sanctuary which is the gate through which the prayers and sacrifices ascend to heaven.

(8) See Ramban above, 14:1 and 15:12. The Four Kingdoms represent the great world powers seen in a vision by Daniel (Chapter 7), who in succession will subject Israel until such time when Israel's final and complete deliverance will be effected by the Messiah. The power of the fourth kingdom, that of Rome, is still in sway. See Ramban further at the beginning of *Seder Vayechi.* Jacob, like Abraham, was thus shown the events that will happen to his descendants during all the generations of their exiles. (9) Daniel 10:20. (10) *Ibid.*, Verse 13. Similarly, the angels mentioned in the verse before us are to be understood as the representatives of the various nations. (11) Symbolic of the seventy years of the Babylonian exile. (12) See my Hebrew commentary, (p. 158, n.12), which asserts that the correct reading is: "He showed him the prince of the kingdom of Media going up fifty-two rungs and then descending. And He showed him the prince of the kingdom of Greece going up one hundred-eighty rungs and then descending." The number of rungs represent the amount of years that these kingdoms held sway over Israel. (13) Isaiah 14:15. (14) Obadiah 1:4. *And though thou set it among the stars, I will bring thee down from thence, saith the Eternal.*

Rashi comments, Rabbi Elazar the son of Rabbi Yosei the son of Zimra said, 'This ladder stood in Beer-sheba and its slope [15] reached unto the Sanctuary in Jerusalem. Beer-sheba is situated in the southern part of Judah, and Jerusalem is to its north on the boundary between Judah and Benjamin, and Beth-el was in the northern portion of Benjamin's territory, on the boundary between Benjamin's territory and that of the children of Joseph. It follows, therefore, that a ladder whose base is in Beer-sheba and whose top is in Beth-el has its slope[15] reaching opposite Jerusalem. Now regarding the statement of our Rabbis that the Holy One, blessed be He, said, 'This righteous man has come to the place where I dwell, [namely, the Sanctuary in Jerusalem, and shall he depart without spending the night?'], [16] and with regard to what they also said, 'Jacob gave the name Beth-el to Jerusalem'[17] this place which he called Beth-el was Luz and not Jerusalem! And whence did they learn to say so, [implying that Luz is identical with Jerusalem] ? I therefore say that Mount Moriah [the Temple site in Jerusalem] was forcibly removed from its place and came here to Luz, and this movement of the Temple site is 'the springing of the earth' which is mentioned in Tractate Shechitath Chullin.[18] It means that the site on which the Sanctuary was later to stand came towards Jacob to Beth-el. And this too is what is meant by *vayiphga bamakom (and he met the place)*:[19] [as two people meet, who are moving towards each other]. If you should ask, 'When our father Jacob passed the site of the Sanctuary [on his way from Beer-sheba to Haran] why did He not detain him there?' The answer is: If it never entered his mind to pray at the place where his fathers had prayed, should Heaven make him stop there? He had journeyed as far as Haran, as we say in the chapter of *Gid Hanasheh,*[20] and Scripture itself helps us clarify this point by

(15) "Its slope." In our text of Rashi: "the middle of its slope." Ramban will explain later that the reference is to "the end" of the slope, which is the head of the ladder. (16) Chullin 91 b. (17) Pesachim 88 b. (18) "The slaughtering of unconsecrated beasts." This tractate is now generally called Chullin (Unconsecrated Beasts). 91 b. (19) Verse 11 here. (20) "The sinew of the hip." It is the seventh chapter of Tractate Chullin (see Note 18) 91 b.

saying, *And he went to Haran.*[21] When he arrived at Haran he said, 'Is it possible that I have passed the place where my fathers prayed without praying there myself?' He decided to return and had returned as far as Beth-el, whereupon the ground of the Temple site sprang for him until Beth-el."

All these are the words of the Rabbi.[22] But I do not agree with them at all for 'the springing of the earth' which the Rabbis mention in connection with Jacob is like that which they have said happened to Eliezer, the servant of Abraham, namely, that he reached Haran in one day. As they have said in Tractate Sanhedrin,[23] "The earth sprang for three persons: Eliezer, the servant of Abraham, our father Jacob, and Abishai the son of Zeruiah."[24] And the Rabbis explained: "Eliezer, the servant of Abraham — for it is written, *And I came this day unto the fountain,*[25] which teaches that on that very day he embarked on his journey. Jacob — for it is written, *And he met the place.*[19] When he arrived at Haran he said, 'Is it possible that I have passed the place where my fathers prayed without praying there myself?' As soon as the thought of returning occurred to him, the earth sprang for him, and immediately *he met the place.*" Thus the Rabbis explicitly say that as soon as the thought to return occurred to him in Haran, the earth sprang for him and he met the place where his fathers prayed, but not that he returned to Beth-el, nor that Mount Moriah sprang and came there to Beth-el. In Bereshith Rabbah[26] the Rabbis further equated them both [Eliezer and Jacob] with respect to "the springing of the earth." Thus they said: "*And he arose, and went to Aram-naharaim*[27] — on the very same day. *And I came this day unto the fountain*[25] — this day I embarked on the journey, and this day I arrived." With respect to Jacob the Rabbis interpreted in a similar vein: "*And he went to Haran*[21] — the Rabbis say on the very same day." And furthermore, what reason is there for Mount Moriah to "spring"

(21) Verse 10 here. (22) Rashi. See also Note 139, *Seder Bereshith.* (23) 95 a. (24) II Samuel 21:17. In coming to the rescue of David, a miracle occurred, and he reached him at once though he was far away from him. (25) Above, 24:42. (26) 59:15. (27) Above, 24:10.

and come to Beth-el, as Rashi claims, after Jacob had troubled himself to return from Haran to Beth-el, a journey of many days?[28] Moreover, Beth-el does not lie on the border of the Land of Israel which faces towards Haran for Haran is a land which lies to the east [of the Land of Israel while Beth-el lies in its western part].[29] Additionally, the middle part of a ladder is not referred to as its "slope."[30] And, finally, what reason is there for the middle of the ladder to be opposite Beth-el, [where, according to Rashi, the side of the Sanctuary had been transported], when the middle part of an object does not possess significance beyond that of its whole?

There is, however, another intent to these Midrashim. The Rabbis have said in Bereshith Rabbah,[31] "Rabbi Hoshayah said, 'It has already been stated, *And Jacob hearkened to his father and his mother, and was gone to Paddan-aram.*[32] What then does Scripture teach by repeating, *And Jacob went out from Beer-sheba?*[21] Rather, the redundancy teaches us that Jacob said, "When my father desired to leave the Land of Israel, at what location did he seek permission for it? Was it not in Beer-sheba? I, too, shall go to Beer-sheba to seek this permission. If He grants me permission, I shall leave, and if not, I shall not go." Therefore Scripture found it necessary to state, *And Jacob went out from Beer-sheba.*' "[21]

The intent of this Midrash is that the Rabbis were of the opinion that Jacob was blessed by his father in Hebron, the land of his father's sojournings, and it was to Hebron that he came when he returned to his father from Paddan-aram, as it is said, *And Jacob came unto Isaac his father to Mamre, to Kiriath-arba – the same is Hebron – where Abraham and Isaac sojourned.*[33] Now if so, the verse stating, *And Jacob went out from Beer-sheba*[21] teaches that when his father commanded him to go to Laban[34] he went to Beer-sheba to receive Divine permission, and that is the

(28) If such a miracle was to be performed, why did not Mount Moriah spring all the way to Haran? (29) Above, 12:8. (30) Thus Rabbi Elazar who said that "its slope" reached to the Sanctuary did not refer to its middle, as Rashi has it. (31) 68:6. (32) Above, 28:7. (33) Further, 35:27. (34) Above, 28:5.

place wherein he spent the night and saw visions of G-d, and it was there that He gave him permission to exit from the Land of Israel, even as He said, *And I will keep thee wherever thou goest and will bring thee back unto this land.*[4] And the ladder which he saw, in the opinion of Rabbi Yosei the son of Zimra, he saw with its feet in Beer-sheba, in the very place where he lay, and with the end of its slope which is the top of the ladder reaching to a point opposite the Sanctuary. It was supported by heaven at the gate through which the angels enter and exit. The revered G-d stood over him, and therefore he knew that Beer-sheba was the gate of heaven, suitable for prayer, and the Sanctuary was the house of G-d. And in the morning Jacob continued his journey from Beer-sheba and arrived at Haran on the same day, and this was "the springing of the earth" mentioned with respect to Jacob.

This is the opinion of Rabbi Yosei the son of Zimra who said in Bereshith Rabbah,[35] "This ladder stood in Beer-sheba and its slope reached to the Sanctuary, as it is said, *And Jacob went out from Beer-sheba;*[19] *And he was afraid and said, How fearful is this place.*"[36] And the stone which he erected as a pillar[37] he did not erect in the place where he slept, for Beer-sheba is not Beth-el and it was in Beth-el that he erected it, and there he went upon his return from Paddan-aram, as it is said, *Arise, go up to Beth-el ... and make there an altar unto G-d who appeared unto thee,* etc.[38] But he erected it [after carrying the stone from Beth-el to Jerusalem][39] opposite the slope, at the place where the head of the ladder stood, which he had called the house of G-d, and this is the city which had previously been called Luz.[40]

Thus in the opinion of Rabbi Yosei the son of Zimra, Luz was Jerusalem which Jacob called Beth-el.[40] Possibly this may be so, according to the verses in the book of Joshua.[41] It is certainly true that it is not the Beth-el near Ai[42] for that Beth-el was originally so named in the days of Abraham[42] and prior to that.

(35) 69:5. (36) Verse 17 here. (37) Verse 18 here. (38) Further, 35:1. (39) Thus comments Rabbi David Luria (R'dal) in explanation of Ramban's words. See my Hebrew commentary, p. 160. (40) Verse 19 here. (41) The source intended is not clear to me. See my Hebrew commentary, p. 160, for further discussion of this matter. (42) Above, 12:8. Whereas the Beth-el referred to here had previously been called Luz.

But Rabbi Yehudah the son of Rabbi Shimon differs there[43] with Rabbi Yosei the son of Zimra, and he says: "This ladder stood upon the Sanctuary site and its slope reached to Beth-el. What is his reason? *And he was afraid, and said,*[36] etc. *And he called the name of that place Beth-el.*"[40] Thus in the opinion of Rabbi Yehudah the son of Rabbi Shimon the verse stating, *And he lighted upon the place,*[19] means Mount Moriah. *And he tarried there all night, because the sun was set* for him not at its proper time [so that he should spend the night there], for as our Rabbis have stated:[16] "[The Holy One, blessed be He, said], 'This righteous man has come to the place where I dwell. Shall he then depart without staying there over night?' " And so Jacob saw the ladder with its feet standing in that place, and its slope, which is its top, reached to a point which was opposite that particular Beth-el [which was mentioned in connection with Ai during Abraham's era],[42] and that was the city of Luz. And Jacob said that the very place where he spent the night was the house of G-d, and the slope of the ladder was the gate of heaven, thus Mount Moriah is excellent for prayer, and Beth-el also is a suitable place for the worship of G-d. And he erected the pillar in Beth-el, for in the opinion of all Rabbis he erected it opposite the slope of the ladder.

The opinion of Rabbi Yehudah the son of Rabbi Shimon, [i.e., that Jacob slept on Mount Moriah, and he erected the pillar in Beth-el], is in agreement with the Midrash in the *Gemara* of the chapter concerning *Gid Hanasheh,*[20] and that of Chapter *Cheleck,*[44] which states that Jacob left Beer-sheba and came to Haran, and when he reconsidered and decided to return and pray at Mount Moriah, the place where his fathers had prayed, then the earth "sprang" for him and he lighted immediately upon Mount Moriah. Perhaps it is the Rabbis' opinion that the earth "sprang" for him both when going from Haran to Mount Moriah and when returning from Mount Moriah to Haran. This would be in agreement with the opinion of the Rabbi who says:[45] *"And he*

(43) Bereshith Rabbah 69:8. (44) "Portion," i.e., in the World to Come. This is the tenth chapter of Tractate Sanhedrin, 95 b. (45) Bereshith Rabbah 68:9.

went to Haran[21] – on the same day. *And he lighted upon the place*[19] – at once, very suddenly."

I found it more explicitly in Pirkei Rabbi Eliezer Hagadol:[46] "Jacob was seventy-seven years of age when he left his father's house,[47] and he followed the well that travelled before him from Beer-sheba to Mount Moriah, a two-day journey, and he arrived there at midday, etc. The Holy One, blessed be He, said to him, 'Jacob, you have bread in your travelling-bag, the well is before you, enabling you to eat and drink and lie down in this place.' Jacob replied, 'Master of all worlds, the sun has yet to descend fifty stages, and shall I lie down to sleep in this place?' Prematurely, the sun then set in the west. Jacob looked and saw that the sun had set in the west, so *he tarried there all night, because the sun was set.*[19] Jacob took twelve stones from the stones of the altar upon which his father Isaac had lain bound as a sacrifice[48] and put them under his head. By the fact that his resting-place contained twelve stones, G-d informed him that twelve tribes were destined to be established from him. But then all twelve stones were transformed into one stone to inform him that all twelve tribes were destined to become one nation in the earth, as it is said, *And who is like Thy people, like Israel, a nation one in the earth?*[49] In the morning Jacob awoke with great fright, and said, 'The house of the Holy One, blessed be He, is in this place,' as it is said, *And he was afraid, and said: How fearful is this place!*[36] From here you learn that whosoever prays in Jerusalem is considered as if he prayed before the Throne of Glory, for the gate of heaven is open there to receive the prayer of Israel, as it is said, *And this is the gate of heaven.*[36] Jacob then wanted to collect the stones [which he had used as a resting-place for his head in order to build an altar], but he found them all to be one stone, and so he set it up as a pillar in that place. Thereupon oil flowed down

(46) Chapter 35. (47) He was sixty-three when he was blessed by his father (Megillah 16 a), and for the following fourteen years he was secluded in the house of Shem and Eber for the purpose of studying Torah. This makes Jacob seventy-seven years old when he left Haran. The Pirkei d'Rabbi Eliezer refers to it as "when he left his father's house," but the intent is as explained. (Rabbi David Luria.) (48) Above, 22:9. (49) II Samuel 7:23.

for him from heaven, and he poured it on top of the stone, as it is said, *And he poured oil upon the top of it.*[37] What did the Holy One, blessed be He, do? With His right foot He sank the anointed stone unto the depths of the abyss to serve as the key-stone of the earth, just as one inserts a key-stone in an arch. It is for this reason that it is called *Even Hashethiyah* (The Foundation Stone),[50] for there is the center of the earth, and from there the earth unfolded, and upon it stands the Temple of G-d, as it is said, *And this stone, which I have set up for a pillar, shall be G-d's house.*[51] From there he [Jacob] went on his journey, and in the twinkling of an eye he arrived in Haran." Thus far [extends the quotation from the Pirkei Rabbi Eliezer Hagadol].

Thus, all Midrashim – despite some minor differences among them – acknowledge that "the springing of the earth" occurred to Jacob through which he travelled a journey of many days in the twinkling of an eye. It is possible that all Midrashim concede to one another, and that on all these journeys of his – when going from Beer-sheba to Haran, when he desired to return to Mount Moriah, and when he left there to go to Haran – the earth "sprang" for him. But there is not one of all these Midrashim which says, as Rashi said, [that Mount Moriah was forcibly removed from its location and was transported to meet him in Beth-el].

18. AND HE SET IT UP FOR A PILLAR. Our Rabbis have explained[52] the difference between a pillar and an altar by saying that a pillar consists of one stone while an altar is composed of many stones. It further appears that a pillar is made for pouring

(50) On this stone, the Ark of G-d, which contained the two Tablets of the Law, rested in the Holy of Holies in the Sanctuary in Jerusalem. (Yoma 53 b.) (51) Verse 22 here. The use of the present tense in the Pirkei d'Rabbi Eliezer – "and upon it *stands* the Temple of G-d" – may either be a reference to the remains of the ancient Sanctuary and its environs, which were still visible in the days when the Pirkei d'Rabbi Eliezer was composed, or it may preferably indicate that although the Temple is now in ruins the place thereof is still deemed sacred as in the days when the House of G-d was firmly established on the sacred mountain. (52) Yerushalmi Abodah Zarah IV, 5.

libations of wine upon it and for the pouring of oil upon it, but not for sacrifices and not for offerings, whereas an altar is for bringing Burnt-offerings and Peace-offerings thereon. When Israel entered the Land, the pillar was prohibited to them[53] because the Canaanites had established it as an ordinance of an idolatrous character to a greater extent than the altars. Even though it is written concerning the altars, *Ye shall break down their altars,*[54] [since the altars were not as prevalent as pillars among the Canaanites, He did not prohibit the Israelites from making their own altars]. It may be that He did not want to prohibit all sacrifices, and so He retained the altar as fit for libations and sacrifices.

20. IF ('IM') G-D WILL BE WITH ME. Rashi comments: "If He will keep for me these promises which He made to me." The reason for the condition is lest the sin cause the abrogation of the promises. And so the Rabbis said in Bereshith Rabbah,[55] "Rabbi Huna said in the name of Rabbi Acha, '*And behold, I am with thee,*[56] and yet it is written, *If G-d will be with me*! However, from here you infer that there is no assurance to the righteous in this world.' "

In line with the simple meaning of Scripture it is further possible that the word *im* does not indicate a doubt in the matter, but such is the way of Scripture when referring to future events, such as: *until 'im asithi' (I have done).*[56] And so also: *'Ve'im' there shall be the jubilee of the children of Israel.*[57] In all these cases it means if there will come a time when the condition is satisfied, then the deed will be fulfilled, that is to say, *ve'im* does not mean "*if* it occurs," but rather "*when* it occurs."

21. THEN THE ETERNAL SHALL BE MY G-D. This is not a condition, as Rashi would have it. It is rather a vow, and its purport is as follows: "If I will return to my father's house, I will worship the proper Name of the Eternal in the Chosen Land at the

(53) Deuteromony 16:22. (54) Exodus 34:13. (55) 76:2. (56) Verse 15 here. (57) Numbers 36:4.

location of this stone which will be for me a house of G-d, and there I will set aside the tithe." There is in this matter a secret relating to that which the Rabbis have said:[58] "He who dwells outside the Land of Israel is like one who has no G-d." [Thus, according to the meaning of the above quotation, the Eternal will be Jacob's G-d only when he returns to the Land of Israel.]

29 2. AND HE LOOKED, AND BEHOLD A WELL IN THE FIELD, AND LO THREE FLOCKS OF SHEEP LYING THERE BY IT. Scripture tells this story at length in order to let us know that *they that wait for the Eternal shall renew their strength,*[59] and the fear of Him gives strength. For here our father Jacob is coming from the journey and he is tired, yet he alone rolls away the stone, a task which required all the shepherds. The many shepherds and all the watchmen of the three flocks of sheep could not shift the rock.

With respect to this chapter, our Rabbis in Bereshith Rabbah[60] also have a secret which alludes to the future. For it happened to him that he came to Haran by way of the well, and only three of all the flocks were gathered. He arrived at the time when the stone was yet upon the mouth of the well, and the flocks waited for the water thereof. Likewise, the matter which is narrated here is all for the purpose of letting it be known that Jacob will succeed in this venture and will have children worthy of the fulfillment of this allusion. For the well alludes to the Sanctuary, and the three flocks of sheep are symbolic of the pilgrims ascending to the Sanctuary during the three festivals.[61] The expression, *For out of that well they watered the flocks,* alludes to the fact that they drew holy inspiration from the pilgrimages to the Sanctuary. It may be that it alludes to the verse, *For out of Zion shall go forth Torah*[62] – which has been likened to water,[63] *and the word of the Eternal from Jerusalem.*[62] – *And thither were all the flocks*

(58) Kethuboth 110 b. (59) Isaiah 40:31. (60) 70:8. (61) *Pesach, Shevuoth,* and *Succoth.* See Deuteronomy 16:16. (62) Isaiah 2:3. Thus both prophecy and law emanated from the Sanctuary. (63) *Ibid.,* 55:1, Baba Kamma 17 a.

gathered[64] – *from the entrance of Hamath unto the Brook of Egypt.*[65] – *And they rolled the stone from the well's mouth and watered,*[64] for they drew holy inspiration therefrom. *And they put the stone back*[64] to lie dormant until the next festival.

5. KNOW YE LABAN THE SON OF NAHOR? Laban was recognized and known by the name of his father's father Nahor since Nahor was more important than Laban's father [Bethuel], and he was the head of their family, as it is written, *the G-d of Abraham and the G-d of Nahor.*[66] [Thus, Laban being the son of Bethuel,[67] was nevertheless known by his father's father's name, Nahor.][68] It is possible that Bethuel was a dishonorable person, and Laban wanted people to ascribe his lineage only to his father's father, for so we find, *And Laban and Bethuel answered.*[69] [Laban is thus mentioned before his father, which indicates that Bethuel was not regarded as the head of the family.] Perhaps all this is in honor of Abraham for [by virtue of Laban's being known by Nahor's name], the whole family traced its lineage to *Nahor the brother of Abraham,*[70] [and thus demonstrated its connection with its illustrious relative Abraham].

9. FOR SHE WAS A SHEPHERDESS. The intent of this is to relate that Laban's sheep had no shepherd other than Rachel, since her father turned over the flock to her alone. She alone tended them all the days, and Leah did not go with the flock at all. The matter was thus unlike that of the daughters of Jethro, where all seven daughters tended the flock simultaneously, as it is said, *And they came and drew water.*[71] Perhaps due to Leah's eyes being tender,[72] the rays of the sun would have hurt her, or because Leah was older and of marriageable age, her father was more concerned about her. Jethro however was honored in his community and he was the priest of the country, and he was confident that people would be afraid of approaching his daughters. It may be that Laban was more modest than Jethro for

(64) Verse 3 here. (65) I Kings 8:65. The verse refers to the gathering of pilgrims for the festival of *Succoth.* (66) Further, 31:53. (67) Above, 28:5. (68) *Ibid.,* 22:22. (69) Above, 24:50. (70) *Ibid.,* 22:23. (71) Exodus 2:16. (72) Further, Verse 17.

Abraham's family was proper and modest, but Rachel was yet young and there was no concern for her. This is the sense of the verse, *And Jacob kissed Rachel.*[73] It may be as Rabbi Abraham ibn Ezra said that where the Hebrew word for "kissing" is followed by the letter *lamed* – [as here: *Vayishak Yaakov l'Rachel,* instead of the word *eth*] – it means not on the mouth, but that he kissed her on her head or on her shoulder.

12. AND SHE TOLD HER FATHER. Rashi comments: "Her mother was dead." And so it is stated in Bereshith Rabbah.[74] But according to the plain meaning of Scripture, Rachel related it to her father in order to inform him of the arrival of his relative and so that he should go forth to meet him and honor him. For, as regards her mother, what was Jacob to her and what could she do for him? However, Rebekah did show her mother the jewels which Eliezer gave her,[75] as is the custom of maidens.

15. IS IT BECAUSE THOU ART MY BROTHER, THAT THOU SHOULDEST SERVE ME FOR NOUGHT? Scripture did not relate that Jacob served Laban. It is possible that from the time Scripture stated, *And he watered the flock of Laban his mother's brother,*[76] the flock never left his care, for when he saw that Rachel was a shepherdess, Jacob had compassion for her and desired that she no longer tend the sheep. So, out of his love for her, he tended them.

It is also possible to say that Laban spoke with cunning. First he said to him that he is his bone and his flesh,[77] and that he will have compassion for him as a man has compassion for his own bone and flesh, but when he saw that Jacob tarried there, supporting himself from Laban's belongings, he said to him, "*Is it because thou art my brother, that thou shouldest serve me for nought?* For I know that you will henceforth serve me for you are an ethical man, and you will not support yourself from the property of others. Nor do I desire that the labor you perform for me be free without full compensation. Therefore tell me what you

(73) Verse 11 here. (74) 70:12. (75) Above, 24:28. (76) Verse 10 here. (77) Verse 14 here.

want for your hire, and I will give it." Jacob then discerned Laban's mind, and he told him that he would serve him for seven years for Rachel. Undefined, "serving" here means tending the sheep, for this is what was needed and this was the subject of their conversation.

21. FOR MY DAYS ARE FULFILLED. This means "the time which my mother told me to remain away from home." Another explanation is: *For my days are fulfilled* – "I am now eighty-four years old and when shall I beget twelve tribes?" These are the words of Rashi.

27. FULFILL 'SHVUA' (THE WEEK OF) THIS ONE. The word *shvua* is in the construct state for it is punctuated with a *sheva*. It thus means the seven days of this wife, referring to the seven days of the wedding feast. These too are the words of Rashi.

But if so, [i.e., if Rashi interprets *shvua* as referring to the seven days of the wedding feast rather than, more simply, the seven years of labor, thus implying that the seven years of work had been completed], why did not the Rabbi [Rashi] explain the verse above, *my days are fulfilled,* as referring to the years of work and the condition which were completed, as Onkelos has it,[78] and which is the true sense of the verse, [instead of explaining it as referring to the length of time his mother told him to remain there or to his advanced age]? For merely because the days his mother told him to remain with him were completed or because of his advanced age, Laban would not give him his daughter before the mutually agreed time, and it is enough to expect of Laban that he fulfill his condition. It is according to Onkelos, [who says that Jacob's seven years of work had been completed], that we are bound to explain, *fulfill 'shvua' this one,* as referring to the seven days of the wedding feast for as Jacob had told him, the days of work had already been completed. So also did Rabbi Abraham ibn Ezra explain it. And I do not know [how the reference here could be to "the seven days of the marriage feast," as Rashi claims], for

(78) The days of my work are fulfilled. (Onkelos, Verse 27.)

"the seven days of the wedding feast" is an ordinance established for Israel by our teacher Moses.[79]

Perhaps we may say that the dignitaries of the nations had already practiced this custom of old, just as was the case with mourning, as it is written, *And he made a mourning for his father seven days.*[80] And that which the Rabbis have deduced from here in the Yerushalmi[81] and in Bereshith Rabbah,[82] "One must not mix one rejoicing with another," that is merely a Scriptural intimation based upon the customary practices of the ancient ones prior to the giving of the Torah. But in our *Gemara,*[83] the Rabbis did not derive it from here, [i.e., from Laban's statement], but instead they deduced it from the verse, *And Solomon held the feast* etc.[84]

Now it is possible to say that this was part of "the changing of the hire ten times"[85] of which Jacob accused Laban. For Jacob told Laban originally that the days were fulfilled, and Laban kept quiet and gave him Leah. Later, Laban told him, "*Fulfill 'shvua' this one*, for the work period for Leah has not been fulfilled, and I gave her to you before the time I had agreed upon." And Jacob listened to Laban and completed the days as defined by Laban, for he desired Rachel, and what could he do? Therefore, Scripture does not say at first, "And it came to pass when the days were fulfilled, and Jacob said, etc.," [for this would have indicated mutual agreement concerning the completion of the work period, whereas Laban, as explained, claimed that that time had not yet arrived].

(79) Yerushalmi Kethuboth I, 1. (80) Further, 50:10. Thus the seven-day period of mourning was already an established practice in the days of the patriarchs. (81) Moed Katan I, 7. (82) 70:18. (83) Moed Katan 9 a. (84) I Kings 8:65. The verse reads: *And Solomon held the feast at that time ... seven days and seven days, even fourteen days.* The Rabbis explain that the first seven days were a feast of dedication of the new Temple, and the second seven days were the feast of Tabernacles, and he did not combine the two festivities into one because "we must not mix one rejoicing with another." – The explanation for this principle is stated by Tosafoth Moed Katan 8 b. "For just as we must not perform religious duties bundle-wise, but pay exclusive attention to each singly, so must we turn our heart completely toward one rejoicing only, without interference from another." (85) Further, 31:41.

It is also possible to say that when the seventh year arrived, Jacob said to Laban, *Give me my wife, for my days are fulfilled,* meaning that this is the year in which the days will be fulfilled. Similarly, *The aged with him that is full of days,*[86] which means, "he who is attaining his final year." Similarly, *Until the day of your consecration be fulfilled,*[87] which means, "until the seventh day in which the days of your consecration will be fulfilled." It is possible that Jacob said, *My days are fulfilled,* because they were about to be fulfilled and are considered as if fulfilled. There are many similar examples in Scripture. Likewise, in the next *Seder* (portion of the Torah), *As her soul was departing, for she died,*[88] which means, "when she was near death, and was considered as if she had already died." And this is the meaning of the expression, *that I may come unto her,*[89] that is to say, Jacob said, "My request is not that you give her to me and I will then leave, but rather that I marry her and complete the few days which are still obligatory upon me for now that the period is almost over, you will not be afraid that I might leave you." Our Rabbis have given a Midrashic interpretation to the words, *that I may come unto her,*[90] because it is not the ethical way to mention it in this manner, the more so with righteous people, but the intent is as I have said.

Laban then told Jacob, "Fulfill the seven years of this one, Leah, for perhaps since I transgressed your will by giving you Leah instead of Rachel you will not fulfill them." Perhaps he mentioned it in order that it be known when the days of work for Rachel begin, and then he told him, "I will give you the other daughter, Rachel, *for the service which thou shalt serve with me* after the wedding."

'VENITNAH' (AND WE WILL GIVE) THEE. The verb is plural, as in, *Let us go down, and let us confound there;*[91] *And let us*

(86) Jeremiah 6:11. (87) Leviticus 8:33. (88) Further, 35:18. (89) Verse 21 here. (90) Bereshith Rabbah 70:17; also mentioned in Rashi, Verse 21: his mind was intent upon having children and rearing them in the religious traditions of his fathers. (91) Above, 11:7.

burn.[92] Here too it is a form of *venitein* (and we will give). This is Rashi's comment, but he did not say why an individual person [Laban] would use the plural form. Perhaps Rashi thought that this is the manner in which dignitaries speak in the Sacred Language, i.e., as if others are speaking. And Rabbi Abraham ibn Ezra said here that *nitnah* is in the (*niphal*) passive tense and the prefix *vav* converts it from the past to the future, thus meaning, "and it shall be given to you."

The correct interpretation appears to me to be that Laban's words were spoken with cunning. He said to Jacob, *"It is not so done in our place,*[93] for the people of the place will not let me do so, [i.e., to marry off the younger before the firstborn], for this would be a shameful act in their eyes. But you *fulfill the week of this one,* and we – I and all the people of the place – will give you also this one, for we will all consent to the matter, and we will give you honor and a feast as we have done with the first one."

30. AND HE LOVED RACHEL MORE THAN LEAH. The reason why Scripture mentions that he also loved Rachel more than Leah is that it is natural for a man to have more love for the woman with whom he first had relations, just as the Sages have mentioned with reference to women:[94] "And she makes a firm commitment only to he who marries her first." Thus Jacob's loving Rachel more than Leah was unnatural. This is the sense of the word *gam*: [*and he loved 'gam' Rachel than Leah*].

31. AND THE ETERNAL SAW THAT LEAH WAS HATED. Now Leah had deceived her sister and also Jacob. For even if we were to say that she showed respect for her father, who took her and brought her in to him and she was not rebellious against him, she should have by word or sign indicated that she was Leah. All the more is this so since she feigned herself all night to be another, which was the reason why Jacob did not recognize her until he saw her in the morning. It was for this reason that Jacob hated

(92) *Ibid.*, Verse 3. (93) Verse 26 here. (94) Sanhedrin 22 b.

her. But G-d, knowing that she did so in order to be married to the righteous one, had compassion upon her. And so the Rabbis said in Bereshith Rabbah:[95] "When Jacob saw the deeds by which Leah had deceived her sister, he decided to divorce her. But when the Holy One, blessed be He, remembered her by giving her children, Jacob said, 'Shall I divorce the mother of these children?' " This is the meaning of the expression, *And the Eternal saw*: He had compassion upon her so that Jacob should not leave her. But there are some scholars[96] who say that in the case of two wives, one of whom is loved exceedingly, the second one, who is the less beloved, is called "hated" relative to the first, just as Scripture said, *And he loved Rachel more than Leah,*[97] but not that he hated her. Leah however was ashamed of the matter and so G-d saw her affliction.

30 1. GIVE ME CHILDREN. The commentators[98] said that this means that Rachel asked Jacob to pray on her behalf. *Or else I die* – Rashi comments: "For one who is childless may be considered as dead." This is a Midrash of our Rabbis.[99]

But I wonder. If so, why was Jacob angry with her? And why did he say, *Am I in G-d's stead?*[100] for G-d hearkens to the righteous.[101] [I wonder concerning] that which Jacob said [to Rachel, as quoted in Rashi:[100] "You say that I should do as did my father, who prayed on behalf of Rebekah, but I am not circumstanced as my father was. My] father had no children at all. I, however, have children. It is from you that He had withheld children and not from me." Do not the righteous pray on behalf of others? There were Elijah[102] and Elisha[103] who prayed on behalf of strange women.

It would appear that on account of Jacob's answer, our Rabbis took him to task, saying in Bereshith Rabbah:[104] "The Holy One, blessed be He, said to Jacob, 'Is this the way to answer a woman

(95) 71:2. (96) R'dak in his Commentary on the Torah. (97) Verse 30 here. (98) Rashi and Ibn Ezra. (99) Bereshith Rabbah 71:19. (100) Verse 2 here. (101) See Psalms 69:34. (102) I Kings 18:21. (103) II Kings 4:33. (104) 71:10.

who is oppressed by her barrenness? By your life! Your children are destined to stand before her son Joseph!' "

In line with the plain meaning of Scripture, Rachel asked of Jacob that he give her children, but her intent was truly to say that he should pray on her behalf and continue indeed to pray until G-d would, in any case, grant her children, and if not, she would mortify herself because of grief. In her envy she spoke improperly, thinking that because Jacob loved her he would fast, put on *sackcloth with ashes,*[105] and pray until she would have children, so that she should not die of her grief.

2. AND JACOB'S ANGER WAS KINDLED. It is not in the power of the righteous that their prayer be heard and answered in any case, and because she spoke in the manner of yearning women who are loved, thus attempting to frighten him with her death, his anger was kindled. Therefore, he said to her that he is not in G-d's stead that he should remember the barren ones by giving them children in any case, and he does not care about it since it is from her that children were withheld and not from him. He said this in order to admonish her and shame her. Now the righteous woman Rachel, seeing that she could not rely upon Jacob's prayer, then went to pray on her own behalf to Him Who hears the cry of those in trouble. This is the sense of the verse, *And G-d hearkened to her.*[106]

Perhaps we can rectify Jacob's retort in consonance with the opinion of our Rabbis [who related that Jacob said to Rachel, "It is from you that he has withheld children and not from me,"] for it is impossible to think that Jacob did not pray on behalf of his beloved wife who was barren, however his prayer was not accepted.

Now Rachel came to him with a pretext saying that he should, in any case, give her children through his prayer for he is not of less stature than his father who did so. At this, his anger was kindled and he said to her that the matter is up to G-d and not to him, and that his father's prayer was heard because he was a

(105) Esther 4:1. (106) Further, Verse 22.

righteous man and was destined to have children, but here it is from her that He has withheld children. This is a correct interpretation.

5. AND SHE BORE 'L'YAAKOV' (TO JACOB) A SON. In the case of all the handmaids Scripture mentions the phrase, *to Jacob* [in connection with the birth of their children], in order to relate that Jacob desired and acknowledged them and that they were not called by him "sons of the handmaids," but "sons of Jacob," just like the sons of the mistresses who traced their lineage to him. In the case of the fifth and sixth sons of Leah it also says, *to Jacob,*[107] since due to her abundance of sons, Scripture deems it necessary to say that Jacob desired and befriended all of them. This is not mentioned in connection with the birth of the first [four sons of Leah because it is obvious that Jacob desired them].

9. WHEN LEAH SAW THAT SHE HAD LEFT OFF BEARING SHE TOOK ZILPAH HER HANDMAID, etc. I do not know what motivated this deed of Leah and why she gave her handmaid to her husband for she was not barren that she should hope to have children through Zilpah, and it is not natural for women to increase the number of their husbands' wives. We must, however, say that the matriarchs were prophetesses,[108] who knew that Jacob was destined to establish twelve tribes, and Leah desired that the majority of his sons be from her or from her handmaid, who was in her power, so that her sister Rachel would not prevail over her with respect to the number of her sons. Therefore, she said, *G-d hath given me my share, because I have given my handmaid to my husband.*[109] Jacob also came unto her on account of this, i.e., that he raise many sons for he knew it to be so, as our Rabbis have said.[110]

It is possible that knowing that the Land had been given to their children, and realizing that Abraham and Isaac had not had many

(107) *Ibid.*, Verses 17 and 19. (108) Bereshith Rabbah, end of Chapter 72. (109) Verse 18 here. (110) Bereshith Rabbah 70:17. Jacob was also aware that he was destined to establish twelve tribes.

children, Jacob wanted to have many wives in order to increase his progeny so as to inherit the Land, for *a fourth generation shall come hither again,*[111] and so Leah wanted to give him her handmaid so that he would not wed a stranger.

14. 'DUDA'IM.' These are *'sigli'* (violets). In Arabic it is called *jasmin.* So I found in Rashi's commentary. But this is not so for the Arabic jasmin bears the same name in the words of our Rabbis, as they say in the chapter *Bameh Tomnin:*[112] "Poppy pomace flavored with jasmin may be used [as a lotion on the Sabbath]," while they say *sigli* is an odorous herb concerning which they have said[113] that on smelling it, one recites the blessing: "Blessed art Thou... who createst odorous plants." However, their season is not *in the days of the wheat,* but perhaps Reuben found them there by chance. It is best to accept Onkelos' opinion concerning the translation of *duda'im,* which he rendered as *yavruchin* (mandrakes). In Bereshith Rabbah[114] it is also explained similarly: "Rabbi Chiya the son of Rabbi Abba said, '*Yavruchin,*' " and these are *yavruach* in Arabic.

Now Rabbi Abraham ibn Ezra wrote: "Onkelos translated *duda'im* as 'mandrakes,' and so they are called in Arabic. They have a good odor. And it is so written: *The mandrakes give forth fragrance.*[115] They resemble the human form as they have the shape of the human head and hands. Now some say that they are an aid to pregnancy, but I do not know it since their effect is to produce the cold fluid in the body." These are Ibn Ezra's words.

The correct interpretation is that Rachel wanted the *duda'im* for delight and pleasure, for Rachel was visited with children through prayer, not by medicinal methods. And Reuben brought the branches of *duda'im* or the fruit, which resemble apples and have a good odor. The stem, however, which is shaped in the form of the human head and hands, he did not bring, and it is the stem which people say is an aid to pregnancy. And if the matter be true, it is

(111) Above, 15:16. (112) "With What May They Cover Up" hot food, the fourth chapter in Tractate Shabbath. 50 b. (113) Berachoth 43 b. (114) 72:2. (115) Song of Songs 7:14.

by some peculiar effect, not by its natural quality. But I have not seen it thus in any of the medicinal books discussing mandrakes.

15. IS IT A SMALL MATTER THAT THOU HAST TAKEN AWAY MY HUSBAND? The intent thereof is as follows: "Is it a small matter that you take my husband unto yourself as if you are his wife and I am the handmaid? Will you now also make yourself the mistress to take the mandrakes in whose odor I delight?"

It is possible that Rachel wanted the mandrakes in honor of Jacob to perfume his couch. Leah had done in the customary way of women, just as it is written, *I have perfumed my bed with myrrh, aloes and cinnamon.*[116] Therefore, Leah said, *Is it a small matter that thou hast taken away my husband* from me that you now also take my son's mandrakes to win him over with them?

And some scholars say[117] that *duda'im* are herbs, which act as a male aphrodisiac, the word being derived from the expression, *the time of 'dodim' (love).*[118] Therefore Leah said, *Is it a small matter that thou hast taken away my husband?* as I have mentioned.

20. G-D HATH 'Z'VADANI' (ENDOWED) ME WITH A GOOD 'ZEVED' (DOWRY). The commentators have not found the source of this word in the Sacred Language.

We could perhaps say that *zeved* is a composite word formed from *zeh bad*, just as is the word *madua*, [which is composed of the two words, *mah dua*, meaning "what is the opinion of this matter" or simply "why"] or the word *bagad*[119] in its written form. [It is read, however, as two words: *ba gad* (good luck cometh.)] Since the vowel signs *segol* and *patach* interchange in many places, particularly in composite words, [the second *segol* in *zeved* could have come from the *patach* of *bad: zeh bad*]. So also in the word *tzalmaveth*, [which consists of the two words: *tzeil maveth* (the shade of death)], and the word *biladai*, [composed of

(116) Proverbs 7:17. (117) I have not been able to identify them. However, see R'dak. (118) Ezekiel 16:8. (119) Verse 11 here.

bal ad (except unto, except unto me, or except me)]. And the second part (*bad*) of the word *zeved* comes from the word *badim* (branches), as in, *'badei' (staves) of accacia-wood;*[120] *And it brought forth 'badim' (branches), and shot forth sprigs.*[121] The thick branches of a tree are called *badim*, and then the word was appropriated to mean "children," as in, *The first-born of death shall devour 'badav' (his sons);*[122] *His ill-founded 'badav' (sons).*[123] Therefore Leah said that this son whom G-d had given her would be a good son for he will cause her husband to reside in her shadow, as "he will now *'yizbleini' (dwell with me)* in my shadow." Similarly, *I have surely built Thee a house 'z'vul' (of habitation),*[124] meaning "in order to abide in His shadow." This was said in this fashion out of respect for the Supreme One, just as Solomon said, *Behold, heaven and the heaven of heavens cannot contain Thee, how much less this house that I have builded!*[125] Likewise, *The sun and moon stand still 'z'vulah' (in their habitation),*[126] meaning "stand still in the place where they abide," as it is said, *In them* [the heavens] *hath He set a tent for the sun.*[127]

Now Onkelos translated *zeved tov* as a good portion. I did not understand his reasoning until I saw in the Jerusalem Targum:[128] "The word of G-d has outfitted me (*zavad*) with good provision." [*Zavad* is written here with two *vavim* instead of the *beth* with which the word *zeved* is written in the Torah.] From this I learned that both Onkelos and the Jerusalem Targum considered the word *zeved* of the Torah, which is spelled with the letter *beth*, as if it were written with the letter *vav*, and they connected it to the Aramaic language which translates the Hebrew word *tzeidah* (provision) as *zvadim* (provisions). Leah thus said that G-d had made this son a good provision and a good portion for her because

(120) Exodus 25:13. (121) Ezekiel 17:6. (122) Job 18:13. (123) Isaiah 16:6. See Rashi there, who explains the verse as follows: *for most of Moab's sons are illegitimate*, etc. (124) I Kings 8:13. (125) *Ibid.*, Verse 27. (126) Habakkuk 3:11. (127) Psalms 19:5. (128) Found in our Targum Yonathan. The traditional *Targumim* (translations) of the Pentateuch are *Onkelos, Yonathan,* and *Yerushalmi.* The latter has not reached us in its entirety.

her husband, due to her many children, will now live mainly with her, and thus she will be supported together with him when it is well with him. The *vav* and the *beth* are used interchangeably in our language in many places, such as: *ta'avah* (desire) written with a *vav,*[129] and *ta'avah*, written with a *beth;*[130] *geivi (My back)* – [written with a *vav*] – *I have given to the smiters,*[131] and, *Upon 'gabi' (my back)* – [written with a *beth*] – *the plowers plowed.*[132] So also, *'Lekitzvei' (To the bottoms)* – [written with a *beth*] – *of the mountains I went down,*[133] is as if it were written, *lekitzvei* with a *vav*. Also, *'Laparbor' (For the precinct)* – [written with a *beth*] – *westward, four at the causeway,*[134] serves as the basis of the word *parvor*, written with a *vav*, as it is written, *By the chamber of Nethan-melech the officer, which was 'baparvorim' (in the precincts),*[135] written with a *vav*, and the meaning of both forms, [whether written with a *beth* or *vav*] is the Court which is outside the wall. *'Umigrash' (And open land) round about the cities,*[136] is rendered by the Jerusalem Targum as, *uparvor.* And so did the Jonathan Targum translate *migrashoth* (open lands) as *parvoraya.*[137] In the Mishnah we also find the *vav* and the *beth* interchange: "A *tarvad* (spoon)-full," written with a *vav,*[138] and in some editions it is written, *tarbad*, with a *beth*; "A board which has no *levazbiz* (edges)," written with a *beth,*[139] and in certain places they use the word *lazbiz,* written with a *beth,*[140] while in other places they use *lazviz* written with a *vav.*[141] Also, *itztaba* (a balcony), written with a *beth,*[142] and *itztava,* written with a *vav,*[143] and many other similar words. In the Jerusalem Talmud they also write *avir* (space)[141] with a *beth* in place of the usual *vav,* as they were not particular about that.

23. G-D 'OSAPH' (HATH TAKEN AWAY) MY DISGRACE. I.e., "He has laid it up somewhere where it cannot be seen." Similar examples are: *And it shall not 'yei'aseph' (have been taken away)*

(129) Above, 3:6. (130) Psalms 119:20. (131) Isaiah 50:6. (132) Psalms 129:3. (133) Jonah 2:7. (134) I Chronicles 26:18. (135) II Kings 23:11. (136) Numbers 35:2. (137) Ezekiel 27:28. (138) Nazir VII, 2. (139) Pesachim 48 b. (140) Kelim II, 3. (141) Source is unknown to me. (142) Shabbath 7 a. (143) Eirubin 77 b.

into the house;[144] *And the stars 'asphu' (withdraw) their shining;*[145] *Neither shall thy moon 'yei'aseph' (withdraw itself),*[146] meaning it shall not hide itself. This is the language of Rashi. But Rabbi Abraham ibn Ezra said that *asaph* has the same meaning as "vanish," as in, *'Vene'esaph' (And vanish) will joy and gladness.*[147]

The correct opinion is that of Onkelos, who made them all expressions of gathering and assembling, as is their plain sense, derived from the verses: *'Vaya'asphu' (And they gathered) the quails;*[148] *But 'me'asphav' (they who have garnered it) shall eat it.*[149] Death is called *asiphah*[150] because the dying person is gathered to his dead ancestors. *And it shall not 'yei'aseph' into the house*[144] means to be gathered to his household. *And the stars 'asphu' their shining*[145] means that they will gather the light within them and not give forth their light outside, or that they will be gathered into their tent, which is in the firmament of the heaven.[151] The word *asiphah* is used in connection with disgrace, meaning that the disgraced person should be gathered and not spread among people, i.e., to be discussed further in the streets.

27. 'NICHASHTI' I HAVE OBSERVED THE SIGNS AND THE ETERNAL HATH BLESSED ME FOR THY SAKE. That is, "on account of you and your merit for you are a righteous man." The word *nichashti* means "I have tested," and every form of *nichesh* connotes testing. And some say[152] that Laban was a diviner with teraphim.[153]

Jacob, however, said, *And the Eternal hath blessed thee 'leragli' (since my coming),*[154] but, in a humble manner, he did not want to say "for my sake." Thus, he said *leragli*, meaning that "from the time I set my foot in your house, you have been blessed."

29. AND HOW THY CATTLE HAVE FARED WITH ME. "You know the number of your few cattle that were entrusted to me at

(144) Exodus 9:19. (145) Joel 2:10. (146) Isaiah 60:20. (147) *Ibid.*, 16:10. (148) Numbers 11:32. (149) Isaiah 62:9. (150) Above, 25:8. (151) See Psalms 19:5, mentioned above, Note 127 (152) Ibn Ezra. (153) See Ramban further, 31:19. (154) Verse 30 here.

first." These are Rashi's words. That is to say, "You know how few your cattle were when they were entrusted to me." But according to Rashi's interpretation, it would have been more proper had he said, "and your cattle which were with me:" you know *for it was little which thou hadst* before I came, *and it hath increased abundantly.*[154] Or, we shall explain: "*Thou knowest how I have served thee* since I have done it with all my strength, and thou knowest *how thy cattle have fared with me,* for a long time has passed since then, and thou knowest *for it was little which thou hadst before I came, and it hath increased abundantly,* in an unnatural way. It is only *The blessing of the Eternal* [that] *maketh rich,*[155] which came from the time I set foot in your house." This is the correct interpretation.

30. WHEN SHALL I PROVIDE 'GAM' (ALSO) FOR MINE OWN HOUSE? "At present, my sons alone provide for my needs, but I also ought to work together with them and assist them." This is the force of the word *gam* (also). These are Rashi's words. But we do not find that Jacob had his own sheep, nor do we find mentioned anywhere that his young children — the oldest of whom was six years or less — tended them. It was possible that before Jacob came, Laban had children younger than Rachel[156] and now they were fit to tend the flock. [However, Jacob's children were still very young.] Perhaps Jacob referred to his wives and servants, who he said did his work for him. But all this is not correct. The meaning of, *When shall I provide also for mine house?* is: "When shall I provide for my house just as I have also done for your house." Similarly, *And he loved also Rachel from Leah,*[157] means "And he loved Rachel also more than he loved Leah." And similarly, *Also thee I would have slain,*[158] means "Also I would have slain thee." And there are many other such verses.

(155) Proverbs 10:22. (156) This is a reference to what Rashi explained in Verse 27 that since Jacob's arrival, a blessing came upon Laban and he begot sons, "for is it possible that if he previously had sons, he would have let his daughter Rachel go among the shepherds?" Yet he had sons, as it is said, *And he* [Jacob] *heard the words of Laban's sons,* (further, 31:1). We must say that these sons were born to him after Jacob came. (157) Above, 29:30. (158) Numbers 22:33.

32. SPECKLED AND SPOTTED. This means speckled *or* spotted. *And every 'chum' among the sheep* – commentators have explained[159] *chum* as meaning "black," since blackness comes from heat (*cham*). But this does not appear to me to be correct since most sheep are black, particularly in the eastern countries where it is warm, and if so, all sheep would then belong to Jacob.

The correct interpretation is the rendition of Onkelos, namely, that *chum* is reddish or brownish, called *rouge* in Old French, and so did Rashi explain it. *Chum* would then be from the root; *the light of 'hachamah' (the sun),*[160] since it is like the sun which is somewhat red.

AND OF SUCH SHALL BE MY HIRE. Rashi comments: "Those which from now on will be born speckled and spotted among the goats, and the brownish ones amongst the sheep shall belong to me." And so also is the opinion of Rabbi Abraham ibn Ezra. The meaning of the expression, *every one among the flock speckled and spotted,* is that it refers to the he-goats; *and the spotted and speckled among the goats* refers to the she-goats, just as Scripture said, *And he removed that day the he-goats ... and all the she-goats.*[161] And the meaning of the expression, *every one that had white in it,*[161] is that it refers to those mentioned, [namely, the spotted and the speckled among the he-goats and the she-goats], *and all the brownish among the sheep.*[161] [Thus, according to Rashi and Ibn Ezra, Jacob's hire was to be all spotted and speckled he-goats and she-goats that will henceforth be born, and also the reddish ones among the sheep, but not the spotted and speckled among the sheep.]

In my opinion, all the spotted and speckled among the sheep, as well as all brownish ones, were to be Jacob's hire since he did not make among his sticks any with a brownish color, in which case he caused himself the loss of his hire from among the sheep, which are the best of the flock. Similarly, in his dream, he was shown *the rams which went up on the flocks were ringstraked, speckled,*[162]

(159) Ibn Ezra and R'dak. (160) Isaiah 30:26. (161) Verse 35 here. (162) Further, 31:10.

there being no brownish ones among them. And the meaning of the verse before us is: removing from there every one of the flock speckled and spotted and all brownish ones among the sheep, and removing the spotted and the speckled among the goats, *and they shall be my hire,* namely, the three colors among the sheep – speckled, spotted, and brownish – and two among the goats – spotted and speckled. And he further said, *So shall my righteousness answer for me in time to come,* that *everyone that is not speckled and spotted among the goats, and* all *brownish among the sheep, that shall be accounted stolen with me.*[163]

35. AND HE REMOVED THAT DAY THE HE-GOATS. The meaning thereof is that Scripture relates that Jacob had said in a general way, *removing from there ... the spotted and the speckled among the goats,*[164] [which, according to Ramban's opinion explained above, refers only to the she-goats], but Laban was afraid of the influence of the male seed, and so he removed the he-goats that were even ringstraked, having a little white on their feet at the spot where they are bound, and he removed from the sheep *every one that had white in it* together with *all the brownish ones.* Now if *every one that had white in it* means that he removed from among the he-goats and she-goats all that had any white color in them, whether ringstraked or grizzled, in that case, *and all brownish among the sheep* is in addition to the colors mentioned [for, as we have seen, Ramban is of the opinion that Jacob's hire from the sheep was from all three colors]. The reason why they added the brownish color to the hire from the sheep is that it is not in their nature to be born with the same colors as he-goats and she-goats, and it is not in the nature of goats to be brownish.

37. AND JACOB TOOK HIM STICKS OF POPLAR. As soon as they agreed that his hire would be these colors it was permissible for Jacob to do whatever he could to cause them to give birth in this manner. Perhaps Jacob had made a condition that he may do with them whatever he wants since Laban did not know of the

(163) Verse 33 here. (164) Verse 32 here.

ramifications of this measure, nor did Laban's shepherds sense anything when they saw the sticks in the gutters once a year during the days of Nisan. For *When the flocks were feeble*[165] in the days of Tishri, *he did not put them in*, otherwise not a hoof would have remained for Laban.

Now some commentators[166] say that the first year [Jacob did not make use of these sticks, but] there were born to him many speckled and spotted ones by virtue of G-d's blessing which the angel showed him.[167] And then he put the sticks in front of those which were his so that they should give birth in their form. This would prevent Laban from saying that their offspring was stolen by Jacob, [as he would have claimed had they given birth to other colored offspring].

This is the meaning of *whensoever the stronger flocks became heated,*[168] referring to those that had been born to Jacob by way of G-d's blessing; *but when the flocks* of Laban *were feeble, he put them not in; so that the feebler were Laban's,* for they did not give birth to speckled ones, *and the stronger* were all *Jacob's,*[165] including their offspring, for they gave birth to speckled ones.

40. AND JACOB SEPARATED THE LAMBS. Rashi comments: "Those sheep that were thus born spotted on the ankles and speckled, he separated and set apart by themselves, thus forming them into a separate flock. The spotted flock he led in front of the ordinary sheep so that the faces of the sheep that followed behind them were gazing at them. This is what Scripture means in saying, *And he set the faces of the flocks towards the spotted;* the faces of the sheep were directed towards the spotted animals and towards all that were brownish which were found amongst Laban's sheep. *And he put his own droves by themselves, and set them not with Laban's flocks,* as I have already explained." This is the Rabbi's [Rashi's] language. But his words here are not correct. For why did Jacob separate the spotted lambs so that there did not remain in Laban's flock any speckled or brownish ones, neither in

(165) Verse 42 here. (166) R'dak. (167) Further, 31:12. (168) Verse 41 here.

the sheep nor in the goats? And if those that he separated were the ringstraked, speckled and spotted which the sheep had given birth to and which belonged to him, and it was from them that he made this spotted flock, why did he separate only the lambs and did not take also the he-goats and she-goats which were born spotted and make from all of them this spotted flock which he led before the sheep? Moreover, Scripture makes no mention of the fact that brownish ones were born. And again, according to the opinion of the Rabbi [Rashi], there were no ringstraked and spotted among the lambs for these were not his hire. Only the brownish were, and for the brownish he had made no sticks.

But the explanation of the verse is that Jacob separated the lambs from the goats and made from them a separate flock. Now he had a flock of brownish lambs and a flock of spotted and speckled goats. He then had the faces of all the flocks – of the lambs and of the goats – directed towards the ringstraked and towards all the brownish which were in the flock of Laban, since he put the ringstraked before the goats and all the brownish before the lambs, this being in accordance with the opinion of the earlier Rabbis, [Rashi and Ibn Ezra, as explained above], or, according to [Ramban's] opinion, the ringstraked and all the brownish before the lamb.For the purpose of the separation of the lambs from the goats was on account of the brownish which were his hire from the lambs alone.

The correct interpretation appears to me to be that Scripture is saying, *Jacob separated* [only] *the lambs and set the faces of the flocks,* which refer to the above mentioned lambs, *to the ringstraked and all the brownish in the flock of Laban, and he put his own droves* of the ringstraked and the brownish *by themselves, and he set them not with Laban's flocks,* for these, [the ringstraked and the brownish], were his hire. And the meaning of the expression, *in the flock of Laban*, is that he did so with all of Laban's flocks but not that they belonged to Laban since the ringstraked among the lambs were Jacob's.

Now do not ask why Scripture at first says "lambs" and then says "the faces of the flocks" rather than "the faces of the lambs", for it is normal for Scripture to express itself this way. In this section there is a similar case in connection with the mountain of Gilead.[169] And the reason Jacob did this with the lambs more than with the goats is that there were no brownish ones among the sticks he put up. It is possible that he knew that because of their heaviness, it is natural for lambs to require many signs to arouse them – more than the light-weight he-goats require.

41. THE FLOCKS 'HAMEKUSHAROTH.' The correct interpretation of this expression appears to me to be that they are the flocks in which the males follow the females at all times, never leaving them due to their abundant desire, as in the expression, *Seeing that his soul is 'keshurah' (bound up) with the lad's soul.*[170] This is also found in the language of our Sages: "a swine *karuch* (clinging) to a ewe;"[171] "clinging to her."[172] And the offspring born at that time are called *hakeshurim* after the name of their father.

But many authorities say[173] that *keshurim* are "the strong ones" whose limbs are firmly attached to each other with a strong tie, as this is the basis of health, while *atuphim*[165] are "the weak ones" whose *soul 'tithataph' (fainted) in them,*[174] and who have no desire, as in the expression, *'ha'atuphim' (that faint) for hunger.*[175] Onkelos translated *hamekusharoth* as the early-bearing sheep, and *atuphim* as the late-bearing ones, for such is the fact: [the early-bearing sheep are the stronger ones, and the late-bearing ones are weaker].

31 6. THAT WITH ALL MY POWER I HAVE SERVED YOUR FATHER. That is, "from the outset, and he has been blessed since my coming." It is possible that Laban's flocks had been many, but that even the feebler ones were blessed since Jacob came, for

(169) Further, 31:25. *Now Jacob had pitched his tent in the mountain, and Laban with his brethren pitched in the mountain of Gilead.* "The mountain" mentioned at the beginning of the verse is the "mountain of Gilead" mentioned at the end. (170) Further, 44:30. (171) Bechoroth 24 a. (172) Kiddushin 79 b. (173) P'sikta Zutrata on this verse. (174) Psalms 107:5. (175) Lamentations 2:19.

Laban's sons complained only out of jealousy of Jacob that *he had gotten all this wealth.*[176]

7. AND YOUR FATHER HATH MOCKED ME, AND CHANGED MY WAGES TEN TIMES. This was true, even though Scripture did not previously relate it. And so too did Jacob tell Laban: *And thou hast changed my wages ten times.*[177] There are many similar places in the Torah. For example, in this earlier section, Scripture did not relate that Leah gave the mandrakes to Rachel [although the event is referred to later in Verse 16: *for I have hired thee with my son's mandrakes*].

8. IF HE SAID THUS: THE SPECKLED SHALL BE THY WAGES. The meaning thereof is that at first Laban agreed to give Jacob the two appearances the speckled and the spotted – also the brownish lambs. Then he retracted and agreed to give him another color, and thus he changed it every year. The flocks, however, gave birth accordingly. This was not due to the power of the sticks, for he was telling them of the deed of the Great G-d who treated him wondrously each and every year, just as he said, *But G-d suffered him not to do me evil.*[178]

It is also possible that Laban changed his wages after the flocks became pregnant and gave birth in accordance with Jacob's will, it pleasing the Creator to do so. [In this case, it clearly was not due to the power of the sticks.] And so we find in Bereshith Rabbah:[179] "The Holy One, blessed be He, foresaw what Laban was destined to do to our father Jacob, and He created the form of the sheep to conform to the colors Laban was to stipulate. Thus, it is not written here, 'If he said (*amar*) thus,' but it is written, 'If he will say (*yomar*) thus,'" [indicating that G-d foresaw what Laban was destined to stipulate to Jacob].

10. AND IT CAME TO PASS AT THE TIME THAT THE FLOCK CONCEIVED. This was after Laban changed his wages, and therefore the angel said to Jacob, *For I have seen all that Laban does unto thee.*[180]

(176) Verse 1 here. (177) Further, Verse 41. (178) Above, Verse 7. (179) 74:2. (180) Verse 12 here.

AND, BEHOLD THE HE-GOATS WHICH WENT UP ON THE FLOCKS [WERE RINGSTRAKED, SPECKLED, AND GRIZZLED]. The meaning thereof is that it was shown to Jacob in a dream that the he-goats which mounted the flocks were all ringstraked, and afterwards they were all speckled, and still later they were all grizzled. And the angel told him that in view of the injustice which Laban does him by changing his wages, the future offspring will have the appearance which Jacob will need, and that henceforth Jacob should not make the sticks, for *Whoso putteth his trust in the Eternal shall be set up on high.*[181]

AND, BEHOLD, 'HA'ATUDIM' WHICH WENT UP ON THE FLOCKS. He-goats and rams are called *atudim* for all the adults in the flocks are so called. This applies also to the mighty ones among men, as in: *'atudei' (the chief ones) of the earth.*[182]

And Rashi comments: "Although Laban had separated all these so that the sheep should not give birth to young marked similarly to them, angels brought them from the flock which had been placed in charge of Laban's sons to the flock in Jacob's charge."

In line with the simple meaning of Scripture this was a vision assuring Jacob that the flocks would give birth to young similar to the marked rams and he-goats, and the proof of it is the word *vehinei* (and behold), for this expression is used with respect to all dreams, indicating that it is as if the action is in the presence of the dreamer. In Bereshith Rabbah,[183] the Sages did not mention the angels [bringing the marked ones from the flocks of Laban], but it may be inferred by exegesis. Thus they said: "It is not written here *olim* (went up) but *ha'olim* (those that mounted)," [meaning those which actually mounted. Thus the dream only indicated the action of the *atudim* which came from Laban's flocks and that they were ringstraked, speckled, etc. However, the fact that they came was not part of the dream. This really occurred since the angels brought them]. But the plain sense of the verse is as we have said.

(181) Proverbs 29:25. (182) Isaiah 14:9. (183) 73:7.

13. I AM THE G-D OF BETH-EL. Jacob related to his wives all that G-d's angel had told him in the dream, all this serving to persuade them to go with him. However, what he told did not consist of one dream. The statement, *Lift up now thine eyes, and see, all the he-goats*[180] was made to him when he served Laban for his flock, *at the time the flock conceived*[184] in one of the first years.[185] The statement, *I am the G-d of Beth-el* was made to him after that, at the time of the journey, for after He said to him, *Now arise, get thee out from this land,*[186] he no longer remained in Haran to further tend Laban's flocks so that the he-goats would mount the flocks and the flocks would give birth to speckled and spotted. But on the morrow of the dream, he sent for Rachel and Leah and told them his dream, and they left Haran.

I am 'ha'e-il' (the G-d) of Beth-el. The meaning thereof is, as Rashi explained it, that the letter *hei* in *ha'e-il* is redundant and is the same as if it were written: "I am *e-il* Beth-el (the G-d of Beth-el)." Similarly, *To 'ha'aretz' (the land) of Canaan;*[187] [the *hei* is redundant and is the same as if it were written: "to *eretz* Canaan (the land of Canaan)."] Grammarians[188] adjusted it by saying that it is as if it were written, "I am the G-d, who is the G-d of Beth-el." Similarly, *And the tree of the knowledge of good and evil,*[189] [which is as if it said: "and the tree of the knowledge, namely the knowledge of good and evil"]; *the cords of gold,*[190] [which is as if it said, "the cords, which are cords of gold]. And the angel here speaks in the name of He Who sent him, [therefore, he speaks in the first person and says, "I am, etc."] ....

WHERE THOU DIDST ANOINT A PILLAR, WHERE THOU DIDST VOW A VOW UNTO ME. The meaning thereof is that "you have vowed to worship the Proper Name of the Eternal in the Chosen Land, and that this stone should be to you a house of G-d in which to set aside your tithes,[191] and if you further delay the fulfillment of your vows, G-d might yet be angry at your voice."[192]

(184) Verse 10 here. (185) One of the first of the six years he served for the sheep. See further, 31:41. (186) In Verse 13 here. (187) Numbers 34:2. (188) Ibn Ezra and R'dak. (189) Above, 2:9. (190) Numbers 39:17. (191) Above, 28:22. (192) See Ecclesiastes 5:5.

19. AND RACHEL STOLE THE TERAPHIM. Her intention was to wean her father from idol-worship. This is the language of Rashi.

Now it is possible that Laban used the teraphim for idol worship, as he himself said, *Why hast thou stolen my gods?*[193] But not all teraphim were for the purpose of worship, for how could one find idolatry in the house of our lord David.[194] That which the commentators[195] say seems reasonable, namely, that these are vessels to receive[196] a knowledge of the hours, and they divine with them in order to gain knowledge of future events. The word *teraphim* is derived from the expressions: *'rephai' (weak) handed;*[197] *'nirpim' (idle) ye are, idle.*[198] They are called "teraphim" in order to hint by their name that their words are like a weak prophecy, usually occurring as a prophecy *for many days hence*[199] and turning out to be false, just as the prophets have said, *For the teraphim have spoken vanity.*[200] People of little faith set them up for themselves as gods. They do not seek to know by the glorious name of the Eternal, nor do they offer their prayers to Him. Rather, their deeds are guided by divination revealed to them by the teraphim. Thus it is written, *And the man Micah had a house of G-d, and he made an ephod, and teraphim,*[201] and it is further written there, *Ask counsel, we pray thee, of G-d that we may know whether our way which we are going shall be prosperous,*[202] for they used to ask of the teraphim. Such also was the case in Israel with the ephod, for, having been accustomed to the sacred ephod[203] they made something similar in form, and they would seek guidance of it, believe in its words, and blunder after it. Even in sickness they sought not G-d but only them.[204] This is the meaning of the verse, *And Gideon made an ephod thereof, and put it in his city, even in Ophrah; and all Israel went astray after it there; and it became a snare unto Gideon, and to his*

(193) Further, Verse 30. (194) See I Samuel 19:13, where it states that there were teraphim in David's house. (195) R'dak, in his Commentary on the verse here. (196) "Receive." According to the Tur, "determine." (197) II Samuel 17:2. (198) Exodus 5:17. (199) Ezekiel 12:27. (200) Zechariah 10:2. (201) Judges 17:5. (202) *Ibid.*, 18:5. (203) See Exodus 25:6-12. (204) See II Chronicles 16:12.

house,[205] for they turned aside from following the Eternal. Now Laban was a diviner and an enchanter, just as he said, *I have divined.*[206] His country, too, was ever a land of diviners, as it is written, *For they are replenished from the east, and with soothsayers like the Philistines,*[207] and Balaam the son of Beor the diviner was from his city.[208] And this is the meaning of, *Why hast thou stolen my gods?*[193]

22. ON THE THIRD DAY. For there was a journey of three days between them. *Seven days' journey—*[209] throughout these three days during which the messenger had travelled to tell Laban that Jacob had proceeded on his journey, Jacob was consequently a six days' journey distance from Laban. On the seventh day, [that is, on the day during which Jacob covered the stretch of ground which made him seven days' journey distance from Laban's starting point, Laban] overtook him. We may thus infer that the entire distance which Jacob covered in six[210] days, Laban covered in one day. These are the words of Rashi quoting Bereshith Rabbah.[211] It is correct that Laban should proceed *as a strong man to run his course,*[212] for such is the way of pursuers. However, Laban *had set a three days' journey*[213] between his flock and the flock which was in Jacob's care, not between the city and his flock. Thus if Laban tended his flocks to the east of the city, Jacob did so to the west, and between them there was *a three days' journey.*[213] Now Jacob began his journey from the city, in which were his wives, sons and daughters, and all his belongings with the exception of the flocks. The fact of his flight was told to Laban on the third day since they were not aware of it on the first day, and then Laban returned to his nearby city and took his brethren[209] from there, and starting from his city he pursued him for seven days. [Hence, it should have been said that what Jacob covered in ten days Laban covered in seven days!] We must say then, according

(205) Judges 8:27. (206) Above, 30:27. (207) Isaiah 2:6. Laban's city Haran was in the land of the children of the east (above, 29:1). (208) See Numbers 23:7. (209) Verse 23 here. (210) "Six." In our Rashi we have "seven," which seems to fit the calculation better. (211) 74:4. (212) Psalms 19:6. (213) Above, 30:36.

to the opinion of Bereshith Rabbah, that it was from the field where the flocks were that Jacob left for the journey, and that Laban took his brethren with him from the shearers of his flocks. [Since there was a three days' journey between them at the outset and Jacob had already travelled for three days, they were thus six travel days apart. On that day Laban was informed, and the following day he pursued him and overtook him. Jacob meanwhile had covered an additional day's distance, with the result that the distance Jacob travelled in seven days, Laban covered in one day].

In Pirkei d'Rabbi Eliezer[214] it appears that Laban returned to his city, and from there he took all mighty men and all valiant ones, and he pursued Jacob from there.

23. AND HE OVERTOOK HIM IN THE MOUNTAIN OF GILEAD. For on the eve of the seventh day Laban reached the base of the mountain, and he saw Jacob encamped at a distance. That night he slept below Jacob's camp and the dream came to him.

24. LABAN THE ARAMEAN. The intent of this is to relate that even though he was an Aramean, and the people of his place used teraphim *and were soothsayers like the Philistines,*[215] yet the prophetic dream came to him in honor of the righteous one [Jacob]. Similarly, *And Jacob outwitted Laban the Aramean:*[216] [the epithet "Aramean" is mentioned in order to indicate that] even though Laban was the Aramean, the diviner and owner of teraphim, [he was still outwitted by Jacob].

EITHER GOOD OR BAD. [Why should he not speak good?] Because all the good that the wicked do is looked upon by the righteous as bad. This is Rashi's language. But the plain meaning thereof is as follow: "Take heed that you speak not to Jacob and promise to treat him well if he will return with you from his journey, or lest you threaten to do him evil if he will not come with you, for it is I Who commanded him to return to his land."

(214) Chapter 36. (215) Isaiah 2:6. (216) Verse 20 here.

33. IN THE TENT OF JACOB AND IN THE TENT OF LEAH. Rashi comments: "*In the tent of Jacob* – this was Rachel's tent, for he was constantly with her. And so also Scripture says, *The sons of Rachel Jacob's wife,*[217] while in the case of the other wives it does not say 'Jacob's wife.' *And he entered into Rachel's tent.* When Laban left Leah's tent he returned again to Rachel's tent before he searched the tent of the two maid-servants. And why did he feel compelled to do all this? Because he knew her to be inclined to touch everything." But in line with the plain meaning of Scripture, it is not correct for the same tent to be called by two names, [i.e., "the tent of Jacob" and "the tent of Rachel"] in one verse.

And Rabbi Abraham ibn Ezra said that Laban entered into the tent of Jacob, the tent of Leah, and the tent of the two maid-servants [the singular form "tent" being used] since one tent served both. Afterwards he came back a second time to Leah's tent, and after that he entered into Rachel's tent. But this too is incorrect.

Rabbi Abraham ibn Ezra further wrote: "The feasible interpretation appears to me to be that Scripture followed here a way of brevity and delayed mentioning the tent of Rachel in order to state concerning all of the others, *but he found them not,* as they were not there. Scripture then returns and explains that when he went out of Leah's tent he came into Rachel's tent where the teraphim were." That is the correct interpretation.

It is true that there were separate tents for all of the wives for this was due to the righteous man's regard for modesty. Thus each one of the wives[218] had a separate tent so that one should not know when he came to the other. It is also a matter forbidden by Torah law, as the Sages have mentioned in Tractate Niddah.[219] And Jacob had a special tent, in which he would eat at his table with his children and people of the household. And the reason why Scripture mentions *Jacob's wife*[217] in connection with Rachel

(217) Further, 46:19. (218) The above mentioned opinion that one tent served the two maid-servants was that of Ibn Ezra; Ramban however differs. (219) 17 a.

in my opinion, according to its simple sense, is that she is mentioned in that chapter among the concubines. For this reason Scripture does not say so in the *Seder Vayishlach Yaakov,*[220] for there it mentions Leah and Rachel and then the maid-servants.

35. LET NOT MY LORD BE ANGRY THAT I CANNOT RISE UP BEFORE THEE. I do not understand what kind of an apology this is. Do women in that condition not rise or stand? Perhaps she said that her head and limbs feel heavy, and she was sick on account of the menstruation, for such is the customary way among them, and all the more among those such as Rachel, whose birth-giving powers are diminished since they have little blood,[221] and menstruation presses very heavily upon them.

The correct interpretation appears to me to be that in ancient days menstruants kept very isolated for they were ever referred to as *niddoth* on account of their isolation since they did not approach people and did not speak with them. For the ancients in their wisdom knew that their breath is harmful, their gaze is detrimental and makes a bad impression, as the philosophers have explained. I will yet mention[222] their experiences in this matter. And the menstruants dwelled isolated in tents where no one entered, just as our Rabbis have mentioned in the *Beraitha*[223] of Tractate Niddah:[224] "A learned man[225] is forbidden to greet a menstruant. Rabbi Nechemyah says, 'Even the utterance of her mouth is unclean.' Said Rabbi Yochanan: 'One is forbidden to walk after a menstruant and tread upon her footsteps, which are as unclean as a corpse; so is the dust upon which the menstruant stepped unclean, and it is forbidden to derive any benefit from her

(220) Further, 35:23-26. (221) See Kethuboth 10 b. (222) See Ramban Leviticus 18:19. (223) "Exterior," a teaching of the *Tannaim* that for some reason had not been included in the Mishnah by Rabbi Yehudah Hanasi. The collection of *Beraithoth* was compiled by Rabbi Chiyah and Rabbi Oshayah. They are generally found in the *Tosephta*. which follows the order of the Mishnah. (224) There are differences of opinion among scholars concerning this *Beraitha.* See my Hebrew commentary, p. 177, and commencing with the second edition also on p. 548, column 2, top of page. (225) The meaning of the word *talmid* or *talmud* here is not clear.

work.' " Therefore Rachel said, "It would be proper for me to rise before my lord to kiss his hands, but *the way of women is upon me,* and I cannot come near you nor walk at all in the tent so that you should not tread upon the dust of my feet." And Laban kept silent and did not answer her, as it was customary not to converse with them at all because the speech of a menstruant was unclean.

36. AND JACOB WAS WROTH, AND QUARRELLED WITH LABAN. Jacob had originally given him permission to search the tents, for he said, *With whomsoever thou findest thy gods,*[226] and he further said, *before our brethren recognize what is thine with me,*[226] and how could Laban find it if not by searching and handling? At first, however, Jacob feared lest one of the wives or servants had stolen Laban's gods, and now that he saw that they were not with them his anger was aroused, for he said, "He did not lose his gods, only *he is seeking a quarrel with me.*"[227] So he said, "*Why have you hotly pursued after me* as one pursues a thief? You have not found in my possession anything *of all thy household stuff*[228] though I was entitled to take from you all I could for you have *changed my hire ten times,*[229] and you demanded of me recompense for the animals that were torn by beasts,[230] and I paid you, though not legally by law required to do so."

42. AND THE FEAR OF ISAAC HAD BEEN ON MY SIDE. "He did not want to say "G-d of Isaac" because G-d does not associate His name with the righteous during their lifetime. Although G-d said to Jacob when he was departing from the Land of Israel, *I am the Eternal, the G-d of Abraham thy father and the G-d of Isaac,*[231] this was because Isaac's eyes were dim, and he might therefore be regarded as dead. Jacob, however, feared to say so, [and instead said, 'the Fear of Isaac']." Thus the words of Rashi. It is also the opinion of Onkelos that *pachad Yitzchak* means "his G-d," for he translated it as: "He Whom Isaac fears."

(226) Verse 26 here. (227) Judges 14:4. (228) Verse 37 here. (229) Verse 41 here. (230) Verse 39 here. (231) Above, 28:13.

And Rabbi Abraham ibn Ezra said: "Isaac's fear of G-d helped me, for the merit of the father helps the son. *And Jacob swore 'bepachad' of his father Isaac,*[232] – by Him Whom Isaac fears." Ibn Ezra's explanations of the same expression are thus not alike. Ibn Ezra further wrote,[232] "And there are some who say[233] that this 'fear' is an allusion to the day of Isaac's Binding." This is not far fetched.

By way of the Truth [namely, the mystic lore of the Cabala] the language fits its plain meaning and intent, that is, it refers to the attribute of Justice on high.[234] Based on this, Scripture says: *Afterward shall the children of Israel return, and seek the Eternal their G-d, and David their king; and shall come trembling unto the Eternal and to His goodness in the end of days.*[235] The verse is stating that they will seek the Merciful One and the attribute of Justice on earth, and bring the Fear of Isaac to G-d and His goodness mentioned.

'VAYOCHACH' YESTERNIGHT. "The word here has the meaning of 'reproof' [*and he reproved*] and not of 'clarification.' " These are the words of Rashi. But is is more correct to say that it is an expression meaning "clarification." Since Jacob said above, *'veyochichu' (that they may judge) between us both,*[228] he now said that it is G-d, Who knows the hidden secrets, Who should clarify the dispute between the two of them. This is why Jacob did not say, *vayochach othcha emesh,* [which would mean, "and He reproved 'thee' yesternight," for the meaning of the word is not "rebuke" but "clarify"].

43. AND TO MY DAUGHTERS, WHAT CAN I DO TO THESE TODAY? Commentators have said[236] that it is as if it were written, "And to my daughters, what could I do to *them* today?" and the word "them" constitutes additional clarification. Likewise, *As we both of us have sworn,*[237] [the word "we" serving as

(232) Further, Verse 53. (233) Found in R'dak. (234) See Ramban above, 9:12. (235) Hosea 3:5. (236) Ibn Ezra and R'dak. (237) I Samuel 20:42.

additional clarification]; *We, our sons and our daughters,*[238] [the word "we" is here too mentioned for the greater clarity].

But it appears to be more correct that this is said in a compassionate way: "*And to my daughters, what can I do to these* who are before me, for I am deeply stirred for them, *or unto their children,* who have been born in my house, and they are to me as my children?" This is also the meaning of *whom they have borne.* Laban thus said this as if defending himself against Jacob's words by claiming: "I have come after you to see my daughters, and to determine what favor I can do for them or their children. Now I can do them this good by seeing that you make me a covenant that you will not afflict them and will take no other wives in addition to them."[239]

44. 'VEHAYAH' FOR A WITNESS. This means, "And let the Holy One, blessed be He, serve as a witness." These are the words of Rashi. But this is not the usual sense of the expression. Rather, Laban is saying, "And let the covenant be for a witness between us, for he who violates it should be cursed with all *the curses of the covenant,*"[240] similar in meaning to the verse, *And they shall be upon thee for a sign and for a wonder.*[241] The meaning of the verse here may be: "Let us establish a covenant by a permanent thing which will serve as a witness between us." For this reason, Jacob set up a stone as a pillar, and this is the meaning of that which he said, *This stone-heap be witness, and this pillar be witness.*[242] A similar meaning is found in the verse, *And Joshua said unto all the people: Behold, this stone shall be a witness against us.*[243]

46. AND JACOB SAID UNTO HIS BRETHREN. I.e., to Laban's brothers mentioned above,[244] who had accompanied him, as Jacob did not want to say it to his father-in-law whom he treated with respect. Likewise, the verse, *And he* [Jacob] *called his brethren to*

(238) Nehemiah 5:2. (239) Verse 50 here. (240) Deuteronomy 29:20. (241) *Ibid.*, 28:46. (242) Verse 52 here. (243) Joshua 24:27. (244) Verse 23 here.

eat bread,[245] also refers to Laban's brothers, and he did not invite Laban to eat bread as an act of respect, as if everything is under his authority and is all his. A similar case is the verse, *And Pharaoh said unto his brethren: What is your occupation?*[246] [which means he said it to Joseph's brethren]. But Rashi explained: "*And Jacob said unto his brethren* – to Jacob's brothers, [meaning, his sons, who were like brothers to him since they stood by him in trouble and in battle]." However, those that came with Laban, whom Scripture calls "his brethren", were really his friends and companions.

It is possible that that which is said concerning Laban, *And he took his brethren with him,*[244] refers to his kinsmen, members of his family from the seed of Nahor the brother of Abraham. He did this because he did not want to bring against Jacob strangers lest they fight with him intensely, or covet, rob and steal his belongings. Thus these men were kinsmen to Jacob just as to Laban, and therefore they are called "brethren" of both.

And some say[247] that Jacob ethically referred to them as "my brothers," just as he said to the shepherds, *My brethren, whence are ye?*[248] And in Bereshith Rabbah, the Sages have said:[249] "*And Jacob said unto his brethren* – these are his sons, whom, in a respectful manner, he called his brothers." However, with respect to the verse, *And he called his brethren to eat bread,*[245] the Midrash did not explain [that "his brethren" refers to his sons]! The correct interpretation is the one I wrote at the outset.

AND THEY DID EAT THERE UPON THE STONE-HEAP. They ate a little there as a remembrance. Perhaps it was customary for both of those who made a covenant to eat from one bread as a sign of love and companionship. After having entered into an oath and a covenant, they offered sacrifices and made a great feast. It is possible that the verse stating, *and they did eat there upon the stone-heap*, refers to the offerings mentioned below,[250] for he said

(245) Verse 54 here. (246) Further, 47:3. (247) P'sikta Zutrata above on Chapter 29, Verse 4. (248) Above, 29:4. (249) 74:11. (250) Verse 54 here.

to them, "*Gather stones*[251] and we will make a heap to eat thereon, and it will also serve as a witness when we make the covenant," and afterwards they ate the offerings upon it. And the meaning of the verse, *And they did eat bread,*[250] is that Jacob made them a great feast, and not just a party, in order that they should tarry with him all night.

48. AND LABAN SAID, THIS STONE-HEAP IS A WITNESS. After Jacob had called it Galed,[252] Laban spoke in Jacob's language, *This stone-heap is a witness*, and therefore its name was called Galed, for they mutually agreed upon this name. It may be that Laban's words are translated into the Sacred Language, [but he himself did not use the term Galed].

49. AND MITZPAH. Rashi comments that the meaning of the verse is: "And the Mitzpah which is on Mount Gilead, as it is written, *And he passed over Mitzpah of Gilead.*[253] Why was it called Mitzpah? Because each of them said to the other, *The Eternal 'yitzeph' (watch).*" And if so, Mitzpah is the name of a high place on top of the mountain. In my opinion, however, Mitzpah is the stone which Jacob set up for a pillar[254] and is connected with the above verse: *Therefore was the name of it called Galed,*[255] *and he* also *called it the Mitzpah because he said, The Eternal watch between me and thee.* It is possible that this stone is Mitzpah of Gilead,[253] for the place was always called by the name of this stone.

32 2. AND THE ANGELS OF G-D MET HIM. Rashi comments: "The angels who minister in the Land of Israel came to meet him. *And he called the name of that place Mahanaim*: the plural form implies two camps, one consisting of the angels ministering outside of the Land of Israel who had accompanied him thus far, the other consisting of those ministering in the Land of Israel who had come forth to meet him."

(251) Verse 46 here. (252) Verse 47 here. (253) Judges 11:29. (254) Verse 45 here. (255) Verse 48 here.

But I wonder at this, for Jacob had not yet reached the Land of Israel and was still distant from there for he sent messengers to Esau from afar. And then it says there, *And he passed over the ford of the Jabbok,*[256] which is *the river Jabbok which is the border of the children of Ammon.*[257] This is to the southeast of the Land of Israel, and he still had to pass the boundary of the children of Ammon and Moab, and then the land of Edom, and his first entry into the Land was at Shechem, as it is said, *And Jacob came in peace to the city of Shechem, which is in the land of Canaan.*[258] Instead, we must say this vision came to Jacob as he arrived in enemy territory in order to inform him that "they that are with him are more than they that are with them."[259] And the name of the place was called "Mahanaim" in the plural, for such is the way of Scripture with names.[260] It may be that "Mahanaim" refers to His camp and the camp of the higher beings,[261] that is to say that His camp on earth is as the camp of the angels, all of them being camps of G-d, blessing Him and confessing His Unity, may His name be blessed forever.

(256) Further, 32:23. (257) Deuteronomy 3:16. (258) Further 33:18. This poses a difficulty to Rashi's interpretation of "Mahanaim." (259) See II Kings 6:16. (260) For a single event or person, a plural name is given, as for example, "Mitzraim". (261) In that case the plural in the word Mahanaim is naturally justified.

Vayishlach

This section was written in order to inform us that the Holy One, blessed be He, delivered His servant, *and He redeemed him from the hand of him that is stronger than he,*[1] *and he sent an angel*[2] and saved him, and in order to further teach us that Jacob did not place his trust in his righteousness and that he strove for delivery with all his might. There is yet in this section a hint for future generations, for everything that happened to our father with his brother Esau will constantly occur to us with Esau's children, and it is proper for us to adhere to the way of the righteous[3] by preparing ourselves in the three things for which he prepared himself: for prayer, for giving him a present, and for rescue by methods of warfare, to flee and to be saved. Our Rabbis have already derived this hint from this section, as I shall mention.

4. TO ESAU HIS BROTHER UNTO THE LAND SE'IR. Since the southern part of the Land of Israel adjoins Edom, and Jacob's father *dwelt in the land of the South,*[4] he had to pass through Edom or near there. Therefore, he feared lest Esau hear of it, and he took the initiative by sending messengers to him in his country. But the Sages have already taken him to task for this, saying in Bereshith Rabbah:[5] "*Like one that taketh a dog by the ears is he that passeth by, and meddleth with a strife not his own.*[6] The Holy One, blessed be He, said to Jacob, 'Esau was going his way, and you send him messengers, and say to him, *Thus saith thy servant Jacob!*'"[7]

(1) Jeremiah 31:11. (2) Numbers 20:16. (3) See Job 17:9. (4) Above, 24:62. (5) 75:2. (6) Proverbs 26:17. (7) Verse 5 here.

In my opinion this too hints at the fact that we instigated our falling into the hand of Edom [Rome] for the Hasmonean kings during the period of the Second Temple entered into a covenant with the Romans,[8] and some of them even went to Rome to seek an alliance. This was the cause of their falling into the hands of the Romans. This is mentioned in the words of our Rabbis,[9] and is well publicized in books.[10]

5. THUS SHALL YE SAY UNTO MY LORD ESAU: THUS SAITH THY SERVANT JACOB. He commanded them that they should say "to my lord Esau we belong," or "we were sent to him,"[11] and to say to him, *Thus saith thy servant Jacob: I have sojourned with Laban.* A similar example in this section is the verse: *When Esau my brother meeteth thee, and asketh thee, saying, Whose art thou?*[12] It may be that in their presence Jacob called Esau "my lord Esau" in order to caution them not to mention Esau in any other but a respectful way even when not in his presence, inasmuch as their lord calls him "my lord."

Know that this respect which Jacob showed for his brother by fearfully saying "my lord" and "thy servant" was due to it being the custom of the younger brother to give recognition and respect to the firstborn as if he were his father, just as the Torah also hints to us on this matter:[13] "This includes your oldest brother." Now Jacob had taken his birthright and his blessing, for which Esau hated him, and now he is acting towards Esau as if the effect

(8) In Maccabees, I, 8, it is related how Judah Maccabee sent a delegation to Rome to establish a political alliance with the Romans. (9) Abodah Zarah 8 b. (10) Ramban is undoubtedly referring to the history book of Josippon, or Joseph ben Gorion, a medieval work regarded as the Hebrew version of Josephus Flavius. It was a popular work with the people of the Middle Ages. See also Ramban on Leviticus 26:16. (11) The intent of Ramban is to state that Jacob, speaking to his servants, did not refer to Esau as "my lord Esau," but rather he commanded them to use the expression in Esau's presence. (12) Further, Verse 18. The verse concludes that they are to tell him that it is a gift "to my lord Esau." Again Jacob is telling them what to say. (13) Kethuboth 103 a. Commenting on the letter *vav* in the expression, *ve'eth imecha* ("honor thy father *'and' thy mother*"), our Rabbis said: "This includes your oldest brother!"

of that sale was nil as far as he was concerned, and he is conducting himself towards him as to a firstborn and father in order to remove the hatred from his heart.

6. AND I HAVE SENT TO TELL MY LORD. I.e., "to announce that I am coming to you. *That I may find favour in thy sight* for I am at peace with you and seek your friendship." These are Rashi's words. Rashi's intent is that the verse; *I have sent to tell my lord,* does not refer to the previous verse, *I have sojourned with Laban,* etc. but, instead, it says, "*And I have sent to tell my lord* that I have come *to find favour in thy sight* and to do whatever my lord will command."

But it is more correct to say that it refers to the verse above: "*And I have sent to tell my lord* that I have wealth, belongings, and precious things, to do with them according to your desire and will." He thus hinted to him that he would send him a present from them, or that Esau may take from him whatever he desires. And so, when Esau asked Jacob, *What meanest thou by all this camp which I met? he* [Jacob] *said: To find favour in the sight of my lord.*[14]

7. AND THE MESSENGERS RETURNED TO JACOB, SAYING. These messengers had fulfilled their mission, but Scripture did not relate this for it would serve no purpose. The meaning of the expression, *And moreover he cometh to meet thee,* is that "even as you go to meet him, so he goes to meet you, and you will quickly encounter one another."

8. THEN JACOB WAS GREATLY AFRAID. This was because they told him that Esau had gone forth from his city and was coming to meet Jacob, and moreover, that he took along many men — four hundred. He thus greatly feared for his life, for he said, "He has not taken all these men except for the purpose of waging war against me."

(14) Genesis 33:8.

It appears to me in this matter that Esau did not receive the messengers properly and paid them no heed. Perhaps they did not even come before him for he did not at all give permission for them to come before him and speak to him for otherwise, Scripture would have related that Esau questioned them concerning his brother's welfare and about his circumstances and those of his household and children. [Scripture further would have told how Esau requested] that they convey greetings to Jacob and tell him that he is proceeding towards him to see him, and they would have told it thus to Jacob. Scripture, however, does not narrate that the messengers transmitted a word in Esau's name. Instead, he [Esau] kept his wrath in his heart,[15] and he came with his army for the purpose of doing Jacob evil. Now the messengers had investigated the matter in the camp, and they knew that he was going to meet Jacob. This is the meaning of the word *vegam* (and moreover) [in the verse, *and moreover he goeth to meet thee*], for they said, "*We came to thy brother Esau,*[16] but he did not answer us a word, and he sent you no greeting, *and moreover, he goeth to meet thee* with might and an army." This was why he added fear to his fear, as Scripture says, *And Jacob was greatly afraid, and was distressed.* And so our Rabbis said that the messengers recognized hatred in him[Esau]. Thus they said:[17] "*We came to thy brother Esau.* You behave towards him like a brother, but he behaves towards you like Esau the villain." However, in the end, when Esau saw the great honor that Jacob bestowed upon him and how he prostrated himself before him, bowing to the ground seven times[18] from the distance until he approached him, his mercy was aroused, and he thought that Jacob is recognizing his birthright and his pre-eminence, as I have explained.[19] And with this he was comforted, for the hearts belong to G-d, Who turns them whither He will.[20]

9. THEN THE CAMP WHICH IS LEFT SHALL ESCAPE. In line with the simple meaning of Scripture, Jacob stated this as a possibility. He said that perhaps one camp shall escape, for during

(15) See Amos 1:11. (16) Verse 7 here. (17) Bereshith Rabbah 75:7. (18) Genesis 33:3. (19) Above, Verse 5. (20) See Proverbs 21:1.

the time he [Esau] smites one, the other will flee, or perhaps his anger will subside or deliverance will come to them from G-d. And so the Rabbis said in Bereshith Rabbah,[21] "The Torah teaches you proper conduct: a man should not leave all his money in one corner." And Rashi wrote: " '*Then the camp which is left shall escape* in spite of him for I will fight against him.' He prepared himself for three things: for prayer, for giving Esau a gift, and for war." And I have seen in the Midrash:[22] "What did Jacob do? He armed his people underneath, and clothed them in white from outside, and he prepared himself for three things." And this is the most correct [interpretation, in line with Rashi and the Midrash, who say that he prepared himself also for war, as opposed to the simple meaning first mentioned].

The intent of this is that Jacob knew that all his seed would not fall into Esau's hands. Therefore, in any case, one camp would be saved. This also implies that the children of Esau will not formulate a decree against us designed to obliterate our name entirely, but they will do evil to some of us in some of their countries. One of their kings will formulate a decree in his country against our wealth or our persons while simultaneously another king will show compassion in his place and save the refugees.[23] And so the Rabbis said in Bereshith Rabbah,[24] "*If Esau come to the one camp, and smite it* — these are our brethren in the south. *Then the camp which is left shall escape* — these are our brethren in the Diaspora." Our Rabbis thus saw that this chapter alludes also to the future generations.

11. 'KATONTI' OF ALL THE MERCIES, AND OF ALL THE TRUTH. "My merits have diminished as a consequence of all the kindness and truth which You have already shown me. For this reason I am afraid lest I have become depraved by sin since the time You made these promises to me, and this may cause me to be

(21) 76:2. (22) Tanchuma, Buber, Vayishlach 6. (23) A clear echo of Ramban's times is hereby heard. While waves of persecution, expulsions and massacres were a steady feature of Jewish life in most European countries, refuge was always found in some country. At the time of Ramban, Spain was a place of relative relief for Jews from France and Germany. (24) 76:3.

delivered into the hand of Esau." This is Rashi's language. But it is not a correct interpretation because it does not fit into the language of the verse, [for *katan* refers to size, not quantity]. Furthermore, Jacob said afterwards, *And Thou saidst: I will surely do thee good and make thy seed as the sand of the sea,*[25] but of what efficacy would this promise be if subsequent sin caused him to be deprived of it? Moreover, Jacob mentioned two promises which the Holy One, blessed be He, had made him – one in Beth-el,[26] and one in Haran[27] – and he first stated the promise given to him in Haran, *O Eternal, who saidst unto me: Return unto thy country, and to thy kindred, and I will do to thee good,*[28] this being what was said to him when he was about to leave the house of Laban: *Return unto the land of thy fathers, and to thy kindred, and I will be with thee.*[27] Now following this promise, G-d did not bestow good upon Jacob to account for all these mercies and truths of which Jacob mentioned that his merits should be diminished on account of them.

The word *katonti* rather means that he is too small to have been worthy of all the mercies which He had done for him. Likewise, *How shall Jacob stand? for he is small,*[29] that is, too small to be able to bear all that was decreed against him. And so the Rabbis said in Bereshith Rabbah,[30] "*Katonti.* Rabbi Abba said that it means 'I am not worthy.'" Now *hachasadim* (the mercies) are the kindnesses which G-d did for him without having vowed to do them, and *ha'emeth* (the truth) is the kindness which He promised him and fulfilled. Jacob thus said that he was unworthy of G-d's promising him and performing those kindnesses which He promised him, nor was he worthy of those other many kindnesses which He did for him without having promised to do them.

But I have not understood the opinion of Onkelos who translated, "from all the mercies and all the good," when he is accustomed to translate *chesed ve'emeth* as "mercy and truth." Perhaps Onkelos is rendering *chasadim* here as referring to Jacob's rescue, that is, the many times He had saved him from his

(25) Verse 13 here. (26) Above, 28:15. (27) *Ibid.*, 31:3. (28) Verse 10 here. (29) Amos 7:2. (30) 76:4.

troubles. Onkelos rendered *emeth* as referring to all this good which Jacob possessed, for G-d had given him sons and daughters, wealth and belongings, and honor.

The correct interpretation appears to me to be that long-lasting kindnesses such as children and wealth are called *emeth*, which is from the root of *emunah* (faith), just as: *'Vene'eman' (and confirmed shall be) thy house and thy kingdom forever,*[31] which connotes assured existence; *His bread shall be given, his waters 'ne'emanim' (shall be sure),*[32] just as the prophet said, *Wilt thou indeed be unto me as a deceitful brook as waters that are not 'ne'emanu' (sure)?*[33]

12. AND HE SMITE ME, THE MOTHER WITH THE CHILDREN. Commentators[34] have explained it as meaning. "And he smite me and smite the mother with the children." There are many similar verses.

13. AND THOU SAIDST: I WILL SURELY DO THEE GOOD. Even though he was afraid lest the sin cause him to lose that which he was promised, Jacob said: "You have done great kindnesses for me even though I was unworthy of them. Certainly You will do for me this undeserved kindness which You have promised me, namely, that You will bestow good upon me and increase my seed. My sin should not withhold from me the good You have promised me, for in the beginning I was also unworthy of it had You marked against me mine iniquities.[35] And You did not promise it to me on account of my deeds, but only out of Your abundant mercies."

And some commentators say[36] that Jacob had compassion for his children and household lest Esau smite them, because he did not know whether the promise, *And thy seed shall be as the dust*

(31) II Samuel 7:16. This was said to David, whose kingdom was assured of existence. (32) Isaiah 33:16. (33) Jeremiah 15:18. (34) Mentioned in Ibn Ezra. The verb "smite" thus applies to the beginning and end of the sentence. (35) See Psalms 130:3. (36) Ibn Ezra. Thus Jacob's fear was not lest his sin cause him to lose that which he was promised, but because he did not know, etc., as explained in the text.

of the earth,[37] applied to these or to others, it being possible that he himself would escape and have additional children. But in my opinion this is not correct, for if this was his thought, how did he say in his prayer, *And Thou saidst: I will surely do thee good and make thy seed as the sand of the sea?* Moreover, it was told to him in Beth-el, *And behold, I am with thee, and will keep thee whithersoever thou goest, and I will bring thee back into this land.*[26] If his children were to fall before his brother's sword, this promise would not be fulfilled, and it is to this promise that Jacob alluded when he said, *And Thou saidst: I will surely do thee good.* Similarly with the promise, *And I will do thee good:*[28] all this Jacob said on the basis of it having been said to him, *And I will be with thee.*[27] But all his misgivings were on account of the fear of sin, for it is the way of the righteous to be always fearful. Thus Jacob was fearful that perhaps even after he left Haran, he sinned by entering into a covenant with Laban, who was an idol-worshipper, or in some other matter, and *Who can discern errors?*[38]

14. OF THAT WHICH HE HAD WITH HIM A PRESENT. Scripture states that he composed a gift out of that which he had since his wealth consisted of flocks and herds, and it was from them that Jacob sent a gift, for he was en-route and he had no opportunity to send him *vessels of silver, and vessels of gold... and precious things.*[39]

17. AND PUT A SPACE BETWEEN DROVE AND DROVE. I.e., in order to satisfy the covetous eye of that wicked man and to amaze him by the size of the gift. In Bereshith Rabbah[40] the Rabbis express the opinion that there is an allusion to the future in this matter: "Jacob said before the Holy One, blessed be He, 'O Master of the universe! If troubles will come upon my children, do not bring them one after another, but allow them intervals from their troubles.' " On the basis of this verse, the Rabbis thus hinted that the tributes and taxes which the children of Esau will collect from Jacob's seed will have intervals and cessations between one another.

(37) Above, 28:14. (38) Psalms 19:13. (39) Above, 24:53. (40) 75:13.

21. 'ACHAPRAH' (I WILL APPEASE) HIM WITH THE PRESENT. I.e., "I will dissipate his anger." Similarly: *'Vechupar' (and annulled shall be) your covenant with death;*[41] *Thou shalt not be able 'kaprah' (to put it away).*[42] I am of the opinion that whenever the word *kaparah* is used in association with iniquity and sin and in association with the word *panim* (anger), it always signifies erasing and removing. It is an Aramaic expression occurring frequently in the Talmud: "He wished to wipe his hands on that man."[43] In Biblical Hebrew, also, the bowls in the Sanctuary are called *'Kipurei' of gold*[44] because the priest wiped his hand on them, that is, on the rims of the bowl. These are the words of our Rabbi Shlomo [Rashi]. And so also did Onkelos translate: "I will calm his anger." If so, the explanation of the verse will [not] be that Jacob said these words, but that Jacob thought to himself, "I will appease him." It is Scripture that tells us this [but it is not part of Jacob's instructions to his messengers], for it would have been improper for the messengers to do so and thereby remind Esau of his antagonism towards Jacob. And so did Rabbi Abraham ibn Ezra explain it.

But it does not appear to me to be correct that Scripture should find it necessary to tell us Jacob's thought at this time when it is a well known matter pertaining to all who send presents. Besides, if it were so, Scripture should have mentioned this originally [in connection with the first drove, in Verse 19], *And, behold, he is also behind us,* for he thought, "I will appease him with the present," for now [when commanding the leaders of the second and third droves] he did not add to that instruction [which he gave the leader of the first drove].

However, the correct interpretation is that now Jacob additionally explained to them that they should say in a respectful manner, *Behold, he is also behind us,* that is to say, "Behold, your servant Jacob is also behind us, and he has sent us before him in order to give *a ransom for his life,*[45] using this present as a means of seeing your honor's face, just as servants present their ransom

(41) Isaiah 28:18. (42) *Ibid.*, 47:11. (43) Gittin 56 a. (44) Ezra 1:10. (45) Exodus 30:12.

when they are given permission to see the king's face. *And afterward I will see his face*, for *perhaps he will accept me* and honor me by permitting me to be among those *who see the king's face."*[46] This was a way of expressing Esau's exalted status and was due to Jacob's fear of him. The expression *achaprah panav* is then being used as it is used in the verse, *The wrath of a king is as messengers of death; but a wise man 'yechaprenah,'*[47] meaning he will give ransom to allay the wrath. And the connotation of "wiping away" attached to forgiveness is not valid in the Sacred Language but rather in the Aramaic tongue. Similarly, *'kipurei' of gold*[44] is the Babylonian name for bowls, for the word *kaparah* is never used in association with "sin," meaning "wipe away," but instead Scripture says: *'lechapeir' (to make atonement) for your souls;*[48] *'lechapeir' (to make atonement) for him, and he shall be forgiven,*[49] i.e., for his soul. And Scripture also says: *'achaprah' (I shall make atonement) for your sin.*[50] All of these are related to the expression, *Then shall they give every man 'kopher' for his soul,*[45] which means a ransom.

22. AND HE HIMSELF LODGED THAT NIGHT IN THE CAMP. Scripture states that he did not enter his tent that night but lodged in the camp together with his servants and the shepherds of the flocks, *set in array, as a man for war,*[51] lest his brother come at night and attack him.

23. AND HE TOOK HIS TWO WIVES, AND HIS TWO HANDMAIDS. There is no significance to being mentioned earlier or later in this verse with respect to rescue work. [Hence even though his wives are mentioned here first, from which you might infer that they appeared before Esau first, Scripture later states – 33:6 – that the handmaids came first.] Instead, Scripture states that he gathered his wives and handmaids and children at the edge of the brook, and he alone traversed the ford of the Jabbok to see if the waters were high, and then he returned and took them all

(46) Esther 1:14. (47) Proverbs 16:14. (48) Exodus 30:15. (49) Numbers 15:28. (50) Exodus 32:30. (51) Jeremiah 6:23.

with him at one time *and made them pass the brook,*[52] and after that *he made pass that which was his,*[52] namely, his camp and his belongings.

25. AND JACOB WAS LEFT ALONE. That is, for he had forgotten some small jars, and he returned for them. These are the words of Rashi. But in line with the plain meaning of Scripture, the verse, *And he took them, and made them pass the brook,*[52] means that he made them [his family] pass together with him, *and he made pass that which was his*[52] – [i.e., his camp and his belongings] – by commanding others to do it. He returned [to his camp after ferrying his family across], and he commanded that all others pass over the brook before him, and so he remained behind them.

'VAYEI'AVEIK' A MAN WITH HIM, A man covered himself with dust. So Menachem ben Saruk explained it, being derived from the word *avak* (dust); by their movements, they were raising dust with their feet. I, however, am of the opinion that it means "and he attached himself to," and that it is an Aramaic word, as in, "After they have joined (*aviku*) it;"[53] "And they twined the Fringes with loops."[54] This is all the language of Rashi.

In the language of the Sages, *avikah* is often used to convey the sense of *chavikah* (loop), as in: "There are *avkso* (loops) in the punishing scourge;"[55], "A couch is called *dargesh* when it is set up and taken apart by means of loops, through which the cords are fastened."[56] Similarly the word *avukah* (a torch) is so called in the language of the Sages because it is made up of small pieces of wood which are tied and bound together. This is because the letter *cheth* is difficult to pronounce in their language and so they used the easier *aleph*. Many times the *cheth* disappears completely as in *tuteich*[57] (underneath) in place of *techuteich; mesuta*[58] (a bath) in place of *maschuta; asita*[59] (a mortar) in place of *chasita*. And it

(52) Verse 24 here. (53) Sanhedrin 63 b. (54) Menachoth 42 a. (55) Makkoth 23 a. (56) Nedarim 56 b. (57) Chullin 7 b: *metutei* (from beneath her feet). (58) Kiddushin 33 a. (59) Shabbath 77 b.

is possible that the word *vayei'aveik* is actually *vayeichaveik,* as *vayechabkeihu (and he embraced him),*[60] for perhaps it is the way of the Hebrew language to interchange the *aleph* and *cheth.* Thus we find: *And in the fourth chariot grizzled 'amutzim' horses,*[61] which is the same as *chamitzim,* derived from the expression, *'chamutz' (crimsoned) garments.*[62] Commentators[63] have said that *'va'aruzim' for thy merchandise*[64] is like *vecharuzim,* derived from the expression, *thy neck 'bacharuzim' (with beads).*[65] So too did they say concerning the word *vate'altzeihu*[66] that it is like *vatechaltzeihu (and she pressed him),* this being an inverted form of *vatilchatzeihu,* [the root of which is *lachatz* (oppression)]. Perhaps this is the opinion of Onkelos who said, in translation of the word *vayei'aveik, ve'ishtadeil,* and so also he translated the expression, *And if a man 'yephateh'*[67] "as if *yeshadeil,*" if he embraces and kisses which is the manner of seduction. It may be that Onkelos found no word comparable to *vayei'aveik,* and so he considered it a matter of cunning, for all effort implies cunning and a clarification of circumstances. In Bereshith Rabbah[68] the Sages said: "Who became filled with dust? The man that was with him." This agrees with the words of Menachem [ben Saruk, who said that *vayei'aveik* means "he covered himself with dust]", and this is the correct interpretation.

26. AND HE SAW THAT HE PREVAILED NOT AGAINST HIM. *Ye angels of His, ye mighty in strength, that fulfill His word.*[69] Because of this[70] the angel could not prevail against him to harm him for it was not permitted to him to do other than that which he did to him, namely, to disjoint the hollow of his thigh. Now the Rabbis have said in Bereshith Rabbah:[71] "He touched all the righteous people who were destined to come from Jacob. This refers to the generation of religious persecution."[72] The purport of

(60) Genesis 33:4. (61) Zechariah 6:3. (62) Isaiah 63:1. (63) R'dak in his Book of Roots, under the root *erez.* (64) Ezekiel 27:24. (65) Song of Songs 1:10. (66) Judges 16:16. (67) Exodus 22:15. (68) 77:3. (69) Psalms 103:20. (70) Although the angel's strength was superior to Jacob's, he was restrained by G-d from harming him. (71) 77:4. (72) This refers to the religious persecution during the reign of Emperor Hadrian, 117-138 Common Era.

this Midrash is that this entire event constitutes a hint to his generations, indicating that there will be a generation from the seed of Jacob against whom Esau [Rome] will prevail to the extent of almost uprooting his seed. This occurred in one generation during the period of the Sages of the Mishnah, which was the generation of Rabbi Yehudah ben Baba[73] and his companions.[74] As they said:[75] "Rabbi Chiya bar Abba said, 'If a person were to tell me, "Give your life for the sanctification of the Name of the Holy One, blessed be He," I would give it, providing only that they slay me immediately. But in the generation of religious persecution I could not endure!' And what did the Romans do in that generation? They would bring iron balls and heat them in fire and then place them under their arm-pits and cause their death." And there are other generations in which they have done to us such things as these and even worse, but we have endured and it has passed over us, just as it is hinted in the verse, *And Jacob came in peace.*[76]

30. WHY IS IT THAT THOU DOST ASK AFTER MY NAME? The angel said: "There is no advantage to you in knowing my name for no one possesses the power and the capability other than G-d alone. If you will call upon me I will not answer you, nor will I save you from your trouble. However, I will now bless you, *for so I am commanded.*"[77] But Scripture does not explain the contents of the blessing. That which our Rabbis have said[78] is most probable, namely that the angel, despite himself, conceded to him at that place the legitimacy of his father's blessings, as Jacob did not wish to wait for him until he arrived at Beth-el.

(73) In Sanhedrin, 13 b, it is recounted how this Sage suffered martyrdom for the sake of ordaining his disciples, an act which the Romans had forbidden. (74) Possibly a reference to the *Assarah harugei malchuth*, the Ten great Rabbis who endured martyrdom rather than abide by the Hadrianic regulations. (75) Shir Hashirim Rabbah 2:18. (76) Further, 33:18. (77) Leviticus 8:35. (78) Mentioned in Rashi, Verse 27. See also the explanatory note on this verse in my Hebrew commentary, p. 186.

33 5. WHO ARE THESE WITH THEE? Esau inquired about the women and children, and Jacob modestly answered, *The children whom G-d hath graciously given thy servant,* as he did not want to say that they were his wives. Esau thereby understood that they were the mothers of the children.

8. WHAT MEANEST THOU BY ALL THIS CAMP WHICH I MET? Now Jacob's servants did everything he had commanded them, but Esau refused to accept the explanation from them. Perhaps due to his haughtiness and his arrogance he did not speak to them and did not ask them, *Whose art thou? and whither goest thou?*[79] and they were afraid to approach him. And so he now said, *What meanest thou by all this camp?* for he thought that they belonged to Jacob on the basis of the words of the first messengers [whom Jacob had originally sent to inform Esau of his coming]. It may be that these messengers had so related in Esau's camp, and it was then conveyed to Esau. Perhaps because there was no other individual on that road that had these things, [he assumed that they belonged to Jacob]. The intent of *What meanest thou by all this camp?* is: "Who is this person to you that you send him all these?" That is to say, "Who is this superior of yours that you send him all these?" And he answered him, "*To find favour in the sight of my lord,* for in my eyes, you are the superior and lord."

10. FORASMUCH AS I HAVE SEEN THY FACE. Jacob said to him: "Take my present from me because I have seen your face, which to me is *as one seeth the sight of an angel, 'vatirtzeini' (and thou wast pleased with me)*, as you indicated by accepting the present," just as *G-d 'rotzeh' (taketh pleasure) in them that fear Him,*[80] by accepting their offerings and sacrifices. This is similar to the verses: *'Venirtzah' (And it shall be favourably accepted) for him;*[81] *Their burnt-offerings and their sacrifices shall be 'leratzon' (acceptable) upon Mine altar,*[82] this being associated with the

(79) Above, 32:18. (80) Psalms 147:11. (81) Leviticus 1:3. (82) Isaiah 56:7.

expressions: *Let him be 'retzui' (the favoured) of his brethren,*[83] *And the light of Thy countenance, for 'ratzitham' (Thou wast favourable to them),*[84] *For Thy servants 'ratzu' (take pleasure) in her stones.*[85] All these forms of *ratzah* connote desire and pleasure in a matter. But Rashi wrote, "Because you have agreed to pardon my offense. *Vatirtzeini,* you are reconciled with me." But I have already said[86] that it was not advisable for Jacob to bring iniquity to remembrance.[87]

11. TAKE, I PRAY THEE, MY BLESSING. I.e., the gift. Likewise, *Make your blessing with me*[88] means "bring me a gift" or "make your peace with me." So also, *Take a blessing of thy servant*[89] means "take a present from thy servant." They called a gift which a man sends of his own free will "a blessing" because he sends it from that with which G-d had blessed him, just as the verse states, *Wherewith the Eternal thy G-d hath blessed thee thou shalt give unto him,*[90] and just as Scripture said above, *And he took of that which he had with him.*[91] However, a specific gift of that which has been agreed upon as due the king is called *mas* (tribute).

13. AND ALL THE FLOCKS WILL DIE. Jacob said this in a compassionate manner for he should have said, "And they will all die," but he would not express himself this way about the children. Neither did he wish to say, "and they will die," with reference to the herds and the flocks, because he had compassion on the children lest they be included by implication. He also did not want to be verbose and say, "and all the flocks and herds will die." It may be that the explanation of the verse is that "*the children are tender – even the youths shall faint and be weary*[92] – and they will not want to go, *and that the flocks and herds giving suck are a care to me,* and if they will be overdriven the flocks will die, as they are small cattle, but the herds [signifying larger cattle] will not die although they will be harmed."

(83) Deuteronomy 33:24. (84) Psalms 44:4. (85) *Ibid.*, 102:15. (86) Above, 32:21. (87) See Ezekiel 21:28. (88) II Kings 18:31. (89) *Ibid.*, 5:15. (90) Deuteronomy 15:14. (91) Above, 32:14. (92) Isaiah 40:30.

14. UNTIL I COME UNTO MY LORD UNTO SE'IR. In returning to his land Jacob could have gone by way of the land of Se'ir. Now Esau told him, *And I will go before thee,*[93] meaning that he will not be separated from him until Jacob returns to his father in order to honor him when he comes into his land. But Jacob said, "I will proceed slowly and let my lord return to the city of his rule, and if I will return by way of his city, he will honor me and go with me as he desires." This was not a vow on the part of Jacob that he will come to him, for Esau did not need him. Our Rabbis have further said[94] that Jacob had no intention of returning by way of Se'ir, and his desire was to remove himself from him as much as possible, but he mentioned *until I come ... unto Se'ir* in order to extend the length of his journey [so that if Esau meant to do him harm he would wait until Jacob reached his abode at Se'ir]. This also was wise counsel. The Rabbis have yet another Midrash,[95] which states that Jacob will fulfill his word in the days of the Messiah, as it is said, *And saviours shall come up on mount Zion to judge the mount of Esau.*[96] Scripture is saying that the saviors [i.e., the judges of Israel][97] who are on Mount Zion shall come up to judge the mount of Esau.

15. WHY THIS? LET ME FIND FAVOUR IN THE EYES OF MY LORD. *Why this,* that you should do me a favor which I do not need? *Let me find favour* in your eyes, and do not give me any recompense at present [for the gift which I have presented to you]. This is the language of Rashi. Now Jacob's meaning was that he did not want them and their company at all, the more so since he intended to go another way.

Our Rabbis have further seen an advisory aspect in this entire chapter. Thus they have said:[95] "Before embarking on a journey to the Roman ruler, Rabbi Yanai would peruse this section of the Torah, and he never took Romans with him as an escort on the return journey. One time he did not peruse this section and he took Romans with him, and he had not yet reached Acco when he

(93) Verse 12 here. (94) Abodah Zarah 25 b, and mentioned here by Rashi. (95) Bereshith Rabbah 78:18. (96) Obadiah 1:21. (97) See Judges 2:16.

was compelled to sell his travelling cloak for bribery money." [The significance attached to this chapter] was because of the Rabbinical tradition that this was the section of the exile. Therefore when Rabbi Yanai entered Rome, in the court of the kings of Edom, [on a mission] concerning public matters, he would peruse this section of the Torah in order to follow the advice of the wise patriarch, for it is he that the generations are to see and emulate. Thus he would not accept the company of the Romans as an escort for they draw no man near to them except for their own interest[98] and take liberties with people's belongings.

17. AND HE BUILT FOR HIMSELF A HOUSE. It is possible that the place was a location which had no city, and he therefore found it necessary to build for himself a house and make booths for his cattle. Or it may be that the expression, *and he built for himself a house,* means that he built for himself a large house with a strong tower to fortify himself against Esau.

18. AND JACOB CAME IN PEACE ... FROM PADDAN-ARAM. [This is stated here in the same manner] as a person says to his friend, "That man there has come from between the teeth of the lions and has arrived unhurt." Similarly here, *And Jacob came in peace,* i.e., from Laban and from Esau. This is the language of Rashi. But Rabbi Abraham ibn Ezra explained that the sense of the verse is that Jacob arrived in peace from his lengthy journey and nothing happened to him, as Scripture now begins to narrate the event of Dinah.

In my opinion Scripture speaks thus since for the length of his sojourn in Succoth[99] he was fearful of Esau. Succoth—if it be the one mentioned in the book of Joshua[100] — was east of the Jordan, in the kingdom of Sihon, and if it be another city by that name, it was nearer to Se'ir. Thus until he entered the land of Canaan Jacob did not feel safe, for only then did he know that Esau would not touch him for his father was nearby, or because the people of the land would help him as his father was a prince

(98) Aboth 2:3. (99) Verse 17 here. (100) Joshua 13:27.

of G-d in their midst, or because the merit of having entered the land would save him. And therefore, Scripture now said that he came in peace into the land of his father's sojourning[101] since G-d delivered him in his travels *out of the hand of all his enemies.*[102] And the Rabbis have said in Bereshith Rabbah[103] that during all these months that our father Jacob stayed in Succoth he honored Esau with that present enumerated above[104] by Scripture for he was afraid of him there, and monthly or annually he would send him a comparable present.

AND HE ENCAMPED BEFORE THE CITY. He did not wish to be a transient lodger in the city, but rather he wished that his inaugural entrance into the land should be into his own property. Therefore he encamped in the field and bought a place for the purpose of taking possession of the land. This action constituted a hint that this place will be conquered by him first[105] before the dwellers of the land would be driven from before his seed, just as I have explained in the case of Abraham.[106] And our Rabbis have said:[107] "He arrived on Friday close to sundown [and was therefore compelled to encamp *before the city* as there was no time left to enter the city], and he set Sabbath limits [while it was yet day." The verse thus teaches us that Jacob observed the Sabbath before it was declared on Sinai]. Now according to this opinion of the Rabbis the act of Jacob encamping there first was unintentional. However, in any case, the event hinted to the future as we have said. Rabbi Abraham ibn Ezra however said that Scripture mentions this in order to inform us that there is great excellence to the Land of Israel, and he who owns a part thereof has it considered as a portion in the World to Come.

20. AND HE CALLED 'LO' (IT) E-IL-ELOKEI-ISRAEL. It does not mean that the altar was called "The G-d of Israel," but because the Holy One, blessed be He, had been with him to deliver him, he named the altar in honor of the miracle so that the praise

(101) Further, 37:1. (102) II Samuel 22:1. (103) 78:20. (104) 32:14-15. (105) Further, 34:28. (106) Above, 12:6. (107) Bereshith Rabbah 79:7.

of the Holy One, blessed be He, would be recalled when people referred to the altar. Thus it would mean, "He Who is *E-il* is the G-d of me whose name is Israel." Similarly we find in the case of Moses: *And he called its* [the altar's] *name Adonai-nissi.*[108] It is not that the altar was called by the Divine Name *Adonai* but rather that he named the altar in honor of the miracle so that the praise of the Holy One, blessed be He, might be mentioned: "G-d – He is my banner." Our Rabbis expounded that the Holy One, blessed be He, called Jacob *eil* (a great and mighty man). [According to this, the verse should be interpreted as follows: "And the G-d of Israel called Jacob *eil*]." The words of the Torah are thus as a hammer splitting the rock into many different pieces, admitting many different explanations. I, however, make it my aim to render the plain sense of Scripture. All of this is the language of Rashi.

Now the words of the Rabbi [Rashi] are correct as regards the plain sense of Scripture. And the meaning of the word *lo* will then be [not "it," which would refer to the altar, but "him," which refers to Jacob], just as is the meaning of the same word in the verses: *And his father called 'lo' (him) Benjamin;*[109] *'Vekarei lecha' (and thou shalt be called) The repairer of the breach.*[110]

Know that it was the custom in Israel that names be called which are indicative of the praises of G-d, such as *Zuriel*[111] (G-d is my rock), *Zurishaddai*[112] (The Almighty is my rock), for the one who calls that name declares that G-d is his rock and the Almighty is his rock. Likewise, *Immanuel*[113] (G-d is with us). And so also the name of the Messiah, who will be called, *The Eternal is our righteousness,*[114] and the name of Jerusalem will be, *The Eternal is there.*[115] And so did they do with the names of the angels: *Gabriel*[116] (G-d is my strength), *Michael*[117] (Who is like unto G-d?), for because of their great power they proclaim with their very name that the strength belongs to G-d and who is like unto Him!

(108) Exodus 17:15. (109) Genesis, 35:18. (110) Isaiah 58:12. (111) Numbers 3:35. (112) *Ibid.*, 7:36. (113) Isaiah 7:14. (114) Jeremiah 23:6. (115) Ezekiel 48:35. (116) Daniel 8:16. (117) *Ibid.*, 10:13.

Onkelos however said: "And he worshipped on it before G-d, the G-d of Israel." In that case the meaning of the word *lo* will be as *bo* ("in it" or "on it"), in the same manner as: *That thou hast chosen 'l'ben' (the son) of Jesse;*[118] *And he took hold 'lo' (of him);*[119] *'L'mei' (In the waters) of Meribah.*[120] It may be that Scripture is saying, "And he called Him G-d, the G-d of Israel," and the meaning of the word *lo* is similar to the usage in these verses: *I will get me unto the great men;*[121] *Get thee out of thy country.*[122]

And by way of the Truth, [that is, the mystic lore of the Cabala, the verse is to be understood] as being in accord with the Midrash which the Rabbis have expounded in Tractate Megillah:[123] "Whence do we know that the Holy One, blessed be He, called Jacob *eil*? It is said, *And He – the G-d of Israel – called him 'eil.'*" There is in this matter a great secret, which the Sages have additionally mentioned in Bereshith Rabbah[124] in another way: "Jacob said to G-d, 'Thou art the G-d of those on high, and I am the master of those down below.'" The Sages thereby alluded to that which they constantly say: the likeness of Jacob is engraved in the Heavenly Throne.[125] The intent [of Jacob's statement quoted in the Midrash – "I am the master of those down below"] – is that the Divine Glory rests in the Land of Israel. The student learned in the mystic lore of the Cabala will understand.

34 1. THE DAUGHTER OF LEAH, WHOM SHE HAD BORNE UNTO JACOB. The reason [Scripture specifies *the daughter of Leah*] is to state that she was the sister of Simeon and Levi, who were envious for her sake and avenged her cause. And Scripture mentions further, *whom she had borne unto Jacob,* in order to allude to the fact that all the brothers were envious for her.

2. AND HE LAY WITH HER, AND HE AFFLICTED HER. *He lay with her* in natural gratification; *and he afflicted her*

(118) I Samuel 20:30. (119) II Samuel 15:5. (120) Numbers 20:24. (121) Jeremiah 5:5. (122) Above, 12:1. (123) 18 a. (124) 79:10. (125) Tanchuma Numbers 19.

unnaturally. This is Rashi's language. But Rabbi Abraham ibn Ezra said: *And he afflicted her* naturally because she was a maiden." But there is no need for this for all forced sexual connection is called "affliction." Likewise, *Thou shalt not deal with her as a slave, because thou hast afflicted her.*[126] And so also: *And my concubine they afflicted, and she is dead.*[127] Scripture thus tells – in Dinah's praise – that she was forced, and she did not consent to the prince of the country.

7. AND THUS IT OUGHT NOT TO BE DONE. I.e., to do violence to maidens, for the nations "had fenced themselves round" against unchastity as a result of the Flood. This is Rashi's language. But I do not know this, for the Canaanites were immersed in unchastity with women, beasts and males, as it is written, *For all these abominations have the men of the land done, that were before you,*[128] and they did not begin such practices in that generation [but rather it was their traditional behavior], and even in the days of Abraham and Isaac, the patriarchs feared lest they kill them in order to take their wives. Instead, the expression, *and thus it ought not to be done,* refers back to the word *beyisrael* (in Israel): *because he had wrought a vile deed in Israel... and thus it ought not to be done* among them. This is why Scripture said *in Israel* for it was not a base deed among the Canaanites. And Onkelos translated: "It is not proper that it be done," meaning that it is forbidden, and that is why it was a base deed in Israel.

12. 'MOHAR' (DOWRY) 'UMATAN' (AND GIFT). *Mohar* [refers to the bridal gifts given at the time of] the marriage-contract which is given to maidens, as it is written, *according to the dowry of virgins,*[129] these being the presents which the young men send to the maidens whom they marry. *Umatan* are garments or silver and gold which the groom sends to her father and her brothers. In Bereshith Rabbah the Rabbis said:[130] "*Mohar* is *parnon* (the wife's settlement); *matan* is *parapurnon* (the additional

(126) Deuteronomy 21:14. (127) Judges 20:5. (128) Leviticus 18:27. (129) Exodus 22:16. (130) 80:7.

settlement above the usual dowry)," these being in the language of the Jerusalem Talmud [131] "the regular dowry" and "the usufruct estate," that is to say, that which he gives her of his properties to be accounted as if she had brought them from her father's house, the produce of which belongs to him.

The reason for this conciliatory gesture is in order that they willingly give her to him as a wife, as the maiden did not consent to him and she steadily protested and cried. This is the sense of the verse, *And he spoke comfortingly unto the damsel.* [132] Therefore Shechem said, *Take me this young maiden to wife,* [133] as she was already in his house and in his power, and he feared not her brothers because he was the prince of the country and how could they take her by force out of his house? Now Shechem's great desire was because the maiden was very beautiful. However, Scripture did not narrate her beauty as it did in the case of Sarah, Rebekah and Rachel because it did not want to mention that which was to her *a stumbling-block of iniquity,* [134] while Scripture speaks only in praise of the righteous women but not of this one. Similarly, Scripture does not mention what happened to her after her rescue from Shechem's house. In line with the simple meaning of Scripture she stayed with her brothers, "shut up, living as widows," [135] as she was considered defiled in their sight, as it is written, *Because he had defiled Dinah their sister.* [136] Our Rabbis have differed on this matter. [137] The most feasible opinion is that of he who says [137] that Simeon took her, and upon her death, he buried her in the land of Canaan, this being in agreement with what we have said, i.e., that she was with him in his house as a widow, and she went down with them to Egypt, and there she died but was buried in the Land of Israel. Her grave is known by tradition to this day as being in the city of Arbel with the grave of Nitai the Arbelite. [138] It is possible that Simeon brought up her

(131) Yerushalmi Kethuboth 5:8. (132) Verse 3 here. (133) Verse 4 here. (134) Ezekiel 18:30. (135) See II Samuel 20:3. (136) Verse 13 here. (137) Bereshith Rabbah 80:10. (138) Aboth 1:7. He was a leader of the Sanhedrin in the early days of the Hasmoneans. As for Dinah's grave being near that of Nitai the Arbelite, see my Hebrew commentary, p. 190, for data from other medieval itinerants. Ramban's testimony though is that of an eye-witness when he travelled through the land.

remains from Egypt out of pity for her while the Israelites were still in Egypt or that the children of Israel brought them up together with the bones of her brothers — all the tribes — just as our Rabbis have mentioned.[139]

13. AND THE SONS OF JACOB ANSWERED SHECHEM AND HAMOR HIS FATHER WITH SUBTLETY. Now Hamor and Shechem spoke to her father and her brothers,[140] but the patriarch did not answer them at all as his sons spoke in his place on this matter out of respect for him for since the affair was a source of shame to them, they did not want him to speak about it at all.

There is a question which may be raised here. It would appear that they answered with the concurrence of her father and his advice for they were in his presence, and it was he who understood the answer which they spoke with subtlety, and, if so, why was he angry afterwards?[141] Moreover, it is inconceivable that Jacob would have consented to give his daughter in marriage to a Canaanite who had defiled her. Now surely all the brothers gave that answer with subtlety, while Simeon and Levi alone executed the deed, and the father cursed only their wrath.[142] [But if all the brothers shared responsibility for the answer and the plan, why did Jacob single out only Simeon and Levi for chastisement?] The answer is that the craftiness lay in their saying that every male of theirs be circumcised,[143] as they thought that the people of the city will not consent to it. Even if perchance they will listen to their prince and they will all become circumcised, they will come *on the third day, when they were in pain,*[144] and will take their daughter[145] from the house of Shechem. Now this was the advice of all the brothers and with the permission of their father, but Simeon and Levi wanted to take revenge of them and so they killed all the men of the city.

It is possible that Jacob's anger in cursing their wrath[142] was because they killed the men of the city who had committed no sin

(139) Mechilta, Exodus 13:19. (140) Verse 11 here. (141) Further, Verse 30. See also Ramban further, 49:5. (142) Genesis 49:7. (143) Verse 15 here. (144) Verse 25 here. (145) "Daughter." in Tur: "sister."

against him; they should have killed Shechem alone. It is this which Scripture says, *And the sons of Jacob answered Shechem and Hamor his father with subtlety, and spoke, because he had defiled Dinah their sister*, for they all agreed to speak to him craftily because of the base deed which he had done to them.

Now many people ask: "But how did the righteous sons of Jacob commit this deed, spilling innocent blood?" The Rabbi (Moshe ben Maimon) answered in his Book of Judges,[146] saying that "sons of Noah"[147] are commanded concerning Laws, and thus they are required to appoint judges in each and every district to give judgment concerning their six commandments[148] which are obligatory upon all mankind. "And a Noachide who transgresses one of them is subject to the death-penalty by the sword. If he sees a person transgressing one of these seven[148] laws and does not bring him to trial for a capital crime, he who saw him is subject to the same death-penalty. It was on account of this that the people of Shechem had incurred the death-penalty because Shechem committed an act of robbery and they saw and knew of it, but they did not bring him to trial."

But these words do not appear to me to be correct for if so, our father Jacob should have been the first to obtain the merit of causing their death, and if he was afraid of them, why was he angry at his sons and why did he curse their wrath a long time after that and punish them by dividing them and scattering them in Israel?[142] Were they not meritorious, fulfilling a commandment and trusting in G-d Who saved them?

In my opinion, the meaning of "Laws" which the Rabbis have

(146) Hilchoth Melachim, IX, 14, with slight textual changes. The Book of Judges is the last of the fourteen books which comprise Maimonides' great life work: The Mishneh Torah, or Yad Hachazakah. (147) Or "a Noachide," a term denoting the human race. See *Seder Bereshith*, Note 222. (148) The six commandments prohibit idolatry, blasphemy, bloodshed, incest, robbery, and eating a limb or flesh which was cut from a living creature. The seventh one is the commandment to establish courts to enforce these laws. Together, these laws are generally referred to as "the seven Noachide laws." Ramban will later set forth his thesis that the seventh commandment also requires that they establish laws regulating all civil matters such as damages, business regulations, labor laws, etc.

counted among their seven Noachidic commandments[148] is not just that they are to appoint judges in each and every district, but He commanded them concerning the laws of theft, overcharge, wronging, and a hired man's wages; the laws of guardians of property, forceful violation of a woman, seduction, principles of damage and wounding a fellowman; laws of creditors and debtors, and laws of buying and selling, and their like, similar in scope to the laws with which Israel was charged, and involving the death-penalty for stealing, wronging or violating or seducing the daughter of his fellowman, or kindling his stack, or wounding him, and their like. And it is also included in this commandment that they appoint judges for each and every city, just as Israel was commanded to do,[149] but if they failed to do so they are free of the death-penalty since this is a positive precept of theirs [and failing to fulfill a positive precept does not incur the death-penalty]. The Rabbis have only said:[150] "For violation of their admonishments there is the death-penalty," and only a prohibition against doing something is called an "admonishment." And such is the purport of the Gemara in Tractate Sanhedrin.[151] And in the Jerusalem Talmud[152] they have said: "With respect to Noachide laws, a judge who perverts justice is to be slain. If he took a bribe he is to be slain. With respect to Jewish laws, [if after having heard both parties] you know perfectly well what the proper legal decision should be, you are not permitted to withdraw from the case without rendering a decision, and if you know that it is not perfectly clear to you, you may withdraw from the case. But with respect to their laws, even though you know the law perfectly well you may withdraw from it." From this it would appear that a non-Jewish judge may say to the litigants, "I am not beholden to you," for it is only in Israel that there is an additional admonishment – *"Lo thaguru' (ye shall not be afraid) of the face of any man,*[153] meaning, "You shall not gather in, [i.e., restrain], your words before any man"[154] – and surely he is not to be slain

(149) Deuteronomy 16:18. (150) Sanhedrin 57 a. (151) 58 b. See my Hebrew commentary, p. 192. (152) Not found in our editions. See my Hebrew commentary, *ibid.* (153) Deuteronomy 1:17. (154) Sanhedrin 6 b. This explanation is based upon the common root of the words *thaguru* and *ogeir* (gathering) as in the expression, *gathering in summer*, (Proverbs 10:5).

for failing to make himself *chief, overseer, or ruler* [155] in order to judge superiors. [Ramban thus disagrees with Rambam, who writes that the people of Shechem had incurred the death-penalty by not having brought Shechem to justice.] Moreover, why does the Rabbi [Moshe ben Maimon] have to seek to establish their guilt? Were not the people of Shechem and all seven nations [156] idol worshippers, perpetrators of unchaste acts, and practitioners of all things that are abominable to G-d? In many places Scripture loudly proclaims concerning them: *Upon the high mountains, and upon their hills, and under every leafy tree,* etc.;[157] *Thou shalt not learn to do after the abominations,* etc.?[158] *For all these abominations have the men of the land done,* etc. [159] However, it was not the responsibility of Jacob and his sons to bring them to justice.

But the matter of Shechem was that the people of Shechem were wicked [by virtue of their violation of the seven Noachide laws] [148] and had thereby forfeited their lives. Therefore Jacob's sons wanted to take vengeance of them with a vengeful sword, and so they killed the king and all the men of his city who were his subjects, obeying his commands. The covenant represented by the circumcision of the inhabitants of Shechem had no validity in the eyes of Jacob's sons for it was done to curry favor with their master [and did not represent a genuine conversion]. But Jacob told them here that they had placed him in danger, as it is said, *You have troubled me, to make me odious,*[160] and there,[142] [i.e., at the time he blessed the other children], he cursed the wrath of Simeon and Levi for they had done violence to the men of the city whom they had told in his presence, *And we will dwell with you, and we will become one people.* [161] They would have chosen to believe in G-d and trust their word, and perhaps they might have indeed returned to G-d and thus Simeon and Levi killed them without cause for the people had done them no evil at all. It is this which Jacob said, *Weapons of violence are their kinship.* [162]

(155) Proverbs 6:7. (156) Deuteronomy 7:1. (157) *Ibid.*, 12:2. (158) *Ibid.*, 18:9. (159) Leviticus 18:27. (160) Verse 30 here. (161) Verse 16 here. (162) Genesis, 49:5.

And if we are to believe in the book, 'The Wars of the Sons of Jacob,'[163] their father's fear was due to the fact that the neighbors of Shechem gathered together and waged three major wars against them, and were it not for their father who also donned his weapons and warred against them, they would have been in danger, as is related in that book. Our Rabbis have mentioned something of this conflict in their commentary on the verse, *Which I took out of the hand of the Amorite with my sword and with my bow.*[164] They said,[165] "All the surrounding nations gathered together to join in battle against them, and Jacob donned his weapons to war against them," just as Rashi writes there.[164] Scripture, however, is brief about this because it was a hidden miracle,[166] for the sons of Jacob were valiant men, and it appeared as if *their own arm saved them.*[167] Scripture is similarly brief about the matter of Abraham in Ur of the Chaldees,[168] and it did not at all mention Esau's wars with the Horites. Instead, Scripture mentions here that *there was the terror of G-d upon the cities that were round them,*[169] and they did not all assemble to *pursue after the sons of Jacob*[169] for they would have fallen upon them *as the sand which is on the sea-shore in multitude.*[170] And this is the meaning of *the terror of G-d,*[169] for the terror and dread[171] of the military prowess they had seen fell upon them. Therefore Scripture says, *And Jacob came to Luz... he and all the people that were with him,*[172] in order to inform us that not one man among them or their servants was lost in warfare.[173]

21. THESE MEN ARE PEACEABLE WITH US. The men of the city thought that they hated them as they saw them dejected, and it angered them very much. Perhaps they guarded themselves against them and installed in their city bars and doors, for Jacob's

(163) This is the Midrash *Vayisu*. See Eisenstein, Otzar Midrashim, p. 157, and L. Ginzberg's, The Legends of the Jews, Vol. I, pp. 404-411. (164) Further, 48:22. (165) As quoted here, the comment appears in Rashi, *ibid.* See also Bereshith Rabbah 80:9. (166) See Ramban above, 17:1. (167) Psalms 44:4. (168) See Ramban above, 11:58. (169) Further, 35:5. (170) I Samuel 13:5. (171) See Exodus 15:16. (172) Further, 35:6. (173) See Numbers 31:49.

sons were mighty men *and valiant men for the war.*[174] But now Hamor and his son Shechem told them, "Do not fear and do not keep distant from them for they are whole-hearted with us."

23. 'MIKNEIHEM' AND THEIR SUBSTANCE AND ALL THEIR BEASTS. The reason for referring to cattle by the word *mikneihem* is that beasts of the herds which are in the field are called *mikneh* – [from the root *kanah,* which means "acquire"] – because whether they are clean or unclean, they are the mainstay of a man's substance, just as it is written, *Behold, the hand of the Eternal is 'b'miknecha' (upon thy cattle) which are in the field, upon the horses, upon the asses, upon the camels, upon the herds, and upon the flocks.*[175] And those which do not constitute a herd, as, for example, single beasts in the house, are not called *mikneh,* and they are included in the term, *and all their beasts.* It may be that [*mikneh* and "all their beasts" both refer to the same cattle], and the redundancy is for the purpose of emphasis, meaning, *and all their beasts* which were very numerous.

35 1. GO UP TO BETH-EL AND ABIDE THERE, AND MAKE THERE AN ALTAR. I do not know the significance of the expression, *and abide there.* Now it is possible that G-d commanded him to abide there at first in order to purify the camp from the idols taken from Shechem or from the dead they had touched, similar to, *And encamp ye without the camp seven days,*[176] since they had not yet been commanded concerning the Waters of Sprinkling,[177] and afterwards they were to make the altar. But Jacob was zealous in observing the commandment to be purified before he came to Beth-el. It may be that Jacob's words, *And let us arise, and go up to Beth-el,*[178] actually preceded the purification mentioned in the previous verse. And perhaps the command, *and abide there*, means that he was to direct his thought to cleaving to G-d.[179]

(174) Jeremiah 48:14. (175) Exodus 9:3. (176) Numbers 31:19. Said to the soldiers who returned from the war against the Midianites. (177) *Ibid.*, 19:17-19. Used in purification from the defilement of touching a dead body. (178) Verse 3 here. (179) See Ramban, Deuteronomy 11, for further elucidation of this matter.

4. AND JACOB HID THEM. An idol and the things that pertain to it are not in the category of objects that require burial and for which burial suffices, but instead they are to be crumbled up and scattered to the wind or thrown into the sea.[180] It appears to me that the sons of Jacob did not take the idols and the things that pertain to them from Shechem until they had been nullified and had thus become permissible to them, for a heathen can nullify an idol against its worshipper's will,[181] thus making it permissible to them. Jacob, however, for the sake of the purity of holy things, commanded that they remove it so that they should be fit to worship G-d and sacrifice before Him, just as He had commanded them concerning immersion and the changing of garments.[182] Burial was thus sufficient for the idols, and therefore *he hid them under the terebinth* in a location which will neither be tilled nor sown.

8. AND DEBORAH REBEKAH'S NURSE DIED. I do not know why this verse has been placed between the verse, *And he called the place El-beth-el*[183] and the following verse, *And G-d appeared to Jacob again.*[184] Scripture thus interrupts one subject which occurred at one time and in one place for when Jacob came to Luz, *that is Beth-el,*[185] he built an altar there *and he called the place El-beth-el,*[183] and G-d appeared to him there *and He blessed him.*[184] Why then was this verse concerning Deborah's death placed in the midst of one subject?

A feasible answer is that which our Rabbis have said,[186] namely that the verse alludes to the death of Rebekah, and therefore Jacob called the name of that place, *Alon-bachut* (the oak of weeping), for the weeping and anguish could not have been such for the passing of the old nurse that the place would have been named on account of it. Instead, Jacob wept and mourned for his righteous mother who had loved him and sent him to Paddan-aram

(180) Abodah Zarah 43 b. And if so, why did Jacob bury the idols when they should have been destroyed? (181) *Ibid.*, 52 b. (182) Verse 2 here. (183) Verse 7 here. (184) Verse 9 here. (185) Verse 6 here. (186) Bereshith Rabbah 81:8.

and who was not privileged to see him when he returned. Therefore G-d appeared to him and blessed him, in order to comfort him, just as He had done to his father Isaac following the death of Abraham. [187] With reference to both of them the Sages have said [188] that He gave them the blessing of consolation addressed to mourners. Proof for this is that which is said below, *And Jacob came unto Isaac his father to Mamre,* [189] for had Rebekah been there, Scripture would have mentioned "unto his father and unto his mother" for it was she who sent him to Paddan-aram and caused him all the good, for Isaac commanded him to go there at her advice.

Now Rashi commented: "Because the time of her death was kept secret in order that people might not curse her – the mother who gave birth to Esau – Scripture also does not make mention of her death." This is a Midrash of the Sages. [190] But neither does Scripture mention the death of Leah! Instead, we must say that the intent of the Sages was to explain why Scripture mentions Rebekah's death by allusion, connecting the matter with her nurse. Since Scripture did refer to it, they wondered why the matter was hidden and not revealed. And the justification for the curse stated by Rashi is not clear since Scripture mentioned Esau at the death of Isaac, *And Esau and Jacob his sons buried him.* [191]

It is, however, possible to say that Rebekah's death lacked honor, for Jacob was not there, and Esau hated her and would not attend; Isaac's eyes were too dim to see, [192] and he did not leave his house. Therefore, Scripture did not want to mention that she was buried by the Hittites.

I found a similar explanation in Eileh Hadvarim Rabbah, [193] in the section of *Ki Theitzei Lamilchamah,* [194] where the Sages say: "You find that when Rebekah died, people said, 'Who shall go before her? Abraham is dead. Isaac is confined to the house and his eyes are dim. Jacob is gone to Paddan-aram. If wicked Esau

(187) Above, 25:11. (188) Sotah 14 a; Bereshith Rabbah 82:4. (189) Verse 27 here. (190) Tanchuma Ki Theitzei 4. (191) Verse 29 here. (192) Above, 27:1. (193) I found this not in Midrash Rabbah but in Tanchuma Ki Theitzei, 4. (194) Deuteronomy 21:10.

shall go before her, people will say, "Cursed be the breast that gave suck to this one.' " What did they do? They took out her bier at night. Rabbi Yosei bar Chaninah said, 'Due to the fact that they took out her bier at night the Scriptures mentioned her death only indirectly. It is this which Scripture says, *And he called its name Alon-bachut,* two weepings, [one for Deborah and one for Rebekah]. Thus Scripture says, *And G-d appeared unto Jacob... and blessed him.* [184] What blessing did He give him? He gave him the blessing of consolation addressed to mourners.' " Thus far the Midrash. Now because Esau was the only one present at her burial, they feared the curse, and they did not view the burial as an honor to her, this being the significance of the Scriptural hint.

Deborah was in Jacob's company because after accompanying Rebekah to the land of Canaan, she had returned to her country, and now she was coming with Jacob in order to see her mistress. It may be that she was engaged in raising Jacob's children out of respect for Rebekah and due to her love for her, and thus she resided with him. Now it is possible that she is not "the nurse" of whom it is said, *And they sent away Rebekah their sister, and her nurse,* [195] but that she was another nurse who remained in the house of Laban and Bethuel, and now Jacob brought her with him to support her in her old age out of respect to his mother, for it was the custom among the notables to have many nurses. It is improbable that the old woman would be the messenger whom his mother had dispatched to Jacob [to have him return to the Land of Israel], as Rabbi Moshe Hadarshan would have it. [196]

10. THY NAME IS JACOB. G-d is saying, "Now you are still called Jacob even though the lord of Esau has changed your name [197] because he was not sent to you to change your name.

(195) Above 24:59. (196) Mentioned by Rashi in this verse. A preacher in the city of Narbonne, Provence, France, who lived in the second half of the eleventh century, Rabbi Moshe Hadarshan, compiled a collection of Agadic material on the book of Genesis. The book itself, which had a great influence upon Rashi and other writers, has been lost except for the quotations made by other scholars. (197) Above, 32:29. See Rashi, *ibid.*, Verse 24, that it was "the lord of Esau" who strove with Jacob and then finally blessed him.

However, from now on, *thy name shall not be called any more Jacob, but Israel shall be thy name*," this being the meaning of the end of the verse, *and He called his name Israel.* It may be that it alludes to the fact that He called his name Israel in addition to the name Jacob, but not that it be forbidden for him to be called Jacob.

12. AND THE LAND WHICH I GAVE UNTO ABRAHAM AND ISAAC, TO THEE I WILL GIVE IT. "As I have given it to them so will I give it to you." This alludes to an oath, for the land was given to them with an oath so that sin should not cause annulment of the gift, but to Jacob it was originally given without an oath. It is this which Scripture refers to when it says in all places, *the land of which I swore unto Abraham, to Isaac, and to Jacob.* [198] It may that the repetition of the prophecy, [mentioned above, 28:13, and repeated here], constitutes an oath, as I have already explained. [199]

13. AND G-D WENT UP FROM HIM. I.e., just as it said with respect to Abraham, *And G-d went up from Abraham.* [200] In both cases, it serves to inform us that this was no mere vision or prophetic dream alone, or something like, *And it brought me in the visions of G-d to Jerusalem,* [201] but that the Divine Presence rested upon him in the place where he stood. And by way of the Truth, [that is, the mystic lore of the Cabala], "G-d went up from him," from the place where He spoke with him, this being similar in purport to that which is said, *Blessed be the glory of the Eternal from His place.* [202] Scripture is thus stating that which the Sages have mentioned: [203] "It is the patriarchs that constitute the Divine Chariot."

14. AND JACOB SET UP A PILLAR. Rabbi Abraham ibn Ezra explained it as meaning: "And Jacob had previously [204] *set up a*

(198) Exodus 33:1. and elsewhere. But nowhere do we find that G-d swore to Jacob, except as implied in this verse. (199) Above, 26:3. (200) 17:22. (201) Ezekiel 8:3. (202) *Ibid.*, 3:12. (203) See Ramban above, 17:22. (204) See above, 28:18; also Ramban, *ibid.*, Verse 17.

pillar, and now he poured out a drink-offering thereon, and poured oil thereon." This is correct.

15. AND JACOB CALLED THE NAME OF THE PLACE... BETH-EL (HOUSE OF G-D). He called it so time after time [since he had previously [205] called it by that name]. This is to inform us that it is truthfully and properly a House of G-d, and there the Divine Presence will ever be. The same was true with the name of Beer-sheba, [which was so called by both Abraham and Isaac. [206] Here too it could not refer to naming the city but rather to calling it by its name.]

16. A 'KIVRATH' OF LAND. Menachem ben Saruk [207] explained the word as having the meaning of *kabir* (much), i.e., great distance. A Midrashic explanation is: "At the time when the ground is full of holes like a sieve, when there was plenty of ploughed ground. The winter was past, but the dry season had not yet come." This, however, cannot be the literal sense of the verse, for in the case of Naaman we find, *And he departed from him a 'kivrath' of land,* [208] [which cannot possibly have this meaning since the sense there is that he had walked away but a small distance from Naaman when Gehazi immediately ran after him]. I think that it is a name for a measure of land. This is Rashi's language.

The correct interpretation is that which Rabbi David Kimchi [209] has advanced, i.e., that the letter *kaph* in the word *kivrath* is the *kaph* of comparison and is not a root letter of the word, the basic word being as in the verses: *They were their 'levaruth' (food);* [210] *'Vethavreini' (and give me to eat) bread,* [211] meaning a small amount of food in the morning. [212] And here the meaning of

(205) Above, 28:19. (206) *Ibid.*, 21:31; 26:33. (207) See Note 347, *Seder Noach.* (208) II Kings 5:19. (209) An elder contemporary of Ramban, Rabbi David Kimchi, wrote extensive commentaries upon most of the books of the Bible which are deemed classical to this day. He also wrote a Hebrew grammar and lexicography. Ramban was influenced by his works. (210) Lamentations 4:10. (211) II Samuel 13:5. (212) R'dak's commentary on this verse is found in his Book of Roots under the root *barah,* and here in his commentary.

kivrath is the distance a pedestrian covers from morning to the time of eating, for all travellers measure distances in this manner.

This I originally wrote when still in Spain, but now that I was worthy and came to Jerusalem[213] – praise to G-d Who is kind and deals kindly! – I saw with my eyes that there is not even a mile between Rachel's grave and Bethlehem. This explanation of Rabbi David Kimchi has thus been refuted, as have the words of Menachem [ben Saruk, who said that there was a great distance between the grave and Bethlehem]. Rather *kivrath* is a name for a measure of land, as Rashi has said, and there is no adjectival part in the word but only a substantive as in most nouns, with the *kaph* serving a formative purpose to indicate that it was not an exact measure. And if the word be adjectival, modifying *eretz*, it is possible that *brath* is like *bath*, as in the expression, *What 'brie' (my son)? and what "bar" (O son) of my womb?*[214] The word *bath* is thus the name for a small measure of land by which travellers measure the way, similar to the present day mile. It is called "*bath* of the land" for this small measure is as "a daughter" to the Persian mile or some other measure known in those days.

And I have also seen that Rachel's grave is not in Ramah nor near it, [as the plain meaning of the verse in Jeremiah, 31:15, would seem to indicate: *A voice is heard in Ramah... Rachel weeping for her children*]. Instead, Ramah which is in Benjamin is about four Persian miles distant from it, and Ramah *of the hill-country of Ephraim*[215] is more than two days' travel from it. Therefore, I say that the verse stating, *A voice is heard in Ramah,*[216] is a metaphor, in the manner of rhetorical expression, meaning to say that Rachel wept so loudly and bitterly that her voice was heard from afar in Ramah, which was on top of the mountain of [the territory of] her son Benjamin. [She cried for her children who went into exile] *because they were not*[216] there,

(213) Ramban arrived in Jerusalem on the ninth day of Ellul in the year five thousand twenty-seven (1267). See my biography of Ramban (Hebrew, pp. 194-5; English p. 14 and 117). See also Note 361, *Seder Noach* and Note 25 in *Seder Lech Lecha*. (214) Proverbs 31:2. (215) I Samuel 1:1. (216) Jeremiah 31:15.

and she was desolate of them. Thus Scripture does not say, "In Ramah, Rachel weeps for her children." but it says that the voice was heard there.

It appears to me that Jacob buried Rachel on the road and did not bring her into Bethlehem in Judah, which was near there, because he saw by the prophetic spirit that Bethlehem Ephrathah will belong to Judah, [217] and he wished to bury her only within the border of her son Benjamin, and the road on which the monument over Rachel's grave stands is near to Beth-el in the border of Benjamin. And so the Rabbis have said in the Sifre: [218] "Rachel died in the portion of Benjamin," as it is found in the *Parshath V'zoth Habrachah.* [218] Now I have seen in the Targum of Yonathan ben Uziel [219] that he discerned this, and he translated: "A voice is heard high in the world." [He thus interpreted *Ramah*, not as the name of a place, since Rachel was not buried in Ramah, as explained above, but rather on the basis of its root *ram* (high)], and he thus translated the whole verse [216] as applying to the congregation of Israel rather than Rachel.

18. 'BEN ONI' (THE SON OF MY SORROW). I am of the opinion that he was so called because he alone was born in the land of Canaan which lies to the south (*yamin*) as one comes from Aram-naharaim, just as it is said: *In the south, in the land of Canaan;* [220] *Going on still toward the south.* [221] *Binyamin* thus means a son of the south, just as in the verse: *The north 'v'yamin' (and the south) Thou hast created them.* [222] For this reason the name *Binyamin* is here written "full" [with a *yud* after the *mem* to indicate that the name is derived from the word *yamin* (south)]. This is Rashi's language.

But I do not understand this claim that the Land of Israel lies to the south of Aram-naharaim for Aram is eastward of the Land of Israel, as it is written, *And he came to the land of the children*

(217) Micah 5:1. (218) Sifre, Deuteronomy 33:12. (219) The standard Targum on the books of the Prophets. See Tractate Megillah 3 a. See also Note 128, *Seder Vayeitzei*, on the three Targumim of the Pentateuch. (220) Numbers 33:40. (221) Above, 12:9. (222) Psalms 89:13.

of the east,[223] and it is further written, *From Aram Balak bringeth me, the king of Moab from the mountains of the East,*[224] and Jacob crossed the Jordan which is to the east of the Land of Israel, and he returned by way of Edom which is south of the Land of Israel. Thus you find that Aram is south-east of the Land of Israel, and the Land of Israel is to its north. However, if Benjamin was born within the border of Bethlehem Ephrathah which is in the land of Judah – as it is written, *Bethlehem in Judah,*[225] and it is further written, *But thou, Bethlehem Ephratha, which art little to be among the thousands of Judah*[217] – this was in the south of the Land of Israel, and he was thus born between Beth-el and Bethlehem Ephrath. And if the place was in the hill country of Ephraim, then it is in the north of the Land of Israel, as it is written, *Judah shall abide in his border on the south, and the house of Joseph shall abide in their border on the north.*[226] And if it was in the portion of Benjamin, it was also not in the south, for it is written, *And their border was on the north side.*[227] Thus in any case there was no reason to call Benjamin "a son of the south."

The correct interpretation appears to me to be that his mother called him *ben oni*, and she meant to say, "the son of my mourning, similar in expression to: *bread of 'onim' (mourners);*[228] *I have not eaten thereof 'b'oni' (in my mourning).*[229] And his father understood the word *oni* in the sense of "my strength," similar in expression to: *the first-fruits of 'oni' (my strength);*[230] *And to those who have no 'onim' (power).*[231] And therefore he called him *Binyamin*, "the son of power" o. "the son of strength," for in the right hand (*yamin*) there is strength and success, just as it is written: *A wise man's understanding is at his right hand;*[232] *Thy right hand shall overtake* all *those that hate thee;*[233] *The right hand of the Eternal is exalted.*[234] Jacob wanted to call him by the name his mother had called him, for all his children were called by

(223) Above, 29:1. (224) Numbers 23:7. (225) Judges 19:2. (226) Joshua 18:5. (227) *Ibid.*, Verse 12. (228) Hosea 9:4. (229) Deuteronomy 26:14. (230) Genesis 49:29. (231) Isaiah 40:29. (232) Ecclesiastes 10:2. (233) Psalms 21:9. (234) *Ibid.*, 118:16.

the names their mothers had called them, and he thus rendered it to good and to strength.

Now I have seen in Bereshith Rabbah:[235] *"Ben oni*, 'the son of my sorrow.' *And his father called him Benjamin*, i.e., in the Sacred Language." I do not know what this means for it is all the Sacred Language, and so are the names of all his sons in the Sacred Language. However, the Rabbis have alluded to that which I have said, namely, that Jacob rendered the expression so that it signified good.

22. AND ISRAEL HEARD OF IT. Scripture relates Jacob's humility. He heard that his son had profaned his couch, but yet he did not command them to remove him from his house and from inclusion among his sons so that he should not inherit with them. Instead, he is counted among them, as it is written, *And the sons of Jacob, were twelve,* and he is counted first. It is for this reason that Scripture has combined the two sections of the Torah[236] through one verse. For although this is the beginning of a subject wherein Scripture commences to count the tribes now that they were all born, it hints that Reuben was not rejected on account of his deed.

In line with the simple meaning of Scripture it is possible that Reuben disturbed the couch of Bilhah [Rachel's handmaid] because he feared that she might give birth again from Jacob, for he, being the first-born and thinking of taking two portions of the inheritance, would thus lose more than all the brothers. He had no fear of his mother for she was elderly. Zilpah had perhaps died, or it may be that he had concern for his mother's honor, and since Zilpah was her handmaid, he did not disturb her. It was for this reason that the right of the first-born was taken away from Reuben, measure for measure. And this is the purport of the verse, *And the sons of Jacob were twelve,* meaning that he did not beget children after that.

(235) 82:10. (236) In the written Torah the upper section concludes with the words, *And Israel heard of it*. Then a new section begins, *And the sons of Jacob were twelve*. Ramban explains why the Masorah combines them into one verse.

28. AND THE DAYS OF ISAAC WERE. There is no strict chronological order in the narrative of the Torah. The sale of Joseph preceded Isaac's death. This is Rashi's language. Now I have already written [237] that such is the customary way of Scripture with respect to all generations: it tells of a person and his children and his death and then begins with the account of the next generation even though the generations overlapped.

Now it would have been proper for Scripture to present Isaac's death prior to the experiences of Jacob, just as it did in the case of Abraham and all former generations. But by this delay, Scripture intended to state that Isaac died *in a good old age, an old man, and full of years* [238] – [just as is said of Abraham] – after his blessed son Jacob, the inheritor of his high rank, returned to him, and his sons Esau and Jacob, great men of the world, buried him. [239] It was not necessary for Scripture to mention that they buried him in the cave of Machpelah since it mentioned that Isaac was in the city of Hebron, [240] and where should they bury him if not near the gravesite of his father?

36 2. ADAH THE DAUGHTER OF ELON. She is identical with Basmath the daughter of Elon, [241] and she was called Basmath because she burned incense (*besamim*) to the idols. And Oholibamah, (mentioned here), is identical with Judith. [241] In order to deceive his father, the wicked Esau changed her name to *Judith* (Jewess) to suggest that she had abandoned idol-worship.

3. BASMATH ISHMAEL'S DAUGHTER. But elsewhere Scripture calls her Mahalath! [242] I have found in the Agadic Midrash on the Book of Samuel: [243] There are three persons all of whose sins are pardoned: a proselyte on conversion, one who is exalted to a high position, and a man on his marriage. It derives the proof for the latter case from here. The reason she was called Mahalath, [from the word *mechilah* (pardon)], is that Esau's sins were pardoned when he married her. All this, [including the comment on Verse 2 above], is the language of Rashi.

(237) Above, 11:32. (238) *Ibid.*, 25:8. (239) Verse 29 here. (240) Verse 27 here. (241) Above, 26:34. (242) *Ibid.*, 28:9. (243) Chapter 17.

But Rashi has not explained the reason why the father of Oholibamah, who, according to Rashi, is identical with Judith, is there[241] called Be'eri and here called Anah. And *Basmath Ishmael's daughter* is here a proper name while there,[241] according to Rashi, is an adjectival noun on account of her burning the incense! And in Bereshith Rabbah, the Sages have said: [244] "Esau set his mind to repent. *Mahalath* means that the Holy One, blessed be He, did pardon him for his sins. *Basmath* means that he was content [with his well-born wives and his decision to repent]." Thus according to the Midrash, both names (Mahalath and Basmath) are descriptive, and their proper names are unknown. For this reason Rabbi Abraham ibn Ezra has said that she had two names, Adah and Basmath. Also in the case of Abijah, [king of Judah, we find that his mother had two names, Micaiah – II Chronicles 13:2 – and Maacah – *ibid.*, 11:20].

It is possible to say that those two women [mentioned above, 26:34, i.e., Judith and Basmath], died childless perhaps as a punishment because *they were a bitterness of spirit unto Isaac and to Rebekah.* [245] Esau then married his wife's sister Adah, the daughter of Elon, and another woman by the name of Oholibamah, the daughter of Anah. But as regards *Ishmael's daughter, sister of Nebaioth*, [who was originally called Mahalath],[242] because of the repugnance of her name, [which suggests *choli*, (sickness)] in the Sacred Language, Esau called her by the honorable name of his first wife Basmath, derived from the word *besamim* (spices). This was because she was beloved by him since she was of his family and was not *evil in the eyes of Isaac his father.* [246]

6. AND ESAU TOOK HIS WIVES, AND HIS SONS, AND HIS DAUGHTERS. This journey took place after his brother had returned from Haran and established himself in the land of Canaan, as it says here, *and he went into a land away from his brother Jacob.* It is possible that this was also after the death of their father. Now when his brother Jacob was still in Haran, Esau was

(244) 67:10. (245) Above, 26:35. (246) *Ibid.*, 28:8.

already in Se'ir, as is written above![247] But the explanation of the matter is that Esau went to Se'ir in the days of the chieftains of *the Horites, the inhabitants of the land,*[248] and he became a lord with a following of four hundred men[249] while his children and family remained in the land of Canaan. It is possible that Esau had some land there in another location, in the plain, not on mount Se'ir. Therefore Scripture speaks of him as living in *the land of Se'ir, the field of Edom.*[247] And after his brother returned to the land of Canaan he vacated before his coming for he knew that the land of Canaan was the inheritance of his brother which his father had given him in his blessing. So he took *his sons... and all the souls of his house* — a multitude of people — and went to Se'ir to settle there. He then fought with *the sons of Se'ir the Horite, the inhabitants of the land,*[248] for perhaps they feared him, and they did not permit him to enter their territory into mount Se'ir, where the fortifications were. However, he settled in the field of Edom, in his original location, *and the Eternal destroyed them from before them, and they succeeded them, and dwelt in their stead,* as it said in Mishneh Torah.[250] It therefore says there, *Because I have given mount Se'ir unto Esau for a possession.*[251]

AND HE WENT INTO A LAND. According to Onkelos, the meaning of this expression is "into another land." But Rashi explained, "He went to stay wherever he could find room" for he went to no particular country but sought a country where he would find room to settle, until he came to mount Se'ir and settled there. In my opinion, the correct interpretation is that Scripture is saying: "And he went to the land of Se'ir," the name of the place being omitted from the verse as it is self-understood since it has already been mentioned that he dwelled in the land of Se'ir, and it is understood that he led his family there, and right nearby, it is mentioned, *And Esau dwelled in mount Se'ir.*[252] A similar case is found in this verse: *He went into the castle of the king's house, and burnt the king's house over him with fire,*[253]

(247) 32:4. (248) Verse 20 here. (249) Above, 32:7. (250) Deuteronomy 2:21. (251) *Ibid.*, 2:5. (252) Verse 8 here. (253) I Kings 16:18.

which means that house of the king in which he was. Similarly, *And he burned the high place and stamped it small to powder, and burned the Asherah,*[254] which means the high place which belonged to Jeroboam, who was mentioned in the beginning of the verse. So also: *And Joab said to the Cushite: Go tell the king... And Cushite bowed down to Joab,*[255] [which means "the Cushite" mentioned]; *And an ass and the lion,*[256] [which means "the ass" mentioned above in Verse 24]. So also: *For ships were broken at Etzion-geber,*[257] which means "the ships" [mentioned in the beginning of that verse]; and there are many similar verses. Here also the expression, *And he went into a land,* is as if it said, "into the land," i.e., the land of Se'ir which was mentioned.

7. AND THE LAND OF THEIR SOJOURNINGS. The meaning thereof is "the city of their sojournings," *which is Hebron, where Abraham and Isaac sojourned,*[258] for the land of Canaan could support a thousand times more than Jacob and Esau. But when Esau saw that he could not stay in his city and in his place, he left the entire country to his brother and went his way.

9. AND THESE ARE THE GENERATIONS OF ESAU THE FATHER OF EDOM. Scripture comes to mention the generations which his children begot after they went with him to Se'ir for Esau did not beget there. Thus Scripture begins from him by saying that he had already begotten Eliphaz and Re'uel,[259] and they begot these children in the land of Se'ir. It also mentions together with them the children of Oholibamah,[260] who were born in the land of Canaan,[261] even though it does not mention any children that were born to them in the land of Se'ir,[262] so that they be counted together with their brothers, the sons of Esau, mentioned in the beginning of the section. It is also mentioned because they became chieftains in Se'ir since Scripture mentions all their chieftains.

(254) II Kings 23:15. (255) II Samuel 18:21. (256) I Kings 13:28. (257) *Ibid.*, 22:49. (258) Above, 35:27. (259) Verse 10 here. (260) Verse 14 here. (261) Verse 5 here. (262) According to Ramban above, the justification for mentioning the birth of Eliphaz and Re'uel was in order to mention their offspring. Why then was the birth of Oholibamah's children mentioned? The answer is: "in order that they, etc."

12. AND TIMNA WAS CONCUBINE TO ELIPHAZ ESAU'S SON. Because Scripture was not particular to tell us the names of the mothers of all the others, our Rabbis have interpreted that this was to tell us of the esteem in which Abraham our father was held, i.e., how eager people were to attach themselves to his descendants. This Timna was a descendant of chieftains, as it is said, *And Lotan's sister was Timna,*[263] [and Lotan was one of the chieftains of Se'ir]. She said to Eliphaz, "If I am unworthy to become your wife, would that I might become your concubine," as Rashi has written.

It is possible that the five sons of Eliphaz, mentioned in the preceding verse, were generally known as his children since he had begotten them from his wives. But Amalek, [born of Timna, the concubine of Eliphaz], was not known among his brothers, [who were the recognized children of Eliphaz], and he might have been included among Esau's children because he was his descendant. Therefore, Scripture found it necessary to say that his mother so-and-so, to whom Amalek was known to have belonged, bore him to Eliphaz, but he is not listed among the descendants of Esau and did not dwell with them on mount Se'ir. Only the sons of the mistresses, and not the son of a concubine, are called Esau's seed, since the son of the handmaid will not be heir with his sons, in keeping with the practice of his father's father.[264]

Now concerning the descendants of Esau, we have been commanded not to abhor them[265] or take their land.[266] This refers to all his known sons who dwell in Se'ir, as they are called Edomites by his name, but the son of the concubine is not part of the descendants of Esau, and he did not inherit together with them in their land, and in fact with respect to him we have been commanded to the contrary, i.e., to abhor him and blot out his name.[267]

Now Rashi wrote further: "In the book of Chronicles[268] Scripture enumerates Timna among the children of Eliphaz! This

(263) Verse 22 here. (264) Above, 21:10. (265) Deuteronomy 23:8. (266) *Ibid.*, 2:5. (267) *Ibid.*, 25:19. (268) I Chronicles 1:36.

implies that he lived with Se'ir the Horite's wife and from this union Timna was born. When she grew up she became his concubine. And this is why Scripture says, *And Lotan's sister was Timna,*[263] [since Lotan's father was Se'ir the Horite]. And the reason why Scripture does not enumerate her among Se'ir's children is that she was Lotan's sister maternally but not paternally."

But I do not agree with this since in the book Chronicles, it should have said, "and Timna his daughter."[269] Why should Scripture enumerate the woman among the sons? Perhaps Scripture is not particular about this when a matter is known for so we find there in Chronicles: *And the sons of Amram: Aaron and Moses, and Miriam. And the sons of Aaron: Nadab and Abihu,* etc.[270] [Scripture thus enumerates a woman among the sons.] If so, it is fitting that we say that this Timna was the daughter of Eliphaz, who had been born to him of the wife of Se'ir the Horite after the death of her husband, and she was thus Lotan's sister from one mother. Eliphaz took her as a concubine, this being permissible to an idolater.[271] Or we shall say, in accordance with the opinion of our Rabbis [that Timna was illegitimate, as explained above in the words of Rashi], that the Timna mentioned in Chronicles[268] is identical with Timna the chieftain mentioned further on,[272] for he is enumerated there in Chronicles[268] among the sons of Eliphaz, just as Korah is enumerated there[273] among the sons of Esau [while here in Verses 15-16 Korah is listed among the sons of Eliphaz. You must therefore conclude that he was illegitimate, as was Timna]. Furthermore, Korah is listed here in Verse 5 as the son of Oholibamah [and Esau, and further in Verse 16 he is enumerated among the sons of Eliphaz. You must therefore conclude] that both Korah and Timna were illegitimate, born of one father, and enumerated with the children of another, for it is far-fetched to say that the woman Timna was enumerated among the sons, as was suggested above.

(269) See further, 46:15: "and Dinah his daughter." (270) I Chronicles 5:29. (271) Sanhedrin 55 b. (272) Verse 40 here. (273) I Chronicles 1:35.

In line with the simple meaning of Scripture it is feasible to conjecture that Timna, the concubine of Eliphaz, after having given birth to Amalek [as stated in our present verse], gave birth to a son, and she had hard labor and died. As her soul was departing she called his name Timna so that her name be remembered, while his father Eliphaz called him Korah. Scripture, however, does not ascribe this son Timna to Timna his mother in order not to prolong the account for the intent is only to enumerate Amalek by himself. However, the sons of Eliphaz were seven, [as they are enumerated here in Verses 15-16, and Korah is among them]. Now Scripture enumerates there the chieftains who were the sons of Eliphaz in the order of their importance. Therefore, it gave Kenaz and Korah precedence over Gatam [although the order of their birth as stated in Verse 11 was: Zepho, and Gatam, and Kenaz].

I have an additional opinion concerning this verse in connection with that which our Rabbis have said in the Midrash of "Thirty-two Rules by which Agadah [274] is explained." There they mentioned this rule: "There should have been one arrangement for [two verses, meaning that there are verses which should really be combined] but the prophets divided them for some reason! An example is the verse which says, *For a multitude of the people,* etc." [275] Those who pursue the plain meaning of Scripture apply this to other verses. And so too this verse says: (*And*) *the sons of*

(274) The part of Rabbinic teaching which explains the Bible homiletically, as opposed to the Halachic (or legal) interpretation, which is governed by the famous thirteen principles of interpretation mentioned by Rabbi Ishmael. This Midrash of "Thirty-two Rules" for Agadah was collated by Rabbi Eliezer the son of Rabbi Yosei the Galilean. (275) *For a multitude of the people... had not cleansed themselves, yet did they eat the passover otherwise that it is written. For Hezekiah had prayed for them, saying: The good Lord pardon,* (II Chronicles 30:18). And then in Verse 19 it continues: *His whole heart he hath set to seek G-d, the Eternal, the G-d of his fathers, though not according to the purification that pertaineth to holy things.* Now Verse 18 does not explain whom G-d should pardon, while Verse 19 does not explain "who set his heart, etc." Combining the two verses makes the sense clear. Hezekiah prayed that the good Lord pardon every one who, though he had not cleansed himself according, etc., had set his whole heart to seek G-d.

Eliphaz were Teman, Omar, Zepho, and Gatam and Kenaz, [276] *and Timna.* Then Scripture returns to say, *there was a concubine to Eliphaz Esau's son, and she bore to Eliphaz Amalek,* but Scripture does not mention the name of the concubine. But in truth she was Timna, as it is said, *Lotan's sister was Timna,* [263] and this is the reason that Scripture did not mention her name here since it did not want to say "and Timna" twice, once in reference to the male chieftain and once in reference to the female concubine. Thus Eliphaz had seven sons, [who are enumerated in Verses 11-12: Teman, Omar, Zepho, Gatam, Kenaz, Timna, and Amalek], and they are the same chieftains ascribed to Eliphaz in Verses 15-16, but they changed the name of this youngest son of Eliphaz – namely Timna – to Korah because his name was like that of the concubine and so that he should not be thought of as her son. He was named Korah upon his ascending to the position of chieftain.

Now Rabbi Abraham ibn Ezra said that Korah the son of Esau's wife Oholibamah is counted twice; [in Verse 5 he is mentioned as Oholibamah's son while in Verse 16 he is listed as Adah's son], because he was the youngest of Oholibamah's sons, [as indicated in Verse 5 where he is mentioned last. Upon his mother's death] Adah raised him, [which explains why he is mentioned among Adah's children in Verse 16]. So also the verse, *the five sons of Michal the daughter of Saul,*[277] as our Rabbis have said.[278]

According to this opinion [of Ibn Ezra, i.e., that because Adah raised Korah he is counted among her children], the explanation of Scripture in the book of Chronicles (I, 1:36), [where it mentions *seven* sons of Eliphaz, and among them, *and Timna and Amalek*, while here in Verses 11-12, it mentions only *six* sons of Eliphaz, is as follows: The expression in Chronicles, *and Timna and Amalek*, means] that Timna gave birth to Amalek, the sense of the verse thus being, "and to Timna, Amalek." The letter *lamed*

(276) This concludes Verse 11, while *And Timna* begins Verse 12. Ramban combines the two verses into one, with the result that Timna is also enumerated among the sons of Eliphaz. (277) II Samuel 21:8. (278) Sanhedrin 19 b: "But they were really Merab's children! [See I Samuel 18:19.] It is because Merab gave birth to them. However Michal raised them; therefore, they are called by her name."

meaning "to" is missing just as in the verse: *And there were two men that were captains of bands Saul's son,*[279] which means "to Saul's son." [Thus it was Timna who was his mother, but because Adah raised him he is enumerated here in Verse 12 among the sons of Adah].

The correct interpretation however is, as I have suggested, [that Timna, Lotan's sister, bore Amalek to Eliphaz], and the verse stating, *And these are the sons of Adah* – [namely, Verse 16, which mentions Amalek among them], refers to the majority of the names mentioned there, for Amalek was not her son. Similarly the verse, *These are the sons of Jacob, who were born to him in Padan-aram,*[280] does not apply to Benjamin, [who was born in the Land of Israel, although he is mentioned in the enumeration which follows].

20. THESE ARE THE SONS OF SE'IR 'HACHORI' (THE HORITE). *Hachori* was the name of a man who was the father of an ancient nation which was called by his name, just as the Amorite and the Perizzite, as it is said, *When He destroyed the Horites from before them.*[281] And he was called Se'ir because of the name of the land which was Se'ir – a name derived from Esau who was *a hairy man*[282] – from the day Esau came there. The name Edom likewise stemmed from Esau. However, Scripture seems to distinguish between "Se'ir" and "Edom" for it says, *These are the sons of Se'ir the Horite* who were *the inhabitants of the land* from the first, not the sons of Se'ir the Edomite who came there. With the help of G-d, I will yet explain the genealogy of the Horite in the book of Mishneh Torah.[283]

Rabbi Abraham ibn Ezra wrote: "Scripture mentions this in order to delineate the genealogy of Se'ir and Esau since Israel was to be commanded, concerning the sons of Esau, [not to abhor them or take their land]."[284] And Rashi wrote: "It would have been unnecessary to write the genealogy of the Horites had it not been that Scripture wishes to mention Timna, thereby showing the esteem in which Abraham was held."

(279) II Samuel 4:2. (280) Above, 35:26. (281) Deuteronomy 2:22. (282) Above, 27:11. (283) Deuteronomy 2:10. (284) *Ibid.*, 23:8; 2:5.

22. AND LOTAN'S SISTER WAS TIMNA. This is analogous to the verses: *And the sister of Tubal-cain was Naamah;*[285] *And their sisters were Zeruiah and Abigail;*[286] *And Tamar was their sister;*[287] *and Serah their sister.*[288] It is the custom of Scripture to trace the genealogy of a daughter through the brothers. Now it would have been proper that Timna be enumerated above with the sons of Se'ir by saying, "*And Dishon, and Ezer, and Dishan*[289] and their sister Timna." But since she was Lotan's sister both paternally and maternally, and not the maternal sister of the other brothers, Scripture therefore wanted to trace her genealogy through Lotan. It may be that she was Lotan's maternal but not paternal sister and she was not the daughter of Se'ir the Horite, [and therefore could not be listed among his children].

24. AND THESE ARE THE CHILDREN OF ZIBEON: AND AJAH, AND ANAH. The letter *vav* in the word *v'ayah* – (and Ajah) is redundant. Similarly: *Thy father's servant 'va'ani' (and I) have been in time past, so 'va'ani' (and I) will now be thy servant.*[290] In both cases the *vav* is redundant, and the meaning of the word is *ani* (I). *And there were the heads of their fathers' houses: 'va'epher' (and Epher), and Ishi*[291] – here too the *vav* is redundant. And there are many others like them.

Now this Zibeon was the third son of Se'ir the Horite,[292] and he begot these two children, Ajah and Anah, and Scripture relates that this Anah, Zibeon's son, *was that* same *Anah who found the mules in the desert as he fed the asses of Zibeon his father,* to differentiate between him and his uncle Anah,[292] the brother of his father, Zibeon. This Anah, Zibeon's son, was Esau's father-in-law.[293]

WHO FOUND THE 'YEIMIM' IN THE DESERT. In the opinion of some of our Rabbis in the Talmud,[294] the *yeimim* are mules,

(285) Above, 4:22. (286) I Chronicles 2:16. (287) *Ibid.*, 3:9. (288) Genesis, 46:17. (289) Verse 21 here. (290) II Samuel 15:34. (291) I Chronicles 5:24. (292) Verse 20 here. (293) Verse 2: *Oholibamah the daughter of Anah.* (294) Pesachim 54 a.

and this man discovered that an ass and a mare, even though they were unlike species, could breed together as opposed to other unlike species. Scripture says that he found them *in the wilderness as he fed the asses*, for he had there in the desert many asses seeking she-asses and he mated them with mares, and they begot offspring. It would appear that in his generation it was accounted to him as an act of wisdom in that he knew the various species which are nearly alike in nature and thus can produce offspring by cross-breeding. He was thus known by this deed, and therefore Scripture described him by it. And Onkelos translated *yeimim* as valiant men. It would appear from his opinion that this Anah was attacked by people from a nation called Emim, as it is said, *The Emim... a people great, and many and tall as the Anakim,*[283] and they wished to rob him of the asses of Zibeon his father. He was in the desert with no one to help him, but he overtook them and saved the asses from their hand. The word *matza* in *matza eth hayeimim* is thus to be associated with these expressions: *Thine hand 'timtza' (shall overtake) all thine enemies;*[295] *And I have not delivered thee into the hand of Saul.*[296] It may be that the word *matza* means that he found them and they were thus saved, and he came to be known for this prowess. This is correct.

25. AND THESE ARE THE CHILDREN OF ANAH: DISHON AND OHOLIBAMAH THE DAUGHTER OF ANAH. Such is the way of Scripture when referring to daughters, as in the expression, *and his daughter Dinah.*[297] Now this Anah was the fourth son of Se'ir the Horite, enumerated above,[292] after Zibeon his brother, for the section enumerates seven sons[298] of Se'ir the Horite in the order of their birth. This Anah had another son also called by the name Dishon as was his uncle,[299] and he had a daughter called Oholibamah, which was also the name of her relative, *the daughter of Anah the daughter of Zibeon.*[300] This is why Scripture says concerning Esau's wife, *Oholibamah the daughter of Anah, the*

(295) Psalms 21:9. (296) II Samuel 3:8. "Saul." In the verse: "David." (297) Further, 46:15. (298) Verses 20-21 here. (299) Verse 21 here. (300) Verse 2 here.

daughter of Zibeon, [300] in order to relate that she was the daughter of Anah who had found the mules, and granddaughter of Zibeon, not Oholibamah the daughter of Anah, the son of Se'ir the Horite, Zibeon's brother. However, in the opinion of some of our Rabbis [294] there is in this entire section only one man called Anah, and he was Zibeon's son. [301] Since Zibeon committed incest with his mother, the wife of Se'ir the Horite, Scripture thus enumerates Anah among Se'ir the Horite's sons [292] because people considered him as Se'ir's son and called him "Anah the son of Se'ir," and he grew up among his sons because Se'ir thought he was his son. Scripture, however, enumerates him a second time as Zibeon's son [301] in keeping with the true facts. This is the interpretation of the symbolizing interpreters as is mentioned in Tractate Pesachim, [294] but it is not the consensus of opinion in the Gemara and is not at all the plain meaning of Scripture.

26. AND THESE ARE THE CHILDREN OF DISHAN: HEMDAN AND ESHBAN. This Dishan is identical with Dishon, the fifth son of Se'ir, [299] it being of no consequence whether he is called Dishan or Dishon, except when both names are mentioned in one verse [299] in order to distinguish between them. Similarly, *And Hirom made the pots...* [302] *So Hiram made an end of doing all the work.* [303] It was necessary for Scripture to call him Dishan here so that it should not be thought that he is identical with Dishon the son of Anah mentioned nearby [in Verse 25] for the purpose of ascribing his children to him, for so it would have appeared.

31. AND THESE ARE THE KINGS THAT REIGNED IN THE LAND OF EDOM. This was written in order to relate that the blessing of Isaac was fulfilled in Esau. He had said to him, *And by thy sword shalt thou live,* [304] and they prevailed over the sons of

(301) Verse 24 here. (302) I Kings 7:40. (303) In the same verse. Since Hirom and Hiram refer to the same person, there is no objection even if both names are used in the same verse. The case is different with Dishon and Dishan, who are two persons. (304) Above, 27:40.

Se'ir the Horite and reigned over them in their land. These cities mentioned here were provinces in the land of Edom, for Bozrah [305] belonged to Edom, as it is written, *For the Eternal hath a sacrifice in Bozrah, and a great slaughter in the land of Edom.* [306] Similarly, *the land of the Temanites,* [307] is also of Edom, as it is said concerning it, *And thy mighty men, O Teman, shall be dismayed, to the end that every one may be cut off from the mount of Esau,* [308] as are all the cities mentioned here. Scripture, however, relates that these kings did not succeed their fathers, as was the case in Israel.

The expression, *Before there reigned any king,* means "many years before." But *before there reigned any king* does not mean that these kingdoms of Edom continued to exist until the kingdom of Israel. Instead, it means to say that at that time the Edomites will not have sovereignty, in order to fulfill Isaac's words, *and thou shalt serve thy brother.* [304] It is possible that all these kings had already passed away in the days of Moses [309] as they were old when they crowned them, and their lives were not prolonged.

35. WHO SMOTE MIDIAN IN THE FIELD OF MOAB. The intent thereof is to tell of Hadad's prowess, for the Midianites had come into the field of Moab to overpower them, but he was victorious over them all.

Baal-hanan the son of Achbor [310] was of the same place as *Shaul of Rehoboth by the River,* [311] in whose stead he reigned, and therefore Scripture does not ascribe another city to him. It is possible that "Hanan" is the name of a place, and he was the master thereof, which accounts for his name Baal-hanan, and afterwards he became king.

40. AND THESE ARE THE NAMES OF THE CHIEFS THAT CAME TO ESAU. At first [312] Scripture enumerated Esau's

(305) Verse 33 here. (306) Isaiah 34:6. (307) Verse 34 here. (308) Obadiah 1:9. (309) Ramban here implies that the expression *before there reigned any king,* refers to Moses. This coincides with the opinion of Ibn Ezra expressed in his commentary on Verse 31. (310) Verse 38 here. (311) Verse 37 here. (312) Verses 15-19 here.

grandsons who were chieftains in that generation, and afterwards some of his descendants succeeded in attaining sovereignty. After that their kingdom ceased, and the Edomites once again appointed these chieftains as their head. And so it is said in the book of Chronicles: [313] *And Hadad died. And the chiefs of Edom were: the chief of Timna.* So did Rashi explain it here in his commentary on this verse.

And that which Scripture says here, *according to their families, after their places, by their names,* [and in Verse 43], *after their habitations in the land of their possessions* means that among the previous chiefs, [mentioned above in Verses 15-19], all the brothers who were the chiefs dwelled in one city, ruling one people, or their position was analogous to the princes of the tribes and the heads of families [in Israel]. But these latter ones were chiefs *according to their families*, meaning that each one was chief of all the families of Esau's descendants, and in all of their dwelling places, for in that generation he alone was called "chief," no other person being so called in all the land they possessed. Thus they were as kings in their countries, but they were not enthroned, and the glory of royalty was not bestowed upon them.

In the opinion of many commentators [314] this section was written as a prophecy. But this is not correct. Why should prophecy mention these kings, and until what point in time was Scripture to enumerate them and stop? Rather the correct interpretation is that all these ruled before the Torah was given in the days of Moses. Now we may say that they all ruled in one time, and then the explanation of *after their places* would be that each one ruled in his place, or else their rule lasted but a short time, as Scripture says, *But the years of the wicked shall be shortened.* [315]

43. MAGDIEL. This is Rome. Thus the words of Rashi. But I have not understood this. If we say that this is a prophecy *for*

(313) I, 1:51. (314) See Rashi on Verse 31. In his opinion, *before there reigned any king* (Verse 31) refers to Saul, king of Israel. Moses who wrote the Torah could therefore know it only by prophecy. (315) Proverbs 10:27.

many days to come, and of times that are far off, [316] then many Roman kings have ruled over the Roman kingdom, and Rome is not a chieftaincy, but rather it is a great empire, *terrible, and strong exceedingly,* [317] there never having been her like among kingdoms. However, the Rabbis have said in Pirkei d'Rabbi Eliezer, [318] "In reward for having cleared out his utensils in the face of our father Jacob, [319] G-d granted him one hundred provinces, from Se'ir to Magdiel, and Magdiel is Rome, as it is said, *The chief of Magdiel, the chief of Iram.*" By this the Rabbis intended to say that of which I have already informed you several times, i.e., that that which occurred with the first ones contains allusion to their descendants. Now these last ten chiefs, together with Magdiel who is the tenth, allude that there will be ten Edomite kings [320] in their sovereignty during the Fourth Kingdom [320] who will rule over Edom, and the tenth of these will rule over Rome, and from there their kingdom will spread over the whole world. It is to this that the name Magdiel – [from the words *gadol* and *el*] – hints that he will magnify himself above every power, as it is said concerning him, *And the king shall do according to his will, and he shall exalt himself, and magnify himself above every power.* [321] And it is this which is written, *And as for the ten horns,* [which were on the head of the fourth beast], *out of this kingdom shall ten kings arise; and another shall arise after them, and he shall be diverse from the former.* [322] And the Rabbis have said in Bereshith Rabbah, [323] "All of the chiefs mentioned by Scripture are descendants of Esau." And the Rabbis have further interpreted: [324] *"The chief of Iram* – that he is destined to heap up [*l'arom*] treasures for the king Messiah." May he speedily reveal himself.

(316) Ezekiel 12:27. (317) Daniel 7:7. (318) Chapter 38. (319) Above, Verse 6. (320) Daniel 7:23-24. See also Note 8 in *Seder Vayeitzei.* (321) *Ibid.*, 11:36. (322) *Ibid.*, 7:24. (323) It is found in Shmoth Rabbah 15:4. (324) Bereshith Rabbah 83:3.

Vayeishev

37 1. AND JACOB DWELT IN THE LAND OF HIS FATHERS. The meaning of the verse is that since Scripture had said that the chiefs of Esau dwelt *in the land of their possessions*[1] – that is to say, the land which they took to themselves as a possession forever – it now says that Jacob, however, dwelt as his father had, as a stranger in a land which was not their own but which belonged to the Canaanites. The purport is to relate that they[2] elected to dwell in the Chosen Land,[3] and that G-d's words to Abraham, *That thy seed shall be a stranger in a land that is not theirs,*[4] were fulfilled in them but not in Esau, for Jacob alone shall be called their progeny.[5]

2. THESE ARE THE 'TOLDOTH' (GENERATIONS) OF JACOB. And this is an account of the generations of Jacob. These are their settlements and the events which occurred to them until they attained settlement status. The first cause was *Joseph, being seventeen years old,* etc. It was through this incident that it happened that they descended to Egypt. This is the literal explanation of the text, which permits each detail to fall into its place. These are the words of Rashi. But the word *toldoth* cannot apply to a settlement.[6]

(1) Above, 36:43, the concluding verse in the previous *Sedra.* (2) Isaac and Jacob. (3) A term denoting the Land of Israel. See Ramban above, 19:5. (4) Above, 15:13. (5) "Their": Abraham and Isaac. (6) Ramban thus understood the above text of Rashi as interpreting the word *toldoth* as having reference to Jacob's settlement. Mizrachi, however, points out that Rashi's intent is that the word *Eileh* (these are) refers to the settlements,

And Rabbi Abraham ibn Ezra said [that the verse should be interpreted thus]: "These are the events which happened to him, and the occurrences which befell him. This is similar in meaning to the usage in the verse, *For thou knowest not what a day may bring forth.*[7] But a person is not said to bring forth his events; it is only to days that events can be ascribed.[8] Now perhaps the verse, according to Ibn Ezra, is saying, "These are the events which the days of Jacob brought forth."

The correct interpretation in my opinion is as follows: "These are the generations of Jacob: Joseph and his brothers, whom Scripture will mention further on." Scripture here adopts a concise approach to their names since it already mentioned them above.[9] But the intent of the verse is to say that these are the generations of Joseph and his brothers to whom the following happened. It is also possible that the word *Eileh* (these are) alludes to all those mentioned in this book: *Thy fathers went down into Egypt with threescore and ten persons.*[10] Just as in the chapter, *These are the generations of Esau,*[11] Scripture mentioned sons and sons' sons, kings and chiefs, including all that there had been among them up to the time the Torah was given,[12] so will Scripture count the generations of Jacob, his sons and grandsons, and all his seed, mentioning only the outstanding details in their generations.

AND THE LAD WAS WITH THE SONS OF BILHAH. His actions were those of youth: he would touch up his eyes and dress his hair. *With the sons of Bilhah,* that is to say, he associated with

while the word *toldoth* is to be understood in its usual sense as meaning "children." The sense of the verse thus becomes: "These are the settlements of the children of Jacob." (7) Proverbs 27:1. The Hebrew is *yolad yom* (a day may bring forth). Similarly, according to Ibn Ezra, the word *toldoth*, which has the same roots as *yolad*, here means the events which evolved. (8) Ramban makes the point that *toldoth* can mean events when it modifies a period of time. However, when referring to a person, as in the present verse, it cannot have this meaning. Ramban thus takes issue with Ibn Ezra's interpretation. (9) Above, 35:23-26. (10) Deuteronomy 10:22. The listing of the names of sixty-nine of these seventy people is found further on "in this book," 46:8-27. Jochebed, who was born as they entered Egypt, is the seventieth. (11) Above, Chapter 36. (12) See Ramban above, 36:40.

the sons of Bilhah because his brothers slighted them as being the sons of handmaids, and he therefore befriended them. *Their evil report* – he told his father about every wrong which he discerned in his brothers, the sons of Leah. This is the language of Rashi.

But if this be so, why did the children of the handmaids not save him later on, inasmuch as he loved and befriended them, and told his father about his brothers' slighting them. And if we say that they feared their brothers, they were four,[13] and Reuben was with them,[14] and, with Joseph himself, [they made a total of six]. Surely they would have prevailed against them especially when considering that the remaining five sons of Leah would not wage war against them. Moreover, it appears from Scripture that all [15] of the brothers concurred in the sale of Joseph. However, according to our Rabbis in Bereshith Rabbah,[16] he uttered slander against all of them.[17]

In my opinion the correct interpretation is that this verse returns to explain that which it mentioned above, and its purport [is as if the phrases in the verse were transposed as follows]: Joseph being a lad of seventeen years, was feeding the flock together with his brothers, the sons of Bilhah and the sons of Zilpah, his father's wives. A similar case requiring transposition of phrases is found in this *Seder:*[18] *And they dreamed a dream both of them in one night, each man according to the interpretation of his dream, the butler and the baker of the king of Egypt, who were bound in the prison.*[19] The verse returns to explain the word *shneihem* (both of them) which it had mentioned at the outset. Its purport, [after the phrases have been suitably transposed, is as follows]: And both of them dreamed a dream, the butler and the baker of the king of Egypt, who were bound in the prison, each man according to the interpretation of his dream. There are many similar verses. It may be that the word *v'hu* (and he was) requires

(13) Dan, Naphtali, Gad, and Asher. (14) As expressly stated further on in Verses 21-22. (15) "All," except Reuben, the eldest, and Benjamin, the youngest, (Rabbeinu Bachya, p. 306, in my edition.) (16) 84:7. (17) And not, as Rashi has it, that the evil report concerned only the sons of Leah. (18) *Sedrah* or *Parsha* (section). (19) 40:5.

another similar word, as if it were written: "and he was a lad, and he was with the sons of Bilhah and with the sons of Zilpah, who were his father's wives." The verse thus states that because he was a lad he was constantly with the sons of Bilhah and the sons of Zilpah, his father's wives, never being separated from them on account of his youth, for their father had commanded them to watch over him and serve him, not the sons of the mistresses, and he brought an evil report concerning them [20] to their father. It was for this reason that these four brothers [13] hated Joseph. Following that, the verse says that his father loved him. Now when the other brothers [21] saw that their father loved him more than all, they became jealous of him and they hated him. Thus Joseph is found to be hated by all: the sons of the mistresses were jealous of him because Jacob loved him more than them although they were also sons of a mistress as he was, and the sons of the handmaids, who would otherwise not have been jealous of his superior position over them, hated him because he brought their evil report to their father.

The purpose of the redundant expression, *dibatham ra'ah* (their evil report), is to magnify, [22] for *dibah* itself connotes evil.[23] Now according to the opinion of Rashi it is possible for *dibah* to be a good report. Thus when Scripture uses the expression, "he brings *dibah*", it means that he tells what he sees,[24] but when it uses the term, *he bringeth forth 'dibah,'* it refers to the fool who speaks falsehood.[25]

In line with the literal meaning of Scripture, the fact that it calls one a *na'ar* (lad) when he was seventeen years of age [26] presents no difficulty for since he was the youngest among them, it calls him by that name, indicating that he was not as sturdy as his brothers

(20) The sons of Bilhah and Zilpah. (21) The sons of Leah. (22) I.e., to indicate that the report was of an exceedingly evil nature. (23) Otherwise, why does Scripture add the word *ra'ah* (evil)? It does so in order to magnify the evil nature of the report. (24) He reports the truth. (25) This opinion that *dibah* connotes evil only when used in conjunction with the word *motzi* (bring forth) is borne out by Numbers 13:32. (26) Ramban's intent is to disagree with Rashi's interpretation of *na'ar,* which is that his actions were those of a youth.

and therefore needed to be with the sons of Bilhah and Zilpah on account of his youth. Now of Rehoboam, Solomon's son, it is written, *And Rehoboam was young and faint-hearted and could not withstand them,* [27] yet he was *forty-one years old when he began to reign.* [28] Similarly the verse: *Is it well with the lad Absalom?* [29] And Benjamin, upon going down to Egypt, was older than Joseph was now, [30] and yet Scripture frequently refers to him as *na'ar.* [31]

Now Onkelos translated *v'hu na'ar* as "*he grew up* with the sons of Bilhah." Thus the verse states that from the time he was a lad he was in their company. They raised him as a father would, and they served him. This interpretation is also correct according to the literal interpretation of Scripture, which I offered as an explanation, namely that Scripture relates that he brought evil report concerning [the sons of the handmaids, who, according to Onkelos, raised him. This is why they hated him, whereas] the sons of the mistresses hated him because of their jealousy, as explained above. [32]

The meaning of the expression, *His father's wives,* is that they were his "wives" for he took them as such. Scripture calls them "handmaids" only when they are mentioned together with Rachel and Leah, who were their mistresses. Similarly, *And he put the handmaids and their children foremost,* [33] as if to say that because they were handmaids of Rachel and Leah, Jacob placed them before them in a more exposed position. Similarly, *And he lay with Bilhah, his father's concubine.* [34] [The word "concubine" is

(27) II Chronicles 13:7. (28) *Ibid.*, 12:13. (29) II Samuel 18:32. Now although Scripture does not state how old Absalom was at the time of his death, it would appear certain that he was about thirty years old since he was born to David in Hebron (*ibid.*, 3:3-5), and David ruled thirty-three years in Jerusalem. The rebellion of Absalom occurred three years before David's death (see Seder Hadoroth, year 2921). Hence Absalom, at his death, was at least thirty years old, yet David calls him *na'ar.* (30) For Joseph was separated from his father for twenty-two years. Therefore Benjamin must have been at least thirty years old at the time he went down to Egypt. (31) Further, 44:31 and 33. (32) Ramban thus indicates that the authoritative interpretation of Onkelos is here consistent with his own. (33) Above, 33:2. (34) Above, 35:22.

used to indicate] that if she were a mistress it would not have occurred. It is possible that during the lifetime of Rachel and Leah, Scripture calls them "handmaids" and "concubines," but now that they had died [Jacob] took them as wives.

3. BECAUSE HE WAS THE SON OF HIS OLD AGE. That is, he was born to him during his old age. Onkelos translated: "he was a wise son to him," for all that he had learned from Shem and Eber [35] he transmitted to him. Another interpretation is that the facial features of Joseph were similar to those of Jacob. This is Rashi's language. Rabbi Abraham ibn Ezra also explains it in this way: "*Because he was the son of old age*— for he begot him in his old age when he was ninety-one [36] years old. They likewise called his brother Benjamin *a little child of his old age.*" [37]

But in my opinion this is not correct for the verse states that Jacob loved Joseph more than all his children because he was the son of his old age, whereas all his children were born to him during his old age! Issachar and Zebulun were not more than a year or two [38] older than Joseph.

The correct interpretation appears to me to be that it was the custom of the elders to take one of their younger sons to be with them to attend them. He would constantly lean on his arm, never being separated from him, and he would be called *ben z'kunav* because he attended him in his old age. Now Jacob took Joseph for this purpose, and he was with him constantly. He therefore did not accompany the flock when they went to pasture in distant places. And Onkelos who translated, "he was a wise son," intended to say that in his father's eyes, Joseph was a knowledgeable and

(35) The traditional masters who taught Torah to Jacob during the fourteen years he hid from Esau (Megillah 17 a). This source, however, mentions only Eber. See Bereshith Rabbah 84:8, where Shem is also mentioned. (36) For when Jacob stood before Pharaoh at the end of two of the lean years he was one hundred and thirty years old (47:9). Now when Joseph stood before Pharaoh he was thirty years old. Therefore after the seven years of plenty, and the two lean years he was thirty-nine. Subtract his age from Jacob's age and there remain ninety-one years. This was Jacob's age when Joseph was born. (Ohel Yoseph.) (37) Further, 44:20. (38) See Seder Olam Rabbah, 2.

wise son, and his understanding was as that of elders.[39] However in the case of Benjamin, who is called *yeled z'kunim (a little child of his old age),* Onkelos translated: *bar savtin*[40] (a son of old age). [The explanation of Onkelos in the case of Joseph becomes clear] because the verse here does not state, "Joseph *hayah* (was) a son of old age;" instead, it says, *hu lo* (he was unto him), meaning that in his eyes he appeared to be [a *ben z'kunim*, and consequently it must mean *bar chakim*, a wise son].[41] This is the intent of the Sages when they said:[42] "Whatever Jacob had learned from Shem and Eber[35] he transmitted to him," meaning that he passed on to him wisdoms and the secrets of the Torah, and that the father found the son to be intelligent and profound in these areas as if he were an elder and a man of many years.

7. MY SHEAF AROSE, AND ALSO PLACED ITSELF UPRIGHT, AND, BEHOLD, YOUR SHEAVES SURROUNDED. The purport of the dream concerning the sheaves is that Joseph was shown that through the sheaves and the produce they will prostrate themselves to him. The matter of "surrounding" – [*your sheaves surrounded*] – is to indicate that they will surround him as they dc a king arrayed for battle, around whom his subjects encamp.

8. SHALT THOU INDEED REIGN OVER US? OR SHALT THOU INDEED HAVE DOMINION OVER US? Rabbi Abraham ibn Ezra explained: "Shall we voluntarily make you king over us, or will you rule over us by force?" The opinion of Onkelos appears to be more correct.[43] He rendered it: "Shall you be king

(39) See the interpretation of Ramban on Leviticus 19:32. (40) Rather than *bar chakim*, as in the case of Joseph. (41) For if the sense of the verse is to be understood literally as meaning that "he was a son of his old age," why specify "to Jacob?" Hence Onkelos correctly translated it as *bar chakim*, which means that Joseph was a wise son in his father's estimate. (42) In the Rashi quoted above. The original source is Bereshith Rabbah 84:8. (43) Since the authority of a king is essentially the same whether he rules by consent or force, Scripture should not change the expression from *malach* (reign) to *mashal* (dominion) if the explanation of Ibn Ezra is correct. Hence Ramban prefers Onkelos' explanation which follows.

over us or some authority ruling us?" For people prostrate themselves before both. The verse thus means, "You will never be king or any kind of authority over us."

The meaning of the expression, *And they continued to hate him still more for his dreams, and for his words,* is that they hated him for the dreams and for relating the dreams to them in a boastful manner, even as it says, *Hear, I pray you, this dream which I have dreamed.*[44]

10. AND HE RELATED IT TO HIS FATHER. He told his father of this dream concerning the sun, moon and stars, but not of the first one concerning the sheaves because he himself recognized its interpretation and knew that the sun alluded to his father, and his father rebuked him.[45]

The meaning of the expression, *And he related it to his father and to his brothers,* is that he related it to them a second time,[46] as he told it to his father in their presence, and his father rebuked him in order to dissipate their anger towards him.

The meaning of the expression, *What is this dream that thou hast dreamed?* is the same as, *What is man that Thou shouldst take cognizance of him?*[47] That is to say, "What is this dream? It is nothing that you should relate for it is nothing but idle talk." Alternatively, the meaning of the rebuke may be: "How dare you dream such a dream? It is but your conceit and youth that bring up such matters in your heart," just as it says concerning dreams, *Thy thoughts came upon thy bed;*[48] *And imaginings upon my bed.*[49]

(44) Verse 6 here. (45) Ramban's intent is to say that the father's rebuke is proof that he knew that Joseph understood the meaning of the dream. (46) Since it is already stated in Verse 9 that he related this dream concerning the sun, moon and stars to his brothers, it must mean here in Verse 10 that he related it to them a second time. (47) Psalms 144:3. (48) Daniel 2:29. Here understood literally: "The thoughts you entertained during the day came with you to bed, and you dreamed about them." (49) *Ibid.*, 4:2. Understood in the same sense as above.

SHALL I AND THY MOTHER AND THY BRETHREN INDEED COME TO PROSTRATE OURSELVES TO THEE TO THE EARTH? "Is not your mother long since dead?" Jacob, however, was not aware that the matter alluded to Bilhah who had raised him as if she were his mother. From here, our Rabbis derived the principle that there is no dream that does not contain invalid matters. Jacob's intention in pointing out the invalidity of the dream was to cause his sons to forget the matter so that they should not be envious of him because of it. Jacob said to Joseph: "Just as it is impossible for the dream to be fulfilled with respect to your mother, so is the remainder invalid." Thus the language of Rashi.

In my opinion, at the time when Jacob went down to Egypt, Bilhah and Zilpah had already died [50] since, in enumerating the seventy souls that went down to Egypt, Scripture states, *Besides Jacob's sons' wives,* [51] and it does not say "besides Jacob's wives and his sons' wives." [52] And if you say that because they were concubines Scripture does not want to say "besides Jacob's sons' wives and his concubines," yet we find that they are referred to as *his father's wives.* [53] Besides, it is unlikely that "the moon" in the dream alludes to his concubine. Instead, my opinion concerning the matter of the dream is that the sun is an allusion to Jacob, and the moon alludes to the children of his household and all his wives, which comprised Jacob's seed. Thus, the moon alludes to the fact that all his seed will prostrate themselves to Joseph, these being all the seventy souls that issued from his loins, since they all prostrated themselves when they came before him. The eleven stars represent the brothers who bowed down before him separately, [54]

(50) See Ramban 46:15. (51) Further, 46:26. (52) Thus, there is proof that Bilhah had already died at the time Jacob went down to Egypt. So how then could Rashi say that the mother in the dream, symbolized by the moon, who was to bow before Joseph in Egypt, referred to Bilhah? (53) Above, Verse 2. Why then does Scripture not say "besides Jacob's wives and his sons' wives?" Thus it is clear that they had already died. (54) This explains why the brothers are singled out from all of Jacob's seed, alluded to by the moon.

before their father arrived, as it is written, *And when Joseph came into the house, they brought him the present which was in their hand into the house, and prostrated themselves to him to the earth.*[55]

14. AND HE SENT HIM OUT OF THE VALLEY OF HEBRON. Scripture mentions the place from which Joseph was sent, in order to indicate that there was a great distance between father and son, and that this was the reason why the brothers did him evil: they were distant far from their father. It also serves to relate that Joseph, out of respect for his father, strengthened himself to go after them to a distant place, and he did not say, "How shall I go when they hate me?". Our Rabbis yet have a Midrash concerning this matter, in which they say, "It was to fulfill the profound thought of the 'seemly companion'[56] who was buried in Hebron."[57]

15. AND A MAN FOUND HIM, AND BEHOLD, HE WAS STRAYING IN THE FIELD. The verse is stating that Joseph was straying from the road, not knowing where to go, and he entered a field since he was looking for them in a place of pasture. Scripture mentions this at length in order to relate that many events befell him which could properly have caused him to return, but he endured everything patiently for the honor of his father. It also informs us that the Divine decree is true and man's industry is worthless. The Holy One, blessed be He, sent him a guide without his knowledge in order to bring him into their hands. It is this that our Rabbis intended when they said[58] that these men[59] were

(55) Further, 43:26. (56) Abraham. The Midrash thus explains the word *Chevron* (Hebron) as if it consisted of the two words: *chever na'eh* (seemly companion). Thus it refers to Abraham who walked before G-d (above 17:1). The Midrash is in Bereshith Rabbah 84:13. (57) Reference is to the covenant — which G-d made with Abraham — that his seed will be a stranger in a land that is not their own (above, 15:13). The idea expressed is that Jacob's act of sending Joseph to his brethren was thus the beginning of a cycle of events which would fulfill the covenant made with Abraham. (58) Bereshith Rabbah 84:13. (59) *And 'a man' found him ... and 'the man' asked him ... And 'the man' said ...* (Verses 15, 17).

angels, for these events did not occur without purpose, but rather to inform us that *It is the counsel of the Eternal that shall stand.*[60]

17. THEY HAVE JOURNEYED HENCE. "They have departed from any feeling of brotherhood. '*Let us go to Dothan,* that is, let us go to seek pretexts of *dathoth* (laws) with which to put you to death.' According to the literal sense, however, *Dothan* is the name of a place, and Scripture never sheds its literal sense." This is Rabbi Shlomo's [Rashi's] language.

Now it was not the intent of our Rabbis to say that the man expressly told him, "They have departed hence from any feeling of brotherhood, and they have gone to stir up charges and pretexts against you," for if so, he would have avoided going there and would not have endangered himself. Instead, their intent is to say that "the man" – Gabriel[61] – who told it to him told the truth, but he spoke words having a double meaning, both of them true. Joseph, however, did not grasp the hidden meaning therein, and he followed the obvious. He thus followed his brothers and found them in Dothan, as he had told him. The Rabbis expounded this on the basis of the fact that the "man" referred to was an angel, and if so, he knew where the brothers were. Why then did he not say, "They are in Dothan," instead of speaking as if he was in doubt, i.e., that he heard from them that they were going to Dothan but he does not know where they are at present. It is for this reason that they expounded the above Midrash concerning his words.

FOR I HEARD THEY ARE SAYING. "I heard that they were saying."[62] Similarly the expression, *Rebekah hears,*[63] means that she heard. It is possible that he is saying: "The shepherds have

(60) Proverbs 19:21. (61) So identified in Rashi (Verse 15), and the source thereof is Pirkei d'Rabbi Eliezer, Chapter 38. (62) Ramban's intent is to explain that the Hebrew *shamati omrim,* literally, "I heard they are saying," is as if it were written, *shamati shehayu omrim,* "I heard that they were saying," thus referring to a past event. (63) Above, 27:5.

gone from here for I heard people saying, [64] 'Let us go to Dothan.' Perhaps they were your brothers." The man thus spoke with him as if he were avoiding the subject.

18. AND THEY CONSPIRED AGAINST HIM TO SLAY HIM. They thought to kill him with their subtle intrigues by which they had conspired against him before he drew near to them [65] so that they would not have to spill his blood with their own hands. Thus did the Rabbis say in Bereshith Rabbah: [66] "Let us set the dogs against him." And perhaps they did so but did not succeed. Now, when they saw that he was approaching them and they could not kill him with their intrigues, they said to each other, "Behold, he has come to us, so let us kill him ourselves."

20. AND WE SHALL SEE WHAT WILL BECOME OF HIS DREAMS. This is a derisive metaphor: "We shall see after his death if we shall prostrate ourselves before him."

The correct interpretation appears to me to be that they said, "Now we shall see *what will become of his dreams,* for if he shall be rescued from our hands he will surely reign over us." But our Rabbis said: [66] "It is the *Ruach Hakodesh* [67] that says, *We shall see what will become of his dreams,*[68] as if to say; 'We shall see *whose words shall stand, Mine or theirs.*' "[69]

22. SHED NO BLOOD. Reuben said to them: "I would have been tolerant of you when you thought to kill him by your subtle intrigues, for I too hated him and desired that he be killed by others. But do not spill blood with your hands. Far it be from you!" And Reuben's intent in all this was to rescue him and restore him to his father. Now Scripture relates that which Reuben told them when they paid heed to him. However, originally he told them other

(64) According to this interpretation, Gabriel spoke concerning people in general as if he did not recognize that these shepherds were his brothers. (65) According to Tur this refers to attempting to kill him with arrows. (66) 84:13. (67) See *Seder Toldoth,* Note 90. (68) The intent is to say that it is the *Ruach Hakodesh* which completes the sentence, and not Joseph's brothers. (69) Jeremiah 44:28.

things which they did not accept, as he said to them afterwards, *Spoke I not unto you, saying: Do not sin against the child and you would not hear?*[70] Now when he saw that they would not listen to the extent of releasing him, he said to them, "If so, *shed no blood* with your own hands."

Now Reuben did not say, "Shed not *his* blood," [but instead, he said, "*Shed no blood,*"] in order to make it appear that he is not saying it because he loves him, but in order that they should not spill blood. Thus he taught them that the punishment of he who indirectly causes death is not as great as that of he who personally spills blood.

The meaning of the expression, *This pit that is in the wilderness,* is that this pit is deep and he will not be able to get out of it, and it is in the desert, and if he cries for help there is no one to rescue him as no one passes by there.

Now Scripture relates that the pit was empty and did not contain water.[71] Had there been water in it they would not have drowned him as they had already avoided spilling his blood. Now Rashi writes: "Since it states that *the pit was empty,* do I not know that there was no water in it? Why then does it say that *there was no water in it?* It means to state that water indeed was not in it, however it did contain serpents and scorpions." This is Rashi's language quoting from the words of our Rabbis.[72] If so, the serpents and scorpions must have been in the cracks of the pit, or it was deep and they did not know about them. Had they seen them and known that they did not harm Joseph, it would have become clear to them that a great miracle had been done to him, and that he was indeed a perfectly righteous man. They would then have known that his merits would save him from all evil, and how would they touch the anointed one of G-d in whom He delights and whom He saves, even as it says, *My G-d hath sent His angel, and hath shut the lions' mouths, and they have not hurt me; for as much as before Him innocency was found in me.*[73] But, we must therefore conclude, they did not know anything about it.

(70) Further, 42:22. (71) Verse 24 here. (72) Shabbath 27 a. (73) Daniel 6:23.

In line with the simple meaning of the verse, it states that the pit was empty and completely devoid of water, for even if there were a little water in it, it would still be called "empty."[74] Similarly, *For thou shalt die and not live,*[75] which means "not live at all, under any circumstances." Such redundancies are all for the purpose of clarification and emphasis.

25. AND, BEHOLD, A CARAVAN OF ISHMAELITES CAME FROM GILEAD. When they looked up and saw at a distance men approaching from the direction of Gilead,[76] they recognized them as a camel caravan of Ishmaelites on their way to Egypt, for it was from Gilead that balms and spices came, and it was their custom to bring it to Egypt. This was why Judah said to them, "Behold these men come from afar and are travelling to a distant country. Let us sell him to them so that the matter should not become known." And when they came near they discovered them to be merchants of spices and balms – *Midianites, merchantmen*[77] – who had hired the camels from the Ishmaelites. They sold Joseph to the Midianites who purchased him for profit, but the company of Ishmaelites, the lessors of the camels, would not purchase him for their own investment purposes. The verse which states, *And they sold Joseph to the Ishmaelites,*[77] means that it was to them that the Midianites who bought him turned him over, for they were the ones who transported the merchandise to Egypt. This is also the meaning of the verse, *From the hand of the Ishmaelites, that had brought him down thither,*[78] for he was in their care. But the Midianites were his masters, and they made trade with him. This is the sense of the verse, *And the Midianites sold him to Egypt.*[79]

All stories in Scripture are written in this manner: sometimes it is told in the name of the authority who commands that it be

(74) Therefore, the verse specifies that *there was no water in it* to indicate that there was no water at all in it. (75) II Kings 20:1. (76) Ramban's intent is to explain why Scripture refers to these men first as Ishmaelites, then as Midianites (Verse 28), and again as Ishmaelites (*ibid.*), and finally as Midianites (Verse 36). (77) Verse 28 here. (78) 39:1. (79) Verse 36 here.

done, and other times in the name of the agent who performs the act. Such a case is the verse, *All the great work of the Eternal which He did,* [80] while elsewhere it states, *Which Moses did in the sight of all Israel.*[81] Similarly it says, *Thus all the work that king Solomon did in the house of the Eternal was finished,*[82] but it was Hiram that did it, as it is written, *And he came to king Solomon, and wrought all his work.* [83] In the case of Joseph himself, the verse says, *And whatsoever they did there, he was the doer of it,* [84] thus ascribing the action both to he who commanded it and the one who did it.

Rabbi Abraham ibn Ezra says that the Midianites are called Ishmaelites, just as Scripture, in speaking of Midianite kings, says, *Because they were Ishmaelites.* [85] But the matter is not as Ibn Ezra considered it to be since the verse which states, *For they had golden ear-rings, because they were Ishmaelites,* [85] alludes to "the children of the east" whose war it was, as it is written, *Now all the Midianites and Amalekites and the children of the east assembled themselves together,* [86] and "the children of the east" are Ishmaelites, for concerning all the sons of the concubines that Abraham had, it is said, *And he sent them away from Isaac his son, while he yet lived, eastward, unto the east country.* [87] It is also possible that the kings were Ishmaelites who ruled over Midian. Otherwise, why should "kings of Midian" [88] be called by the name of Ishmael their brother?

In line with the literal sense of Scripture the correct interpretation concerning the sale of Joseph is as we have said. But our Rabbis have said [89] that he was sold several times [and have thereby explained why his captors are alternately referred to as Midianites and Ishmaelites].

26 AND WE SHALL CONCEAL HIS BLOOD. "We shall hide the fact of his death." This is Rashi's language. And Onkelos similarly says, "and we shall cover up his blood."

(80) Deuteronomy 11:7. (81) *Ibid.*, 34:12. (82) I Kings 7:51. (83) *Ibid.*, Verse 14. (84) Further, 39:22. (85) Judges 8:24. (86) *Ibid.*, 6:33. (87) Above, 25:6. (88) Judges 8:26. (89) Bereshith Rabbah 84:2.

The correct interpretation is as its literal sense indicates. It is the custom of those who kill in secret to slay the victim, bury him, and conceal his blood in the earth, even as it says, *And he hid him in the sand.*[90] This was why Judah said to them, "By casting him into the pit we shall kill our brother and cover his blood with dust, for it will so be accounted to us."[91]

Now Reuben had instructed them not to spill blood with their hands. Rather, they should throw him into the pit and let him perish there, since the punishment of he who causes bloodshed is not the same as the punishment of one who actually commits the murder. Judah now came and said, "This too will be accounted to us as murder, as if we had killed him." Such indeed is the truth, as the verse says, *And him* [Uriah] *thou hast slain with the sword of the children of Ammon.*[92] The difference between actual murder and causing death is that there is a greater punishment for a murderer and a lesser punishment for the one who indirectly causes death. Thus, the two of them [Reuben and Judah] spoke the truth.

32. AND THEY SENT THE COAT OF MANY COLORS, AND THEY BROUGHT IT TO THEIR FATHER. I.e., by command.[93] Perhaps the word *vayavi'u* (and they brought) refers to the messengers who brought the coat, for the brothers dispatched it when they were still in Dothan, and it was the messengers who said, *This we have found; recognize now.* It may be that they sent the coat to Hebron, to one of their homes, and when they arrived they brought it before their father, and said to him, *This we have found.* They did all of this in order to feign ignorance of the matter, for had they remained quiet, he would have suspected them, saying; "You killed him," for he knew that they were jealous of him.

(90) Exodus 2:12. (91) Judah was arguing against throwing him into the pit, for this act would also be accounted to them as murder. This explanation is developed further on in the text. (92) II Samuel 12:9. (93) Ramban's intent is to resolve the following difficulty: The verse, *And they sent the coat of many colors,* clearly indicates that they did not bring it themselves. Ramban answers that the second half of the verse means that they commanded others to bring the coat to their father.

And some scholars[94] explain the word *vayeshalchu* – ordinarily translated as "and they sent" – to mean that they pierced the coat with a sword in order to tear it in many places, to give the appearance of having been torn by the teeth of animals. The word *vayeshalchu* would thus be derived from the verse, *By the sword ('b'shelach') they shall perish.*[95] The significance of the word *hapasim* (many colors) is that they sent him the coat so that he might recognize it by the colors which he had made for him.

35. AND ALL HIS DAUGHTERS. This refers to his daughter and his son's daughter.[96] Now it is possible that his daughters-in-law are also included in this category, for in Scripture they too are called "daughters," or as the saying of the Sages has it:[97] "A person does not refrain from calling his daughters-in-law 'daughters.'" So did Naomi say to her daughters-in-law: *Go, turn back, my daughters;*[98] *Nay, my daughters;*[99] *Go, my daughter.*[100] It is nothing but an expression of love, just as, *Hearest thou not, my daughter?*[101]

36. OFFICER OF 'HATABACHIM.' This means the slaughterers of the king's animals. This is the language of Rashi. Similarly, it says, *And the 'tabach' (cook) took up the thigh;*[102] *For perfumers and for cooks 'tabachoth'.*[103]

Closer to the meaning of the word *hatabachim* is the opinion of Onkelos who says that since the prison house was under his charge, [he was called the officer of the *tabachim,* since] we find the word *t'vichah* in connection with the killing of people. *Prepare ye the slaughter ('matbiach') for his children;*[104] *Thou hast slaughtered ('tavachta') unsparingly.*[105] The verse in the book of

(94) Mentioned in R'dak in the name of "some" scholars. (95) Job 36:12. (96) Since Jacob had only one daughter, Dinah, the expression "and his daughters" in the plural must include some other person. Ramban first suggests that the term includes his granddaughter, Serach the daughter of Asher. See also my Hebrew commentary, pp. 211-2. (97) Bereshith Rabbah 84:19. (98) Ruth 1:8 and 12. (99) *Ibid.*, Verse 13. (100) *Ibid.*, 2:2. (101) *Ibid.*, Verse 8. This was said by Boaz to Ruth and can certainly not indicate the relationship of daughter or daughter-in-law. (102) I Samuel 9:24. (103) *Ibid.*, 8:13. (104) Isaiah 14:21. (105) Lamentations 2:21.

Daniel is proof of the validity of Onkelos' interpretation: *To Arioch the captain of 'tabachaya' of the king, who was gone forth to slay the wise men of Babylon.* [106]

38 2. A DAUGHTER OF A CERTAIN CANAANITE. [In translating "Canaanite," Onkelos said "merchant." That is to say, a merchantman who came to dwell in the land of Canaan for business reasons. His intent is to say that Jacob's sons guarded themselves from marrying Canaanitish women, as Isaac and Abraham, their fathers, had commanded. [107] And thus did the Sages mention in the *Gemara* of Tractate Pesachim. [108] They took as wives women from Egypt, Ammon, Moab, and from the noble families of the children of Ishmael and the sons of Keturah. It is for this reason that Scripture singles out Shaul, the son of Simeon, as the son of a Canaanitish woman, [109] as he was the only one among them. And even there the Rabbis expounded [110] that the reference is to Dinah who had relations with a Canaanite [Shechem].

Our Rabbis, however, have differed in this matter. Thus they have said: [111] "Rabbi Yehudah says, 'Twin sisters were born with each of Jacob's sons, and they took them as wives.' Rabbi Nechemyah says, 'Their wives were Canaanitish women.' " It is possible that Rabbi Nechemyah was not particular about [the term "Canaanitish" and did not mean it to indicate] their genealogy. He meant to say only that they took women from the land of Canaan as wives. However, they were from among the strangers and the sojourners who had come there from all lands, either Ammonite or Moabite women, and other peoples. His purpose [112] was only to differ with Rabbi Yehudah and say that they did not marry their sisters, since a maternal sister is forbidden to the sons of Noah. But according to Rabbi Yehudah it will be necessary to

(106) Daniel 2:14. The word *tabachaya* or *tabachim* is thus clearly associated with the slaying of people. See my Hebrew commentary, Note 77, pp. 211-212. (107) Above, 28:1. 24:3. (108) Pesachim 50 a. (109) Further, 46:10. (110) Bereshith Rabbah 80:10. (111) *Ibid.*, 84:19. (112) Ramban is pointing out that Rabbi Nechemyah agrees with the Talmudic sages who said that Jacob's sons did not marry Canaanitish women. See Note 108.

say that the sons of Leah married the twin sisters of the six other brothers, [113] and they in turn wed the twin sisters of the sons of Leah. It may be that Rabbi Nechemyah does not at all admit the existence of these twins, with Jacob not having any daughter other than Dinah, as the literal interpretation of Scripture would indicate.

It is not logically correct to say that they all married Canaanitish women since there would then have been descendants of Canaan, the accursed servant, among those who inherited the land, just as there were representatives of the seed of Abraham, and Scripture has commanded that he be destroyed until neither remnant nor survivor remain.

In any case, [114] this man [the Canaanite referred to here] was a merchant, for why should Scripture find it necessary to state that he was a Canaanite by descent when all people of the land were Canaanites, of the Perizzites and Jebusites and their brothers, as all of these traced their genealogy to Canaan? Adullam, [from where this man came] furthermore, was in the land of Canaan. [115] It would then have been proper for the verse to say: "And Judah took there a wife with such-and-such a name," just as it mentions the names of the women in the case of Tamar, and Esau's wives, [116] and others. But the true explanation is that he was a merchant, not of the land of Canaan, which belonged to the Hivite or the Amorite. This then is the meaning of the verse: *And Judah saw there a daughter of a certain Canaanite,* implying that he married her on account of her father. [117] And concerning the verse

(113) This is because "the sons of Noah" were forbidden to marry a maternal sister. Prior to the giving of the Torah on Sinai, our ancestors had the status of *b'nei Noach* (sons of Noah). Consequently they could marry a paternal sister but not a maternal sister. See Sanhedrin 58 a; Rambam, Hilchoth Melachim 9:5. (114) I.e., whatever the correct opinion be in the matter discussed above. (115) In Joshua 12:15, the king of Adullam is mentioned among the kings of Canaan. Thus if the word "Canaanite" is to be understood literally, why should Scripture have even mentioned it? (116) Above, 26:34. (117) This is implied in the expression, *And he saw there,* meaning that he saw a man there who was not of the regular community. The word "Canaanite" must therefore mean merchant, for they were all Canaanites, and if "Canaanite" were to refer to his genealogy it would not be significant enough to be mentioned.

which states, *The sons of Judah: Er, and Onan, and Shelah; which three were born unto him of Bath-shua the Canaanitess,* [118] this is due to the fact that being the daughter of the man called "the Canaanite," she was also so called, since this man was called "the merchant" by them as he was known for, and expert in, his trade, on account of which he settled there.

Rabbi Abraham ibn Ezra says [119] that because this woman was a Canaanitess, and Judah had transgressed the opinion of his fathers, her children were evil and they died. And this is why concerning Shaul, [109] Scripture mentions only that he was the son of a Canaanitish woman, but with respect to Shelah the son of Judah it was not necessary for Scripture to mention it [120] [when enumerating the descendants of Jacob who entered Egypt].

If so, [121] the expression, *And Judah saw there a daughter,* would mean that he saw her and desired her, even as it says of Samson, *And he saw a woman in Timnah.* [122] And in the *Parshah* of *Vayechi Yaakov,* Rashi wrote: *"And his sons bore him,* [123] but not his sons' sons. For thus indeed did Jacob command them; 'My bier shall not be borne by any of your sons since they are children of Canaanitish women.' " [124]

It may be that, according to Rashi, Jacob said this of Shaul the son of Simeon, and Shelah the son of Judah, who were of the daughters of Canaan, and therefore Jacob excluded all the other [grandsons although their mothers were not Canaanitish]. However, in all of our texts of Bereshith Rabbah [125] we find this version: "My bier shall not be borne by any of your sons' sons, as

(118) I Chronicles 2:3. This would seem to indicate that she was indeed a Canaanitess. (119) In his commentary on Genesis 46:10. (120) Since it is so stated in this present chapter. Shaul, on the other hand, was not mentioned above. Hence in mentioning the seventy souls, it states that he was of a Canaanitish woman (46:10). These are the words of Ibn Ezra, and Ramban now proceeds to comment upon them. (121) If Judah, according to Ibn Ezra, went against the command of Abraham and Isaac. (122) Judges 14:1. (123) Further, 50:13. (124) Now this text of Rashi would apparently contradict the opinion of Ibn Ezra who states that only Shaul the son of Simeon, and Shelah the son of Judah, were born of Canaanitish women. Ramban, however, proceeds to reconcile the position of Rashi with that of Ibn Ezra. (125) Mentioned in Yalkut Shimoni 161.

there is among them of the daughters of Canaan."[126] Tamar likewise was the daughter of one of the strangers living in the land, not the daughter of a man who was a Canaanite by descent. Far be it that our lord David [127] and the Messiah our just one, who will speedily reveal himself to us, be of the seed of Canaan, the accursed servant. Our Rabbis have also said [128] concerning Tamar that she was the daughter of Shem, of whom it is said, *And he was a priest of the most high G-d.*[129]

3. AND HE CALLED HIS NAME ER. Judah called his son Er, said name being derived from the expression, *Stir up ('Or'rah') Thy might.* [130] His wife called the name of the second son Onan,[131] but Scripture does not relate the reason for this name. Now it is possible that she experienced difficult labor, for it is customary for women to name their children after such an experience, as did the mother of Jabez who so named him, *saying: Because I bore him with pain.* [132] And so did Atarah, the mother of Onam, [133] [call him by the name Onam on account of her difficult labor], the name being derived from the expression, *And the people were 'k'mithon'nim' (as murmurers);* [134] *Wherefore doth a living man 'yithonen' (complain)?* [135] This is similar in expression to *ben oni* (the son of my sorrow) [136] mentioned in the case of Rachel. Judah was not particular about changing Onan's name as his father Jacob had done. [136]

In Bereshith Rabbah[137] our Rabbis said, by way of explaining the name Er, that he was destined to be thrown off (*she'hu'ar*)

(126) The Midrash there concludes: "For it is said, *And Shaul the son of a Canaanitish woman* (46:10)." Thus it is clear from this Midrash that only Shaul was born of a Canaanitish woman, but not Shelah the son of Judah. (127) He was a descendant of Tamar and Judah through Peretz, who was the ancestor of David. See Ruth 4:15-22. (128) Bereshith Rabbah 85:11. (129) Above, 14:18. (130) Psalms 80:3. (131) A word which suggests grief and mourning. Ramban makes the point that the name Judah chose for his son can easily be surmised, as it suggests strength. But why his wife should choose a name like "Onan" is not indicated. (132) I Chronicles 4:9. The name "Yavetz" contains the Hebrew letters of *atzev* (pain). (133) *Ibid.*, 2:26. (134) Numbers 11:1. (135) Lamentations 3:39. (136) Above, 35:18. (137) 85:5.

from the world.[138] Now this is not to say that such was Judah's intent. However, the Rabbis made their exposition since the names indicate the future.

5. AND SHE CALLED HIS NAME SHELAH, AND HE [Judah] WAS AT CHEZIB, WHEN SHE BORE HIM. Rashi wrote: "I am of the opinion that because it was there that she ceased bearing children, the place was called *Chezib* (deceit). It is similar in expression to the verse, *Wilt thou indeed be unto me as a deceitful ('achzav') brook.*[139] If this be not so, what is the verse teaching us by mentioning that Judah was in Chezib?"

Now I do not know why a place should be named for that reason, [i.e., because there she ceased bearing children], there being nothing outstanding in such an event as three sons were sufficient for her.[140] Moreover, at the time she gave birth to the third son it was not yet known whether she had ceased bearing or would give birth afterwards. Only at the time of her demise did it become established [that she had ceased bearing with the third son].[141]

Now some scholars[142] say that it was their custom for the father to name the firstborn, and the mother the second one. It is for this reason that Scripture states concerning the first son, *And he called his name,*[143] and concerning the second one, *And she called.*[144] Now concerning the third son, [the naming of whom was the father's prerogative, Scripture nevertheless] says, *And she called,* explaining that this was because Judah was in Chezib when she gave birth to him, and he was not there to name him. This interpretation lacks rhyme or reason.

(138) Since, as Scripture relates, he died on account of his sin. (Verse 7, and see Ramban there.) (139) Jeremiah 15:18. (140) Had she been barren that would be a tragedy of some significance. (141) Why then would the place have been called Chezib at the time she gave birth to the third son? (142) R'dak in his commentary. Also in Da'ath Z'keinim ba'alei Tosafoth. (143) Verse 3 here. (144) Verse 4 here.

In the opinion of Rabbi Abraham ibn Ezra Scripture relates where they were born; the statement, *when she bore 'him,'* is as if it had said 'them,' as all three sons were born in one place.

In my opinion, the name Shelah is an expression meaning a thing which stops and deceives. Thus, *do not 'thashleh' (deceive) me,* [145] which the Targum there renders as, "Let not your word deceive your handmaid." Perhaps it is related to the concept of error, for he who commits an error deceives his thinking. Thus Scripture is saying that she called him Shelah, [a word which is traceable to the root of the Hebrew word meaning 'error,'] because of the name of the place, as *he was in Chezib* – [a word which means 'deceive'] – *when she bore him.* And [the word *v'hayah* (and he was), although it should really be saying, *v'haytha,* (and *she* was), is identical with the expression *'V'hayah hana'arah'* (And the damsel shall be). [146] This is the intent of the saying of the Rabbis in Bereshith Rabbah: [137] "Paskath was the name of the place." [147]

7. AND ER, JUDAH'S FIRSTBORN, WAS WICKED IN THE SIGHT OF THE ETERNAL. Scripture does not specify the nature of his wickedness as it did in the case of his brother.[148] Instead, it simply states that he died for his own sin. It informs us that this was not by way of punishment of Judah for his role in the sale of Joseph, since the saving of Joseph's life by Judah compensated for his role in the sale. There was no case of death of a child in the house of the patriarchs except this one who *was wicked in the sight of the Eternal,* since the race of the righteous is blessed. This is why Jacob mourned many days for his son Joseph, *and he refused to comfort himself,* [149] for he considered this to be a great punishment to himself, quite apart from his love for him.

(145) II Kings 4:28. (146) Above, 24:14. There, too, it should be saying, *v'haytha hana'arah* in the feminine, except that the word *v'haya* does not refer to *na'arah* but to the event itself and is therefore to be understood as: "And it shall come to pass that the damsel, etc." Here, likewise, it is to be so understood. (147) This contradicts the opinion of Rashi, who maintains that it was the mother who named the place Chezib because she ceased bearing children. (148) Verse 9 here. (149) Above, 37:34-35.

8. AND MARRY HER AS BROTHER-IN-LAW, AND RAISE SEED TO THY BROTHER. The son will be called by the name of the deceased. This is Rashi's language.

But this is not true, for in the same commandment of the Torah it likewise says, *And it shall be, that the firstborn that she beareth shall succeed in the name of his brother that is dead, that his name be not blotted out of Israel,* [150] and yet the brother-in-law is not commanded to call his son by the name of his dead brother.[151] In the case of Boaz it says, *Moreover Ruth the Moabitess, the wife of Machlon, have I acquired to be my wife, to raise up the name of the dead upon his inheritance, that the name of the dead be not cut off from among his brethren, and from the gate of his place,* [152] and yet she called him Obed,[153] not Machlon. Moreover, it says here, *And Onan knew that the seed would not be his.* [154] Now what misfortune would have befallen him – to the point that he wasted his seed from before her – if his son was to be called by the name of his dead brother? Most people even desire to do so. Again, Scripture does not say, "And Onan said," but instead it says, *And Onan 'knew' that the seed would not be his.* [154] This would indicate that Onan had some definite kind of knowledge in this matter which made him certain *that the seed would not be his.*[154]

The subject is indeed one of the great secrets of the Torah,[155] concerning human reproduction, and it is evident to those observers who *have eyes to see, and ears to hear.*[156] The ancient wise men who were prior to the Torah knew of the great benefit in marrying a childless dead brother's wife, and that it was proper for the brother to take precedence in the matter, and upon his failure to do so, his next of kin would come after him, for any kinsman who was related to him, who would inherit his legacy, would derive a benefit from such a marriage. And it was customary for the dead man's wife to be wed by the brother or father or the

(150) Deuteronomy 25:6. (151) Yebamoth 24 a. (152) Ruth 4:10. (153) *Ibid.*, Verse 21. (154) Verse 9 here. (155) Ramban here hints to the mystic doctrine of the transmigration of souls. Onan "knew" that when he married his brother's wife his brother's soul would become incarnate in his son. Therefore Onan did not consider the child to be his own. See my Hebrew commentary, pp. 214-5. (156) Deuteronomy 29:3.

next of kin in the family. We do not know whether this was an ancient custom preceding Judah's era. In Bereshith Rabbah[157] they say that Judah was the one who inaugurated the commandment of marrying a childless person's widow, for since he had received the secret [155] from his ancestors he was quick to fulfill it. Now when the Torah came and prohibited marrying former wives of certain relatives, it was the will of the Holy One, blessed be He, to abrogate the prohibition against marrying a brother's wife in case he dies childless, but it was not His will that the prohibition against marrying a father's brother's wife or a son's wife or similar wives of relatives be set aside. It was only in the case of a brother that the custom had established itself, [158] and the benefit is likely with him and not with the others, [159] as I have mentioned. Now it was considered a matter of great cruelty when a brother did not want to marry his dead brother's wife, and they would call it *the house of him that had his shoe loosed,*[160] for [after his dead brother's wife had performed *Chalitzah* (the loosening of the shoe) of the brother-in-law], he[161] was now removed from them, and it is fitting that this commandment be fulfilled through the loosening of the shoe. Now the ancient wise men of Israel, having knowledge of this important matter, established it as a custom to be practised among all those inheriting the legacy, providing there is no prohibition against the marriage, and they called it *Ge'ulah* (Redemption).[162] This was the matter concerning Boaz, and the meaning of the words of Naomi and the women neighbors.[163] The man of insight [164] will understand.

(157) 85:6. (158) Prior to the giving of the Torah. (159) Ramban's intent is that when two brothers come from one father, the soul of the dead one finds closer identification with the child that his brother will beget rather than with that of any of the other relatives. (Abarbanel; see my Hebrew commentary, p. 215). (160) Deuteronomy 25:10. (161) The soul of the dead brother. The Cabala has considered the subject of Chalitzah, as one of profound mystery. (162) Ruth 4:7. (163) Reference is to what the neighbors said; *There is a son born to Naomi* (Ruth 4:17), meaning that she was thereby given back the son Machlon whom she had lost. This explains why the women did not say, "There is a son born to Ruth or Boaz." (164) A term denoting the student of the Cabala, the mystic doctrine of the Torah.

11. ABIDE A WIDOW AT THY FATHER'S HOUSE. The meaning thereof is that "you should conduct yourself there as a widow until Shelah be grown up." He suggested to her: "Place yourself in mourning, put on mourning garments, do not anoint yourself with oil, as a woman *girded with sack-cloth for the bridegroom of her youth,*[165] until Shelah be grown up and he will marry you." Such was the custom of a widow waiting to be married: she who desires to be married to a stranger wears mourning garments only for a short period as is the custom, and then feigning comfort arrays herself in scarlet. *And she covered herself with a veil,* [166] until she be married to a man.

FOR HE SAID, LEST HE ALSO DIE, LIKE HIS BRETHREN. That is to say, he dismissed her with a paltry reply because he never intended to give her to him in marriage. *For he said, Lest he also die, like his brethren,* for she has established herself as one whose husbands die young. This is Rashi's Language.

Now I do not know why Judah, a ruler of his generation, should be shy towards this woman and not tell her, "Go in peace from my house," and why should he mislead her when she is even forbidden to Shelah, just as the Rabbis have said concerning a married woman: [167] "Twice establishes a presumption [that the woman is a *katlanith* — a woman whose husbands die]." However since Judah was angered by her harlotry to the extent of condemning her to be burned, it would appear that he originally did wish her to remain in his family. It is also unreasonable to say that Judah did not hear about how his children sinned against G-d, thus causing Him to deliver them into the hands of their fate, while Tamar was guiltless in their death.[168]

(165) Joel 1:8. (166) Verse 14 here. Ramban thus interprets the verse; *And she removed the garments of her widowhood, and covered herself with a veil,* as an indication that she was no longer mourning. See Ramban further, Verse 16. (167) Kethuboth 43:2. (168) Ramban thus raises two questions against Rashi's interpretation. It is obvious that Judah did care to have Tamar in the family, and as for her part in the death of Er and Onan, did not Judah hear how his sons had sinned against G-d, and that Tamar was guiltless?

The correct view appears to me to be that Shelah was fit for the marriage, but his father did not want him to marry Tamar while he was still a youth, lest he commit some sin with her as had his brothers who died young, for they were boys, none of them having attained twelve years [169] of age. His intention was that when he would mature and would listen to the instruction of his father, he would then give her to him as a wife. But when she had waited a long time and it appeared to her that Shelah had grown up – although in the eyes of his father he was still a boy as he was not yet ten years old and therefore his father was bent on waiting longer – then Tamar, in her craving to give birth from the sacred race, hastened and did this deed.

12. AND JUDAH, WENT UP UNTO HIS SHEEP-SHEARERS. He would go there continually to console himself after his wife's death so that he may turn his attention to the sheep *and forget his poverty.* [170] Now when it was told to Tamar that he goes up there daily without fail, she waited for him on one of those days. It may be that since Judah was prominent in the land, people would assemble there to make a feast at the time of the shearing, similar to a royal feast, and the poor would go there, and it was told to her before he went up there.

15. AND HE THOUGHT HER TO BE A HARLOT. This was because she was sitting at the cross-roads. *For she had covered her face,* and he could not see her. A Midrash of our Rabbis explains: *For she had covered her face,* i.e., that when she stayed in Judah's house, she had acted modestly, always covering her face, and therefore he did not suspect her. This is Rashi's language.

Now the Rabbi's [Rashi's] [171] literal interpretation is feasible since it was the way of the harlot to sit at the cross-roads, just as it is written, *And she sitteth at the door of her house, on a seat in the high places of the city, to call to them that pass by,* etc. [172]

(169) Seder Olam 2. See my Hebrew commentary, p. 216. (170) Proverbs 31:7. [and remember his trouble no more.] (171) See Note 139, *Seder Bereshith.* (172) Proverbs 9:14-15.

Accordingly, the verse states that because her face was veiled he did not recognize her. But according to the Midrash of our Rabbis which states that she covered her face in her father-in-law's house, meaning that she hid herself from him while being in his house and that he never saw her face, how would he recognize her even if she were not veiled?

It further appears to me to be correct, in line with the literal sense of Scripture, that the verse is stating that he thought her to be a harlot because her face was veiled, since afterwards it states, *For he knew not that she was his daughter-in-law.*[173] The reason for the covering of the face is that it was the way of the harlot to sit at the cross-roads wrapped up in a veil, with part of the face and hair uncovered, gesticulating with the eyes and lips, and baring the front of the throat and neck. Now since she would speak to the by-passer in an impudent manner, catching him and kissing him,[174] she therefore veiled part of the face. Furthermore, harlots sitting by the roadside veil their faces because they commit harlotry even with relatives. Sodomites still do it to this day in our countries, and when they return to the city they remain anonymous.

Thus we have learned in a Mishnah:[175] "There are three kinds of head-nets: that of a girl, which is susceptible to *midras*[176] uncleanness; that of an old woman, which is susceptible to the uncleanness of a corpse, while that of a *yotza'ath chutz,* [literally, 'she who goes outside'], is not susceptible to any uncleanness." Now a *yotzath chutz* refers to the harlot, the *nafkat bro* of Onkelos[177], who places the head-net on part of the head. It does

(173) Verse 16 here. This indicates that if her face were not veiled, he would have recognized her to be his daughter-in-law. This again is at odds with the Midrash which states that he never saw her face. (174) See Proverbs 7:13. (175) Keilim 24,16. (176) A term applied to the uncleanness conveyed by a *Zav* or *Zavah* – (see Leviticus 15:2-6; 25-26) – to an object which is used as a seat. An object not so used, but which serves as a garment or a container, is susceptible only to corpse-uncleanness (see Numbers 19:14-17). If it serves none of these purposes, it is not susceptible to any uncleanness. (177) Verse 15 here. This is the Aramaic form of the Hebrew term, *yotza'ath chutz* (she who goes outside).

not serve her the purpose of lying on it, for in that case it would be susceptible to *midras*-uncleanness.[176] Nor does she cover her head with it, for in that case it would be susceptible to corpse-uncleanness. Instead, she uses it to dress up the ends of her hair, in order that it be partly visible from beneath the net, and this is why it is not susceptible to any uncleanness.

18. THY SIGNET 'UP'THILECHA.' Onkelos renders it as "thy signet and thy cloak," meaning "the ring which you use as a seal, and the cloak with which you cover yourself." This is Rashi's language.

But it is not correct to say that he would give his cloak, and go away from her unclothed. And how is it that a cloak is called *p'thil* in the Hebrew language? And how can it be referred to later on as *p'thilim,*[178] in the plural? Now should you say that on account of its fringed strings (*p'thilim*), the garment was called *p'thil,* far be it that Judah should fulfill the Commandment of *Tzitzith* (Fringes),[179] yet treat it so lightly as to give it away in unchastity! Perhaps, he had with him a small scarf which he occasionally wound around part of the head, and which was called *p'thil* because it was short as a *p'thil* (fringe), and it is this which the Targum [Onkelos] rendered as *shashifa*, [which Rashi incorrectly took to mean "a cloak"]. Now you will not find that Onkelos will translate *simlah* (a garment) as *shashifa* wherever it is found in the Torah. Instead, he translates it throughout by a term denoting "cover" or "garment," excepting the verse, *And they shall spread the 'simlah'* (garment),[180] concerning which he says, "And they shall spread the *shashifa*," because this is the *sudar* referred to in the Talmud[181] through which virginity is established. So did Jonathan ben Uziel translate *hama'ataphoth*[182] (the mantlets) as *shashifa*, these being small scarfs which they wound around the head, and distinguished persons spread them over their bonnets and headbands. This custom still prevails in eastern countries.

(178) Verse 25 here. (179) See Numbers 15:38. (180) Deuteronomy 22:17. (181) Kethuboth 10 a: "Bring me the *sudar*." See also Ramban to Deuteronomy 22:17. (182) Isaiah 3:22.

It is further possible that Judah possessed a seal impressed with the form of a lion or some other known figure, as rulers do, and he also had fringes in his hand, woven in the same design, with which to stroll about, as well as a rod in his hand, as becomes a ruler or lord, even as it is written, *A strong rod, to be a sceptre to rule,*[183] and it is further written, *The sceptre shall not depart from Judah.*[184] It was these that he gave into Tamar's hand.

24. AND JUDAH SAID: BRING HER FORTH, AND LET HER BE BURNT! Ephraim Makshoah,[185] a disciple of Rabbi Meir, said in the name of Rabbi Meir: "Tamar was the daughter of Shem who was a priest.[186] They therefore sentenced her to be burnt."[187] Rashi quoted this Midrash but did not explain it. And I do not know this law, for a priest's daughter is not liable to be burned except for harlotry in conjunction with a binding relation to a husband, either espoused or married, as is explained in the *Gemara* in Tractate Sanhedrin.[188] However, a priest's daughter who is waiting to be married by a brother-in-law is not at all liable to death for harlotry. Whether she is an Israelite's daughter or a priest's daughter, her punishment is only that of having violated a simple negative precept.[189] And should you say that marrying a childless brother's wife was customary among the Sons of Noah, and that she was regarded by them as having the status of a married woman, and that their prohibitions were punishable by death, it would not be correct. The Rabbis say in Bereshith Rabbah[157] that Judah was the one who first inaugurated the observance of the commandment that a brother marry a childless brother's widow. And again, in the *Gemara* in Tractate Sanhedrin,[190] it is made clear that a childless brother's widow of the Sons of Noah is not at all liable to any punishment for harlotry.

(183) Ezekiel 19:14. (184) Further, 49:10. (185) There are two interpretations for the name 'Makshoah': (a) he was a watchman in a cucumber field (*kishuim*); (b) he was a scholar famous for his great ability in debate (*kasheh*). See Commentaries to Bereshith Rabbah 84:11. (186) See Ramban above, 14:18. (187) See Leviticus 21:9. (188) Sanhedrin 51 b. (189) This would be stripes, but not the death penalty. (190) Sanhedrin 58 a.

It appears to me that since Judah was a chief, an officer, and a ruler of the land, his daughter-in-law who committed harlotry against him was not judged by the same law as other people, but as one who degraded royalty. It is for this reason that it is written, *And Judah said: Bring her forth, and let her be burnt,* for the people came before him to do unto her in accordance with his command, and he declared her guilty of a capital crime because of the superior rank of royalty. Thus he judged her as if she had profaned her father in respect of his priesthood, but this was not the judgment meted out to commoners.

In line with the literal interpretation of Scripture, it is possible that their law was similar to that which is presently customary in some of the countries of Spain, i.e., that a married woman who commits a faithless act is turned over to her husband who decrees death or life for her, as he wishes. Now Tamar was designated for his son Shelah, and in the eyes of their laws she was considered as a married woman.

26. SHE IS RIGHTEOUS FROM ME. "*She is righteous* in her words. *From me* is she with child. Our Rabbis expounded that a *bath kol* (a Divine voice) came forth and said the word *mimeni*, i.e., 'From Me and from My authority did these events unfold.' " This is Rashi's language.

The correct interpretation is that it is similar to the verses: *Men more righteous and better than he;*[191] *And he* [Saul] *said to David, Thou art more righteous than I; for thou hast rendered unto me good, whereas I have rendered unto thee evil.*[192] Here too the meaning is: "She is more righteous than I, for she acted righteously and I am the one who sinned against her by not giving her my son Shelah." The purport of the statement is that Shelah was the brother-in-law, [hence he was the first designated to marry her], and if he did not wish to take her as his wife, his father is next in line to act as the redeemer, as I have explained above[193] when I discussed the law of marrying a childless brother's widow.

(191) I Kings 2:32. (192) I Samuel 24:18. (193) In Verse 8 here.

AND HE KNEW HER AGAIN NO MORE (*'v'lo yasaph'*). After having established progeny for his children, he did not wish to be with her again even though this was dependent upon his wish as she was not forbidden to him, being, in fact, considered as his wife, as is the law when the widow of a childless man has relations with a relative. This is the reason for the explanation given by a certain Sage,[194] who explains the verse as saying, "And he did not *cease* to know her,"[195] since here the expression used is, *v'lo yasaph,* and elsewhere it is written, *A great voice 'v'lo yasaph'.*[196]

29. HOW HAST THOU BURST FORTH? THIS BURSTING UPON THYSELF ('PARATZTA ALECHA'). "What a strong effort you have made!" thus the language of Rashi.

But the word *paretz,* wherever used, signifies the breaching of a fence and passing through, just as: *I will break down ('p'rotz') the fence thereof;*[197] *Why hast Thou broken down ('paratzta') her fences?*[198] And in the language of the Rabbis: "*Pirtzah* (a breach in a wall) calleth forth to the thief."[199] Indeed, the Sacred Language[200] uses the term *p'rotz* when referring to anything that oversteps its boundary: *And thou shalt break forth ('upharatzta') to the west, and to the east;*[201] *And the man broke forth ('vayiphrotz') exceedingly.*[202] It is for this reason that the verse here is saying, at the time that the first child drew back his hand, and this one hurriedly came out, "What great breach hast thou made in the fence in order to hurry out before him?" The verse

(194) Shmuel the Elder (Sotah 10 b). (195) Since Tamar did in fact become his legitimate wife, as explained above, he did not cease living with her. (196) Deuteronomy 5:19. Reference there is to the Divine Voice that came forth from Mount Sinai, concerning which Scripture says, *v'lo yasaph* [with a *kamatz*], meaning "and it did not cease," or "it did not diminish in strength," unlike the human voice which decreases and eventually stops completely. Here also the identical expression, *v'lo yasaph* [with a *patach*], means "and he did not cease." (197) Isaiah 5:5. (198) Psalms 80:13. (199) Sotah 26 a. (200) Hebrew. See Ramban on Exodus 30:13, as to why Hebrew is called "a sacred" language. (201) Above, 28:14. Here referring to the conquest of land. (202) *Ibid.*, 30:43. Here referring to an unusual increase in wealth. It is thus clear that the word *p'rotz* is used to refer to anything which breaks forth from its normal boundary.

says, *alecha* (upon thee), to indicate that 'the fence' was upon him, and he was imprisoned in it. The sense of the verse is thus: "What great breach did you take upon yourself to make in the fence, with the result that you came out of it?"

Rabbi Abraham ibn Ezra said in explanation of the verse: "*Mah paratzta*? What have you broken, in the manner of a man who makes a breach in a fence and exits through it, and now the responsibility for this breach is upon you." [203]

There is no point to this interpretation. In the Midrash of Rabbi Nechunya ben Hakaneh [204] there is mentioned a mystic principle in connection with the name of these children, Peretz and Zerach. Thus they said: "He was called *Zerach* (shining) on account of the sun which always shines, and *Peretz* (breaking) on account of the moon which is sometimes dismantled [205] and sometimes whole. Now was not Peretz the firstborn, and yet the sun is greater than the moon? [206] This presents no difficulty, for it does indeed say, *And he* [Zerach] *put out his hand,* [207] and it is further written, *And afterwards came out his brother.*" [208] Now according to their opinion, the moon is associated with the name Peretz on account of the kingdom of the House of David. [209] Peretz and Zerach were born twins since the moon functions by means of the sun. Thus Peretz is the twin of Zerach who gives forth the hand, while he [210] is the firstborn by virtue of the power of the Supreme One, as is said, *I also appoint him first-born.* [211] This is the purport of

(203) That is, "if in the process of your hurried exit you would have caused harm or death to your brother, you would have been held responsible." (204) Sefer Habahir, 196. See Note 42, *Seder Bereshith.* (205) Referring to the days when the moonlight decreases, and to the end of the month when its light completely disapppears. (206) In which case Zerach, whose name is symbolic of the sun, should have been the first born. (207) Verse 28 here. Thus Zerach was indeed the firstborn. (208) Verse 30 here, referring to Zerach. And the verse concludes; *that had the shining red thread upon his hand,* thus indicating the importance of his having put out his hand first. (209) Having gone through various periods of ascendancy and decline in its history, the kingdom of the House of David resembles the light of the moon which is constantly changing. (210) That is, Peretz. In other words, by putting forth his hand, Zerach indicated that the birthright was to have been his, but Peretz, by coming out first, indicated the consent of the Supreme One to his being appointed the firstborn. (211) Psalms 89:28.

the saying of the Sages with respect to the Sanctification of the Moon: "David King of Israel lives and exists."[212] The man learned [in the mystic teachings of the Cabala] will understand.

39 3. THAT THE ETERNAL WAS WITH HIM. The name of G-d was a familiar word in his mouth. This is Rashi's language. But it does not appear to be correct.[213] Instead, *And his lord saw that the Eternal was with him,* means that he saw that his endeavors were always more successful than that of anyone else, so he knew that success came to him from G-d. In a similar sense is the verse, *We have surely seen that the Eternal was with thee.*[214] Thus Joseph found favor in his lord's eyes, and he appointed him as his personal attendant and overseer of his house.

4. AND ALL THAT HE HAD HE GAVE INTO HIS HAND. I.e., to be overseer and officer in charge of all that he had in the house and in the field. Our Rabbis have a Midrash on this verse. Thus they say:[215] "He would whisper[216] whenever he entered and whenever he left. If his master said to him, 'Mix a hot drink,' it was hot immediately in Joseph's hands and if he said, 'Mix it lukewarm,' it was lukewarm. [Because he suspected Joseph of witchcraft, his master said to him,] 'What is this, Joseph? Bringing witchcraft to Egypt is like importing straw to Ofraim!'[217] How long did his master suspect him of practicing witchcraft? It was until he saw the Divine Presence standing over him. This is the meaning of the words, *And his lord saw that the Eternal was with him.*"[218]

(212) Rosh Hashanah 25 a. Ramban's meaning is that since the kingdom of David evolved from Peretz, and Peretz is symbolized by the moon, the Sages of the Talmud, when wishing to inform the Jews in other countries that the New Moon had appeared and been sanctified by the Great Court, would use this message: "David, king...." This they did in order to circumvent a prohibition by the Romans against transmitting news regarding the times set for the festivals. See Ramban above, 32:26. (213) For, according to Rashi, the text should have read: "that the name of the Eternal was familiar in his mouth" (214) Above 26:28. (215) Bereshith Rabbah 86:6. (216) His father's instructions. (*Ibid.*, Commentaries.) (217) "Straw to Ofraim" is the Midrashic equivalent of the present day expression, "coals to Newcastle." (218) Verse 3 here.

The point of this Midrash is that because his lord was an Egyptian who did not know the Eternal, the Sages in the Midrash said that when he saw Joseph's great success he suspected that it was done by witchcraft, as was the case with his countrymen, until he saw in a vision which was shown to him in a dream, or, when awake, in the form of a cloud of glory or the like, that his success came from the Supreme One. This was done in honor of the righteous Joseph.

6. SAVE THE BREAD WHICH HE DID EAT. In the words of our Rabbis, this is a refined expression which refers to his wife.[219]

Rabbi Abraham ibn Ezra said in interpretation of the verse that whatever Potiphar possessed was left in the hands of Joseph excepting the bread which he ate. This he did not even permit him to touch since he was a Hebrew. It was the customary behavior of the Egyptians towards the Hebrews that they not permit the Hebrews to touch their food, *because that is abhorrent to the Egyptians.*[220]

Possibly this is so. Perhaps the interpretation of the verse is that his lord did not know of Joseph taking anything from him save only the bread which Joseph ate, but no other pleasures as young people are wont to do. Nor did he gather wealth and property, just as it is said of David, *And I have found no fault in him since he fell unto me unto this day.*[221] Now the verse, *Having me, he knoweth not what is in the house,*[222] expresses another matter, namely, that he [Joseph's lord] did not trouble himself to know about anything inside the house. But the present verse, *Having him, he knew not aught,* is an expression of negation; he knew that nothing in the house is [taken by Joseph except the bread which he eats].[223]

AND JOSEPH WAS HANDSOME AND GOOD-LOOKING. The verse mentions this here in order to indicate that it was on account

(219) Bereshith Rabbah 86:7. (220) Further, 43:32. (221) I Samuel 29:3. (222) Verse 8 here. Joseph speaking to Potiphar's wife. (223) See my Hebrew commentary, pp. 219-220.

of his good looks that his master's wife cast her eyes upon him. And Rashi wrote that because he saw that he was ruler of the house, he began to eat and drink, and curl his hair, etc.[224]

8. BUT HE REFUSED, AND SAID UNTO HIS MASTER'S WIFE. Scripture relates that he refused to do her will even though she was his mistress, i.e., his master's wife, and he feared her, for he feared G-d more. This is the meaning of the expression, *unto his master's wife.*

9. AND I SHALL SIN AGAINST G-D. The Sons of Noah[225] were commanded concerning forbidden relations. This is Rashi's language.

This is correct. It is only due to the feminine lack of knowledge that he first told her that the act would constitute a betrayal of his master who trusted him, and following that he added that it also involves a sin against G-d.

It is possible to further explain the verse, *And I shall sin against G-d,* by this betrayal, since "it would be a matter of great evil consequence which would be accounted to me as a sin against G-d since His eyes are *upon the faithful of the land,*[226] and no traitor dare come before Him." Joseph spoke the truth. However he did not mention the prohibition of the illicit relation[227] because he spoke in language suitable to women.

10. TO LIE 'ETZLA' (BY HER). The meaning of this expression is as Rabbi Abraham ibn Ezra interpreted it: "even to lie near her, each in their garment, or to be with her for general conversation." This interpretation is correct since we do not find the word *etzla* (near her) in Scripture in connection with sexual intercourse, only the word *ima* (with her) or *othah* (with her), as for example: *Lie*

(224) "The Holy One, blessed be He, said to Joseph: 'Your father is mourning for you, and you curl your hair. I will incite a bear against you.'" (Rashi.) That is, "I shall let temptation loose against you." (225) See Note 113 above. (226) Psalms 101:6. (227) According to this interpretation.

'imi' (with me); [228] *And if any man lie 'othah' (with her);* [229] *And the women ravished ('tishachavnah').* [230]

12. AND HE LEFT HIS GARMENT IN HER HAND. Out of respect for his mistress he did not wish to take the garment from her hand with his superior strength, and he removed it from upon himself, as it was a garment which one wears as a robe and headdress. But when she saw that he left his garment in her hands she feared lest he expose her to the people of the household or his master, and so she preceded him to them, saying that he had removed his garment to lie with her, but "when he saw that I screamed he fled in confusion." This is the meaning of the verse, *And it came to pass, when she saw that he had left his garment in her hand.* [231] This is also why she did not say, "And he left his garment in my hand," but she instead told the men of her house and her husband, *And he left his garment 'etzli' (with me).* [232]

14. SEE, HE HATH BROUGHT IN A HEBREW UNTO US. The meaning thereof is that the Hebrews were hated by the Egyptians. They did not eat with them, this being a matter of abhorrence to them. [233] They did not purchase them as servants except as vinedressers and plowmen, but they would not permit them to come into their homes. This is why she said: "Behold, the master has done us evil by bringing a Hebrew into our home, and he has further appointed him as overseer and ruler, and now he has fittingly seen to mock us." [The point of her statement] is similar to that which is said in the verse, *He that delicately bringeth up his servant from a child shall have him become a master at the last.* [234] This is the meaning of her saying, *Whom thou hast brought unto us,* [235] as his being brought into their house was in itself embarassing to them.

(228) Verse 12 here. (229) Leviticus 15:24. (230) Zechariah 14:2. In *tishachavnah*, the plural form of *othah* is implicit. (231) Verse 13 here. (232) The word *etzli* (with me) indicates that he himself had removed his garment, as explained above. (233) See further, 43:32. (234) Proverbs 29:21. (235) Verse 17 here.

In the verse before us, the expression, *He has brought us,* refers to her husband. She does not mention him by name out of respect,[236] or perhaps because such is the ethical way for women to speak, or perhaps because it is known who brought Joseph into the house. Similarly, in many places in the book of Job it speaks of Almighty G-d anonymously because the conversants know that they are speaking of Him. Similarly, in the verse, *And he said to Abner, Why hast thou gone in unto my father's concubine?*[237] the name of the speaker is not mentioned, and no reference is made to him at all in the above verse because it is known that he was Ish-bosheth.[238]

19. AND IT CAME TO PASS, WHEN THE MASTER HEARD. She told him about it at the time of conjugal intimacy. *Matters such as these did your servant to me,* i.e., matters of intimacy such as these. So says Rashi.

So also did they say in Bereshith Rabbah:[239] "Rabbi Abahu said, 'She said it to him at the time of conjugal relations.' "

Now I wonder. Joseph's master was a castrate,[240] who had married his wife during his youth, and the Rabbis expounded, " *'Sris' (a captain of) Pharaoh*[241] – this teaches us that he bought Joseph for carnal purposes only, but the Holy One, blessed be He, caused Joseph's master to become castrated."[242] Moreover, how would she dare discredit herself and become loathsome in the eyes of her husband by telling him that she had committed adultery, whether by force or with acquiescence, which would have merited mortal punishment, for why did she not cry out at the outset, so that he should run away, as she did at the end? Now to the men of her house she said, *He came unto me to lie with me,*[243] but not that he lay with her, only that he came to do so, but she cried

(236) In view of the fact that she blames him for what happened. (237) II Samuel 3:7. (238) Of "the house of Saul," mentioned there in Verse 6. And it is already self-understood that the speaker in Verse 7 is Ish-bosheth, as he was the leader of the house of Saul. (R'dak.) (239) 87:10. (240) Sotah 13 b. (241) Above, 37:36. (242) The Hebrew word for castrate is *saris*, the same word mentioned in the verse above. (243) Verse 14 here.

out and he fled. And surely she would hide the matter from her husband. And should you say that she told him so in order that his anger be kindled against him and that he should kill him, [it would have been sufficient for this purpose that she say that he attempted to violate her, for] any servant that attempts to violate his master's wife deserves the death penalty!

It is possible that they intended to explain the expression, *Matters such as these,* as meaning matters of intimacy, meaning, exposing and caressing but not actual intimacy, as his master had become physically castrate, having been visited by a disease which resulted in a lack of desire for conjugal relations, as is the case with a *shachuf.* [244]

In line with the literal interpretation of Scripture there is no need for all this, for the Hebrew letter *kaph,* in the word *kadvarim,* is not for the purpose of expressing comparison to other matters. Instead its meaning is "these things." [245] A similar usage [of the letter *kaph* is found in these verses]: *And she told her mother's house 'kadvarim ha'eileh' (according to these words);* [246] *And when he had spoken unto me 'kadvarim ha'eileh' (according to these words) I set my face toward the ground.* [247] There are many similar verses. It may be that the verse is saying that when his master heard his wife's words which she told him – "Your servant did unto me such matters as these which I had immediately related to the men of the house" – then his anger was kindled.

It is possible that the *kaph* is here used for exaggeration, similar to its use in the verses: *Why speaketh my lord 'kadvarim ha'eileh' (such words as these)?* [248] *And there have befallen me such things as these ('ka'eileh')?* [249]

Now due to his master's love for Joseph he did not kill him, or it was a miracle of G-d, or knowing Joseph's righteousness, he doubted her words. Similarly the Rabbis said in Bereshith Rabbah: [250] "The master said to Joseph, 'I know this charge

(244) One whose genitals are atrophied. (245) I.e., only to indicate approximation, and here meaning: "matters as these, more or less." (246) Above, 24:28. (247) Daniel 10:15. (248) Further 44:7. (249) Leviticus 10:19. (250) Bereshith Rabbah 87:10.

against you is false, but lest a stigma fall on my children, [251] [I will put you in prison].' "

20. AND HE PUT HIM INTO PRISON, THE PLACE WHERE THE KING'S PRISONERS WERE BOUND. Rabbi Abraham ibn Ezra says that the verse itself explains that a *beth haso'ar* (prison) is "a place where the king's prisoners were bound." The reason this is stated in the verse itself is that *beth haso'ar* is an Egyptian word, for it is the style of Scripture to explain foreign words just as, *they cast pur, that is the lot.* [252]

This interpretation is of no significance. Rather, *And he put him into the prison,* means that he put him into a certain prison recognized as the royal prison, which was the place where the king's prisoners were bound. The sense of the verse is thus to state that this was the cause of the butler and the baker being imprisoned with him.

It is possible that the term, "the king's prisoners," means his servants and attendants who have sinned against him in matters of state, as other prisoners of the people sentenced by judges and officers were placed in another prison house. Scripture relates that they placed Joseph in the king's prison because of his master's love for Joseph, all of which was caused by G-d.

Linguists [253] explain *sohar* as an arched chamber, similar in expression to, *agan hasohar* (a round goblet). [254] In my opinion it is an underground house having a small opening above ground, through which the prisoners are lowered and from which they have light. The word *sohar* is thus derived from the word *sihara* (light) in Aramaic, just as in Hebrew, Scripture says; *A transparency ('tzohar') shalt thou make to the ark,* [255] the word *tzohar* being derived from *tzaharayim* (mid-day – when the light reaches its zenith). The difference between *tzohar* and *sohar* is that *tzohar* connotes an abundance of light, while *sohar* connotes minimal light.

(251) Lest people say; "Just as she was free with you, so she was with others, and the children she had are not his." (252) Esther 3:7. (253) Here referring to R'dak, who so writes in his Book of Roots, under the term *sohar.* (254) Song of Songs 7:3. (255) Above, 6:16.

40 2. AGAINST TWO 'SARISAV' (OF HIS EUNUCHS). These two lords were both castrates, for as they also acted as the chiefs of the butlers and bakers in the women's quarters in the royal apartments, the kings would customarily castrate them. Onkelos' opinion though is that *sarisim* means lords and chiefs. Thus he says of Potiphar, who is called *sris par'oh,*[241] "the officer of Pharaoh," and in the present verse he similarly translates, "against his two officers." And so did the Targum Yonathan translate: *And they shall be 'sarisim' in the palace of the king of Babylon.*[256]

5. EACH MAN ACCORDING TO THE INTERPRETATION OF HIS DREAM. The expression "interpreting dreams" means relating the events which will happen in the future, and he who foretells that future is called *potheir* (interpreter). In the opinion of many scholars the word *pithron* signifies "meaning."[257] And the interpretation of the verse, *Each man according to the interpretation of his dream,* is that each dreamed a dream consistent with the interpretation[258] which foretold the future that was to befall them. This is Rashi's language.

Now what sense does it make for Pharaoh's chief butler to say, "We have dreamed a dream consistent with the interpretation," thereby minimizing the wisdom of the interpreter. Besides, Pharaoh's dream [related later on] may not have been so, [that is, consistent with the interpretation], and Joseph would not know it.[259]

Rabbi Abraham ibn Ezra says in explanation of the verse that each saw in his dream the truth concerning the future as the interpretation would indicate, meaning that it was a true dream, not the kind which comes from many worries, of which only a part is fulfilled. This is the correct interpretation.

(256) II Kings 20:18. Yonathan translated this as: "And they shall be officers." (257) But it does not signify the foretelling of future events. (258) The butler dreamed of wine, the symbol of joy, while the baker dreamed of a bird snatching the food he was bringing to the king, an event which signifies grief. (Tur.) (259) Why then did he recommend Joseph as being able to interpret the king's dream? The king had not yet related his dream, and it could be that that dream might not be consistent with its interpretation, as was the case in his own dream. Why then did he not fear for his life in recommending Joseph to the king?

7. AND HE ASKED PHARAOH'S OFFICERS THAT WERE WITH HIM IN THE WARD OF HIS MASTER'S HOUSE. It would be proper for Scripture to say; "And he asked them, saying." Instead, Scripture speaks at length about it for its desire is to speak in praise of Joseph. Here is a servant lad who is enquiring of two great officers who are wards in the house of his master who hates him, [260] and each of whom could command his hanging. [261] Yet he was not afraid of them, and asked them their dreams and told them his opinion with respect to the interpretation because he trusted in his wisdom. Had the lord of the bakers been saved and restored to his position by the king, he would have hung him for his false interpretation.

8. AND THERE IS NO INTERPRETER OF IT. The meaning thereof is that "there is no one to inform us concerning the future which can be derived from the dream."

It is possible that they sent for some magicians in the morning, or that there were people with them in the prison, but no one could interpret it. It may be that they said; "There is no one in the world, in our opinion, who can interpret it, for it is very obscure."

DO NOT ('HALO') INTERPRETATIONS BELONG TO G-D? Rabbi Abraham ibn Ezra explained it as saying that "future events destined to come as indicated in dreams belong to G-d, for He alone brings on the dream and lets the future be known, and it is He *who makes peace, and creates evil,* [262] but in my speaking to you there is neither benefit nor loss." This he said so that they should not punish him if evil should befall them, or so that they should tell him the dreams and not scorn him. [263]

(260) "Who *hates* him." Ramban is here writing from the standpoint of the butler and the baker, who must have thought that Joseph's master imprisoned him because he hated him, not being aware, as explained above, that he did so to protect his family's reputation. (261) If his interpretation of the dreams would turn out to be incorrect. Thus, as explained further on by Ramban, if the baker had been restored to his position, he would have seen to it that Joseph pay for his mistake with his life. (262) Isaiah 45:7. (263) Thus far the comment of Rabbi ibn Ezra.

But if so, there is no sense for the word *halo* (do not) in this context.[264] Perhaps its meaning is the same as that of the word *hinei* (behold). Thus Joseph is saying, "Behold, to G-d alone belong interpretations, but not to man the interpreter."

In my opinion the correct interpretation is that Joseph is saying; "Do not interpretations of all dreams which are obscure and confined belong to G-d? He can make known the interpretation of your dreams. Now if it is obscure to you tell it to me; perhaps He will be pleased to reveal His secret to me."

10. AND IT WAS AS THOUGH IT BUDDED AND ITS BLOSSOM WENT UP. "It seemed as though it budded. *And it was as though it budded,* i.e., it seemed to me in my dream as though it budded, and after the bud its blossom shot up, and after that it brought forth the clusters and then the ripe grapes. Onkelos translates: 'And, when it buddeth, it brought forth sprouts.' These words are the translation of the word *porachath* alone."[265] Thus far the words of Rashi.

This is not correct. If he is speaking in terms of appearances because they are matters of a dream, he should say, "Behold, *like* a vine was before me, and on the vine *like* three shoots."[266] This *kaph* of comparison is found neither in the dream of the chief of the bakers nor in the dream of Pharaoh. Why then should the chief of butlers use the comparative form more than the others? Instead, in all three dreams it says *v'hinei* (and behold).[267] It is this word which indicates comparison, for its meaning is "as if."

(264) Since Joseph is stating it all in the affirmative; "dreams belong to G-d, etc." the interrogative form of the word *halo* is out of place. (265) The Hebrew states: *V'hi keporachath althah nitzah.* Rashi's intent, in quoting the Targum, is to say that Onkelos' words, *apeikath lavlevin* (brought forth sprouts), is an expression which Onkelos appended to his translation of the Hebrew word *porachath.* Ramban will later differ with this opinion, holding that it constitutes Onkelos' rendition of the Hebrew word *althah*, and signifies: "And it, when it budded, *immediately* brought forth sprouts." See below, Note 271. (266) Instead, Scripture states: "Behold, a vine was before me. And on the vine were three shoots."(Verses 9-10.) (267) Verse 9, in the dream of the butler; Verse 16, in the dream of the baker, and in Chapter 41, Verse 3, the word *v'hinei* is used in connection with Pharaoh's dream.

But the explanation of the verse before us, *And it was 'keporachath' its blossoms shot up,* is that he saw that immediately as it budded, its blossoms shot up and its clusters ripened into grapes. This was to indicate that G-d was hastening to do it. This is how Joseph recognized that the "three shoots" indicated three days, and not months or years, and he himself deduced that on the same day the two will be summoned before the king. It may be [that this was also indicated by the dreams] because both of them dreamed in one night. Thus there is no need for the words of Rabbi Abraham ibn Ezra, who says that Joseph knew of Pharaoh's birthday.

This usage of a *kaph* to indicate immediacy is found in many places: *And it came to pass, 'k'meishiv' (as he drew back) his hand;* [268] *'k'vo Avram' (as Abram came);* [269] *'uk'eith' (and at the time) of her death the women that stood by her said,* [270] and many others.

Onkelos' rendition into Aramaic stating, "And when it budded, it brought forth sprouts," [means to say that the expression "brought forth sprouts"] is a translation of the Hebrew word *althah,* meaning that it immediately brought forth sprouts of the vine. That is, as soon as it budded, it brought forth large sprouts, its blossoms shot up, and its clusters ripened into grapes. [271] Onkelos would not apply the word *althah* (shoot up) to *nitzah* (sprouts), as they do not "shoot up."

(268) Above, 38:29. (269) *Ibid.*, 12:14. (270) I Samuel 4:20. (271) Rashi is of the opinion that Onkelos' expression, *va'aneitzath neitz,* (not mentioned by Ramban, but appearing in the Targum, following *apeikath lavlevin,* mentioned above in Note 265), is the Aramaic equivalent of the Hebrew *althah nitzah.* Ramban however says that it is the translation only of the word *nitzah,* for *althah* (shoot up) could not refer to *nitzah* (sprouts). This is why, according to Ramban, Onkelos translated the word *althah* as *apeikath lavlevin* (it brought forth sprouts). In brief, according to Rashi's understanding of the Targum, the Hebrew *v'hi keporachath* is rendered by the Targum as *kad aphrachath apeikath lavlevin.* The Hebrew *althah nitzah* is rendered *va'aneitzath neitz.* In the opinion of Ramban, *v'hi keporachath* is rendered by the Targum as *kad aphrachath;* the Hebrew *althah* is rendered *apeikath lavlevin,* and the Hebrew *nitzah* has its equivalent in Onkelos' *va'aneitzath nitzah.*

14. BUT HAVE ME IN THY REMEMBRANCE. "If you will remember me when it will be well with you, I now pray for the kindness and truth you will do to me by making mention of me to Pharaoh." And if the word *na* [272] is to be understood as expressing supplication, the sense of the verse is: "If you will remember me and would, in your mercy, do me a kindness, I beg that you remember me to Pharaoh."

The sense of the word *itcha* (with thee) is that "you should remember to show me mercy in the very same way that it has been shown to you, i.e., that you went out from prison." The interpretation may be that "you should remember me in your heart as if I am with you."

The purport of mentioning him before Pharaoh is that he should praise him by saying, "Now in the house of the chief of the officers there is an excellent servant fit to enter the service of kings."

It further appears to me correct that Joseph is saying: "If you will remember me to be with you when all goes well with you and you return to your high position, and you should want to do me this kindness, then make mention of me to Pharaoh, saying to him, 'I remember a lad who served me in the prison; give him to me to be my servant.' *And bring me out of this house* for it is a great sin to those who retain me here."

It may be that the meaning of the expression, *And make mention of me to Pharaoh,* is that "Pharaoh saw me when I was a servant to his minister, in charge of all he had and performing my duties before him, [273] and if you will remember me before him you will bring about my release from here. I have committed no sin, and it is befitting the king to release me and thereby save me from the hands of my oppressors, for *there is no matter hid from the king* [274] if he desires."

(272) *V'asitha 'na' imadi chesed.* In the explanation above the Hebrew word *na* was understood in the sense of 'now': "If you will remember me then... I *now* pray for the kindness and truth you would show me." But according to the second interpretation, the word *na* is understood as supplication, as explained in the text. (273) Thus, the sense of the verse is to state that "all you need do is mention my name to Pharaoh, as he knows me already." (274) II Samuel 18:13.

15. THE LAND OF THE HEBREWS. This means the land of Hebron, wherein dwelt Abraham, Isaac, and Jacob. Abraham, the head of the lineage, was called "Abraham the Hebrew" [275] since he came from across the River Euphrates, and he was honored among the nations for in him was fulfilled the blessing, *And I will make thy name great.* [276] It is for this reason that all of his seed are called *Ivrim* (Hebrews). They hold on to this name in order not to intermingle with the various peoples in the Canaanite lands, and this name has been established as the name for all Israel's seed forever. This is the meaning of the verse, *He hath brought in a Hebrew unto us,* [277] since Joseph told them "I am a Hebrew," and he did not want them to take him as a Canaanite. And the land where they resided was called "the land of the Hebrews," that is to say, the land in which the Hebrews are. [278] It may be that it was so called because they were its leaders and nobles, even as it says, *Thou art a prince of G-d in the midst of us,* [279] and it is further written, *Touch not My anointed ones.* [280]

16. THAT THE INTERPRETATION WAS GOOD. Onkelos rendered it that he interpreted it well. A similar use is found in the verses: *Teach me fair discernment and knowledge;* [281] *That they were 'tovoth' (fair),* [282] which means "pretty." The intent of the verse is to state that this man [the lord of the bakers] had scorned Joseph, thinking of him as not ever knowing how to interpret the dream, and he would never have told him the dream had he not seen that he interpreted for his friend in a fair and proper manner. It may be that the verse is saying: "And the lord of the bakers saw that he gave a favorable interpretation to the lord of the butlers and he rejoiced. He then told him his own dream which had caused him more anguish than that of his friend."

BASKETS OF 'CHORI.' "Baskets made of peeled willows, made so that they have many holes." This is Rashi's language.

(275) Above, 14:13. (276) *Ibid.*, 12:1. (277) *Ibid.*, 39:14. (278) But not that it is theirs. (279) Above, 23:6. (280) Psalms 105:15. (281) *Ibid.*, 119:66. (282) Above, 6:2.

Rav Saadia Gaon [283] interpreted it as "baskets of white bread," white as befits the king's bread, with the word *chori* being derived from the Hebrew, *Neither shall his face now wax white ('yechvaru'),* [284] as well as from the Aramaic where the word *chivar* means "white." This is the correct interpretation, for all the baskets in the dream contained the king's bread, and in the uppermost basket there were all manner of baked goods for Pharaoh.

You find it similarly in the language of our Rabbis in the Mishnah: [285] "Large loaves and white cakes (*v'chivri*) [may be baked on a Festival Day]." And in the Jerusalem Talmud on this Mishnah: "The Rabbis [in discussing the permissibleness of baking extra fine white breads on the Festival Day even though they require more work than ordinary bread] derived the meaning of *chori* from this verse: *And, behold, I had three baskets of 'chori' on my head.*" [286]

(283) See the Commentary of Abraham ibn Ezra. (284) Isaiah 29:22. (285) Beitzah 2:6. (286) This establishes that the word *chori* in the verse and *chivri* in the Mishnah were considered by the Rabbis of the Talmud as identical. For just as in the case of the king's bread it means "large and white," as befits such bread, so does it have a similar meaning in the Mishnah. It is thus obvious that the Rabbis understood the word *chori*, as did Rav Saadia Gaon, to mean "white."

Mikeitz

41 1. BY THE 'YE'OR' (RIVER). With the exception of the Nile, none of the other rivers is called *ye'or*, a word signifying "canal," because the entire country consists of artificially constructed canals, and the waters of the Nile[1] flow into them. This is the language of Rashi.

Onkelos however did translate the word *ye'or* here as "river," but in the book of Exodus he translated *al ye'oreihem*[2] as "on their canals," as he had to distinguish between *nahar* and *ye'or* since they are both mentioned in the same verse: *'al naharotham ve'al ye'oreihem' (on their rivers and on their canals).* Thus, according to Onkelos, all rivers are called *ye'orim,* with the large ones being called both *n'haroth* and *ye'orim* while those canals constructed by man are also called *ye'orim.*[3] Thus we find that the Tigris, besides being called *nahar*, is also called *ye'or*, as it is written, *I was by the side of the great 'nahar' (river), which is Tigris... and behold a man clothed in linen,*[4] and it is further written there: *And, behold, there stood other two, the one on the bank of the 'ye'or' (river) on this side, and the other on the bank of the 'ye'or' on that side. And one said to the man clothed in linen, who was above the waters of the 'ye'or' (river).*[5] In my opinion the fact is as Onkelos said,[6] as both *ye'or* and *nahar* convey the same concept, both being an expression for *orah*

(1) "Rain does not fall in Egypt, but the Nile rises and irrigates the land." (Rashi, Exodus 7:17). (2) Exodus 7:19. (3) Thus the word *nahar* applies only to a natural river, while the word *ye'or* applies to both a natural river and a man-made canal. (4) Daniel 10:4-5. (5) *Ibid.*, 12:5-6. (6) When he said that *ye'or* and *nahar* are both terms for rivers.

(light). The rain, likewise, is called *or* (light), as it is said: *He spreadeth 'oro' (His light) upon it;*[7] *He spreadeth abroad the cloud of 'oro' (His lighting);*[8] and as Rabbi Yochanan said,[9] "All verses in Elihu's speech in the book of Job containing the word *orah* refer to the coming down of rain." Perhaps this is because the rains are influenced by the luminaries,[10] and the rivers which are formed by the rains are thus related to their first cause,[11] the luminaries.

2. AND BEHOLD, THERE CAME UP OUT OF THE RIVER. Since the land of Egypt is irrigated by the river, and it is from the river that abundance or famine befalls them, the king saw the cows coming up out of the river. The cows symbolize plowing, and the ears of corn symbolize the harvest, just as Joseph said, *in which there shall be neither plowing nor harvest.*[12] He saw that the river rose only slightly and there would thus be no plowing, and the little which will be planted in moist places, *a wind blowing from the east, a wind from the Eternal*[13] would burn them, even as he saw the ears of corn *parched with the east wind.*[14]

It would appear to be implied in the verses that the abundance was only in the land of Egypt, even as it said, *Seven years of great plenty throughout all the land of Egypt;*[15] likewise the verse, *And he stored up all the food of the seven years which was in the land of Egypt.*[16] But the famine, on the other hand, was in all the lands. And so did Joseph interpret it when he said, *And there shall arise after them seven years of famine,*[17] and did not mention the land of Egypt. It was for this reason that in the other countries

(7) Job 36:30. (8) *Ibid.*, 37:11. (9) Bereshith Rabbah 26:18. (10) "Luminaries." In his commentary to Job 36:30, Ibn Ezra writes: "For the rain is called *or* (light) on account of the small luminary (the moon), since its movements, by command of the Creator, cause the rain." An identical explanation is also found in R'dak's Sefer Hashorashim, under the root *or*. (11) This explains why rain is referred to in Elihu's speech as *or* (light), since the rain is caused by the movement of the luminaries, as explained above. (12) Genesis 45:6. Thus it is obvious that Joseph understood the characters in the dreams — i.e. the cows and the ears of corn — as symbolizing plowing and harvesting. (13) Hosea 13:15. (14) Verse 6 here. (15) Verse 29 here. (16) Verse 48 here. (17) Verse 30 here.

they were unable to store up food even if they had heard about it, as they undoubtedly did, for the matter was well known throughout their lands. Perhaps this was alluded to in the dream since with respect to the fat cows, it mentions, *And they fed in the reed-grass,* for it was there in Egypt that they fed and stood, but the lean ones, after they consumed the fat ones, *walked to and fro through the earth,*[18] and Pharaoh did not know where they had gone.

BA'ACHU. Meaning "in the marshy land," as in the verse, *Can 'achu' grow?*[19] This is the language of Rashi.

This is not correct, as *achu* is the name of the grass which grows, [and not the land upon which it grows, as Rashi explained it], just as in the verse, *Can the rush shoot up without mire, can the 'achu' (reed-grass) grow without water? It withereth before any other herb.*[20] Thus it is obvious that the word *achu* is not the marsh land. Perhaps Rashi's intent is that the grass which grows in the marsh-lands is called by the name of the land upon which it grows.

The correct interpretation is that *achu* is the generic name for all vegetation and grass which grow on the banks of the rivers and the marsh-lands. In that case, the letter *beth* in *ba'achu* would be as the *beth* in the verse, *Come, eat 'b'lachmi' (of my bread), and drink of the wine which I have mingled,*[21] for they were feeding on the bank of the river, just as it is said, *near the cows upon the bank of the river.*[22] Now perhaps the word *achu* is a derivative of *achvah* (brotherhood), since many varieties of grass grow together.

3. AND THEY STOOD BESIDE THE COWS. I.e., by their side and near them. This was a sign that there would be no lapse of time between the years of plenty and the years of famine even

(18) Zechariah 6:7. (19) Job 8:11. (20) *Ibid.*, Verses 11-12. (21) Proverbs 9:5. Ramban's intent is to say that if *achu* is the name of the grass, as he said in attempting to vindicate Rashi's explanation, the verse before us should have said *achu*, rather than *ba'achu*. But if *achu* is a generic name, the term *ba'achu* is correct, and the verse would mean that they fed in the green foliage or vegetation which was upon the bank of the river. (22) Verse 3 here.

though Pharaoh did not relate this to Joseph.[23] But perhaps the vision which Pharaoh saw and the relating of the dream to Joseph were really alike, except that Scripture did not concern itself [with mentioning all the details Pharaoh told Joseph], just as it added into the story [details not mentioned in the actual dream, as for example], *And it could not be known that they had eaten them up,* [24] and also, *the ears of corn came up on one stalk,* [25] which was a sign that the seven years will occur consecutively.

4. AND THE COWS ATE UP. In my opinion [26] this is a sign that the years of famine shall consume the years of plenty. It is from this that Joseph inferred that he should tell Pharaoh, *And let them store up all the food of those good years,*[27] *And the food shall serve as a reserve for the land against the seven years of famine,*[28] as he saw that the healthy cows and ears of corn were absorbed by the lean ones. [29] This was no mere counsel which Joseph proposed, for was he appointed to be a counselor of the king? [30] It was only in connection with the interpretation of the dream that he said thus: *And the plenty shall be forgotten,* [31] *And the plenty shall not be known.* [32] These words of Joseph constitute the interpretation of: *It could not be known that they had eaten them up, their appearance being bad as previously,*[33] for Joseph saw that by their consumption of the fat cows, the lean ones did not become fine and plump. They served them for subsistence only, for had they not eaten them they would have died in their lean state. This is unlike Rashi, who says that *the plenty shall be forgotten* [31] is the interpretation of the eating itself. [34]

(23) See Verse 19 here. (24) Verse 21 here. (25) Verse 5 here. (26) Ramban's interpretation differs from Rashi, who writes that the eating up of the fat by the lean indicates that all joy occasioned by the years of plenty would be forgotten in the days of the famine. His own opinion is presented in the text. (27) Verse 35 here. (28) Verse 36 here. (29) The fact that the fat ones were absorbed by the lean ones was a sign to Joseph that the food from the seven years of plenty should be kept as a reserve for the years of famine. (30) See II Chronicles 25:16. (31) Verse 30 here. (32) Verse 31 here. (33) Verse 21 here. (34) But according to Ramban, Joseph's words, *And the plenty shall be forgotten,* are the interpretation of the aspect of the dream expressed by: *It could not be known that they had eaten them up.*

Vayigash

18. LET THY SERVANT, I PRAY THEE, SPEAK A WORD. The intent thereof is to say that he [Judah] will speak but a few words which will not burden Joseph. In my opinion, the correct interpretation is that "a word" refers to the exchange concerning which he is to plead before him, namely, that Joseph exchange him for his brother Benjamin, for he will not ask any other thing of him, and all of the rest of his words are an appeasement and a plea for this exchange.

AND LET NOT THINE ANGER BURN AGAINST THY SERVANT. Judah is saying: "Do not be angry at me for speaking before you."

FOR THOU ART EVEN AS PHARAOH, i.e., "it is with great fear that I speak before you, as if I was speaking before Pharaoh."

19. MY LORD ASKED HIS SERVANTS. I know no reason for this lengthy speech of Judah in which he relates that which has already transpired between them. And that which the Rabbis, of blessed memory, have said in interpretation of Judah's words: [1] "Is this the 'setting your eyes upon him' to which you referred when you said, *That I may set mine eyes upon him?"* [2] – does not make it a valid argument, for a ruler who commands that a person be brought before him does not do so

(1) Bereshith Rabbah 93:5, quoted here by Rashi. (2) Verse 21 here.

on condition that he be freed from the consequences of the evils he would commit, and the more so for a theft in which the goblet from which he drinks was stolen from the king's house. And originally he had favorably cast his eyes upon Benjamin, greeting him by saying *G-d be gracious unto thee, my son,*[3] and he made all a party before him in the palace in Benjamin's honor, and he gave them presents[4] and gave them corn *as much as they can bear*[5] in excess of the money they had brought him, as I have explained, and what else was he to do for him!

It therefore appears to me, in line with the plain meaning of Scripture, that Judah's words are nought but supplications to bestir Joseph's compassion, for Judah thought that he was a man who fears G-d, as he had told him,[6] and since he had conducted himself mercifully towards them in the manner of one who fears sin, by consoling them for the trouble he had caused them.[7] And this is the purport of the story. Judah said to him: "As a consequence of my lord's inquiry, we were forced to tell you about this brother of ours, and we also did not consent to bring him down before you as you commanded at first, but we said that *the lad cannot leave his father.*[8] However, at the peril of our lives, *because of the burning heat of famine,*[9] we brought him, for you said, *Ye shall see my face no more.*[10] But our father did not want to listen and permit us to return to buy a little food until we were all in danger, and then he consented with fear and worry. But now *when he seeth that the lad is not with us,*[11] he will die *in bitterness of soul.*[12] Therefore, *let my supplication, I pray thee, be presented before thee,*[13] to have pity upon us and the aged father, and take me in place of the lad as a permanent servant, for I am better than he, *and it shall be righteousness unto thee.*"[14] This is the purport of the entire section.

It is possible that the expression, *and thy servants will bring down the gray hairs of thy servant our father,*[11] is a euphemism

(3) Above, 43:29. (4) *Ibid.*, Verse 34. (5) *Ibid.*, 44:1. (6) *Ibid.*, 42:18. (7) *Ibid.*, 43:23. (8) Verse 22 here. (9) Lamentations 5:10. (10) Verse 23 here. (11) Verse 31 here. (12) Job 21:25. (13) Jeremiah 37:20. (14) Deuteronomy 24:13.

out of respect [for Joseph, and Judah's intent was to say], "and *you* will bring down the gray hairs of thy servant our father." Similarly, *But this thing brings sin upon thy people.*[15] [The officers meant to say, "This thing brings sin upon you."]

It may further be said, in line with that which our Rabbis have said: "Is this the 'setting your eyes upon him' to which you referred?"—that Judah said, *For thou art even as Pharaoh,*[16] meaning "it behooves you to stand by your word and your inquest, for it was on account of you that we have brought the lad under great duress," as he [Judah] mentions, and he feared to be more explicit. But hidden in his words is the hint that the goblet affair was a scheme of his to have a pretext against them, for why should Joseph have wanted to see Benjamin to begin with, against their will. And so the Rabbis said in Bereshith Rabbah:[17] "Judah said to him, 'I will prove to you that you moved against us with a pretext. The people of how many countries have come down to buy food? Have you interrogated them as you have interrogated us? Were we perhaps asking for your daughter in marriage or were you seeking to marry our sister?' " The Rabbis are saying that this was hinted at in his words.

21. THAT I MAY SET MINE EYES UPON HIM. Rabbi Abraham ibn Ezra said that the meaning thereof is "that I may see him." But I have not found "setting of eyes" in Scripture in reference to just seeing. Thus: *And I will set Mine eyes upon them for good;*[18] *Take him, and put your eye upon him, and do him no harm,*[19] for Nebuchadrezzar did not command Nebuzaradan to merely see Jeremiah after he took him into custody, but to watch him and treat him well. But the meaning here is that Joseph had vowed to them to have pity on the lad and to guard him, even though it is not mentioned explicitly [in the narrative of the original confrontation between Joseph and his brothers], just as Scripture is concise there about all these matters which Judah related in Joseph's presence. Now Judah did not mention the

(15) Exodus 5:16. (16) Verse 18 here. (17) 93:8. (18) Jeremiah 24:6. (19) *Ibid.*, 39:12.

imprisonment of Simeon and the pretext that *Ye are spies,*[20] out of respect or out of the fear of majesty.

22. AND WE SAID UNTO MY LORD: THE LAD CANNOT LEAVE HIS FATHER; FOR IF HE SHOULD LEAVE HIS FATHER, HE WOULD DIE. Rabbi Abraham ibn Ezra explained this to mean "and his father would die." But if so, Judah would have said: "Our father cannot leave his son, for if he should leave his son, he [the father] would die." Or he should have said, "We cannot bear that the lad leave the father," for they would not make the plea for compassion for their father dependent upon the lad, [saying, as the verse has it. *'The lad' cannot leave his father for if he should leave his father, he would die*], since they considered him as a child who did not know the difference between good and evil. [Therefore, if it be as Ibn Ezra says, i.e., that the concern in this verse is lest the father die, they would have said, "We cannot bear that the lad should leave his father," or "Our father cannot leave his son."] Rather, the meaning is: *The lad cannot leave his father* on account of his youth and his being the darling son in the lap of his father who loves him, and if he should leave him and come on the journey the lad would die.

24. WHEN WE CAME UP UNTO THY SERVANT MY FATHER, WE TOLD HIM THE WORDS OF MY LORD. Judah said that immediately upon coming to their father, they told him that they will not see the ruler's face again without their younger brother, but he refused to send him, and would have left Simeon to him in his prison. This is the meaning of the verse, *And our father said: Go again, buy us a little food,*[21] for he did not consent to send Benjamin in spite of all we said, until forced to by the famine.

27. YE KNOW THAT MY WIFE BORE ME TWO SONS. If we say [that Jacob's intention was to point out] that Benjamin is the only one left to his mother, why is this a reason [for his saying

(20) Above, 42:9. (21) Verse 25 here.

that if some harm will befall him] it will bring down his *gray hairs with sorrow to the grave?* [22] After all, he has many sons and grandchildren, and Benjamin's mother has already died, and she would no longer weep over him in Jacob's presence. The meaning of the verse, however, is that Jacob took only Rachel as a wife on his own initiative. This is the sense of the words, *my wife bore me*: "for from a woman that was my wife of my own will there have been only two sons born to me, and I have bestowed my love upon them as if they were my only ones, the rest being to me as if they were children of concubines. And with his brother Joseph dead, this one alone is my only son whom I have loved." It is for this reason that Scripture mentions Rachel before Leah: *Like Rachel and like Leah, which two did build the house of Israel;* [23] *And he called Rachel and Leah to the field.* [24] Rachel took precedence in his mind. The commentators [25] have said that the reason why Scripture in this *Seder* says, *The sons of Rachel Jacob's wife,* [26] is that she is called his wife in truth, without any deception. In my opinion, however, this is because Rachel is mentioned there among the handmaids, as I have already so mentioned. [27]

29. AND 'ASON' (HARM) BEFALL HIM, YE WILL BRING DOWN MY GRAY HAIRS. That is, "if harm befall him as it did to his brother Joseph, you will bring down *my gray hairs with sorrow to the grave.*" Perhaps the expression, *and 'ason' (harm) befall him,* means that it will so happen to him on account of his being young and tender and not accustomed to travel on the road, this being analogous to what Jacob said above, *Lest 'ason' (harm) should befall him,* [28] for the meaning of the word *ason* is accidental death, such as those killed by a human or a wild beast or the change of air on the road.

(22) Verse 29 here. (23) Ruth 4:11. (24) Above, 31:4. (25) See Rashi further 46:19. (26) Further, 46:19. (27) Above, 31:33 and 37:2. Ramban agrees with the principle as he himself explains it in connection with the verse above, 31:4. However, he points out that in the verse further, 46:19, the term, *Jacob's wife,* is independently justified. (28) *Ibid.,* 42:4.

32. FOR THY SERVANT BECAME SURETY FOR THE LAD. Judah is saying that his father will go down *with sorrow to the grave*[29] on account of the lad, for "despite all that we have said to him, the aged father did not want to send him until I became surety for him, and he trusted me. Therefore, *let thy servant, I pray thee, abide*[30] in his stead." And if the explanation of the verse, *And thy servants will bring down the gray hairs of thy servant our father...to the grave,*[11] is in line with the plain meaning thereof, [namely, that the responsibility will fall upon the brothers, as opposed to Ramban's previous interpretation that "thy servants" is a euphemism for Joseph,[31] then Judah] is saying that "we will have caused the death of the aged father by sorrow, for I was surety for the lad." He said, *For how shall I go up to my father,*[32] in order to let him [Jacob] know that he [Judah] would choose to be a permanent servant rather than go up to his father without the lad for he could not bear to see his sorrow, as he would constantly weep and mourn for him all day. Judah mentioned this so that he should not suspect him of planning some deceit since he would know how to escape better than the lad.

45 1. THEN JOSEPH COULD NOT 'L'HITHAPEIK' (REFRAIN HIMSELF) BEFORE ALL THEM THAT STOOD BY HIM. He could not bear that the Egyptians should stand by him witnessing how his brothers would be put to shame when he makes himself known to them. This is the language of Rashi. But Rabbi Abraham ibn Ezra said that *l'hithapeik* means "to bear." The expression *Before all them that stood by him,* means until all that stood by him would go out, and so it was necessary that he call out that they be removed. Onkelos, however, translated *l'hithapeik* as meaning "to strengthen himself." Similarly: *'Va'ethapak" (And I forced myself) and offered the burnt-offering.*[33] Every other form of *hithapkuth* in every place is likewise an expression of strengthening.

The correct interpretation in my opinion is that there were present many people of Pharaoh's house and other Egyptians,

(29)Verse 31 here. (30) Verse 33 here. (31) See Ramban above, Verse 19. (32) Verse 34 here. (33) I Samuel 13:12.

pleading with Joseph to pardon Benjamin, for their compassions were deeply stirred by Judah's pleas, and Joseph could not overcome them all. He then called forth to his servants, *"Let every* strange *man go out from me,* because I will speak to them." And when they had gone out, *he wept aloud; and the Egyptians heard, and* the people of *the house of Pharaoh,* [34] who had been expelled from his presence, for they were still in the outer court.

It is possible that the expression, *'hanitzavim' (them that stood) by him,* means his servants who stood before him, just as: *The servant 'hanitzav' (that was set) over the reapers;* [35] *'sarei hanitzavim' (chief officers);* [36] *'L'hithyatzeiv' (To present themselves) before the Eternal.* [37] And the meaning of *Vayikra* (and he called) is that he raised his voice with anger and said to his servants, *"Cause every man to go out from before me,* except these men." And the reason for the removal is that he expelled them from there so that they should not hear when he mentions the matter of the sale to his brothers because it would be a source of distress to them and also to himself, for the servants of Pharaoh and the Egyptians will say of them: "These are treacheous people who must not live in our land, nor tread in our palaces. They have acted treacherously against their brother, and also dealt treacherously with their father. What will they do to the king and his people?" They would also no longer believe in Joseph.

6. FOR THESE TWO YEARS HATH THE FAMINE BEEN IN THE LAND. The reason why he mentioned to them what had transpired, which they themselves also knew, was to state that a land which has gone through two years of famine, in which the people had consumed all which they possessed, resulting in exceedingly high prices, and which was destined to experience five more years of famine, could offer them no sustenance whatsoever – had G-d not dispatched me before you.

10. AND THOU SHALT DWELL IN THE LAND OF GOSHEN. Joseph knew that his father would not want to stay in that part of

(34) Verse 2 here. (35) Ruth 3:6. (36) I Kings 5:30. (37) Job 1:6.

the land of Egypt where the royal palace was. Therefore he now informed him that he will settle him in the land of Goshen. The meaning of the expression, *Thou and thy children,* is that it is connected with the previous verse: *Come down unto me...*[38] *thou and thy children, and thy children's children, and thy flocks, and thy herds, and all that thou hast.*

11. LEST THOU COME TO POVERTY, THOU, AND THY HOUSEHOLD. Joseph said this by way of respect for his father. To his brothers he said, *For G-d did send me before you to preserve life,* [39] and *to give you a remnant,* [40] but to his father he did not want to say so. Instead, he said, "that if you will delay in the land of Canaan you will be impoverished for I could not send you much food from the royal storehouse as they will suspect me of selling it there in order to accumulate treasures of money and then return to my land and to my birthplace. But when you come here, and they will know that you are my father and brothers, the king will give me permission to sustain you."

12. THAT IT IS MY MOUTH THAT SPEAKETH UNTO YOU. I.e., in the Holy Language. This is the opinion of the commentators, [41] and it is also the translation of Onkelos. It is possible that Joseph said so to them for plausibility and in order to be conciliatory, for the fact that a person in Egypt speaks the Holy Language is not proof that he is Joseph. It is my opinion that the Holy Language was the language of Canaan for Abraham did not bring it there from Ur of the Chaldees or Haran, as they spoke Aramaic there, as is attested to by "the heap." [42] Now it was not the language of one man alone; rather, it was the language of the entire land of Canaan, and many people in Egypt knew it, since Canaan was nearby. We would particularly expect knowledge of languages in the case of a ruler for it is usual for kings and rulers to be linguistic. It is just as you see in the case of

(38) Verse 9 here. (39) Verse 5 here. (40) Verse 7 here. (41) Rashi, Ibn Ezra and R'dak. (42) Above, 31:47. In Aramaic, Laban named it *Yegar-sahaduth* (the heap of witness). Thus it is clear that Aramaic was the spoken language in Abraham's birthplace.

Nebuchadnezzar who said in the Holy Language, *I have dreamed a dream, and my spirit is troubled to know the dream,*[43] because there were *the magicians, and the enchanters, and the sorcerers, and Chaldeans,*[44] people of many languages, as well as from Israel, and they all would understand him. They, however, answered him in Aramaic, as it says, *Then spoke the Chaldeans to the king in Aramaic,*[45] as they were close to him, *and sat first in the kingdom,*[46] and they had the permission to speak to the king. Moreover, just as Joseph came from Canaan to Egypt, many others also came. Besides, the brothers had greater proof that he was Joseph when he mentioned his name and the circumstance of the sale, saying, *I am Joseph your brother, whom ye sold into Egypt.*[47]

The correct interpretation in my opinion is that Joseph is saying: *"And, behold, your eyes see, and the eyes of my brother Benjamin,* that I, the ruler and lord of all Egypt, am the one telling you with my mouth that I am your brother, and command you to bring down my father to me in order to sustain him. This being so, you will tell my father of all the glory in Egypt, *and of all that you have seen*[48] with your eyes, and you will hurry and bring him down to me for the words I have spoken are true, and I have the power to deliver him and to keep him alive in the famine."[49] This is analogous to saying, "for I have spoken my word." In the *Gemara* of Tractate Megillah,[50] the Rabbis have said: "As my mouth, so is my heart," [meaning: "Just as I indicate no hatred against you in my speech, so is my heart free of hatred against you]."

16. JOSEPH'S BRETHREN ARE COME. The intent thereof is that Joseph told the house of Pharaoh that he had honorable brothers in the land of the Hebrews, for he had been stolen away from there,[51] and now the Egyptians heard that Joseph's brothers had come as he said.

(43) Daniel 2:3. (44) *Ibid.*, Verse 2. (45) *Ibid.*, Verse 4. (46) Esther 1:14. (47) Verse 4 here. (48) Verse 13 here. (49) See Psalms 33:19. (50) 16 b. (51) See above, 40:15.

AND IT PLEASED PHARAOH WELL, AND HIS SERVANTS. For it was a disgrace to them to be ruled by a stranger, a servant [of whom it is said], *out of prison he came forth to be king,* [52] and now when his honorable brothers came to him, and it became known that Joseph was worthy to stand before kings,[53] they all rejoiced in the matter.

19. NOW THOU ART COMMANDED, THIS DO YE. Pharaoh stated the matter in the form of a directive to him because his knowledge of Joseph's integrity assured him that he would not stretch forth a hand to take from the king's fortune, *and having him, he gave no concern to anything.* [54] Therefore Pharaoh thought that perhaps Joseph would not want to send his father anything. Hence he said to him, "I command you that you do this in any case."

23. AND TO HIS FATHER HE SENT 'KAZOTH' (IN LIKE MANNER). I.e., according to this amount. And what was the amount? *Ten asses,* etc. This is the language of Rashi. It is not correct that *kazoth* should refer to the amount [for if it refers to *cheshbon* (amount), it should have said *kazeh* in the masculine, and not *kazoth* in the feminine]. But it is possible that Scripture says, *in like manner,* meaning "according to this gift," [with the word *minchah* matching the feminine gender of *kazoth*] The purport thereof is, "and to his father he sent this gift: ten asses, etc.," [with the word *kazoth* being understood as if it were written *zoth*], and the letter *kaph* in the word *kazoth* is considered redundant. However, it is the way of the Sacred Language to express it in this way, just as, *And she spoke to him,* [saying]: *'ka'dvarim ha'eileh' (after the manner of these things) did thy servant do to me.* [55] It may be that Scripture is saying: "and to his father he sent provision *(tzeidah),* [which is also in the feminine gender], which was like this provision which he gave to his brothers." But the intent of the expression is not to make them equal, but only to say that just as he gave them provision for the

(52) Ecclesiastes 4:14. (53) See Proverbs 22:29. (54) Above, 39:6. (55) *Ibid.,* Verses 17 and 19.

road when they went to Canaan, so did he send his father *corn and bread and sustenance* for his journey towards Egypt. And this is the correct interpretation. Scripture mentions asses and she-asses to inform us that he sent him both the provisions and the animals that carried them, and it was customary to send males and females, as his father had done.[56]

24. DO NOT 'TIRG'ZU' BY THE WAY. *Rogez* is an expression of trembling and movement, and is usually applied when the trembling is a result of fear, as for example, *a heart 'ragaz' (that is trembling);*[57] *'V'ragzu' (and they shall tremble), and be in anguish;*[58] *And where I stand 'ergaz' (I tremble);*[59] *And drink thy water 'b'ragzah' (with trembling) and with anxiety.*[60] Therefore, the correct interpretation of this verse is, in my opinion, that Joseph said to them, "Do not fear by the way," and the purport thereof is that since they were carrying *corn and bread and sustenance*[61] and the best of Egypt in the days of the famine, they might fear lest robbers attack them while they travelled on their journey to Canaan, and the moreso when they return to Egypt with all their possessions, and thus they will not hasten the matter.[62] Therefore he told them that they should go quickly and hurry to come there, as it is said, *Hasten ye, and go up to my father,*[38] and they should have no fear at all on the way as his name is upon them. Since he is the ruler of the entire land of Egypt, and the lives of the peoples of those countries are in his hand, and all are fearful of his awe, they will travel and arrive in peace.

26. 'VAYAPHAG' HIS HEART. His heart passed away and ceased to believe; his heart took no notice of their words. The word *vayaphag* has the same meaning as the Mishnaic expression: "The fragrance of all spices *m'phigin* (escape)."[63] Similar is the verse, *Without any 'haphugoth' (intermission).*[64] The verse, *And*

(56) *Ibid.,* 32:16. (57) Deuteronomy 28:65. (58) *Ibid.,* 2:25. (59) Habakkuk 3:16. (60) Ezekiel 12:18. (61) Verse 23 here. (62) See II Chronicles 24:15. (63) Beitza 14 a. (64) Lamentations 3:49.

his scent is not 'namar,'[65] is rendered in the Targum: "and his scent is not *pag* (passing away)." This is the language of Rashi. But it is not correct, for *phugah* is an expression of cessation and abolition, just as : *give thyself no 'phugath' (respite).*[66] So also, *Mine eye is poured out, and ceaseth not, without any 'haphugoth,'* [64] meaning "mine eye pours out tears steadily without cessation or intermission." And so likewise, "*m'phigin* (their fragrance)" [63] means that the spices scatter the fragrance and it is voided. So also, *Therefore the law is 'taphug,'*[67] that is, voided and ceased. In this verse also, *'vayaphag' his heart* [thus means that the beat of] his heart was suspended and his breathing ceased, for the movement of the heart ceased and he was as dead. This condition is known when joy suddenly comes upon one, and it is mentioned in the books of medicines that old or feeble persons cannot withstand the shock, for many of them faint when joy comes to them very suddenly. The heart widens and opens suddenly, and its natural heat goes out and scatters throughout the outer parts of the body, and the heart thus ceases to function because of its coolness. Thus the patriarch fell as dead. Scripture says, *for he believed them not,* in order to relate that he remained in that condition a great part of the day, and he lay so without movement because he did not believe them.

Concerning such fainting it is known that people shout to the fainting person and accustom him to that joyful event gradually until he accepts it with a tranquil spirit. And this is the meaning of the verse, *And they told him all the words of Joseph, which he had said unto them, and when he saw the wagons [which Joseph had sent to carry him, the spirit of Jacob their father revived]*,[68] for they shouted into his ears the words of Joseph and brought the wagons before him. Then did his spirit return to him, and his breathing began and he was revived. It is this which Scripture says, *And the spirit of Jacob their father revived.* Now Onkelos translated: "The Divine Presence, [which had departed from him when he was in mourning], again rested upon him." Onkelos

(65) Jeremiah 48:11. (66) Lamentations 2:18. (67) Habakkuk 1:4. (68) Verse 27 here.

added this because the thing is true, and he expounded this interpretation from the word *ruach* (spirit), since Scripture does not say, "and Jacob their father revived," [but rather, *and the spirit of Jacob their father revived*]. He thus explained the verse here as being analogous to these verses: *The spirit of the Eternal G-d is upon me;*[69] *And now the Eternal G-d hath sent me and His spirit;*[70] *A man in whom is spirit.*[71]

27. AND THEY TOLD HIM ALL THE WORDS OF JOSEPH. It is my opinion, in line with the plain meaning of Scripture, that it was never told to Jacob throughout his entire lifetime that the brothers had sold Joseph. Rather he thought that Joseph had strayed in the field, and those who found him took him and sold him into Egypt. The brothers did not want to tell him of their sin, being afraid for their lives lest he be wroth and curse them as he did to Reuben, Simeon and Levi,[72] while Joseph in his good ethical conduct did not want to tell him. It is for this reason that it is said, *And they sent a message unto Joseph, saying: Thy father did command before he died,* etc.[73] And had Jacob known of this matter, it would have been proper for them to plead before their father at the time of his death to command Joseph by word of his mouth, for he would have granted his father's request and not rebelled against his word, and they would not have been in danger, nor would they need to feign words out of their own hearts.[74]

46 1. AND HE OFFERED SACRIFICES UNTO THE G-D OF HIS FATHER ISAAC. The duty of honoring one's father is more imperative than that of honoring one's grandfather. Therefore the sacrifices are associated with the name of Isaac, and not with that of Abraham. Thus the language of Rashi. But this is not sufficient, for it would have been proper for Scripture to say, "and he offered sacrifices unto the G-d of his fathers," without singling out any one person, just as Jacob said, *The G-d before whom my fathers Abraham and Isaac did walk;*[75] and in his prayer he said, *O*

(69) Isaiah 61:1. (70) *Ibid.*, 48:16. (71) Numbers 27:18. (72) Further, 49:3-7. (73) *Ibid.*, 50:16. (74) See Nehemiah 6:8. (75) Further 48:15.

G-d of my father Abraham, and G-d of my father Isaac. [76] Or Scripture should have said, "and he offered sacrifices to the Eternal," just as it says in the case of Abraham, *And he built there an altar unto the Eternal.* [77] And what need was there to explain it further?

However, this verse contains a secret, which the Rabbis revealed to us there in Bereshith Rabbah: [78] When Jacob was about to go down to Egypt he saw that the exile was beginning for him and his children, and he feared it, and so he offered many sacrifices to *the Fear of his father Isaac* [79] in order that Divine judgment should not be aimed against him. This he did in Beer-sheba which was a place of prayer for his father, and from there he had taken permission when he went to Haran. [80]

Now Scripture uses the word *z'vachim,* [a term connoting peace-offerings], to inform us that they were not burnt-offerings as were his fathers', as Abraham offered burnt-offerings. Our Rabbis have said [81] that Noachides [82] did not offer peace-offerings; they offered burnt-offerings. And concerning Noah it is clearly written, *And he offered burnt-offerings on the altar.* [83] But on account of his fear of the Eternal, Jacob offered peace-offerings in order to bring all Divine attributes into accord towards him, even as the Rabbis have expounded: [84] "They are called *sh'lamim* (peace-offerings) because they bring *shalom* (peace) into the world." Now his original intent was directed at the Divine attribute of power, this being nearest to Isaac. This is the explanation of that which the Rabbis mentioned in Bereshith Rabbah,[78] i.e., that the duty of honoring one's father is more imperative than that of honoring one's grandfather. This explanation applies to that which the Rabbis have said there in yet another form: "First you greet the pupil and afterward you greet the Rabbi." [85]

(76) Above, 32:10. (77) *Ibid.,* 12:7. (78) 94:5. (79) Above, 31:53. (80) See Ramban above, 28:17. (81) Zebachim 116 a. (82) See Note 148 in *Seder Vayishlach,* also Note 222 in *Seder Bereshith.* (83) Above 8:20. (84) Torath Kohanim Vayikra 16:1. (85) The case refers to a procession of a Rabbi and his pupils on the road. Since the pupils travel in advance of the Rabbi, a person coming from the opposite direction would first meet the pupils and then the Rabbi. Similarly, Isaac is the pupil and Abraham is the Rabbi. Hence Jacob offered sacrifices to the G-d of his father Isaac.

I have seen this text in the Midrash of Rabbi Nechunya ben Hakanah: [86] "*And Jacob swore by the Fear of his father Isaac.* [79] Is there any one who swears by the belief of the Fear of his father? However, it was because Jacob was not yet given strength, and so he swore by the power given to his father, as it is said, *And Jacob swore by the Fear of his father Isaac.* [79] And what is this? It is this concerning which Scripture writes, *Then the fire of the Eternal fell, and consumed the burnt-offering,* [87] and it is further written, *For the Eternal thy G-d is a devouring fire,* etc." [88] Thus far the Midrash. From the words of the Rabbis of this Midrash, we learn that it was for this reason that it does not say here, "and he offered sacrifices to the Eternal," [but instead it says, "to the G-d of his father Isaac]," because now in Beer-sheba Jacob had already become privileged to possess his own portion [and needed only to bring all Divine attributes into accord towards him], [89] as it is said, *Thou wilt give truth to Jacob, mercy to Abraham, as Thou hast sworn unto our fathers from the days of old.* [90] It was therefore necessary to explain it now. Thus by the merit of the sacrifices, the G-d of his father Isaac appeared to him *in the visions of the night* [91] with an ameliorated Divine attribute of justice. It is this which Scripture says concerning them, *in the visions of the night,* complementing that which He said, *I am G-d, the G-d of thy father,* [92] for He is the G-d of Beth-el Who said to him in Haran, *I am the G-d of Beth-el, where thou didst anoint a pillar;* [93] it is He Who is *the G-d of thy father.* This is the Name and this is the attribute. And He assured him that he should have no fear in Egypt for he will be found righteous in Divine judgment, and he will be redeemed after the affliction. This is the meaning of the Divine promise, *And I will also surely bring thee up again.* [94]

Now the Rabbi [Moshe ben Maimon] has written in the twenty-seventh chapter of the first part of the Moreh Nebuchim (Guide of the Perplexed) concerning Onkelos' translation of the

(86) Sefer Habahir, 135. See Note 42 in *Seder Bereshith.* (87) I Kings 18:38. (88) Deuteronomy 4:24. (89) The words in the brackets are from the Commentary of Lvush to the Rekanati on the Torah, who quotes these words of Ramban. (90) Micah 7:20. (91) Verse 2 here. (92) Verse 3 here. (93) Above, 31:13. (94) Verse 4 here.

verse, *I will go down with thee into Egypt, and I will also surely bring thee up again,* [94] [which Onkelos rendered here literally]: "I will go down with thee...and I will bring thee up." And the Rabbi was amazed at the opinion of Onkelos, [namely, that the literal translation should be used], saying that Onkelos had exerted all his effort to remove any implication of G-d's corporeality from all narratives in the Torah. Accordingly, in the case of any expression found in the Torah implying any mode of motion that refers to G-d, Onkelos ascribed the action to a certain glory that had been created for the occasion, or a manifestation of Divine Providence. Thus he translated *And G-d came down* [95] as "and G-d manifested Himself;" *I will go down now and see* [96] as "I will manifest Myself now and see." And if so, why did Onkelos here translate literally, "I will go down"? And so the Rabbi explained that since Scripture said at the outset of the matter, *And G-d spoke unto Israel in the visions of the night,* [91] thus indicating that it is an account of what Jacob was told and not what actually took place, Onkelos therefore did not hesitate to literally translate the words as they were addressed to Jacob in the visions of the night, for the words in question represent an account of what Jacob was told, not what actually took place. There is thus a great difference between a communication transmitted in a dream or a vision of the night, or a communication designated as having been made in a vision or manifestation, and a communication given clearly, [not in a dream, such as communications introduced by phrases like these]: "And the word of the Eternal came unto me, saying," or "And the Eternal spoke unto me, saying." These are the words of Rabbi Moshe ben Maimon.

Similarly he said [97] that Onkelos never translated expressions of "hearing" literally [when the Scriptural references were to G-d], but instead explained them as expressing that a certain matter reached the Creator, or that He accepted a prayer. Thus Onkelos translated *the Eternal heard* [98] as "it was heard before the Eternal;" he translated the verse, *I will surely hear his crying* [99] as "I will surely accept his complaint."

(95) Exodus 19:20. (96) Above, 18:21. (97) Moreh Nebuchim I, 48. (98) Above, 29:33. (99) Exodus 22:22.

But if the matter is as the Rabbi [Moshe ben Maimon] said, why does Onkelos shun literal translations of expressions of movement, and also avoid literal expressions of hearing due to his fear that they might indicate corporeality, but he does not in any place shy away from literally expressing "saying," "speaking" or "calling," whether the communication was in a dream or manifestation or overt speech, for in every case he translates: "and G-d said," "G-d spoke," "and G-d called unto Moses"? These expressions likewise signify corporeality, and Onkelos should have translated, "and it was said from before G-d," or "and the glory of G-d said," or "and G-d willed," as is appropriate in each case, just as the Rabbi has explained [100] with reference to the terms "speaking" and "saying" when they refer to G-d. And why did Onkelos avoid literal translation in the case of "hearing" and did not do so with respect to "seeing," which he translated as: "and the Eternal saw"? [101] And that which the Rabbi has said [102] that "seeing" indicates mental perception as well as the sensation of sight, this applies all the more to "hearing" for it is employed in many places to indicate mental perception and will, such as: *And Abram hearkened to the voice of Sarai;* [103] *Hear the voice of my supplications;* [104] *Yea, when ye make many prayers, I will not hear;* [105] *And it shall come to pass, if thou shalt hearken diligently unto the voice of the Eternal thy G-d.* [106] And so also, *leiv shomei'ah* [107] (literally: a hearing heart, an understanding heart), and so also in the case of most of [the verses cited by Rabbi Moshe ben Maimon]. So Onkelos should not have been apprehensive of expressions of "hearing" as they only indicate acceptance of a matter by G-d and His being pleased with it, for he does not avoid literal translations of expressions of sight any place, but translates it literally in all cases even when seeing alone is involved. However, where a matter is not conceived by sight alone, but requires attention and discernment, Onkelos renders it as befits the subject. For example, when Scripture says, *Because the Eternal hath looked upon my affliction,* [108] [Onkelos rendered it as, "because my

(100) Moreh Nebuchim I, 65. (101) Above, 6:5. (102) Moreh Nebuchim I, 48. (103) Above 16:2. (104) Psalms 28:2. (105) Isaiah 1:15. (106) Deuteronomy 28:1. (107) I Kings 3:9. (108) Above, 29:32.

affliction is manifested before the Eternal"]. The verse, *I have surely seen the affliction of My people,*[109] [was rendered by Onkelos as, "the enslavement of my people is manifest before me," and the verse], *And G-d saw the children of Israel,*[110] [he rendered as, "and the enslavement of the children of Israel was manifest before G-d]," since His seeing them was not just as a matter of perceiving their bodies but of His attention to their situation and His knowledge thereof. This is Onkelos' method throughout the Torah, and not as the Rabbi's opinion would have it, as a consquence of which opinion he had to declare [our version of Targum Onkelos] erroneous[111] in [the following three places: the verse mentioned above, namely, *And the Eternal saw*],[101] and two other verses,[112] which Onkelos translated as, "and He saw," since these translations do not fit his theory.

With reference to expressions of "passing" Onkelos paraphrased and thus translated the expression, *And the Eternal passed by before him,*[113] as, "and He caused His Presence to pass before his [Moses'] face." He did this so that the passing object would be, in accordance with Onkelos' opinion, something created, as he would not ascribe any expression of motion to the Creator in accordance with what the Rabbi has mentioned.[114] But if this is so, why did

(109) Exodus 3:7. (110) *Ibid.*, 2:25. (111) Ramban refers here to Chapter 48 of the first part of the Moreh Nebuchim mentioned above, in which Rabbi Moshe ben Maimon (Rambam) sets forth the theory that Onkelos always renders "seeing" literally except where it is connected with wrong, injury or violence, in which cases he expresses it as "It was manifest before the Eternal." Onkelos is thus consistent with the prophetic phrase, *Thou canst not look on iniquity* (Habakkuk 1:13). However, Rambam mentions that he found three passages which contradict his theory. One is the verse, *And the Eternal saw that the wickedness of man was great upon the earth,* (above, 6:5), and the other two are mentioned in the following note. In these three cases which are connected with wrong and violence, Onkelos should have expressed "seeing" in the form of "being manifest before the Eternal," and yet he translated them literally! Rambam then concludes that our version of Onkelos is inaccurate in those three cases! It is this conclusion of Rambam with which Ramban takes issue in the text before us. (112) *And G-d saw the earth, and behold it was corrupt,* (above, 6:12). *And the Eternal saw that Leah was hated,* (above, 29:31). (113) Exodus 34:6. (114) Moreh Nebuchim I, 21.

Onkelos literally translate the verse, *The Eternal thy G-d, He will go over before thee?* [115] This is a form of motion occurring in a narrative [116] and yet Onkelos was not apprehensive about it! Similarly, Onkelos translated the verse, *And Israel saw the great hand,* [117] as, "and Israel saw the power of the great hand." He added the term "power" due to the subsequent expression, *that the Eternal did,* [117] yet he left intact the expression, "the great hand" and was not apprehensive and fearful of the term "hand" being ascribed to G-d and did not paraphrase it at all! He did the same in literally translating, *written with the finger of G-d.* [118] The Rabbi's answer [119] that Onkelos thought that "the finger" was a created instrument which, by the will of the Creator, engraved the writing on the tablets, is not the truth. There is the verse, *At His right hand was a fiery law unto them,* [120] in translation of which Onkelos wrote, "His right hand," and he was not apprehensive of "the right hand writing," that is lest it indicate corporeality, and such is the case also with "the finger" as mentioned above. He furthermore literally translated: *Thou stretchest forth Thy right hand* [121] as, "Thou raisest Thy right hand." So also the verses: *Thy right hand, O Eternal, dasheth in pieces the enemy;* [122] *Thy strong hand;* [123] *By a mighty hand, and by an outstretched arm;* [124] *And My hand take hold on judgment;* [125] *The eyes of the Eternal thy G-d are always upon it.* [126] [Onkelos literally translated all of these verses without fear that the terms "hand" and "eyes" might indicate corporeality.] Now in the case of Jacob, the Scriptural narrative begins, *And he dreamed, and behold a ladder set up on the earth,*etc., and yet Onkelos, fearing corporeality, translated [the verse, *And, behold, the Eternal stood beside him*], [127] as "and, behold, the Glory of G-d stood beside him," and he did not translate literally, "and, behold, the

(115) Deuteronomy 31:3. In our version of Onkelos, the text reads, "His word will go over." Ramban's objection is thus removed. (116) As opposed to "the visions of the night." See the beginning of the section where Ramban explains this distinction which Rambam makes. (117) Exodus 14:31. (118) *Ibid.,* 31:18. (119) Moreh Nebuchim I, 66. (120) Deuteronomy 33:2. (121) Exodus 15:12. (122) *Ibid.,* Verse 6. (123) Deuteronomy 3:24. (124) *Ibid.,* 4:34. (125) *Ibid.,* 32:41. (126) *Ibid.,* 11:12. (127) Above, 28:12-13.

Eternal" although it was in a dream.[128] He further translated the expression, *And, behold, I am with thee,*[129] as "and, behold, My word will be in thy help," and did not say literally, "and, behold, I am with thee," just as he literally translated, "I will go down with thee," even though the story of the ladder is a statement of what Jacob was told, [not a narrative of what took place], and is completely analogous to the narrative of the dream here. Again, Onkelos literally translated the expression, *And I will be with thy mouth,*[130] [even though the story there is not introduced as a vision of the night or a dream], and on the other hand he translated the verse, *And He said, Certainly I will be with thee, and this shall be the token unto thee,*[131] as "behold, My word will be with thee." Furthermore, Onkelos does not always translate literally in the case of dreams. Thus he rendered the verses, *And G-d came to Abimelech in a dream of the night,*[132] *And G-d came to Laban in a dream,*[133] as "and the word came from before G-d." Should you say that Onkelos paraphrased it there because he was concerned lest one think that G-d came to them before the dream, and one might thus think that G-d's appearance actually took place, [this would still not justify his using the expression, "and the word came,"] for in the case of Solomon it is written, *In Gibeon the Eternal appeared to Solomon in a dream,*[134] and yet Jonathan ben Uziel[135] translated it as, "G-d revealed Himself to Solomon," even though, according to Rabbi Moshe ben Maimon, a narrative introduced as a dream is rendered by Onkelos and Jonathan as it was actually said. They find no difficulty in translating such a statement literally, even though the expression connotes corporeality, because since it occurs in a dream, they understand that it is inexact. Thus in the case of Solomon, since the Eternal appeared to him in a dream, it was proper for Jonathan

(128) Rabbi Moshe ben Maimon's thesis is that the reason Onkelos did not paraphrase the verse, *I will go down with thee into Egypt,* but translated it literally, is that the narrative begins with a statement that it was in a vision of the night. Ramban questions this thesis, for in the story of the ladder, which is also introduced as a dream, Onkelos avoided possible indications of corporeality, and accordingly he paraphrased the verses. (129) Above, 28:15. (130) Exodus 4:12. (131) *Ibid.*, 3:12. (132) Above, 20:3. (133) *Ibid.*, 41:22. (134) I Kings 3:5. (135) See Note 152 in *Seder Noach.*

to give a literal account of the occurrence, for since Scripture relates that it was *in a dream by night,* [134] one would himself infer that it was not real but only a dream in which the person dreaming imagined it to be so. [Now since Jonathan did not paraphrase the account of Solomon's dream, although Onkelos did so in the case of the dreams of Abimelech and Laban, it thus helps to disprove the thesis of Rabbi Moshe ben Maimon that accounts of what occurred in man's imagination are not paraphrased by the Targum.] Now do not think that Jonathan ben Uziel did this because the term "seeing" in reference to dreams is not found in Aramaic – for the verse, *And I saw in my dream,* [136] is indeed translated [in Targum Onkelos] as "I saw," and in the case of the dream of Nebuchadnezzar, it likewise says in Aramaic, *Thou O King, sawest.* [137]

And so did Onkelos translate the verse, *Your murmurings are not against us, but against the Eternal,* [138] as "but against the word of G-d." Onkelos thus paraphrased here even though there is no fear or apprehension of corporeality connoted by literal translation. Likewise, he translated *And the people spoke against G-d, and against Moses* [139] as, "and the people murmured against the word of G-d." So also the verses, *Between Me and you,* [140] and *Between G-d and every living creature,* [141] were translated by Onkelos as: "between My word and you," "between the word of G-d and every living creature." There are many similar examples [of verses which he paraphrased in spite of the fact that there would have been no apprehension of intimating corporeality had he translated literally]. And so also he translated *The Eternal watch* [142] as "the word of G-d watch;" *G-d is witness* [143] as "the word of G-d is witness." Yet there would be no apprehension of corporeality had those expressions been literally translated. Besides, what sense is conveyed here by the expression, "the word of G-d' watch or witness"? Similarly the verse, *Swear unto me here by G-d,* [144] is rendered by Onkelos as "swear unto me by the word of G-d," although people who swear do not mention, "I swear by the word of G-d." There are many other such cases in Onkelos, and their secret meaning is known to the learned students [of the mystic lore of the Torah].

(136) Above, 41:22. (137) Daniel 2:31. (138) Exodus 16:8. (139) Numbers 21:5. (140) Above, 9:12. (141) *Ibid.,* Verse 16. (142) *Ibid.,* 31:49. (143) *Ibid.,* Verse 50. (144) *Ibid.,* 21:23.

Likewise, with respect to the term "standing" when applied to G-d, the Rabbi said[145] that Jonathan ben Uziel's intent was to explain it as meaning "to endure permanently," and therefore he translated the expression, *And His feet shall stand,* [146] as "and He will appear in His might." So also all expressions denoting contact and motion were rendered by him as "the might of G-d." Yet Onkelos had no apprehension of the term "standing." and he translated it literally: *Behold, I will stand before thee there upon the rock.*[147]

And concerning that which the Rabbi has said[148] that all expressions denoting any mode of motion are rendered by Onkelos as the revelation of the Divine Presence, or the manifestation of a certain Glory that had been created for the occasion, now Onkelos avoids even literal translation of verses which mention "seeing" the Glory [of G-d, and would certainly oppose using it to denote expressions of motion]. Thus he translates the verse, *And the glory of the Eternal appeared unto all the congregation,* [149] as "and the glory of G-d was manifested," just as he said in translation of the verse, *And the Eternal came down,* [150] "and the Eternal manifested Himself," and did not translate it literally as "and the glory of the Eternal appeared." He also likewise translates "seeing," when referring to angels, as "and he manifested himself." [151] Now if it is as the Rabbi [Moshe ben Maimon] said [148] that in the case of angels, or manifestation of a certain glory that had been created for the occasion, Onkelos does not hesitate to literally translate expressions denoting corporeality, it would have been proper for him not to avoid expressions of literal "seeing" of angels by man, and should there [151] translate it as "and he appeared," just as he has literally rendered the verse, *For I have seen 'Elokim' face to face,* [152] as "for I have seen an angel of G-d." Heaven forbid that the Divine Presence or the Glory created for the occasion be anything except the glorious Divine Name, blessed be He, as the Rabbi has expressed himself here [148] and in many chapters of his book. Thus Onkelos translated

(145) Moreh Nebuchim I, 28. (146) Zechariah 14:4. (147) Exodus 17:6. (148) Moreh Nebuchim I, 27. (149) Numbers 16:19. (150) Exodus 19:20. (151) Onkelos, *ibid.*, 3:2. (152) Above, Verse 32.

the expression, *If Thy face go not,* [153] as "if Thy Divine Presence go not among us." Now, other than the glorious Divine Name, blessed be He, Moses did not want a special Glory created to go with him, since the Holy One, blessed be He, had already told him, *Behold Mine angel shall go before thee,* [154] and Moses was not pleased with it. He instead wanted that G-d in His own glory should go with him. Also, after G-d heard his plea and told him, *I will do this thing also that thou hast spoken,* [155] Moses said, *Let the Lord, I pray thee, go in the midst of us,* [156] and this Onkelos rendered as "let now G-d's Divine Presence go among us." [157] He similarly translated the expression, *Thou canst not see My face,* [158] "thou cannot see the face of My Divine Presence, for man shall not see Me." [In translating the verse in the book of Ezekiel, *Blessed be the glory of the Eternal from His place,*] [159] Jonathan ben Uziel said, "Blessed be the glory of the Eternal from the region of His Divine abode." Now if by this "Glory," [which is mentioned in the book of Ezekiel] Scripture refers to the Creator in His true essence, analogous to the verse, *Show me, I pray Thee, Thy glory,* [160] which the Rabbi has indeed so interpreted, [161] then how did [Jonathan ben Uziel] in translating the verse mention "the region of His Divine abode" [when the terms "region," "abode," etc., indicate corporeality]? And if one would say that the verse in Ezekiel refers to a certain glory that had been created for the occasion, as is the opinion of the Rabbi with respect to the verse, *And the glory of the Eternal filled the tabernacle,* [162] and other similar verses, then how did the angels direct their words, "Blessed, etc.," towards it when he who blesses and prays to a glory created for an occasion is as he who worshipped idols? The teachings of our Rabbis also contain many texts which indicate that the name *Shechinah* (Divine Presence) is identical with G-d, blessed be He. But all these subjects, [some of which are rendered literally and some of

(153) Exodus 33:15. (154) *Ibid.*, 32:34. (155) *Ibid.*, 33:17. (156) *Ibid.*, 34:9. (157) We thus see that even here, where it is clear from the context that the verse refers to G-d and not an angel, Onkelos does not hesitate to translate "going" literally. (158) *Ibid.*, 33:20. (159) Ezekiel 3:12. (160) Exodus 33:18. (161) Moreh Nebuchim I, 54 and 64. (162) Exodus 40:35. Moreh Nebuchim I, 64.

which are paraphrased, are not influenced by a fear of using terms denoting corporeality but rather by secrets] of the Cabala [163] known to Onkelos and Jonathan ben Uziel, and the secrets thereof are revealed to those who know the mystic lore of the Torah. Thus in the Revelation on Mount Sinai, wherever *Elokim* is mentioned in that section, Onkelos renders it as "the Glory" or "the Word of G-d," but when Scripture mentions the Tetragrammaton he does not so render it. All this is done by Onkelos with extraordinary care and wisdom, and I will yet mention [164] this with the help of G-d, blessed be He. Now the reason that Onkelos literally translated the verse, *And 'Elokim' spoke all these words, saying,* [165] [rather than render it, "and the Glory of G-d spoke," as he usually does wherever *Elokim* is mentioned], is that it is said, *Face to face the Eternal spoke* [166] *unto your whole assembly.* [167] The student learned [in the mystic lore of the Cabala] will understand.

However, the reason why Onkelos here literally translated, *I will go down with thee to Egypt,* [and did not paraphrase it as "My Glory will go down with thee]," is that he wanted to allude to that which the Rabbis have said: [168] "When they were exiled to Egypt, the Divine Presence went with them, as it is said, *I will go down with thee to Egypt.* When they were exiled to Elam, the Divine Presence went down with them, as it is said, *And I will set My throne in Elam.*" [169] Thus both the verse which speaks of G-d "saying" [namely, *And He said, I am G-d, the G-d of thy father, etc.*], [170] and [the verse which speaks of G-d] "going down," [namely, *I will go down with thee*], are alike [for they both refer to the Creator in His true essence], as I have explained above, and therefore he could not, under any circumstances, have translated in any other way, as I have hinted. But there in the case of Jacob's dream, Onkelos could not have literally translated, "and behold I am with thee," [and was forced to paraphrase it as, "and My word will be in thy help]," [129] because it is written there, *And, behold, the Eternal stood beside*

(163) See Note 56 in Introduction to *Sefer Bereshith.* (164) See Ramban on Exodus 20:19. (165) *Ibid.*, 20:1. (166) Deuteronomy 5:4. (167) *Ibid.*, Verse 19. (168) Mechilta Shirah 3. See also Megillah 29 a. (169) Jeremiah 49:38. (170) Verse 3 here.

him. [171] The student learned [in the mystic lore of the Cabala] will understand. And due to the fact that Onkelos found the meaning of this verse not to be in line with its plain meaning, he therefore spurned [literally translating the rest of the verse, and rendered it as referring to assistance], and thus he said, "My word will be in thy help," instead of saying "My word will be with you," as he said in the case of Moses. [131] And may G-d show us wonders in His Torah.

2. AND HE SAID, JACOB, JACOB. After G-d had told him, *Thy name shall not be called any more Jacob, but Israel shall be thy name,* [172] it would be proper that He call him by this glorious name, and so he is indeed mentioned three times in this section. [173] However, He called him Jacob in order to hint that now he will not contend with G-d and men and prevail, [as the name Israel indicates], [174] but he will be in a house of bondage until He will also bring him up again, since the exile now begins with him. This is the meaning of the verse, *And these are the names of the children of Israel who came into Egypt, Jacob and his sons,* [175] for they would come there with the appellation, "children of Israel," since the children would multiply and increase there and their name and glory would extend. However, he is "Jacob" when descending thereto.

The reason why Scripture mentions Er and Onan [176] together with *the children of Israel who came into Egypt,* [177] [although they had already died, as clearly stated in Verse 12]; is due to a secret which can be known from the words we have already written. [177] The learned student [of the mystic lore of the Cabala] will understand this, as well as the meaning of the entire Verse [12]. Scripture

(171) 28:13. Since the Tetragrammaton ("the Eternal") represents the attribute of mercy, had Onkelos literally translated Verse 15, "and, behold, I am with thee," it would have indicated that this attribute would follow Jacob into exile since at the outset of this matter in Verse 13, Scripture uses the Tetragrammaton. Hence Onkelos translated Verse 15 as, 'and My word will be in thy help,' which is a reference to the attribute of judgment. (Bei'ur Ha'lvush to Rekanati on the Torah, who quotes the words of Ramban.) (172) Above, 35:10. (173) In Verses 1, 2 and 5. (174) Above, 32:29. (175) Verse 8 here. (176) Verse 12 here. (177) See Ramban above, 38:8.

likewise mentioned them among those numbered [178] in the desert: *The sons of Judah: Er and Onan; and Er and Onan died in the land of Canaan. And the sons of Judah after their families were,* etc. [179] And there, in the book of Chronicles, Scripture enumerates them in another count: *The sons of Judah: Er, and Onan and Shelah; which were born unto him of Bath-shua the Canaanitess...And Tamar his daughter-in-law bore him Perez and Zerah. All the sons of Judah were five.* [180]

7. AND HIS SONS' DAUGHTERS. These were Serah, the daughter of Asher, and Jochebed, the daughter of Levi. This is the language of Rashi. But what will Rashi include in the term, *his daughters,* [which is also plural, although Jacob only had one daughter, Dinah]? Rather, it is the way of Scripture, when mentioning the genealogy of many people, to refer to an individual in the plural form, as for example, *And the sons of Dan: Hushim;* [181] *And the sons of Palu: Eliab.* [182] The same is true here: "daughters" refer to Dinah. "His sons' daughters" refers to Serah the daughter of Asher, but Jochebed [Moses' mother] is not mentioned by Scripture [as being among the persons who went down to Egypt], as it is said, *All the souls were threescore and six.* [183] She is, however, hinted at, according to the opinion of our Rabbis. [184]

15. THIRTY AND THREE. But in the above enumeration you will find only thirty-two. However, the one whose name is omitted is Jochebed who was born as they entered the border city, as it is said, *Jochebed, the daughter of Levi, whom* [her mother] *bore to Levi in Egypt.* [185] She was born in Egypt, but she was not conceived in Egypt. This is the principle of our Rabbis.[184]

(178) The intent of the Hebrew text may also be that Scripture likewise mentions them "in the book of Numbers," thus giving this sentence the same format as Ramban's next sentence, "And in the book of Chronicles...." (179) Numbers 26:19-20. (180) I Chronicles 2:3-4. This is difficult to understand. Since two of his sons died prior to the birth of the youngest two, how does Scripture conclude that they totalled five? Thus there is here also an allusion to that which was referred to above. (181) Verse 23 here. (182) Numbers 26:8. (183) Verse 26 here. (184) Baba Bathra 123 a. See also Ramban, next Verse. (185) Numbers 26:59.

But Rabbi Abraham ibn Ezra replied, saying that "this is surprising. For if so, why did Scripture not mention the wonder that befell her, for she gave birth to Moses when she was one hundred and thirty years old? [186] And why did it mention the case of Sarah who gave birth when she was ninety years old? This distress was not yet sufficient for us so that the poets came and composed liturgic poems for the day of *Simchath Torah,* [187] wherein they state, 'Jochebed, my mother, will be comforted after me,' [implying that Jochebed survived her son], and thus she was two hundred and fifty years old at the death of Moses! [188] Is the proof of the poets for this longevity of Jochebed because Ahijah the Shilonite [189] lived a life of great duration? [190] [If so, this is not a proof, for his longevity is but] an Agadic tradition or the opinion of a single authority." [191] These are the words of Rabbi Abraham ibn Ezra.

Now lest he be wise in his own eyes [192] in contradicting the words of our Rabbis, I must answer him and say that in any case, there is in the matter of Jochebed a great wonder of the hidden miracles [193] which constitute the foundation of the Torah. Jochebed was Levi's actual daughter, and not merely his offspring, as it is written, *Jochebed, the daughter of Levi, whom* [her mother[*bore to Levi,* [185] and it is furthermore written, *And Amram took himself Jochebed his father's sister for a wife.* [194] [Thus Amram, Levi's

(186) Israel stayed in Egypt two hundred and ten years. Since Moses was eighty years old when he stood before Pharaoh, he was thus born one hundred and thirty years after they entered Egypt. (187) Literally, "Rejoicing of the Law." On this festival day, which marks the last day of the festival of Succoth, the concluding chapter of the life of Moses is read in the Synagogue. The joyous celebrations on this day are due to the annual completion of the reading of the Torah, as well as to the fact that it is commenced anew. (188) Her age when Moses was born added to Moses' life span of one hundred and twenty totals two hundred and fifty. (189) I Kings 11:29. (190) According to an Agadic tradition, Ahijah the Shilonite was among those who went out of Egypt, and lived to the days of Jeroboam I, king of Israel, a period of about four hundred and fifty years. (Baba Bathra 121 b.) On the basis of this tradition, the poets claimed that since longevity was possible for Ahijah, it was possible also for Jochebed, Moses' mother. (191) The source for Ahijah's longevity is the Seder Olam, Chapter 1. This book is a chronicle of Biblical times, composed by Rabbi Yosei ben Chalaphtah, a disciple of Rabbi Akiba. (192) Proverbs 26:5. (193) See Ramban, above, 17:1. (194) Exodus 6:20.

grandson, married Jochebed, Levi's daughter.] Now if we would say that Levi begot Jochebed in his younger years, just as he begot all his sons, this would place her birth soon after his descent into Egypt, and she would have been very old at the time of Moses' birth,[186] at or near the age stated by our Rabbis.[195] And if we would say that he begot her after he resided in Egypt for many years – say, for a period of fifty-seven years – then Levi would have been one hundred years old at Jochebed's birth, for when he went down to Egypt he was forty-three years[196] of age. In that case, there were two great wonders! [Levi, at the time he begot Jochebed], was as old as Abraham, concerning whom Scripture mentions, *Shall a child be born to him who is a hundred years old?*[197] and it is further written, *And my lord is old also,*[198] while Jochebed would still have been an elderly woman of seventy-three when Moses was born! And should we further postpone Jochebed's birth to the end of Levi's days, the wonder of his begetting a child will be greater than that of Abraham!

But I will tell you a true principle, clearly indicated in the Torah. Scripture mentions miracles performed through a prophet and which he previously prophesied, or performed by an angel who is revealed in the course of a Divine mission, but those effected naturally in order to help the righteous or destroy the wicked are not mentioned in the Torah or in the books of the prophets. May this be "hot gold poured into the mouth"[199] of this wise man who refuted the words of our Rabbis in the matter of Phinehas[200] and similar matters in many places. Why should Scripture mention hidden miracles when all the foundations of the Torah are hidden miracles. In the entire scope of the Torah there are only miracles, and no nature or custom. All assurances of the Torah are in the form of signs and wonders, as it is not natural that he who has connection with one of the forbidden

(195) In that case the wonder would have been only on the part of Jochebed. (196) Jacob married Leah when he was eighty-four years old. (Bereshith Rabbah 68:5). When Levi, her third son, was born, Jacob was thus eighty-seven. When he stood before Pharaoh, Jacob said that he was one hundred and thirty years old (47:9). Thus Levi was forty-three at that time. (197) Above, 17:17. (198) *Ibid.*, 18:12. (199) Sanhedrin 92 b. (200) In his Commentary to Numbers 25:12, Ibn Ezra brushes aside the tradition that Phinehas is identical with Elijah.

degrees of marriage or he who eats forbidden fat suffers excision or death.[201] Nor is it by nature that the heavens become as iron[202] because we have sowed our fields in the Sabbatical year. Similarly, all the assurances of the Torah concerning those blessings [which will result from our observance of the law], and all the good fortune of the righteous ones because of their righteousness, as well as all the prayers of our king David [in the book of Psalms] and all our prayers, all are founded upon miracles and wonders, except that there is no heralded change in the nature of the world, as I have already mentioned,[193] and I will yet explain it further,[203] with the help of G-d.

I will give you faithful testimony to that which I have said. We know that from the time Israel came into the Land until the birth of our lord David, about three hundred and seventy years elapsed.[204] These years are to be divided among four generations: Salmon, Boaz, Obed, and Jesse [David's father],[205] each one being allotted ninety-three years. Thus when they begot children they were all approximately as old as Abraham was when he begot Isaac. Furthermore, each one begot his son in the year of his death, a most unusual thing, since in their era the general span of life was not a hundred years. And if one of them begot his son in his younger years, as is usual, the others would have had to be much older than Abraham, and thus the wonder concerning them would be exceedingly great since people in the generation of Abraham lived long, and in the days of David the average lifespan was reduced to a half. And perhaps these four generations lived longer than their contemporaries for it is possible that Salmon was already advanced in years when he entered the Land of Israel. It is for this reason that the masters of Tradition, who are the true Sages, have attributed longevity to Obed,[206] this being a covert miracle which was done to

(201) Ramban here refers to death by heavenly punishment. See, for example, Leviticus 20:17. (202) Leviticus 26:19. (203) *Ibid.*, Verse 11. (204) From the Exodus to the building of the Temple, four hundred and eighty years elapsed (I Kings 6:1). Deduct the forty years spent in the desert and the seventy years of David's lifespan, and the remainder is three hundred and seventy. (205) Ruth 4: 21-22. (206) Bereshith Rabbah 96:4: "The Sages have said, Obed lived more than four hundred years."

the ancestor of the kingdom [of the house of David], the son of the righteous one [Ruth], who had come to take refuge under the wings of the Divine Presence.[207] The Sages similarly mention longevity in connection with Obed's mother, Ruth.[208] Now I have already explained[197] that the wonder in the case of Abraham was not as the above-mentioned Sage [Rabbi Abraham ibn Ezra] and other masters of the Scriptures have thought.[209] Abraham begot Isaac seventy-five years before his death, prior to the completion of two-thirds of his lifespan, and in all generations, old age does not affect people until three quarters of their lives have passed, just as the doctors have considered the divisions of life to be: childhood, youth, manhood, and old age. In these generations, when the lifespan is about seventy years, doctors do not consider a person aged until after sixty. Moreover, Abraham begot many children[210] forty years after the birth of Isaac, and the wonder is thus manifoldly miraculous! And should we say that G-d caused Abraham to revert to his youthful days, it may be asked why Scripture does not mention this great wonder when it was an open and known miracle which is contrary to nature. Moreover, it is known that in this present generation some men beget children until they are full seventy or eighty years old and more, depending upon the extent to which they retain their natural vitality. Women also have no specific time [for ceasing to conceive], as long as they have their period they can give birth. However, the wonder in the case of Abraham and Sarah, as I explained there,[197] was due to the fact that they had not begotten children in their younger years, and now together they begot a child. In the case of Sarah there was an additional wonder, i.e., *that the manner of women*[211] had ceased with her, and after this happens, women no longer give birth. Now if Jochebed lived as many years as her father Levi had,[212] and if her vitality remained with her until near her old age, as is the way of women, it would be no wonder if she gave birth

(207) See Ruth 2:12. (208) In Baba Bathra 91 b, it is stated that Ruth was still alive in the days of Solomon. (209) That the wonder was due to Abraham's advanced age. (210) Above, 25: 1-2. (211) *Ibid.,* 18:11. (212) One hundred and thirty-seven years (Exodus 6:16).

at the time set forth by our Rabbis, [namely, at one hundred and thirty years of age]. It is because G-d wanted to redeem Israel though the brothers [Moses and Aaron], and since the time of the redemption had not yet come, He delayed their birth many years until their mother was old. Nothing is too difficult for the Eternal.[213]

Rabbeinu Shlomo [Rashi] wrote:[214] "According to the view that a twin-sister was born with each of Jacob's sons, we must say that they died before Jacob and his sons went down to Egypt because they are not enumerated here." There is no necessity for this conclusion, for the Rabbis have said:[215] "Rabbi Yehudah says that Jacob's sons married their sisters." These twin-sisters were thus the wives of Jacob's sons, concerning whom Scripture says, *besides Jacob's sons' wives.*[214] In fact, Rabbi Yehudah arrived at this opinion on the basis of this verse, since if it refers to Canaanitish women what reason is there for Scripture to say, *besides Jacob's sons' wives,* after it had already said, *that came out of his loins?*[214] It is only because his sons' wives were also of those "that came out of his loins" that Scripture refers to them. It does not, however, divulge them here, just as it did not mention them explicitly when they were born together with Jacob's sons. Furthermore, Scripture mentions here only those who begot children and increased in Egypt, in order to make known the great miracle which was performed in the mighty increase which they effected in Egypt, for at this juncture, they numbered seventy souls. Thus their wives were not counted because a man and his wife are one.

18. THESE ARE THE SONS OF ZILPAH, etc. 19. THE SONS OF RACHEL JACOB'S WIFE, etc. It is customary for Scripture to first enumerate the sons of the mistresses together, just as it said in the *Seder Vayishlach Yaakov*[216] and in the *Seder V'eileh Shmoth bnei Yisrael,*[217] or else to enumerate them according to the order of their birth, *the firstborn according to his birthright and the youngest according to his youth,*[218] as Scripture did when they were blessed

(213) See above, 18:14. (214) Verse 26 here. (215) Bereshith Rabbah 84:19. See also Ramban, above, 38:2. (216) Above, 35: 23-26. (217) Exodus 1: 2-4. (218) Above, 43:33.

by Jacob in the *Seder Vayechi Yaakov.* [219] Here, however, because Scripture's purpose was to enumerate their numbers and to state that with seventy souls they went down to Egypt, it gave precedence to those who were more numerous. This was why Scripture mentioned Rachel among the concubines, and hence it was necessary to mention her with respect, saying, *Jacob's wife,* as I have mentioned above. [220]

29. AND HE APPEARED BEFORE HIM. Joseph appeared before his father. *And he wept on his neck a good while.* The phrase *vayeivk od* signifies "weeping copiously." Jacob, however, did not fall upon the neck of his son Joseph, nor did he kiss him. Our Rabbis said that this was because he was reciting the *Shema,* (the affirmation of G-d's Unity). This is the language of Rashi. But [according to this interpretation, which says that it was Joseph who fell on his father's neck and wept], I know of no reason for the statement, *And he appeared before him,* since it is understood that Joseph appeared before Jacob since he fell upon his neck. Moreover, it is not respectful for Joseph to fall upon his father's neck. He should rather bow before him or kiss his hands, as it is written, *And Joseph brought them out from between his knees, and he fell down on his face.* [221] And at the present moment, it was more fitting that he bow to him [than at the time referred to in the aforementioned verse]. [221] So also, every term *'od'* in Scripture indicates an addition to the original but does not imply copiousness. Thus: *He doth not set a stated time 'od' for a man,* [222] which means, "He sets a stated time for a man in accordance with his transgression, and nothing is added." [223]

The correct interpretation appears to me to be that Israel's eyes were already slightly dim from age, [224] and when Joseph arrived *in the carriage of the second in rank,* [225] with a mitre on his head as

(219) See my Hebrew Commentary (p. 295) where the point is made that Ramban refers only to Joseph and Benjamin. Either Scripture mentions them at first together with the sons of Leah, as it did in *Seder Vayishlach* and in *Shmoth,* or according to their age, as it did in *Vayechi.* Ramban is attempting to explain why they are mentioned here after Zilpah's children. (220) Above, 37:2. (221) Further, 48:12. (222) Job 34:23. (223) We thus see that *od* can refer to a slight increase. (224) See further, 48:10. (225) Above, 42, 43.

was the custom of the Egyptian kings, his father did not recognize him. His brothers also had not recognized him.[226] Therefore Scripture mentioned that when he appeared before his father, who stared at him and finally recognized him, his father fell on his neck and cried again over him, even as he had continually cried over him to this day when he had not seen him after his disappearance, and then Jacob said, *Now let me die, since I have seen thy face.*[227] It is a known matter as to whose tears are more constant: that of an old father who finds his son alive after having despaired of him and having mourned for him, or that of a grown-up son who reigns. Do not be concerned [lest this interpretation be open to question] because Scripture immediately says, *And Israel said,*[228] [thus implying that the previous subject is not Israel but Joseph], whereas according to our interpretation Scripture is speaking of Jacob and then mentions his name once again in the following verse. A similar case is found in these verses: *And he gathered up all the foods of the seven years,* etc.,[229] [where Joseph is the subject of the verse, and yet Scripture mentions his name in the succeeding verse], *And unto Joseph were born two sons.*[230] There are constantly many similar places in the Torah and in the other books of Scripture.

32. AND THE MEN ARE SHEPHERDS, FOR THEY HAVE BEEN KEEPERS OF CATTLE. Joseph told them that they are shepherds but that they do not tend to the cattle of others because even with respect to their own cattle, they have servants and attendants to pasture them. It is only that their wealth consists of cattle. This is the sense of the expression, *they have been keepers of cattle,* and had wealth, *and a very great household*[231] by virtue of the great multitude of cattle which they possessed. It was Joseph's intention to mention them in an honorable way.

47 4. TO SOJOURN IN THE LAND ARE WE COME; FOR THERE IS NO PASTURE FOR THY SERVANTS' FLOCKS. I wonder about this reason which they told to Pharaoh, for there was also no pasture in Egypt; the famine was as severe in the land of

(226) *Ibid.,* 42:8. (227) Verse 31 here. (228) Verse 30 here. (229) Above, 41:48. (230) *Ibid.,* Verse 50. (231) Job 1:3.

Egypt as it was in the land of Canaan, or even more so, for it was against Egypt that the main decree was directed. Perhaps they said that in the land of Canaan, due to the severity of the famine, people were eating the grass of the field and were not leaving any sustenance for the cattle. However, in the land of Egypt where there is corn, people subsist on that, and thus in Egypt there is a little pasture left. It is possible that in the land of Egypt there was a little pasture in the reedgrass on account of the rivers and the ponds.

5. THY FATHER AND THY BRETHREN ARE COME UNTO THEE. This introduction is as if to say: "Now I have heard that your father and your brothers have come, and the land of Egypt is before you." The correct interpretation appears to me to be that Pharaoh said to Joseph: "Your father and your brothers have come to you because they have heard of your glory, and it is upon you that they have cast their burden. See that you treat them well for it is your responsibility and it is within your power."

7. AND JACOB BLESSED PHARAOH. This refers to a salutation, as is customary for all who are granted an occasional interview with kings. Thus the language of Rashi. But this does not appear to be so, for it is not royal protocol for a person to greet the king, and the Rabbis have similarly said: [232] "May a servant greet the king?" Instead, it refers to a real blessing which Jacob bestowed upon Pharaoh, for it is customary for aged and pious people who come before kings to bless them with wealth, possessions, honor, and the advancement of their kingdom, even as Scripture says, *Let my lord king David live forever.* [233] Upon his taking leave of Pharaoh, Jacob again blessed him [234] in order to take permission to leave. Our Rabbis have said [235] that he blessed him that the Nile might rise at his approach.

9. FEW AND EVIL HAVE BEEN THE DAYS OF THE YEARS OF MY LIFE. I know no reason for this comment by our aged patriarch. Is it ethical for a person to complain to the king? And

(232) Shabbath 89 a. (233) I Kings 1:31. (234) Verse 10 here. (235) Tanchuma Naso 26, and mentioned here by Rashi.

what sense is there in saying, *and they have not attained unto the days of the years of the life of my fathers?* He may yet possibly attain them and live even longer than they did!

It appears to me that our father Jacob had turned gray, and he appeared very old. Pharaoh wondered about his age, for most people of his time did not live very long as the lifespan of mankind had already been shortened. [236] He therefore asked him, "*How many are the days of the years of thy life,* [237] as I have not seen a man as aged as you in my entire kingdom?" Then Jacob answered that he was one hundred and thirty years of age, and that he should not wonder at the years he had lived for they are few when compared with the lifespans of his fathers who had lived longer. However, on account of their having been hard years of toil and groaning, he had turned gray and he appeared extremely old.

11. AND JOSEPH SETTLED HIS FATHER AND HIS BRETHREN AND GAVE THEM A POSSESSION, etc. The meaning thereof is that he settled them in the choicest land and with the possession which he gave them since he did not want them to be as strangers in the land. Thus he bought them houses and gave them *an inheritance of fields and vineyards.* [238] This he did with the permission of Pharaoh because they had said, "*To sojourn in the land are we come,* [239] not to live, and when the famine will pass we will return to our land." But Pharaoh said to Joseph, *Settle thy father,* [240] meaning that he settle them in the manner of citizens of the land who reside in the land of Goshen.

14. AND JOSEPH GATHERED UP ALL THE MONEY, etc. Scripture relates this and goes on to complete the subject in this entire section in order to make known Joseph's excellence *in wisdom, in understanding, and in knowledge,* [241] and that he was *a faithful man* [242] in that he brought all money into Pharaoh's house and did not accumulate for himself treasures of money and secret

(236) See Ramban, above, 5:4. (237) Verse 8 here. (238) Numbers 16:14. (239) Verse 4 here. (240) Verse 6 here. (241) Exodus 31:3. (242) Proverbs 20:6.

hiding places for wealth in the land of Egypt, or send it to the land of Canaan. Instead, he gave all money to the king who trusted him and purchased the land for him, and even the bodies of the Egyptians. Through this endeavor, he found grace even in the eyes of the people, for it is G-d Who causes those who fear Him to prosper.

15. AND WHEN THE MONEY WAS ALL SPENT IN THE LAND OF EGYPT, AND IN THE LAND OF CANAAN, ALL THE EGYPTIANS CAME UNTO JOSEPH, etc. Scripture mentions that the money in the land of Canaan had been exhausted because when the Egyptians came before Joseph they reminded him of this, for they said: "Since the money is also exhausted in the land of Canaan, and since they will no longer come to buy food, *why should we die in thy presence? For the money is at an end,* and you will cause our death in vain, for the food will remain in your hand, and no man shall buy it."

18. THEY CAME UNTO HIM IN THE SECOND YEAR. I.e., the second year of the years of the famine. Now although Joseph had said, *And there are yet five years when there will be no plowing and sowing,* [243] as soon as Jacob came to Egypt a blessing came with his arrival, and they began to sow and the famine came to an end. And thus we read in the Tosephta of Tractate Sotah.[244] Thus the language of Rashi. And it is similarly mentioned in Bereshith Rabbah: [245] "Rabbi Yosei the son of Rabbi Chanina said that the famine lasted for two years, for when our father Jacob went down to Egypt the famine ceased. When did it return? In the days of Ezekiel, etc." But if so, then Joseph's words regarding his interpretation of [Pharaoh's dream which predicted the seven years of famine] were not fulfilled, and would thus cause people to doubt his wisdom! Perhaps we shall say that the famine continued in the land of Canaan as Joseph had said, but in Egypt our father Jacob went down to the

(243) Above, 45:6. (244) 10:9. *Tosephta* means "addition." This is a collection of Tannaitic teachings compiled by Rabbi Chiya and Rabbi Oshayah soon after the Mishnah was completed by Rabbi Yehudah Hanasi. (245) 89:11.

river in the presence of Pharaoh and all of Egypt, whereupon all his people saw that the waters in the Nile rose as he approached it, and thus they knew that G-d's blessing was due to the prophet's arrival. In that case, the verse stating, *And Joseph sustained his father, and his brethren, and all his father's household, with bread, according to the want of their little children,*[246] applies to the remainder of the seven years and for as long as his father lived,[247] for even after his father's death, Joseph said, *I will sustain you and your little ones.*[248]

Yet, with all this, I wonder: for if so, then Pharaoh's dream was not true since it only revealed the decree to him but not what would ultimately become of those seven years! Now I have seen there in the Tosephta of Tractate Sotah:[244] "Rabbi Yosei said that as soon as our father Jacob died, the famine reverted to its former condition, etc." We have further been taught in the Sifre:[249] *"And Jacob blessed Pharaoh.*[234] How did he bless him? [His blessing was] that the years of famine should cease. Nevertheless they were completed after Jacob's death, as it is said, *Now therefore fear ye not; I will sustain you.*[248] Now just as 'sustaining' mentioned above[250] by Scripture refers to years of famine, so also 'sustaining' mentioned here[248] refers to years of famine. Rabbi Shimon says, 'It is not a sanctification of G-d's Name for the words of the righteous to be effective as long as they live, and then to be removed after their death.' Rabbi Eleazar the son of Rabbi Shimon said, 'I accept the opinion of Rabbi Yosei rather than that of my father, for it is indeed a sanctification of G-d's Name for there to be a blessing in the world for the period that the righteous are in the world, and for the blessing to remove from the world when they leave.'" Thus far the text of the Tosephta. Thus the remaining five years of the famine were completed.

The opinion of Rabbi Abraham ibn Ezra is that these two years, [recounted in Verses 14-20, during which the Egyptians gave their money and cattle to Joseph in exchange for food], occurred after

(246) Verse 12 here. (247) According to the Tur's version of Ramban, this passage reads: "applies to the years of plenty of his father's entire lifespan." (248) Further, 50:21. (249) Sifre Eikev, 38. (250) Above, 45:11. *And there I will sustain thee, for there are yet five years of famine.*

Jacob had come to Egypt, [and since there were two years of famine before he came to Egypt, this accounts for four of the seven years of famine]. And Ibn Ezra wrote as follows: "We find in homiletic texts of the Rabbis that the famine was removed by the merit of Jacob. It is also possible that there were three more years of famine, but that they were not as severe as the first four years which had passed." But Ibn Ezra's words are not at all correct. The account of the dream and its interpretation make all seven years alike, and, had it been as he said, Scripture would have mentioned the different nature of these three last years.

In line with the plain meaning of Scripture, Joseph gathered up all the money that was found in the land of Egypt and in the land of Canaan during a period of five years, and he brought it to Pharaoh, for how is it possible for the money and cattle to be exhausted in one year? Rather, the money sufficed them for the entire five years, as is the usual way of the world. [251] Now since nothing was initiated, and no change of any kind occurred during all these years, Scripture relates nothing about them except, *And Joseph gathered up all the money,* etc. [252] When the money was exhausted, Scripture relates that they came to Joseph – this was in the sixth year of the famine – and he gave them bread in exchange for their cattle. He fed them with bread only to the extent of sustaining them, but not to satiety. *And when that year was ended,* [253] in which he had vowed to them that he would feed them with bread in exchange for their cattle–which was the sixth year–*they came unto him the second year,* [i.e., the year following the sixth year of famine being discussed], and they told him that he should purchase them and their land for the bread which he will feed them during that seventh year, and since the land will then belong to Pharaoh, he should give them seed so that the land will not be desolate, for they knew that when the seven years of famine will be completed, they will have planting and reaping. The verse stating, *And Joseph sustained his father...with bread, according to the want of their little ones,* [246] thus means that he furnished them with bread sufficient for their needs during the famine, as the expression, *according to the want of their little ones,* indicates.

(251) In a time of famine, people conserve money and make it last for a long period of time. (252) Verse 14 here. (253) Verse 18 here.

19. BUY US AND OUR LAND. Now they said to him that he should also purchase their bodies as servants for Pharaoh, and thus did Joseph say, *Behold, I have bought you this day and your land.* [254] However, Scripture records, *And Joseph bought all the land of Egypt for Pharaoh; for the Egyptians sold every man his field,* [255] but it does not say that he bought their bodies, only the land. The reason for it is that the Egyptians told Joseph that he should purchase them as servants to perform the king's business as he pleases. But Joseph wanted to buy only the land, and he made a condition with them that they work on it forever, thus becoming Pharaoh's family tenants. Afterwards he said to them, *"Behold, I have bought you this day and your land for Pharaoh,* [254] not as servants as you told me, but you will belong to him with the land. Now it is proper that the king, who is now lord of the land, take four parts of the harvest and that you take the remaining fifth, but I will deal kindly with you in that you will take the portion due to the owner of the land, and Pharaoh will take the portion due the tenant. However, you will be sold to him in that you will not be able to leave the fields." This is the meaning of that which they vowed to him, *And the land will not be desolate* [256] meaning that it will never be desolate. For this reason they said to Joseph, *"We have found favor in the sight of my lord,* [257] for you have been lenient with us by permitting us to take four parts of the harvest so that we may use them to live, *and we will be Pharaoh's servants,* [257] as we have vowed, in that we will work the ground in accordance with his will."

(254) Verse 23 here. (255) Verse 20 here. (256) Verse 19 here. (257) Verse 25 here.

Vayechi

28. AND JACOB LIVED IN THE LAND OF EGYPT SEVENTEEN YEARS. I have already mentioned [1] that Jacob's descent into Egypt alludes to our present exile at the hand of the "fourth beast,"[2] which represents Rome. [There are many parallels,] for it was Jacob's sons themselves who, by the sale of their brother Joseph, caused their going down there. Jacob, moreover, went there on account of the famine, thinking to find relief with his son in the house of his son's friend, for Pharaoh loved Joseph and considered him as a son. It was their hope to ascend from there as soon as the famine would cease in the land of Canaan, just as they said, *To sojourn in the land we have come, for thy servants have no pasture for their flocks, for the famine is heavy in the land of Canaan.* [3] But then they did not come up, but instead the exile prolonged itself upon Jacob and he died there, and his bones ascended from there accompanied by all the elders and courtiers of Pharaoh, who instituted severe lamentation for him. Our relationship with our brothers Rome and Edom is similar. We ourselves have caused our falling into their clutches, as they [4] made a covenant with the Romans, and Agrippa, the last king during the Second Temple, fled to them for help. It was due to famine that Jerusalem was captured by the Romans, and the exile has exceedingly prolonged itself over us, with its end, unlike the other

(1) Above, 43:14. (2) In Daniel's vision concerning the Four Kingdoms, the fourth beast symbolizes Rome. See Daniel 7:7, also Note 8 in *Seder Vayeitzei.* (3) Above, 47:4. (4) The Hasmonean rulers during the Second Temple era. See Abodah Zarah 8 b.

exiles, [5] being unknown. We are in it as the dead, who say, "Our bones are dried up, we are completely cut off." [6] But in the end they will bring us from all the nations as *an offering to the Eternal,* [7] and they will be in deep sorrow as they will behold our glory, and we will see the vengeance of the Eternal. *May He raise us, that we may live in His presence.* [8]

29. AND WHEN THE DAYS OF ISRAEL DREW NEAR TO DIE. This means when the time for Israel's death approached, which was during the last year of his life, [9] he called his son Joseph. The purport of it is that he felt exhaustion and undue weakness in himself, but he was not sick. Rather, he knew that he would not live much longer, and therefore he called his son Joseph. Now after Joseph returned to Egypt [from visiting with his father who lived in Goshen, Jacob] became ill, whereupon Joseph was informed, and he came before him with his two sons so that he [Jacob] would bless them.

In a similar sense is the verse, *Now the days of David drew near that he should die,* [10] and there it says, *I go the way of all the earth,* [11] [which clearly indicates that the meaning of the first verse is] that David knew in his heart that his end was approaching.

31. SWEAR UNTO ME. AND HE SWORE UNTO HIM. Jacob did not suspect that his righteous and beloved son would disobey his father's command and renege on the matter which he had promised him by saying, *I will do according to thy words.* [12] But Jacob did so in order to strengthen the matter in the eyes of Pharaoh, as perhaps he might not give Joseph permission to leave him, and he would instead say to him, "Send your brothers and

(5) It was known that the Babylonian Exile would last for a period of seventy years, (Jeremiah 25:12; II Chronicles 36:21). There was also a terminus known for the Egyptian Exile, (above 16:13). (6) See Ezekiel 37:11. (7) Isaiah 66:20. (8) Hosea 6:2. (9) Ramban's intent is to say that the verse does not refer to Jacob's day of death but to the general period in his life when he felt his powers beginning to ebb. (10) I Kings 2:1. There too the sense of the verse is that this occurred some time before David's death. (11) *Ibid.*, Verse 2. (12) Verse 30 here.

your servants, and they will bring him up there." It may be that Pharaoh would want the prophet [13] to be buried in his country as an honor and privilege to them. It was for this reason that he made him swear for it would not then be proper for him to force Joseph to violate his oath, and Joseph too would feel more obligated to fulfill his father's wish on account of the oath. Such indeed was the case, as Pharaoh said, *Go up, and bury thy father, as he made you swear.* [14]

48 6. AND THE CHILDREN THAT WERE BORN TO YOU AFTER THEM. "If you beget any more children, they will not be numbered among my sons, but they will rather be included among the tribes of Ephraim and Menasheh. Nor shall they have a name amongst the tribes as far as inheritance in the Land of Israel is concerned." Now even though the Land of Israel was divided according to the number of persons, as it is written, *To the more thou shalt give the more inheritance,* [15] and each person received an equal share except for the first-born, who received a double share, [16] nevertheless only these sons were designated as "tribes." This is the language of Rashi.

Now this is not correct, for if so, [17] then Jacob's granting of the birthright to Joseph was just nominal, its only effect being that Joseph's sons would be called "tribes," whereas the verse states, *in their inheritance.* [18] In the *Gemara,* [19] the Sages have said: "I have likened Ephraim and Menasheh to Reuben and Simeon with respect to the matter of inheritance, but not with respect to other

(13) Jacob. – Rashi quotes Hilchoth Gedoloth in Megillah 14 a that Jacob was one of the forty-eight prophets that arose in Israel. (14) 50:6. (15) Numbers 26:54. (16) Deuteronomy 21:17. (17) If, as Rashi says, Joseph's designation as firstborn meant only that Joseph's two sons shall be counted as separate tribes, but not that they shall receive a double share in the Land, then it follows that, etc. (18) At the end of the verse before us: *And the children that were born to you after shall be counted to you; they shall be called after the name of their brethren 'in their inheritance.'* This indicates that the two sons of Joseph were to be given the extra right of the firstborn in the matter of inheritance. (19) Horayoth 6 b.

matters,"[20] as is stated in Tractate Horayoth.[19] Our Rabbis have mentioned in many places[21] that Joseph was the first-born as far as inheritance was concerned, and that he received a double share in the Land, as is the rule of every first-born,[16] but not that his being first-born consisted merely of his sons being called "tribes," as the Rabbi [Rashi] would have it.

From this we further learn that the Land was not divided among all the tribes of Israel according to their populations for if so, what was the significance of this primogeniture with respect to inheritance? If we would say it meant that each and every individual offspring of Joseph was given double that of each person of all other tribes, this is not mentioned at all in Scripture, and we do not find Jacob giving the birthright to Joseph except by what he said here, *As Reuben and Simeon shall they be to me,*[22] and based upon this, Scripture states, *His* [Reuben's] *birthright was given to the sons of Joseph the son of Israel.*[23] If so, then Ephraim and Menasheh were fully considered as two tribes, and it was this which constituted Joseph's birthright, and the words of the Sages indeed corroborate this everywhere.

Thus the matter is not at all as the Rabbi[24] stated it. Instead, the Land of Israel was divided according to tribes. They made twelve equal parts of it, with Simeon, the least populous of the tribes, taking a share equal to that of Judah, the most populous of the tribes, and thus, Ephraim and Menasheh took exactly the same amount of land as Reuben and Simeon. This is the conclusion of the *Gemara* in the chapter, *Yesh Nochalin.*[25] Scripture also states,

(20) As, for example, the case of a Sin-offering which is brought by the great Sanhedrin for an erroneous decision, followed by *most of the tribes* even though they did not constitute an actual majority of the entire population. In that case Ephraim and Menasheh are considered part of the tribe of Joseph. (21) Baba Bathra 123 a. (22) Verse 5 here. (23) I Chronicles 5:1. (24) Rashi. Rashi's premise that the Land was divided according to population is disputed by Ramban. Since, according to Ramban, each tribe received an equal portion, he proceeds to differ with Rashi and says that Joseph received twice as much land as any other tribe since Ephraim and Menasheh were considered separate tribes. (25) Baba Bathra 121 b. *Yesh Nochalin* ("There are some that inherit,") the eighth chapter of that tractate, deals with all problems of personal inheritance, as well as with the whole range of problems connected with the original division of the Land by Joshua.

Ye shall divide the land for inheritance according to the twelve tribes of Israel, Joseph receiving two portions. [26] So too does Onkelos say, [27] "Two tribes shall come forth from his sons. They shall receive *chulka ve'achsanta* (portion and inheritance)," which means that they shall be equal to the other tribes with respect to inheritance received. Now *chulka* (portion) refers to the extra share of the first-born, and *achsanta* (inheritance) refers to ordinary inheritance. In the verse stating, *To the more thou shalt give the more inheritance, and to the fewer thou shalt give the less inheritance,* [28] Scripture refers to the paternal families mentioned there in the chapter. [29] Scripture is stating that the tribe divides its share of the land among the paternal families that left Egypt by giving a larger portion to a more populous family and a smaller portion to a less populous family, with the dead becoming heirs of the living, as is explained in the Sifre [30] and is mentioned by Rashi in the *Parshah* of *Pinchas.* [31] Thus the general principle with respect to Joseph was that he was the first-born as regards inheritance, and if, as mentioned in the *Gemara,* [25] the land was divided according to the number of tribes, they gave the children of Joseph portions equal to those of Reuben and Simeon.

And even if we were to say that the land was divided according to the number of persons, as is apparent from the verse, [32] then we would say that they gave them double portions commensurate with their numbers — an ordinary share as large as all the other people, and a second portion for the birthright. In that case, the meaning of Jacob's words, *As Reuben and Simeon shall they be to me,* [22] is that they should receive as many shares as twice their number of people. But that Joseph should be as the other tribes with respect to inheritance, with the birthright consisting of his two sons being

(26) Ezekiel 47:13. (27) In translating the blessing bestowed upon Joseph by Jacob. Further, 49:22. (28) Numbers 26:54. This verse, which seems to indicate that the Land was divided according to population, as Rashi taught, is explained by Ramban as referring to the internal division within each tribe. (29) *Ibid.*, Verses 8-50. (30) Sifre Pinchas 132. See also Ramban on Numbers 26:54. (31) Rashi, *ibid.* (32) *To the more thou shalt give the more inheritance,* etc. (Numbers 26:54.)

called "tribes," as the Rabbi [33] stated, this is impossible under any circumstance.

7. AND I BURIED HER THERE. In Rashi's commentary it is written, "And I did not transport her for burial even to Bethlehem to bring her into the Land."

Now I do not know the meaning thereof. Was Rachel buried outside of the Land? Forbid it! She died within the Land, and she was buried there, just as it says here in the *parshah: Rachel died by me in the land of Canaan.* [34] And there in the narrative of her death it is still more clearly written, *And Jacob came to Luz, which is in the land of Canaan – the same is Beth-el,* [35] and it is further stated, *And they journeyed from Beth-el and there was still some way to come to Ephrath,* [36] and Rachel died on the way between Beth-el and Bethlehem Ephratha in the Land of Israel.

AND I BURIED HER THERE. "Now I know that there is some resentment in your heart against me [for not having brought her into the city]. But you should know that I buried her there by the word of G-d, that she might help her children when Nebuzaradan [37] would exile them," for when they passed along that road, Rachel came forth from her grave and stood by her tomb beseeching mercy for them, as it is said, *A voice is heard in Ramah, lamentation and bitter weeping, Rachel weeping for her children,* [38] and the Holy One, blessed by He, answered her, *Thy work shall be rewarded ... and the children shall return to their own border.* [39] This is the language of Rashi.

Now in any case there should be some allusion in Scripture to this interpretation which is stated in this Agadah. Perhaps this is alluded to in the expression of the verse, *She died by me ... in the*

(33) Rashi. In his commentary to Numbers 26:54, Ramban further discusses this problem at great length. (34) In the verse before us. (35) Above, 35:6. (36) *Ibid.*, Verse 16. (37) Chief general of Nebuchadnezzar, king of Babylon, who destroyed the city of Jerusalem, burned the Temple, and led the people into captivity (II Kings 25:8-21). (38) Jeremiah 31:15. (39) *Ibid.*, Verses 16-17.

way ... And I buried her in the way,[40] that is to say, "She died on the road which her children would pass, and I buried her there for her advantage." She did not die on the road, but in Ramah,[41] a city in the land of Benjamin, and there she was buried. [Thus, according to the Midrash, Scripture is implying that] she died on the road which her children were destined to pass in the future, as Scripture does not fully explain future events but only alludes to them in a general manner.

In line with the plain meaning of Scripture, it is likewise understood that Jacob spoke to Joseph in an apologetic vein so that when he discerned his father's wish to be buried in the cave of Machpelah, Joseph should not be angered about his failure to bury his mother there just as he buried Leah there. It was for this reason that Jacob told him that she died in the land of Canaan, and she was not buried outside of the Land in the manner in which an Egyptian burial would befall Jacob. Furthermore, she died on the road suddenly, and he could not bury her in the cave of Machpelah for how could he leave his children and his flocks on the road and hurry with her body to the cave of Machpelah? And where could he find doctors and medicines to embalm her? This is the meaning of the word *alai* (by me) [in the verse, *Rachel died by me*]. Even though the cave of Machpelah is but a half-day's distance from the place of her death, Jacob was heavily laden with much cattle and family, and he would not arrive there for many days. Thus he did indeed spend many days on that road until he came to his father. Our Sages have further taught:[42] "The bier of a woman may never be set down, out of respect."

Now it is my opinion that these are but words of apology as Joseph already knew that Rachel died on the road and was buried in the Land, and that honor was paid to her when she died. But the reason Jacob did not transport Rachel to the cave of Machpelah was so that he should not bury two sisters there,[43] for

(40) The second *baderech* (in the way) is unnecessary except as an allusion to "the way" which Rachel's children were destined to use when they went into captivity. (Bachya. See my Hebrew commentary on Ramban, p. 261.) (41) See Ramban, above, 35:16. (42) Moed Katan 27 a. (43) For being married concurrently to two sisters was later prohibited by the Torah (Leviticus 18:18). See also Ramban above, pp. 330-2.

he would be embarassed before his ancestors. Now Leah was the one he married first, and thus her marriage was permissible, while he married Rachel out of his love for her and because of the vow he made to her.[44]

9. WHOM G-D HATH GIVEN ME HERE. It was really not necessary for Joseph to inform his father that his two sons were born to him in Egypt since when Joseph left him he had no wife and children, and Jacob himself had previously said to him, *Thy two sons, who were born unto thee in the land of Egypt.*[45] It appears to me that the meaning of the word *bazeh* (here) is "in this matter concerning which you have spoken," i.e., "G-d gave them to me before you came to Egypt to me, and they are the ones concerning whom you have said that they are yours."[46] A similar use of the word *bazeh* is found in the verse, *In this way ('u'bazeh') the maiden came to the king.*[47] Now Joseph said, *G-d hath given me,* meaning that "G-d had performed miracles for me until the king gave me this wife, and I have these children from her."

15. AND HE BLESSED JOSEPH, AND SAID. The meaning of this verse[48] is that in order to bless Joseph, out of his love for him, he blessed his sons. Scripture is relating that Joseph had no other children and his entire blessing was inherent in the blessing of these boys. It may be that [the blessing here was directed at Joseph himself, stating that] the other children who will be born to him in the future[49] shall be called by the name of their brothers and be blessed with their blessing.

(44) Since he married her while already married to Leah, the wedding to Rachel would have been forbidden according to the Torah's later prohibition. Hence her burial place could not be in the cave of Machpelah. See my Hebrew commentary, p. 262. (45) Verse 5 here. Why then was it necessary for Joseph to tell his father, *They are my sons, whom G-d hath given me here?* (46) See Verse 5 here. (47) Esther 2:13. Meaning that she came in this manner specified above. (*Ibid.*, Verse 12). (48) The verse begins by stating that Jacob blessed Joseph, and the blessing that follows refers only to his sons. Ramban is attempting to resolve this difficulty. (49) Verse 6 here.

In my opinion this latter interpretation is correct since the prophet Jacob said, *And the children that were born ('holad'to')* [50] *after them, shall be thine,* and his word would not be in vain. [51] However, Joseph did beget children after that, just as is the opinion of Onkelos, who translated: "And the children that you *will beget* after them." And thus, *asher holad'to* is a past tense replacing a future, just as in the verse, *Which I took out of the hand of the Amorite,* [52] and many additional verses besides. Even in line with the literal interpretation of Scripture it would appear that Joseph had children that he had begotten after his father came to him in Egypt. This is obvious from the fact that Jacob found it necessary to elaborate rather than say, "And now thy sons, Ephraim and Menasheh, who were born to thee, shall be mine as Reuben and Simeon, and the children that will be born shall be thine." This is the reason why Scripture states, *And unto Joseph were born two sons before the year of famine came,* [53] since after the famine additional children were born to him, but Scripture does not mention them as there is no need for us to know of them [since they were absorbed into the tribes of Ephraim and Menasheh].

THE G-D, BEFORE WHOM MY FATHERS, ABRAHAM AND ISAAC, DID WALK, THE G-D WHO HATH BEEN MY SHEPHERD ALL MY LIFE LONG UNTO THIS DAY. The prophet [54] calls upon the G-d of his fathers Who [has] the greatness and the power and Who did great and tremendous things

(50) *Holad'to* is in the past tense and means "were born to you." Ramban will explain that Jacob's words are to be understood as if they were in the future tense: "And the children that *will be born to you* after them shall be thine." Joseph thus had other children besides Ephraim and Menasheh, whom Scripture does not record, as they were counted among the tribes of his first sons. (51) As it would be if we interpret the verse literally as referring to the past for Joseph did not as yet have any children other than Ephraim and Menasheh. (52) Verse 22 here. Here again, *lakachti* (I took) is to be understood as if it were in the future tense. (53) Above, 41:50. (54) Jacob. Ramban is here explaining the double use of *Elokim* (G-d) in this blessing: *The G-d before Whom ... the G-d who hath been my shepherd.*

for them, and [after that he refers to Him in a synonymous way and] he calls upon the true G-d, Who had been his shepherd all his life.

It is possible that the word *haro'eh* (shepherd) – in the phrase, *Who hath been my shepherd* – is derived from the word *rei'ah* (friend), as in the verse, *Thine own friend ('rei'acha'), and thy father's friend, forsake not,* [55] for in that attribute there is peace and friendship. Do not find difficulty with the expression, *all my life unto this day,* in connection with that which we have written on the verse, *And he offered sacrifices unto the G-d of his father Isaac,* [56] for from his very inception He did indeed lead him in the true path, but His attribute of truth was not brought to bear upon him completely until he returned to the land of his ancestors as he was outside of the Land, and also because he was constrained to conduct himself in a crafty manner towards Laban, and that was not the path of truth.

16. AND LET MY NAME BE CALLED ON THEM. Rabbi Abraham ibn Ezra said that it means that all Israel be called by the name Ephraim, [57] just as they are called "the children of Abraham, Isaac, and Jacob."

This is not correct for Scripture uses the word *bahem (on them),* [thus referring to both Ephraim and Menasheh], and they were not called by the name of Menasheh. But perhaps this is because they were called *the house of Joseph.* [58]

The correct interpretation though is that their race and their name will exist forever, and the name of Abraham, Isaac and Jacob will forever be upon them.

(55) Proverbs 27:10. (56) Above, 46:1. The difficulty is that the verse here indicates that the attribute of peace was forever directing Jacob's life, while in the verse above (46:1) Ramban explained that this attribute did not come into his life until that time. (Tziyoni. See my Hebrew commentary, p. 263.) (57) As in the verse: *Is Ephraim a darling son unto me?* (Jeremiah 31:19), the reference there being to all Israel. (58) Zechariah 10:6. *And I will help the house of Joseph.*

17. IT DISPLEASED HIM. Perhaps Joseph loved Menasheh more on account of his being the first-born. Hence it displeased him. The correct interpretation in my opinion is that he thought that his father had made a mistake concerning them, and if his blessing will be without true knowledge it will never be fulfilled upon them as it will not have been done with the proper *Ruach Hakodesh* (holy spirit). But when his father told him, *I know it, my son, I know it,* [59] he was reconciled.

20. AND HE BLESSED THEM THAT DAY. The meaning of *that day* is that since Joseph had urged him to give Menasheh precedence, the verse declares that Jacob did not wish to remove his right hand from Ephraim's head to that of Menasheh. Moreover, he expressly reiterated on that occasion, in Joseph's presence, when he blessed them by saying, *As Ephraim and Menasheh. And he put Ephraim before Menasheh* in all his blessings.

BY THEE SHALL ISRAEL BLESS. Jacob addressed this to Joseph. It means that the nation of Israel will bless with your children and say to those being blessed, *God make thee as Ephraim and Menasheh.*

22. MOREOVER I HAVE GIVEN TO THEE ONE PORTION ABOVE THY BRETHREN. After he had blessed Joseph's children and made them two tribes, he returned to Joseph and said to him: "*Behold, I die; but G-d will be with you* [60] in exile in order to save you from all trouble, and you will increase and multiply exceedingly, and He will bring you back to the land of your fathers to inherit it. I have already given you the one portion in my power to bestow – namely, the portion of the birthright – to be yours above that of your brothers, right from the day that *I took it out of the hand of the Amorite with my sword and with my bow.*" All this is a conciliation to Joseph and a manifestation of his love for him, for he informed him that he gave him the

(59) Verse 19 here. (60) Verse 21 here.

birthright, meaning that his sons will henceforth be blessed by becoming two tribes, also in the banners which were assigned in the desert, [61] and in the dedication of the Tabernacle by the princes of the tribes. [62] He also gave him his portion in the inheritance which he would acquire when the children of Israel will conquer the Land by sword and bow and war. Jacob thus told him: "I have done for you all the good which I was able to do for you as long as it was in my power to do it." Jacob's right in the Land was but one portion for he had no right to divest any of his sons of his inheritance. Only the birthright was his to give to whomever he pleased, and it was to Joseph that he gave it.

OUT OF THE HAND OF THE AMORITE. The meaning of this is that Israel first took the Land from the hand of the Amorite. Sichon and Og were two Amorite kings, and the first great war in the conquest of the Land took place between the children of Joseph and the Amorites. This was the war of Joshua [63] with the Amorites, and it was in the course of the war with them that the great miracle took place, as it is written, *Then spoke Joshua to the Eternal in the day when the Eternal delivered up the Amorites before the children of Israel,* etc. [64] And it was out of the hand of the Amorites that the children of Joseph took their portion and inheritance in the Land, as it is written, *And the children of Machir the son of Menasheh went to Gilead, and took it, and dispossessed the Amorites that were there.* [65] The children of Ephraim likewise inherited in the territory of the Amorites, as it is written, *But the Amorites were resolved to dwell in Har-cheres, in Ayalon, and in Shaalbin; yet the hand of the house of Joseph prevailed, so that they became tributary.* [66]

WITH MY SWORD AND WITH MY BOW. The meaning thereof is that the Land was captured by them only through the sword and bow. This alludes to that which Scripture states, *There was*

(61) See Numbers, Chapter 2. (62) *Ibid.*, Chapter 7. (63) Joshua belonged to the tribe of Ephraim, Joseph's son. See Numbers 13:8, and 16. (64) Joshua 10:12. (65) Numbers 32:39. (66) Judges 1:35.

not a city that made peace with the children of Israel, save the Hivites the inhabitants of Gibeon; they took all in battle. For it was of the Eternal to harden their hearts, to come against Israel in battle, that they might be utterly destroyed.[67] He attributes the sword and bow to himself[68] for it was his merit which waged war for them and fought on their behalf, not they themselves, even as the verse states it, *For not by their own sword did they get the land in possession, neither did their own arm save them, but Thy right hand, and Thine arm, and the light of Thy countenance, because Thou wast favorable unto them.*[69] This is a reference to the merit of the patriarchs, for by way of the truth,[70] *Thy right hand* [is a reference to the merit of] Abraham, *Thine arm* to that of Isaac, and *the light of Thy countenance* to that of Jacob.

It further appears reasonable to me that Jacob did as the prophets later on were wont to do. He inclined his hand with a sword towards the land of the Amorites and cast arrows there to symbolize that the land would be captured by his children, even as Elisha did: *And he laid his hands upon the king's hands, and Elisha said, Shoot; and he shot.*[71] Now even though Scripture does not relate it here, it is alluded to in this verse. It is possible that this is the meaning of Jacob's saying, *lakachti* (I took),[72] for from that moment on the Land was taken for his sons.

49 1. IN THE END OF DAYS. These are the days of the Messiah, for Jacob alludes to him in his words, even as he said, *Until Shiloh come, and his be the obedience of peoples.*[73] Now our Rabbis have said[74] that Jacob wished to reveal the end of Israel's exile, but the *Shechinah* (the Divine Presence) departed from him. Thus in the opinion of all scholars, *the end of days* is a reference to the days of the Messiah.

(67) Joshua 11:19-20. (68) Saying, *with 'my' sword and with 'my' bow.* (69) Psalms 44:4. (70) The teaching of the Cabala. (71) II Kings 13:16-17. (72) This explains the use of the past tense "I took," although the land was not actually captured until the time of Joshua. (73) Verse 10 here. (74) Pesachim 56 a.

3. REUBEN MY FIRSTBORN THOU ART.[75] The sequence of this verse is, "Reuben, thou art my firstborn, my might, and the first-fruits of my strength, the excellence of majesty, and the excellence of power," and its purport is as follows: "You are the first-born of my might and the first-fruits of my strength when I was the excellence of majesty (*se'eith*) and position" – the expression being similar to that found in the verses: *Shall not his excellency ('se'eitho') make you afraid?*[76] *When he raiseth himself up ('mise'eitho') the mighty are afraid,*[77] *'mise'eitho'* meaning ascendancy and power – "and when I was at the height of strength (*oz*) for war" – the expression being similar to that found in the verses: *And He will give strength ('oz') unto His king;*[78] *And the strength ('ve'izuz') of battle.*[79]

4. UNSTABLE ('PACHAZ') AS WATER, YOU HAVE NOT THE EXCELLENCY. *Pachaz* is a noun, derived from the expression, *Vain and reckless ('upachazim') fellows,*[80] meaning "hasty and impulsive people." Our Rabbis have made steady use of this word: "I was looking at my image in the water and my evil inclination rose (*pachaz*) within me,"[81] that is "my evil inclination leaped upon me" They said further: "It is their recklessness (*apichzeihu*) which they are revealing,"[82] meaning their impulsiveness. "A reckless (*p'chizah*) people, who spoke before listening, you still retain your recklessness (*'b'pachzuteich'*),"[83] meaning "hasty and impulsive." It is possible that this word *pachaz* is a permutation of the word *chipazon* (hurry).[84] Jacob was thus saying: "Since you burst forth as water, you shall no longer excel *for thou wentest up to thy father's place of repose* in thy haste and impulsiveness. *Then didst thou profane* them,[85] when your

(75) This is the order of the Hebrew words: *Reuven b'chori atah.* Ramban will transpose the order of the words for the purpose of deriving the meaning of the verse. (76) Job 13:11. (77) *Ibid.*, 41:17. (78) I Samuel 2:10. (79) Isaiah 42:25. (80) Judges 9:4. (81) Nedarim 9 b. (82) Sanhedrin 57 a. See Note 63 in my Hebrew commentary, p. 265. (83) Shabbath 88 a. (84) As is the case with the words; *keves* and *kesev*, both of which mean "lamb," and other similar words. (85) The Hebrew is *mishk'vei* (places of repose), which is in the plural form. Hence Ramban writes *otham* (them).

recklessness ascended my couch like the rising and gushing water." This is similar to the Scriptural description of water: *Now, therefore, behold, the Lord bringeth up upon them the waters of the river, mighty and many, even the king of Assyria and all his glory; and he shall come up over all his channels, and go over all his banks; and he shall sweep through Judah, overflowing as he passeth through.*[86]

Our Rabbis have said:[87] "*Then didst thou profane He Who hovered over my couch,* meaning the *Shechinah*" that used to abide above my [Jacob's] couch. Yet the verse says, *Forasmuch as he* [Reuben] *defiled his father's couch,*[88] thus clearly stating that it was the couch which was defiled! But perhaps [out of respect for the Divine Presence, Scripture] modifies the expression there.

But if [we accept the explanation that Scripture modifies the expression], it is possible that the word *alah* (going up) refers to [Jacob, thus saying, "then didst thou profane my couch upon which I used to go up]," just as in the verse, *Nor go up into the bed that is spread for me.*[89] Thus Jacob's intent is to say: "Then thou didst defile me;" He spoke in the third person[90] only as a matter of respect. Similarly, the verse, *Forasmuch as he defiled his father's couch,*[91] is a Scriptural modification, meaning "forasmuch as he [Reuben] defiled the one who goes up[92] upon his father's couch."

From the literal meaning of this verse it would appear as I have explained it in *Seder Vayishlach,*[93] i.e., that it was Reuben's intention to disqualify Bilhah from his father so that she should no longer give birth to children, thus lessening his share as the firstborn. It was for this reason that Jacob said to him that it was

(86) Isaiah 8:7-8. (87) Shabbath 55 b. It is found here in Rashi in the form mentioned by Ramban. (88) I Chronicles 5:1. This clearly shows that it was "the couch" which was defiled and not, as the comment of Rashi would have it, the *Shechina.* Ramban proceeds to answer that Scripture modifies the expression out of respect for the Divine Presence. (89) Psalms 132:3. (90) *Alah,* "he" went up. (91) I Chronicles 5:1. (92) I.e., Jacob. His name though is not mentioned directly, as a matter of respect. (93) Above, 35:22.

reckless and impulsive to think that he would gain thereby, whereas he had no profit from it but only loss.

5. SIMEON AND LEVI ARE BRETHREN. Jacob is saying that they possess the attribute of kinship for their hearts were inflamed concerning their sister.[94] He is thus stating in their defense that they acted as they did out of their brotherly zeal, thus suggesting [that were it not for this extenuating circumstance], they would have been deserving of great punishment and their sin would have been unforgivable since what they did to the people of Shechem was an act of violence.

The correct interpretation appears to me to be that he is saying that Simeon and Levi are real brothers, uniting in fraternity and brotherhood in counsel and deed. Now I have already explained[95] that Jacob was angry with Simeon and Levi for having committed violence when they killed the people of the city of Shechem, for they[96] had not sinned against them at all. They even made a covenant with them and they were circumcised, thus being enabled to return to G-d and become included within the people of the household of Abraham, part of *the souls that they had gotten in Haran.*[97] Jacob was additionally angry with them lest people say that the matter was done at his suggestion, thus creating a profaning of G-d's Name, as people will say that the prophet has committed violence and plunder. This is the intent of the verse, *Let my soul not come into their council*—[98] this is an excuse for he was not in their council when they answered the people of Shechem *with subtlety,*[99] and he was not united *in their assembly* when they came upon the people of the city and killed them. It was for this reason that he cursed their anger and wrath.[100] And so did Onkelos translate: "My soul was not in their council when they assembled to strike, etc."

(94) *Ibid.*, 34:25-26. (95) *Ibid.*, 34:13. (96) The people of the city committed no wrong. It was Shechem who violated Dinah, and the people were not in a position to protest his action. (97) Above, 12:5. A reference to the proselytes whom Abraham and Sarah had brought "beneath the sheltering wings of the *Shechina*" (Rashi, *ibid.*) (98) Verse 6 here. (99) Above, 34:13. (100) Verse 7 here.

INSTRUMENTS OF VIOLENCE 'M'CHEIROTHEIHEM.' According to Onkelos and all commentators, [101] the meaning of the verse is as if it were written: *instruments of violence 'm'garotheihem'* (in their sojournings). This is similar to the verses: *Thy sojourning ('m'chorothayich') and thy nativity,* [102] *into the land of their sojourn ('m'churatham').* [103] Thus the commentators said that the meaning of the verse is that they did violence in the land of their sojourn. [104] Now if so, the approximate sense of the verse is as follows: "They had instruments of violence in the land of their sojournings," it being referred to as "the land of their sojournings" since they lived there afterwards. [105]

But in my opinion Jacob is saying that "the instruments of violence are their dwelling places," i.e., the essence of their lives, even as the expression, *the days of my pilgrimage ('m'gurai').* [106] He is thus saying that the very instruments of violence are their dwelling places for they live and sustain themselves by them. A similar expression is found in the verse: *The desert yieldeth them bread for their children.* [107] And it is on account of this that their father *divided them in Jacob* [100] so that they should not unite *and scattered them in Israel* so that they should not assemble. This was indeed so, for Simeon's inheritance in the Land was contained in the inheritance of the children of Judah, as it is written, *And their inheritance was in the midst of the inheritance of the children of Judah,* [108] with the cities of Simeon set apart from one another throughout the entire tribe of Judah. And Levi's

(101) Rashi and R'dak. (102) Ezekiel 16:3. There too *m'chorothayich* is as if it were written *m'gorothayich.* (103) *Ibid.*, 29:14. (104) That is, the people lived with them in peace, and they did not act accordingly. (105) At the time when Simeon and Levi wrought punishment upon the city of Shechem, they had just entered the land. How then could Jacob refer to the event as having taken place in the land of their sojourning? Ramban answers that this is a reference to the future. (106) See above, 47:9. (107) Job 24:5. The word "yieldeth" is not in the Hebrew text. Ramban interprets the meaning of the verse as follows: "The desert is to him bread for his children," for there he has the opportunity to rob and plunder. Similarly, the verse here says that the sword is their livelihood. Ramban's interpretation of the above verse in the book of Job is also found in his commentary to that book. See Kitvei Haramban, I, p. 80. (108) Joshua 19:1.

inheritance consisted of the Cities of Refuge,[109] which were scattered through all Israel.[110]

6. FOR IN THEIR ANGER THEY SLEW A MAN AND IN THEIR SELF-WILL THEY DISABLED AN OX ('SHOR'). The meaning of this is that they committed violence in their wrath in that they were angry at Shechem, and it was to satisfy their own desire and not because of the guilt or sins of the slain.

Now Onkelos says that the word *shor* (ox) should be understood as *shur* (wall) with a *shuruk,*[111] as in the verse, *Daughters treaded on the wall ('shur').*[112] Thus Onkelos translated the word *shor* in the present verse as "the wall of the enemy," similar in expression to the verse: *Mine eye also hath gazed on them that lie in wait for me ('b'shuroi').*[113] The meaning of the verse is thus: "and they uprooted a city surrounded with a wall, slaying their children and women after having killed the men of the city." The word *ikru* (disabled) would then be similar in use to the verse, *Ekron shall be rooted up ('tei'akeir').*[114]

Others[115] have explained that the ox, which is the largest of cattle, is an allusion to Hamor and his son Shechem, the prince of the country,[116] just as in the verses: *His firstling bull, majesty is his;*[117] *Ye kine of Bashan, that are in the mountain of Samaria.*[118] Similarly do the verses surname the great princes "rams"[119] and "he-goats."[120]

(109) See Numbers 35:1-8. (110) See Joshua, Chapter 21. (111) The phonetic equivalent *oo*. Thus the word should be understood as *shur* (wall) rather than *shor* (ox). The Torah-script has no vowel signs, and for the sake of interpretation, a difficult word may sometimes be interpreted as if it were vowelled differently than the traditional reading. (112) Verse 22 here. (113) Psalms 92:12. Ramban is thus suggesting that the enemy lies in wait for me behind his fortified walls. (114) Zephaniah 2:4. (115) Mentioned in the commentary of R'dak in the name of Rabbi Yaakov the son of Rabbi Elazar. (116) Above, 34:2. (117) Deuteronomy 33:17. (118) Amos 4:1. (119) Exodus 15:15. *Eilei Moab* is generally translated, "the mighty men of Moab," but literally it means "the rams of Moab." (120) Isaiah 14:9. *Atudei eretz* is generally translated, "the chief ones of the earth," but literally it means "the he-goats of the earth."

The correct interpretation appears to me to be that the verse is to be understood in its usual sense as stating that *in their anger they killed* each *man* of whom they were wrathful; *and in their self-will,* after their anger had been calmed by the slaying of the men, *they uprooted* all *oxen,* this being an allusion to their cattle and their possessions, including everything that was in the home and everything in the field. Now Jacob mentioned this in order to state that he had no part in all these secret deliberations of theirs, even in the removal of the cattle and possessions, or any aspect of the spoiling and plundering of the people of the city of Shechem. The word *ikru* [in the expression, *ikru shor*], has the same meaning as in the verse: *Thou shalt hemstring ('te'akeir') their horses.* [121] But the expression and purport is all one.

10. THE SCEPTRE SHALL NOT DEPART FROM JUDAH. Its purport is not that the sceptre of royalty shall never depart from Judah, for it is written, *The Eternal will bring thee, and thy king whom thou shalt set over thee, unto a nation that thou hast not known, thou nor thy fathers,* [122] with the result that the people and their king will be in exile, devoid of royalty and nobility, and for a long time there has not been a king in Israel! The prophet Jacob did not assure Israel that they would not enter captivity under any circumstances because Judah would rule over them. Instead, the purport of the verse before us is that the sceptre shall not depart from Judah to any of his brothers, for the king of Israel, who will rule over them, will be from the tribe of Judah, and none of his brothers will rule over him. The same meaning applies to the expression, *there shall not depart a lawgiver from between his feet,* which means that every lawgiver in Israel who carries the king's signet shall be from Judah. It is he who will rule and command in all Israel, and he will have the seal of royalty until the coming of his son, who [will have] the obedience of all people, to do with all as he pleases, this being a reference to the Messiah. "The sceptre" is thus an allusion to David, who was the first king to have the sceptre of royalty, and "Shiloh" [123] is his son, who will have the obedience of the peoples.

(121) Joshua 11:6. (122) Deuteronomy 28:36. (123) *Ad ki yavo Shiloh,* "until Shiloh come, and his be the obedience of peoples."

Rabbi Abraham ibn Ezra's assertion that "Shiloh" is a reference to David is impossible for Judah never possessed a royal sceptre prior to David. And even though the tribe of Judah was honored and marched first in the desert,[124] the word *sheivet* (sceptre) applies only to a king or prince, as it is written: *A sceptre ('sheivet') of equity is the sceptre of thy kingdom;*[125] *the sceptre of the rulers;*[126] *a sceptre to rule.*[127]

Now this verse before us alludes to the fact that Jacob made the tribe of Judah king over his brothers and bequeathed to Judah sovereignty over Israel. This is what David said: *And the Eternal, the G-d of Israel, chose me out of all the house of my father to be king over Israel forever; for He has chosen Judah to be prince, and in the house of Judah, the house of my father, and among the sons of my father He took pleasure in me to make me king over all Israel.*[128]

Jacob said, *It shall not depart,* in order to allude to the fact that another tribe[129] will rule over Israel, but once the sceptre of royalty comes to Judah it will not depart from him to another tribe. This is the intent of the verse, *For the Eternal, the G-d of Israel, gave the kingdom over Israel to David forever, to him and to his sons.*[130] The reason for Saul [being appointed the first king over Israel] was that the request for royalty at that time was distasteful to the Holy One, blessed be He.[131] He did not wish to appoint a king over them from the tribe to whom royalty belonged and from whom it was never to depart. He therefore granted them a temporary royalty. It is this which Scripture alludes to when it says, *I give thee a king in Mine anger, and take him away in My wrath.*[132] Having given him unwillingly, He therefore removed him in His wrath, as he and his children were killed[133] and his royal line was interrupted. The reason for all this was that at this time Samuel was judge and prophet who was fighting their battles

(124) See Numbers 2:9. (125) Psalms 45:7. (126) Isaiah 14:5. (127) Ezekiel 19:14. (128) I Chronicles 28:4. (129) Benjamin, for Saul was from the tribe of Benjamin. (130) II Chronicles 13:5. (131) See I Samuel 8:5-9. Ramban will explain why the people's request for a king was unpleasing to G-d "at that time." (132) Hosea 13:11. (133) I Samuel 31:6.

according to the word of G-d, saving them in times of trouble, and it was improper for them to request a king during his lifetime, even as Samuel said to them, *And the Eternal your G-d is your king,* [134] and Scripture further states, *They have not rejected thee, but they have rejected Me, that I should not be king over them.* [135] It was for this reason that He did not grant them permanent royalty. The verse stating, *Thou hast done foolishly; thou hast not kept the commandment of the Eternal thy G-d, which He commanded thee; for now would the Eternal have established thy kingdom upon Israel forever,* [136] means that had not Saul sinned, his descendants would have had sovereignty over some part of Israel, but not over all. This is the meaning of [the expression], *upon Israel,* [rather than "upon *all* Israel]." Perhaps Saul would have reigned over the tribes that were descended from his mother, [137] namely, Benjamin, Ephraim and Menasheh, as Judah and Ephraim were considered as two nations in Israel. [138] Or again, Saul might have been king, subject to the king of Judah.

In my opinion, the kings from other tribes, who ruled over Israel after David, went against the wish of their father Jacob by diverting the inheritance of Judah to another tribe. Now they relied on the word of Achiyah the Shilonite, the prophet who anointed [139] Jeroboam, who said, *And I will for this afflict the seed of David, but not forever.* [140] But when [the ten tribes of] Israel continued to crown kings one after another of the rest of the tribes, and they did not revert to the kingdom of Judah, they transgressed the testament of the ancestor, and they were accordingly punished, just as Hosea said, *They have set up kings, but not from Me.* [141]

(134) *Ibid.*, 12:12. (135) *Ibid.*, 8:7. (136) *Ibid.*, 13:13. This verse clearly indicates that had Saul not sinned, his kingdom would have endured forever, which seems contrary to Ramban's above thesis. Ramban's answer is stated in the text. (137) Rachel. Joseph and Benjamin were her sons, and the tribes of Benjamin, Ephraim and Menasheh were her descendants. (138) There would then have been no contradiction between the permanent sovereignty of both Saul and David, as Judah and Ephraim are separate nations. (139) We do not find in Scripture that Jeroboam was anointed king. But see Horayoth 11 b, where it is stated that kings of Israel were anointed although not with the Oil of Anointment prepared by Moses. (140) I Kings 11:39. (141) Hosea 8:4.

This was also the reason for the punishment of the Hasmoneans, who reigned during the Second Temple. They were saints of the Most High, without whom the learning of Torah and the observance of Commandments would have been forgotten in Israel, and despite this, they suffered such great punishment. The four sons [142] of the old Hasmonean Matithyahu, saintly men who ruled one after another, in spite of all their prowess and success, fell by the sword of their enemies. And ultimately the punishment reached the stage where our Rabbis, of blessed memory, said: [143] "He who says, 'I come from the house of the Hasmoneans,' is a slave," as they were all destroyed on account of this sin. [144] Now although among the children of Shimon, there was cause for punishment on account of the Sadducees,[145] all the children of the righteous Matithyahu the Hasmonean were deposed for this only: they ruled even though they were not of the seed of Judah and of the house of David, and thus they completely removed "the sceptre" and "the lawgiver" from Judah. And their punishment was measure for measure, as the Holy One, blessed be He, caused their slaves [146] to rule over them, and it is they who destroyed them.

It is also possible that, [in addition to the Hasmoneans having sinned for assuming royalty when they were not of the tribe of Judah], they sinned in ruling on account of their being priests, who have been commanded: *Guard your priesthood in everything that pertaineth to the altar, and to within the veil; and ye shall serve; I give you the priesthood as a service of gift.* [147] Thus it was not for them to rule, but only to perform the Service of G-d.

(142) Judah the Maccabee, Elazar, Jonathan and Shimon, were all slain by the sword. (143) Baba Bathra 3 b. (144) The Hasmoneans were priests of the tribe of Levi. By assuming the crown of royalty, they transgressed the command of Jacob, who said as long as royalty exists in Israel it should not be removed from the tribe of Judah. All this is elucidated by Ramban further in the text. (145) Reference here is to Yochanan Hyrcanus, son of Shimon, who towards the end of his long reign became a member of the sect of the Sadducees, who, in opposition to the Pharisees, denied the Oral Traditions. See Kiddushin 66 a. (146) A reference to King Herod. (147) Numbers 18:7.

In Tractate Horayoth of the Jerusalem Talmud [148] I have seen the following text: "We do not anoint priests as kings. Rabbi Yehudah Anturya said that this is on account of the verse, *The sceptre shall not depart from Judah.* Rabbi Chiya the son of Rabbi Abba said [that Scripture states concerning the king], *To the end that he may prolong his days in his kingdom, he and his children, in the midst of Israel.* [149] Now what is written afterwards? *The priests the Levites ... shall have no portion."* [150] Thus the Sages have taught here that kings are not to be anointed from among the priests, the sons of Aaron. Now at first the above text explains that this is out of respect for the tribe of Judah since sovereignty is not to depart from that tribe. Therefore, even if Israel, out of temporary necessity, raises a king over itself from the other tribes, he is not to be anointed so that the glory of royalty should not be upon him. Instead, such kings are to be merely as judges or officers. The reason for mentioning "priests" [when the same stricture applies to all tribes other than Judah] is that even though the priests as such are suited for anointment, [151] we are not to anoint them as kings, and the moreso the rest of the tribes. It is as the Rabbis said in the *Gemara:* [152] we are to anoint only the kings of the house of David. [153] And Rabbi Chiya the son of Rabbi Abba, [who in the above text from the Jerusalem Talmud based the law upon a verse in the book of Deuteronomy], explained that anointing priests as kings is forbidden by a law of the Torah, which says that *the priests the Levites, even all the tribe of Levi, shall have no portion nor inheritance* [154] in royalty. This comment is a matter which is fitting and proper.

AND UNTO HIM SHALL BE AN ASSEMBLAGE ('YIKHATH') OF PEOPLES. *Yikhath amim* means an assemblage of peoples, as it is said with reference to the Messiah, *Unto him shall the nations*

(148) 3:2. (149) Deuteronomy 17:20. (150) *Ibid.*, 18:1. Thus taeching by juxtaposition that the priests are not to act as kings. (151) For any priest who is designated as the High Priest enters upon his new duties through anointment (Horayoth 11 b). (152) Horayoth 11 b. The principle is mentioned there, but Ramban's quote follows the text of Rambam (Mishneh Torah, Hilchoth Melachim I, 10). (153) See Note 139 above. (154) Deuteronomy 18:1.

seek. [155] Of similar meaning is the verse, *The eye that mocketh at his father, and despiseth 'likhath eim,'* [156] meaning "the gathering of wrinkles in his mother's face due to her old age." In the Talmud [157] we find a similar expression: "They gathered assemblies *(d'makhu k'hiatha)* in the streets of Nehardea." It could also have said here in the verse, *kehiyath amim,* instead of *yikhath amim.* This is the language of Rashi.

Now it does not appear to me to be correct to explain, as Rashi does, *likhath eim* to mean the gathering of wrinkles in the mother's face. And the expression, *makhu k'hiatha,* is nothing but a phrase to express disputes and questions, suggesting that the matter was disputed with many questions and interrogations, for in the language of the Sages, one who finds difficulty with a certain point of law is referred to as *kohah.* Such an example is found in the Midrash Chazit: [158] *"They all handle the sword,* [159] as they all study the Law with minds sharpened as a sword, so that if any problem comes before them, the law should not be moot (*kohah*) to them." There are many other similar examples of the usage of this word there in the Midrash Chazit. This is also the origin of the expression in the *Gemara:* [160] "Rabbi Yehoshua *kihah* and declared it to be clean," meaning that he asked many questions and refuted all arguments of those who held it to be unclean until he was compelled to pronounce it to be clean. In many old texts in the *Gemara Baba Metzia* [161] we also find the saying: "He who *d'kohi* on coins is called a malevolent soul," meaning that he who is strict and causes difficulty in accepting a coin from another [on the grounds that it is slightly worn shows himself to be stingy in his dealings].

(155) Isaiah 11:10. (156) Proverbs 30:17. (157) Yebamoth 110 b. Nehardea was a town in Babylonia, renowned as the seat of the academy founded by Shmuel. His colleague Rav was head of the academy in Sura. (158) Another name for Shir Hashirim Rabbah. The name Midrash Chazit is derived from the first word of the opening of this Midrash. It begins with the verse in Proverbs 22:29: "*Chazita* (Seest thou a man....)" The Midrash quoted here is in 3:13. (159) Song of Songs 3:8. (160) Negaim 4:11. See also Tosafoth Yebamoth 110 b. (161) 52 b.

Grammarians [162] have said concerning *yikhath* that its root is *yakah,* thus explaining it in the sense of obedience and acceptance of a command. Hence *yikhath amim* would mean that the peoples would listen to him and do whatever he commands them to do; and *despiseth 'likhath eim'* [156] means "despising accepting her command."

The correct interpretation appears to me to be that the word *yikhath* is similar in expression to the verse, *He that eateth the sour grapes his teeth 'tikhenah' (shall be set on edge),* [163] and its root is *kahah,* with the letter *yud* in the word *yikhath* being similar to the *yud* in the word *yitzhar.* The purport of all words having the root *kahah* is weakness and collapse. The verse before us is thus stating that the rod of the oppressor will not be removed from Judah until his son, who will bring about the meakness of the peoples and their collapse, will come, as he will weaken them all by sword. Similarly, the verse, *If the iron be 'keihah,'* [164] means "if the iron be dull and unable to cut" – similar to [the expression] in the language of the Sages, *sakin she'amda,* [165] (a knife which has become dull) "or has been partly broken and contains notches."

Again I found a similar use of the word *kohah* there in Midrash Chazit, [166] [with reference to the period of the Exodus when Israel was to eat of the Passover-offering]: "The Holy One, blessed be He, directed at them a most pleasant odor from the Garden of Eden, and their souls were *koheh,* to eat. They said to Moses: 'Our master Moses, give us something to eat.' He answered them: 'So did the Holy One, blessed be He, say to me: *There shall no alien eat thereof.'* [167] So the Israelites arose and separated the aliens from among them. Now their souls were *koheh* to eat, etc." The purport of the word *koheh* here is that their souls were weakened and their bodies overcome on account of their desire to eat of the Passover-offering to which there had been attached this good odor from the Garden of Eden. In a similar vein are the expressions

(162) R'dak in his Book of Roots, under the root *yakah.* (163) Jeremiah 31:29. (164) Ecclesiastes 10:10. (165) Beitza 28 b. Literally, "a knife which has stood." (166) 1:57. See Note 158 for derivation of the name Midrash Chazit. (167) Exodus 12:43.

mentioned above: "The Law should not be *kohah* to them,"[158] meaning "faint and deficient in their hand"; the expression, *makhu k'hiatha*,[157] means that they were asking questions which induce a weakening of the soul from the great pressure and concentration. It may be that it is an expression of disproof and smashing refutation, such as, "*Parich* Rav Acha."[168] They similarly use the expression [in connection with the question of the wicked son in the Passover Hagaddah]: "You too *hakheih* his teeth,"[169] meaning "break them or weaken them by your words," for with respect to the flesh you can only use the term "weaken" but not "break" although the intent of weakening and breaking is alike, and the word *kehiyah* includes both.

12. HIS EYES ARE 'CHACHLILI' (FROM WINE). The Commentators[170] say that the word *chachlili* denotes redness, and it means that his eyes will become red from drinking much wine. Of similar meaning is the verse, *Who hath 'chachliluth' (redness) of the eyes?*[171]

Now it appears to me that this is a case of a word whose letters are transposed,[172] it being derived from the expression, *Thou didst paint ('kachalt') thine eyes.*[173] The *lamed* is doubled –[*chachlili*]– as is customary in many places, and it denotes the process of painting eyes which is known and frequently mentioned in the words of our Rabbis. In Arabic also its name is "al kachul." The verse is thus stating that Judah's eyes are colored with wine for just as others paint them with *puch* (eye-paint),[174] which is the Arabic "al kachul," so does he paint them with wine, and just as others whiten their teeth with ointments, so does he whiten them with milk, the comparison indicating the abundance of wine and milk in Judah's land, just as Onkelos mentioned.[175] Similar in

(168) Kiddushin 13 a. "Rav Acha objected" Ramban is suggesting that it means: "Rav Acha asked a crushing question." (169) Mechilta Bo 18, toward the end. (170) Rashi, Ibn Ezra, and R'dak. (171) Proverbs 23:29. (172) Thus, instead of the order of the letters being *cheth, kaf, lamed*, it should be understood as if it were written: *kaf, cheth, lamed*, suggesting the act of painting, as will be explained further. (173) Ezekiel 23:40. (174) Jeremiah 4:30. (175) "His mountains will be red with his vineyards, and his wine-presses will drip with wine" (Onkelos).

meaning is the verse, *Who hath 'chachliluth' of eyes,* [171] [the letters in the word *chachliluth* are to be transposed to read] *kachliluth"* (paint), with the verse stating that the drunkard has his eyes painted by wine and he cannot hide his drunken state. It is possible that the verse is stating, "Who has coloring of eyes?" meaning "who needs to paint his eyes always? *They that tarry long at the wine,* [171] since the wine dims their eyes, causing them to tear, *and be consumed away in their sockets,* [176] thus making it necessary for him to have his eyes constantly painted." Scripture, in the book of Proverbs, is thus speaking of the disgrace of wine and the external evils of contentions and wounds which befall he who drinks it in abundance, while in his house there will always be the cry of "Woe" and "Alas." [171] It then also mentions this specific harm which affects his body, namely, the dimming of his vision, and many other sicknesses. This is a correct interpretation and elucidation of the subject.

16. DAN SHALL JUDGE 'YADIN' HIS PEOPLE. This has the same meaning as in the verse, *For the Eternal 'yadin' His people,* [177] which Onkelos translates as, "For the Eternal will judge the judgment of His people," [178] just as in the expressions: *Be thou my judge, O G-d, and plead my cause against an ungodly nation;* [179] *The cause of the widow.* [180] The verse is thus stating that Dan will avenge the cause of his people, all the tribes of Israel, as one. [181] And the purport of it is as follows: The

(176) Zechariah 14:12. (177) Deuteronomy 32:36. (178) Here also, the sense of the verse is: "Dan will judge the judgment of his people." (179) Psalms 43:1. (180) Isaiah 1:23. The reference should rather be to Verse 17 there: *rivu almanah* (plead for the widow), which means *rivu riv almanah* (plead the plea of the widow). Here, likewise, the sense of the verse is: "Dan will judge the judgment of his people." (T'chelet Mordechai. See my Hebrew commentary, p. 270, Note 39.) (181) As explained further in the text, it is clear that Ramban is transposing the words of the verse and interpreting it in the following way: "Dan will judge his people," that is, Samson, a descendant of the tribe of Dan, will avenge the cause of his people from the hands of the Philistines. And who are "his people?" All "the tribes of Israel." And how will that help affect them? "As one," that is, as one whole nation, for when, at the time of Samson's death, the Philistines' temple collapsed, all the lords of the Philistines (Judges 16:27) died, and thus all "the tribes of Israel as one" were delivered from their hands.

Philistines wronged all Israel many times. In the days of Shamgar the son of Anath [182] they began their oppression of Israel, and in the days of Jephthah it is written, *And He gave them over into the hand of the Philistines,* [183] and after the days of Abdon the son of Hillel, [184] it is also written, *And the Eternal delivered them into the hand of the Philistines forty years.* [185] There was none among the Judges who subdued them or had any victory at all over them. Now although it is written concerning Shamgar, *And he smote the Philistines six hundred men with an ox-goad,* [182] this was not "vengeance," relatively speaking, as it was not *a great slaughter.* [186] This is why it is written concerning Samson, *And he shall begin to save Israel out of the hand of the Philistines,* [187] and he avenged the cause of Israel from them for he slew many people and killed all the lords of the Philistines. [188] Scripture mentions *yadin* (he will judge), since this avenger was a judge, not a king. It is possible that this interpretation coincides with the opinion of Onkelos, who translated: "In his days his people will be delivered." [189]

It is possible that the expression, *as one of the tribes of Israel,* means "as the outstanding one of the tribes," namely, Judah, concerning whom it is said, *Thy hand shall be on the neck of thine enemies,* [190] thus implying that this one also [191] will be victorious over his enemies and subdue them.

17. SH'PHIPHON (SERPENT) [192] is the name of a snake which bites at the heel, with the second root-letter [193] being doubled. [194] In the Jerusalem Talmud, Tractate Terumoth [195] the Rabbis said, "It is a small kind of serpent, its name is *sh'phiphon*, and it is as thin as a hair," with the earth being permitted to crack before it. Samson is compared to a snake because Samson did not wage war

(182) Judges 3:31. (183) *Ibid.*, 10:7. (184) *Ibid.*, 12:13. (185) *Ibid.*, 13:1. (186) II Chronicles 13:17. (187) Judges 13:5. (188) See *ibid.*, 16:27 and 30. (189) Thus it is clear that Onkelos also explained the word *yadin* as meaning "will avenge." See also my Hebrew commentary, p. 270. (190) Above, Verse 8. (191) The judge from the tribe of Dan, namely, Samson. (192) Verse 17 here: *Dan shall be a serpent by the way, a 'sh'phiphon' on the path, that biteth the horse in the heels, so that his rider falleth backward.* (193) Namely, the *pei.* (194) Ramban is suggesting that the root of *sh'phipon* is *shapha* which means "hissing while biting," except that the letter *pei* is here doubled. (195) 8:3.

against his enemies as did the other judges and kings. Rather he alone went out against them, just as the viper which leaves his hole to attack travellers on the road, or the small species of serpent of which the traveller is not at all aware.

THAT BITETH THE HORSE'S HEEL.[192] This alludes to the two pillars[196] upon which the house of Dagan, the Philistine god, rested, whereas the three thousand people who were upon its roof[197] are "the rider that falleth backward,"[198] for when the snake bites the horse's heels, the horse lifts its head and his forefeet, causing the rider to fall backward.

18. I HOPE FOR THY AID, O ETERNAL. Among all the judges of Israel there was none who fell into the hands of his enemies except Samson, who is this "snake" [referred to in Jacob's prophecy], just as it is written, *Then the Eternal was with the judge, and saved them out of the hand of their enemies all the days of the judge,*[199] and Samson was the last of the judges since his successor Samuel was a prophet and he did not conduct war on the people's behalf, and in his days the kings [Saul and David] reigned. Now when the prophet Jacob saw that the deliverance which was to come through Samson ceased [when he died together with the Philistines], he said, "*I hope for Thy aid, O Eternal,* not for the aid of 'the snake' or 'the serpent,' for it is by Thee that I will be helped, not by a judge, as Thy salvation is 'an everlasting salvation.' "[200]

19. 'GAD G'DUD Y'GUDENU.' Rashi, in accordance with Onkelos, explained it as follows: A troop will troop out of him, and that troop will troop back upon its footsteps, meaning it will return in its own track back to its territory in peace [and not one of them will be missing].[201]

(196) Judges 16:29. (197) *Ibid.*, Verse 27. (198) See Note 192. (199) *Ibid.*, 2:18. (200) See Isaiah 45:17. (201) Reference here, according to Rashi and Onkelos, is to the time when the armed Gadites will cross the Jordan with their brethren, and they will remain with them until the land will have been conquered. When they will return to their land on the east side of the Jordan not one of them will be missing.

The correct interpretation [appears to be that the word *y'gudenu* here] is as in the verse: *When he cometh up against the people that he invadeth ('y'gudenu').*[202] The verse is thus stating that a troop will always assail Gad, that he will have many wars, with enemy troops spreading out over his land, and that he will follow the enemy in his track and be victorious over him and pursue him, returning on the heel of those who shame them. Jacob thus praised the Gadites for their valor and for their victory over all those who enter into battle against them. This is similar to the blessing which Moses our teacher gave them, as it is said, *Blessed be He that enlargeth Gad; he dwelleth as a lioness.*[203] Since Gad inherited a very wide and large land which was across the Jordan, bands from Ammon and Moab, his evil neighbors, would always descend upon him, claiming the land and invading it. Yet Gad lurked like a lioness over its prey, fearing not their noise, nor showing any dismay at their shouting.

This fitting interpretation I learned from the Jerusalem Talmud, where in Tractate Sotah[204] they say: "*Gad g'dud y'gudenu,* a troop will come trooping upon him, but he shall troop upon it;" that is to say, bands will come to gather wealth and assail him, but he shall troop upon them and bring his troops into their land.

Perhaps the prophet Jacob was alluding to the war of Jephthah the Gileadite against the children of Ammon, as the children of Gad inherited all the cities of Gilead, and half of the land of the children of Ammon. The children of Ammon were always warring against the men of Gilead, and Jephthah scarcely passed over them and he smote them and their cities [with] *a very great slaughter.*[205] This event was indeed a great miracle, and so the prophet Jacob mentioned it, even as he mentioned the matter of Samson.

21. NAPHTALI IS A HIND SENT FORTH. It was a custom among the rulers of countries to send hinds to one another, and

(202) Habakkuk 3:16. Thus, "the troop" mentioned in the prophecy of Jacob is not a friendly troop, as Rashi and Onkelos would have it, but the enemy, as explained further. (203) Deuteronomy 33:20. (204) 8:10. (205) Judges 11:33.

this was the manner in which it was done: Hinds which were born in the territory of the king of the north country would be raised in the palaces of the king of the south country. They would attach a written message to its horns, and it would run speedily and return to its original habitat, and in this way the king of the north country would be apprised of the news. This is the meaning of the phrase, *He giveth goodly words,* meaning that he is a dispatched hind sent who bears good tidings.

This practice is known, and it is mentioned in the Jerusalem Talmud, in Tractate Shevi'ith:[206] "They said,[207] 'If they go they will return, and if you wish to prove it, bring deer and send them to a land far away, and in the end they will return.' He did so. He brought deer and covered their horns with silver[208] and sent them to Africa, and at the end of thirteen years they returned to their place." That is, they freed them after thirteen years, and they returned at once. The analogy is that *Naphtali is satisfied with favor, and full*[209] with all good things, and from him tidings will come forth to all Israel that his land has produced fruits abundantly, even as our Rabbis have mentioned concerning the fruits of Genothar.[210]

22. 'BEIN PORATH YOSEPH.' A graceful son. It is an expression used in Aramaic: "*Apiryon namtui* (Let us gracefully treat) Rabbi Shimon."[211] *Bein porath alei ayin.* His gracefulness attracts the eye that sees him. This is the language of Rashi.

Now it is farfetched to base the interpretation of the word *porath* upon this Aramaic expression, for such expressions in the

(206) 9:2. (207) In our Jerusalem Talmud the text reads: "The officers said to him." The story told there is about Diocletian, the emperor who oppressed the people of a certain city with heavy taxes. When the people threatened to leave the place the officers said to Diocletian: "If they go they will return, for it is in the nature of people to return to their birthplace. And if you wish to prove it, etc." (208) So that they would be recognized upon their return. (209) Deuteronomy 33:23. (210) Berachoth 44 a. The fruits of Genessar (a district around the Sea of Kinnereth) were considered more nourishing than bread, so that if one eats them together with bread he recites the Benediction over the fruits, as they are the main food. (211) Baba Metzia 119 a.

Talmud — be they Greek, Persian, or other languages — have no kinship with the Sacred Language. Moreover, each example found of this word is only an expression of blessing and praise, not grace, and the letter *nun* [in the word *apiryon*] is a root letter.[212] It is so mentioned in Bereshith Rabbah:[213] *"And they blessed Rebekah.*[214] They were depressed and mean. They were *m'pharnin* (blessing) only with their mouth."

It appears to me that the meaning of *porath* is as in the expression, "*Purna* belongs to the orphans,"[215] where *purna* means the improvement in the value [of the orphans' portion of the dowry which] belongs to the orphans. The Rabbis further called the *kethubah* (the written marriage-contract) *purna*, saying, "A woman collects the *purna* from them,"[216] meaning the *kethubah* which constitutes the benefit from her father's house. They similarly said that "*mohar*[217] (dowry) means *pranun.*"[218]

But *bein porath* in the present verse is to be interpreted either as Onkelos has it as being an expression of fruitfulness and abundance, or as the grammarians[219] — who derived the word *porath* from the phrase, *And its branches ('p'orothav') became long*[220] — would have it. They further said that the word *bein* is similar in meaning to "a plant" or "branch", and they bring a similar verse as proof: *And of the stock which Thy right hand hath planted, and the branch ('bein') that Thou madest strong for Thyself.*[221] Thus the purport of the verse is as if Jacob had said: "Joseph is a planting containing many branches."

In my opinion, the word *bein* is to be understood in its ordinary sense, namely, "son," with the verse stating that Joseph is a son who is similar to a many branched tree, planted beside a spring whose waters fail not, and whose branches in turn gave forth

(212) Whereas the Hebrew *porath* has no *nun*. How then can Rashi explain the word *porath* as being similar to *apiryon* in which the *nun* is a root letter? (213) 60:13. (214) Above, 24:60. (215) Kethuboth 54 a. (216) *Ibid.*, 67 a. (217) Exodus 22:16. (218) It is so rendered there in Targum Jonathan. (219) Rabbi Yonah and Rabbi Yehudah, mentioned by R'dak in his Book of Roots, under the root *banah.* (220) Ezekiel 31:5. (221) Psalms 80:16.

offspring, [i.e., other boughs]. [On account of their heaviness] these tread upon the sky-high walls.[222] He called the boughs which come forth from the branches as *banoth* (daughters), for they are "the daughters" of the great branches. This is stylistic elegance for the expression, *bein porath.* The word *bein,* accordingly, is not in the conjunctive mode to the word *porath,* but instead is like: *The Assyrian was a cedar in Lebanon;*[223] *Naphtali is a hind sent forth;*[224] *Benjamin is a wolf.*[225] It is for this reason that it is vowelled with a *tzeirei* – [*bein*] – for if its interpretation were "a plant of boughs,"[226] the word *bein* should have been vowelled with a *segol,* [thus rendering it *ben* rather than *bein*]. The reason he uses the term *bein* (son) is to show affection, just as: *From the prey, my son, thou art gone up.*[227]

In general it is proper to interpret Joseph's blessing as alluding to the two tribes which came from him, and this could be based upon the words *porath* (branches) and *banoth* (boughs). However, since he mentioned Levi, and the tribes of Israel number only twelve, he did not treat them as two separate tribes in his blessing, but he does allude to them. Moses our teacher, likewise, in his blessing, compared Joseph to the bullock and the wild-ox, and mentioned "the horns"[228] in connection with him as each one constitutes a distinct body from which two horns branch out. There, however, because Moses our teacher did not mention Simeon by name, he explicitly said, *And they are the ten thousands of Ephraim, and they are the thousands of Menasheh.*[228]

24. BY THE HANDS OF THE MIGHTY ONE OF JACOB. This befell him from the Holy One, blessed be He, Who is the Mighty One of Jacob. And from there [from his position as viceroy], he became worthy to be *the feeder of the foundation stone of Israel,*

(222) For lacking such support they would break under the weight of their abundant fruit. (223) Ezekiel 31:3. (224) Above, Verse 21. (225) Further, Verse 27. (226) As "the grammarians," whose interpretation was discussed previously, would have it. See text above. According to their interpretation, since the two words *bein porath* are in the constructive mode ("a plant of..."), the word should have been *ben* and not *bein*, as is the rule. (227) Above, Verse 9. (228) Deuteronomy 33:17.

that is, the source of the tribes of Israel. The word *"even"* (stone) has the same meaning here as the word *"even"* in the expression, *the chief stone,*[229] [where it means high position]. This is the language of Rashi. "*From the G-d of thy father* did this befall you, and He will help you. [*And with the Almighty,* i.e.,] and your heart was with the Holy One, blessed be He, when you did not hearken to the words of your mistress, and He will bless you." This is also the language of Rashi.

Rabbi Abraham ibn Ezra said that the letter *mem* in the expression, *mei'e-il avicha ('from' the G-d of thy father),* is also to apply to the expression, *ve'eith Sha-dai,* [as if it read, *umei'eith Sha-dai (and 'from' the Almighty)*], *and He will bless thee....*

29. BURY ME 'EL AVOTHAI.' With my fathers. This is the language of Rashi. However, Rashi did not explain the expression *el hame'arah* as meaning *'with' the cave.*[230]

It is possible that the expression of this verse is concise [and should be understood as if it said], "Bury me and carry me to my fathers to the cave," for so Jacob said, *And thou shalt carry me out from Egypt,*[231] and it further says, *And his sons carried him.*[232]

It is possible that the word *el* serves here to indicate many meanings:[233] *Bury me 'with' my fathers,* just as in the verse, *And thou shalt not take a woman 'el' her sister,*[234] meaning "*with* her sister." *El hame'arah* means "in the cave," just as in the verses: *'Ve'el' (And in) the ark thou shalt put the testimony that I shall give thee;*[235] *Behold, he hath hidden himself 'el' (among) the baggage.*[236] Of similar usage is the expression, *And after this, Abraham buried Sarah his wife 'el' (in) the cave.*[237]

(229) Zechariah 4:7. (230) Ramban's intent is to point out that the word *el* in the second expression could not mean "with," which confronts us with the difficulty of having the same word assume different meanings in the same verse. Ramban will suggest various ways of resolving this difficulty. (231) Above, 47:30. (232) 50:13. (233) Since Ramban cites Scriptural references to justify each usage, he finds no difficulty in the fact that the word is used differently in the same verse. (234) Leviticus 18:18. (235) Exodus 25:21. (236) I Samuel 10:22. (237) Above, 23:19.

Rabbi Abraham ibn Ezra said that the meaning of the expression, *Bury me*[238] *with my fathers,* is that the brothers should go with Joseph.

Now Jacob really did not need to do that. However, he now commanded all of them to bury him in the cave, just as he had sworn Joseph, because he feared that Pharaoh might not give Joseph permission to leave the land lest he remain in his land [Canaan].[239] Do you not see that it was necessary for Joseph to plead with the house of Pharaoh[240] that they should request Pharaoh to let him go, and he answered, *Go up, and bury thy father, as he made thee swear,*[241] as he agreed to it only on account of the oath!

31. THERE THEY BURIED ISAAC AND REBEKAH. The reason for saying this rather than saying, "I buried," was that Esau was with him at the burial of their father,[242] and he did not wish to mention him now. Furthermore, [he did not mention Esau's name] as he would have been forced to extend the account, saying, "there *we* buried Isaac, and there *they* buried his wife Rebekah," since Jacob was not present at the burial of his mother.

Now in his testament, Jacob mentioned the cave and those who were buried in it to his children on account of the eminence of the place so that they make a zealous effort to bury him there.

Which Abraham bought with the field... for a possession of a burying-place.[243] He said this in order to let it be known that Abraham commanded that that place be their burial ground as an everlasting possession. However, further on, when it says, *And they*

(238) *Kivru* (bury me) is in the plural form. (239) Abarbanel comments that the reason Pharaoh sent a group of Egyptians to accompany the burial party was that he feared lest Joseph and his brothers be influenced by the attachment to Canaan demonstrated by their father in both life and death and decide to stay there. (240) Further, 50:4-5. (241) *Ibid.*, Verse 6. (242) Above, 35:29. (243) Verse 30 here. To emphasize his thought on the eminence of the place, Ramban reverts to explain the preceding verse in the same light.

buried him in the cave of the field of Machpelah, which Abraham bought with the field for a burying-place,[244] the intent of the verse is to allude that the intention of the righteous one [Abraham] was completed with Jacob's being buried there as he had bought it for the three of them, and no other person was to be buried there. It is for this reason that Joseph did not command that they bury him in the cave with his fathers.

Now I have seen in the Mechilta of Rabbi Shimon ben Yochai[245] that Joseph said to them: "And when you bring me up to the land of Canaan bury me anywhere you wish. I have received a tradition that I will not be buried with my fathers for no one is permitted there for burial except the three patriarchs and the three matriarchs, as it is said, *There they buried Abraham,* etc., and it further says, *In my burying-place which I digged for me,*[246] as he [Jacob] terminates [the group of people who are to be buried there].

It is possible that by saying, *And there I buried Leah,* Jacob hinted to them that he had already taken possession of the cave. This he said with respect to Esau, lest he and his children protest his [Jacob's] being buried there by claiming that the cave is his as he was the firstborn and he is deserving of being buried with his ancestors. Now even though Esau had already left for another country,[247] his sons might transport him from there, just as Jacob's sons carried him. Jacob longed to be buried with his sacred ancestors and to be united with them in burial, and if Esau were to be buried there, Jacob could not be buried there for one burial-place does not serve two families. This is also the purport of his words, *In my burying-place which I digged for me,*[246] meaning that he had already dug the grave in order to take possession of it.

(244) Further, 50:13. (245) *Beshalach* 19. See also Midrash Hagadol, ed. Shechter, end of *Vayechi* 25, and Notes. – The Mechilta is a Midrash on the Book of Exodus, the standard Mechilta is that of Rabbi Yishmael. Ramban here refers to another Mechilta, namely, that of Rabbi Shimon ben Yochai. That is why he specifies it by name. (246) Further 50:5. (247) Above, 36:6.

This is also the reason that it says, *And there went up with him both chariots and horsemen,* [248] as Joseph knew the presumptuousness of Esau and his sons.

This is actually what occurred. We find in the Book of Chronicles of Joseph ben Gorion [249] and in other books of ancient history that Zepho the son of Eliphaz the son of Esau [250] came and quarrelled with the children of Jacob concerning this burial, with the result that they waged war. But the power of Joseph prevailed, and they captured him together with his choice army, and they brought them to Egypt. There, Zepho remained in prison all the days of Joseph, but upon his death he escaped from there and went to the land of Compagna [in Italy] and there he ruled over the Caetheans in Rome, and ultimately was crowned [ruler] over the land of Italy. It was he who first reigned over Rome, and it was he who built the first and largest palace ever built in Rome.

Our Rabbis also mentioned this matter of the quarrel [251] with Esau at the cave. The verse which states here, *And Joseph returned into Egypt, he and his brethren, and all that went up with him to bury his father, after he had buried his father,* [252] alludes to the fact that not one of them died in the war or on the way, as the merit of the prophet Jacob and the merit of Joseph stood by those who went up with him.

Joseph did not command that he be carried and buried now in the Land as his father had commanded, for the house of Pharaoh would not permit it since he was a source of honor to them. Furthermore, if his brothers and his father's house were to

(248) Further, 50:9. (249) The book is known as Josippon. This was an anonymous popular Hebrew medieval work containing the ancient history of the Jews. It was based in part upon the work of the historian Josephus. The story related here is told at length in Chapter 2. (250) Above, 36:11. (251) Sotah 13a. (252) Further, 50:14. It would appear that Ramban wishes to finish his commentary on the entire book of Genesis with the death of Jacob (for reasons made clear further). Hence Ramban explains first the oath of Joseph, although it is not mentioned in Scripture till further on (at the end of Chapter 50), and then he reverts to Verse 33, (of the present Chapter 49), in order to explain the nature of the demise of the patriarch which mirrors as well the life of the hereafter, thus confirming the statement of the Sages: "Jacob our father did not die." The Commentary thus ends on the high note of the deathlessness of the righteous.

accompany him, the people of the Land would rob and steal whatever they had, and it would not be respectful behavior for others to transport him there.

AND JOSEPH SAID TO HIS BRETHREN, I DIE.[253] All of his brothers were still alive for they all survived him, as you see in the case of Levi.[254] *And Joseph made the children of Israel swear.*[255] Upon seeing that his brothers were old, he made their children and all his father's household swear that they too would command their children's children [to take up his bones with them] at the moment of redemption, as they all knew of the impending exile.

33. AND HE EXPIRED, AND WAS GATHERED TO HIS PEOPLE. But the word "death" is not mentioned in his case. Our Rabbis therefore said, "Jacob, our father, did not die." This is the language of Rashi.

Now according to this opinion of our Rabbis, the difficulty arises: Now Jacob applied the term "death" to himself, as it is written, *Behold, I die, but G-d shall be with you!*[256] Now perhaps he did not know it himself, or it may be that he did not wish to pay honor to himself. Similarly, with respect to the verse, *And when Joseph's brethren saw that their father was dead,*[257] we must say that to them he was dead, or it may be that they did not at all know of this. Now the purport of this Midrash [which states that "Jacob, our father, did not die]," is that the souls of the righteous *are bound in the bind of life with the Eternal,*[258] and his soul *covereth him all the day,*[259] "wearing a scarlet garment"[260] so that she not be stripped naked, as Jacob's [soul

(253) Further, 50:24. Ramban here attempts to remove this difficulty: Why did Joseph address himself first to his brothers, and then made the children of Israel swear to bring his remains to the land of his ancestors (as stated in the following verse.) (254) Seder Olam, Chapter 3: "None among the tribes lived less than Joseph, and none among them lived longer than Levi." (255) Further, 50:25. (256) Above, 48:21. (257) 50:15. (258) I Samuel 25:29. (259) Deuteronomy 33:12. (260) A Cabalistic term indicating "the garment" which the soul dons after the death of the physical body.

was privileged to do continually], or which she dons at certain occasions [as do the souls of lesser righteous individuals]. This matter will be understood in the light of what is told in Tractate Shabbath [261] and Tractate Kethuboth.[262]

Thus concludes the book *Bereshith*, containing the story of the accounts of the patriarchs. It tells of what has occurred and of new things that will occur [263] even before they spring up in the hearts of people.

And to the Creator of all beginnings,
Him that rideth the skies,[264]
Many praises and myriads of thanksgivings.
By Him actions and causes are weighed;[265]
He uncovereth deep things[266] and lofty opinions,
And brings the thoughts to light.
It is He Who leadeth me in the path of righteousness,
In the midst of the path of justice,[267]
Who vouchsafest benefits unto the undeserving."[268]

(261) There (152 b) the story is told of certain grave-diggers who were digging in the ground when they heard the voice of Rabbi Acho'ie the son of Yoshiyahu, who had been buried there previously, rebuking them. He was yet alive in the sense which the Rabbis refer to when they say Jacob did not die. (262) There (103 b) the story is told of Rabbeinu Hakadosh who, after his demise, would come home every Sabbath eve and pronounce the *Kiddush*. (263) Here we have Ramban's recurrent theme that the book of Genesis alludes to the future events in the story of Israel. (264) Psalms 68:5. (265) I Samuel 2:3. (266) Job 12:22. (267) See Proverbs 8:20. (268) From the benediction upon deliverance from peril or recovery from sickness (Berachoth 54 b).

Index

OF NAMES, PLACES, BOOKS AND SUBJECTS

Index

A

Numbers refer to pages. Names and subjects in the Commentary appearing in place of the Biblical text, are not listed.

Abraham ibn Ezra, Bereshith Rabbah, Onkelos and Rashi, because of their constant occurrence, are not listed.

C

D

E

F

G

H

I

J

L

M

N

O

P

R

S

T

V

W